Lecture Notes in Computer Science 3552

Commenced Publication in 1973
Founding and Former Series Editors:
Gerhard Goos, Juris Hartmanis, and Jan van Leeuwen

W0079065

Hermann de Meer   Nina Bhatti (Eds.)

Quality of Service – IWQoS 2005

13th International Workshop, IWQoS 2005
Passau, Germany, June 21-23, 2005
Proceedings

 Springer

Volume Editors

Hermann de Meer
University of Passau
Faculty of Mathematics and Informatics
Innstraße 33, 94032 Passau, Germany
E-mail: demeer@fmi.uni-passau.de

Nina Bhatti
Hewlett-Packard Laboratories
1501 Page Mill Road, Palo Alto, CA 94304, USA

Library of Congress Control Number: 2005927231

CR Subject Classification (1998): C.2, D.4.4, H.3.5-7, H.4, H.5.1, K.4.4, K.6.5

ISSN   0302-9743
ISBN-10   3-540-26294-6 Springer Berlin Heidelberg New York
ISBN-13   978-3-540-26294-7 Springer Berlin Heidelberg New York

Springer is a part of Springer Science+Business Media

springeronline.com

© IFIP International Federation for Information Processing, Hofstrasse 3, A-2361 Laxenburg, Austria 2005
Printed in Germany

Typesetting: Camera-ready by author, data conversion by Scientific Publishing Services, Chennai, India
Printed on acid-free paper   SPIN: 11499169   06/3142   5 4 3 2 1 0

Preface

We welcome you to the proceedings of IWQoS 2005 held at the University of Passau, in the beautiful state of Bavaria, Germany. We hope that all attendees enjoyed their time in that ancient and historic city.

Quality of Service(QoS) continues to be an important area of research. Traditionally very focused on the area of networking, it has grown to include mobile applications, wireless environments, 3G and 4G cellular networks, user experience, overlay networks, large-scale systems and other important areas of application. Six full-paper sessions that comprised selected papers of very high quality were devoted to the above mentioned, cutting-edge topics in this volume. We had a fascinating cross-disciplinary program and hope to have seeded connections between different disciplines and between industry and academia.

In addition to the reviewed paper sessions, we were pleased to present two inspiring keynote speakers in this year's program: *Randy Katz*, University of California, Berkeley, USA, and *Michael Stal*, Siemens AG, Munich, Germany. One speaker being from academia and one from industry, reflected well the balanced view of this workshop. Both keynotes extended the scope of QoS and addressed pressing issues, such as "spam," and leading trends, such as "service orientation," and their relevance to QoS.

We worked towards returning IWQoS back to its roots as a workshop where emerging research can be presented. In addition to the regular paper sessions, we therefore extended the program for inclusion of two short-paper sessions and a panel session. These three extra sessions were designed to be particularly interactive between speakers and audience. The Work in Progress short-paper track featured ideas and early research that is still open for discussion and commentary and therefore was given room to be innovative, provocative and visionary. The Position Papers session featured short papers that investigate the impact of QoS: where industry meets academia. The papers in this session paid tribute to the maturing state of QoS-related research and were intended to expose the community to new applications of QoS and to help understanding the barriers to deployment. The Panel session was devoted to discussing a provocative new paradigm, namely whether QoS can be achieved in a "self-organizing" manner, and brought up a controversial and novel view, which implied a shift away from more traditional paradigms.

As always a great deal of effort went into creating this program. More than 120 submitted papers were received with 317 co-authors from 32 countries belonging to all five continents. We were particularly pleased with the relatively large number of papers received from Asia and South America. The five countries with the most co-authors of the submitted papers were: USA (49), Germany (43), South Korea (31), China (29) and Brazil (20). The best 23 full papers, all of which are technically excellent, were selected after a thorough peer-reviewing process, where each paper was independently evaluated by at least three reviewers. In addition to the full papers, 17 short papers were selected based on their merit for the respective session and their general quality.

We wish to thank the Program Committee for its hard work to ensure that high-quality papers were accepted and that new research was viewed with an open mind. Finally, the authors are to be thanked for their submissions and continuing excellence.

As with any large endeavor, there are many people who managed the computational and physical logistics. We wish to thank Ivan Dedinski for his heroic efforts to manage the IWQoS Web site and online support, and Silvia Lehmbeck for her fabulous organizing efforts. Eva Gutsmiedl did an excellent job with the careful compilation of the camera-ready papers for the preparation and final editing of the proceedings. David Hutchison is to be thanked for his effort and excellence in organizing a fascinating panel, and Georgios Karagiannis, together with François Le Faucheur, helped greatly to shape the industrial session. Jan de Meer excelled in organizing the floor exhibition as an accompanying program. In alphabetic order, many thanks also to Richard Holzer, Alois Höng, Amine Houyou, Anton Kornexl, Elisabeth Loibl, Jens Oberender, Patrick Wüchner and to the other many people who helped with the workshop organization during various phases.

Passau

April – June 2005   Hermann de Meer and Nina Bhatti

Organization

Program Chairs

Hermann de Meer, University of Passau, Germany
Nina Bhatti, Hewlett-Packard Laboratories, Palo Alto, California, USA

Steering Committee

Thomas Gross, ETH Zürich, Switzerland
Kevin Jeffay, University of North Carolina, Chapel Hill, USA
Baochun Li, University of Toronto, Canada
Jörg Liebeherr, University of Virginia, USA
Ion Stoica, University of California, Berkeley, USA
Zhi-Li Zhang, University of Minnesota, Twin Cities, USA

Program Committee

Tarek Abdelzaher, University of Virginia, USA
Eitan Altman, INRIA, Sophia-Antipolis, France
Supratik Bhattacharyya, Sprint ATL, Burlingame, California, USA
Nina Bhatti, Hewlett-Packard Laboratories, Palo Alto, California, USA
Olivier Bonaventure, Université Catholique de Louvain, Belgium
Chen-Nee Chuah, University of California, Davis, USA
Hermann de Meer, University of Passau, Germany
Jan de Meer, IHP Microelectronics, Frankfurt/Oder, Germany
Sonia Fahmy, Purdue University, USA
Jean-Marie Farines, Federal University of Santa Catarina, Brazil
Stefan Fischer, University of Lübeck, Germany
Erol Gelenbe, Imperial College, London, UK
Thomas Gross, ETH Zürich, Switzerland
Abdel Hafid, University of Montreal, Canada
Gísli Hjálmtýsson, Reykjavík University, Iceland
Geoff Huston, Telstra Internet, Australia
David Hutchison, Lancaster University, UK
Georgios Karagiannis, University of Twente, The Netherlands
Gunnar Karlsson, Royal Institute of Technology (KTH), Kista, Sweden
Magnus Karlsson, Hewlett-Packard Laboratories, Palo Alto, California, USA
Jasleen Kaur, University of North Carolina, Chapel Hill, USA
Srinivasan Keshav, University of Waterloo, Canada

Reviewers

Tarek Abdelzaher
Eitan Altman
Attila Báder
Supratik Bhattacharyya
Nina Bhatti
Thomas Bohnert
Olivier Bonaventure
Claude Chaudet
Kai Chen
Chen-Nee Chuah
Florence Clévenot-Perronnin
Pieter-Tjerk de Boer
Hermann de Meer
Jan de Meer
Daniel Dietterle
Elias Doumith
Avadora Dumitrescu
Roman Dunaytsev
Antonio Estepa Alonso
Sonia Fahmy
Jean-Marie Farines
Stefan Fischer
Erol Gelenbe
Michael Gellman
Thomas Gross
Abdel Hafid
Jarmo Harju
Boudewijn Haverkort
Gísli Hjálmtýsson
Richard Holzer
Amine Houyou
Geoff Huston
David Hutchison
Georgios Karagiannis
Gunnar Karlsson
Magnus Karlsson
Jasleen Kaur
Kalevi Kilkki
Ram Keralapura
Srinivasan Keshav
Eckhart Körner
Yevgeni Koucheryavy

Andrey Krendzel
Geng-Sheng Kuo
Olaf Landsiedel
Guy Leduc
Baochun Li
Raymond Liao
Jorg Liebeherr
Peixiang Liu
Claudia Linnhoff-Popien
George Loukas
Bryan Lyles
Abdelilah Maach
David Mayer
Jogesh Muppala
Klara Nahrstedt
Elie Najm
Srihari Nelakuditi
Arturo Núñez
Jens Oberender
Konstantina Papagiannaki
Leo Petrak
Krzysztof Piotrowski
Simon Richie
Sambit Sahu
Georgia Sakellari
Jens Schmitt
Samarth Shah
Raghupathy Sivakumar
Michael Smirnov
Ralf Steinmetz
Burkhard Stiller
Pu Su
Joseph Sventek
Vanish Talwar
Steve Uhlig
Remco van de Meent
Hans van den Berg
Peter van der Stok
Srivatsan Varadarajan
Klaus Wehrle
Yan Wu
Patrick Wüchner

Organizer

Technical Sponsors

Sponsoring Companies and Institutions

Table of Contents

QoS in Wireless Environments

The User Experience of QoS

QoS in Large Scale Systems

Stochastic QoS

QoS in $3^{rd}/4^{th}$ Generation Mobile Systems

III   Short Papers

Work in Progress - Innovative, Provocative and Visionary Statements

The Impact of QoS - Where Industry Meets Academia

QoS in Wireless and Wired Networks - Why Is This Needed?

Stateful QoS Versus Overprovisioning

Part I

Invited Program

COPS: Quality of Service vs. Any Service at All

Randy Katz, George Porter, Scott Shenker, Ion Stoica, and Mel Tsai

637 Soda Hall, CS Division, EECS Department,
University of California, Berkeley, CA 94270, USA
{randy, gporter, istoica, shenker, mtsai}@cs.berkeley.edu
http://www.cs.berkeley.edu/~randy

Abstract. Todays networks are awash in illegitimate traffic: port scans, propagating worms, and illegal peer-to-peer transfers of materials [8]. This "noise" has created such a crescendo that legitimate traffic is starved for network resources. Essential network services, like DNS and remote file systems, are rendered unavailable. The challenge is no longer "quality of service" but rather "any service at all". Techniques must be developed to identify and segregate traffic into good, bad, and suspicious classes. Quality of Service should now protect the good, block the bad, and slow the ugly when the network is under stress of high resource utilization. We discuss the research challenges and outline a possible architectural approach: COPS (Checking, Observing, and Protecting Services). It is founded on *"Inspection-and-Action Boxes"* (iBoxes) and *packet annotations*. The former are middlebox network elements able to inspect packets deeply while performing filtering, shaping, and labelling actions upon them. The latter is a new layer between routing and transport that tags packets for control purposes while also providing an in-band control plane for managing iBoxes across a network.

1   Introduction

Networks have become critical for the proper functioning of modern enterprises. An enterprise must be able to depend on its networkthe part it operates, as well as the rest to which it interfacesto provide reliable end-to-end connectivity between consumers, suppliers, and for wide-area applications. Dependability encompasses *reliability* (i.e., a path can always be established between end-points even in the face of link and router failures) and *trustability* (i.e., reachability can be achieved even in the face of incorrect or malicious behaviour within the network). One down hour of access to Amazon.com results in an estimated loss of revenue of $600,000 [5]. Being able to depend on the network when you need it is a critical requirement for modern network-based applications.

Traditional quality of service methods focus on improving network performance by managing latency and bandwidth. Little effort has been directed towards improving the dependability of networked systems. Yet weaknesses in dependability seriously impacts performance. For example, denial of service attacks generate so much traffic that the normal functioning of the network collapses,

H. de Meer and N. Bhatti (Eds.): IWQoS 2005, LNCS 3552, pp. 3–15, 2005.

yielding link resets and the melt-down of routing protocols in the wide-area. In the local-area, critical applications services like name servers and remote file systems are rendered inaccessible. Poor reliability and poor trust translate into poor performance and poor service.

The critical performance challenge is no longer service differentiation; rather, it is to enhance the dependability of networked applications while protecting the network-based services upon which they rely. Any method likely to succeed must be able to detect unusual network behaviourslike unanticipated traffic surgesand perform actions to correct or recover from these. Our approach is founded on two components. First, we introduce *Inspection-and-Action Boxes* (iBoxes): network elements able to observe traffic and act upon it by filtering and shaping traffic. iBoxes are built from *programmable network elements* (PNEs)–Layer 2 and 3 devices with enhanced packet processing via flexible packet classification, transformation, and action while operating at network line speeds. Second, we introduce a new *Annotation Layer* between routing and transport to enable information sharing among iBoxes. Together these provide the essential foundation for (enterprise) network-wide Observe-Analyze-Action.

The rest of the paper is organized as follows. First we present some background on the causes of network failures and prior work on extensible networking. In Section 3, we introduce COPS, our conceptual approach for checking-observing-protecting network services. Section 4 describes our Inspection-and-Action Boxes, which provide the observation-and-action points within the network to implement COPS. We introduce the annotation layer in Section 5, and illustrate its use in Section 6 for a network management and protection application. Our summary and conclusions are in Section 7.

2 Background and Related Work

2.1 Network Protection and Quality of Service

A key challenge for the administrators of the Berkeley Campus Network, a diverse edge network with up to 40,000 active ports on an average day, is dealing with unanticipated traffic surges that render the network unmanageable [3]. These surges can be due to a denial of service attack, the outbreak of the latest Internet worm, or a new file sharing protocol recently discovered by the students. While the source of the surge is often difficult to determine initially, the way it leads to service failure is remarkably similar: the in-band control channel is starved, making it difficult to manage and recover the network exactly when you most need to do so.

Another example is offered by the administrators of our departmental network. In mid-December 2004, largely after the students had left for Christmas break, traffic surges rendered DNS and remote file systems unusable [4]. While the administrators suspected a denial-of-service attack against DNS at the time, another possible source was a poorly implemented and configured spam appliance that generates DNS queries for every email message it examines. Even to this day, and after extensive examination of system logs, the administrators have yet to identify the true source of the surge.

Traditional security tools like intrusion detection systems, firewalls, and virus detection software offer only limited protection in the situations suggested by the above. The signature of events that generate the surge are unlikely to be found in the existing fault databases of these systems. The source of the surge is as likely to be inside the network as outside, and so boundary methods like firewalls are insufficient in any event. Furthermore, the root cause of the surge may be difficult to identify, and need not have anything to do with overtly malicious attacks against the network.

Traditional QoS mechanisms, like DiffServ and IntServ, allocate network resources like bandwidth to statically identified traffic classes [2]. An example is rate-limiting UDP traffic to reserve sufficient bandwidth for TCP traffic. In our view, since the threats are evolving too quickly for static traffic characterization and blocking, protecting networks from unanticipated surges isnt about strict reservations and resource allocation policies. Rather, we need survival policies when the network is under stress.

2.2   Active Networking and Commercial Network Appliances

There is a comprehensive research literature on *active networking*, first proposed by David Tennenhouse [12]. Active networks allow third parties to inject their own functionality into distributed network nodes. The concept remains highly controversial, because of the numerous performance and access control challenges it raises. From our perspective, we are not concerned with running arbitrary application code inside the network. Others have focused on applying programmable networks for network management [6]. Our focus is on protective mechanisms to defend critical network services.

As evidenced by the emergence of *network appliances* for network functions like firewalls, intrusion detection systems, network address translation, traffic blocking and shaping, spam filtering, storage virtualization, and server load balancing, deep packet analysis and processing at the network layer is a commercial reality. Unfortunately, existing appliances focus on point functionality, and they do not offer a network-wide platform upon which to develop a comprehensive architecture for network protection.

We are interested in network management and control mechanisms that become operational when the network detects that it is under stress. We believe that we can build such a capability on top of commercially available PNEs. We concentrate on enterprise-area network management, where the services to be protected are simpler to identify and the policies for their protection can be easily specified.

2.3   Extensible Routing

Extensible routing provides one method for adding capabilities to the network. *Click* is a modular software router developed at MIT [7] and extended by the *XORP* open source effort [1]. A Click router is a collection of modules called *elements*. These control a routers behaviour, including operations like packet modification, packet queuing, packet dropping and packet scheduling. A new router is implemented by gluing together elements using a simple configuration language. Click/XORP provides a powerful framework for developing new and extended software-based implementations of network protocols, but it provides no particular platform support for network-wide protection. It is an excellent prototyping environment for packet processing experimentation, but it lacks an implementation path to performance commensurate with the gigabit and higher line speeds of modern local-area networks.

3   COPS Paradigm

The Internet's protocols were designed to tolerate point failures, such as a broken router or link. Failures induced by syntactically well-formed traffic that is otherwise badly behaved were never formally considered. Protocols are vulnerable to easy exploitation, through Denial of Service attacks that overwhelm a service, inducing traffic loads that starve the control plane of legitimate service requests. While the phenomenology of failure is complex, the recent Berkeley experience discussed in Section 2 suggests that it is the effect of unanticipated traffic surges that render enterprise networks unusable.

What is needed is a comprehensive architecture for network protection. Under times of high utilization, our approach prioritizes network resources for good traffic, blocks known bad traffic, and slows suspicious traffic until it can be further classified. To succeed, it is crucial that the behaviour of the network be checkable and observable. Network protocols are *checkable* if their behaviour can be verified as being well-formed and semantically consistent. This simplifies the job of identifying good traffic. Most existing behaviours have not been designed to be checkable, so we must *observe* them over time to infer their good or bad qualities. Once classified as good, bad, or ugly (i.e., still to be determined), we *protect* network resources by limiting ugly flows while guaranteeing bandwidth to control plane messages. We describe our approach in more detail in the following subsections.

3.1   Checking

Protocols whose behaviour can be characterized by an invariant can be checked by network entities. An invariant is not foolproof, so there is no guarantee of correct protocol behaviour even if it holds. Rather, our goal is to provide significant but imperfect protection against misconfigurations or malicious attacks. The approach uses a network entity to observe a protocols traffic, perhaps using statistical sampling. It checks the protocol invariant to determine if the protocol is semantically-consistent and well-behaved. It protects well-behaved traffic, by lowering the priority of suspect traffic.

Checkable protocols often require new protocols or significant changes to the end-points. Due to limited space, we do not present our approach to the design of checkable protocols in detail. However, we have developed checkable versions of BGP called Listen and Whisper [11] and QoS-based Traffic Rate Control [10].

These designs offer significant building blocks that can be used in constructing checkable protocols: observable protocol behaviour, cryptographic techniques, and statistical methods.

3.2 Observing

Achieving protection of network services requires "in-the-network" observation and control points. Such protocol-aware observation points can detect inappropriate traffic, such as a SYN flood or a DNS smurf attack. When traffic is too high, thus threatening critical services, these points invoke protective mechanisms. At a basic level, observation points passively collect data and calculate statistics to distinguish between normal operation and a network under stress. While this is not unlike existing network tools for data collection, we can combine observation with some analysis to enable management actions. Because we can inspect packets, thus achieving a degree of protocol awareness, these are points "inside-the-network" to verify checkable protocol invariants. A checkable protocol flow for which an observation point has detected an invariant violation can either restore the invariant (e.g., "punish" the flow by restoring it to a fair rate) or even drop it before its reaches a vulnerable network service.

Beyond filtering and traffic shaping, these points can perform deeper actions on packets. For example, they can add annotations to support new network controls, like inserting labels in packets entering the enterprise at the Internet edge to distinguish among outside packets and those generated internally. This enables a spectrum of new protective actions beyond traditional firewalls or traffic managers: e.g., when a critical resource is overloaded, they preferentially queue local traffic, thereby deferring resources from external traffic. This will be described in more detail in Section 5.

3.3 Protecting

The conventional approach to avoiding attacks is to identify and then block bad traffic. Such distinctions are difficult. To be effective, almost all bad traffic must be identified. To make the defense acceptably tolerant, almost all good traffic must be passed. This sets an impossibly high bar for classification, as very few mistakes can be tolerated. We adopt a different approach: protect crucial network services (e.g., DNS, a network file system, etc.) for use by crucial and trusted clients (e.g., authenticated end-hosts of the organization versus outside sources). Identifying a set of trusted clients beforehand, and verifying that identity, simplifies the task of characterizing traffic into "known good and important", "known bad", and "unknown".

We block "known to be bad" traffic but also ensure that "known to be good" traffic receives sufficient resources at critical services. Ugly traffic is not blocked, but network resources are allocated so they cannot prevent good traffic from getting their required services. This triage simplifies the problem. The identification of bad traffic can be conservative, since very high accuracy isnt needed to preserve the networks functioning. We can use explicit signals to identify good traffic, based on the annotation layer. This relieves the network from making real-time judgments about the nature of the traffic; instead, decisions about goodness can be based on long-standing and operator-tunable policies. We do not seek perfect protection; instead, we only minimize and mitigate the effect of attacks or other traffic surges that can affect the availability of network services. With our approach, attacks may cripple non-essential services and/or block non-essential users, but the use of crucial services by essential users is protected.

4   Inspection-and-Action Boxes

4.1   Programmable Network Elements

While specific PNEs vary in architecture, there is much they share in common. Figure 1 offers a generic block diagram consisting of input and output ports and buffer memories interconnected by a high speed interconnection fabric, and Classification (CP) and Action (AP) Processors. Packets are presented at an input port, where they are staged into a buffer memory. One of several classification processors examines the packet based on a set of specified pattern matching and sequencing rules. The multiple CPs operate in parallel. They can inspect packet fields beyond headers. The complexity of the classification rules depends on how deep within protocol layers the packet analysis requires. Once a classification decision is made, tagging information is associated with the packet in a Tag Memory (TM). An AP can now process the packet and its tags. It moves the packet to an output queue, modifying specific fields or generating new packets in response to detecting this particular packet, either to be queued for transmission to the sender or to be forwarded on to the receiver. It retains information about the packet and the session or flow to which it belongs. Finally, the packet

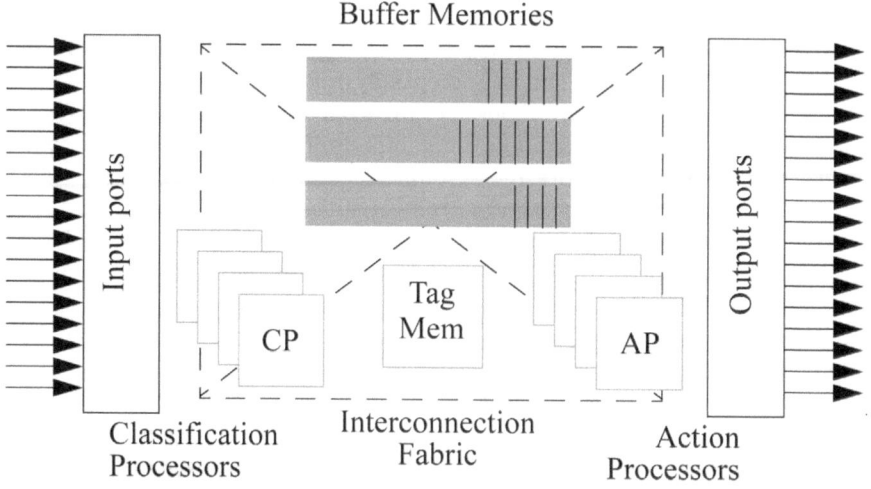

Fig. 1. Generic Internal Organization of a Programmable Network Element

is queued for output to a particular port, based on the policies and processing done at the APs.

4.2   RouterVM

RouterVM is our mechanism for specifying packet processing [13]. It is constructed from cascaded generalized packet filters, a bundling of *patterns* for packet classification and *actions* for manipulating packets that match these patterns. Figure 2 illustrates the concept with the user interface used to specify GPFs. A GPF can specify packet contents beyond IP headers, allowing the GPF author to express higher level protocol patterns, such as the embedded *bittorrent* file sharing protocol headers in the figure (this is accomplished via a regular expression found in an attached library). An action language allows us to further control packet flow. In the example action list shown in the figure, packets for IP address 192.168.0.2 are dropped, while the remaining packets are directed to port 6666 and rate-limited to 256 kbps.

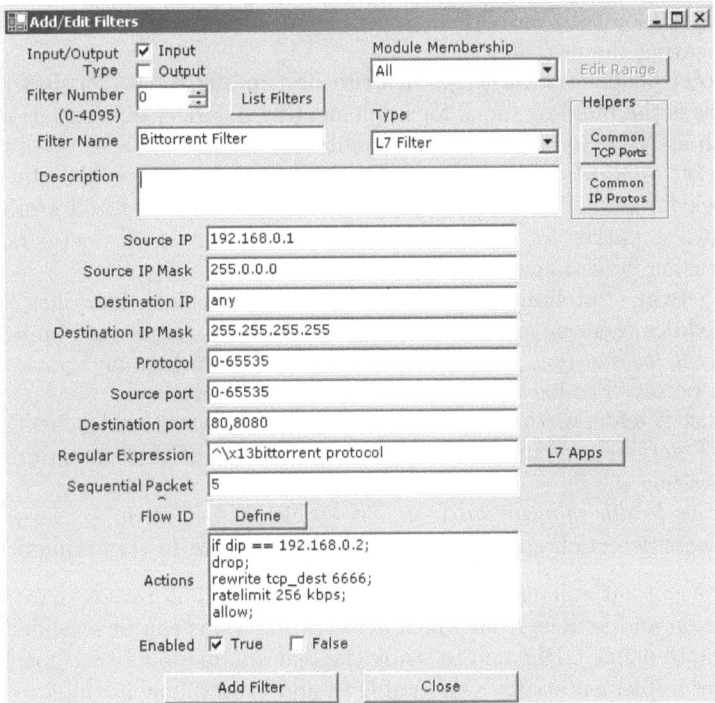

Fig. 2. Generalized Packet Filters

To test the generality and flexibility of GPFs, and to develop a better understanding of how state needs to managed in such an environment, we have written proof-of-concept specifications for several network observe-analyze-act functions.

These include traffic shaping and monitoring, layer 7 traffic detection (e.g., recognizing Kazaa, HTTP, AIM, POP3, etc. traffic flows), quality of services and packet scheduling, network address translation, intrusion detection, protocol conversion (e.g., IPv6-to-IPv4 interworking), content caching, server load balancing, router/server health monitoring, storage networking (including iSCSI management), fibre channel to IP interworking, iSCSI, XML preprocessing, TCP offloading, mobile host management (e.g., 802.11), encryption/decryption for virtual private networks, and network data structures (e.g., multicast, overlays, and distributed hash tables).

The essential building blocks within GPF specifications to implement these functions are illustrated with the following examples:

- *Programmatic decision making* (e.g., "if dest_ip == 127.0.0.0 then drop;"). An essential feature of GPFs is the ability to perform an action based on a general classification of a packets content.
- *Server load balancing* (e.g., "loadbalance table SLB_Table;"). Tables are GPFs data structure for maintaining state. An element of the loadbalance action is to examine the server load balance (SLB) table to assess currently assigned loads to individual servers as an input to the decision process of allocating the next flow.
- *Packet field rewriting* (e.g., "rewrite dest_ip 192.168.0.1;"). Rewriting actions is the building block for implementing a variety of translation actions such as NAT and support for mobility.
- *Packet duplication* (e.g., "copy;"). Packet duplication is a useful building block for numerous operations, such as updating mirrored storage or to spawn a packet for redirection to another point in the network, like an intrusion detection system.
- *QoS* (e.g., "ratelimit 1 Mbps;"). This building block identifies flows and schedules them in such a fashion as to achieve a target rate limit.
- *Packet logging* (e.g., "log intrusion_log.txt;"). Packets and packet subsets can be saved to log data structures for later analysis.
- *Network address translation* (e.g., "nat dir=forward, table=NAT_table;"). NAT actions are constructed as a combination of table look-up and field re-writing.
- *Server health monitoring* (e.g., "if 192.168.0.5 is alive;"). Network node liveness detection can be used as a building block in triggering actions.

This is not an exhaustive description of GPFs, but rather a taste of the classification and actions from which network functions can be specified. We are continuing to define GPFs and to study the issues in mapping such specifications into target implementations. Our goal is to understand how flexibility of expression influences implementation cost, and how such costs could be mitigated by underlying hardware support.

4.3   iBox Placement

To emphasize how PNEs form a foundation for implementing inspection and action at critical points within edge networks, we call them *iBoxes* when used in

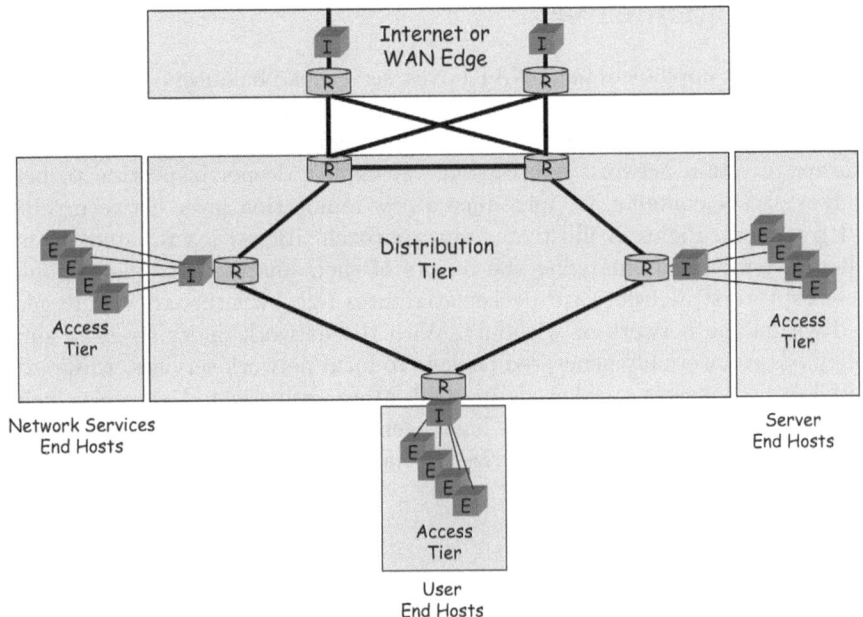

Fig. 3. Enterprise Network Placement of iBoxes

this way. Figure 3 illustrates the most likely places for iBoxes within an Enterprise network. The server and user edges are interconnected by the Distribution tier to the Internet edge, providing connectivity to the network outside of the immediate administrative control of the enterprise. Rs are routers, Es are end nodes, and Is represent iBoxes. iBoxes are placed between existing routers and in front of network and user services, like DNS and file servers.

There is value in off-loading "observation" from routers, thus allowing existing routers to be extended by cascading them with iBoxes. Because commercial network appliancesupon which iBoxes are ultimately implementedhave been "built" for inspection and analysis, this helps iBoxes avoid denial of service attacks based on traffic diversity/slow path processing known to plague conventional routers. Since iBoxes seek to detect traffic surges, statistical sampling techniques offer a feasible approach for reducing the classification load during periods of high traffic. However, as an edge network technology, iBoxes cannot help an enterprises flooded Internet connection.

iBoxes perform management actions through coordination and sharing of information. Observations are summarized and statistical abstracts shared among iBoxes within a given network. Whether a distributed localized algorithm for action decision-making is sufficient, or a centralized/hierarchical scheme scales better is under investigation. A mechanism is needed to allow iBoxes to intercommunicate. This is the essential functionality provided by the Annotation Layer, presented next. iBoxes assign a high priority and reserve bandwidth for their own signalling annotations to insure that the network remains manageable even in the face of surging traffic.

5   Annotation Layer

Many network appliances (e.g., NAT boxes, server load balancers), rewrite packet headers, thus violating the Internets end-to-end principle. Encryption/decryption devices change packet contents, as do compression/decompression boxes. Given a desire to retain network layerization, yet exploit deeper inspection to better analyze packet contents, we introduce a new annotation layer between routing and transport. Figure 3 illustrates our approach. iBoxes insert annotation labels into packets summarizing the results of their analyses. At their simplest, these capture straightforward packet attributes (e.g., whether they were generated within the network or without). With the network under stress, a simple policy passes internally generated packets to local network services, while externally labelled packets are slowed/dropped. More sophisticated examples include the summarization of how packets have been classified into good, bad, and ugly along with statistics that characterize the nature of the flow to which it belongs.

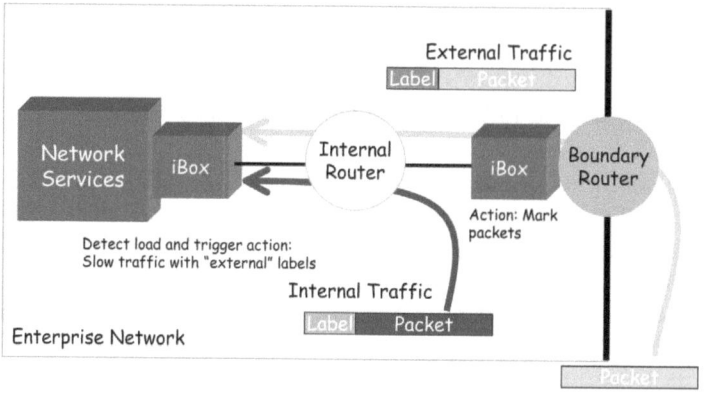

Fig. 4. iBox Annotation using Labels

A possible impediment to in-depth packet inspection is the widespread deployment of IP security. One possibility is to make iBoxes part of the trusted infrastructure, with access to end-host keys. iBoxes could then decrypt, inspect, reencrypt, label, and pass packets on. Such an approach may not be feasible in all networks (in addition to the processing overheads). In that case, inspection and subsequent labelling can be performed for those coarse attributes gleaned from the packet flows, such as packet size, packet interarrival times organized by sources and destinations, and frequency of encountering given source and IP address ranges. This is not an exhaustive list, but rather represents the kinds of attributes that can be extracted even from encrypted streams. We plan to demonstrate how to distinguish and protect the good flows, even if it becomes more difficult to identify the bad flows.

6   Network Management and Service Protection

6.1   General Approach

Better network reliability is founded on mechanisms monitoring network performance, and rapidly detecting and reacting to failures. One approach is *active probing*, a technique that periodically sends requests to a server or network element to measure the network-level response time. However, this does not scale due to the overhead of injecting measurement traffic. Passive monitoring is more attractive. It is inherently scalable and it detects network failures more quickly in parts of the network more frequently accessed. These usually represent the more critical network paths. Previous work on passive monitoring was limited by the weak support provided by network hardware [9]. PNEs provide a new platform for deploying passive monitoring within edge networks. Their positioning within edge networks is an advantage; they are easier to control, and when multiple devices cooperate, it is possible to better pinpoint network failures.

We are developing a shared monitoring infrastructure to improve network reliability. This is based on applying statistical learning theory [14] to build models of expected performance, using passive measurements collected over time. Such a performance profile consists of a distribution of network and application-level measurements like roundtrip time, packet loss, throughput, and application requests, organized according to network address prefix. We use this to detect performance degradation by calculating the probability of consecutive network events. A small probability implies a performance change, which may indicate failed or failing network paths. We are also investigating how various monitoring points can share their measurements via the annotation layer, thus accelerating learning while also correlating observations for fault diagnosis.

6.2   A Scenario: DNS Service Degradation and Protection

In this subsection, we describe how the December 2004 loss of service experienced at Berkeley could have been mitigated by the COPS approach, and in so doing, illustrate the concepts we have presented above. First we consider the case of an externally generated DoS attack against the DNS service and then we examine the alternate case of the misconfigured spam appliance.

Figure 5 shows the network topology, with iBoxes placed at the Internet, Access, and Server edges of the network (labelled I_I, I_A, and I_S respectively). Through protocol-aware packet inspection and statistics collection, I_S detects an unusual increase in latency between the arrival of DNS queries and their response. As other services are within normal ranges, it can pinpoint the problem to the DNS server. It exchanges information with I_I via the annotation layer to determine if the number of external DNS queries is high. If so, I_I negotiates with I_S to slow these requests to a level that insures that internally generated requests receive adequate service. Alternatively, I_S can load balance requests to the Primary and Secondary DNS servers, redirecting external requests to the latter while local requests are sent to the former. Such a strategy only works

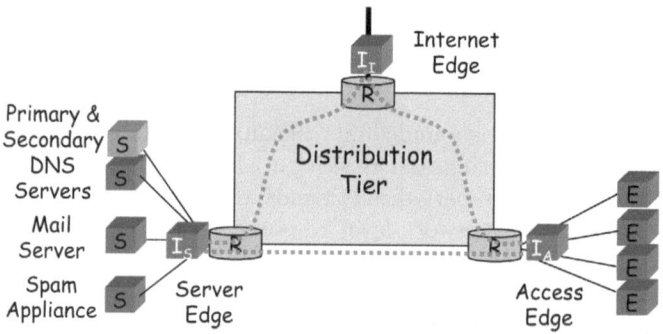

Fig. 5. Network Topology for Scenario

if indeed it is the server rather than the server network segment that is the performance bottleneck.

Another theory for our DNS failure is that our third party spam appliance generated a large number of DNS requests to verify mail domain validity during an email flood. An unusual increase in email traffic positively correlates with increased DNS latencies, thereby affecting the performance of web access and network file system access in a completely unexpected way. Yet even in this difficult case for human diagnosis, the iBoxes can detect such correlations, pinpoint the email surge as the root cause of the problem, and slow email delivery to regain control of the DNS service.

The scenario illustrates some points about network protection. Slowing email to restore DNS availability is a policy decision that must be determined in advance, or presented to the network administrators for their adjudication. Observability also affects the network topology design. Our iBox placement makes it difficult to observe/act on the traffic between the spam appliance and the mail and DNS servers. Had the network been designed so that orthogonal services were placed in different segments visible to iBoxes, the infrastructure could then detect the unusual number of DNS queries originating at the spam appliance. Given sufficient protocol awareness, one possible action is to bypass the spam appliance altogether. A better alternative is to spawn a new DNS server in response to the increased demand for domain name lookups, while redirecting to it some of the traffic load. Our administrators essentially did this by hand: our surge problems went away when they dedicated a new DNS server to the spam appliance.

7   Summary and Conclusions

With the emergence of a broad range of network appliances for diverse packet processing, it is clear that the active networking promise of Processing-in-the-Network is now a reality. While these devices succeed in integrating networking and processing, they still lack a unified framework for specifying and extending their functionality. We have been developing such a framework based on *RouterVM*, to describe packet filtering, redirection, and transmission, and *cPredicates* to enable session extraction and packet execution based on session-level context.

We believe that the challenge of protecting network services when the network is under stress can be met by harnessing these programmable network elements for a pervasive infrastructure for observation and action at the network level. In implementing the Check-Observe-Protect paradigm, PNEs form the foundation of *iBox*-based "inside the network" observation and action points, and the *Annotation Layer* provides the mechanism for inter-iBox coordination. While for todays Internet, we have introduced iBoxes as standalone networks elements, there is no reason to believe that their functionality could not eventually be migrated into future router architectures.

References

[1] *http://www.xorp.org.*
[2] *RFC 2998 A Framework for Integrated Services Operation over Diffserv Networks.*
[3] *Personal Communication.* Berkeley IS&T Staff, Aug 2004.
[4] *Personal Communication.* Berkeley EECS Network Administrators, Feb 2005.
[5] A. Fox and D. Patterson. Self-repairing computers. In *Scientific American*, June 2003.
[6] A. Galis, S. Denazis, C. Brou, and C. Klein, editors. *Programmable Networks for IP Service Deployment.* Artech House Publishers, London, 2004.
[7] E. Kohler, R. Morris, B. Chen, J. Jannotti, and M. F. Kaashoek. The click modular router. In *ACM Transactions on Computer Systems*, volume 18, November 2000.
[8] R. Pang, V. Yegneswaran, P. Barford, V. Paxson, and L. Peterson. Characteristics of internet background radiation. In *ACM Internet Measurement Conference*, Taormina, Sicily, October 2004.
[9] M. Stemm, S. Seshan, and R. H. Katz. A network measurement architecture for adaptive applications. In *IEEE Infocomm 2000 Conference*, Tel Aviv, Israel, March 2000.
[10] I. Stoica, H. Zhang, and S. Shenker. Self-verifying CSFQ. In *Proceedings of INFOCOM'02*, pages 21–30, New York, June 2002.
[11] L. Subramanian, V. Roth, I. Stoica, R. H. Katz, and S. Shenker. Listen and whisper: Security mechanisms for BGP. In *USENIX/ACM Symposium on Networked System Design and Implementation (NSDI'04)*, San Francisco, CA, March 2004.
[12] D. L. Tennenhouse and D. J. Wetherall. Towards an active network architecture. In *Computer Communications Review*, volume 26, April 1996.
[13] Mel Tsai. *The Design and Implementation of RouterVM.* PhD thesis, U. C. Berkeley, Aug 2005 (Expected).
[14] A. X. Zheng, M. I. Jordan, B. Liblit, and A. Aiken. Statistical debugging of sampled programs. In *Advances in Neural Information Processing Systems (NIPS)*, 2003.

Beyond Middleware and QoS - Service-Oriented Architectures - Cult or Culture?

Michael Stal

Siemens AG, Munich, Germany

Abstract. State-of-the-art middleware such as CORBA, RMI or .NET Remoting represents a stack of interoperability layers to connect different islands of code. While all these existing solutions are widely used for the development of commercial and industrial software, they still lack essential features: First of all, there is no accepted middleware standard to connect different technology platforms with each other. And second, standard middleware promotes a tight coupling between peers. SOA principles introduce loose coupling which is important when even small parts of a distributed system are not under control of the developers. One implementation of these principles, XML Web services, are capable of bridging heterogeneous languages, platforms, and middleware. On the other hand, complain about immature, missing or even competing standards for XML Web services. And it still seems unclear how component-based technologies and services fit together. The keynote tries to illustrate how the upcoming universe of middleware, services and components could look like. Not only from a functional perspective but also keeping quality of service issues in mind.

H. de Meer and N. Bhatti (Eds.): IWQoS 2005, LNCS 3552, p. 16, 2005.
© IFIP International Federation for Information Processing 2005

Would Self-organized or Self-managed Networks Lead to Improved QoS?

David Hutchison[1,*], Gísli Hjálmtýsson[2,**], James P.G. Sterbenz[3,**],
Giorgio Ventre[4,**], and John Vicente[5,**]

[1] Lancaster University, UK
[2] Reykjavik University, Iceland
[3] University of Massachusetts, Amherst, USA
[4] University of Napoli, Italy
[5] Intel Corporation, USA

Background

Quality of Service (QoS) is an often misunderstood term. The International Standardisation (ISO) efforts of the early 1990s on a QoS Framework showed that there are several QoS aspects, the most significant being performance, availability and security. Ultimately, the most important consideration is that the service provided (by whatever system is providing it) is for the benefit of the user. Most of the research effort in the subsequent decade has been on the performance aspect (including, rightly, perceptual QoS), but unfortunately the other aspects have largely been ignored or overlooked. Both availability and security have a central role to play in ensuring the overall QoS of a networked system. Should either of these be compromised, there will be a fairly direct and negative impact on the system performance: this is a particularly topical issue.

In recent years several events have shown how current networked systems are vulnerable to a wide variety of threats and failures. Malicious and terrorist attacks (hits to telecommunication and IT infrastructures, worms and Denial of Service attacks) as well as failures related to external events (natural disasters, major outages of electrical power) can lead to critical situations for the life of the current and the future Information Society. The interdependencies existing across all the components (hardware, software, support infrastructure) of complex networked systems demand a new approach to the definition of proper design and evaluation methodologies of fault and attack **resilience** capabilities. Even router mis-configurations may be a major source of disruption in the network, emphasising the urgent need for appropriate resilience mechanisms.

Resilience – the ability of a system to recover to acceptable levels of operation following failures or attacks – is therefore a key QoS characteristic that has a direct impact on the system's performance.

---

* Panel Convener.
** Panellists.

H. de Meer and N. Bhatti (Eds.): IWQoS 2005, LNCS 3552, pp. 17–18, 2005.

The Proposition

This panel debates the following proposition: *self-organization or self-management can help implement networked systems resilience and therefore provide improved QoS for end-users.*

Related issues likely to be covered include:

- what is our *definition of QoS* and *which layer(s)* are significant?
- what is the difference between *self-organization* and *self-management* in this context?

Part II

Full Papers

Overlay Networks with Linear Capacity Constraints

Ying Zhu and Baochun Li

Department of Electrical and Computer Engineering,
University of Toronto
{yz, bli}@eecg.toronto.edu

Abstract. Previous work have assumed an independent model for overlay networks: a graph with independent link capacities. We introduce a model of overlays (LCC-overlay) which incorporates correlated link capacities by formulating shared bottlenecks as linear capacity constraints. We define metrics to measure overlay quality. We show that LCC-overlay is perfectly accurate and hence enjoys much better quality than the inaccurate independent overlay. We discover that even the restricted node-based LCC yields significantly better quality. We study two problems in the context of LCC-graphs: widest-path and maximum-flow. We also outline a distributed algorithm to efficiently construct an LCC-overlay.

1   Introduction

The proliferation of research on overlay networks stems from their versatility, ease of deployment, and applicability in useful network services such as application-layer multicast [1, 2], media streaming and content distribution [3]. Previous studies have uniformly taken the view of an overlay network as merely a weighted network graph; the nodes are end systems, the links are unicast connections, and the links are weighted by unicast delay and bandwidth. Overlay networks are therefore treated exactly as a flat single-level network, in which the overlay links are independent. In particular, link capacities are independent of each other. This model is inaccurate as the overlay network encompasses two levels: a virtual network of end systems residing on top of an underlying IP network. An overlay link maps to a path, determined by the routing protocols, in the underlying network. When two or more overlay links map to paths that share an underlying link, the sum of the capacities of the overlay links are constrained by the capacity of the shared link, i.e., these overlay links are *correlated* in capacity. This obvious but crucial observation leads us to conclude that an accurate model of overlay networks must include *link correlations*.

In this paper, we propose the model of overlay network with linear capacity constraints (LCC). An LCC-overlay is a network graph in which the capacities of overlay links are represented by variables and link correlations are formulated as linear constraints of link capacities (i.e., LCC). The LCC-overlay model is a succinct way to accurately represent the true network topology with all its link correlations, requiring only the addition of a set of linear capacity constraints to the simple overlay graph.

We address the following questions. How do we qualitatively measure the quality of an overlay? Why do we prefer LCC-overlays instead of a simple network graph with independent links? Our analysis and simulations reveal the necessity of LCC-overlay in assuring the quality of overlay networks and we introduce two qualitative

H. de Meer and N. Bhatti (Eds.): IWQoS 2005, LNCS 3552, pp. 21–36, 2005.

metrics — accuracy and efficiency — to measure overlay quality. We also study a restricted class of LCC, node-based LCC, that is more efficient and of a distributed nature. Surprisingly, we find that even with such restricted and incomplete LCC, the accuracy and efficiency are much better than overlays with no LCC, and they are close to overlays with complete LCC. We propose a distributed algorithm for constructing an LCC-overlay based on node-based LCC. We further study two network flow problems, widest-path (i.e., maximum-bandwidth single-path unicast) and maximum-flow (i.e., maximum-bandwidth multiple-path unicast), with the addition of LCC. Traditional algorithms cannot be used to solve them in a network graph with LCC. We show that widest-path with LCC is NP-complete. We formulate the problem of maximum-flow with LCC as a linear program and propose an efficient algorithm for solving it.

The remainder of the paper is organized as follows. Sec. 2 will introduce the concept of overlays with LCC; provide formal definitions of the LCC-overlay and the quality metrics; and show the necessity of LCC-overlay in ensuring high overlay quality, through analysis and simulations. In Sec. 3, we present the problem of widest-path with LCC and show that it is NP-complete. In Sec. 4, the problem of maximum-flow with LCC is presented and formulated using linear programming; an efficient algorithm for solving it is proposed. Then, in Sec. 5, we outline an algorithm for constructing an LCC-overlay. Sec. 6 describes the related work and Sec. 7 concludes the paper.

2 Overlay with Linear Capacity Constraints

In this section, we will define an overlay with linear capacity constraints (LCC), and two metrics for measuring overlay quality — accuracy and efficiency. We will moreover demonstrate through analysis and simulation that LCC are necessary for ensuring high quality of overlay networks.

As a result of the two-level hierarchical structure, overlay links are virtual links that correspond to paths in the lower-level network. We define *link correlation* as follows: Overlay links are correlated if they map to underlying paths that share one or more physical links. Link correlation is a fundamental property of overlay networks. Yet, in the current prevailing independent overlay model of a graph in which each link is weighted by its unicast capacity, the underlying assumption is that overlay links have independent capacities. Suppose two overlay links both map to a bottleneck physical link of capacity c, then each has the unicast bandwidth c; however, when data flows on these overlay links simultaneously, each has a capacity of only $c/2$. Thus, the independent overlay may be egregiously inaccurate in representing the network in reality.

We propose an overlay model, *LCC-overlay*, that accurately represents the real network topology, by using linear capacity constraints to succinctly formulate link correlations. Essentially, it is a regular overlay graph, but the link capacities are variables, and a set of LCC express the constraints imposed by shared bottlenecks. The formal definition will be presented in Sec. 2.2.

2.1 Worst-Case Analysis of Overlays with No LCC

For the purpose of illustration, we examine a simple example of a two-level network, as seen in Fig. 1(a). The mapping of overlay links to physical paths is the obvious one in

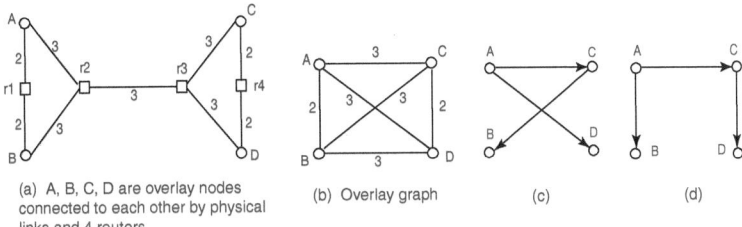

(a) A, B, C, D are overlay nodes connected to each other by physical links and 4 routers.

(b) Overlay graph

(c)

(d)

Fig. 1. A simple example of the detrimental effect that the independent model of overlay has on the overlay quality

the graph. We adopt a simplified overlay construction algorithm, denoted by OC, that is nevertheless representative of such algorithms proposed in previous work. In OC, every node selects d neighbors to which it has links with the highest bandwidth.[1] With $d = 3$, the overlay graph for our example network is shown in Fig. 1(b); it is not hard to see that the results we reach below hold for $d = 2, 1$. The highest-bandwidth multicast tree for this overlay graph, denoted T_{OC}, is given in Fig. 1(c). Although the *predicted* bandwidth of T_{OC} in the overlay is 3, the actual *achievable* bandwidth of T_{OC} is only 1 because all three tree links share the physical link (r_2, r_3) of capacity 3.

In contrast, under the LCC-overlay model, capacities of overlay links are variables and link correlations are captured by *linear capacity constraints*. For instance, the four links $(A, C), (A, D), (B, C), (B, D)$ are correlated, hence the sum of their capacities is constrained by the capacity of shared physical link (r_2, r_3), i.e., $x_{AC} + x_{AD} + x_{BC} + x_{BD} \leq c(r_2, r_3)$. The linear capacity constraints for the overlay graph in Fig. 1(b) are given below in matrix form:

$$\begin{pmatrix} 1 & 0 & 0 & 0 & 0 & 0 \\ 0 & 1 & 1 & 1 & 1 & 0 \\ 0 & 0 & 0 & 0 & 0 & 1 \end{pmatrix} \begin{pmatrix} x_{AB} \\ x_{AC} \\ x_{AD} \\ x_{BC} \\ x_{BD} \\ x_{CD} \end{pmatrix} \leq \begin{pmatrix} 2 \\ 3 \\ 2 \end{pmatrix} \qquad (1)$$

The overlay graph together with the linear capacity constraints (LCC) form an LCC-overlay. For the LCC-overlay in our example, the highest-bandwidth multicast tree is shown in Fig. 1(d), obtained by a greedy algorithm that is a variation of the one for regular graphs, modified to take LCC into consideration. In this case, the predicted tree bandwidth is equal to the achievable bandwidth; both are 2.

Taking a cue from the above simple example, we arrive at the following.

Proposition: For any fixed number of overlay nodes n, there exists a lower-level network G such that the bandwidth of an optimal multicast tree in any overlay graph constructed by OC residing over G is asymptotically $1/(n - 1)$ of the bandwidth of an optimal multicast tree obtained in the LCC-overlay.

---

[1] Though fictitious, this is only a slightly simpler variation of the neighbor selection rule in [4].

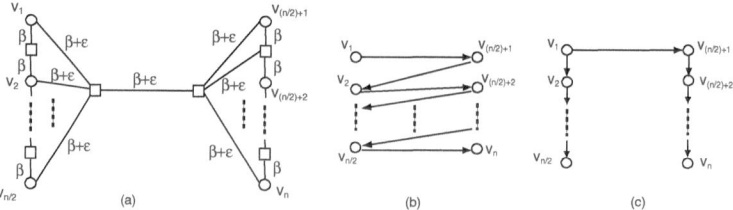

Fig. 2. A worst-case example of the poor quality of an overlay with no LCC

Proof: Consider a generalized graph $G = (R \cup S, E)$ of the one in Fig. 1(a), with n overlay nodes, shown in Fig. 2(a). Any overlay graph constructed by OC will contain the middle $(\beta + \epsilon)$-link for every overlay link between the partitions, see Fig. 2(b). An optimal multicast tree in the OC graph must include only the $(\beta + \epsilon)$-links, because otherwise its predicted bandwidth would be suboptimal. However, its achievable bandwidth is only $(\beta + \epsilon)/(n-1)$ since all $n-1$ tree links traverse the same $(\beta + \epsilon)$-link in the middle. In the LCC-overlay, the optimal tree has bandwidth β, as shown in Fig. 2(c). With ϵ approaching 0, the OC tree asymptotically achieves $1/(n-1)$ of β.   □

2.2   Formal Definitions of LCC-Overlay and Quality of Overlay

From the above analysis, we observe that the extreme poor performance of the overlay with no LCC (No-LCC overlay) is a consequence of its *inaccuracy* in representing the true network topology. The LCC-overlay, on the other hand, represents the network with perfect accuracy, and hence achieves the optimal bandwidth. Two questions now arise naturally. (1) How do we quantitatively measure the quality of overlay networks? (2) How does the quality (i.e., accuracy, performance) of LCC-overlays compare with that of No-LCC overlays in realistic networks?

Before we directly address these questions, we must first formally define the LCC-overlay and the metrics to measure overlay quality. We also will make more precise the notions of predicted and achievable bandwidth of overlay flows.

The two-level hierarchy of an overlay network can be formulated as consisting of: a low-level (IP) graph $G = (V, E)$, each link $e \in E$ has a capacity of $c(e) \geq 0$; a high-level (overlay) graph $\widehat{G} = (\widehat{V}, \widehat{E})$, where $\widehat{V} \subset V$; a mapping P of every overlay edge $(\widehat{v}_1, \widehat{v}_2) \in \widehat{E}$ to a low-level path $P(\widehat{v}_1, \widehat{v}_2) \subset G$ from $\widehat{v}_1$ to $\widehat{v}_2$.

The formulation of capacity constraints in the overlay graph $\widehat{G}$ is where LCC-overlay departs from No-LCC overlay. The No-LCC overlay is a pair $(\widehat{G}, \widehat{c})$, where $\widehat{c}$ is a capacity function such that each link $\widehat{e} \in \widehat{E}$ has a capacity $\widehat{c}(\widehat{e}) \geq 0$. The LCC-overlay is defined as follows.

Definition 1 (LCC-Overlay): The *LCC-overlay* is a triplet $(\widehat{G}, C, b)$, where the capacity of each link $\widehat{e}$ in $\widehat{G}$ is a variable $x_{\widehat{e}}$; and (C, b) represent a set of m linear capacity constraints $Cx \leq b$: C is a 0-1 coefficient matrix of size $m \times |\widehat{E}|$, x is the $|\widehat{E}| \times 1$ vector of link capacity variables, $b \in \mathbb{R}^m$ is the capacity vector. Each row i in (C, b) is a constraint of the form $\sum_{\widehat{e}:C(i,\widehat{e})=1} x_{\widehat{e}} \leq b(i)$.

A flow f from s to t in $\widehat{G}$, is an assignment of bandwidth to every link in $\widehat{E}$ subject to capacity constraints and flow conservation; the flow rate, $|f|$, is the total outgoing bandwidth of s. We denote the *achievable flow* of $f \subset \widehat{G}$ in the low-level G by $\sigma_G(f)$ and the *achievable bandwidth* of f by $|\sigma_G(f)|$. We now describe the procedure for obtaining these.

Let f be a flow from node A to node C in the No-LCC overlay shown in Fig. 1(b), with $f(A, C) = 3, f(A, B) = 2, f(B, C) = 3$, hence $|f| = 3$. The low-level graph $G = (V, E)$ is shown in Fig. 1(a). Suppose low-level link (r_1, r_2) is in $P(A, C) \cap P(B, C)$, then the true capacity of overlay links (A, C) and (B, C) in f is a fair share of the bottleneck capacity, denoted by $\gamma_f(A, C) = \gamma_f(B, C) = c(r_1, r_2)/2$. For link (A, B), $P(A, B) = \{(A, r_1), (r_1, B)\}$, thus $\gamma_f(A, B) = f(A, B)$. Using the true capacities of these three links with respect to f, a maximum flow from A to C can be obtained. This is the achievable flow of f, $\sigma_G(f)$, in which a flow of 1.5 is assigned to all three links, and $|\sigma_G(f)| = 1.5$ is the achievable bandwidth of f.

In general, given G and a flow $f \subset \widehat{G}$, the procedure of determining $\sigma_G(f)$ is shown in Fig. 3.

```
for each e ∈ E
    use max-min fairness to allocate c(e) among
        {ê : e ∈ P(ê) and f(ê) > 0},
    let each allocation be denoted by γ_f^e(ê)
    for each ê ∈ Ê
        if f(ê) > 0    γ_f(ê) ← min{γ_f^e(ê) : e ∈ P(ê)}
        else           γ_f(ê) ← 0
    σ_G(f) ← maximum-flow in (Ĝ, γ_f),    |σ_G(f)| ← bandwidth of σ_G(f)
```

Fig. 3. The procedure of determining $\sigma_G(f)$

We introduce two metrics for measuring overlay quality: *accuracy* and *efficiency*. With respect to a maximum flow f in the overlay, accuracy is the predicted flow rate over its achievable bandwidth; it measures the degree to which the overlay over-estimates a maximum flow. Efficiency is the achievable bandwidth of f divided by the low-level maximum flow bandwidth; it measures how good an overlay maximum flow performs in comparison with the low-level optimum (which cannot be attained in overlays). The formal definitions are as follows.

Definition 2 (Accuracy): Accuracy of a maximum-flow f in overlay network $\widehat{G}$ residing over G, is $\alpha_{\widehat{G}}^f = |\text{ maximum-flow } f \subset \widehat{G}| / |\sigma_G(f)|$.

Definition 3 (Efficiency): Efficiency of a maximum-flow f in overlay network $\widehat{G}$ residing over G, is $\varepsilon_{\widehat{G}}^f = |\sigma_G(f)| / |\text{ maximum-flow } \bar{f} \subset G|$.

The overall accuracy and efficiency of an overlay are better measured by taking the average of accuracy and efficiency over all possible maximum-flows.

Definition 4 (Accuracy and Efficiency of Overlay): Accuracy of an overlay $\widehat{G}$ is the *mean* of $\{\alpha_{\widehat{G}}^f : s\text{-}t \text{ maximum-flow } f, \forall s, t\}$. Efficiency of an overlay $\widehat{G}$ is the *mean* of $\{\varepsilon_{\widehat{G}}^f : s\text{-}t \text{ maximum-flow } f, \forall s, t\}$.

2.3   Comparing the Quality of No-LCC Overlay and LCC-Overlay in Realistic Internet-Like Topologies

In practical terms, to discover a complete set of LCC incurs high cost, and also requires centralized operations. Motivated by this, we consider a restricted class of LCC that is naturally distributed: *node-based LCC*. A node-based LCC contains only capacity variables of links that are adjacent to a single node. Therefore, we simulate three types of overlays: No-LCC, All-LCC, and Node-LCC. Through simulations with realistic network topologies, we compare the quality of all three types of overlays, using the accuracy and efficiency metrics defined above. We use an Internet topology generator, BRITE [5], which is based on power-law degree distributions.[2]

First, we compare the accuracy and efficiency of the three overlays with various overlay sizes relative to the low-level network size. We fix the number of low-level nodes to 100 and vary the number of overlay nodes from 10 to 90; the data are averaged over numerous maximum flows with randomly selected source and destination nodes. In Figure 4(a), accuracy is plotted against ratio of overlay over low-level size. The All-LCC overlay always achieves its predicted maximum flows (accuracy of 1) because it has all the bottleneck information. As the number of overlay nodes increases, the accuracy of Node-LCC only deviates negligibly from 1. No-LCC fares much worse, with much higher values for the accuracy metric, which indicate that it over-estimates in predicting maximum flow values and the achievable bandwidths are substantially lower than predicted.

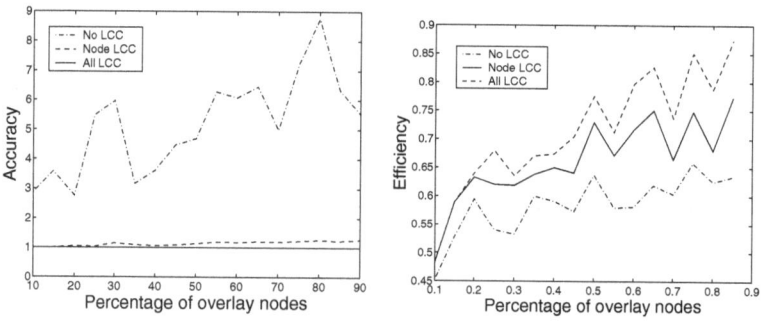

(a) Accuracy of No-, All- and Node-LCC overlays, versus % overlay nodes

(b) Efficiency of No-, All- and Node-LCC overlays, versus % overlay nodes

Fig. 4. Overlay quality versus ratio of overlay size to low-level size

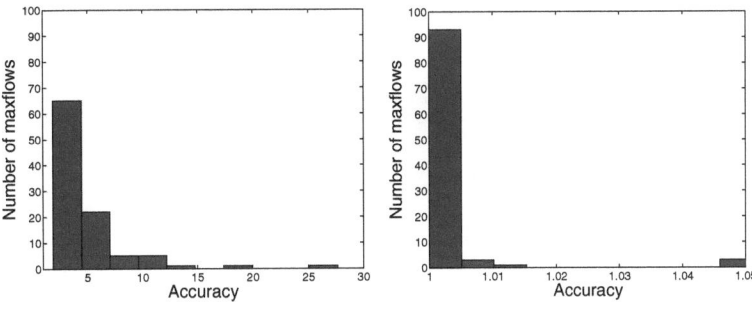

(a) Accuracy distribution for No-LCC, for fixed % overlay nodes

(b) Accuracy distribution for Node-LCC, for fixed % overlay nodes

Fig. 5. Accuracy distributions for No-LCC (a) and Node-LCC (b), with the fixed ratio 30% of overlay to low-level size

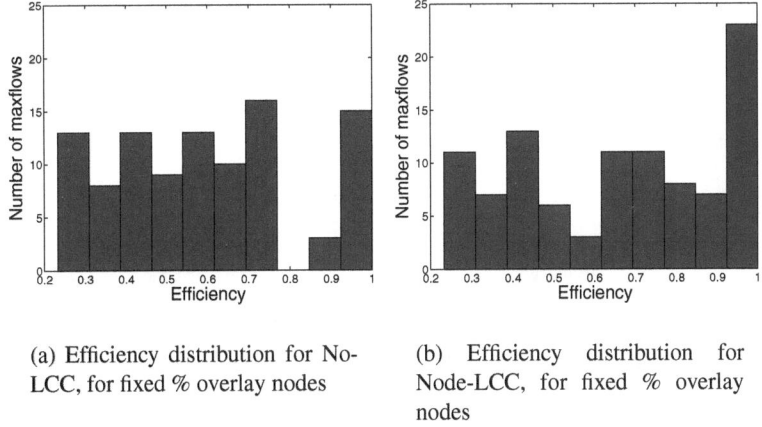

(a) Efficiency distribution for No-LCC, for fixed % overlay nodes

(b) Efficiency distribution for Node-LCC, for fixed % overlay nodes

Fig. 6. Efficiency distributions of No-LCC (a) and Node-LCC (b) for fixed ratio 30% of overlay to low-level size

Figure 4(b) shows efficiency versus overlay-to-low-level ratio for the three overlays. All-LCC has the highest efficiency, as expected, since it has the optimal overlay efficiency, i.e., higher efficiency cannot be achieved by only using overlay links. The surprise here is how closely the Node-LCC efficiency curve follows that of All-LCC for all realistic overlay ratios (less than 65%). No-LCC has much lower efficiency than both All-LCC and Node-LCC. It should be noted that No-LCC efficiency is not as poor as its accuracy, relatively to the two LCC. This can be explained by the fact that No-

---

[2] A seminal paper [6] revealed that degree distribution in the Internet is a power-law.

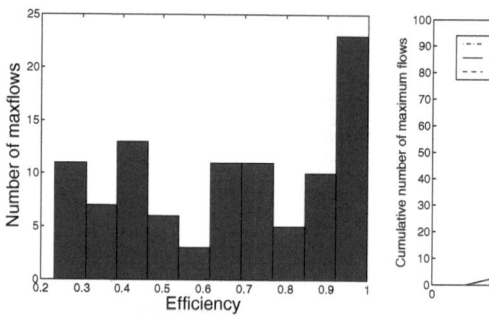 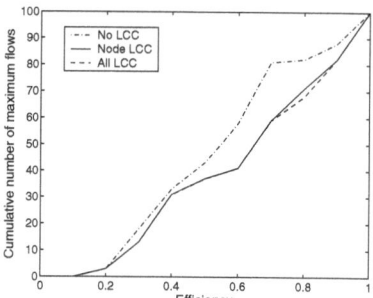

(a) Efficiency distribution for All-LCC, for fixed % overlay nodes

(b) Cumulative distribution of efficiency for No-, All- and Node-LCC

Fig. 7. Efficiency distribution of All-LCC (a) and the cumulative distributions for the three overlays (b), for the fixed ratio 30% of overlay to low-level size

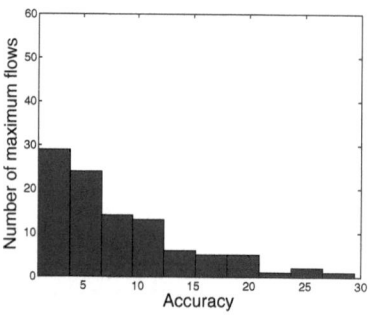 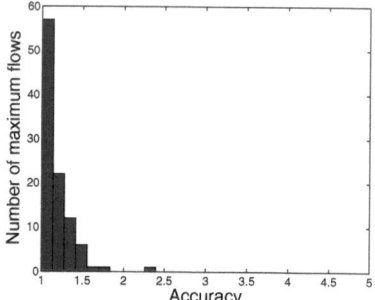

(a) Accuracy distribution for No-LCC, for network size 500

(b) Accuracy distribution for Node-LCC, for network size 500

Fig. 8. Accuracy distributions for No-LCC (a) and Node-LCC (b), for network size 500

LCC heavily over-estimates (indicated by its poor accuracy) link capacities, and thus overloads low-level links to their full capacity and thereby benefiting the efficiency. But overloading some low-level links results in other links being under-utilized, because it was not foreseen that they were needed. This is why No-LCC is still significantly less efficient than Node-LCC.

Next, we evaluate the accuracy and efficiency of maximum flows with a fixed overlay-to-low-level ratio of 30%. The distributions of accuracy over 100 maximum flows for No-LCC and Node-LCC are given in Fig. 5(a) and (b), respectively. As above, effectively all Node-LCC maximum flows have perfect accuracy, while No-LCC is remarkably inaccurate.

The distributions of efficiency are more interesting. In No-LCC, shown in Fig. 6(a), only a small fraction of maximum flows are efficient. It is quite different for All-LCC,

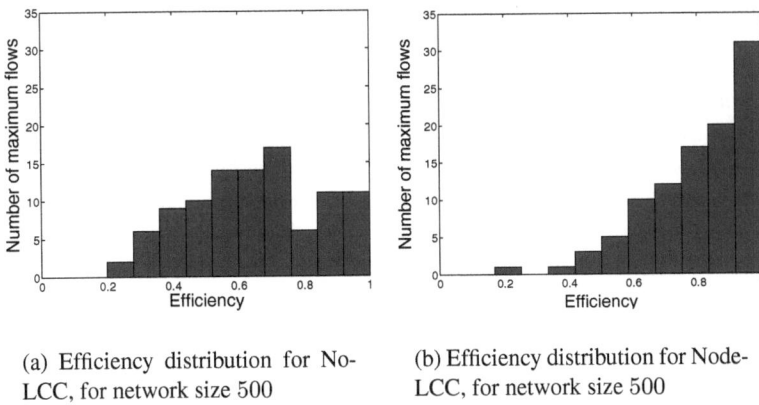

(a) Efficiency distribution for No-LCC, for network size 500

(b) Efficiency distribution for Node-LCC, for network size 500

Fig. 9. Efficiency distributions for No-LCC (a) and Node-LCC (b) for network size 500

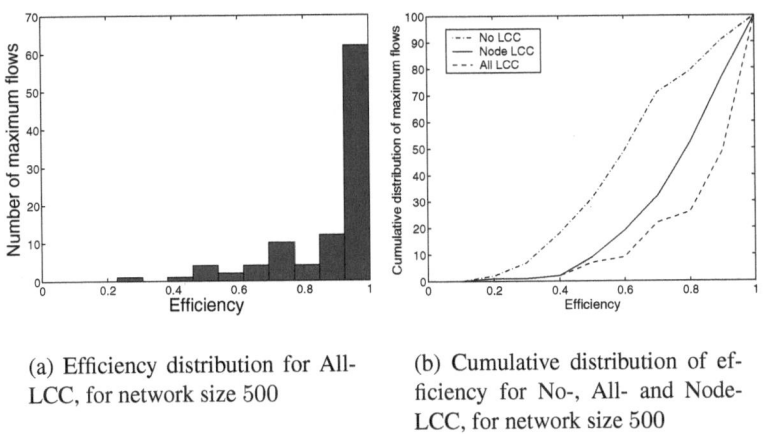

(a) Efficiency distribution for All-LCC, for network size 500

(b) Cumulative distribution of efficiency for No-, All- and Node-LCC, for network size 500

Fig. 10. Efficiency distribution for All-LCC (a) and cumulative distributions for the three overlays (b), for network size 500

seen in Fig. 7(a), where a majority of maximum flows have high efficiency. The Node-LCC distribution in Fig. 6(b) looks almost the same as All-LCC. The coinciding of Node-LCC efficiency with All-LCC efficiency is confirmed in their cumulative distributions in Fig. 7(b), where the two curves are almost the same.

We examine the impact of larger network sizes on accuracy and efficiency, by increasing the network size to 500 nodes and keeping the percentage of overlay nodes at 30%. Figure 8 shows the accuracy distributions of No-LCC and Node-LCC. No-LCC accuracy is much worse than for the previous smaller network size. However, the increased network size causes only a tiny change in Node-LCC accuracy, which is still almost perfect. The efficiency distribution for All-LCC, given in Fig. 10(a), shows extremely high efficiency for almost all the maximum flows sampled. All-LCC efficiency has significantly improved for increased network size. The reason, we conjecture, is that the low-level maximum flows have to travel longer paths in the larger network, thus they are more similar to the paths that overlay flows map to, which means that both overlay and low-level maximum flows encounter much of the same bottlenecks. The same reasoning explains the improved efficiency for Node-LCC in this larger network; Fig. 9(b) shows its efficiency distribution. As can be seen in Fig. 9(a), No-LCC efficiency is more inferior compared to Node-LCC than in the smaller network.

The cumulative distribution graph in Fig. 10(b) illustrates that the gap in efficiency between Node-LCC and All-LCC is smaller than the gap between Node-LCC and No-LCC. In Node-LCC, most of the maximum flows have high efficiency. Moreover, Node-LCC is (like All-LCC) more efficient for the larger network size than for the smaller one. We conclude that increasing network size causes significant deterioration in No-LCC quality, but actually improves significantly the quality of All-LCC and Node-LCC.

3   Widest-Path with LCC Is NP-Complete

The LCC-overlay is an entirely different type of network graph than traditional network graphs. Existing algorithms for network flow problems may not work in the LCC-graph. In this section, we consider the problem of widest-path with LCC, i.e., finding a highest-bandwidth path from source to destination. Widest-path can be solved by a variation of Dijkstra's shortest-path algorithm, however, this algorithm does not in general find a widest path in an LCC-graph.

We are given an LCC-graph $\{G = (V, E), C, b\}$, as defined above in Sec. 2.2. The width of a path $p = \langle e_1, e_2, \ldots, e_k \rangle \subset G$, $w(p)$, is defined as: maximize x_{e_1} subject to $x_{e_j} = 0, \forall e_j \notin p, Cx \leq b$, and $x_{e_1} = x_{e_2} = \ldots = x_{e_k}$. This can be computed by assigning 1 to $x_{e_i}, \forall e_i \in p$, and 0 to the remaining variables; and obtain $\min\{b_j/x_j : j \text{ s.t. } x_j = 1\}$. We define Widest-Path with Linear Capacity Constraints (WPC) as a decision problem: INSTANCE: An LCC-graph (G, C, b), where $G = (V, E)$ and (C, b) are a set of LCC, specified s and t, a positive integer $K \leq \max\{b_i\}$. QUESTION: Is there a directed path p from s to t whose width is no less than K?

Theorem: WPC is NP-complete.

Proof: WPC is in NP because a nondeterministic algorithm need only guess a subset of E and check in polynomial time whether these edges form a path p with $w(p) \geq K$.

We transform the Path with Forbidden Pairs (PFP) [7] to WPC. The PFP problem is defined as follows. INSTANCE: Directed graph $G = (V, E)$, specified vertices $s, t \in V$, collection $F = \{(a_1, b_1), \ldots, (a_n, b_n)\}$ of pairs of vertices from V. QUESTION: Is there a directed path from s to t in G that contains at most one vertex from each pair in F?

Let G, s, t, F be any instance of PFP. We must construct a graph $G' = (V', E')$, $s, t \in V'$, a set of linear capacity constraints $Cx \leq b$ for edges in E', and an positive integer $K \leq \max_i\{b_i\}$ such that G' has a directed path from s to t of width no less than K if and only if there exists a directed path from s to t in G that contains at most one vertex from each pair in F.

Any vertex $v \in V$ not in F and any edge $e \in E$ not incident to a vertex in F remain unchanged in V' and E', respectively. For every vertex u in F, we replace it with vertices u', u'' and a directed edge e_u from u' to u'', called u's replacement edge. For every edge $e = (v, u) \in E$ that enters u, an edge $e' = (v, u'$ is added to E'; similarly, for every edge $e = (u, v) \in E$ that exits u, we add $e' = (u'', v)$. Now we form the linear capacity constraints. Each non-replacement edge $e \in E'$ gives rise to a one-variable constraint $x_e \leq 1$. For each pair $(a, b) \in F$, having replacement edges e_a and e_b in G', respectively, we form a two-variable constraint $x_{e_a} + x_{e_b} \leq 1$. Finally we set $K = 1$. Clearly the construction can be accomplished in polynomial time.

Suppose there exists a directed path p from s to t in G containing at most one vertex from each pair in F. A corresponding path p' can be obtained in G' by substituting all p's constituent vertices that appear in F by their replacement edges in G'. All non-replacement edges in p^{prime} are assigned 1. The PFP condition ensures that for each replacement edge e_a, where $(a, b) \in F$, e_b is not in p'; thus $x_{e_a} = 1, x_{e_b} = 0$. It is easy to see that all the one-variable and two-variable constraints are satisfied, and $w(p^{prime}) = 1$, hence a solution of WPC.

Conversely, let p' be an $s - t$ path in G' satisfying all the constraints and having width no less than 1. The width of no less than 1 and every two-variable constraints being satisfied imply that at most one edge from any two-variable constraint appears in p'. Collapsing p' to a path $p \in G$ by shrinking the replacement edges into corresponding vertices, it is obvious that p satisfies the PFP condition. □

Even though the WPC problem is NP-complete, we discovered through simulations that widest paths obtained without considering LCC can usually achieve optimal bandwidth. The reason is that it is highly unlikely for links in a single path to correlate heavily. Therefore traditional widest-path algorithm suffices in realistic overlay topologies. In general, however, the WPC problem — with consideration of all possible pathological cases — is still NP-complete.

4   Maximum Flow with LCC

In this section we study the problem of maximum flow in an LCC graph. The traditional maximum flow algorithms such as Ford-Fulkerson and Push-Relabel cannot solve the maximum flow with LCC problem. We first formulate the problem as a linear program and then propose an algorithm for it based on Lagrangian relaxation and existing algorithms for minimum cost flow.

Maximum Flow with LCC Problem (MFC): Input : $\widehat{G} = (\widehat{V}, \widehat{E}), C, b$. Output: A flow $f \subset \widehat{G}$ satisfying LCC constraints (C, b). Goal : Maximize $|f|$.

Like the maximum flow problem, the MFC problem can be viewed naturally as a linear program. A variable v is used to indicate the total flow out of s and into t. In the flow conservation constraint, A is the node-arc adjacency matrix for $\widehat{G}$,[3] and d is a vector with a 0 for every node, except $d(s) = -1$ and $d(t) = 1$.

---

[3] Rows are nodes; columns are edges; for each directed edge $e = (i \to j)$, $A(i, e) = 1, A(j, e) = -1$, otherwise entries of A are zero.

$$\text{Maximize} \qquad v$$
$$\text{subject to} \quad Af + dv = 0, \ Cf \le b, \ f \ge 0$$

The MFC linear program can be solved by general linear programming algorithms, such as the simplex method. However, due to their general nature, they may not be as efficient as algorithms that are tailored to the problem. We propose such an alternative algorithm.

Note that the MFC linear program only differs from the generic maximum flow linear program in having $Cf \le b$ (LCC) as the inequality constraint instead of $f \le b$. MFC can be seen as a generalized maximum flow problem; maximum flow is a special case of MFC with the identity matrix as C. With that observation, we modify the linear program slightly to reveal even more clearly the embedded maximum flow structure. We do this by sieving (uncorrelated) link capacity constraints from (C, b): for each link e, add the constraint $f(e) \le b_l(e)$, where $b_l(e) = \min\{b(j) : C(j, e) = 1\}$, that is, minimize over all constraints in C involving $f(e)$. The additional $f \le b_l$ constraints do not change the feasible flow region, therefore the new linear program is equivalent to the original one. The objective function is expressed in a different form for convenience.

$$z^* = \text{Minimize} - v \quad \text{subject to} \quad Af + dv = 0, \ f \le b_l, \ Cf \le b, \ f \ge 0. \quad (2)$$

It is now evident that MFC is a maximum flow problem with some additional constraints $Cf \le b$(i.e., the LCC). We apply the decomposition solution strategy of Lagrangian relaxation [8] to the MFC problem, by associating nonnegative Lagrange multipliers $\mu = [\mu_i]_1^m$ with the LCC constraints ($Cf \le b$), and creating the following Lagrangian subproblem:

$$L(\mu) = \min \quad -v + \mu(Cf - b) \quad \text{subject to} \quad Af + dv = 0, \ f \le b_l, \ f \ge 0. \quad (3)$$

For any given vector μ of the Lagrangian multipliers, the value $L(\mu)$ of the Lagrangian function is a lower bound on the optimal objective function value $z^* = \min -v$ of the original problem (3). Hence, to obtain the best possible lower bound, we need to solve the Lagrangian multiplier problem

$$L^* = \max_{\mu \ge 0} L(\mu). \quad (4)$$

Note that for the our Lagrangian subproblem (3), for any fixed value of Lagrangian multipliers μ, $L(\mu)$ can be found by solving a minimum cost flow problem. A polynomial-time minimum cost flow algorithm is the cost scaling algorithm, with a running time of $O(n^3 \log(nC))$, where n is the number of nodes and C is the upper bound on all the coefficients in the objective function. Since the objective coefficients are 1 or -1, the time complexity in this case is $O(n^3 \log(n))$. We choose the cost scaling algorithm precisely because its running time depends neither on m (number of rows in C), nor on U (upper bound on values in b_l), which may have large values, whereas C is a constant here.

Now that we can solve the Lagrangian subproblem for any specific μ, we can solve the Lagrangian multiplier problem (4) using the subgradient optimization technique.

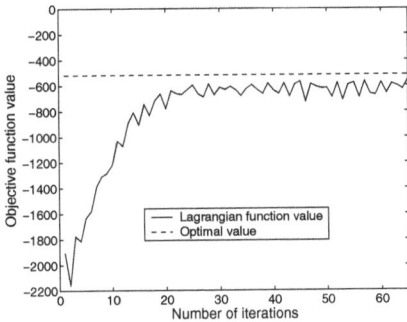

Fig. 11. Shows the convergence of Lagrangian function values (or Lagrangian subproblem solutions) $L(\mu)$ (in Problem 3) to a value near to the true optimal value z^* (in Problem 3), after a relatively small number of iterations

It is an iterative procedure: begin with an initial choice μ^0 of Lagrangian multipliers; the subsequent updated values μ^k are determined by $\mu^{k+1} = [\mu^k + \theta_k(Cx^k - b)]^+$. Here, the notation $[.]^+$ means taking the maximum of 0 and each vector component; x^k is a solution to the Lagrangian subproblem when $\mu = \mu^k$; θ_k is the step length at the kth iteration. The step length is selected to be a popular heuristic, $\theta = \frac{\lambda_k(UB - L(\mu^k))}{\|Cx^k - b\|^2}$, where $0 < \lambda_k < 2$ and UB is any upper bound on the optimal value of (4).[4]

We show in Fig. 11 that for MFC in a simulated network in which 30% of the nodes are overlay nodes, the Lagrangian function values converge to near optimal value in around 65 iterations.

5   Constructing an LCC Overlay

In this section, we present a distributed scheme for constructing an LCC overlay. In Sec. 2, we showed that node-based LCC exhibits notably better quality than no-LCC. The advantage of node-based LCC is that they are naturally distributed. In our scheme, an overlay node first determines a conservative set of node-based LCC; it then *successively refines* the LCC.

The input is a set of overlay nodes, each possessing a list of other known nodes; the list may not be complete at first, but it is periodically disseminated and updated. Existing methods make use of unicast probes to estimate link bandwidth. Independent unicast probes cannot yield shared bottleneck information. Therefore, the probing tool we use in our scheme is an efficient and accurate technique for detecting shared bottlenecks (DSB), proposed by Katabi et al. in [9, 10]. This technique is based on the entropy of the inter-arrival times of packets from flows. A set of flows are partitioned into groups

---

[4] It should be noted that sometimes there may be a gap between the optimal Lagrangian multiplier objective function value and the optimal value for the original problem, the branch and bound method can be used to overcome the gap. We do not go into the details here.

of flows, each group of flows share a bottleneck, and the bottleneck capacities are also measured. We refer to this probing tool for detecting shared bottlenecks as DSB. Every time DSB is executed with the input of a set of flows, the output is a collection of groups of flows with their corresponding bottleneck capacities. Prior to determining LCC, a node selects k neighbors; for our simulation, the k highest bandwidth links are selected.

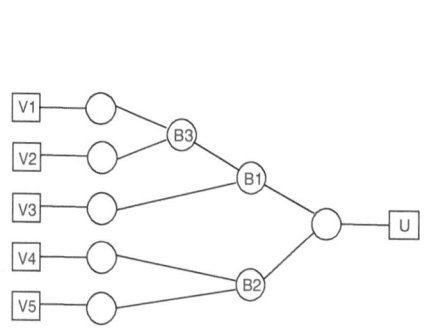

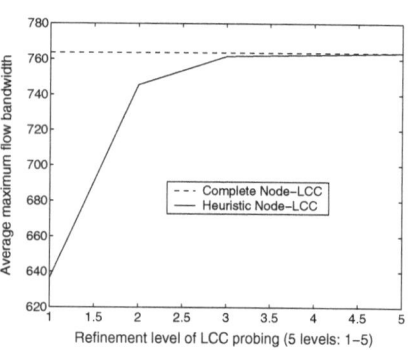

(a) Illustrates the phenomenon of hidden bottlenecks

(b) The rapid convergence of the accuracy of discovered node-based LCC

The node-based LCC are obtained in iterations of increasing refinement. In the first stage, the least refined set of LCC is determined. A node executes DSB once with the input of the set of k flows to all its neighbors. The k flows are partitioned into n bottleneck-sharing groups of flows, $g_1, g_2, \ldots, g_n$, with the respective bottleneck capacities $b_1, b_2, \ldots, b_n$. The LCC obtained are thus $C_1 = \{\sum_{e \in g_i} x_e \leq b_i\}_{i=1}^n$. Since DSB detects only the dominant bottlenecks, some bottlenecks cannot be discovered in the first stage. We give an example of this in Fig. 5(a); assume that node U is using DSB to probe for bottlenecks, and assume that bottleneck $B1$ has a smaller capacity than $B3$. When node U executes DSB with all 5 flows from its neighbors ($V1, \ldots, V5$), only the most dominant bottlenecks $B1$ and $B2$ can be discovered. To determine more refined LCC, node U must execute DSB with the input of only the flows from $V1$ and $V2$. This will be done in the second iteration of LCC refinement.

In order to guarantee that all bottlenecks are found, all possible subsets of flows in each group must be probed separately. However, the brute-force search is exponential in computational complexity and hence infeasible. We maintain a low complexity by randomly dividing each group g into two subsets and execute DSB on each subset. Our simulation results show that this non-exhaustive approach is not only efficient but also able to quickly find LCC that are negligibly close to the complete LCC.

The entire procedure of discovering node-based LCC is summarized as follows:

1. Start with G containing one single group including all k flows.
2. Execute DSB with each group g from G separately.
3. Every group g is partitioned into n sub-groups, from which n LCC derive; add to C (the growing set of LCC) those LCC not redundant with ones already in C.
4. Each sub-group of > 2 flows is randomly divided into two groups, add to G.
5. Repeat step 2 as long as more LCC can be found.

The simulation results for a network of 100 nodes with 30% overlay nodes are given in Fig. 5(b). In our simulation, LCC obtained at successive stages of refinement are used to compute maximum flows, and maximum flows are also computed from the complete node-based LCC. A large number of source and destination pairs are randomly chosen to compute maximum flows and the maximum flow bandwidths are averaged over all such pairs. In Fig. 5(b), the average maximum flow bandwidths for successive stages of LCC refinement are plotted, and compared to the average maximum flow bandwidth computed using complete node-based LCC. After only 5 refinement stages, the DSB LCC are as good as complete node-based LCC. The number of stages required for such accuracy may have something to do with the node degree limit, which is set at 6 in this simulation, because the node degree limit determines the maximum size of the groups given by DSB.

The complexity of the procedure depends on two factors: number of executions of DSB and number of flows probed. A reasonable estimate of the number of packets per DSB flow, based on reported empirical results in [9], is a few hundred packets. In our simulation, to obtain LCC that are 98% accurate of complete node-based LCC, DSB is executed a few times and the number of flows probed is around 10, on average. This translates to a total of a few thousands of probes used. It is worth noting, though, that the probing can be done passively. The overlay can begin data transmission without knowledge of LCC. The data transmission acts as passive probing and is used to determine more and more refined node-based LCC over time. The data dissemination topology can adapt to the discovered LCC.

6   Related Work

To the best of our knowledge, there has not been previous work on overlays with LCC. Prior work have without exception assumed an overlay model of independent link capacities, with no correlation. To alleviate overloading of shared underlying bottlenecks, the typical approach is to limit overlay node degrees. Several projects based on Distributed Hash Tables, e.g., CAN [11] and Chord [12], designed structured overlay networks. Distributed algorithms for general-purpose overlay construction were proposed by Young et al. in [13] and by Shen in [4], using heuristics of minimum spanning trees and neighbor selection based on unicast latency and bandwidth. Application-specific proposals have been made for overlay multicast [1], content distribution [3] and multimedia streaming [2]. Also relevant is work by Ratnasamy et al. [14]. A distributed binning scheme is designed to build unstructured overlays; the aim is to incorporate more topological awareness. This work differs from ours in focusing exclusively on latency. Due to the additive nature of the latency metric (the bandwidth metric is concave), overlay links are essentially independent of each other in latency. We focus on overlay link capacity correlation.

Common to all these proposals are heuristics that use unicast probing to select overlay routes with low latency or high bandwidth. They view and treat overlay links as independent. However, we propose a new overlay model and hence work upon a premise distinct from previous work.

7   Conclusions

We have introduced a new overlay model, LCC-overlay, that uses linear capacity constraints to efficiently and accurately represent real networks with link correlations. We showed that LCC-overlay has optimal quality, and even the restricted node-based LCC yields good quality, while overlays with no LCC has poor quality which deteriorates as network size increases. We proposed a distributed algorithm for LCC-overlay construction. We also studied the problems of widest-path and maximum-flow with LCC.

References

1. Y. Chu, S. G. Rao, S. Seshan, and H. Zhang, "A Case for End System Multicast," *IEEE Journal on Selected Areas in Communications*, pp. 1456–1471, October 2002.
2. M. Castro, P. Druschel, A.-M. Kermarrec, A. Nandi, A. Rowstron, and A. Singh, "Split-Stream: High-Bandwidth Multicast in Cooperative Environments," in *Proc. of the 19th ACM Symposium on Operating Systems Principles (SOSP 2003)*, October 2003.
3. J. Byers and J. Considine, "Informed Content Delivery Across Adaptive Overlay Networks," in *Proc. of ACM SIGCOMM*, August 2002.
4. K. Shen, "Structure Management for Scalable Overlay Service Construction," in *Proc. of NSDI*, 2004.
5. A. Medina, A. Lakhina, I. Matta, and J. Byers, *BRITE: Boston University Representative Internet Topology Generator*, http://www.cs.bu.edu/brite.
6. C. Faloutsos, M. Faloutsos, and P. Faloutsos, "On Power-Law Relationships of the Internet Topology," in *Proc. of ACM SIGCOMM*, August 1999.
7. M.S. Garey and D.S. Johnson, *Computers and Intractability: A Guide to the Theory of NP-Completeness*, W. H. Freeman, New York, 1979.
8. R.K. Ahuja, T.L. Magnanti, and J.B. Orlin, *Network Flows: Theory, Algorithms, and Applications*, Prentice-Hall, Englewood Cliffs NJ, 1993.
9. D. Katabi and C. Blake, "Inferring Congestion Sharing and Path Characteristics from Packet Interarrival Times," Tech. Rep., Laboratory of Computer Science, Massachusetts Institute of Technology, 2001.
10. D. Katabi, I. Bazzi, and X. Yang, "A passive approach for detecting shared bottlenecks," in *Proc. of ICCCN '01*, 2001.
11. S. Ratnasamy, M. Handley, R. Karp, and S. Shenker, "A Scalable Content-Addressable Network," in *Proc. of ACM SIGCOMM*, August 2001, pp. 149–160.
12. I. Stoica, R. Morris, M. F. Kaashoek, and H. Balakrishnan, "Chord: A scalable peer-to-peer lookup service for internet applications," in *Proc. of ACM SIGCOMM*, 2001.
13. A. Young, J. Chen, Z. Ma, A. Krishnamurthy, L. Peterson, and R. Wang, "Overlay Mesh Construction Using Interleaved Spanning Trees," in *Proc. of INFOCOM*, 2004.
14. S. Ratnasamy, M. Handley, R. Karp, and S. Shenker, "Topologically-Aware Overlay Construction and Server Selection," in *Proc. of the IEEE INFOCOM*, 2002.

A High-Throughput Overlay Multicast Infrastructure with Network Coding

Mea Wang, Zongpeng Li, and Baochun Li

Department of Electrical and Computer Engineering,
University of Toronto
{mea, arcane, bli}@eecg.toronto.edu

Abstract. Network coding has been recently proposed in information theory as a new dimension of the information multicast problem that helps achieve optimal transmission rate or cost. End hosts in overlay networks are natural candidates to perform network coding, due to its available computational capabilities. In this paper, we seek to bring theoretical advances in network coding to the practice of high-throughput multicast in overlay networks. We have completed the first real implementation of network coding in end hosts, as well as decentralized algorithms to construct the routing strategies and to perform random code assignment. Our experiences suggest that approaching maximum throughput with network coding is not only theoretically sound, but also practically promising. We also present a number of unique challenges in designing and realizing coded data dissemination, and corresponding solution techniques to address them.

1   Introduction

In recent years, application-layer overlay networks have emerged as important directions to evolve future network architectures, due to the *flexibility* of programming overlay nodes to execute any application-layer algorithm one has designed. This is in sharp contrast with the lack of flexibility at the IP layer. Regardless of the approach taken, most of the previous work in overlay or peer-to-peer networks focuses on accessing or disseminating information more efficiently over the current-generation Internet. We may attempt to find unicast paths with higher throughput or lower latency by passing through other overlay nodes, or to construct a high-quality overlay multicast tree from one source to multiple receivers [1, 2]. Depending on the applications, we may be disseminating bulk data, or streaming multimedia with stricter throughput and timing constraints [3].

Despite the contributions of existing work, we have still not answered one fundamental question: what is the maximum throughput one can achieve using overlay networks, given a single source with information to be disseminated, and a set of interested receivers? With the intuition of constructing an overlay multicast tree, it is easy to show that we still have residual idle network capacities after the tree is formed. In this paper, we consider the problem of distributing large volumes of data across overlay networks, and seeks to design and implement the best strategy to disseminate data from the source to the receivers with maximized throughput, even with the presence of the dynamic nature of overlays.

H. de Meer and N. Bhatti (Eds.): IWQoS 2005, LNCS 3552, pp. 37–53, 2005.
© IFIP International Federation for Information Processing 2005

One naturally starts with constructing multiple multicast trees from the source to the destinations with the best possible performance [4]. The fundamental advantage of multicast over unicast is that multicast employs intermediate nodes to *replicate* data packets to achieve higher transmission performance. It's a unique property of information flows to be replicable. In fact, we can do better than transmitting along multiple trees, by also taking advantage of another fundamental property of information flows: we can *code* multiple streams of information into one stream. In contrast, none of the normal commodity flows may be coded. *Network coding* extends the capabilities of network nodes in a communication session: from basic data forwarding (as in all unicast) and data replication (as in IP or overlay multicast), to *coding in finite fields*. It has been shown that, with linear codes, we may be able to achieve surprising results with respect to optimizing throughput for both delay-sensitive and delay-insensitive applications [5, 6, 7]. As overlay nodes can afford to code data flows computationally, they are ideal candidates to execute network coding based algorithms and protocols.

In this paper, we bring theoretical advances in network coding to realistic implementations, and present a complete set of network infrastructure and distributed protocols for coded data flow dissemination, which is ready to serve overlay applications that may benefit from high end-to-end transmission rate without high cost. Towards a realistic implementation of coded overlay flows, we present our algorithms for the construction of a transmission topology for network coding, and for randomized code matrix generation. Based on observations and experiences from our prototype system, we argue that network coding enables a more efficient way to compute the best transmission topologies to maximize session throughput and to utilize residual network capacities. Overlay multicast systems implemented in previous work generally employ a multicast tree or a multicast mesh (multi-tree) as the transmission topology, with encoding at source node only or no coding at all. To the best of our knowledge, our real-world implementation of multicast flows with network coding is the first in the research community. It is also the first real multicast system that targets mathematically provable near-optimal throughput, as contrasted to heuristically high throughput. We believe it is instrumental to develop additional insights of the practical implications of network coding and high-throughput data networking.

The remainder of this paper is organized as follows. In Sec. 2, we review related past research. In Sec. 3, we propose our decentralized algorithm to compute optimal routing strategies with network coding. We present our real-world implementation of both our algorithms and network coding itself in Sec. 4, followed by observations and experiences with such an implementation (Sec. 5). We conclude the paper in Sec. 6.

2   Related Work

Recent work on high-bandwidth data dissemination in overlay networks has focused on constructing multiple multicast trees or an overlay mesh, as exemplified by *SplitStream* [4], *Bullet* [8], as well as Digital Fountain [9]. In SplitStream, the original data is split into multiple stripes and is sent among interior-node-disjoint multicast trees to improve the throughput, such that all nodes share the burden of duplicating and forwarding data. Digital Fountain and Bullet uses source erasure codes and reconciles missing data among peers. This effectively leads to a topological overlay *mesh*. The designs depend on strong buffering capabilities to tradeoff end-to-end latency for achievable throughput. They work well on bulk data downloading or delay-insensitive streaming of media.

Another category of proposals have each overlay node establish k links to other overlay peers. Links established may be shortest (smallest latency), widest (highest bandwidth), randomly chosen, or a combination of the above. Previous experiences show that, always selecting the k best links may result in poor connectivity and a large diameter in the resulting mesh. This problem may be resolved by selecting some best links mixed with a small number of random links [10]. Young *et al.* [11] proposed a distributed algorithm to compute k Minimum Spanning Trees (k-MST), where edge weights correspond to the latency or loss rate. The k-MST mesh ensures the existence of k edge disjoint overlay paths between any pair of nodes.

If we assume an overlay node may encode and decode data using linear codes in Galois fields, we may then take advantage of the recent theoretical advances in *network coding* [12, 13]. As opposed to source coding, where data is encoded and decoded only at the source and destinations, respectively, network coding allows *every* node in the network to encode and decode data streams as necessary. The coding process uses *linear codes* in the Galois field, and includes two basic operations: the $+$ and $\cdot$ operations in the Galois field $GF(2^k)$. Since elements in a Galois field have a fixed-length representation, bytes in flows do not increase in length after being encoded.

While information flows differ from normal commodity flows in that they may be replicated and encoded, the transmission of information flows still exhibits an underlying network flow structure. Ahlswede *et al.* [12] and Koetter *et al.* [13] prove that, a multicast rate χ can be achieved for the entire multicast session if and only if it can be achieved from the sender to each of the multicast receivers independently. With this theorem, computing the routing strategy to maximize session throughput can be transformed into a sequence of maximum flow computations, which is not only polynomial-time solvable, but also allows fully distributed solutions. If flows to different receivers share some links in the network, the conflict may be resolved through network coding.

Recently, a number of multicast algorithms [6, 7, 14, 15] have been proposed to utilize the underlying network flow structure of coded multicast to efficiently achieve high transmission rate or low cost. Gkantsidis *et al.* [16] also propose to employ network coding in large-scale content distribution in peer-to-peer networks, to eliminate the need of strategic peer reconciliation. Our work in this paper focuses instead on high-throughput with controlled delay.

3   Computing the Optimal Routing Strategy

In this work, we achieve the objective of maximizing end-to-end session throughput in two phases: constructing the transmission topology, and designing the suitable coding strategy for data dissemination using a randomized code assignment algorithm. The network coding theorem reviewed in Sec. 2 establishes the underlying connection between multicast flow routing and network flows. Consequently, the computation of the multicast rate and the optimal multicast transmission topology is separable into a number of maximum flow computations. The maximum achievable throughput of a multi-cast session is the smallest throughput among all source-destination pairs. Given such a transmission topology, the final question is how data should be disseminated and coded. In this section, we present algorithms for all phases that may be realistically applied to compute the optimal transmission topology for coded overlay flows.

3.1   The Maximum Flow Problem

Maximum flow is a well studied problem in the theory of network flows. Given a directed network $G = (V, A)$ and nodes $u, v \in V$, the maximum flow from u to v is the maximum rate at which flows can be shipped from u to v along capacitied arcs in G. In the *min-cost flow* problem, which is a more general version of the max-flow problem, a cost is associated with every unit flow shipped through an arc, and a given flow rate is to be achieved while introducing minimum link costs. A min-cost flow algorithm may be used to compute the maximum flow, by inserting a virtual arc (*a feedback link*) from receiver v to sender u with cost -1, while setting other arc costs to zero. We employ an ϵ-relaxation based algorithm [17] to compute the max-rate multicast topology with minimum bandwidth consumption. Our algorithm is amenable to fully distributed and fully asynchronous implementations.

In our notation, each link $(i, j) \in A$ is associated with bandwidth capacity b_{ij}. f_{ij} is the flow rate from node i to node j, c_{ij} is the cost of transmitting a unit flow via link (i, j), g_i is the flow excess on node i, and p_i is the dual variable acting as unit price charged for flow excess at node i.

3.2   Computing the Transmission Topology

The first step towards maximum-rate multicast transmission is to compute a routing topology indicating the amount of bandwidth required on each link in the network. Given this topology, we assign flows on each link according to the allocated bandwidth and eventually transmit the data. In this section, we focus on computing the transmission topology and bandwidth allocation.

Unicast Sessions. In the case of unicast sessions, each link $(i, j) \in A$ is initialized with flow $f_{ij} = 0$ and cost $c_{ij} = 0$. We then add a feedback link with $b_{ds} = f_{ds} = \alpha$, and $c_{ds} = -|D|$, where α is a constant with any value known to be larger than the achievable maximum flow rate and $|D|$ is the maximum diameter of the network (in number of hops). For each node i, the flow excess g_i is calculated as $\sum_{(j,i) \in A} f_{ji} - \sum_{(i,j) \in A} f_{ij}$, and the price p_i is initialized to 0. After initialization, each node with a positive flow excess ($g_i > 0$) executes the algorithm in the Table 1. The algorithm terminates when every node has zero flow excess [17].

Multicast Sessions. We are now ready to generalize the algorithm to compute a transmission topology that seeks to achieve maximized throughput for any communication session. In a multicast session, data are sent from the source to a group of interested receivers at the same rate in the overlay. To achieve maximized multicast throughput, we first need to identify the maximum achievable throughput between each source-destination pair, using the previously described algorithm for unicast sessions. Given

Table 1. The ϵ-relaxation based min-cost max-flow algorithm

Each node i maintains a price vector of its direct upstream and
downstream nodes and a capacity vector of incident links, and execute:

1 **while** $(g_i > 0)$
2   Scan all links for an outgoing links (i, j) such that
         $p_i = p_j + c_{ij} + \epsilon$ and $f_{ij} < c_{ij}$,
         or an incoming link (j, i) such that
         $p_i = p_j - c_{ji} + \epsilon$ and $f_{ij} > 0$.
3   **if** (such outgoing link (i, j) is found)
         Decrease excess by increasing f_{ij}
4          $\delta = \min(g_i, c_{ij} - f_{ij})$;
5          $f_{ij} = f_{ij} + \delta$;
6          $g_i = g_i - \delta$;
7          $g_j = g_j + \delta$;
8   **else if** (such incoming link (j, i) is found)
         Decrease excess by reducing f_{ji}
9          $\delta = \min(g_i, f_{ji})$;
10         $f_{ji} = f_{ji} - \delta$;
11         $g_i = g_i - \delta$;
12         $g_j = g_j + \delta$;
13   **else**
         Increase price of node i
14         $p_i = \min_{\xi \in R^+ \cup R^-} \xi$,
         where,
           $R^+ = \{p_j + c_{ij} + \epsilon\}|(i, j) \in A$ and $f_{ij} < b_{ij}\}$,
           $R^- = \{p_j - c_{ji} + \epsilon\}|(j, i) \in A$ and $f_{ij} > 0\}$,

the maximum achievable throughput for each destination, the throughput of a multicast session corresponds to the smallest throughput achievable to all destinations [12, 13]. Since the maximum throughput for each destination may be different from each other, they need to be reduced to match the prevailing multicast flow rate.

We introduce a set of variables to maintain the status of each link with respect to each destination. The cost and bandwidth capacity are still denoted by c_{ij} and b_{ij} respectively on each directed link (i, j). We let f_{ij}^k be the flow rate on arc (i, j) serving destination k, g_i^k be the flow excess on node i in serving destination k, and p_i^k be the price on node i in serving destination k. The min-cost flow algorithm remains unchanged, except that we apply the algorithm independently for each source-destination pair.

When the min-cost flow algorithm terminates for all destinations, the maximum achievable throughput f_k of a source-destination pair is the flow rate on the feedback link. The maximum achievable throughput is $f_{\max} = \min\{f_k\}$. To tune the transmission topology to conserve unnecessary bandwidth, we reduce the flow from the source to destination k by $\delta = f_k - f_{\max}$. We initiate the flow reduction process by reducing the flow on each feedback link by δ. The reduction algorithm is presented in Table 2.

Table 2. The flow reduction algorithm for multicast sessions

	for (each destination k)
1	$I_i = \phi$
2	Scan all incoming links (j, i) such that link (j, i) serve flows for destination k
3	$I_i = I_i \cup (j, i)$
4	$I_{total} = \sum_{j \in I_i} f_{ji}$
5	$O_i = \phi$
6	Scan all outgoing links (i, j) such that link (i, j) serve flows for destination k
7	$O_i = O_i \cup (i, j)$
8	$O_{total} = \sum_{j \in O_i} f_{ij}$
9	$D = O_{total} - I_{total}$
10	**while** $(D > 0)$
11	Scan all links (j, i) in O_i such that $f_{ij} > 0$
12	$\delta = min\{f_{ij}, D\}$
13	$f_{ij} = f_{ij} - \delta$
14	$D = D - \delta$

3.3   Data Dissemination

Each transmission topology computed by the min-cost flow algorithm provides information not only on the maximum achievable throughput of a multicast session, but also on the amount of bandwidth to be reserved on each link. Notice that these topologies are computed independently based on the assumption that each topology has the privilege to utilize up to 100% of the currently available link capacity. Bandwidth contention problem occurs when two or more transmission topologies share links. For instance, we require $b_1 + b_2$ units of bandwidth on the link shared by two destinations, where b_1 and b_2 are the amount of bandwidth required by each destination. We are pushing the limit of the link capacity if $b_1 + b_2 > b_{ij}$. Fortunately, network coding resolves this issue by allowing coexistence of multiple flows. The coded flow requires no more than $max\{b_1, b_2\}$ units of bandwidth on such link.

There are still a few remaining problems to be addressed. First, the transmission topology specifies only the amount of flows to be assigned on each link, but not the actual coded flows. We thus need an algorithm to perform flow assignment. Second, if each node simply forwards all flows that it has received, with high probability the destinations are unable to successfully reconstruct the original data. Though there exist centralized polynomial time algorithms that guarantee optimal code assignment [18], it is not desirable in a realistic implementation of network coding due to their high complexity. We propose a randomized and distributed algorithm to assign codes on each overlay node, so that flows may be encoded and decoded appropriately, with significantly less complexity.

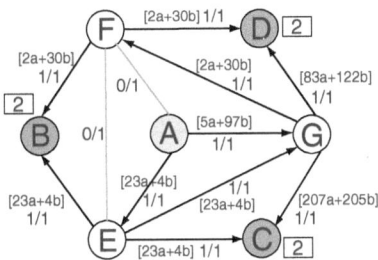

Fig. 1. Illustration of randomized code assignment

Without loss of generality, we explain the algorithm with an example shown in Fig. 1. Each link is labeled with both its capacity and the reserved bandwidth, as computed by algorithms proposed in Sec. 3.2. Before disseminating data, the source node A needs to determine how many *original flows* (the maximum achievable throughput) the transmission topology can handle. In our example, we have two original flows, labeled a and b, since the intended throughput of this transmission topology is 2.

First, each node generates a code matrix in a randomized fashion, which remains static unless the network environment changes. The number of rows and columns correspond to the number of incoming and outgoing flows at this node, respectively. Each entry in the matrix is independently and uniformly taken from $GF(2^8)$. Next, the source node initiates the computation of flow content on each link, which is determined by both incoming flows and the code matrix at its tail node. Therefore at each node, the outgoing flows can be determined by taking a production of the incoming flow coefficient matrix and the code matrix. For example, at node G we have:

$$M_O = C_D \cdot M_I = \begin{pmatrix} 27 & 173 \\ 112 & 85 \\ 98 & 164 \end{pmatrix} \begin{pmatrix} 23 & 4 \\ 5 & 97 \end{pmatrix} = \begin{pmatrix} 207 & 205 \\ 2 & 30 \\ 83 & 122 \end{pmatrix}$$

Matrix operations are all computed over the Galois field GF(2^8). More detailed discussions on performing finite field operations can be found in [19]. Note that such matrix production needs to be performed only once upon session set-up, unless network dynamics occur. After successful execution of the algorithm, each destination should receive exactly n flows if there are n original flows. The coefficient matrix of incoming flows is then inverted at each receiver to serves as its decoding matrix. The product of the decoding matrix with each incoming flow yields the original flow.

3.4   Coding Challenges

So far, we have implicitly assumed links selected by the optimal routing strategy form a directed acyclic graph. However, a cycle in the routing topology may introduce a deadlock for code generation. An simple example is shown in Fig. 2(a), in which nodes B and C each expects a flow description from the other.

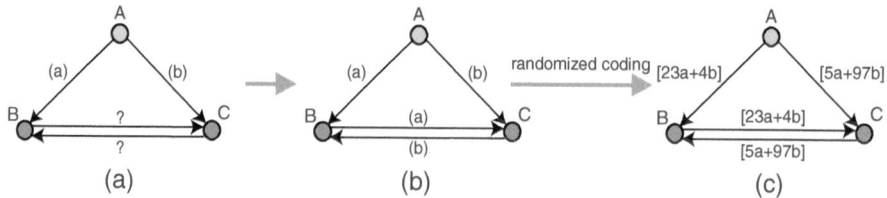

Fig. 2. An example of avoiding coding cycles

To address this problem, we label each link with a list of receivers it is serving, during the max-flow computation phase. Consequently, each node constructs a $0, 1$-matrix representing the input-output dependence relation among its incident flows. Only entries with value 1 will then be replaced by a uniform random symbol taken from $GF(2^8)$. The new solution applied to the previous example is shown in Fig. 2(b) and (c).

3.5   Adapting to Dynamic Variations

Our algorithms are based on the knowledge of link capacity. Any realistically measured link capacities, however, may not reflect the actual link capacities between two nodes in the underlying physical network. For example, if two overlay links share the same physical link in the IP network, results from independent available bandwidth probes will not be accurate when both links are utilized by the overlay mesh. Furthermore, even if all overlay link capacities are independent, they may still fluctuate over time, due to cross traffic beyond the control of the overlay.

We highlight the fact that our algorithms naturally adapt to such uncertainty and network dynamics very well. If a certain link capacity turns out to be different than what was expected, the ϵ-relaxation algorithm may resume with cached states, including flow rates and node prices. Since the new optimal state is usually not far from the old one, convergence speed is much higher than re-computing the new multicast topology.

4   Implementation

We have experimentally implemented all the algorithms proposed in Sec. 3. To the best of our knowledge, this work represents the first work on a realistic implementation of network coding. In this section, we discuss our observations, experiences and challenges encountered during this implementation. We have implemented two main components, as illustrated in Fig. 3: (1) a generic application-layer message switch, with the multi-threaded capability of handling and switching multiple incoming and outgoing flows; and (2) an implementation of the architectural design supporting coded overlay flows.

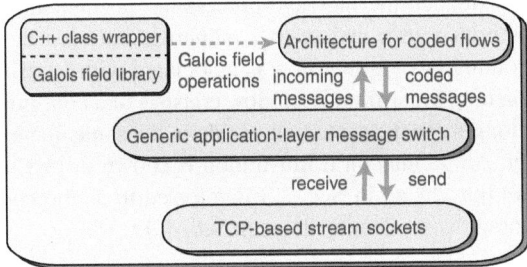

Fig. 3. The overlay network infrastructure

4.1   Infrastructure

To simplify the implementation of both the algorithms for routing strategy and network coding, we have developed an infrastructure to reduce the mundane work. These include multi-threaded programming for message forwarding engines, failure detection and reaction, measurement of delay and throughput, as well as monitoring and deploying facilities.

To facilitate the switching of application-layer messages from multiple incoming connections to multiple outgoing connections, we have designed a high-performance application-layer message processing facility in UNIX, to support live data sessions from the source to the receivers.

The salient capabilities of the application-layer switch are three-fold: (1) *Message processing*. The application-layer message switch is able to efficiently switch data from upstream nodes to downstream nodes, and process each of them using algorithm-specific implementations. (2) *Measurements of performance metrics*. Important performance metrics such as per-link throughput and latency are measured by the switch. (3) *Emulation of bandwidth availability*. To verify correctness of the algorithm implementations, we sometimes prefer to perform preliminary tests of the algorithm under controlled environments, in which node and link characteristics are more predictable. The switch supports precise emulations of bandwidth availability on each overlay link. For detailed discussions on the switch design and implementation, we refer the readers to our recent work on *ioverlay* [20].

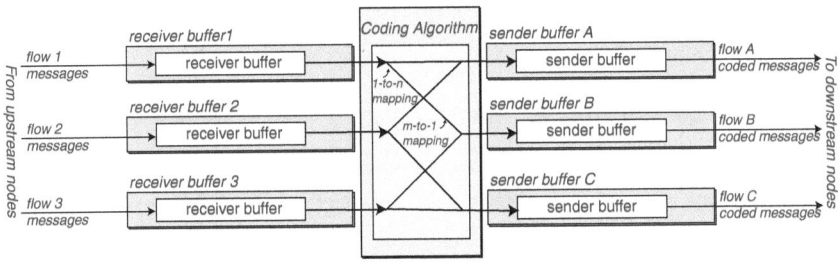

Fig. 4. Switch design: m-to-m mapping among input and output coded flows

We have further extended the message processing mechanism to support network coding, by allowing both 1-to-n and m-to-1 mappings between incoming and outgoing flows. Each incoming or outgoing flow is associated with a buffer managed by our customized FIFO queuing algorithm. Each flow consists of a continuous stream of messages. Messages belonging to the same flow reside in the same queue and are processed in their arrival order. An architectural illustration is shown in Fig. 4, in which the design for coded flows introduced in Sec. 3.3 is referred to as the *coding algorithm* for simplicity. We discuss how to identify flows in Sec. 4.3.

4.2   Routing Strategy

In computing the routing topology, the minimum assumption is that each node is aware of its one overlay-hop neighbors as well as the cost and capacity on its incident links. For any multicast session with m destinations, each node maintains m sets of local information. These information include node price p_i^k, flow excess g_i^k, and flow rate f_{ij}^k as defined in Sec. 3.

During the initialization phase of a multicast session, the source node s sends a fInitiate message to each destination d_k directly. On receipt of the fInitiate message, the node d_k adds to the source node s an outgoing link with $b_{ds} = f_{ds}^k = \alpha$, and $c_{ds} = \gamma$. In other words, the destination node d injects flows into the source to start the min-cost flow algorithm. For each neighbor, the source node then computes δ and sends the results in a fPush message to the corresponding neighbor. When a node receives the fPush message, it applies the min-cost flow algorithm to update all its local variables, and sends the value of δ in an fPush message to push flows on each link. The destination nodes never push any flow away. The flows on each link converge once the number of flows received by the destination and the number of flows sent by the source are the same. Links that are not selected by the algorithm will have *zero* flows on them. Eventually, the links with a positive flow rate form the transmission topology with the maximized throughput.

After determining the maximum flow between each source-destination pair, we need to perform flow reduction if max-flow rates toward different receivers do not agree. A few additional control messages are introduced into the implementation of our distributed algorithm. We explain the implementation with a representative example in Fig. 5(a), in which each link is labeled with the flow rates it's serving for destination B, C, and D respectively. The source collects the optimal throughput from each destina-

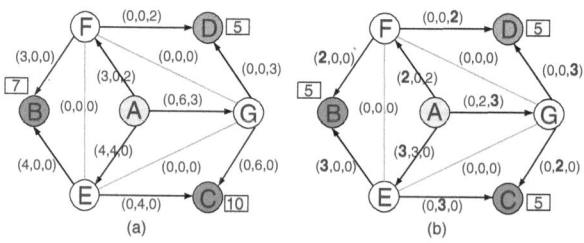

Fig. 5. Reducing flows

tion using the `fReport` message, and compute the maximum multicast throughput as $\min(7, 10, 5) = 5$.

The source node sends a `fReduce` message along each network flow, with the appropriate value for flow reduction (initially 2 in the flow to B and 5 in the flow to C). If a node i can not reduce the specified amount by reducing flow rate at a single outgoing link, it reduces rates on more than one outgoing links, and relay a `fReduce` message along each of them, with the total flow reduction amount sum up to the amount being reduced at i. Result of this reduction procedure is shown in Fig. 5(b). The numbers in bold face indicate the amount of flows each link must serve. Again, the computation of the optimal multicast transmission topology is based on the assumption that each node can support network coding. In Fig. 5(b), the optimal throughput 5 can be achieved for each of the destinations.

4.3   Network Coding

The randomized network coding algorithm presented in Sec. 3.3 is almost ready for direct implementation. Several challenges are still worth mentioning, though. We continue to use our network coding example, as shown in Fig. 1. The first problem is flow identification at each node. Recall that each flow in the transmission topology is a linear combination of the original flows, in the form of $\sum_i \lambda_i f_i$. Hence, each flow can be uniquely identified by the coefficient vector λ, referred to as the *flow description*. The flows are designed to be *self-explanatory*, in that the flow description of the flows are stored in the application-layer header of data messages, as an array of bytes, each byte representing one coefficient. In our example, the flow $23a + 4b$ can be represented by an array of two bytes $[23, 4]$.

Each data message may be coded with several other messages, from the same queue or other queues, to produce a message of an outgoing flow. Our second challenge is to keep the message in the queue long enough for each outgoing flow, while controlling the size of the queue as small as possible at all time. To this end, we modify the message buffer by attaching a reference counter, initialized to n, to each message as it is queued into the appropriate buffer. Every time a message is used to code a new outgoing message, its reference counter is decremented by 1. A message is deleted as soon as the its reference counter reaches zero. For the jth incoming flow on a node, the value of n is the number of nonzero entries in the jth column of the code matrix. More precisely, a positive value presented at the (i, j) cell in the code matrix means that the jth incoming flow is required to produce the ith outgoing flow.

Conventionally, only the message at the front of a FIFO queue is available to the algorithm. This raises the message blocking problem, which causes the algorithm to serve either all outgoing flows or nothing. Consider two outgoing flows: flow Out_1 requires coding messages from all incoming flows A, B, and C; and flow Out_2 is just a duplication of flow A. Thus, the reference counters for messages of flow A are initialized to 2, whereas the reference counters for messages of flow B and C are initialized to 1. In the case where the buffer for flow A contains several messages, and the buffers for flow B and C are empty, this node is ready to serve flow Out_2, but not flow Out_1. Consequently, none of the messages, except the first one in A can be forwarded to Out_2 until messages become ready in B and C. The same problem occurs, but to a less extent, when the arrival rate varies among different flows. To overcome this problem, we allow algorithms to peek any message in the queue, but must process them in a sequential order.

The third challenge is to ensure the correctness of the decoded messages received at the destinations. At each node, the actual outgoing data messages are computed as linear combinations of the incoming messages, using the code matrix, and over GF(2^8). In Fig. 1, the outgoing message of node G $m_{out}^j(j = 1, 2, 3)$ is produced by taking a message $m_{in}^i(i = 1, 2)$ from each incoming flow i as input, and compute $m_{out}^1 = 27 \cdot m_{in}^1 + 173 \cdot m_{in}^2$, $m_{out}^2 = 112 \cdot m_{in}^1 + 85 \cdot m_{in}^2$, and $m_{out}^3 = 98 \cdot m_{in}^1 + 164 \cdot m_{in}^2$. Since TCP connections preserve message ordering as they are originally generated, the incoming messages are coded in the same order as they are received. For example, the ith message of flow $23a + 4b$ is always coded with the ith message of flow $5a + 97b$. Otherwise, the destination node will not be able to decode and restore the original messages correctly.

5   Evaluation

In this section, we perform an empirical study of various performance aspects of coded flows. we have completed a realistic implementation of our proposed algorithms, and conducted a series of experiments on a cluster of dual-CPU Pentium 4 Xeon 2.4GHz servers. The topology of the test networks are generated using the BRITE topology generator [21], with up to 100 overlay nodes.

The parameters we use include: (1) The number of original flows from the source to all receivers in the optimal routing strategy, henceforth referred to as *maxflow*. (2) The message size, which is the number of data bytes in typical messages of a particular flow, and (3) The session size, which is the number of sender and receivers in a session.

For the purpose of comparison, we implemented an alternative of the k-MST algorithm: rather than computing k minimum spanning trees, we devise and implement a distributed algorithm to compute k spanning trees with the maximum bandwidth, referred to as k-*MaxST*. Since we seek to maximize the throughput of data dissemination rather than minimizing latency, we naturally would like to employ the *widest* selection criterion, in order to achieve high throughput.

5.1   Performance of Routing Strategy Computation

The message overhead introduced by our protocol for computing the optimal routing strategy is less than 12KB per node on average. Such low overhead is due to the reason that messages are passed between nodes only when the prices of flows and nodes are being updated. Fig. 6(a) illustrates the message overhead required to compute the optimal routing strategy is closely related to both the network size and session size. As the network size increases, the message overhead grows linearly. The optimal routing strategy between each pair of source and destination nodes are computed separately. For every additional destination, the message overhead is increased.

The message overhead is also affected by the network topology. Depending on the number of nodes involved in the optimal transmission topology, the message overhead may vary. As shown in Fig. 6(a), the total message overhead is increased by 400KB in

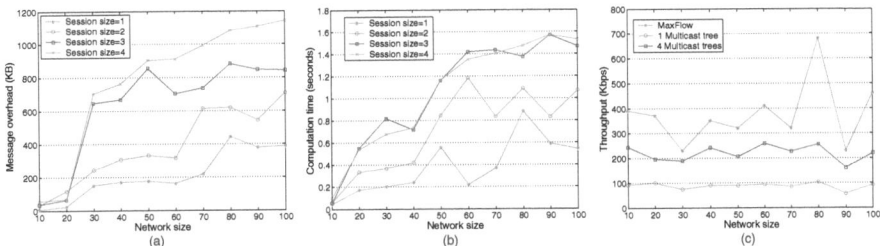

Fig. 6. (a) Messages required to compute the optimal strategy for different session sizes and network sizes; (b) computation time for the routing strategy over networks of different sizes; and (c) the throughput of the optimal strategy in comparison with k multicast trees for the session size of 3 in networks of various sizes

the network of size 30 when the session size is increased from 2 to 3. This is mainly because the optimal routing strategy between the source and the third destination introduces a number of new nodes to the final optimal routing strategy.

We count the computation time of the algorithm from the time a request is sent to the source node until the time the routing strategy is fully established, *i.e.*, when all nodes have no excess flows. The time plotted in Fig. 6(b) shows that the computation time again depends on both the network size and the session size. With more destinations, a larger number of messages are exchanged and processed. Note that the delay of less than 1.6 seconds is introduced only once upon session set up, and does not apply to the transmission of data messages.

The theoretical achievable throughput of the routing strategy is presented in Fig. 6(c) in comparison with single multicast tree and four multicast trees. We observe that our routing strategy always enjoys the highest throughput regardless of the network size.

5.2 Coding Delay

In coded overlay flows, the end-to-end delay depends on not only the TCP delay, but also the coding delay introduced at each routing hop. Therefore, we measure the coding time on each node and the end-to-end delay. We present the average coding time per node and and the code-delay ratio under various parameter settings. The *code-delay* ratio is the ratio between the sum of the coding time on all nodes and the end-to-end delay. This sum is the upper bound of the end-to-end coding time since non-sequential nodes perform coding in parallel.

To quantitatively evaluate the average coding time per node, we vary the size of the application-layer data messages from 1KB to 35KB, and measure the time to code each message. The results are presented in Table 3. We observe that the computation time increases linearly as the data size increases, but they are all on the order of microseconds, which is insignificant compared to typical end-to-end latencies over wide-area networks.

To evaluate the code-delay ratio, we set the available bandwidth on each link in the overlay within the range (1KB, 10KB). In order to achieve the optimal throughput,

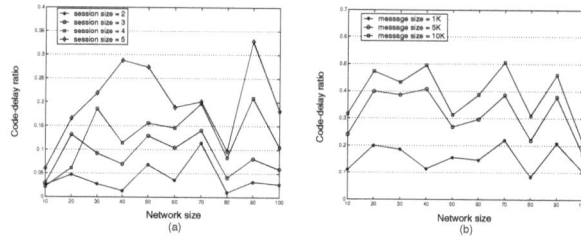

Fig. 7. The code-delay ratio of: (a) sessions with different sizes; and (b) sessions with different message sizes

Table 3. Average computational overhead for coding one message at one node over different message sizes

Size	1	5	10	15	20	25	30	35
Computation time (μsec)	224	1057	2194	3288	4447	5374	6256	7664

the message size is set to 1KB so that each link can accommodate as many flows as possible. We start the experiment by selecting a pair of source and destination node. One additional receiver node is added to the session for each repetition of the experiment. We set the maxflow of each session to be within the range (11, 20). In each experiment, we collect the times that each node has spent on performing Galois field coding as well as the end-to-end delay.

Nodes in larger networks spend less time on network coding since the flows are scattered in the network. In other words, network coding is performed in a more distributed fashion in larger networks. In Fig. 7(a), we have observed that the coding time becomes more significant as the session size increases. This is because each additional receiver requires at least k more flows in the network, where k is the maxflow from the source to all receivers.

We further investigate the effect of message size in various network settings. We vary message size from 1KB to 5KB and then to 10KB. The session size is set to 4, and the maxflow is within the (11-20) range throughout this experiment. We compare the coding and end-to-end delay of sessions with different message sizes. As shown in Fig. 7(b), the larger message sizes introduce higher coding time at each node, but the amount of increase is rather moderate, which is consistent with the results in Table 3.

5.3   Throughput

The key advantage of coded overlay flows is the improvement in end-to-end throughput. Theoretically, the throughput achieved by coded overlay flows approaches mathematically-provable optimality. In order to evaluate the achievable throughput of our algorithms, especially the optimal routing strategy, we conduct a set of experiments under various settings.

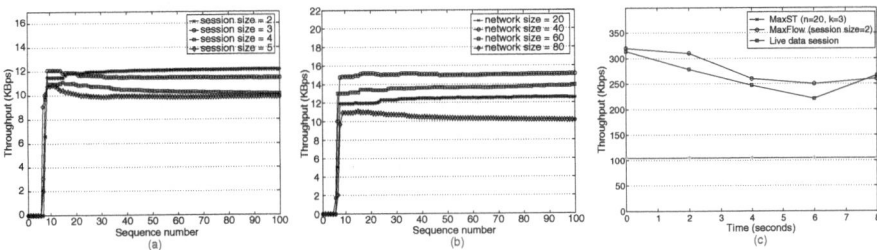

Fig. 8. The throughput of (a) sessions with different sizes; (b) sessions with size = 4, message size = 1KB, and maximum achievable throughput = $(11 - 20)$KBps in different networks; and (c) coded overlay flow in comparison with 1-MaxST and maxflow

To see how the multicast throughput computed by our algorithm varies with more nodes joining the multicast session, we test the algorithm with increasing session sizes. For each network size, we select one node as the source node and add one new destination node to multicast group as the session size increases. The throughput performance over time (in increasing order of the sequence number) under different parameter settings is shown in Fig. 8(a). These throughput are collected from a network of size 80. The optimal throughput of the session of size 2 is 12Kbps. We observe that the throughput of a session quickly converges to the optimal throughput after starting up, and remains stable throughout the session. The throughput decreases only when the newly added destination has lower end-to-end throughput with the source node than the throughput of the smaller session size. Such situation arises when a node with a small incident link capacity joins the multicast group. Otherwise, a high flow rate to each destination can be concurrently achieved, without interference with each other, thanks to network coding.

To further verify the scalability of coded overlay flows in terms of network sizes, we run experiments in various networks, and evaluate the throughput measurement of the first 100 messages of sessions with fixed size in different networks. For fair comparison, we control the maximum achievable throughput of the multicast session to be within the range 11Kbps and 20Kbps. Fig. 8(b) provides additional evidence for the optimality of the throughput achieved by coded overlay flows. Therefore, we claim that the coded overlay flows can achieve maximized throughput with minimum tradeoff of end-to-end delay.

Finally, we show the performance of all three algorithms working together over time. We start with a network of size 20, and select two links to decrease their bandwidth every 2 seconds. As shown in Fig. 8(c), the maximum throughput of the single multicast tree remains unchanged. It is because the bandwidth on the selected links are not decreased below the bottleneck link bandwidth of the corresponding tree. However, the throughput of a multicast session of size 2 is indeed affected by the bandwidth variation. The actual throughput for a *live data streaming session* with randomized network coding of this multicast session is also given in Fig. 8(c). We observe that the throughput of a *live coded data session* is rather close to the optimal throughput estimated by the optimal routing strategy. This justifies the case for coded overlay flows in realistic experiments.

6   Concluding Remarks

In this paper, we have established the case for coded overlay flows, which uses network coding to achieve maximized end-to-end throughput in multicast sessions. We propose distributed algorithms to construct the optimal transmission topology, and design corresponding coding strategies for data dissemination. Our main contribution is the implementation of coding in the Galois field and all our proposed algorithms in a realistic overlay testbed, which suggests that using coded overlay flows to maximize throughput is not only theoretically sound, but realistically feasible. To our knowledge, this is the first attempt towards implementing network coded flows in overlay networks.

References

1. Y. H. Chu, S. G. Rao, and H. Zhang, "A Case for End System Multicast," in *Proceedings of the ACM SIGMETRICS*, June 2000, pp. 1–12.
2. S. Banerjee, B. Bhattacharjee, and C. Kommareddy, "Scalable Application Layer Multicast," in *Proceedings of the ACM SIGCOMM*, August 2002, pp. 205–217.
3. S. Banerjee, C. Kommareddy, K. Kar, B. Bhattacharjee, and S. Khuller, "Construction of an Efficient Overlay Multicast Infrastructure for Real-Time Applications," in *Proceedings of IEEE INFOCOM*, 2003.
4. M. Castro, P. Druschel, A.-M. Kermarrec, A. Nandi, A. Rowstron, and A. Singh, "Split-Stream: High-Bandwidth Multicast in Cooperative Environments," in *Proceedings of ACM SOSP*, October 2003.
5. S. Y. R. Li, R. W. Yeung, and N. Cai, "Linear Network Coding," *IEEE Transactions on Information Theory*, vol. 49, pp. 371, 2003.
6. Z. Li, B. Li, D. Jiang, and L. C. Lau, "On Achieving Optimal Throughput with Network Coding," in *Proceedings of IEEE INFOCOM*, March 2005.
7. Z. Li and B. Li, "Efficient and Distributed Computation of Maximum Multicast Rates," in *Proceedings of IEEE INFOCOM*, March 2005.
8. D. Kostic, A. Rodriguez, J. Albrecht, and A. Vahdat, "Bullet: High Bandwidth Data Dissemination Using an Overlay Mesh," in *Proceedings of ACM SOSP*, October 2003.
9. J. Byers, J. Considine, M. Mitzenmacher, and S. Rost, "Informed Content Delivery Across Adaptive Overlay Networks," in *Proceedings of ACM SIGCOMM*, 2002.
10. K. Shen, "Structure Management for Scalable Overlay Service Construction," in *Proceedings of NSDI*, 2004.
11. A. Young, J. Chen, Z. Ma, L. Peterson A. Krishnamurthy, and R. Y. Wang, "Overlay Mesh Construction Using Interleaved Spanning Trees," in *Proceedings of the IEEE INFOCOM*, March 2004.
12. R. Ahlswede, N. Cai, S. R. Li, and R. W. Yeung, "Network Information Flow," *IEEE Transactions on Information Theory*, vol. 46, no. 4, pp. 1204–1216, July 2000.
13. R. Koetter and M. Médard, "An Algebraic Approach to Network Coding," *IEEE/ACM Transactions on Networking*, vol. 11, no. 5, pp. 782–795, October 2003.
14. D. Lun, N. Ratnakar, R. Koetter, M. Médard, E. Ahmed, and H. Lee, "Achieving Minimum-Cost Multicast: A Decentralized Approach Based on Network Coding," in *Proceedings of IEEE INFOCOM*, March 2005.
15. Y. Wu, P. A. Chou, Q. Zhang, K. Jain, W. Zhu, and S. Kung, "Network Planning in Wireless Ad Hoc Networks: A Cross-Layer Approach," *IEEE Journal on Selected Areas in Communication*, vol. 23, no. 1, January 2005.

16. C. Gkantsidis and P. Rodriguez, "Network Coding for Large Scale Content Distribution," in *Proceeding of IEEE INFOCOM*, March 2005.
17. D. P. Bertsekas and J. N. Tsitsiklis, *Parallel and Distributed Computation: Numerical Methods*, Prentice Hall, 1989.
18. P. Sanders, S. Egner, and L. Tolhuizen, "Polynomial Time Algorithm for Network Information Flow," in *Proceedings of the 15th ACM Symposium on Parallelism in Algorithms and Architectures*, 2003.
19. J. S. Plank, "A Tutorial on Reed-Solomon Coding for Fault-Tolerance in RAID-like Systems," in *Software - Practice & Experience*, September 1997, pp. 27(9):995–1012.
20. B. Li, J. Guo, and M. Wang, "iOverlay: A Lightweight Middleware Infrastructure for Overlay Application Implementations," in *Proceedings of the 5th ACM/IFIP/USENIX International Middleware Conference (Middleware)*, October 2004.
21. A. Medina, A. Lakhina, I. Matta, and J. Byers, *BRITE: Boston University Representative Internet Topology Generator*, http://www.cs.bu.edu/brite.

On Topological Design of Service Overlay Networks

Arunabha Sen[1], Ling Zhou[1], Bin Hao[1], Bao Hong Shen[1], and Samrat Ganguly[2]

[1] Dept. of Computer Science,
Arizona State University, Tempe, AZ 85287, USA
{asen, ling.zhou, binhao, bao}@asu.edu
[2] Dept. of Broadband & Mobile Networks,
NEC Laboratories, USA
samrat@nec-lab.com

Abstract. The notion of *service overlay network* (SON) was proposed recently to alleviate difficulties encountered in providing end-to-end *quality of service* (QoS) guarantees in the current Internet architecture. The SONs are able to provide QoS guarantees by purchasing bandwidth from individual network domains and building a logical end-to-end data delivery infrastructure on top of existing Internet. In this paper, we consider a generalized framework for SON, which is categorized based on three different characteristics: a) single-homed/multi-homed end-system b) usage-based/leased cost model and c) capacitated/uncapacitated network. We focus on the algorithmic analysis of the topology design problem for the above generalized SON. We prove that for certain case, polynomial-time optimal algorithm exists, while for other cases, the topology design problem is NP-complete. For the NP-complete cases, we provide approximation algorithms and experimental results.

1 Introduction

The Internet today comprises multiple independently operated networks (autonomous systems or domains) joined at the peering points. The independently operated networks (often Internet Service Providers, ISPs) may have an interest in providing QoS guarantees within their own network, but they do not have any incentive to provide service guarantees to customers of other remote ISPs. The notion of *service overlay network* (SON) was proposed in [3] to overcome this problem, so that end-to-end guarantees can be provided to the customers of different ISPs. Service overlay network is an outcome of the recent studies on overlay networks such as Detour [10], Resilient Overlay Network [1] and Internet Indirection Infrastructure [11].

The SONs are able to provide end-to-end QoS guarantees by building a logical delivery infrastructure on top of the existing transport network by purchasing bandwidth from individual network domains. The SONs provide various flexibilities in deploying and supporting new services by allowing the creation of

H. de Meer and N. Bhatti (Eds.): IWQoS 2005, LNCS 3552, pp. 54–68, 2005.

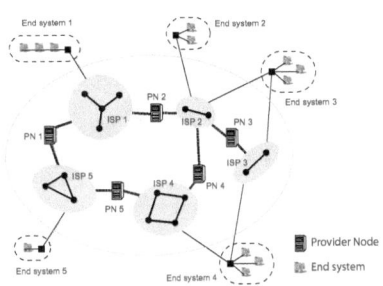

Fig. 1. Service Overlay Network Model

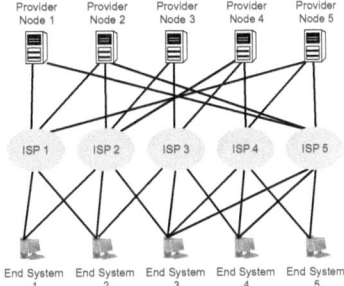

Fig. 2. Relationship between Provider Nodes, End-systems and ISPs

service-specific overlay network without incorporating changes in the underlying network infrastructure. This mechanism can be utilized to support applications for fault-tolerance, multi-cast communication, security, file sharing and QoS [1, 2, 7].

We consider the SON model described in [8], where it is constructed on top of an infrastructure of ISPs and is capable of providing QoS guarantees to a set of customers. Because of this capability, the network is referred to as a QoS Provider Network or *Provider Network*. The provider network comprises a collection of *provider nodes*, and a set of customers referred to as the *end-systems or enterprises*. The provider nodes and the end-systems gain access to the Internet through ISPs. An illustration of the SON is given in Figure 1. The provider nodes are connected to each other through ISPs and the end-systems are also connected to the provider nodes through ISPs. Two provider nodes are said to be connected to each other, if they are connected to the same ISP. Similarly, an end-system is said to be connected to a provider node if they are connected to the same ISP. Figure 2 illustrates the relationships between provider nodes, ISPs and end-systems. The provider node buys services (guaranteed bandwidth) from ISPs and sells them to the end-systems with end-to-end service guarantees. Currently, there exists at least one commercial service overlay network (Internap [6]) that closely resembles the model used in this paper as well as in [8].

The topology design problem of a SON can be described as follows: Given a set of end-systems, provider nodes, access cost of traffic from an end-system to a provider node, transport cost of traffic among provider nodes, traffic demand for each pair of end-systems, find the least cost design that satisfies the traffic bandwidth demand between each pair of end-systems. Our work is motivated by the recent study done by Vieira *et.al.* [8] on topology design problem for a specific SON model. In this paper, we introduce a generalized framework for SON, which provides a comprehensive view of the overall topology design space. We categorize the generalized SON model based on the following scenarios:

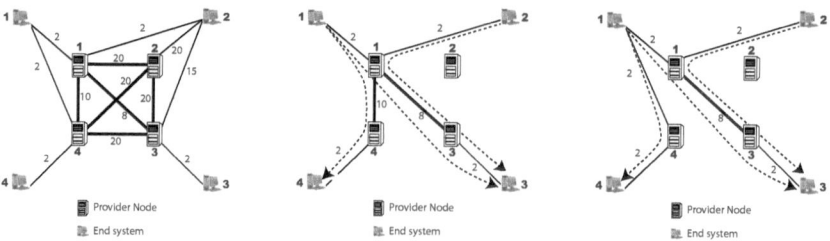

Fig. 3. Service Overlay Net- **Fig. 4.** Single-homed Solu- **Fig. 5.** Multi-homed Solu-
work Model   tion for SON Design   tion for SON Design

- **Single-homed vs multi-homed:** The term *multihoming* is generally used
  to indicate that an end-system is connected to multiple ISPs [12]. In the
  context of SON, we extend this notion and let *multihoming* refer to the
  scenario where one end-system can be connected to multiple *provider nodes*
  instead of multiple ISPs. In a multi-homed environment, an end-system has
  more flexibility in connecting to a set of provider nodes. This flexibility
  enables the designer to find a lower cost solution. Figures 4 and 5 show the
  solution of the same problem in single-homed and multi-homed scenarios,
  where the cost of the single-homed design is 26 and that of the multi-homed
  is 18.
- **Usage-based vs leased(fixed) cost model:** In the usage-based cost model,
  the cost of the link is proportional to the volume of data sent through the
  link. In a leased or fixed cost model, we assume that each link has an associated cost that is independent of the traffic sent through it. Such fixed cost
  scenario is often applicable to enterprises who buy leased lines from ISPs at
  a flat rate.
- **Capacitated vs uncapacitated network:** In case of a capacitated network, we assume that any link in the SON has a capacity bound that cannot
  be exceeded. While in an uncapacitated case, there exist no such constraints.

It may be noted that the authors in [8] provide solution only for the single-
homed, uncapacitated network with usage-based cost model. In this paper, we
provide results of our comprehensive study of the SON design problem. The key
contributions of this paper are as follows:

- We prove that the SON topology design problem with (a) multi-homed enterprise, (b) usage-based cost model and (c) uncapacitated network can be
  solved in *polynomial* time.
- We prove that the SON topology design problem with (a) single-homed
  enterprise, (b) usage-based cost model and (c) uncapacitated network is NP-
  Complete.
- We prove that the SON topology design problem with (a) single-homed/multi-
  homed enterprise and (b) fixed cost model is NP-Complete in both capaci-

Table 1. Complexity results for different versions of SON design problem

Cost Model	Uncapacitated Network		Capacitated Network	
	Single-homed	Multi-homed	Single-homed	Multi-homed
Usage-based cost	NPC	Poly. Solution	NPC	NPC
Fixed cost	NPC	NPC	NPC	NPC

tated and uncapacitated network scenarios. We present approximation algorithms for the solution of uncapacitated version of these problems.

– We show that all the four problems in the capacitated version of the SON design problem are NP-Complete.

A summary of the complexities involved in the topology design problem for the various cases is shown in Table 1.

2   Problem Formulation

The optimal topology design problem of a SON is described in the previous section. We consider different versions of the problem based on different application environments: (i) *single-homed* or *multi-homed* end-system, (ii) *usage-based* or *fixed* cost model [9], and (iii) *finite* or *infinite* capacity links. The notations used in this paper are same as in [8] and are given in Table 2.

The *access cost* α_{ij} of an *access link* connecting an end-system ES_i to a provider node PN_j refers to the cost of transmitting one unit of data over that

Table 2. Basic Notations

ES_i	end-system i
PN_j	Provider node i
M	Number of end-systems
N	Number of provider nodes
α_{ij}	Access cost (per unit of reserved bandwidth) for traffic from ES_i to PN_j
α	Access cost matrix for traffic from all ES_i to all PN_j
l_{ij}	Transport cost (per unit of reserved bandwidth) for traffic on the transport link from PN_i to PN_j
L	Transport cost matrix for traffic on the transport link from all PN_i to all PN_j
b_{ij}	Cost of least-cost route (per unit of reserved bandwidth) for traffic between PN_i to PN_j
B	Cost of least-cost route matrix for traffic between all PN_i to all PN_j
ω_{ij}	Reserved bandwidth for traffic from ES_i to ES_j
Ω	Reserved bandwidth matrix for traffic from all ES_i to all ES_j

link in usage-based cost model and the cost of transmitting any number of units of data in fixed cost model. In case ES_i can be connected to PN_j through more than one ISP, α_{ij} represents the cheapest way of connecting ES_i to PN_j. If ES_i cannot reach PN_j through any ISP, access cost $\alpha_{ij} = \infty$. The *transport cost* l_{ij} of a *transport link* connecting PN_i to PN_j refers to the cost of transmitting one unit of data over that link in usage-based cost model and the cost of transmitting any number of units of data in fixed cost model. In case PN_i can be connected to PN_j through more than one ISP, l_{ij} represents the cheapest way of connecting PN_i to PN_j. If PN_i cannot reach PN_j through any ISP, transport cost $l_{ij} = \infty$.

From the set of input data, we construct a graph $G_{ESPN} = (V_{ESPN}, E_{ESPN})$, where the vertex set V_{ESPN} consists of two different types of nodes, V_{PN} and V_{ES}, representing the provider nodes and the end-systems respectively. Similarly, the edge set E_{ESPN} consists of two different types of edges, $E_{PN,PN}$ and $E_{ES,PN}$. For any $v_i, v_j \in V_{PN}$, there is an edge in $E_{PN,PN}$ connecting them with an associated weight l_{ij}. l_{ij} values for all pairs of provider nodes are denoted by matrix L. The length of the shortest path between v_i and v_j is denoted by b_{ij}. b_{ij} values for all pairs of provider nodes are denoted by matrix B. For any $v_i \in V_{ES}$ and $v_j \in V_{PN}$, there is an edge in $E_{ES,PN}$ connecting them with an associated weight α_{ij}. α_{ij} values for all end-system to provider node pairs are denoted by matrix α. For any $v_i, v_j \in V_{ES}$, there is a traffic demand ω_{ij} associated with this ordered pair of nodes (ω_{ij} may be zero). Traffic demands for all pairs of end-systems are denoted by matrix Ω. An illustration of such a graph is shown in Figure 3. In this example, there is a non-zero traffic demand for the pairs (ES_1, ES_3), (ES_1, ES_4) and (ES_2, ES_3). In the fixed cost model, the actual bandwidth request by each pair is not relevant. The optimal solutions for the single-homed and multi-homed versions of the SON design problem are shown in Figures 4 and 5 respectively. The optimal cost of the single-homed version is 26, whereas the multi-homed version is 18.

The main difference between usage-based model and fixed cost model is how the access and transport costs are calculated, especially when the same edge appears on more than one path between end-system pairs. For example, if an edge $e_{pq} \in E_{ES,PN}$ is used for transferring $\omega_{i,j}$ amount of data from ES_i to ES_j and also used for transferring $\omega_{i,k}$ amount of data from ES_i to ES_k, then the cost of using this link will be $\alpha_{pq}(\omega_{i,j} + \omega_{i,k})$ in usage-based cost model and only α_{pq} in the fixed cost model. Similarly, If an edge $e_{pq} \in E_{PN,PN}$ is used for transferring $\omega_{i,j}$ amount of data from ES_i to ES_j and $\omega_{r,s}$ amount of data from ES_r to ES_s, then the cost of using this link will be $l_{pq}(\omega_{i,j} + \omega_{r,s})$ in usage-based cost model and only l_{pq} in the fixed cost model.

3   SON Topology Design - Algorithms and Complexities

We consider eight different versions of the SON topology design problem. We show that only one of the four different versions with uncapacitated network model is polynomial-time solvable, and the other three are NP-complete. Since uncapacitated version of the problem is just a special case of the capacitated version, the NP-Completeness of the capacitated version will follow from the NP-Completeness of the uncapacitated version. The complexity results of various versions are summarized in Table 1.

3.1 SON Design Problem with Multi-homed Enterprise, Uncapacitated Network and Usage-Based Cost Model (SONDP-MHE/UN/UBC)

Instance: Given a graph $G_{ESPN} = (V_{ESPN}, E_{ESPN})$ with matrices L, α, Ω, and a positive integer K.

Question: Is it possible to construct a SON topology with total cost less than or equal to K so that all traffic demands given in matrix Ω are satisfied?

Theorem 1. *SON design problem with MHE/UN/UBC can be solved in polynomial time.*

Proof: From the special properties of this problem, it is no hard to see that the cost of establishing a path to transmit w_{ij} units of data from ES_i to ES_j is independent of the cost of establishing paths for other pairs. Therefore, we can minimize the total cost by establishing a shortest path for each pair of end-systems separately in G_{ESPN}, and thus obtain the optimal solution for this problem.

The computation complexity of this algorithm is $O(k(|V_{ESPN}| \ log \ |V_{ESPN}| + |E_{ESPN}|))$, where k is the number of end-systems pairs that need to transfer data between each other.

3.2 SON Design Problem with Single-Homed Enterprise, Uncapacitated Network and Usage-Based Cost Model (SONDP-SHE/UN/UBC)

From the transport cost matrix L (in Table 2), we compute the least-cost route matrix B. The problem instance is described in terms of matrix B.

Instance: Given a graph $G_{ESPN} = (V_{ESPN}, E_{ESPN})$ with matrices B, α, Ω, and a positive integer K.

Question: Is it possible to construct a SON topology with total cost less than or equal to K so that all traffic demands given in matrix Ω are satisfied, and meanwhile each end-system is connected to only one provider node?

Theorem 2. *SON design problem with SHE/UN/UBC is NP-complete.*

Proof: We can restate the question more formally in the following way:

Question: Is there a function $g : \{1, 2, ..., M\} \to \{1, 2, ..., N\}$, such that

$$\sum_{i=1}^{M} \sum_{j=1}^{M} w_{ij}(\alpha_{ig(i)} + b_{g(i)g(j)} + \alpha_{jg(j)}) \leq K? \tag{1}$$

Clearly SONDP-SHE/UN/UBC is in NP. We prove its NP-Completeness by reduction from the Matrix Cover problem [4]. The reduction maps a Matrix Cover instance (an $n \times n$ matrix $A = \{a_{ij}\}$, K) to a SONDP-SHE/UN/UBC instance (Ω, B, α, K'), so that there is a function $f : \{1, 2, ..., n\} \to \{-1, +1\}$ such that $\sum_{i=1}^{n} \sum_{j=1}^{n} a_{ij} f(i) f(j) \leq K$ if and only if there is a function $g : \{1, 2, ..., M\} \to \{1, 2, ..., N\}$ such that $\sum_{i=1}^{M} \sum_{j=1}^{M} w_{ij} (\alpha_{ig(i)} + b_{g(i)g(j)} + \alpha_{jg(j)}) \leq K'$. Given any instance of Matrix Cover: An $n \times n$ matrix $A = \{a_{ij}\}$ with nonnegative integer entries, and an integer K, we construct the instance for SONDP-SHE/UN/UBC problem as follows:

1. Let $M = n$. For the $M \times M$ bandwidth reservation matrix $\Omega = \{w_{ij}\}$, $\forall 1 \leq i \leq M, 1 \leq j \leq M$, let $w_{ij} = 1$.

2. Let $N = 2M$. For the $N \times N$ transport matrix $B = \{b_{ij}\}$, $\forall 1 \leq k \leq M, 1 \leq l \leq M$, let

$$b_{2k,2l} = \frac{a_{kl} + a_{lk}}{2} + max; \qquad b_{2k-1,2l-1} = \frac{a_{kl} + a_{lk}}{2} + max;$$

$$b_{2k,2l-1} = -\frac{a_{kl} + a_{lk}}{2} + max; \qquad b_{2k-1,2l} = -\frac{a_{kl} + a_{lk}}{2} + max; \tag{2}$$

where max is the maximum element of matrix A in the instance of Matrix Cover. It is added to make sure that b_{ij} is nonnegative.

3. For the $M \times N$ Access Cost matrix $\alpha = \{\alpha_{ij}\}$, $\forall 1 \leq i \leq M$

$$\alpha_{ij} = \begin{cases} 0 & \text{if } j = 2i - 1, \text{ or } 2i \\ \infty & \text{otherwise} \end{cases} \tag{3}$$

4. Let $K' = K + M^2 \cdot max = K + n^2 \cdot max$.

The construction can be done in polynomial time. To complete the proof, we show that this transformation is a reduction. Suppose for the instance of matrix cover problem, there is a function $f : \{1, 2, .., n\} \to \{-1, +1\}$ such that $\sum_{i=1}^{n} \sum_{j=1}^{n} a_{ij} f(i) f(j) \leq K$, then we can build the corresponding $g : \{1, 2, .., M\} \to \{1, 2, ..., N\}$ for the instance of SONDP-SHE/UN/UBC as follows:

$$\forall 1 \leq i \leq M (M = n, N = 2M)$$

$$g(i) = \begin{cases} 2i & \text{if } f(i) = +1 \\ 2i - 1 & \text{if } f(i) = -1 \end{cases} \tag{4}$$

Due to the process of construction, there exists a relationship between the objective functions of the two problems, as shown in the following table. Therefore, given the g function we have build, it is true that

Table 3. Relationship between two objective functions

$f(i)$	$f(j)$	$a_{ij}f(i)f(j)$	$a_{ji}f(j)f(i)$	$g(i)$	$g(j)$	$b_{g(i)g(j)}$	$b_{g(j)g(i)}$
$+1$	$+1$	a_{ij}	a_{ji}	$2i$	$2j$	$\frac{a_{ij}+a_{ji}}{2}+max$	$\frac{a_{ij}+a_{ji}}{2}+max$
-1	-1	a_{ij}	a_{ji}	$2i-1$	$2j-1$	$\frac{a_{ij}+a_{ji}}{2}+max$	$\frac{a_{ij}+a_{ji}}{2}+max$
$+1$	-1	$-a_{ij}$	$-a_{ji}$	$2i$	$2j-1$	$-\frac{a_{ij}+a_{ji}}{2}+max$	$-\frac{a_{ij}+a_{ji}}{2}+max$
-1	$+1$	$-a_{ij}$	$-a_{ji}$	$2i-1$	$2j$	$-\frac{a_{ij}+a_{ji}}{2}+max$	$-\frac{a_{ij}+a_{ji}}{2}+max$

$$
\sum_{i=1}^{M}\sum_{j=1}^{M} w_{ij}(\alpha_{ig(i)} + b_{g(i)g(j)} + \alpha_{jg(j)})
$$

$$
= \sum_{i=1}^{M}\sum_{j=1}^{M} b_{g(i)g(j)} \qquad (w_{ij}=1, \alpha_{ig(i)} = \alpha_{jg(j)} = 0)
$$

$$
= \sum_{i=1}^{n}\sum_{j=1}^{n} a_{ij}f(i)f(j) + \sum_{i=1}^{n}\sum_{j=1}^{n} max
$$

$$
= \leq K + n^2 \cdot max
$$

$$
= K'
$$

(5)

Conversely, suppose that for the instance we have built for the SONDP-SHE/UN/UBC problem, there is a function $g : \{1, 2, .., M\} \rightarrow \{1, 2, ..., N\}$ such that $\sum_{i=1}^{M}\sum_{j=1}^{M} w_{ij}(\alpha_{ig(i)} + b_{g(i)g(j)} + \alpha_{jg(j)}) \leq K'$. Then $\forall 1 \leq i \leq M$, $g(i)$ must be equal to $2i$ or $2i - 1$, otherwise $\alpha_{ig(i)}$ will be equal to ∞. Then we can build the corresponding $f : \{1, 2, .., n\} \rightarrow \{-1, +1\}$ for the instance of Matrix Cover as follows:

$$
\forall 1 \leq i \leq n(n = M, N = 2M);
$$

$$
f(i) = \begin{cases} +1 \text{ if } g(i) = 2i \\ -1 \text{ if } g(i) = 2i - 1 \end{cases}
$$

(6)

Similarly, due to the relationship shown in Table 3, it is true that

$$
\sum_{i=1}^{n}\sum_{j=1}^{n} a_{ij}f(i)f(j) = \sum_{i=1}^{M}\sum_{j=1}^{M} b_{g(i)g(j)} - \sum_{i=1}^{n}\sum_{j=1}^{n} max
$$

$$
= \sum_{i=1}^{M}\sum_{j=1}^{M} w_{ij}(\alpha_{ig(i)} + b_{g(i)g(j)} + \alpha_{jg(j)}) - \sum_{i=1}^{n}\sum_{j=1}^{n} max \quad (7)
$$

$$
\leq K' - n^2 \cdot max
$$

$$
= K
$$

This proves the theorem.

3.3   SON Design Problem with Multi-homed/Single-Homed Enterprise, Uncapacitated Network and Fixed Cost Model (SONDP-MHE/UN/FC)

In this section we consider both the multi-homed and single-homed versions of the uncapacitated network with fixed cost model, which are described as follows:

Instance: Given a graph $G_{ESPN} = (V_{ESPN}, E_{ESPN})$ with matrices L, α, Ω, and a positive integer K.

Question: Is it possible to construct a SON topology with total cost (under fixed cost model) less than or equal to K so that all traffic demands given in matrix Ω are satisfied?

Instance: Given a graph $G_{ESPN} = (V_{ESPN}, E_{ESPN})$ with matrices L, α, Ω, and a positive integer K.

Question: Is it possible to construct a SON topology with total cost (under fixed cost model) less than or equal to K so that all traffic demands given in matrix Ω are satisfied, and meanwhile each end-system is connected to only one provider node?

Theorem 3. *SON design problems with MHE/UN/FC and SHE/UN/FC are NP-complete.*

Proof. Clearly, the SONDP-SHE/UN/FC problem belongs to NP. We prove its NP-Completeness by reduction from the Steiner Tree Problem. Given any instance of Steiner Tree Problem: undirected graph $G(V, E)$, weights $c : E(G) \to \mathbb{R}_+$, the set of terminals $S \subseteq V(G)$, and a positive integer K, we construct an instance $(G', L, \alpha, \Omega, K')$ for SONDP-SHE/UN/FC problem as follows: $G' = (V \cup U, E \cup E')$, where V is the set of provider nodes; $U = \{u | u$ is new added node adjacent to $v, \forall v \in S\}$ is the set of end-systems; $E' = \{(u, v) | \forall v \in S\}$; $\forall e \in E, l(e) = c(e); \forall e' \in E', \alpha(e) = 0; \forall u_i, u_j \in U, \omega(u_i, u_j) = 1$; and $K' = K$. The construction can be done in polynomial time.

Now we show that this transformation is a reduction. Suppose for the instance of Steiner Tree problem, there is a Steiner tree $T = (V_{ST}, E_{ST})$ for S in G with total cost $c(E_{ST})$ less than or equal to K, then we can construct a solution T' for SONDP-SHE/UN/FC problem as follows: $T' = (V_{ST} \cup U, E_{ST} \cup E')$, where T' connects all the end-systems, which means the bandwidth requirement for each pair of end-systems is satisfied. In addition, each end-system is connected to only one provider node, and the cost of T' is less than or equal to K'. Similarly, given the solution $T' = (V' \cup U, E'' \cup E')$ for the instance of the SONDP-SHE/UN/FC problem, we can construct a corresponding solution T for Steiner Tree problem as $T = (V', E'')$, by removing all the end-systems and the associated edges. T is a solution for the Steiner Tree Problem, since all the terminals are connected and $c(E(T))$ is no greater than K. Therefore, the transformation is a reduction and the SONDP-SHE/UN/FC problem is NP-Complete.

$$\text{Minimize} \sum_{i=1}^{M} \sum_{j=1}^{N} \alpha_{i,j} y_{i,j} + \sum_{i=1}^{N-1} \sum_{j=i+1}^{N} l_{i,j} z_{i,j} \qquad (8)$$

Subject to

$$\sum_{j=1}^{N} q_{i,j}^{k,l} >= 1, \qquad \text{for } 1 \leq i \leq M,\, w_{k,l} > 0;\ (9)$$

$$\sum_{l=1}^{N} x_{i,k}^{j,l} + q_{k,j}^{i,k} - \sum_{l=1}^{N} x_{i,k}^{l,j} - q_{i,j}^{i,k} = 0, \qquad \text{for } 1 \leq j \leq N,\, w_{i,k} > 0;\ (10)$$

$$\sum_{k=1}^{M} \sum_{l=1}^{M} q_{i,j}^{k,l} \leq M^2 \times y_{i,j}, \qquad \text{for } 1 \leq i \leq M,\, 1 \leq j \leq N;\ (11)$$

$$\sum_{i=1}^{N} \sum_{k=1}^{N} \left(x_{i,k}^{j,l} + x_{i,k}^{l,j} \right) \leq 2N^2 \times z_{j,l}, \qquad \text{for } 1 \leq j < l \leq N;\ (12)$$

$$y_{i,j} = 0/1, \qquad \text{for } 1 \leq i \leq M,\, 1 \leq j \leq N;\ (13)$$

$$z_{j,l} = 0/1, \qquad \text{for } 1 \leq j < l \leq N;\ (14)$$

$$q_{i,j}^{k,l} = 0/1, \qquad \text{for } 1 \leq i, k, l \leq M,\, 1 \leq j \leq N;\ (15)$$

$$x_{i,k}^{j,l} = 0/1, \qquad \text{for } 1 \leq i, k \leq M,\, 1 \leq j, l \leq N;\ (16)$$

Fig. 6. ILP for SONDP-MHE/UN/FC Problem

It's true that the instance of SONDP-SHE/UN/FC problem we constructed can also be seen as a special instance for SONDP-MHE/UN/FC problem, since in the problem description, there is no constraint on the number of provider nodes each end-system can connect to. Therefore, a similar proof can show that SONDP-MHE/UN/FC problem is also NP-Complete.

3.4   Optimal Solution for SON Topology Design Using Integer Linear Programming

In this section, we provide a 0-1 integer linear programming formulations for both SONDP-SHE/UN/FC and SONDP-MHE/UN/FC problems. The formulation for multi-homed problem is shown in Figure 6. For single-homed problem, we only need to add one more set of constraints for the ILP to ensure that exactly one access link is used for each end-system, i.e. $\sum_{j=1}^{N} y_{i,j} = 1$ for $1 \leq i \leq M$.

The variable $y_{i,j} = 1$ indicates that bandwidth is reserved on the access link from end-system i to provider node j. The variable $z_{j,l} = 1$ indicates that bandwidth is reserved on the transport link between provider node j and provider node l. The variable $q_{i,j}^{k,l} = 1$ indicates that the traffic from end-system k to end-system l is using the access link between end-system i and provider node j,where i is equal to k or l. The variable $x_{i,k}^{j,l} = 1$ indicates that traffic from end-system i to end-system k is using transport link between provider node j and provider node l.

The objective function in Figure 6 is the sum of the costs of access links and transport links. Constraint (9) ensures that at least one access link is used to connect an end-system to the overlay network. Constraint (10) is for flow conservation at each provider node. No traffic is initiated or terminated at a provider node. Constraints (11) and (12) determine the access links and the transport links used by the solution.

4   Approximate Algorithms for SON Topology Design

In this section we present approximate algorithms for the solution of SHE/UN/FC and MHE/UN/FC problems. It may be noted that we have shown that the MHE/UN/UBC problem is polynomial-time solvable, and approximate solution for the SHE/UN/UBC problem has been presented in [8]. Since in the fixed cost model, the cost of each link is independent of the amount of data transmitted on it, the amount of reserve bandwidth ω_{ij} between end-systems ES_i and ES_j can be ignored. If $\omega_{ij} > 0$, then ES_i and ES_j should be connected in the resulting topology, otherwise, they don't need to be connected. Therefore, from the reserve bandwidth matrix Ω, we construct a connectivity requirement set $R = \{(s_1, t_1), \dots, (s_k, t_k)\}$, where each (s_i, t_i) is an ordered pair of end-systems which has positive bandwidth demand.

We provide three different heuristics for the solution of SHE/UN/FC problem: (i) Randomized Heuristic, (ii) Gain-based Heuristic and (iii) Spanning Tree based heuristic. It may be noted that by shortest path between any two nodes (end-systems or provider nodes), we implies the shortest path that only uses provider nodes as intermediate nodes. In analyzing the computational complexity of each heuristic, M is the number of end-systems, N is the number of provider nodes and k is the number of connections to be established.

Heuristic 1: Randomized Approach

Step 1: Intialize $C_{RH} = \infty$ and $D_{RH} = 0$.
Step 2: Repeat steps 3 to 13 W times (the parameter W is set by the user to determine the number of times the random process is repeated).
Step 3: Set $R = \{(s_1, t_1), (s_2, t_2), \dots, (s_k, t_k)\}$.
Step 4: Randomly choose a pair (s_i, t_i) from R, and remove it.
Step 5: Compute the shortest path from s_i to t_i. Suppose in the computed shortest path, s_i is connected to provider node P_j, and t_i is connected to P_k. Call these provider nodes *gateways* for s_i and t_i, and denote them $G(s_i)$ and $G(t_i)$ respectively.
Step 6: Set $D_{RH} = D_{RH} + \{$weight of the shortest path computed in step 5$\}$.
Step 7: Set the weights of all the links on the computed shortest path zero.
Step 8: Repeat steps 9-12 till R is empty.
Step 9: Randomly choose a pair (s_i, t_i) from R, and remove it.
Step 10: If $G(s_i)$ and $G(t_i)$ are known, compute the shortest path between $G(s_i)$ and $G(t_i)$; else if $G(s_i)$ is known while $G(t_i)$ is not known, compute the shortest path between $G(s_i)$ and t_i; else if $G(s_i)$ is not known

while $G(t_i)$ is known, compute the shortest path between s_i and $G(t_i)$; else if neither $G(s_i)$ nor $G(t_i)$ is known, compute the shortest path between s_i and t_i.

Step 11: Set $D_{RH} = D_{RH} + \{$weight of the shortest path computed in step 10$\}$.

Step 12: Set weights of all the links on the computed shortest path zero.

Step 13: Set $C_{RH} = min(C_{RH}, D_{RH})$.

Step 14: Output C_{RH}. This is the cost of the solution.

Computational Complexity: The computational complexity of the Randomized Heuristic is $O(kW(M + N)log(M + N))$, where W is the number of times the random process is repeated.

Heuristic 2: Gain Based Approach

Step 1: Initailize $C_{GBH} = 0$.

Step 2: Set $R = \{(s_1, t_1), (s_2, t_2), \ldots, (s_k, t_k)\}$.

Step 3: Compute shortest paths for all pairs of end-systems in R.

Step 4: Identify the source-destination pair (s_i, t_i) from R that has the longest path length. Remove this pair from R. Suppose in the computed shortest path, s_i is connected to provider node P_j, and t_i is connected to P_k. Call these provider nodes *gateways* for s_i and t_i, and denote them $G(s_i)$ and $G(t_i)$ respectively.

Step 5: Set $C_{GBH} = C_{GBH} + \{$weight of the path chosen in step 4$\}$.

Step 6: Set the weights of all the links on the path chosen in step 4 zero.

Step 7: Repeat steps 8-12 till R is empty.

Step 8: Compute shortest paths for all the pairs of end-systems in R. If either $G(s_i)$ or $G(t_i)$ is identified in one of the earlier iterations, in the shortest path computation, $G(s_i)$ and $G(t_i)$ should replace s_i and t_i respectively.

Step 9: Note the *gain*, i.e. the change in path length, for all the pairs in the set R.

Step 10: Identify the end-system pair (s_i, t_i) with largest gain. Remove it from R.

Step 11: Set $C_{GBH} = C_{GBH} + \{$weight of the path chosen in step 10$\}$.

Step 12: Set the weights of all the links on the path chosen in step 10 zero.

Step 13: Output C_{GBH}. This is the cost of the solution.

Computational Complexity: The computational complexity of the Gain-based Heuristic is $O(k(M + N)^3)$. A different implementation can realize this in $O(k^2(M + N)^2)$. The implementation should be chosen based on the values of M, N and k.

Heuristic 3: Spanning Tree Based Approach

Step 1: Initialize $C_{STH} = 0$.

Step 2: Set $R = \{(s_1, t_1), (s_2, t_2), \ldots, (s_k, t_k)\}$.

Step 3: Compute the minimum spanning tree MST_{PN} of the subgraph induced by the Provider Nodes. Set $C_{STH} = $ Cost of MST_{PN}.

Step 4: Connect each end-system to its nearest provider node. Update C_{STH} with the additional cost of connecting all the end-systems.

Step 5: Remove those provider nodes from MST_{PN} that are not used to connect any end-systems pair, and also remove the cost used to connecting them from C_{STH}.

Step 6: Output C_{STH}. This is the cost of the solution.

Computational Complexity: The computational complexity of the Spanning Tree based Heuristic is $O((M + N)^2 log(M + N))$.

The approximate algorithms for the multi-homed version are similar to the ones for the single-homed version, except that end-system is no longer required to connect to only one provider node. So the shortest path for each end-system pair should be computed directly, and the *gateway* information is not needed.

5   Experimental Results

In this section, we compare the performance of our three heuristics for the SONDP-SHE/UN/FC problem against the optimal solution obtained by solving ILP. Simulation experiments are carried out using randomly generated input sets. We develop a random graph generator, which takes as input the number of nodes and average degree, and generates connected undirected graphs. It also randomly generates the weights on the links from a uniform distribution over a specified range (we use the ranges of 3 to 8, and 3 to 80 for our experiments). The graphs produced by the generator are used as the network for the provider nodes. The random weights on the edges are the transport cost among provider nodes. Once the network for provider nodes is generated, a specified number of end-systems are connected to the provider nodes in the following way:

Step 1: The degree of an end-system is randomly generated from a uniform distribution over the range of 1 to 10.

Step 2: The provider node neighbors of an end-system are randomly generated with uniform distribution.

Step 3: The access cost from the end-system to the provider node is randomly generated with a uniform distribution over the range of 3 to 8 (small access cost variation) or 3 to 80 (large access cost variation).

Step 4: Communication requests between end-systems are also randomly generated.

In our simulation experiments, we compute the optimal cost of SON design and the costs obtained by three different heuristics. These results are presented in Table 4. The time taken by the optimal solution as well as the heuristic solutions are also presented. In Table 4, M and N represent the number of end-systems and provider nodes respectively. There could potentially be $M(M-1)/2$ possible requests between M end-systems. The term *Req%* represents the percentage of $M(M - 1)/2$ possible requests that is considered for the instance. The term *Cost-variation ratio* is defined to be the ratio of the cost difference between the heuristic solution(s) and the optimal solution to the cost of the optimal solution. The values of cost-variation for three different heuristics are presented. It may be observed that ILP fails to find a solution within a reasonable amount of time when the problem instance increases in size. The heuristics however are able to produce solutions for these instances. As noted earlier, the link cost distribution is taken to be 3 to 8 for some of the instances and 3 to 80 for the rest. We did not notice any perceptible impact of the variation of the link weights on results. From the experiment results, it may be concluded that Heuristic 2 produces the best solution for most of the instances, whereas Heuristic 3 produces the solution

Table 4. Simulation Results for SONDP-SHE/UN/FC Problem

	Instance			Cost				Cost-var. Ratio (%)			Running Time (s)			
#	M	N	Req%	Opt	H1	H2	H3	H1	H2	H3	Opt	H1	H2	H3
1*	10	10	44	124	134	134	142	8.1$^+$	8.1$^+$	14.5	1	< 1	< 1	< 1
2*	12	10	36	93	131	128	141	40.9	37.6$^+$	51.6	< 1	< 1	< 1	< 1
3*	15	10	29	103	141	165	145	36.9$^+$	60.2	40.8	< 1	1	< 1	< 1
4	20	15	53	94	130	124	132	38.3	31.9$^+$	40.4	3	< 1	< 1	< 1
5	25	15	42	102	150	140	144	47.1	37.3$^+$	41.2	2	1	1	< 1
6	30	25	34	143	186	191	202	30.1$^+$	33.6	41.3	40	1	1	< 1
7	35	25	29	129	195	185	205	51.2	43.4$^+$	58.9	14	3	1	< 1
8*	40	30	26	704	1083	1247	1073	53.8	77.1	52.4$^+$	43	3	1	< 1
9	45	35	23	169	301	285	309	78.1	68.6$^+$	82.8	11	3	2	< 1
10*	50	40	20	904	1646	1475	1441	82.1	63.2	59.4$^+$	68	5	3	< 1
11	55	45	19	237	393	364	371	65.8	53.6$^+$	56.5	693	6	4	< 1
12*	60	50	17	1285	2245	2208	2004	74.7	71.8	56.0$^+$	72	6	6	< 1
13	65	55	16	242	408	392	445	68.6	62.0$^+$	83.9	325	8	8	< 1
14*	70	60	14	1464	2038	1962	2248	39.2	34.0$^+$	53.6	578	9	8	< 1
15	75	65	14	295	496	482	548	68.1	63.4$^+$	85.8	422	11	11	< 1
16	85	75	12	313	566	552	594	80.8	76.4$^+$	89.8	176	14	17	< 1
17	95	85	11	N/A	608	592	638	N/A	N/A	N/A	N/A	19	25	< 1
18*	80	70	13	N/A	2721	2851	2726	N/A	N/A	N/A	N/A	13	14	< 1
19	105	95	10	N/A	673	674	729	N/A	N/A	N/A	N/A	23	34	< 1

+: Result with best cost variation ratio
*: Link cost is between 3 and 80; otherwise, it is between 3 and 8.
N/A: ILP failed to find an optimal solution.

in the least amount of time. Clearly, a tradeoff between quality of solution and the time taken to find it exists in these two heuristics. It may be noted that all three heuristics produce a reasonable quality solution in a fraction of time needed to find the optimal solution.

References

1. D. G. Anderson, H. Balakrishnan, M.F. Kaashoek and R. Morris, "Resilient Overlay Network", *Proc. 18th ACM SOSP 2001*, Banff, October 2001.
2. A. Keromytis, V. Mishra and D. Rubenstein, "Secure Overlay Networks", *Proc. of SIGCOMM'02*, pp. 61-72, 2002.
3. Z. Duan, Z. L. Zhang and Y.T. Hou, "Service Overlay Networks:SLAs, QoS and Bandwidth Provisioning", *Proc. 10th IEEE International Conference on Network Protocols*, Paris, France, November 2002. Also in *IEEE/ACM Trans. on Networking*, vol. 11, no. 6, pp. 870-883, 2003.
4. M. Garey and D. Johnson, "Computers and Intractability: A guide to the theory of NP-COmpleteness", W.H. Freeman, 1979.

5. X. Gu, K. Nahrstedt, R. H. Chang and C. Ward, "QoS-Assured Service Composition in Managed Service Overlay Networks", *Proc. of 23rd IEEE International Conference on Distributed Computing Systems*, Providence, May 2003.
6. Internap Network Services Corporation, *http://www.internap.com*
7. L. Subramanian, I. Stoica, H. Balakrishnan and R. H. Katz, "OverQoS: Offereing Internet QoS using Overlays", *Proc. HotNET-I Workshop*, October 2002.
8. S. L. Vieira and J. Liebeherr, "An algorithmic approach to topological design of Service Overlay Networks", *Proc. of IWQoS'04*, 2004, Montreal, Canada.
9. J. Walrand and P. Varaiya, "High Performance Communication Networks", Morgan Kaufman Publishers, 2000.
10. S. Savage, T. Anderson, and et al. "Detour: a case for informed internet routing and transport." *IEEE Micro,* 19(1):5059, January 1999.
11. Ion Stoica, Daniel Adkins, Shelley Zhuang, Scott Shenker and Sonesh Surana, "Internet Indirection Infrastructure," *Proc. of ACM SIGCOMM,* August, 2002
12. A. Akella, J. Pang, A. Shaikh, B. Maggs and S. Seshan, " A Comparison of Overlay Routing and Multihoming Route Control," *In Proc. of ACM SIGCOMM,* 2004

On Transport Layer Adaptation in Heterogeneous Wireless Data Networks

Aravind Velayutham[1], Hung-Yun Hsieh[2], and Raghupathy Sivakumar[1]

[1] Georgia Institute of Technology, Atlanta, GA 30318, USA
[2] National Taiwan University, Taiwan, ROC

Abstract. Numerous transport protocols and protocol enhancements (e.g. TCP-ELN, WTCP, STP, etc) have been proposed for optimal performance in different types of wireless networks. In this paper, we define "transport layer adaptation" as the behavior of the transport protocol, with the goal of obtaining best performance, when a mobile host moves across different wireless networks. While defacto assumptions have been made in related work on the ideal characteristics of such transport layer adaptation, no explicit work has been performed in either identifying the nature of adaptation required, or the granularity at which the adaptation should occur. In this paper, we argue that : (i) Transport mechanism changes are how ideal transport adaptation should be performed. Neither transport protocol nor protocol parameter change is sufficient enough for optimal performance across heterogeneous wireless networks. (ii) Transport adaptation has to be performed at a granularity finer than interface handoffs. Ideal transport adaptation should change mechanisms even when the network characteristics change within the same wireless network. We then present the design and implementation of an adaptive transport layer framework called *TP that accommodates fine-grained runtime adaptation of transport mechanisms to achieve the best performance in a given wireless network.

1   Introduction

A tremendous amount of research has been performed in the area of transport protocols for wireless data networks over the last decade or so. It is well established that appropriately designed wireless transport protocols can substantially improve the performance experienced by mobile users [1–3]. Such protocols are designed specifically to address characteristics of the wireless environment they are targeted for. For example, TCP-ELN uses explicit loss notification to aid its congestion control in lossy networks [1]. WTCP [2] uses techniques specifically targeted to address the challenging characteristics of wireless wide-area networks such as low and variable bandwidth and high and variable delay. Similarly, STP addresses the limited reverse path bandwidth problem by aggregating feedback messages from the receiver [3].

Although, the problem of transport layer design for any given wireless environment is well addressed by existing research, the problem of transport layer behavior when a mobile host moves across different types of wireless networks is relatively unexplored. At the same time, the fact that mobile hosts are increasingly equipped with multiple heterogeneous wireless interfaces has elevated the significance of the issue.

H. de Meer and N. Bhatti (Eds.): IWQoS 2005, LNCS 3552, pp. 69–80, 2005.

In this context, we define *transport layer adaptation* [1] as the behavior of the transport layer protocol, when the mobile host moves across different wireless networks. Appropriately designed transport layer adaptation is critical for achieving the best performance for a mobile host moving across heterogeneous wireless data networks. Toward identifying the ideal transport adaptation behavior required for such mobile hosts, we consider two issues in this work:

1. *What should be the ideal nature of transport adaptation?* Should the adaptation involve changing entire transport protocols at a time, or changing transport mechanisms as required, or simply changing only protocol parameters? We argue that ideal transport adaptation should accommodate changes at the level of transport mechanisms, and that neither transport protocol nor protocol parameter changes are sufficient enough for optimal performance across heterogeneous wireless networks.

2. *At what time granularity will such transport adaptation be required?* Should the adaptation be done only when there is a handoff between network interfaces or will it be required even when network conditions change within the same wireless network? We argue that the transport adaptation has to be performed at a time granularity much finer than that of interface handoffs. Essentially, ideal transport adaptation should change mechanisms even for change in network characteristics within the same wireless network.

We then design and implement a runtime adaptive transport layer framework called *TP [2]. *TP is a transport layer solution that accommodates the ideal nature and granularity of transport adaptation. It allows for the reconfiguration of transport layer behavior, while minimizing the impact of such transformations on applications, and hiding it completely in the best case. Briefly, *TP provides a clear separation in the realization of core and non-core transport functionalities, is fully modular, employs an event-driven execution model, and allows for effective state propagation between different avatars of the transport protocol as it transforms.

The rest of the paper is organized as follows : In Section 2, we present in more detail the transport adaptation issues addressed by this work. In Section 3, we present the design and implementation of the adaptive transport layer framework called *TP. We present case studies to evaluate the performance of the proposed *TP transport layer framework in Section 4 and conclude the paper in Section 5.

2   On Transport Adaptation

In this section, we discuss the two key issues with respect to achieving ideal transport adaptation. The arguments presented serve as the basis for the design and implementation of the *TP transport layer framework presented later in the paper.

---

[1] For purposes of brevity, we refer to transport layer adaptation as simply transport adaptation in the rest of the paper

[2] The "*" in *TP represents a "wild-card" that can take the form of any desired transport protocol solution.

2.1   What Is the Required Nature of Ideal Transport Adaptation?

A transport protocol can be viewed at different levels of complexity and these levels dictate the choices available for transport layer adaptation. The coarsest level of detail is the entire transport protocol consisting of all the mechanisms used to implement the different functionalities. Change at the protocol level would require the replacement of one transport protocol (say TCP-ELN) by another (say WTCP) for optimal performance. At a finer granularity than protocol change, is change of one or more mechanisms used by transport protocols. Examples of transport mechanisms include loss-based congestion detection, rate-based congestion control, self-clocked data transmission and timeout-based loss recovery. We note that this level of adaptation is the most complex because it involves the co-existence of multiple previously unrelated modules. The finest level of detail of transport protocols are the parameter values used by the transport mechanisms. Protocol parameters include increase and decrease values in AIMD congestion control mechanism, the number of SACK blocks used by the SACK acknowledgment scheme, etc. Although protocol parameter change is the finest level of detail within the transport protocol, it is also the easiest level of adaptation wherein the values of variables are changed within the same transport protocol.

We argue that transport mechanism change is the ideal nature of transport adaptation for efficient performance across heterogeneous wireless networks. Varying network characteristics directly impacts the performance of transport mechanisms. For instance, a high wireless loss rate adversely impacts any loss-based congestion detection mechanism. Although the loss-based congestion detection mechanism used by say TCP-ELN is affected adversely under high loss conditions, other transport mechanisms of TCP-ELN such as window-based congestion control might not be affected. Thus change at the granularity of transport protocols is not sufficient for ideal transport adaptation. Protocol parameter change is also not sufficient for achieving optimal performance under all network environments. For instance, under high loss conditions, merely increasing the number of SACK blocks (a protocol parameter) would not achieve efficient congestion detection as long as loss is used to detect congestion. In this case, an alternative mechanism to loss-based congestion detection such as delay-based congestion detection should be used[3]. Thus, any transport adaptation framework should have the ability to change transport mechanisms constituting transport protocols. We incorporate this observation as a design element in the *TP adaptive transport layer framework.

2.2   What Is the Ideal Time Granularity for Transport Layer Adaptation?

The coarsest level of time granularity for transport layer adaptation is across transport layer sessions. This level of adaptation is triggered by application requirements rather than wireless networks. Another level of transport adaptation granularity is change of elements when there is a *vertical handoff* from one wireless network to another. In [5], the authors define a vertical handoff as the shift from one wireless network to another. Another alternative level of granularity for transport layer adaptation is when there is

---

[3] In [4], we present a comprehensive set of simulations based performance results that support the above arguments.

"significant" change of network characteristics within the same wireless network. By "significant" change, we refer to change in network characteristics which would lead to degradation of the performance of the transport protocol currently being used. These can happen due to several reasons including "horizontal handoffs" from one access point (or base station) to another possibly overloaded access point, traveling through a low-signal area like a tunnel, etc.

Any wireless network can be characterized in terms of its bandwidth, loss rate and delay properties. Each transport mechanism has an optimal operating region in this network characteristics space governed by the specific operations of the mechanism. For example, loss-based congestion detection is not efficient under high wireless loss conditions. At the same time, it can be shown that wireless loss rates can vary significantly even within the same wireless network such as WLANs depending on the location of the communicating entities. Similarly, depending on the amount of multiplexing performed at the gateway of a WWAN cell, the delay jitter characteristics of the network can change within the WWAN. Thus we argue that, given the fact that transport mechanisms are effective in specific network conditions and that network conditions can vary even within the same wireless network, transport layer adaptation should be performed when network characteristics change significantly even within the same wireless network[4].

3   *TP: A Unified Transport Layer Framework

In this section, we present the design elements of *TP, an adaptive transport layer framework, that can accommodate the mechanisms used in different transport protocols, and dynamically transform itself to exhibit the behavior of the transport protocol best suited for a given environment. The principal focus of the adaptive framework is the ability to accommodate multiple alternative transport mechanisms that will be absorbed into the framework from different transport layer solutions. Hence, we primarily focus on how the framework supports such dynamic reconfigurability.

3.1   Design Goals

The design goals of the *TP framework reflect the solutions to the transport adaptation problems we have identified. The goals include:

Reconfigurability: A key design goal of *TP is the ability to reconfigure itself to use the transport layer mechanisms best suited for a given environment. The reconfiguration of mechanisms is triggered by changes in network characteristics such as the increase in loss rates and delay jitter, or simply interface handoffs. Unlike other configurable frameworks and protocols proposed in related work [6], *TP is designed to support run-time reconfigurability with minimal application intervention. Note that since most

---

[4] Interested readers are referred to [4] for performance results substantiating the above arguments.

of the changes in network characteristics do not require the awareness of the application, it is desirable to design a transport layer framework that can *seamlessly* perform reconfiguration with minimal disruptions to the application.

Extensibility: *TP is designed as a generic framework that can accommodate various mechanisms used in different transport layer protocols. Therefore, *TP by nature is an extensible framework that can "plug-in" any new or existing transport mechanisms. The performance of *TP is not limited to any specific transport protocol or mechanism. Instead, whenever a better mechanism tailored to the characteristics of a given environment becomes available, *TP can use these protocols for achieving higher baseline performance. The design of *TP ensures that whenever the network characteristics become favorable to any module already registered, it will be invoked to perform the corresponding functionality. Toward this goal, *TP defines a set of interface functions that facilitate new protocols to be incorporated into the *TP framework.

Minimal Overheads: While *TP allows flexible reconfigurability and extensibility of transport mechanisms, it does not trade overheads for the ability of fine-grained transport adaptation. *TP is designed to incur minimal overheads compared to a static transport protocol (e.g. WTCP and STP). The overheads that need to be minimized in a dynamic protocol like *TP include: (i) Complexity: The execution efficiency of *TP should not be sacrificed simply because modules are dynamically composed. In other words, *TP should minimize the computation overheads, such that any host can support as many connections using *TP as connections using a static transport protocol. (ii) Redundancy: The redundancy due to repetitive implementations of any functionality in different modules should be minimized. In other words, the memory footprint of *TP should be kept at a minimum. (iii) Latency: The latency incurred during reconfiguration of mechanisms can cause interruptions or disruptions at the application layer. Since it is possible that reconfiguration occurs several times in a connection, such a "reconfiguration" latency should be kept to a minimum.

3.2 Design Elements

We now present the key design elements in *TP that allow it to meet the design goals described earlier.

Triggers: The reconfiguration of mechanisms in *TP is triggered by changes in one or multiple network parameters pertinent to the transport mechanism in consideration. The transport functionalities have dominating parameters associated with them which influence which strategy to use in specific network conditions. Each potential module to be used by *TP first specifies the network parameters that need to be monitored, as well as the conditions (e.g. threshold values) for triggering the reconfiguration. *TP is responsible for initiating the reconfiguration when the network conditions are met. Whenever a decision is made to swap in a module, the corresponding module is loaded into *TP, replacing the current module in use. The monitoring of the triggers and related parameters is again performed by *TP.

Separation of Core and non-Core Modules: As we mentioned earlier, the *TP framework is invariant and independent of the specific protocols used, while individual mechanisms may be swapped in and out depending on the network characteristics. *TP adopts a structured separation of permanent *core* and configurable *non-core* modules. The core is the the *TP framework itself, and the non-core can be considered as different transport mechanisms that may change across different operating conditions. Since the core does not change, it can be optimized for achieving higher execution efficiency and minimizing overheads. The non-core modules on the other hand consist of all the transport mechanisms implementing various transport functionalities.

Modular Architecture and Execution Model: *TP uses a modular architecture for incorporating the non-core modules.[5] Since the non-core transport mechanisms are those that change across different network environments, the modular design of the non-core mechanisms allows for *fast swapping of modules* in and out of the kernel, and *fine-grained adaptation* of the transport protocol mechanisms. Together with an event-driven execution model, the modular architecture facilitates ease of reconfigurability. In *TP, the core maintains an event queue that is served through the invocation of non-core modules. When modules are invoked, they may in turn register further events in the event queue, thus ensuring the execution of the proper set of mechanisms in the appropriate order. Specifically, the event-driven execution greatly simplifies the reconfiguration process in *TP as it merely involves replacement of appropriate event-handlers.

State Propagation: *TP allows the inheritance of transport layer state from one non-core module to another when a reconfiguration is performed. Examples of states that can be inherited across modules include the data buffer, the SACK scoreboard for reliability, and the advertised window size of the receiver, etc. *TP enables such state propagation by allowing non-core modules to maintain both *public*, and *private* state. Any public state is maintained by the core, while the private state is maintained by the non-core module. Thus, when a non-core module is swapped out, and a new non-core module is swapped in, the new module has access to the public state left behind by the old module.

Mobile-host Centric Operations: *TP allows dynamic switching of different protocols on the fly, and extending the protocol stack when newer protocols are developed. While it is reasonable to assume that the mobile host will need to accommodate these protocols for achieving the best performance in different wireless environments, it may not be the case for the static Internet host. This is because static hosts in such a scenario will have to accommodate *all possible* transport protocols in anticipation of communication from any mobile host in the Internet – which is clearly infeasible given that there can be a multitude of protocols corresponding to the large number of heterogeneous wireless access technologies. Therefore, a setting adopted by *TP is to make the mobile-host the primary seat of transport layer intelligence, irrespective of whether it is acting as a sender or a receiver. In such a setting, any change runtime or otherwise can be performed solely at the mobile host without any intervention at the static host.

---

[5] Note that the *TP core is a static component, and hence does not need to be modular.

3.3   Software Architecture

*TP is a mobile-centric framework with the mobile host being the primary control for the protocol operation. The static host in *TP is very simple. When the static host acts as the receiver, it simply sends feedback information used by the mobile host (sender) such as ACK and SACK information. When the static host acts as the sender, on the other hand, it merely responds to requests from the mobile host for sending data. In other words, the static host plays a passive role responding only to instructions sent by the mobile host. The reconfiguration occurs at the mobile host depending on the network environment.

Figure 1 shows a high level architectural diagram of *TP at the mobile host. We refer to it as *TP for purposes of presentation, and qualify it only when the reference is to the static host. As shown in the figure, the *TP functionality is separated into the fixed *core* and reconfigurable *non-core*.

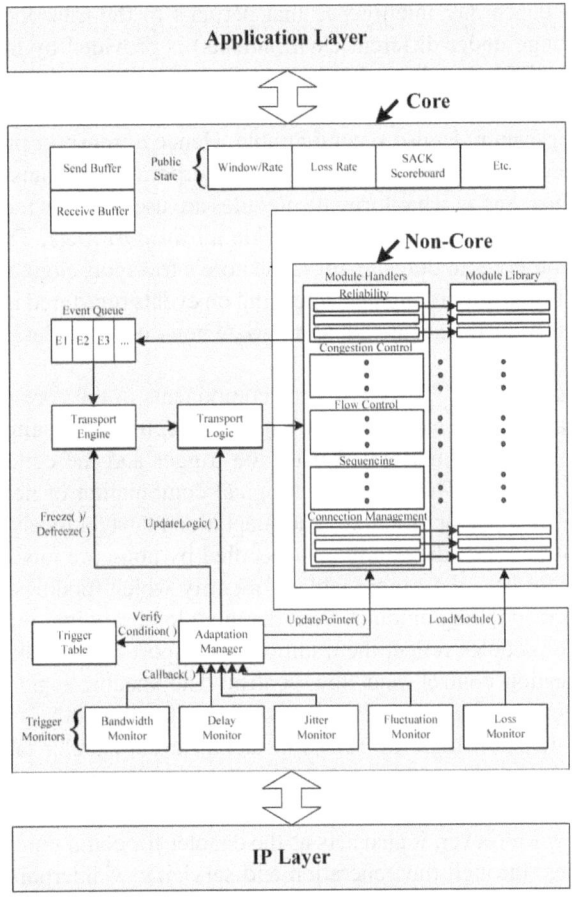

Fig. 1. *TP Framework

The core consists of the following components:

Interfaces with the Application and IP: The core provides a fixed interface for the application layer and the IP layer to communicate with *TP. Any communication coming in from the application including data and control (say, socket options, connection open and close) is handled by the core. Similarly, any communication coming in from the IP layer is handled by the core.

Global Data Structures: The data maintained by the core includes the send and receive buffers, the public state, and the event queue. The handling of the buffers by the core is clear since the reconfiguration of transport modules should not affect the data in the buffer. The public state is used for *state inheritance* and serves as a shared space for non-core modules to communicate with each other. Finally, the event queue is related to *TP's execution model.

Transport Engine: The core in *TP supports the backbone of the transport layer framework, and hence any intelligence that pertains to the transport protocol operations (which change under different environments) is provided by the non-core modules. Note that in *TP, not only the transport modules can be reconfigured, but the *logic* (e.g. sequence of execution) for the execution of these non-core modules (in response to transport layer events) is also reconfigurable. Hence a transport protocol developed in the *TP framework not only can use *TP to incorporate new transport modules, but also can decide how and in what form the modules are used. This is facilitated by allowing the transport protocol developed to provide a *transport logic*. The logic is loaded along with the non-core modules, but it is the core's transport engine that *executes* the transport logic. The transport engine, depending on events registered in the event queue, uses the transport logic to execute the appropriate non-core modules.

Reconfiguration Entities: There are three components in the core that are related to the reconfiguration initiation process: the trigger table, trigger monitors, and the adaptation manager. Non-core modules register the trigger and the condition for module invocation with the core. The trigger is a logical combination of network parameters monitored by various trigger monitors. The adaptation manager receives callbacks from the trigger monitors when the conditions specified by non-core modules are met. The adaptation manager uses the trigger table to identify which modules and logic to use, and loads the corresponding modules from the module library into the non-core.

The non-core modules reflect the traditional transport layer intelligence, including reliability, congestion control, and flow control. The specific logic used to combine the modules together for achieving a transport layer functionality is part of the *transport logic*. The transport logic in *TP is in fact an event/handler table that maps the events registered with the engine and the available non-core modules. Thus, it acts as the liaison between input events to the transport framework, and the actual transport functionality. Moreover, it also acts as the enabler for communication between the non-core modules, through the generation and servicing of internal events. Non-core modules communicate with each other solely through the generation and servicing of events, and the public state maintained by the core. The non-core module can read and write from/into the public state. Non-core modules can interface with the core through registering events in the event queue, and data exchange in the send/receive buffer.

4   Case Studies

In this section, we present case studies to evaluate the performance of the *TP framework in comparison with other transport protocols. The specific transport protocols we compare against are TCP-ELN [1], WTCP [2], STP [3]. We use these protocols as representative tailored protocols for their respective target environments of wide-area, satellite, and local-area wireless networks respectively. The case-studies help in understanding the benefits obtained by using an adaptive transport framework solution, which can perform runtime re-reconfigurability and modular composition of transport mechanisms.

4.1   Experimental Network Topology

Our experimental test-bed consists of Dell Inspiron laptops and Pentium-based personal computers. The static machines are interconnected using 10Mbps WAN connection and the mobile hosts are connected to the base station (access point) using an IEEE 802.11b wireless connection with a raw signaling bandwidth of 2Mbps. The network topology is depicted in Figure 2. We have implemented the three protocols, TCP-ELN, WTCP and STP in the Linux 2.4 kernel. Implementation details about the mechanisms used by each of the protocols can be found in [4].

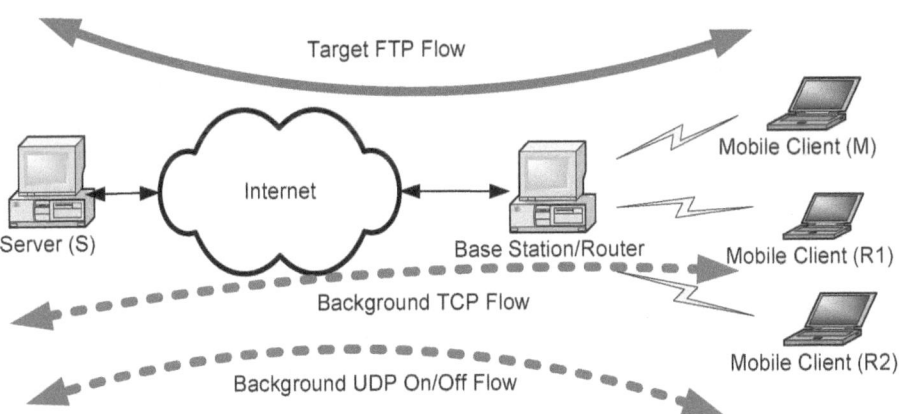

Fig. 2. Network Topology

4.2   Network Environment Parameters

Any network environment can be captured by the bandwidth, packet loss and delay of the network. We use the mean (average) bandwidth, packet loss and delay as well as the variance of the bandwidth and delay to capture the specific wireless environment. Different wireless networks have different values for the above parameters and we analyze the performance of the different transport mechanisms across varying values of the above-mentioned parameters. We use the values given in Table 1 for the different wireless data networks. The data rate is the average bandwidth that the wireless link supports; the fluctuation period is the frequency at which the bandwidth varies (the magnitude of variation is 30% of the mean bandwidth of the link) - the fluctuation period is represented as the percentage of the delay of the link; the packet loss rate is the average drop rate of the uniform loss module. The magnitude of jitter is represented as a percentage of the average one-way delay across the wireless link.

Table 1. Wireless network characteristics

	Data rate (Kbps) (Fluctuation Period)	Average Packet Loss Rate (%)	Delay (ms) (Jitter)
WLAN	2000 (500%)	1	50 (10%)
WWAN	300 (250%)	5	250 (20%)
Satellite network	100 (250%)	5	1000 (30%)

4.3   Lossy WLANs

We know that in WLANs, as the loss rate increases, loss-based congestion detection mechanism degrades in performance. This is due to the inability of the mechanism to detect congestion because of insufficient information about the network at high packet loss rates. We use loss-rate as the trigger parameter for the loss-based congestion detection mechanism and the threshold value is set to 2%. When the *TP trigger module detects that the loss rate increases beyond 2% then it switches the loss-based congestion detection to a delay-based congestion detection mechanism which does not suffer

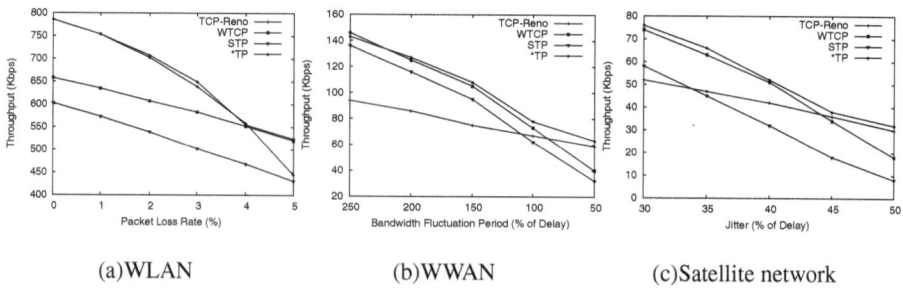

(a)WLAN   (b)WWAN   (c)Satellite network

Fig. 3. Performance study of the *TP framework

much in lossy environments. We can see from Figure 3(a) that *TP performs well even as the loss rate increases within the WLAN environment. We can see that the slope of the curve corresponding to the throughput of *TP follows the best set of mechanisms for the given conditions. This is because of the capability of *TP to choose and use the best available mechanisms at run-time.

4.4   Bandwidth Fluctuation in WWANs

The tuned-rate acknowledgment scheme, such as the one used by WTCP, that performs well in WWAN conditions suffers when the bandwidth fluctuation increases. Since bandwidth fluctuations can be considered to be the norm in both CDPD and higher generation wireless wide area networks, an ideal transport adaptation solution should be able to change the acknowledgment scheme when the bandwidth fluctuation increases beyond a certain threshold value. *TP has the capability to accommodate both the self-clocked (such as the one used in TCP) and tuned-rate acknowledgment schemes and can swap between them depending on the operating conditions. We use bandwidth fluctuation as the trigger for the acknowledgment scheme and the threshold value to be 100% of the delay in the network. We observe from the results in Figure 3(b) that *TP achieves the best performance by swapping the acknowledgment mechanism used when the network conditions degrade. As noted earlier, *TP achieves the best throughput for a given set of transport mechanisms because of its ability to change mechanisms in an intelligent fashion using triggers.

4.5   Jitter in Satellite Networks

Both delay-based and inter-packet separation-based congestion detection mechanisms suffer under high delay variations. Although the delay-based scheme performs well in high-loss satellite environments, it has to be replaced by the loss-based scheme when the jitter increases beyond a threshold. *TP achieves precisely this functionality by swapping the congestion detection mechanisms if the trigger, namely jitter, value is beyond a threshold value. We see from the result in Figure 3(c), that by performing such fine-grained adaptability *TP is able to achieve best performance even in varying network conditions. Here we can see that even as the performance degrades due to the original congestion detection mechanism suffering at high jitter, *TP is able to adapt its behavior to use a different mechanism better-suited for the high jitter conditions.

5   Summary

In this paper, we consider the problem of transport adaptation in heterogeneous wireless data networks. Specifically, we answer the questions relating to the ideal nature and granularity of transport adaptation. We argue that an ideal adaptation solution should be able to change mechanisms at a granularity finer than normal interface handoffs. The change in mechanisms should happen even as the network characteristics change within a single wireless network. We design and implement a runtime adaptive transport layer framework, called *TP, that accommodates the requirements of adaptation determined by the performance evaluation.

Acknowledgment

This work was supported in part by a Motorola UPR grant, and National Science Foundation grants ECS-0225497, CCR-0313005, ANI-0117840, and ECS-0428329.

References

1. H. Balakrishnan and R. Katz, "Explicit loss notification and wireless web performance," in *Proceedings of IEEE GLOBECOM*, Nov. 1998.
2. P. Sinha, T. Nandagopal, N. Venkitaraman, R. Sivakumar, and V. Bharghavan, "WTCP: A reliable transport protocol for wireless wide-area networks," *Wireless Networks*, vol. 8, no. 2-3, pp. 301–316, 2002.
3. T. Henderson and R. Katz, "Trasnport protocols for internet-compatible satellite networks," *IEEE Journal on Selected Areas in Communications(JSAC)*, vol. 17, no. 2, pp. 345–359, Feb. 1999.
4. A. Velayutham, H.-Y. Hsieh, and R. Sivakumar, "*TP : An adaptive transport layer framework for multi-homed mobile hosts," in *GNAN Research Group Technical Report*, 2005.
5. M. Stemm and R. Katz, "Vertical handoffs in wireless overlay networks," *Mobile Networks and Applications*, vol. 3, no. 4, pp. 335–350, 1998.
6. G. Wong, M. Hiltunen, and R. Schlichting, "A configurable and extensible transport protocol," in *INFOCOM*, Apr. 2001, pp. 319–328.

LT-TCP: End-to-End Framework to Improve TCP Performance over Networks with Lossy Channels

Omesh Tickoo[1], Vijaynarayanan Subramanian[1], Shivkumar Kalyanaraman[1], and K.K. Ramakrishnan[2],*

[1] Dept. of ECSE - RPI
{tickoo, subrav, kalyas}@rpi.edu
[2] AT&T Labs Research
kkrama@research.att.com

Abstract. TCP performance over wireless links suffers substantially when packet error rates increase beyond about 1% - 5%. This paper proposes end-end mechanisms to improve TCP performance over lossy networks with potentially much higher packet loss rates. Our proposed scheme separates congestion indications from wireless packet erasures by exploiting ECN. Timeout effects due to packet erasures are combated using a dynamic and adaptive Forward Error Correction (FEC) scheme that includes adaptation of TCP's Maximum Segment Size. Proactive and reactive FEC overhead enhance TCP SACK to protect original segments and retransmissions respectively. Dynamically changing the MSS tailors the number of segments in the window for optimal performance. SACK and timeout mechanisms are used as a last resort. *ns-2* simulations show that our scheme substantially improves TCP performance even for packet loss rates up to 30%, thus extending the dynamic range and performance of TCP over networks with lossy (e.g., wireless) links.

1 Introduction

With the use of WiFi (802.11) hotspot/metro access, WiMax (802.16), 3G, mesh and community wireless networks, end-to-end communication could involve traversal of multiple wireless links. In such links, performance variability is the norm: TCP will see variable capacity and unpredictable *residual* packet erasure rates. Seamless communication under such conditions requires tolerance of such performance variability, especially packet erasures.

TCP depends on packet loss to respond to congestion, and its drawbacks over lossy wireless links are well-known. A key issue is TCP's inability to distinguish

* This work was supported in part by grants from AT&T Labs Research, Intel Corp., NSF (grant number NSF-ITR 0313095) and ARO (grant number W911NF-04-1-0300).

H. de Meer and N. Bhatti (Eds.): IWQoS 2005, LNCS 3552, pp. 81–93, 2005.

between losses due to channel errors and congestion, leading to significant underestimation of the available capacity. This behavior only worsens as the channel error rate increases. It is important to separate TCP's response to congestion from packet erasures.

Explicit Congestion Notification (ECN) is a mechanism that can be used to unambiguously indicate incipient congestion. By sharply reducing congestion loss (due to buffer overflow), it allows us to isolate packet losses as being due, primarily, to channel errors. In this paper, we re-examine TCP's behavior in ECN-enabled networks and propose adaptive mechanisms that allow robust performance even under heavy and persistent erasure conditions (e.g., up to 30% erasure rates). With TCP reacting to ECN [10], packet loss in a network with wireless links would be predominantly due to bit errors. However, the resultant packet erasures stills extract a substantial performance toll through TCP timeouts. We therefore propose a package of complementary and adaptive mechanisms (adaptive MSS and proactive/reactive FEC) to recoup TCP's performance, with minimal end-end extensions.

An interesting question is: Why end-to-end mechanisms for erasure tolerance over-and-above link-level error protection mechanisms? First, link level mechanisms may not be sufficient. Recently, studies by a group of researchers showed substantial *residual* performance variability (e.g., 10-50% packet erasure rates) in 802.11b mesh networks [1]. Emerging high speed LAN standards like 802.11n use adaptive modulation/coding techniques (i.e., variable capacity) targeting a packet error rate of 10%, but these techniques are triggered by low SNR events (i.e., bursty packet erasures). The efficacy of ARQ persistence in 802.11x is countered by the exponential backoff timers, leading to variable capacity/delays. Barakat et al [7, 8] study TCP over links with just FEC or hybrid ARQ/FEC. They find a pure FEC strategy ineffective. Pure ARQ is also shown to fail for high erasure conditions, despite persistent retries. Though link-level hybrid ARQ/FEC is better than either FEC or ARQ alone, its performance also significantly degrades for higher loss rates (5% or more) despite high amounts of ARQ retries, fragmentation of IP packets, FEC overhead and buffering (see Fig. 15/16 in [8]). The situation is complicated further because different link layer standards/implementations have different erasure resilience capabilities.

Second, any appreciable residual erasures may have a disproportionate impact on TCP depending upon *which* packets are lost (e.g., data, acks, or retransmissions). Erasures of retransmissions or segments when TCP's window is small raise the risk of timeouts. In addition, information about the current window size, loss rate and packet size (MSS) can be exploited by TCP to provide the correct and variable amount of error protection when needed. Of course, our design (or the end-end design principle) does not preclude *general-purpose* error mitigation schemes at the link layer, and we remain cautiously optimistic about the potential of link-layer hybrid ARQ.

TCP Performance Enhancing Proxies (PEPs) [6] are TCP-aware mechanisms placed on boundaries where network characteristics change dramatically. PEPs maintain per-flow state and perform layer violations (with implications for security, mobility and scalability). The TCP-PEP technique is less applicable for the emerging regime of variable-performance, high-erasure, highly multiplexed, meshed wireless links.

Rizzo showed the feasibility of transport-layer high-speed FEC computation [5]. Although [5] mentions the idea of FEC in TCP, a specific scheme has not been studied and subsequent researchers' focus has been on multicast transport protocols [2, 4]. Recent attempts at FEC with TCP have met with limited success [3] (for less than 10% erasure rates). Success with higher erasure rates have not been reported to the best of our knowledge. TCP Westwood [9] uses an estimate of output rate to guide congestion control, and has been effective for low erasure rates (under 5%). Presumably all these schemes encounter the risk of increased timeouts mentioned earlier. Overall, despite growing interest, there has been no clear baseline proposal that offers a significant increase in TCP performance over a wide range of erasure rates.

In our scheme, called **Loss-Tolerant TCP (LT-TCP)**, we provision *proactive* FEC in the original window as a function of the estimate of the actual packet erasure rate (PER). *Reactive* FEC is used to mitigate the effect of erasures during the retransmission phase. An adaptive maximum segment size (MSS) component provides a minimum granularity (a minimum number of packets) in the TCP window, again seeking to reduce the risk of timeouts. We seek to adaptively balance the FEC and packetization overhead while reducing the risk of timeouts and also rapidly recovering erased packets. In particular, when the end-to-end path has little or no loss/erasure, LT-TCP introduces negligible overhead. At the same time, we seek to significantly improve the performance of TCP and channel utilization even under packet erasure rates as high as 30-50 percent.

The rest of this paper is organized as follows. Section 2 describes the scheme. Performance results (ns-2 simulations) are presented in Section 3. The last section presents our conclusions and future work.

2   Scheme Description

LT-TCP design focuses on the following key issues:

- **Congestion Response:** How should TCP respond to congestion, but *not* respond to packet erasures. What is the appropriate signal of congestion in an error-prone environment?
- **Mix of Reliability Mechanisms:** What mix of TCP repair mechanisms (ARQ, FEC) should be used to achieve the TCP reliability objectives and how should they be structured?
- **Timeout avoidance:** Timeouts are a final fallback mechanism under significant congestion loss, but truly wasteful otherwise. How can the mix of TCP repair mechanisms be setup to reduce the timeout risk ?

Congestion Response: Our answer to this issue is simple: *react only based upon ECNs, not on detection of packet loss.* This solution would obviously work only in an ECN-enabled network. However, despite this simplifying assumption, timeout risk reduction poses further challenges as discussed below.

Reliability Mix: Error correction packets (a.k.a. FEC packets) have a property unlike regular data packets: if *any* k (out of *N*) packets are received, then it does not matter *which* k packets are received. A *unique* FEC packet can repair any one data packet. In contrast, TCP uses SACK or 3-dupacks to identify and retransmit a packet with a *specific* sequence number. This sequence-agnostic property for FEC-based repair allows a unique FEC packet to be used either in the original window (i.e., in a proactive manner, called **PHASE 1**) or in the retransmission process (i.e., in a reactive manner, called **PHASE 2**). If the *cumulative number* of FEC and data packets in PHASE 1 and PHASE 2 do not meet the threshold of k (out of N), we will fallback to traditional retransmission or timeout. Our mix will first have adaptive amounts of proactive and reactive FEC repair packets, extending the traditional TCP mechanisms (SACK, dupacks, timeouts, retransmissions).

Timeout Avoidance: Timeouts occur for the following key reasons that are exacerbated in a high packet erasure environment:

a) *All* packets in a window are lost.
b) *Three dupacks* do not reach the source (to trigger SACK-based repair).
c) One or more of the retransmitted packets are lost (because dupacks stop arriving).

To overcome each of these issues related to timeout avoidance, we propose to:

a) Granulate the TCP window more finely to increase the number of segments in a window that (due to the self-clocking nature of TCP) are spread over an RTT. Smaller packets also reduce the impact of bit errors (which translate to smaller packet error rates).
b) Use proactive FEC packets in the window based upon an estimate of current erasure rate to reduce the need for dupacks and reduce the burden on SACK retransmissions for recovering lost packets.
c) Use reactive FEC repair packets triggered by dupacks to complement and protect SACK retransmissions.

In summary, we propose the following complementary building blocks to extend TCP-SACK:

ECN-Only: Congestion response only to ECN, since it is the definitive signal of congestion in ECN-enabled networks.

Per-window Erasure Rate Estimate (E). We use an exponential weighted moving average (EWMA), with adaptive parameters (to increase responsiveness and bias towards higher estimates after a spike):

$$E = \alpha \times new_l + \beta \times E \tag{1}$$

$$\alpha = \frac{new_l}{new_l + E}, \quad \beta = 1 - \alpha = \frac{E}{new_l + E} \tag{2}$$

Section 3 shows that Equation 1 tracks the average erasure rate fairly well, although it may overestimate the erasure rate after a spike (burst loss). Under such conditions the proactive FEC algorithm will add deadweight FEC that is either insufficient to provide required protection or is more than the level required. Since previous studies have noted that the erasure rates are relatively stable over intervals as large as a second [1], we feel that the estimate we use will track the actual erasure rate fairly closely over most wireless channels. The erasure rate estimation can be performed equally conveniently at either the receiver or the sender. The receiver can use the information from the packets received to estimate E while the sender can use the ACK information to do the same.

Proactive FEC: The number of FEC packets per window (P) used in PHASE 1 (i.e., Proactive FEC) is a function of the erasure estimate, i.e., $P = f(E)$ The MSS is adjusted to allow one or more FEC packets per window (while maintaining sufficient window granulation). Our initial method divides the erasure rate range into multiple *bins*. Depending on the bin E falls in, we select a hard-coded number of FEC packets that define the minimum number of proactive FEC packets needed. We are investigating alternate methods to better decouple the amount of FEC added from the granulation decision.

Adaptive MSS: Granulate the congestion window to have at least G packets, subject to limits of a minimum and maximum MSS (MSS_{min} and MSS_{max}). Depending on the window size in bytes, the MSS is adjusted to accommodate the required number of FEC packets while providing adequate erasure protection. Thus, the variation in MSS is governed by the following factors:

- The window must be large enough to maintain the minimum granularity, G.
- The window should be able to accommodate at least $f(E)$ proactive FEC packets while providing adequate erasure protection for the estimated erasure rate, E.
- The MSS chosen must be bounded by the MSS_{min} and MSS_{max} values.

Reactive FEC: For every dupack, the sender transmits R reactive FEC packets. R is a function of the erasure rate estimate, E. i.e., $R = g(E)$. Again, R is currently chosen depending on the erasure *bin* that E falls in. The reactive FEC packets will complement and protect data in PHASE 1 and SACK retransmissions in PHASE 2.

The sender module is responsible for adaptive MSS adjustment (i.e. window granulation), computing proactive and reactive FEC packets, and the appropriate transmission of FEC packets.

The receiver implements packet reconstruction (using FEC if and when necessary) and per-window loss-rate estimation. The FEC overhead (proactive and reactive) is computed on a per-window basis using shortened Reed-Solomon (R-S) codes (similar to the method used in CD-ROMs). The proactive FEC is transmitted in the window, but the inventory of excess FEC packets is stored for potential use as reactive FEC.

The tradeoffs of our mechanisms are as follows. Adaptive MSS uses smaller segments when windows are small and therefore the header (or packetization) overhead is larger then, but diminishes as window sizes grow. Proactive FEC may lead to a small deadweight goodput degradation due to over-estimation of erasure rate, and some increased burstiness in the release of dupacks from the destination. Reactive FEC triggered by each dupack leads to a somewhat increased load and burstiness in the retransmission periods. However, since these mechanisms are all adaptive (i.e., they become more active only during higher erasure rate conditions), we argue that the tradeoffs are worth making as they achieve a significant improvement in performance, and enables a wider dynamic range of applicability of TCP.

3   Performance Results

In this section, we present the performance of LT-TCP compared with TCP-SACK (with ECN), the performance of LT-TCP components, comparisons of LT-TCP and two link level schemes (LL FEC and LL Hybrid FEC-ARQ). The link layer schemes are as follows: LL FEC uses FEC to match the average packet erasure rate (PER) on the link and LL Hybrid FEC-ARQ is a hybrid ARQ/FEC scheme that uses 10% FEC protection and has ARQ persistence of 3. LT-TCP performs better than all the schemes compared, especially as the PER increases (up to 30-40%).

We use a single-bottleneck test case (see Fig. 1: 10 Mbps bottleneck, 20 ms one-way delay, 10 TCP flows) with erasure rates varying from 0% to 50% is used. Hosts are ECN-enabled, bottlenecks implement RED/ECN on a 250 KB buffer

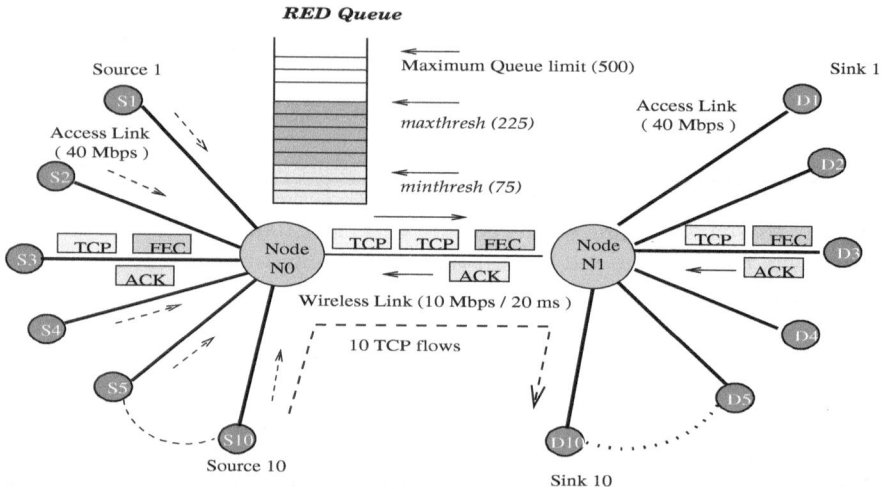

Fig. 1. Single Wireless Bottleneck Setup: RED AQM with ECN

(i.e. upto 500 packet of size 500-bytes). RED *minthresh* and *maxthresh* values
are 75 and 225 packets respectively. The simulations are run for 1000 seconds,
and results are averaged over 5 randomized runs. To assess the contribution of
LT-TCP components, we use a 10% PER test case.

Metrics include aggregate throughput, goodput, congestion window dynamics, number of timeouts, bottleneck queue dynamics, FEC overhead and adaptive
MSS dynamics.

3.1   LT-TCP vs TCP-SACK

Tables 1 and 2 present the performance of TCP-SACK and LT-TCP respectively. TCP-SACK and LT-TCP perform well *without* packet erasures. But TCP-
SACK's performance drops quickly for PER of 10% and higher. LT-TCP outperforms TCP-SACK by a wide margin and its absolute performance (goodput)
is good up to about 30% PER (see Table 2). However, for higher PER (40% and
higher) the goodput drops off, while the number of timeouts goes up, despite
high FEC overhead. This points to room for further improvements to LT-TCP.

In comparison however, TCP-SACK is worse. The congestion window dynamics shown in Fig. 2(b) shows that at 20% PER, TCP-SACK is operating with a
very small window compared to LT-TCP. TCP-SACK sees fewer total number of
timeouts at high erasure rates. But this is due to Karn's exponential timer backoff algorithms (triggered with back-to-back timeouts), and it spends significantly
more time in each timeout period, achieving very little useful goodput.

Table 1. TCP-SACK w/ Erasure Rates (0-50%)

	ERROR RATE					
PARAMETER	0 %	10 %	20 %	30 %	40 %	50 %
Goodput(Mbps)	9.158	1.098	0.233	0.048	0.01	0.003807
Number of Timeouts	0	267	287	135	52	26
Throughput (Mbps)	9.52	1.272	0.306	0.073	0.018	0.007984

Table 2. LT-TCP w/ Erasure Rates (0-50%)

	ERROR RATE					
PARAMETER	0 %	10 %	20 %	30 %	40 %	50 %
Goodput(Mbps)	8.94	5.36	4.086	2.99	0.89	0.3
Number of Timeouts	1	24	19	40	130	243
Throughput(Mbps)	9.53	8.55	9.01	9.06	3.53	1.74
Proactive FEC Overhead (%)	2	29	45	52	53	55
Reactive FEC Overhead (%)	0	3.7	7	11	15	17

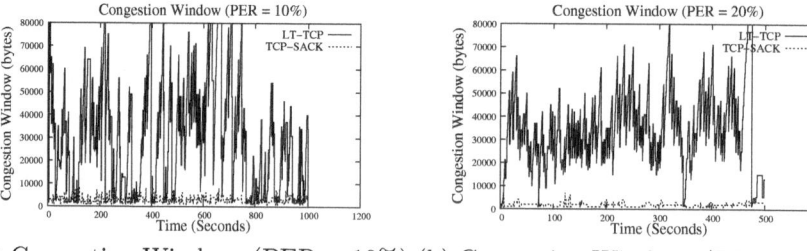

(a) Congestion Windows (PER = 10%) (b) Congestion Windows (PER = 20%)

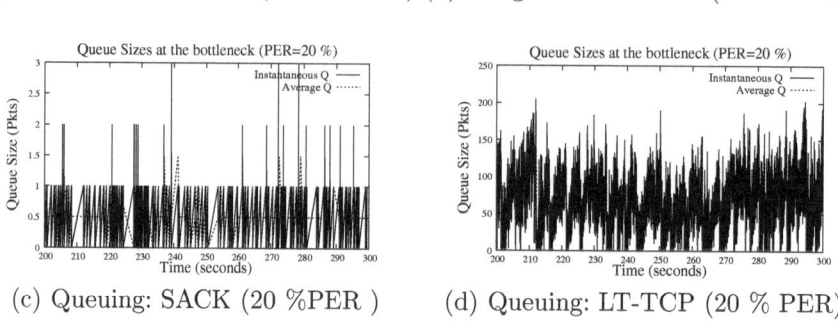

(c) Queuing: SACK (20 %PER)   (d) Queuing: LT-TCP (20 % PER)

Fig. 2. Graphs of Congestion Window (in bytes) and Queue Length (in packets) vs Time for TCP-SACK and LT-TCP

The congestion window (cwnd) and queue graphs reiterate these points. With TCP SACK at high PER (10-20%), cwnd is small and queues are small (i.e. bottlenecks are underutilized). LT-TCP shows fully utilized bottlenecks and well-managed RED/ECN-controlled queue lengths. Congestion window should be deflated by FEC and packetization overheads to reflect true goodput. However, it does reflect the dramatic reduction in timeouts with LT-TCP over these PER regimes.

3.2   LT-TCP Component Performance

The LT-TCP components are evaluated in the following (cumulative) order:

1. TCP-SACK.
2. TCP-SACK with ECN-only (i.e. RED/ECN at bottleneck and congestion response only to ECN marks).
3. TCP-SACK with ECN-only and adaptive MSS.
4. TCP-SACK with ECN-only, adaptive MSS and proactive-FEC (no reactive FEC).
5. TCP-SACK with ECN-only, adaptive MSS and reactive-FEC (no proactive FEC).
6. Full LT-TCP scheme with TCP-SACK, ECN-only, adaptive MSS, proactive and reactive FEC.

The average goodput for the different component bundles is shown in Fig. 3(a). The addition of each component to TCP-SACK consistently improves perfor-

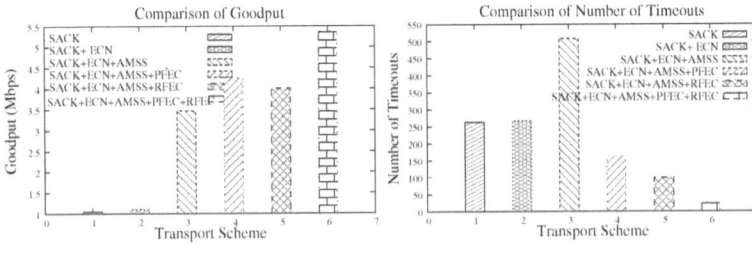

(a) Goodput Comparison   (b) Timeout Comparison

Fig. 3. LT-TCP Component Contributions

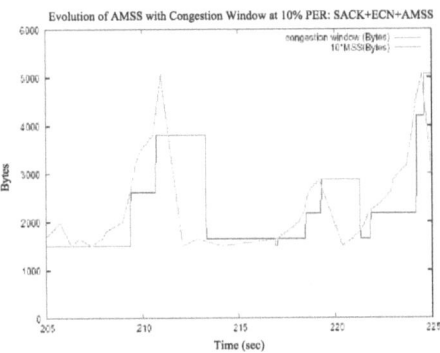

Fig. 4. Effect of Adaptive MSS

mance. The final goodput for LT-TCP is over five times the goodput achieved by TCP-SACK. The overhead due to conservative FEC provisioning is reflected in the difference (throughput = $8.55Mbps$ vs. goodput = $5.36Mbps$). The performance gains of LT-TCP are largely explained through the reduction of timeouts (Fig. 3(b)).

We now examine some of the component-level dynamics. Figure 4 shows the behavior of the adaptive MSS and the resultant effect on congestion window granulation. By varying the MSS with the congestion window, we ensure that a minimum window granulation is maintained, thus increasing the number of dupacks and the effectiveness of SACK. MSS also increases when $cwnd$ increases, to reduce the packetization overhead.

Figures 5(a) and (b) illustrates the FEC-estimation and proactive FEC provisioning. We see that estimator (Equation 1) tracks the average erasure rate well, and responds quickly to spikes, but is biased towards over-estimating after the spike vanishes. This overestimate bias will lead to some excess dead-weight FEC, but it has the potential to reduce effects of sudden erasure bursts that can otherwise lead to timeouts.

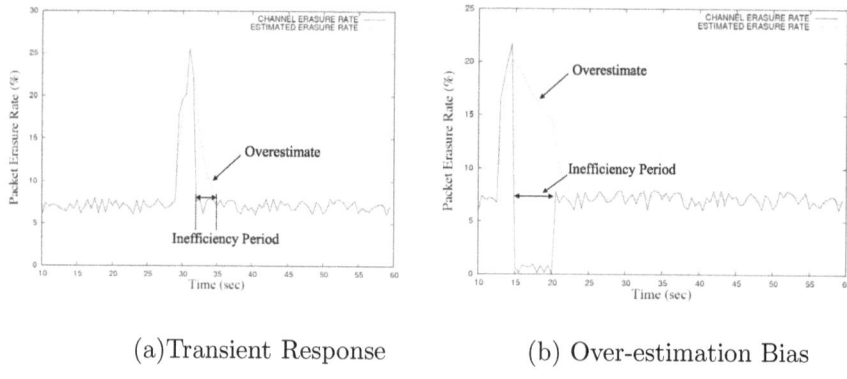

(a)Transient Response   (b) Over-estimation Bias

Fig. 5. Adaptive-Parameter EWMA Erasure Estimator Behavior

3.3   Comparison with Link-Level Schemes

We compare LT-TCP with TCP-SACK and with two other schemes with link layer reliability support: LL-FEC where the link provides FEC to match the average erasure rate on the link, and LL-Hybrid FEC/ARQ where the link provides 10% FEC ($N = 10, K = 9$)and ARQ with a persistence of 3 retries. For LL-FEC, a packet is broken up into N fragments where K units are data units that are protected by $R = N - K$ FEC packets. Each fragment is sent independently on the link. For LL Hybrid FEC/ARQ, we added a realistic mix of ARQ persistency (to not impact latency adversely) and FEC protection that does not assume perfect knowledge of the PER on the channel.

Simulation results [1] for number of timeouts and goodput for four schemes is presented in Figure 6. Surprisingly, the LL-FEC scheme does not perform well even at 10% erasure rates and even underperforms SACK (see Table 3 and Figure 6). This is attributable to the deadweight overheads due to short-term

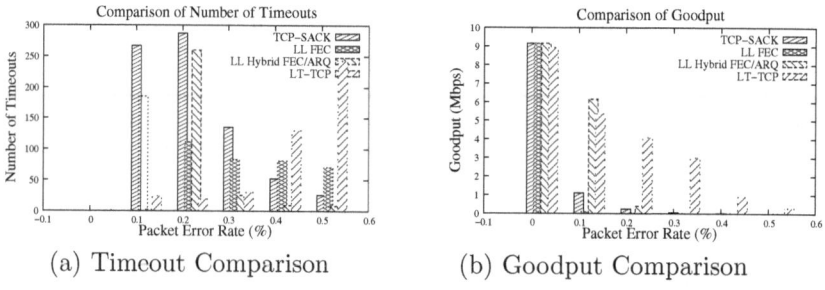

(a) Timeout Comparison   (b) Goodput Comparison

Fig. 6. Comparing LT-TCP with SACK, LL-FEC and LL Hybrid FEC-ARQ

---

[1] Thanks to Dr. Chadi Barakat, INRIA, whose ns-2 source code and model in [8] we simplified.

Table 3. SACK + LL-FEC at (0-50%) PER)

	ERROR RATE					
PARAMETER	0 %	10 %	20 %	30 %	40 %	50 %
Goodput(Mbps)	9.15	0.086	0.034	0.02	0.019	0.015
Number of Timeouts	0	185	111	83	81	71
Throughput(Mbps)	9.52	0.1235	0.053	0.03	0.019	0.026

Table 4. SACK + LL Hybrid FEC/ARQ at (0-50%) PER

	ERROR RATE					
PARAMETER	0 %	10 %	20 %	30 %	40 %	50 %
Goodput(Mbps)	9.15	6.16	0.39	0.002	0.0003	0.0001
Number of Timeouts	0	2	260	25	9	8
Throughput(Mbps)	9.52	6.44	0.49	0.005	0.001	0.0007

mismatches of FEC to erasure rates, even though the long-term average matches the FEC rate.

The LL Hybrid FEC/ARQ with TCP-SACK end-end provides very good performance (Table 4 and Figure 6) when the static FEC protection is matched to the link PER, and backed up by ARQ. However, when the PER exceeds the provisioned FEC value (> 10%), its performance rapidly declines (see Figure 6). Failure to manage timeout risks and limited short-term adaptivity are important reasons for this behavior.

4   Summary and Conclusions

This paper addressed the performance of TCP over networks that include lossy wireless links, where it is well-known that TCP performance suffers substantially when packet erasure rates (PERs) get beyond a small value of about 1% - 5%.

Loss-Tolerant TCP (LT-TCP) contains a complementary set mechanisms for robust TCP performance in ECN-enabled networks, under extreme and highly variable erasure rate conditions (upto 30% PERs). The mechanisms are adaptive and match the amount of error protection and granulation to the conditions of the end-end channel (primarily to reduce retransmissions and avoid timeouts). Thus LT-TCP introduces negligible overhead in the erasure-free case, as one would demand of a transport protocol that needs to operate over wired links that do not have bit errors. LT-TCP does not require any additional router functionality beyond ECN (which has been standardized) As such, it may be easily implemented on an end-to-end basis.

We compared the performance of LT-TCP with TCP-SACK and showed that for the case of 10% packet erasure rate, LT-TCP achieves a factor of 5 better

TCP goodput, while introducing about 30% overhead for FEC on the channel at these error rates. We also demonstrate the better performance of LT-TCP compared to link-level FEC and hybrid ARQ/FEC protection. The reasons lie in limited adaptivity at the link layer and inability to avoid TCP timeouts. LT-TCP can complement existing link layer schemes to overcome the residual PER on wireless channels.

We claim that LT-TCP shows consistent and significant *relative* performance improvement for all non-zero erasure rate cases in comparison to the other approaches. However, its *absolute* performance (especially goodput) still suffers for very high erasure rates (40% and higher). Reasons for this clearly lie at the inability to avoid sharply increased timeouts despite the high and adaptive FEC overhead and adaptive granulation policy, and addressing this will be the focus of our immediate future work. In addition, we are examining the following enhancements to the scheme described in this paper.

- Options for better decoupling between the granularity of packets in a window (MSS adjustment) and the amount of proactive FEC added.
- Upon a timeout, ways of dealing with the transmission of the old FEC block of packets at the sender that that are being retransmitted, and decoding of these blocks at the receiver, in relation to the current FEC block of packets.
- At the receiver, when packets are received out-of-order, we deliver only the in-sequence packets to the receiving TCP (unless we know the remaining packets cannot be recovered). This leads to some burstiness in the generation of acks and dupacks. We are exploring ways to mitigate this.
- We are exploring whether or not to generate dupacks upon reception of reactive FEC packets. Further, we need to ensure that reactive FEC packets also honor the TCP window.

We hope to report results of these enhancements and tradeoffs in an upcoming paper.

References

1. D. Aguayo, J. Bicket, S. Biswas, G. Judd and R. Morris, "Link-level Measurements from an 802.11b Mesh Network",*SIGCOMM 2004*, Aug 2004.
2. J. W. Byers, M. Luby, M. Mitzenmacher and A. Rege, "A Digital Fountain Approach to Reliable Distribution of Bulk Data", pp. 56-67, *SIGCOMM 1998*, Aug.-Sep. 1998.
3. Tal Anker, Reuven Cohen and Danny Dolev, "Transport Layer End-to-End Error Correcting", *Leibniz Center, Technical Report*, The School of Computer Science and Engineering , Hebrew University, Jerusalem, Israel, June 2004.
4. J. Nonnenmacher and E. Biersack, "Reliable Multicast: Where to use FEC," *Protocols for High-Speed Networks*, pp. 134-148, 1996.
5. L.Rizzo, "On the feasibility of software FEC", *DEIT Technical Report*, LR-970131, Available at http://citeseer.ist.psu.edu/rizzo97feasibility.html .
6. J. Border,M. Kojo, J. Griner, G. Montenegro and Z. Shelby, "Performance Enhancing Proxies Intended to Mitigate Link-Related Degradations",*IETF RFC 3135*, June 2001.

7. C. Barakat and E. Altman, "Bandwidth tradeoff between TCP and link-level FEC", *Computer Networks*, vol. 39, no. 5, pp. 133-150, June 2002.
8. C. Barakat and A. A. Fawal, "Analysis of link-level hybrid FEC/ARQ-SR for wireless links and long-lived TCP traffic", *Performance Evaluation Journal*, vol. 57, no. 4, pp. 423-500, August 2004.
9. C. Casetti, M. Gerla, S. Mascolo, M. Y. Sanadidi, and R. Wang, "TCP Westwood: Bandwidth Estimation for Enhanced Transport over Wireless Links", *Proceedings of ACM Mobicom 2001*, pp 287-297, July 2001.
10. K.K. Ramakrishnan, S. Floyd, and S. Black, "The Addition of Explicit Congestion Notification (ECN) to IP", *IETF RFC 3168*, September 2001.

QoS Guarantees in Multimedia CDMA Wireless Systems with Non-precise Network Parameter Estimates

H. Cahit Akin[1], Ozdemir Akin[1], and Kimberly M. Wasserman[2]

[1] University of California at San Diego,
9500 Gilman Drive, La Jolla, California 92093, USA
[2] Cisco Systems, Research Triangle Park,
North Carolina 27709, USA

Abstract. Overwhelming majority of the next generation wireless cellular networks are based on CDMA (Code Division Multiple Access) technologies, with various flavors such as CDMA2000, WCDMA and their variations. Compared to the existing cellular networks which are designed for voice-only applications, the upcoming networks will be capable of providing high throughput and QoS dependent applications such as gaming, real-time streaming media, video conferencing etc., without significant improvements in the overall network capacity. Therefore for satisfactory end-user experiences, efficient use of the scarce network resources is vital. An efficient such algorithm has to depend on the estimates of information gathered from the network, such as the channel gains, received power levels, intercell/intracell interference etc. In such a scheme there are inherent sources for inaccuracies for the estimated values, such as the measurement errors, the delay in the estimates and the inaccuracies in models used for estimation. Implementing a resource allocation scheme which is robust 12to such measurement errors is important. In this paper, we study an optimum resource allocation scheme in a CDMA based cellular network, which is capable of allocating network resources to end-users of multimedia type applications, with QoS guarantees which are robust to inaccuracies in the estimated values, provided that those estimates can be bounded within a certain neighborhood of the real values.

1   Introduction

In cellular wireless communications, the recent worldwide trend has been overwhelmingly towards CDMA (Code Division Multiple Access) based technologies, namely, CDMA-2000 1x, CDMA-2000 HDR, CDMA-2000 EV-DO, CDMA-2000 EV-DV, WCDMA, HSDPA etc. As the deployments of these next generation technologies become more wide-spread, the importance of the efficient use of precious spectrum resources become increasingly vital. Part of this urgency comes

H. de Meer and N. Bhatti (Eds.): IWQoS 2005, LNCS 3552, pp. 94–106, 2005.
© IFIP International Federation for Information Processing 2005

with the introduction and penetration of various applications other than simple voice. Downloading/uploading images, online gaming, video conferencing, streaming media and many upcoming new applications can only succeed if the underlying infrastructure is capable of cramming in enough end-users with minimum network resource expenditure so as to reach and sustain viable economic models for network operators.

With the industry success of Qualcomm's IS-95 CDMA voice system, the resource allocation of voice-only applications has been mainly focused on "perfect-power-control", in the reverse-link which is targeting the lowest level of received powers at the base-station provided that the QoS level of the users are still satisfied. In the last decade, many researchers have attacked various research problems related to power control, majority of which were centered around the idea of achieving perfect-power-control either in a centralized or in a distributed fashion ([1], [2], [3] and references therein). In particular, when communications for real-time applications are considered, the majority of power control research papers have been focused on how to better achieve equal received powers in the uplink, to achieve efficient use of bandwidth. Some distributed algorithms were discussed to achieve the equal received power without a centralized control and the convergence of such methods were analyzed. In [2], an algorithm for handling mobiles' transmitter power levels while explicitly handling their time-varying transmission rates is introduced for future CDMA networks. In [3], the performance of the step size closed loop power control algorithm that is implemented in IS-95 is studied and a new predictive power control algorithm is suggested. In [4] and [5] a truncated channel inversion is studied for non-real time connections where the improvement in throughput and energy efficiency is achieved at the cost of extra queueing delay. In [6], the tradeoff between fairness and throughput is addressed and an extension is given to transmitting a single user at a time to transmitting more than one user at a time. In [7], the power management is done to minimize the power consumption of the wireless network and it is compared to traditional cellular networks.

The limited capacity of wireless telecommunication media, with the expectation of upcoming multimedia applications with different QoS has attracted attention to resource allocation issues in wireless systems. Some of the approaches are listed in [6]-[13]. Specifically, in [8] and [9], the wireless users are classified into real-time users and non-real time users. Then, the optimum spreading gain control is implemented to increase the spectral efficiency and satisfy the QoS of real-time users. The left-over capacity is shared among the non-real time users. Resource allocation in wireless LAN's with QoS requirements is studied in [10]. The coexistence of real-time voice users and high data rate non-real time users is studied in [11]. In [12], the throughput of CDMA-HDR is analyzed.

In recent years, some studies have proven that theoretically the perfect-power-control was indeed not optimum, even for voice-only applications and performed poorly for other QoS depended applications [15], [16].

In practical systems, the chosen resource allocation algorithm will make use of the best available estimates of the parameters in the network which the resource allocation algorithm uses to carry out the resource allocations. As an example, the parameter FER (Frame Error Rate) or the received power levels are both estimated values of the real values which are delayed in time, since estimating some of those values necessitate time averaging so-named values over time. There are also inherent estimation errors attached to each of the parameters caused by the inaccuracies of the methods and circuitries used to obtain those estimates. Given this framework, implementation of a resource allocation algorithm for cellular networks must be able to cope with the inherent inaccuracies of the estimated parameters to be able to implement the resource allocation algorithm it is targeting.

In this paper, we will describe an optimum resource allocation algorithm for a CDMA based wireless multimedia network which achieves the QoS requirements of the end-users even if the estimated parameters are inaccurate, provided that the inaccuracies are bounded within a certain neighborhood of the estimated value. In section II, we will describe the resource allocation algorithm. In section III, we will describe the resource allocation with the assumption of precise parameter estimates. In section IV, we will relax our assumptions to have non-precise parameter estimates and introduce the modified resource allocation algorithm. In section V, we will discuss our results and we will conclude in section VI.

2   Optimum Resource Allocation with Precise Parameter Estimates

2.1   System Model and Analysis

We will focus on the downlink (forward link) in a CDMA based cellular Wireless Wide Area Network (WWAN). We will assume that every wireless station is assigned to a single base station in the network and stays assigned to that base station throughout its connection lifetime. Every wireless station has some latency sensitive data to transmit with different QoS requirements during its connection lifetime. We will further assume without loss of generality that every wireless station has a single connection and the QoS requirement of that connection is not changing over time.

Let M be the number of wireless stations in a particular cell site of interest within a larger network. Let $\mathbf{p(t)} \doteq (p_1(t), p_2(t), \ldots, p_M(t))$ be the powers of the transmitted signals to the wireless stations from the basestation with time dependencies. Also define $\mathbf{g(t)} \doteq (g_1(t), g_2(t), \ldots, g_M(t))$ as the downlink channel gains vector from the base station to the wireless stations.

Define $\mathbf{P} \doteq (P_1, P_2, \ldots, P_M)$ as the maximum allowed transmission powers vector, where P_i is the maximum allowed power from the basestation to wireless station i. Notice that such a power restriction non-explicitly exists for real-time connections with latency requirements. As an example consider a 9.6Kbps realtime connection with 100msec latency tolerance (i.e. voice connection). Then, every 100msecs, there is only 960 bits to be sent. If the smallest granularity of packets is 10 msecs then the maximum needed peak rate is limited by 96Kbps which in turn creates a soft limit on the peak power level needed.

Let I_i denote the intercell interference (interference caused by the neighbor basestations in the adjacent cells) plus the background noise experienced by the wireless station i. In general the value of I_i will be time dependent, but during the initial part of this analysis, for short time durations of our interest, we will assume that I_i is a constant. Later, in the final algorithm, we will relax this assumption as we let I_i vary with time.

There is a unique mapping from the BER requirement of a downlink connection to the required E_b/N_0 value at the wireless station, where E_b is the energy per bit and N_0 is the total noise experienced at the wireless station for that connection. This mapping depends on factors such as the modulation scheme, interleaving method and error-correction scheme. Therefore we will assume that the wireless stations define their QoS requirements in terms of their E_b/N_0 needs. Let $(\kappa_1, \kappa_2, \ldots, \kappa_M)$ be that QoS requirements vector. Then the SNR equation for the wireless station i is:

$$\left(\frac{E_b}{N_0}\right)_i = \frac{W}{R_i} \frac{g_i p_i}{\sum_{j \neq i} g_j p_j + I_i} = \frac{W}{R_i} \frac{p_i}{\sum_{j \neq i} p_j + \frac{I_i}{g_i}}, \quad \forall i \in \{1, 2, \ldots, M\} \quad (1)$$

where R_i is the throughput of the ith wireless station for a unit time duration (*rate*) and W is the bandwidth of the downlink. The last equation follows because $g_i = g_j$ for all $j \in \{1, 2, \ldots, M\}$ in a downlink from the base station to the ith wireless station, in other words both the signal aimed for the ith user and all the other communication that is only interference to user i traverses the same channel.

Notice that the right-hand side of the equation is the processing gain multiplied by the user's received power divided by the total noise power that the user is experiencing. $(E_b/N_0)_i$ and R_i are inversely proportional, therefore the QoS requirements should be met with equality, $(E_b/N_0)_i = \kappa_i$, for throughput maximization; since we can always lower the E_b/N_0, increase R_i and keep every other value constant in equation (1) as long as the E_b/N_0 requirement is satisfied. Therefore the throughput of the ith wireless station in the $[0, t]$ time interval is given by:

$$h_i(0, t) = \int_0^t R_i(t) \, dt = \frac{W}{\kappa_i} \int_0^t \frac{p_i(t)}{\sum_{j \neq i} p_j(t) + I_i/g_i(t)} \, dt \quad (2)$$

Let $\Lambda \doteq (\rho_1, \rho_2, \ldots, \rho_M)$ be the minimum required rates vector. Define the sets $\Phi = \{\mathbf{R} \mid \frac{\int_0^t R_i(t) \, dt}{t} \geq \rho_i, \forall i = 1, 2, \ldots, M\}$ and $\Upsilon(B) = \{\mathbf{p} \mid \mathbf{0} \leq \mathbf{p} \leq \mathbf{P} \text{ and } \mathbf{1}^T \cdot \mathbf{p} = B\}$ as the required rates and feasible powers vector sets respectively[1], where B is the maximum power level that the basestation can transmit. Assume that the connection topology stays the same during $[0, t]$ and further assume that $[0, t]$ is short enough so that the channel gains are constant. If we denote $H(0, t) \doteq \sum_i h_i(0, t)$ as the total throughput then the total downlink throughput maximization problem of the cell is given by:

---

[1] Vector relations are componentwise.

$$\sup_{\mathbf{p}\in\varUpsilon(B):\ \mathbf{R}\in\varPhi} H(0,t) = \sup_{\mathbf{p}\in\varUpsilon(B):\ \mathbf{R}\in\varPhi} \sum_i \frac{W}{\kappa_i} \int_0^t \frac{p_i(t)}{\sum_{j\neq i} p_j(t) + I_i/g_i}\, dt \quad (3)$$

Clearly the set that defines the domain of the optimization (3) is infinite and there is no clear feasible method of finding the best solution.

For a practical system, the transmitted powers are selected from a discrete (quantized) set of power levels. Therefore with a dense enough quantization, the continuous time power allocation and scheduling can be approximated with a power allocation and scheduling with fixed power levels, with arbitrary proximity. For quantization level k (i.e., a transmitted power can take one of the k discrete values), there are only k^M different power allocations possible. Let's associate the time durations $\varGamma_n = (t_n, t_{n+1})$, $n = 1, 2, \ldots, k^M$ to each such distinct power allocation and find the optimum set of $\varGamma_n$'s which maximizes the total throughput of the cell site, i.e.:

$$\max_{\mathbf{p}\in\varUpsilon(B):\ \mathbf{R}\in\varPhi} H(0,t) \cong \max_{\varGamma:\ \sum|\varGamma_n|=t,\ \mathbf{R}\in\varPhi} \sum_i \frac{W}{\kappa_i} \sum_{n=1}^{K} \frac{p_{in}\,|\,\varGamma_n\,|}{\sum_{j\neq i} p_{jn} + \frac{I_i}{g_i}} \quad (4)$$

where the set $\varUpsilon(\alpha) = \{\mathbf{p} \mid 0 \le \mathbf{p} \le \mathbf{P} \text{ and } \mathbf{1}^T \cdot \mathbf{p} = \alpha\}$ and B is the maximum total power the base station is allowed to transmit, $|\,\varGamma_n\,| = t_{n+1} - t_n$ and p_{in} is the fixed transmitted power level of wireless station i in the nth subinterval $\varGamma_n$, i.e. $p_i(t) = p_{in}$ for $t \in \varGamma_n$. $\varGamma_n$'s form a partition of the $[0, t]$ time interval. Notice that the above maximization problem is done over all possible sets of $\varGamma_n$'s and the p_{in} values are constants. Therefore the condition $\mathbf{R} \in \varPhi$ becomes the constraint on the decision variables $\varGamma_n$'s. It is also worth nothing that the RHS of equation (4) can be made arbitrarily close to LHS for large enough k, which in turn requires a large enough K.

Definition 1. *Vertex: A transmitted powers vector is a vertex in a time interval if $p_i = 0$ or $p_i = P_i$ for all $i = 1, 2, \ldots, M$ in that time interval.*

Definition 2. *Vertex-restricted-by-B: A transmitted powers vector is a vertex-restricted-by-B in a time interval if $p_i = 0$ or $p_i = P_i$ for all $i = 1, 2, \ldots, M$ except one $i = k \in \{1, 2, \ldots, M\}$ for which $0 \le p_k \le P_i$ and $\Sigma_i p_i = B$ in that time interval.*

Proposition 3. *In the solution of the optimization problem (4), the transmitted powers vector in subinterval $\varGamma_i$ is either a vertex or a vertex-restricted-by-B, for all $i = 1, 2, \ldots, M$.*

Proof. Assume there exists at least one subinterval $\varGamma_j$ in the optimum solution such that the transmitted power vector is not a vertex nor a vertex-restricted-by-B. This means at least two of the transmitted power values, p_{ij} is neither 0 nor P_i and p_{kj} is neither 0 nor P_k. Assume $p_{ij} > p_{kj}$ without loss of generality. Then one can divide $\varGamma_j$ into two subintervals such that the new value of p_{ij} is

$p_{ij}^1 = p_{ij} - q > 0$ and the new value of p_{kj} is $p_{kj}^1 = p_{kj} + q$ in the first λ portion of Γ_j and the new values are $p_{ij}^2 = p_{ij} + q$ and $p_{kj}^2 = p_{kj} - q$ in the remaining $1 - \lambda$ portion of Γ_j. Let all the other transmitted power values stay unchanged for both subintervals. Then the throughput of the downlinks other than i and k are unchanged in the new power allocation scenario. But for the ith and k^{th} downlink we have an increased throughput in the new power allocation scenario if $\lambda \in (\frac{a+b_2-q}{2(a+b_2)}, \frac{c+b_1+q}{2(c+b_1)})$ where $a = p_{ij}$, $b_1 = (\Sigma_{n \neq i,k} p_{nj}) + \frac{I_i}{g_i}$, $b_2 = (\Sigma_{n \neq i,k} p_{nj}) + \frac{I_k}{g_k}$ and $c = p_{kj}$ since:

$$\lambda < \frac{c+b_1+q}{2(c+b_1)} \Rightarrow \lambda \frac{a-q}{b_1+c+q} + (1-\lambda)\frac{a+q}{b_1+c-q} > \frac{a}{c+b_1} \qquad (5)$$

where the intermediate steps are mundane arithmetics and therefore are skipped. Notice that multiplying each side of the last inequality by $| \Gamma_j |$ proves that the throughput of the ith downlink is improved in the new scenario. Similarly:

$$\lambda > \frac{a+b_2-q}{2(a+b_2)} \Rightarrow \lambda \frac{c+q}{a+b_2-q} + (1-\lambda)\frac{c-q}{a+b_2+q} > \frac{c}{a+b_2} \qquad (6)$$

Again notice that multiplying each side of the last inequality by $| \Gamma_j |$ proves that the throughput of the kth downlink is improved in the new scenario. Finally one can easily verify that $\frac{a+b_2-q}{2(a+b_2)} < \frac{c+b_1+q}{2(c+b_1)}$ to complete the proof. $\square$

Let $\Gamma \doteq (| \Gamma_1 |, | \Gamma_2 |, \ldots, | \Gamma_L |)$, then by proposition 3, the optimization problem in (4) becomes:

$$\max_{\Gamma: \ \sum |\Gamma_n|=t, \ \mathbf{R} \in \Phi} \sum_i \frac{W}{\kappa_i} \sum_{n=1}^{L} \frac{\tilde{p}_{in} | \Gamma_n |}{\sum_{j \neq i} \tilde{p}_{jn} + \frac{I_i}{g_i}} \qquad (7)$$

where the vectors $(\tilde{p}_{1n}, \tilde{p}_{2n}, \ldots, \tilde{p}_{Mn}) \in \varphi$, $n = 1, 2, \ldots, L$ are all distinct, and φ denotes the set of all possible vertices and vertices-restricted-by-B. Also without loss of generality we renamed the partition in which the vertex $(\tilde{p}_{1n}, \tilde{p}_{2n}, \ldots, \tilde{p}_{Mn})$ is employed, to Γ_n, for all $n = 1, 2, \ldots, L$. Unlike the original optimization problem (over the infinite set $\Upsilon(B)$) , after restricting the solution set considerably (to the finite set φ) , we can now solve the optimization problem with Linear Programming (LP). The output of the optimization algorithm will be the $| \Gamma_1 |, \ldots, | \Gamma_L |$ values.

Let $\mathbf{A} = ((a_{ij}))$ where $a_{ij} = \frac{W}{\kappa_i} \frac{\tilde{p}_{in}}{\sum_{j \neq i} \tilde{p}_{jn} + \frac{I_i}{g_i}}$ then the optimization problem can be written as:

$$maximize \ \mathbf{1}^T \mathbf{A}\Gamma \ with \ the \ constraints^2: \ \mathbf{A}\Gamma \geq \Lambda \qquad (8)$$

Notice that although we have found the throughput maximizing scheduling for the duration $(0, t)$, this scheduling will satisfy all the QoS requirements of

---

[2] The inequalities are componentwise.

each wireless user but the extra capacity will be transferred to users with better channel gains which is unfair and unpractical. If we introduce the additional condition that each user will share the extra capacity proportional to their QoS requirements, then it is easy to show that the throughput maximization problem is equivalent to finding the minimum feasible value t, by when all the QoS requirements are satisfied. Therefore we transform the throughput optimization problem to the following minimization problem:

$$minimize \sum_{i=1}^{L} \mid \Gamma_i \mid \; with \; the \; constraints^2: \mathbf{A}\Gamma \geq \Lambda \qquad (9)$$

It is not hard to see that the inequality in the constraint above can be replaced by equality since the optimum solution will satisfy the rate requirements with equality. Let $\mathbf{\Gamma^*} = (\mid \Gamma_1^* \mid, \mid \Gamma_2^* \mid, \ldots, \mid \Gamma_L^* \mid)$ be the solution to the last optimization problem which can be solved by LP. The optimum solution $\mathbf{\Gamma^*}$ will have at least $L - M$ zero values and at most M non-zero values. The efficient LP techniques like *simplex method* can be used in order to achieve fast results. Since in the algorithm we would only have M *basic feasible solutions* at any iteration, we will have $O(ML)$ worst-case time and $O(M^2)$ best-case time. The memory need is only $O(M^2)$.

We can now construct the power allocation and scheduling scheme for precise channel gain and interference estimates. The proposed power allocation scheme will work as follows: As soon as one of the values of measured values of $\mathbf{g(t)}$ or I_i's changes, the base station will run the optimization algorithm and will assign the powers according to the optimization output, meaning for a period of $\mid \Gamma_1^* \mid$, the powers vector $\mathbf{V}_1$ will be transmitted, then for a period of $\mid \Gamma_2^* \mid$, the powers vector $\mathbf{V}_2$ will be transmitted and so forth. As soon as the duration $\mid \Gamma_L^* \mid$ where the powers vector $\mathbf{V}_L$ is assigned elapses, the base station will repeat the exact same assignments until either the value of $\mathbf{g(t)}$ or I_i changes. Remember that there are only at most M non-zero Γ_i^* values, meaning that there will be a time-division round robin between at most M vertices. We named the generic family of this resource allocation method as FiGARO.

For uplink (reverse link) resource allocation problem, most of the analysis follows in a similar fashion. For sake of completeness of the analysis, we will list the results for uplink with some notation abuse. For uplink the Γ' only consists of the 2^M vertices. The minimization problem corresponding to equation (9) is:

$$minimize \sum_{i=1}^{2^M} \mid \Gamma_i \mid \; with \; the \; constraints^2: \mathbf{A}\Gamma \geq \Lambda \qquad (10)$$

where $\mathbf{A} = ((a_{ij}))$ is the matrix with entries $a_{ij} = \dfrac{W}{\kappa_i} \dfrac{g_i \tilde{p}_{ij}}{\sum_{k \neq i} g_k \tilde{p}_{kj} + I_0}$.

3   Optimum Resource Allocation with Non-precise Parameter Estimates

In practical systems the channel gain and interference estimations of the network may not be perfect. If the estimation of the channel gain is different than the actual value, the FiGARO algorithm may result some of the connections to fail to satisfy their QoS guarantees. If the real channel gain is lower than the estimated value, the QoS of the channel will suffer and the connection may eventually be lost. In order to have a robust resource allocation, we will formulate and solve the resource allocation algorithm such that the QoS requirements will be met even if they are off by some amount. To serve this aim we will formulate the resource allocation problem with inexact constraints for the estimated values, namely, the channel gains and the interference estimates will lie within a certain interval, rather than being exact. Then we will use the Inexact Linear Programming (ILP) method to reduce that stochastic LP problem to an ordinary LP and solve it.

3.1   Inexact Linear Programming

In an inexact LP, the usual convex inequalities, $\mathbf{A}\Gamma \geq \mathbf{\Lambda}$, are replaced by the constraint that the sum of a finite number of convex sets is contained in another convex set, in our case, we will restrict the latter to the special form of a polyhedral convex set, i.e.:

$$maximize\ \mathbf{1A}\Gamma\ with\ the\ constraints^3\colon \Gamma_1 G_1 + \Gamma_2 G_2 + \ldots + \Gamma_{\mathbf{L}} \mathbf{G_L} \subseteq \mathbf{G}\ and\ \Gamma_j \geq \mathbf{0} \tag{11}$$

where G_j is a convex set containing $\mathbf{a}_j$, the jth column of the matrix $\mathbf{A}$, and $G = \{\mathbf{y} \in R^{2^M} \mid \mathbf{y} \geq \mathbf{\Lambda}\}$. In (11), Γ' is only a feasible solution if and only if $\Gamma_1\mathbf{a}_1 + \Gamma_2\mathbf{a}_2 + \ldots + \Gamma_L\mathbf{a}_L \geq \mathbf{\Lambda}$ and $\Gamma_i \geq 0$ for all possible sets of activity vectors in G_i's.

Notice that unlike (11), in generalized LP there is freedom to choose any vector $\mathbf{a}_j \in G_j$ for each j to maximize the objective function, i.e.,

$$maximize\ \mathbf{1A}\Gamma\ with\ the\ constraints\colon \Gamma_1\mathbf{a_1} + \Gamma_2\mathbf{a_2} + \ldots + \Gamma_L\mathbf{a_L} \geq \Lambda\ and\ \Gamma_j \geq \mathbf{0}, \mathbf{a_j} \in \mathbf{G_j} \tag{12}$$

In the generalized LP the activity vectors $\mathbf{a}_j$ are decision quantities as are the Γ_j's.

If the convex sets G_i's are equal to single vector, than the inexact LP coincides with regular LP. Therefore the inexact LP [14] applies to problems where the constraint vectors $\mathbf{a}_j$'s are not exactly known but are known to be in a convex set G_j.

Proposition 4. $S = \{\Gamma \mid \Gamma\ is\ feasible\ for\ (11)\ \}$ is a convex set.

---

[3] The inequalities are componentwise and the $+$ refers to addition of sets in this equation.

Proof. Let $(\tilde{\Gamma}_1, \tilde{\Gamma}_2, \ldots, \tilde{\Gamma}_L)$ and $(\hat{\Gamma}_1, \hat{\Gamma}_2, \ldots, \hat{\Gamma}_L) \in S$ and for any $\mathbf{a}_j$, $\forall j = 1, \ldots, n$, and $\lambda \in (0, 1)$ we have $\mathbf{s}_1 = \tilde{\Gamma}_1 \mathbf{a}_1 + \tilde{\Gamma}_2 \mathbf{a}_2 + \ldots + \tilde{\Gamma}_L \mathbf{a}_L$ and $\mathbf{s}_2 = \hat{\Gamma}_1 \mathbf{a}_1 + \hat{\Gamma}_2 \mathbf{a}_2 + \ldots + \hat{\Gamma}_L \mathbf{a}_L \in S$, so $(\lambda \hat{\Gamma}_1 + (1 - \lambda)\tilde{\Gamma}_1)\mathbf{a}_1 + (\lambda \hat{\Gamma}_2 + (1 - \lambda)\tilde{\Gamma}_2)\mathbf{a}_2 + \ldots + (\lambda \hat{\Gamma}_L + (1 - \lambda)\tilde{\Gamma}_L)\mathbf{a}_L = \lambda \mathbf{s}_2 + (1 - \lambda)\mathbf{s}_1 \geq \mathbf{\Lambda}$, which means $\lambda \mathbf{s}_2 + (1 - \lambda)\mathbf{s}_1 \in S$. $\square$

Definition 5. *The support functional of the convex set G_j, denoted as $\delta(\mathbf{z} \mid G_j)$, is equal to $\inf_{\mathbf{a}_j \in G_j} \mathbf{z} \cdot \mathbf{a}_j$.*

For each j define the vector $\bar{\mathbf{a}}_j$ where its ith entry is equal to $\hat{\delta}(\mathbf{e}_i \mid G_j) \doteq \inf_{\mathbf{a}_j \in G_j} a_{ij}$, where $\mathbf{e}_i$ is the vector with its ith entry as 1 and has entry 0 elsewhere. Notice that if the set G_j includes a vector who has an entry equal to $-\infty$, say the ith entry, then $\hat{\delta}(\mathbf{e}_i \mid G_j) = -\infty$ and therefore $\Gamma_1 G_1 + \Gamma_2 \cdot G_2 + \ldots + \Gamma_L \cdot G_L \geq \mathbf{\Lambda}$ necessarily implies that $\Gamma_j = 0$. Therefore we can omit the activity set G_j from our LP without loss of any generality. Therefore we will assume that $\hat{\delta}(\mathbf{e}_i \mid G_j) > -\infty$ for all i and j, from now on. The same restriction is automatically achieved if it is assumed that the sets $\{G_j\}$ are compact [14].

After forming $\bar{\mathbf{A}} = (\bar{\mathbf{a}}_1, \bar{\mathbf{a}}_2, \ldots, \bar{\mathbf{a}}_L)$, consider the following artificial LP problem:

$$maximize\ \mathbf{1}\bar{\mathbf{A}}\Gamma'\ with\ the\ constraints:\ \Gamma_1 \bar{\mathbf{a}}_1 + \Gamma_2 \bar{\mathbf{a}}_2 + \ldots + \Gamma_L \bar{\mathbf{a}}_L \geq \mathbf{\Lambda}\ and\ \Gamma_j \geq 0 \tag{13}$$

In the following paragraphs we will argue that the optimal solution to (13) is also the optimal solution to (11). Let's define the set H, as the set of all possible matrices formed from the convex sets G_i's; i.e.:

$$H = \{(\mathbf{a}_1, \mathbf{a}_2, \ldots, \mathbf{a}_L) \mid \mathbf{a}_i \in G_i, \forall i\} \tag{14}$$

After this definition, it's appropriate to claim that Γ' is a feasible solution to problem (11) if and only if $\mathbf{A}\Gamma' \geq \mathbf{\Lambda}$, $\forall \mathbf{A} \in H$ and $\Gamma' \geq 0$.

Proposition 6. *If $\bar{\Gamma}'$ is a feasible solution to (13) (the artificial ordinary linear optimization problem), then $\bar{\Gamma}'$ is a feasible solution for (11) (the inexact linear optimization problem), and vice versa.*

Proof. Let $\bar{\Gamma}'$ be a feasible solution to our artificial LP (13), then since $\bar{\mathbf{A}}\bar{\Gamma}' \geq \mathbf{\Lambda}$ and $\bar{\Gamma}' \geq 0$, and by construction we have $\mathbf{A} \geq \bar{\mathbf{A}}$. But then $\bar{\Gamma}'$ is a feasible solution for our original inexact LP (11) since $\mathbf{A}\bar{\Gamma}' \geq \bar{\mathbf{A}}\bar{\Gamma}' \geq \mathbf{\Lambda}$ for all $\mathbf{A} \in H$.

Conversely, if $\bar{\Gamma}'$ is a feasible solution for (11), then, $\bar{\Gamma}_1 \mathbf{a}_{i1} + \cdots + \bar{\Gamma}_L \mathbf{a}_{iL} \geq \rho_i$ (where ρ_i is the ith component of the vector $\mathbf{\Lambda}$), where $\mathbf{a}_j \in G_j$, for $i = 1, 2, \ldots, M$. Therefore, for all $i = 1, 2, \ldots, M$ we have

$$\bar{\Gamma}_1 \inf_{a_1 \in K_1} a_{i1} + \bar{\Gamma}_2 \inf_{a_2 \in K_2} a_{i2} + \cdots + \bar{\Gamma}_L \inf_{a_L \in K_L} a_{iL} \geq \rho_i, \tag{15}$$

which is indeed equivalent to $\bar{\Gamma}$ being a feasible solution to (13). $\square$

Corollary 7. *As an immediate result of proposition 6, the sets of the feasible solutions to the two problems are identical, i.e., the solution of (11) can be directly obtained by solving (13), which is a ordinary linear optimization problem.*

3.2   FiGARO with Inexact Estimates

Assume that the FiGARO engine does not have the exact values of the channel gains and the interference values, but rather inaccurate estimates of those variables. Therefore the real values of the estimated variables are only guaranteed to be within a neighborhood of the estimate, i.e. we have:

$$g_i \in [\hat{g}_i - \Delta_i, \hat{g}_i + \Delta_i] \text{ and } I_i \in [\hat{I}_i - \bar{\Delta}_i, \hat{I}_i + \bar{\Delta}_i] \text{ for all } i = 1, \dots, M \qquad (16)$$

These relations translate into the following condition that a_{ij} is guaranteed to be in the interval θ_{ij} where the θ_{ij} is defined by

$$\theta_{ij} = \left[\frac{W}{\kappa_i} \frac{\tilde{p}_{ij}}{\sum_{k \neq i} \tilde{p}_{kj} + \frac{\hat{I}_i + \bar{\Delta}_i}{\hat{g}_i - \Delta_i}}, \frac{W}{\kappa_i} \frac{\tilde{p}_{ij}}{\sum_{k \neq i} \tilde{p}_{kj} + \frac{\hat{I}_i - \bar{\Delta}_i}{\hat{g}_i + \Delta_i}} \right] \qquad (17)$$

If we define the set G_j's, $j = 1, 2, \dots, M$ such that:

$$G_j = \{(a_{1j}, a_{2j}, \dots, a_{Lj})^T \mid \forall i \ a_{ij} \in \theta_{ij}\}, \qquad (18)$$

to satisfy the individual connection requirements under FiGARO, no matter what channel gains and interference values we get (given that they will lie within their allowed intervals) we have to solve (11) with the new values of G_j's. But by corollary, solving that LP is equivalent to solving the following artificial LP:

maximize $\mathbf{1}\bar{\mathbf{A}}\Gamma'$ *with the constraints:* $\Gamma_1\bar{\mathbf{a}}_1 + \Gamma_2\bar{\mathbf{a}}_2 + \dots + \Gamma_L\bar{\mathbf{a}}_L \geq \Lambda$ *and* $\Gamma_j \geq 0$
$$(19)$$

where the vectors $\bar{\mathbf{a}}_j = (\bar{a}_{1j}, \bar{a}_{2j}, \dots, \bar{a}_{Mj})$, the matrix $\bar{\mathbf{A}} = (\bar{\mathbf{a}}_1, \bar{\mathbf{a}}_2, \dots, \bar{\mathbf{a}}_L)$ and

$$\bar{a}_{ij} = \hat{\delta}(\mathbf{e}_i \mid G_j) = \inf_{\mathbf{a}_j \in G_j} a_{ij} = \inf_{a_{ij} \in \theta_{ij}} a_{ij} = \frac{W}{\kappa_i} \frac{\tilde{p}_{ij}}{\sum_{k \neq i} \tilde{p}_{kj} + \frac{\hat{I}_i + \bar{\Delta}_i}{\hat{g}_i - \Delta_i}} \qquad (20)$$

Notice that at this point, we can assign the desired values to Δ_i's and $\bar{\Delta}_i$'s and calculate the output of FiGARO, namely, the vector Γ'.

4   Discussions

Since it leads to a very practical implication, which is a slightly more interesting case, in this section we will present our results for the uplink scenario. In the uplink the θ_{ij}'s are given by

$$\theta_{ij} = \left[\frac{W}{\kappa_i} \frac{(\hat{g}_i - \Delta_i)\tilde{p}_{ij}}{\sum_{k \neq i}(\hat{g}_k + \Delta_k)\tilde{p}_{kj} + (\hat{I}_0 + \Delta_I)}, \frac{W}{\kappa_i} \frac{(\hat{g}_i + \Delta_i)\tilde{p}_{ij}}{\sum_{k \neq i}(\hat{g}_k - \Delta_k)\tilde{p}_{kj} + (\hat{I}_0 - \Delta_I)} \right]$$
$$(21)$$

For the sake of analysis, let's assume that we can foresee and guarantee estimation of the channel gains and the intercell interference values with the same percentage accuracy, i.e.:

Table 1. Increase in Time Requirements with Estimation Errors in Uplink

Estimation Error	1%	2%	3%	5%	10%	20%	25%	33%	50%
Γ'/Γ		1.020	1.041	1.062	1.105	1.222	1.500	1.667	2.000	3.000

$$\frac{\Delta_1}{\hat{g}_1} = \frac{\Delta_2}{\hat{g}_2} = \cdots = \frac{\Delta_M}{g_M} = \frac{\Delta_I}{\hat{I}_0} = c \tag{22}$$

Then,

$$\bar{a}_{ij} = \frac{W}{\kappa_i} \frac{(\hat{g}_i - c\hat{g}_i)\tilde{p}_{ij}}{\sum_{k \neq i}(\hat{g}_k + c\hat{g}_k)\tilde{p}_{kj} + (\hat{I}_0 + c\hat{I}_0)} = \frac{1-c}{1+c} \frac{W}{\kappa_i} \frac{\hat{g}_i\tilde{p}_{ij}}{\sum_{k \neq i}\hat{g}_k\tilde{p}_{kj} + \hat{I}_0} = \frac{1-c}{1+c}\hat{a}_{ij} \tag{23}$$

and therefore, $\bar{\mathbf{A}} = \frac{1-c}{1+c}\hat{\mathbf{A}}$, where $\hat{\mathbf{A}} = (\hat{\mathbf{a}}_1, \hat{\mathbf{a}}_2, \ldots, \hat{\mathbf{a}}_{2M})$. To interpret what this means, we will go over an example. Assume we have the channel gain estimates, $\hat{g}_1, \cdots, \hat{g}_M$, and an estimate for the intercell interference value, $\hat{I}_0$. Additionally, assume that we know that the estimates are guaranteed to be within 5% of our estimated values. FiGARO would calculate the output, Γ' with the input set $\hat{g}_1, \cdots, \hat{g}_M, \hat{I}_0$. But the Quality of Service requirements will not be satisfied unless we are lucky and get exactly the estimated values. If we want the outcome scheduling be optimum and satisfy the individual Quality of Service requirements as long as the estimation errors are within the 5% error margins, then FiGARO should calculate Γ' as if the rate requirements of each of the connections were higher by a multiple of $\frac{1+c}{1-c} = \frac{1+0.05}{1-0.05} \cong 1.105$ and implement the modified output. But this will result in an output of $\Gamma' = \frac{1+c}{1-c}\Gamma'$, where Γ' is the solution to the original situation where we weren't seeking any guarantees for the estimation errors. So if (22) is satisfied, we have a very simple modification to the FiGARO algorithm and that is:

run FiGARO with the input set $(\hat{g}_1, \cdots, \hat{g}_M, \hat{I}_0)$ *to get output* Γ'

implement $\Gamma' = \frac{1+c}{1-c}\Gamma'$ *where c is the percentage error that can be tolerated for estimates.*

In table 1, we tabulated how the time requirements increase with respect to the error margin tolerance. As we become closer to 100% estimate error range, the Γ'/Γ' value reaches ∞ which is expected. The solution of (13), actually provides an ultraconservative strategy for the stochastic LP of the form (11). If we have different estimation error percentages for the different connections, i.e. for example the better channel may be estimated more accurately, then those values should be used to calculate the corresponding $\bar{a}_{ij}$ values. This will improve the performance loss for rate requirement guarantees.

We have simulated a CDMA2000 EV-DV like system in Mathematica. Our system model allows $5msec$ packets on a 1.25MHz channel with Rayleigh distribution on top of a lognormal fading for the channel model. We have soft-limited the peak rates to $200Kbps$ for the multi media type application with a $10Kbps$ minimum rate requirements. We assume each terminal have the same application with the same QoS requirements. Our model also incorporates some technical details such as the need to be connected to the basestation with a bare-minimum rate ($1200Kpbs$) even in case the transmitter is scheduled to be silent, in order to keep the connection alive. The suggested resource allocation scheme with over provisioning for 2%, 5%, and 10% error margins are compared to a theoretical upperbound where the scheduler has perfect knowledge of the parameters and implements the optimum corresponding to those values. Our simulations over many iterations show that the overprovisioning in time was 1.0414, 1.1063, and 1.2266 times more than the theoretical optimum respectively for 2%, 5%, and 10% error margins for the estimated parameters. The theoretical optimum is calculated such that for every iteration, the scheduler calculates the optimum allocation with the perfect knowledge of the parameters. The average additional time required to provision for the estimation errors in simulations are in perfect agreement with the tabulated theoretical data in table1.

5   Conclusion

We proposed a novel power allocation and scheduling scheme for multimedia CDMA based wireless wide area networks with non-precise parameter estimates. Unlike traditional CDMA networks, our proposed algorithm transmits to the wireless stations with certain power levels and durations which is a result of an optimization problem we define and solve. The resulting algorithm dynamically adapts to the changes in the channel gains, intercell interference and background noise levels and guarantees QoS for end-users as along as the estimation errors are within a pre-defined range. Therefore the algorithm FiGARO provides an adaptive resource allocation scheme for cellular wireless networks with fault-tolerance towards parameter estimation errors.

References

1. D. Goodman, N. Mandayam, "Power Control for Wireless Data" *IEEE Personal Communications*,vol. 7, no. 2, pp. 48-54, 2000.
2. D.Kim, "Rate-Regulated Power Control for Supporting Flexible Transmission in Flexible Transmission in Future CDMA Mobile Networks" *IEEE Journal on Selected Areas in Communications*,vol. 17, no. 5, pp. 968-977, May 1999.
3. M. L. Sim, E. Gunawan, B. -H. Soong, C. -B. Soh "Performance Study of Close-Loop Power Control Algorithms for a Cellular CDMA System" *IEEE Transactions on Vehicular Technology*,vol. 48, no. 3, pp. 911-921, May 1999.
4. L. Ding, J. S. Lehnert "Performance Analysis of an Uplink Power Control Using Truncated Channel Inversion for Data Traffic in a Cellular CDMA System" *IEEE Vehicular Technology Conference*,vol. 3, pp. 1673-1677, 2000.

5. L. Ding, J. S. Lehnert "On Uplink Power Control Using Two-Level Channel Inversion: Scheme, Performance, and Optimal Design in a Cellular CDMA System for Data Traffic" *IEEE Vehicular Technology Conference*,vol. 3, pp. 1678-1682, 2000.

6. J. M. Holtzman "CDMA Forward Link Water-filling" *IEEE Vehicular Technology Conference*,vol. 3, pp. 1663-1667, 2000.

7. J. M. Rulnick, N. Bambos "Mobile Power Management for wireless Communication Networks" *Wireless Networks*,no. 3, pp. 3-14, 1997.

8. S. -J. Oh, K. M. Wasserman "Dynamic Spreading Gain Control in Multi-service CDMA Networks" *IEEE Journal on Selected Areas in Communications*,vol. 17, no. 5, pp. 918-927, May 1999.

9. S. -J. Oh, K. M. Wasserman "Adaptive Resource Allocation in Power Constrained CDMA Mobile Networks" *IEEE Wireless Communications and Networking Conference*,vol. 1, pp. 510-514, 1999.

10. S. Lal, E. S. Sousa "Distributed Resource Allocation for DS-CDMA-Based Multimedia ad hoc Wireless LAN's" *IEEE Journal on Selected Areas in Communications*,vol. 17, no. 5, pp. 947-967, May 1999.

11. S. Kumar, S. Nanda "High Data-Rate Packet Communications for Cellular Networks Using CDMA: Algorithms and Performance" *IEEE Journal on Selected Areas in Communications*,vol. 17, no. 3, pp. 472-492, March 1999.

12. A. Jalali, R. Padovani, R. Pankaj "Data Throughput of CDMA-HDR a High Efficiency-High Data Rate Personal Communication Wireless System" *IEEE Vehicular Technology Conference*,vol. 3, pp. 1854-1858, 2000.

13. K. S. Gilhousen, I. M. Jacobs, R. Padovani, A. J. Viterbi, L. A. Weaver, C. E. Wheatley "On the Capacity of a Cellular CDMA System" *IEEE Transactions on Vehicular Technology*,vol. 40, no. 2, pp. 303-312, May 1991.

14. A. L. Soyster "Convex Programming with Set-Inclusive Constraints and Applications to Inexact Linear Programming" *Technical Notes, Pennsylvania State University, University Park, Pennsylvania*, pp. 1154-1157, July 1972.

15. H. C. Akin, K. M. Wasserman, "Resource Allocation and Scheduling in Uplink for Multimedia CDMA Wireless Networks", *Proc. of IEEE Sarnoff Conference*, April 26-27, 2004.

16. H. C. Akin, K. M. Wasserman, "Optimized Resource Allocation and Scheduling in Downlink for Multimedia CDMA Wireless Systems", *Proc. of IEEE WiOpt Conference*, March 24-26, 2004.

Analyzing Object Detection Quality Under Probabilistic Coverage in Sensor Networks*

Shansi Ren, Qun Li, Haining Wang, Xin Chen, and Xiaodong Zhang

College of William and Mary
Williamsburg, VA 23187, USA
{sren, liqun, hnw, xinchen, zhang}@cs.wm.edu

Abstract. Object detection quality and network lifetime are two conflicting aspects of a sensor network, but both are critical to many sensor applications such as military surveillance. Probabilistic coverage is an appropriate approach to balancing the conflicting design requirements of monitoring applications. Under probabilistic coverage, we present an analytical model to analyze object detection quality with respect to different network conditions and sensor scheduling schemes. Our analytical model facilitates performance evaluation of a sensing schedule, network deployment, and sensing scheduling protocol design. Applying the model to real sensor networks, we design a set of sensing scheduling protocols to achieve targeted object detection quality while minimizing power consumption. The correctness of our model and the effectiveness of the proposed protocols are validated through extensive simulation experiments.

1 Introduction

Sensor networks are used for a range of object detection and tracking applications, such as vehicle detection in military surveillance and wild animal habitat monitoring [9]. These applications, by their nature, enforce certain detection quality and lifetime requirements. The first requirement determines how fast a sensor network should detect the intrusion of a moving vehicle, or how often the data about a wild animal should be sampled and collected. The second requirement specifies the working duration a sensor network should sustain. These two requirements, however, are two conflicting optimization goals due to the stringent energy constraints of sensor nodes.

Full sensing coverage is mandatory for sensor monitoring applications that require either immediate response to detected events or information of all points in the sensing field. Full sensing coverage, however, is too restricted and expensive to support long-time monitoring applications. More often those applications do not need zero response time or information at all points of a sensing field. They may be willing to sacrifice some event detection delay or sensing fidelity

---

* This work is supported in part by the U.S. National Science Foundation under grants CNS-0098055, CCF-0129883, and CNS-0405909.

H. de Meer and N. Bhatti (Eds.): IWQoS 2005, LNCS 3552, pp. 107–122, 2005.

to increase the network lifetime. Full sensing coverage gives little leverage to tune object detection quality and battery power consumption. A relaxed sensing coverage—probabilistic coverage where any point in a sensing field is sensed with a certain probability at any time—is a more appropriate approach to balancing object detection quality and battery power consumption.

Probabilistic coverage scheme allows sensor nodes to periodically wake up and go back to sleep. A node in sleep mode cannot sense events; its sensing capability is resumed after it wakes up. Therefore, the sensor network provides only a fraction of the maximal coverage of all the sensors. Battery power, however, is conserved for the nodes in sleep mode. How much time and how frequently a sensor node should stay in active mode determine detection quality and power saving. Our study aims to characterize the interplay among the sensor scheduling, detection quality and power saving.

In this paper, under probabilistic coverage, we present a mathematical model to analyze the object detection quality with respect to various network conditions such as the node density and the object moving speed, and sensor scheduling schemes including random sensing schedules and synchronized sensing schedules. Note that the full coverage can be incorporated into our model since it is just a special case of the probabilistic coverage. We define two metrics to assess the object detection quality: the sensor detection probability (DP), and the stealth distance (SD) that an object can stealthily pass. Applying the model to real sensor networks, we further design distributed random and localized algorithms to achieve targeted object detection quality while minimizing the power consumption. We validate the correctness of our model and the effectiveness of sensing scheduling protocols through extensive simulation experiments.

The contributions of our analytical model are threefold. First, this analytical model gives solid and thorough understanding about various protocols and provides insights into the pros and cons of each protocol. Even if some protocols are not amenable to easy analysis, we can approximate them and incorporate many of them into the model.

Second, the analytical model helps to plan a sensor network with certain object detection quality requirements and power budget. The model is flexible enough to capture the interaction among the system parameters (e.g., sensor density, sensing range, object moving speed, etc.), object detection quality requirements, and network energy constraint. Thus, it can provide accurate guidelines for optimal sensor network deployment, and can also derive the necessary speed of an object wanting to evade sensor detection.

Third, in sensing scheduling protocol design, aside from determining the parameters for sensing scheduling protocols, the analytical model can direct new sensing scheduling protocol design.

The remainder of this paper is organized as follows. Section 2 sketches related work. Section 3 presents the system metrics and parameters. Section 4 details the analytical models. We design a set of sensing protocols in Section 5. Section 6 studies energy consumption and system working time properties of different schedules and protocols. Section 7 shows analytical results and their simulation validations. In Section 8 we apply our model to two formerly proposed protocols in the literature. Finally, we conclude our work in Section 9.

2   Related Work

Detecting and tracking a moving object in sensor networks has been extensively studied from different perspectives: maintaining high tracking precision [2, 5, 11], utilizing node collaborations [8, 15], and reducing energy consumption [10]. A large number of sensing coverage maintenance protocols, aiming to conserve energy under various conditions, have been proposed [1, 6, 12, 13]. The closest previous work to ours is [4], which is the first we believe to consider the trade-off between power conservation and quality of surveillance in target detection and tracking by using non-full coverage. [7] is an interesting work that gives the bound and asymptotic results on detectability. In [3], Cao *et al.* presented an optimized framework for rare event detection that compromises between event detection delay and lifetime while maintaining point coverage.

3   Object Detection Under Probabilistic Coverage

In order to evaluate the object detection quality of a sensor network, we define two metrics detailed as follows:

- *Detection Probability* (DP). The detection probability is defined as the probability that an object is detected in a certain observation time.
- *Stealth Distance* (SD). The stealth distance is defined as the average distance an object travels before it is detected for the first time.

Taking energy constraints into account, we further define other two metrics.

- *Lifetime* (*LT*). The system lifetime is the elapsed working time from system startup to the time when the object detection quality requirement cannot be met for the first time when live nodes continue sensing with their current periods.

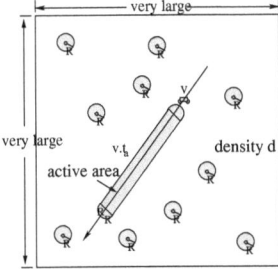

parameter	definition
d	density of sensors
R	sensing radius of a sensor
v	object moving speed
P	sensing period of sensors
f	active ratio of sensors in P
H	active duration $H = f \cdot P$
t_a	observation duration

Fig. 1. An object detection and tracking scenario

Fig. 2. System modeling parameters

- *Maximum Working Time.* The maximum working time is the longest possible working time of the system that satisfies the object detection quality requirement. When some nodes deplete their power, the remaining nodes can adjust their schedules to sustain the object detection quality.

Figure 1 shows a typical scenario of the object detection in a sensor network. A number of sensors with density d are randomly and independently distributed in a sensing field; the sensing radii of sensors have the same value R; the sensors have the same sensing period P and the same active ratio f. There is a small moving object crossing over the field with a constant speed v along a specified direction. Note that the object size can be neglected considering the large dimensions of the sensing field. The observation duration is t_a. These system parameters of a sensor network are summarized in Figure 2.

Object detection applications may have different DP requirements and SD requirements. For given sensing scheduling schemes, we assess their object detection quality using DP and SD with respect to these system parameters. We study how each parameter affects the metrics, and how we can adjust them to reach the object detection quality goal while minimizing the energy consumption. Our simplified theoretical model can be easily applied to real applications because the real moving path can be approximated by a set of line segments, to each of which the analytical results can be directly applied.

4   Detection Quality Analysis Under Different Schedules

In this section, we present the theoretical analyses on how different scheduling schemes affect the object detection quality in terms of DP and SD. More specifically, we study random sensing schedules and synchronized sensing schedules. In a random sensing schedule, a node independently and randomly chooses the starting time of its active duration H in a sensing period P; while in a synchronized sensing schedule, all nodes start their active duration H at the same time in every sensing period P. We compare these two schedules, and find that the random schedule performs better generally, while the synchronized schedule has a better worst case object non-detecting traveling distance in multiple experiments.

4.1   Random Sensing Schedule Analysis

A random sensing schedule is a simple but usually efficient schedule due to its distributed nature. It can serve as a baseline for analysis of and comparison to other schedules.

We first analyze the DP and the SD when sensors have the same sensing period P. Then we study the DP for a special case of fast objects. We introduce this special case analysis because it yields more simplified numerical results, which eases choosing appropriate network parameters to achieve required object detection quality while minimizing energy consumption. Finally we study how nodes can sense with different periods to achieve the same DP as those having the same period for fast objects.

Detection Probability. We study random sensing schedules in which all the nodes have the same sensing period P and the same active duration H.

Consider a moving object moves from left to right on x-axis. Suppose it starts at the point $\frac{-vt_a}{2}$, travels a distance of vt_a, and arrives at the point $\frac{vt_a}{2}$ during the observation duration t_a. Define the *active area AA* of this object as the oblong area in Figure 3, including the rectangle area with length vt_a and width of $2R$, and the two half disks with radius R attached to the rectangle. We can see that $AA = vt_a \cdot 2R + \pi R^2$.

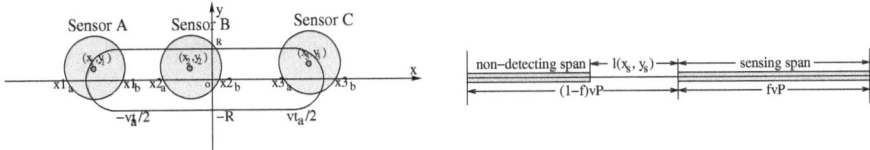

Fig. 3. Three sensors are located in the active area of a moving object

Fig. 4. The distance an object crosses in one sensing period

Proposition 1. *Let $Pr(x_s, y_s)$ denote the detection probability of a sensor located at (x_s, y_s) in the active area within t_a, and $\tilde{P}r$ denote the probability that one single sensor can detect this object within t_a, then*

$$\tilde{P}r = \frac{1}{AA} \int_{-R}^{R} dy_s \int_{-\frac{vt_a}{2}-R}^{\frac{vt_a}{2}+R} Pr(x_s, y_s) dx_s. \tag{1}$$

Proof: For a specific sensor located at position (x_s, y_s) to detect this object, two conditions must be satisfied: the sensor must be in the active area; the sensor must be active when the object crosses its sensing range. The detection probability of this sensor depends on the length of the segment that the object moving path intersects its sensing range. As shown in Figure 3, when the sensor is located at different parts in the active area, the intersecting length $l(x_s, y_s)$ has different representations. Then we have $l(x_s, y_s) = min(\frac{vt_a}{2}, x_b) - max(\frac{-vt_a}{2}, x_a)$, where $x_a = x_s - \sqrt{R^2 - y_s^2}$ and $x_b = x_s + \sqrt{R^2 - y_s^2}$ are the x coordinates of two intersecting points.

According to Figure 4, the detection probability of this sensor is $Pr(x_s, y_s) = f + \frac{t}{P}$ when $l(x_s, y_s) < (1-f)vP$ or $Pr(x_s, y_s) = 1$ when $l(x_s, y_s) \geq (1-f)vP$, where $t = \frac{l(x_s, y_s)}{v}$. Notice that $l(x_s, y_s) = 0$ and $Pr(x_s, y_s) = 0$ when (x_s, y_s) is outside the active area. Then, $\tilde{P}r$ can be obtained by computing the expectation of $Pr(x_s, y_s)$ over the active area as in (1). □

For the case of multiple sensors, since the nodes are randomly deployed, the number of sensors in the active area follows a Poisson distribution with an expected value of $\lambda = d \cdot AA$.

Theorem 1. *The detection probability under the random sensing schedule is*

$$DP = 1 - e^{-\lambda \tilde{P}r}. \tag{2}$$

Proof: The probability that there are k sensors in the active area is $Pr(k) = \frac{e^{-\lambda} \cdot \lambda^k}{k!}$, $k = 0, 1, \ldots, \infty$, while the probability that there exists k sensors in the active area and at least one of them can detect this object is $Pr(dt \wedge k) = \frac{e^{-\lambda}\lambda^k}{k!}[1 - (1 - \tilde{P}r)^k]$. Particularly, when $k = 0$, we have $Pr(0) = \frac{e^{-\lambda} \cdot \lambda^0}{0!} = e^{-\lambda}$. Because $\sum_{k=0}^{\infty} \frac{e^{-\lambda} \cdot \lambda^k}{k!} = 1$, we have $\sum_{k=1}^{\infty} \frac{e^{-\lambda} \cdot \lambda^k}{k!} = 1 - e^{-\lambda}$. Also $Pr(0) = \frac{e^{-\lambda}\lambda^0(1-\tilde{P}r)^0}{0!} = e^{-\lambda}$, and $\sum_{k=0}^{\infty} \frac{e^{-\lambda}\lambda^k \cdot (1-\tilde{P}r)^k}{k!} = e^{-\lambda \tilde{P}r}$. Then, we get $DP = \sum_{k=1}^{\infty} Pr(dt \wedge k) = \sum_{k=1}^{\infty} \frac{e^{-\lambda} \cdot \lambda^k}{k!}[1 - (1 - \tilde{P}r)^k] = (1 - e^{-\lambda}) - (e^{-\lambda \tilde{P}r} - e^{-\lambda}) = 1 - e^{-\lambda \tilde{P}r}$. $\qquad\square$

Stealth Distance. The stealth distance is an important metric to characterize the object detection quality. Here we derive the stealth distance for the random sensing schedule.

Theorem 2. *The stealth distance under the random sensing scheme is*

$$SD = \int_0^{\infty} v e^{-\lambda \tilde{P}r} dt_a. \tag{3}$$

Proof: Denote $cdf(x)$ and $pdf(x)$ as the cumulative distribution function and the probability density function of a numerical random variable x. We know $cdf'(x) = pdf(x)$. Also define $(1 - cdf)(x) = 1 - cdf(x)$.

The DP in (2) is a cdf function that can be written in the form of $Pr(t \leq t_a)$, where t is the point that the object is detected for the first time, and t_a can be viewed as a variable. Thus, $(1 - cdf)(t_a) = Pr(t > t_a) = e^{-\lambda \tilde{P}r}$. Because $lim_{t_a \to \infty} cdf(t_a) = 1$, and $lim_{t_a \to \infty}(1 - cdf)(t_a) = 0$, and they approach their limits exponentially when t_a approaches ∞ linearly, we have the expected detecting time $E(t_a) = \int_0^{\infty} pdf(t_a) \cdot t_a dt_a = \int_0^{\infty}(1 - cdf)(t_a)dt_a$. Therefore, $E(t_a) = \int_0^{\infty} e^{-\lambda \tilde{P}r} dt_a$. Thus, $SD = vE(t_a) = \int_0^{\infty} v e^{-\lambda \tilde{P}r} dt_a$. $\qquad\square$

Detection Probability For Fast Objects. For fast objects, we can have more simplified numerical results for the detection probability, as described in the following corollary.

Corollary 1. *We consider a special case, in which an object moves with a high speed v such that $vt_a > 2R$ and $(1 - f)vP > 2R$. Then, the probability of a single sensor detecting this fast object is*

$$\tilde{P}r = f + \frac{\pi R^2 t_a}{(vt_a \cdot 2R + \pi R^2)P}. \tag{4}$$

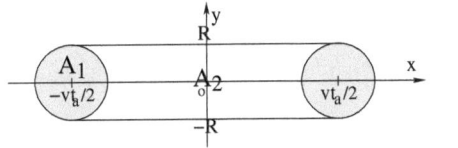

Fig. 5. The active area for detection probability calculation

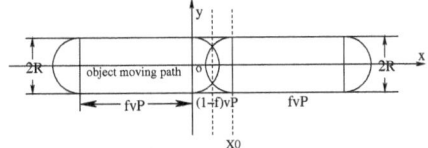

Fig. 6. The active area in the synchronized schedule when R is large

Proof: For this object, we get $\tilde{Pr} = f + \frac{1}{AvP} \int_{-\frac{vt_a}{2}-R}^{\frac{vt_a}{2}+R} dx_s \int_{-R}^{R} l(x_s, y_s)dy_s$ if we simplify (1).

Consider a sensor s located at (x_s, y_s). Denote $\xi_1 = \iint_{A_1} l(x_s, y_s)dx_sdy_s$, and $\xi_2 = \iint_{A_2} l(x_s, y_s)dx_sdy_s$, where A_1 is the circle on the left and A_2 is the unfilled area in the middle as shown in Figure 5. Due to the symmetry of the integrating area, we have $\int_{-\frac{vt_a}{2}-R}^{\frac{vt_a}{2}+R} dx_s \int_{-R}^{R} l(x_s, y_s)dy_s = 2\xi_1 + \xi_2$.

Let x_a and x_b $(x_b > x_a)$ be the x coordinates of the two intersecting points between the object path and the sensing circle of node s. Notice that $l(x_s, y_s) = max(x_b, -\frac{vt_a}{2}) - max(x_a, -\frac{vt_a}{2})$ when $(x_s, y_s) \in A_1$. Now we compute $l(x_s, y_s)$ under following conditions:

- $x_b > x_a > -\frac{vt_a}{2}$. We have $x_s > \sqrt{R^2 - y_s^2} - \frac{vt_a}{2}$ and $l(x_s, y_s) = x_b - x_a = 2\sqrt{R^2 - y_s^2}$.
- $x_b > -\frac{vt_a}{2}$ and $x_a < -\frac{vt_a}{2}$. We have $-\frac{vt_a}{2} - \sqrt{R^2 - y_s^2} < x_s < -\frac{vt_a}{2} + \sqrt{R^2 - y_s^2}$ and $l(x_s, y_s) = x_b + \frac{vt_a}{2} = x_s + \frac{vt_a}{2} + \sqrt{R^2 - y_s^2}$.
- $x_b < -\frac{vt_a}{2}$ and $x_a < -\frac{vt_a}{2}$. We have $l(x_s, y_s) = 0$.
- $x_b < -\frac{vt_a}{2}$ and $x_a > -\frac{vt_a}{2}$. Because $x_b > x_a$, this case is impossible.

We can get $\xi_1 = \int_{-R}^{R} dy_s \int_{-\sqrt{R^2-y_s^2}-\frac{vt_a}{2}}^{\sqrt{R^2-y_s^2}-\frac{vt_a}{2}} (x_s + \frac{vt_a}{2} + \sqrt{R^2 - y_s^2})dx_s = \frac{8R^3}{3}$,

and $\xi_2 = \int_{-R}^{R} dy_s \int_{\sqrt{R^2-y_s^2}-\frac{vt_a}{2}}^{-\sqrt{R^2-y_s^2}+\frac{vt_a}{2}} 2\sqrt{R^2 - y_s^2}dx_s = \pi R^2 vt_a - \frac{16R^3}{3}$. Therefore, $2\xi_1 + \xi_2 = \pi R^2 vt_a$. We can get $\tilde{Pr} = f + \frac{1}{AvP}(2\xi_1 + \xi_2)$, which leads to (4). □

Sequential Schedule and k-Set Schedule. As an extension of our previous results, here we show two equivalent scheduling schemes that can achieve the same detection quality as the random schedule with a constant sensing period P. We assume $2R < (1 - f)vP$, which implies that $l(x_s, y_s)$ is always less than $(1 - f)vP$, and H is a constant. Under these assumptions, according to (2), we know $\tilde{Pr}$ can be written in the form of $\frac{a}{P}$, where a is a variable that is independent of P and λ. In the following analysis, we only vary P and λ while leaving all other system parameters unchanged.

Lemma 1. *Let A be a schedule with sensing period kP and λ, where k is a non-negative value. We randomly divide the nodes into k equal-sized sets, and nodes in* *each set are randomly distributed in the field. Consider a sequential schedule B, where nodes in ith set are active only in the duration of $[(i-1)P+nkP, iP+nkP)$ for $1 \leq i \leq k$, then the schedule A and the schedule B have identical detection probability, i.e., $DP_A = DP_B$.*

Proof: In schedule B, all sets have identical detection probabilities. Consider the ith set S_i, the detection probability is $DP_B(S_i) = 1 - e^{-\frac{\lambda}{k}\tilde{P}r} = 1 - e^{\frac{\lambda a}{kP}}$, which is the same as that of schedule A.   □

Lemma 2. *We randomly divide the nodes into k sets $S_1, S_2, \cdots, S_k$. For any set S_i with density $x_i\lambda$, we associate a sensing period g_iP with it. Let $DP(S_i)$ denote the DP for the nodes in set S_i. If $\frac{x_1}{g_1} + \frac{x_2}{g_2} + \cdots + \frac{x_k}{g_k} = 1$, then the detection probability DP of this k-set schedule is equal to that of the schedule with all nodes having the same period P.*

Proof: We know that $DP(S_i) = 1 - e^{-x_i\lambda \cdot \frac{a}{g_iP}}$. Let $\overline{DP(S_i)}$ be the probability that no node in S_i detects this object, so $\overline{DP(S_i)} = 1 - DP(S_i) = e^{-x_i\lambda \cdot \frac{a}{g_iP}}$. Thus, we have $DP = 1 - \overline{DP(S_1)} \cdot \overline{DP(S_2)} \cdots \overline{DP(S_k)} = 1 - e^{\frac{-\lambda a}{P}(\frac{x_1}{g_1} + \frac{x_2}{g_2} + \cdots + \frac{x_k}{g_k})} = 1 - e^{\frac{-\lambda a}{P}}$.   □

4.2   Synchronized Sensing Schedule Analysis

A synchronized sensing schedule has the benefit that the worst case object non-detecting traveling distance is relatively small. Given that the field is fully covered by all active sensors, the worst case object non-detecting traveling distance is bounded by the maximum distance this object travels in one sensing period. Under synchronized sensing schedule, we first analyze the DP under the given system parameters. Based on the DP analysis, we then derive the SD. Note that all nodes have the same sensing periods here.

Detection Probability. Similar to the random sensing analysis, we study the active area under a synchronized sensing schedule to derive the detection probability.

Consider the traveling distance of a moving object in one sensing period P, we divide it into two parts: the first part is the distance the object travels in the duration $(1-f)P$ when all sensors are asleep; the second part is the distance the object travels when all sensors are active. In the first part, the object cannot be detected by any sensor; however, in the second part, the object can be detected when there are active sensors within a distance of R to it. Define the *active area* AA of a moving object as the set of points that are within a distance of R to the second part traveling segments of this object.

As shown in Figures 6, AA is the set of periodically repeated areas, except the last one when t_a is not multiple times of P. Each repeated area is either a rectangle plus two overlapped half circles (shown in Figure 6), or a rectangle plus two disjoint half circles. Denote $X_0 = (1-f)vP$ as shown in Figures 6. We assume that $t_a > P$.

Let $IA(P)$ be the total covering area of two half disks in one intermediate sensing period P. We consider whether there is overlapping in $IA(P)$. When $R \geq \frac{X_0}{2}$, intersecting points of two half disks are $(\frac{X_0}{2}, -\sqrt{R^2 - \frac{X_0{}^2}{4}})$ and $(\frac{X_0}{2}, \sqrt{R^2 - \frac{X_0{}^2}{4}})$. Then $IA(P) = 4 \int_0^{\frac{X_0}{2}} \sqrt{R^2 - x^2} dx = X_0 \sqrt{R^2 - \frac{X_0{}^2}{4}} + 2R^2 \arcsin \frac{X_0}{2R}$. When $R < \frac{X_0}{2}$, $IA(P) = \pi R^2$. Therefore, the active area in one intermediate sensing period P is $AA(P) = IA(P) + 2RvfP$.

To calculate the detection probability, we have the following theorem.

Theorem 3. *During the observation duration t_a, the active area is $AA(t_a) = \pi R^2 - IA(P) + \frac{t_a IA(P)}{P} + 2Rvft_a$. Let λ_s be the expected number of sensors in the active area, $\lambda_s = d \cdot AA(t_a)$. Then*

$$DP = 1 - e^{-\lambda_s} \tag{5}$$

Proof: The probability that no sensor in the active area is $e^{-\lambda_s}$. So, the detection probability that at least one sensor can detect this object under the synchronized sensing schedule is $DP = 1 - e^{-\lambda_s}$. □

Stealth Distance. Based on the above DP result, we can immediately derive the stealth distance for the synchronized sensing schedule. We have the following theorem.

Theorem 4. *The stealth distance SD under synchronized sensing schedule is*

$$SD = \frac{vP}{d \cdot (IA(P) + 2RvfP)} e^{-d(\pi R^2 - IA(P))}. \tag{6}$$

Proof: Similar to the random sensing analysis, we can view t_a in DP as a variable. We know $(1 - cdf)(t_a) = 1 - DP = e^{-d(\pi R^2 + IA(P))} \cdot e^{-d(\frac{IA(P)}{P} + 2Rvf)t_a}$. Let $F'(t_a) = (1 - cdf)(t_a)$, then $F(t_a) = \frac{-Pe^{-d(\pi R^2 - IA(P))}}{d(IA(P) + 2RvfP)} e^{-d(\frac{IA(P)}{P} + 2Rvf)t_a} + C$, where C is constant.

Let $E(t_a)$ be expected detecting time, we have $E(t_a) = \int_0^\infty (1 - cdf)(t_a) dt_a$, then $E(t_a) = F(t_a)|_0^\infty = \frac{Pe^{-d(\pi R^2 - IA(P))}}{d(IA(P) + 2RvfP)}$. So $SD = vE(t_a) = \frac{vP}{d \cdot (IA(P) + 2RvfP)}$ $\cdot e^{-d(\pi R^2 - IA(P))}$. □

Now we study a special case of $f = 100\%$, which means nodes wake up the whole time and never sleep. We have $(1 - cdf)(t_a) = e^{-d\pi R^2 - 2dRvt_a}$, therefore

$$SD = \int_0^\infty ve^{-(d\pi R^2 + 2dRvt_a)} dt_a = \frac{e^{-d\pi R^2}}{2dR}. \tag{7}$$

5 Design of Power Efficient Sensing Protocols

In this section, we design three practical sensing protocols that ensure: (I) the object detection quality requirement is satisfied; (II) low sensing duty cycles are utilized to save sensing energy; and (III) only moderate communication and computation overhead are incurred. The protocols are detailed as follows. Note that H is fixed in these protocols and there are n sensors in the network.

(I) *Global Random Schedule (GRS)*: The global density d is known to all sensors. According to Theorem 1, each node senses the field with the maximum sensing period P_{max} that satisfies the DP requirement.

(II) *Localized Asynchronous Schedule (LAS)*: This protocol is based on the fact that sensors in a dense region can have a larger P than those in a scarce region to reach the same object detection quality. After a node boots up, it broadcasts beaconing messages and infers the relative distance to its neighbors based on their signal strength. Then, it computes its local node density d_l by dividing the number of nodes in its communication range over the area of that range. According to Theorem 1, each node uses its local density d_l to compute the maximum period P_{max} that meets the object detection quality requirement as its sensing period. So, this algorithm achieves an object detection quality close to the targeted one.

(III) *Power-Aware Asynchronous Schedule (PAAS)*: This protocol takes the diversity of power capacity among sensor nodes into consideration. The whole set of nodes is divided into k sets $S_1, S_2, \cdots, S_k$, such that all nodes in set S_i have approximately the same power capacity E_i, where $1 \leq i \leq n$. Based on Lemma 2, we can set $g_i = \frac{\sum_{i=1}^{k} x_i E_i}{E_i}$ to achieve the same object detection quality as GRS does with a constant sensing period P for each node. If each set has one and only one node, given the sum of the power capacities $E = \sum_{i=1}^{n} E_i$, we can schedule a node that has a power capacity E_i with a sensing period $\frac{E}{nE_i} P$ to achieve the same object detection quality as GRS protocol does.

6   Energy Consumption and Working Time Analysis

We assume in all schedules the active duration H lasts long enough so that we can ignore the wake-sleep transition energy cost. System lifetime is a critical factor that indicates the quality of the sensor network, since the energy resource is an extremely scarce resource in each node. Let T be the continuous working time of a single node, and all nodes have the same T. Under the random sensing schedule and the synchronized sensing schedule, if all nodes have the same P and the same f, then one node spends H energy in a period P. This node will last for $\frac{T}{H}$ periods, thus its working time is $\frac{T}{H} \cdot P = \frac{T}{f}$. Therefore, the system lifetime is $LT = \frac{T}{f}$. Particularly, when H is constant, $LT = \frac{T}{f} = \frac{TP}{H}$, this means that a small f or a large P can yield a long system lifetime.

Define the first failure time and the last failure time as the time when the first live node and the last live node in the system deplete their power. For a sensor network with n nodes, we denote T_i as the time when the ith node runs out of its power for $i = 1, 2, \ldots, n$, and define T_f and T_l as the first failure time and the last failure time of the network. Note that H is fixed here.

In GRS, all nodes have the same sensing period P and the same active ratio f. Therefore, $T_i = \frac{E_i}{f}$ for $i = 1, 2, \ldots, n$. So, $T_f(GRS) = min(T_1, T_2, \ldots, T_n) = min(\frac{E_1}{f}, \frac{E_2}{f}, \ldots, \frac{E_n}{f})$. In PAAS, because nodes have different sensing period, they have different active ratio as well. Let P and f be the fixed sensing period and the fixed active ratio in the GRS protocol, respectively. Denote f_i as the active ratio of the ith node, where $i = 1, 2, \ldots, n$, then we have $f_i = \frac{H}{g_i P}$. On the other hand, because $g_i P = \frac{E}{nE_i} P$, we can get $f_i = \frac{nfE_i}{E}$. Note that in PAAS, all nodes have the same elapsed working time, i.e., $T_f = T_i = T_1 = T_2 = \ldots = T_n$. Therefore, $T_f(PAAS) = \frac{E}{nf}$. Because $\frac{E}{n} \geq min(E_1, E_2, \ldots, E_n)$, we know $T_f(GRS) \leq T_f(PAAS)$. In other words, PAAS has a larger first failure time than GRS.

The maximum working time is always longer than the lifetime in the previous definition, thus it can better characterize the energy consumption property of the network. Here we consider a *simple random sensing schedule*, in which all nodes have identical sensing periods at any moment, and only wake up once in one sensing period. We have the following theorem.

Theorem 5. *With the same DP requirement, the simple random sensing schedule and the PAAS have the same energy consumption rate, thus have the same maximum working time.*

Proof: We know $DP = 1 - e^{-\lambda c/P}$, where c is a constant if H and other detection parameters are fixed. The energy consumption per time unit that meets the required detection quality is fixed and is proportional to λ/P. This is because the number of participating sensors is proportional to λ, and the energy consumption of each sensor is proportional to $1/P$. Therefore, for any simple random sensing schedule with a given detection probability requirement, the energy consumption rate is nf, where n is the total number of nodes and f is the active ratio of each sensor node.

For the PAAS, even though each node sets its P according to its remaining power, the total power consumption of all nodes is still constant. Consider the ith node in all n nodes, where $1 \leq i \leq n$. Its energy consumption rate is $er_i = \frac{H}{P_i}$. Because $P_i = \frac{E}{nE_i}$ and H is constant, then $er_i = \frac{H}{P_i} = \frac{H}{\frac{E}{nE_i}P} = \frac{nHE_i}{EP}$. The total energy consumption rate is $\sum_{i=1}^{n} er_i = \sum_{i=1}^{n} \frac{nHE_i}{EP} = \frac{nfEP}{EP} = nf$. Therefore, the PAAS has the same maximum working time as the simple random schedule, in which all nodes have fixed sensing periods. $\square$

7   Analysis Validation and Protocol Evaluation

In our simulation experiments, we generated a 500×500 grid field, and randomly placed $d \times 250,000$ sensors on it. Sensors use either random sensing schedule or synchronized sensing schedule. A small object moves along a straight line with a constant speed v. We run each simulation scenario for hundreds of times. Then, we use the ratio of detection times over the number of experiments to estimate DP, and use the average non-detecting distance to estimate SD.

7.1   Evaluation of Random and Synchronized Schedules

We plot both analytical curves and simulation results under different combinations of six parameters as shown in Figures 7, 8, and 9, respectively. Our observations are summarized as follows: (I) The simulation results match the analytical curves well, which validates the correctness of our derivations. (II) DP monotonically increases, and SD monotonically decreases with the increase of the parameters, as shown in Figure 10. (III) The random schedule outperforms the synchronized schedule on both DP and SD, which is shown in Figure 9. This is because the synchronized schedule causes more overlapping sensing areas than the random schedule. (IV) The non-detecting distance distributions have long tails: most non-detecting distances are short, while a few have large values. The worst case of non-detecting distance in the random schedule is longer than that of the synchronized schedule.

7.2   Evaluation of GRS, LAS, and PAAS Protocols

We use the DP to evaluate the effectiveness of the GRS, LAS, and PAAS protocols, and use the first failure time, the last failure time, and the system lifetime to compare their power consumption properties.

In our experiments to evaluate these three protocols, each sensor node's energy follows a uniform distribution between $[0, E_{max}]$. We set system parameters as follows: $d = 0.2, R = 0.5, v = 5, t_a = 2, P = 1.1, H = 0.55, r = 3,$ and

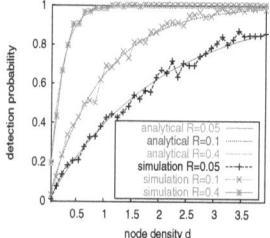 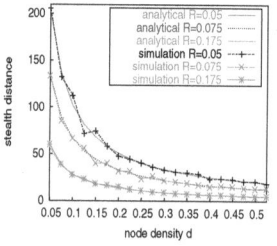 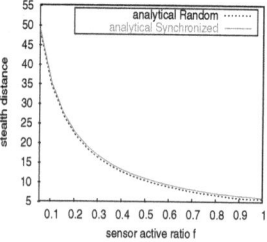

Fig. 7. DP under the random schedule. $v = 1, t_a = 5, P = 0.1, f = 0.5$

Fig. 8. SD under the random schedule, $v = 1, P = 0.1, f = 0.5$

Fig. 9. SD under the two schedules. $d = 0.4, R = 0.2, v = 2, P = 2$

metric	$d \uparrow$	$R \uparrow$	$v \uparrow$	$t_a \uparrow$	$P \uparrow$	$f \uparrow$
DP	$\uparrow$	$\uparrow$	$\uparrow$	$\uparrow$	$\uparrow$	$\downarrow$
SD	$\downarrow$	$\downarrow$	$\uparrow$		$\downarrow$	$\uparrow$

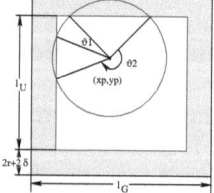

Fig. 10. DP and SD change when system parameters increase

Fig. 11. Uncovered square of one grid in the Mesh protocol

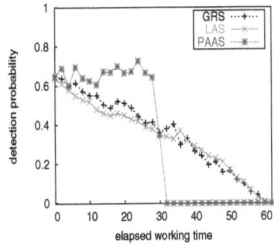 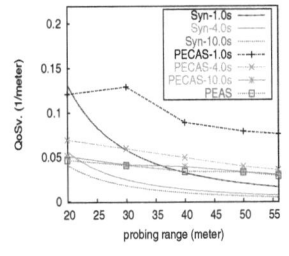 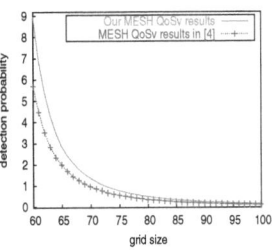

Fig. 12. DP comparison between GRS, LAS, and PAAS

Fig. 13. $QoSv$ under the synchronized schedule compared to that in [4]

Fig. 14. $QoSv$ of the Mesh protocol compared to that in [4]

$E_{max} = 30$. Here r is the range to compute the local density in LAS. Given the requirement of $DP \geq 60\%$, Figure 12 illustrates the degradation of DP as nodes run out of power. Note that every data point in this figure is obtained by averaging hundreds of experiment results.

Based on the simulation results, we have the following observations: (I) GRS, LAS, and PAAS can achieve the same DP at the beginning when no sensor depletes its energy. (II) The first failure time and the last failure time of PAAS are the same; by contrast, GRS and LAS have smaller first failure time and larger last failure time. (III) PAAS has a longer system lifetime than those of GRS and LAS. (IV) The DP degradation curves of GRS and LAS in Figure 12 are exponential, instead of linear. This is because for a sensor whose energy is uniformly distributed in $[0, E_{max}]$, the DP at time t is $DP(t) = 1 - e^{-\lambda(t)\tilde{P}r}$, where $\lambda(t) = \lambda_0 - qt$, q is the death rate, and λ_0 is the initial sensor density. Thus, $DP(t) = 1 - e^{\lambda_0\tilde{P}r} \cdot e^{qt\tilde{P}r}$.

8 Applying the Model to PECAS Protocol and Mesh Protocol

We further apply our analytical model to two sensing schedules in the literature, namely PECAS and Mesh. We show that by choosing appropriate parameters these schedules can be approximated by the random sensing schedule and the synchronized sensing schedule. In particular, we present the analytical $QoSv$ results on the PECAS protocol, while in [4] only simulation results are given.

8.1 Analysis of the PECAS Protocol

The PECAS protocol [4] is an enhanced variance of the Probing Environment and Adaptive Sleeping (PEAS) protocol [14]. In PECAS, each node remains active only for a limited duration. Here we extract the network parameters out of the PECAS experiments in [4]. Let the node density of the field be d, and the probing range of a node be r. In a circle area of πr^2, the expected number of nodes is $d \cdot \pi r^2$. Because $d \cdot f = \frac{1}{\pi r^2}$, on average the active ratio of a node is $f = \frac{1}{d\pi r^2}$. The system parameters in [4] are as follows: $d = \frac{800}{400m \times 400m} = 0.005/m^2$, $R = 20m$, $v = 10m/s$, and r varies from $20m$ to $56m$. Since $f = \frac{1}{d\pi r^2}$, we know f changes from 0.159 (when $r = 20m$) to 0.0203 (when $r = 56m$). The working time duration in the three curves in [4] is 1.0sec, 4.0sec, and 10.0sec, respectively. This duration is H in the random schedule and the synchronized schedule. On the other hand, the $QoSv$ is the reciprocal of the SD, i.e., $QoSv = 1/SD$.

With these parameter settings, we plot the corresponding $QoSv$ under the random and the synchronized sensing schedules as well as the PECAS curves in [4]. A larger probing range r or a larger working time duration results in a smaller $QoSv$. We find that the random sensing schedule has a better $QoSv$ than PECAS for the reason that a small node density d incurs a small chance of nodes being close to each other. On the other hand, the synchronized sensing schedule has a similar $QoSv$ result to that of the PECAS protocol, as shown in Figure 13. In the PECAS, once a node goes into sleep, there are several nodes around it wake up. This is similar to the scenario where nodes all wake up simultaneously in the synchronized schedule.

8.2   Analysis of the Mesh Protocol

In the Mesh protocol [4], nodes at planned locations remain active and form a planned pattern of 2-D mesh by a set of horizontal and vertical solid lines. The distance between adjacent horizontal or vertical lines is L_G. Each uncovered area in this sensor deployment is a square with a side length of L_u, where $L_u = L_G - 2r - 2\delta$, as shown in Figure 11.

If the node density is high, for a randomly chosen point, its probability of not being covered by any active sensor is $Pr_{uc} = \frac{(\lfloor \frac{L}{L_G} \rfloor)^2 (L_G - 2r - 2\delta)^2}{L^2}$. As shown in Figure 11, for the point with coordinate (x_p, y_p) in the uncovered square, we draw a disk centered at it with a radius of vt_a. Denote $\xi = \frac{L_u}{2}$. Suppose there are $2m$ intersecting points between this disk and the four border lines, then the circle is divided into arcs by the intersecting points, interleavingly inside and outside the uncovered square. Let the angles of these arcs inside be $\theta_1(x_p, y_p), \ldots, \theta_m(x_p, y_p)$. By definition, the average DP at the point (x_p, y_p) is $\frac{\sum_{i=1}^{m} \theta_i}{2\pi}$. We integrate the average DP of a point over the whole uncovered square to obtain the DP in t_a:

$$DP_{mesh} = \frac{(\lfloor \frac{L}{L_G} \rfloor)^2 \int_{-\xi}^{\xi} dx_p \int_{-\xi}^{\xi} (\frac{\sum_{i=1}^{m} \theta_i(x_p, y_p)}{2\pi}) dy_p}{L^2}.$$

We use the same parameter settings as that in [4], which are listed as follows: $l = 400m$, $R = 20m$, $v = 10m/s$, l_G varies from $60m$ to $100m$, $l_U = l_G - 10m$, and $2\delta = 10m$. The DP here is a cdf function of the variable t_a. We integrate the $(1 - cdf)$ function over the time span of $[0, \infty)$ to obtain the SD, then $QoSv_{mesh} = \frac{1}{\int_0^\infty DP_{mesh} dt_a}$. The comparison between our results and the results in [4] is illustrated in Figure 14. The close match of the two curves validates the correctness of both analyses.

9   Conclusion

Balancing object detection quality and network lifetime is a challenging task in sensor networks. Under probabilistic coverage, we present an analytical model to fully investigate object detection quality with respect to various network conditions and sensing scheduling protocols. Based on the model, we design and analyze a number of sensing protocols. The correctness of our analytical model and the effectiveness of the proposed scheduling protocols are justified through extensive simulation experiments.

Acknowledgment

We thank the anonymous reviewers for their constructive comments and suggestions. We are also grateful to William L. Bynum for reading an early draft of this paper.

References

1. Z. Abrams, A. Goel, and S. Plotkin. Set K-Cover algorithms for energy efficient monitoring in wireless sensor networks. In *Proceedings of IPSN'04*.
2. J. Aslam, Z. Butler, F. Constantin, V. Crespi, G. Cybenko, and D. Rus. Tracking a moving object with a binary sensor network. In *Proceedings of ACM SenSys'03*.
3. Q. Cao, T. Abdelzaher, T. He, and J. Stankovic. Towards optimal sleep scheduling in sensor networks for rare-event detection. In *Proceedings of IPSN'05*.
4. C. Gui, and P. Mohapatra. Power conservation and quality of surveillance in target tracking sensor networks. In *Proceedings of ACM MobiCom'04*.
5. R. Gupta, and S. R. Das. Tracking moving targets in a smart sensor network. In *Proceedings of IEEE VTC Fall 2003 Symposium*.
6. C. Hsin, and M. Liu. Network coverage using low duty-cycled sensors: random & coordinated sleep algorithms. In *Proceedings of IPSN'04*.
7. B. Liu, and D. Towsley. A study on the coverage of large-scale sensor networks. In *Proceedings of IEEE MASS'04*.
8. J. Liu, J. Liu, J. Reich, P. Cheung, and F. Zhao. Distributed group management for track initiation and maintenance in target localization applications. In *Proceedings of IPSN'03*.
9. A. Mainwaring, R. Szewczyk, D. Culler, and J. Anderson. Wireless sensor networks for habitat monitoring. In *ACM International Workshop on Wireless Sensor Networks and Applications'02*.
10. S. Pattem, S. Poduri, and B. Krishnamachari. Energy-quality tradeoffs for target tracking in wireless sensor networks. In *Proceedings of IPSN'03*.
11. Q. Wang, W. Chen, R. Zheng, K. Lee, and L. Sha. Acoustic target tracking using tiny wireless sensor devices. In *Proceedings of IPSN'03*.
12. X. Wang, G. Xing, Y. Zhang, C. Lu, R. Pless, and C. Gill. Integrated coverage and connectivity configuration in wireless sensor networks. In *Proceedings of ACM SenSys'03*.

13. T. Yan, T. He, and J. Stankovic. Differentiated surveillance for sensor networks. In *Proceedings of ACM SenSys'03*.
14. F. Ye, G. Zhong, J. Cheng, S. Lu, and L. Zhang. Peas: a robust energy conserving protocol for long-lived sensor networks. In *Proceedings of IEEE ICDCS'03*.
15. F. Zhao, J. Shin, and J. Reich. Information-driven dynamic sensor collaboration for tracking applications. In *IEEE Signal Processing Magazine*, March 2002.

A Self-tuning Fuzzy Control Approach for End-to-End QoS Guarantees in Web Servers*

Jianbin Wei and Cheng-Zhong Xu

Department of Electrical and Computer Engineering,
Wayne State University, Detroit, Michigan 48202
{jbwei, czxu}@wayne.edu

Abstract. It is important to guarantee end-to-end quality of service (QoS) under heavy-load conditions. Existing work focus on server-side request processing time or queueing delays in the network core. In this paper, we propose a novel framework eQoS to monitoring and controlling client-perceived response time in Web servers. The response time is measured with respect to requests for Web pages that contain multiple embedded objects. Within the framework, we propose an adaptive fuzzy controller, STFC, to allocating server resources. It deals with the effect of process delay in resource allocation by its two-level self-tuning capabilities. Experimental results on PlanetLab and simulated networks demonstrate the effectiveness of the framework: it controls client-perceived pageview response time to be within 20% of a pre-defined target. In comparison with static fuzzy controller, experimental results show that, although the STFC has slightly worse performance in the environment where the static fuzzy controller is best tuned, because of its self-tuning capabilities, it works better in all other test cases by 25% in terms of the deviation from the target response time. In addition, due to its model independence, the STFC outperforms the linear proportional integral (PI) and adaptive PI controllers by 50% and 75%, respectively.

1 Introduction

In the past decade we have seen an increasing demand for provisioning of quality of service (QoS) guarantees to various network applications and clients. There existed many work on provisioning of QoS guarantees. Most of them focused on Web servers without considering network delays [1, 6], on individual network router [7], or on clients with assumptions of QoS supports in networks [8]. Recent work [11] on end-to-end QoS guarantees in network cores aimed to guarantee QoS measured from server-side network edges to client-side network edges without considering delays incurred in servers.

In practice, client-perceived QoS is attributed by network delays and by server-side request queueing delays and processing time. The objective of this paper is to guarantee end-to-end QoS in Web servers. To provide such QoS guarantees, service quality must be accurately measured in real time so that server resources can be allocated promptly.

---

* This work was supported in part by US NSF grant ACI-0203592 and NASA grant 03-OBPR-01-0049.

H. de Meer and N. Bhatti (Eds.): IWQoS 2005, LNCS 3552, pp. 123–135, 2005.

Most recently, the ksniffer approach presented in [14] realized such on-line real-time measurement and made such guarantees possible.

The first contribution in this paper is a novel *eQoS* framework to monitoring and controlling client-perceived QoS in Web servers. To the best of our knowledge, the *eQoS* is the first one to guarantee client-perceived end-to-end QoS based on the ksniffer ideas of real-time QoS measurement. Moreover, because more than 50% of Web pages have one or more embedded objects [9], the guaranteed QoS is measured with respect to requests for *whole* Web pages that contain multiple embedded objects, instead of requests for a single object [1, 2] or connection delay in Web servers [19].

The second contribution of this paper is a two-level self-tuning fuzzy controller (STFC) that requires no accurate server model to allocate server resources within the *eQoS*. Traditional linear feedback control has been applied as an analytic method for QoS guarantees in Web servers because of its self-correcting and self-stabilizing behavior [1]. It adjusts the allocated resource of a client class according to the difference between the target QoS and the achieved one in previous scheduling epochs. It is well known that linear approximation of a nonlinear system is accurate only within the neighborhood of the point where it is linearized. In fast changing Web servers, the operating point changes dynamically and simple linearization is inappropriate.

In Web servers, resource allocation must be based on accurately measured effect of previous resource allocation on the client-perceived response time of Web pages. According to the HTTP protocol, on receiving a request for the base (or container) of a Web page, the server needs to schedule the request according to its resource allocation. At this point, it is impossible to measure the client-perceived response time of the Web page because the server needs to handle the request and the response needs to be transmitted over the networks. An accurate measurement of resource-allocation effect on response time is thus delayed. Consequently, the resource allocation is significantly complicated because it has to be based on an inaccurate measurement. We refer to the latency between allocating server resources and accurately measuring the effect of the resource allocation on provided service quality as *process delay*.

The STFC overcome the existing approaches' limitations with its two-level self-tuning capability. On its first level is a resource controller that takes advantage of fuzzy control theory to address the issue of lacking accurate server model due to the dynamics and unpredictability of pageview request traffic. On the second level is a scaling-factor controller. It aims to compensate the effect of the process delay by adjusting the resource controller's output scaling factor according to transient server behaviors. We note that fuzzy control theory was recently used by others for QoS guarantees as well [12, 16]. Their approaches, however, are non-adaptive. They cannot guarantee client-perceived pageview response time in the presence of the process delay.

We implement a prototype of *eQoS* in Linux. We conduct experiments across wide-range server workload conditions on PlanetLab test bed [18]. and on simulated networks. The experimental results demonstrate that provisioning of client-perceived QoS guarantees is feasible and the *eQoS* is effective in such provisioning: it controls the deviation of client-perceived average pageview response time to be within 20% of a pre-defined target. For comparison, we also implement three other controllers within the *eQoS* framework: a static fuzzy that uses similar as the one in [12], a linear PI controller, and an adaptive PI controller that bears resemblance to the approach in [10]. Experimental results show that, although the STFC works slightly worse than the non-adaptive fuzzy controller in the environment where the non-adaptive fuzzy controller is best tuned, because of its self-tuning capabilities, it has better performance in all other test cases by 25% in terms of the deviation from the target response time. The STFC outperforms the linear PI and adaptive PI controllers by 50% and 75%, respectively.

The structure of the paper is as follows. Section 2 presents the *e*QoS framework. Section 3 presents the two-level STFC. Section 4 evaluates the performance of the *e*QoS in real-world and simulated networks and compares the performance between different controllers. Section 5 reviews related work and Section 6 concludes the paper.

2   The *e*QoS Framework

The *e*QoS framework is designed to guarantee the average pageview response time of premium clients $W(k)$ to be close to a target $D(k)$ in heavy-loaded servers. Because the server load can grow arbitrary high, it is impossible to guarantee QoS of all clients under heavy-load conditions. Client-perceived response time is the time interval that starts when a client sends the first request for the Web page to the server and ends when the client receives the last object of the Web page. In this work we use the Apache Web server with support of HTTP/1.1. We assume that all objects reside in the same server so that we can control the processing of the whole Web page. The latency incurred in resolving domain name into IP address is not considered because it is normally negligible. As shown in [15], 90% of the name-lookup requests have response time less than 100 *ms* for all of their examined domain name servers except one.

The *e*QoS framework consists of four components: a Web server, a QoS controller, a resource manager, and a QoS monitor. Fig. 1(a) illustrates the components and their interactions. The QoS controller determines the amount of resource allocated to each class. It can be any controller designed for the provisioning of QoS guarantees. In addition to the STFC, current implementation includes three other controllers: a non-adaptive fuzzy, a PI, and an adaptive PI controllers for comparison. The QoS monitor measures client-perceived pageview response time using ideas similar as those presented in [14].

The resource manager classifies and manages client requests and realizes resource allocation between classes. It comprises of a classifier, several waiting queues, and a processing-rate allocator. The classifier categorizes a request's class according to rules defined by service providers. The rules can be based on the request's header information (e.g., IP address and port number). Without the *e*QoS, a single waiting queue is created in the kernel to store all client requests for each socket. In the *e*QoS, requests are stored in their corresponding waiting queues in the resource manager. The requests from the same class are served in first-come-first-served manner. The process-rate allocator realizes resource allocation between different classes. Since every child process in the Apache Web server is identical, we realize the processing-rate allocation by controlling the number of child processes that a class is allocated. In addition, when a Web server becomes overloaded, admission control mechanisms [25] can be integrated into the resource manager to ensure the server's aggregate performance.

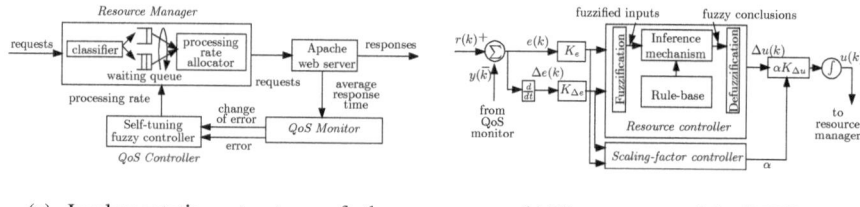

(a) Implementation structure of the eQoS

(b) The structure of the STFC

Fig. 1. The structure of the *e*QoS framework

3   The Self-tuning Fuzzy Controller

To guarantee client-perceived QoS effectively, the QoS controller must address issues of the process delay in resource allocation without any assumption of pageview request traffic model. To the end, we present a self-tuning fuzzy controller, STFC. Fig. 1(b) presents its structure.

3.1   The Resource Controller

As shown in Fig. 1(b), the resource controller consists of four components. The rule-base contains a set of *If-Then* rules about quantified control knowledge about how to adjust the resource allocated to premium class according to $e(k)$ and $\Delta e(k)$ in order to provide QoS guarantees. The fuzzification interface converts controller inputs into certainties in numeric values of the input membership functions. The inference mechanism activates and applies rules according to fuzzified inputs, and generates fuzzy conclusions for defuzzification interface. The defuzzification interface converts fuzzy conclusions into the change of resource of premium class in numeric value.

The resource controller presented in Fig. 1(b) also contains three scaling factors: input factors K_e and $K_{\Delta e}$ and output factor $\alpha K_{\Delta u}$. They are used to tune the controller's performance. The actual inputs of the controller are $K_e e(k)$ and $K_{\Delta e}\Delta e(k)$. In the output factor, α is adjusted by the scaling-factor controller. Thus, the resource allocated to premium class during the $(k+1)$th sampling period $u(k+1)$ is $\int \alpha K_{\Delta u}\Delta u(k)dk$.

The parameters of the control loop as shown in Fig. 1(b) are defined as follows. The reference input for kth sampling period $r(k)$ is $D(k)$. The output of the loop is the achieved response time $W(k)$. The error $e(K)$ and the change of error $\Delta e(k)$ are defined as $D(k) - W(k)$ and $e(k) - e(k-1)$, respectively.

It is well known that the bottleneck resource plays an important role in determining the service quality a class receives. Thus, by adjusting the bottleneck resource a class is allocated, we are able to control its QoS: The more resource it receives, the smaller response time it experiences. The key challenge in designing the resource controller is translating heuristic control knowledge into a set of control rules so as to provide QoS guarantees without an accurate model of continuously changing Web servers.

In the resource controller, we define the control rules using linguistic variables. For brevity, linguistic variables "$e(k)$", "$\Delta e(k)$", and "$\Delta u(k)$" are used to describe

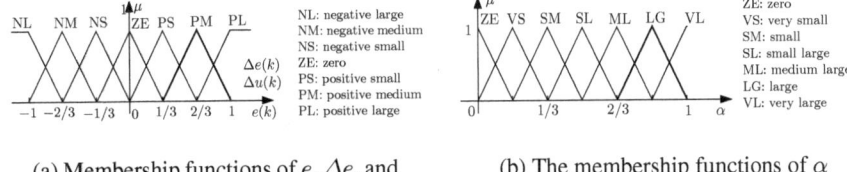

(a) Membership functions of e, Δe, and Δu

(b) The membership functions of α

Fig. 2. The membership functions of the STFC

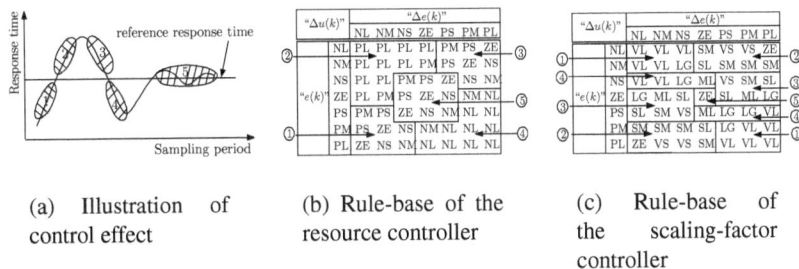

(a) Illustration of control effect

(b) Rule-base of the resource controller

(c) Rule-base of the scaling-factor controller

Fig. 3. Fuzzy control rules in the STFC

$e(k)$, $\Delta e(k)$, and $\Delta u(k)$, respectively. The linguistic variables assume linguistic values $NL, NM, NS, ZE, PS, PM, PL$. Their meanings are shown in Fig. 2(a).

We next analyze the effect of the controller on the provided services as shown in Fig. 3(a). In this figure, five zones with different characteristics can be identified. Zone 1 and 3 are characterized with opposite signs of $e(k)$ and $\Delta e(k)$. That is, in zone 1, $e(k)$ is positive and $\Delta e(k)$ is negative; in zone 3, $e(k)$ is negative and $\Delta e(k)$ is positive. In these two zones, it can be observed that the error is self-correcting and the achieved value is moving towards to the reference value. Thus, $\Delta u(k)$ needs to set either to speed up or to slow down current trend. Zone 2 and 4 are characterized with the same signs of $e(k)$ and $\Delta e(k)$. That is, in zone 2, $e(k)$ is negative and $\Delta e(k)$ is negative; in zone 4, $e(k)$ is positive and $\Delta e(k)$ is positive. Different from zone 1 and zone 3, in these two zones, the error is not self-correcting and the achieved value is moving away from the reference value. Therefore, $\Delta u(k)$ should be set to reverse current trend. Zone 5 is characterized with rather small magnitudes of $e(k)$ and $\Delta e(k)$. Therefore, the system is at a steady state and $\Delta u(k)$ should be set to maintain current state and correct small deviations from the reference value.

By identifying these five zones, we design the fuzzy control rules as summarized in Fig. 3(b). A general linguistic form of these rules is read as: *If* premise *Then* consequent. Let $rule(m, n)$, where m and n assume linguistic values, denote the rule of the (m, n) position in Fig. 3(b). As an example, $rule(PS, PM) = NL$ reads that: *If* the error is positive small *and* the change of error is positive medium *Then* the change of resource is negative large. Note that the control rules are designed based on the analysis of resource-allocation on achieved response time. It avoids the needs of an accurate server model.

In the resource controller, the meaning of the linguistic values is quantified using "triangle" membership functions, which are most widely used in practice, as shown in Fig. 2(a). In Fig. 2(a), the x-axis can be $e(k)$, $\Delta e(k)$, or $\Delta u(k)$. The mth membership function quantifies the *certainty* (between 0 and 1) that an input can be classified as linguistic value m. The fuzzification component translates the inputs into corresponding certainty in numeric values of the membership functions. The inference mechanism is to determine which rules should be activated and what conclusions can be reached. Based on the outputs of the inference mechanism, the defuzzification component calculates the fuzzy controller output, which is a combination of multiple control rules, using "center average" method.

3.2   The Scaling-Factor Controller

To successfully design the resource controller discussed in Section 3.1, the effect of the process delay must be compensated. To the end, we design a scaling-factor controller to adaptively adjust $\alpha K_{\Delta u}$ according to the transient behaviors of a Web server in a way similar to [13]. The selection of output scaling factor $\alpha K_{\Delta u}$ is because of its global effect on the control performance.

The scaling-factor controller consists of the same components as the resource controller. The membership functions of "α" (the corresponding linguistic variable of α) also have "triangle" shape as shown in Fig. 2(b). Because α needs to be positive to ensure the stability of the control system, "α" assumes different linguistic values from "$e(k)$" and "$\Delta e(k)$". Fig. 2(b) also shows the linguistic values and their meanings.

The control rules of the scaling-factor controller are summarized in Fig. 3(c) with following five zones.

1. When $e(k)$ is large but $\Delta e(k)$ and $e(k)$ have the same signs, the client-perceived response time is not only far away from the reference value but also it is moving farther away. Thus, α should be set large to prevent the situation from further worsening.
2. When $e(k)$ is large and $\Delta e(k)$ and $e(k)$ have the opposite signs, α should be set at a small value to ensure a small overshoot and to reduce the settling time without at the cost of responsiveness.
3. When $e(k)$ is small, α should be set according to current server states to avoid large overshoot or undershoot. For example, when $\Delta e(k)$ is negative large, a large α is needed to prevent the upward motion more severely and can result in a small overshoot. Similarly, when $e(k)$ is positive small and $\Delta e(k)$ is negative small, then α should be very small. The large variation of α is important to prevent excessive oscillation and to increase the convergence rate of achieved service quality.
4. The scaling-factor controller also provides regulation against the disturbances. When a workload disturbance happens, $e(k)$ is small and $\Delta e(k)$ is normally large with the same sign as $e(k)$. To compensate such workload disturbance, α is set large.
5. When both $e(k)$ and $\Delta e(k)$ are very small, α should be around zero to avoid chattering problem around the reference value.

The operation of the STFC has two steps. First, we tune the K_e, $K_{\Delta e}$, and $K_{\Delta u}$ through trials and errors. In the step the scaling-factor controller is off and α is set to

1. In the second step, the STFC is turned on to control resource allocation in running Web servers. The scaling-factor controller is on to tune α adaptively. The K_e and $K_{\Delta e}$ are kept unchanged and the $K_{\Delta u}$ is set to three times larger than the one obtained in previous step to maintain the responsiveness of the STFC during workload disturbances.

Finally we remark that the STFC has small overhead because at most eight rules are on at any time in the STFC. In addition, the controller only needs to adjust resource allocation once a sampling period. We conducted experiments with STFC-on and STFC-off and observe their performance difference is within 1%. Furthermore, the implementation of the STFC totaled less than 100 lines of C code.

4   Performance Evaluations

We define a metric of relative deviation $R(e)$ to measure the performance of the eQoS:

$$R(e) = \frac{\sqrt{\sum_{k=1}^{n} (D(k) - W(k))^2 / n}}{D(k)} = \frac{\sqrt{\sum_{k=1}^{n} e(k)^2 / n}}{D(k)}. \tag{1}$$

The smaller the $R(e)$, the better the controller's performance. We have conducted experiments on the PlanetLab test bed to evaluate the performance of the eQoS in a real-world environment. The clients reside on 9 geographically diverse nodes: Cambridge in Massachusetts, San Diego in California, and Cambridge in the United Kingdom. We assume that premium and basic clients are from all these nodes for fairness between clients with different network connections. The Web server is a Dell PowerEdge 2450 configured with dual-processor (1 GHz Pentium III) and 512 MB main memory and is located in Detroit, Michigan. During the experiments, the RTTs between the server and the clients are around 45 ms (Cambridge), 70 ms (San Diego), and 130 ms (the UK).

The server workload was generated by SURGE [3]. In the emulated Web objects, the maximum number of embedded objects in a given page was 150 and the percentage of base, embedded, and loner objects were 30%, 38%, and 32%, respectively. The Apache Web server was used to provide Web services with support of HTTP/1.1. The number of the maximal concurrent child processes was set to 128. In the experiments with two classes, we aimed to keep the average response time of premium class to be around 5 seconds. In the experiments with three classes, we assumed the target of class 1 was 5 seconds and that of class 2 was 11 seconds because they are rated as "good" and "average", respectively [5]. We aimed to provide guaranteed service when the number of UEs was between 500 and 800. When the number of UEs is less than 500, the average response time of all Web pages is around 5 seconds. When the number of UEs is larger than 800, we have observed refused connections using unmodified Apache Web server and admission control mechanisms should be employed.

To investigate the effect of network latency on the performance of the eQoS, we have implemented a network-delay simulator in a similar way to [22]. With the RTT set as 180 ms, ping times were showing a round trip of around 182 ms using the simulator. In the experiments on the simulated networks, the RTT between clients and servers was set to be 40, 80, or 180 ms that represent the latency within the continental U.S., the latency between the east and west coasts of the U.S., and the one between the U.S. and Europe, respectively [20].

4.1   Effectiveness of the eQoS

To evaluate the effectiveness of the eQoS, we have conducted experiments under different workloads and network delays with two and three client classes. In the experiments, the system was first warmed up for 60 seconds and then the controller was on. The size of sampling period was set to 4 seconds. The effect of the sampling period on the performance of the eQoS shall be discussed in Section 4.3. Fig. 4 presents the experimental results. Fig. 4(a) shows the relative deviations of the premium class relative to the reference value (5 seconds). From the figure we observe that all the relative deviations are smaller than 35%. Meanwhile, most of them are around 20%. It means the size of deviations is normally around 1.0 seconds. Fig. 4(b) presents the results with three classes. Because we observe no qualitative differences between the results with different RTTs in the simulated networks, we only present the results where RTT was set to 180 *ms* for brevity. From the figure we see that most of the relative deviations are between 15% and 30%. These demonstrate the effectiveness of the eQoS.

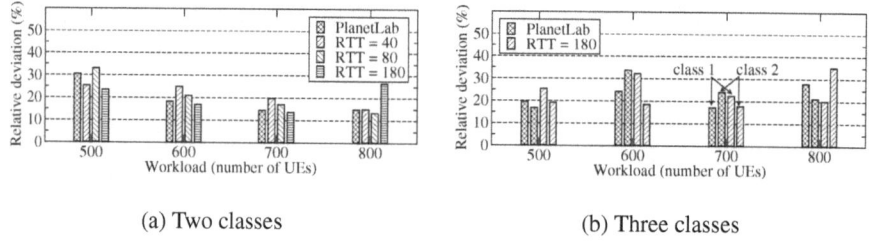

(a) Two classes   (b) Three classes

Fig. 4. The performance of the eQoS with two and three classes

We then investigate why it is feasible to guarantee end-to-end QoS from server side under heavy-load conditions. The pageview response time consists of server-side waiting and processing time and network transmission time. The waiting time is the time interval that starts when a connection is accepted by the operating system and ends when the connection is passed to the Apache Web server to be processed. The processing time is the time that the Apache Web server spends on processing the requests for the whole Web page, including the base HTML file and its embedded objects. The transmission time includes the complete transfer time of client requests and all server responses over the networks. We instrumented the Apache Web server to record the processing time.

Fig. 5 shows the breakdown of response time. From the figure we observe that, when the number of UEs is larger than 400, the server-side waiting time is the dominant part of client-perceived response time. This finding is consistent with those in [4]. It is because that, when the server is heavily loaded, the child processes of the Apache Web server are busy in processing accepted client requests. The newly incoming client

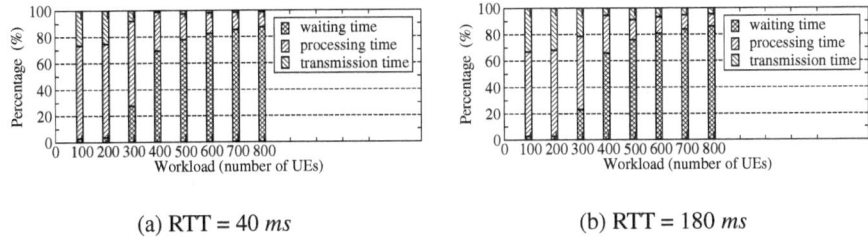

(a) RTT = 40 *ms*   (b) RTT = 180 *ms*

Fig. 5. The breakdown of response time of Web pages under different RTTs

requests then have to wait. Furthermore, we also observe that the transmission time is only a small part of response time when server workload is high. It indicates that, although the service providers have no control over the network transmissions, they can still control the client-perceived response time by controlling the server-side waiting time and processing time.

4.2   Comparison with Other Controllers

Within the *eQoS* framework, we also implement three other controllers: a fuzzy controller without self-tuning, a traditional PI controller, and an adaptive PI controller using the basic idea of [10]. We have specifically tuned the fuzzy and the PI controllers in an environment where the number of UEs was set to 700 and RTT was set to be 180 *ms* on the simulated networks. We define the performance difference *PerDiff* between the STFC and other controller as $(R(e)_{other} - R(e)_{STFC})/R(e)_{STFC}$. The $R(e)_{other}$ and $R(e)_{STFC}$ are the relative deviations of other controller and the STFC, respectively. Fig. 6 presents the performance difference due to compared controllers.

From Fig. 6(b) we observe that the STFC provides worse services than the non-adaptive fuzzy controller when the number of UEs is 700 and the RTT is 180 *ms*. The behavior is expected because a self-tuning controller cannot provide better performance than a non-adaptive controller that has been specifically tuned for a certain environment. Even under such environment, the performance difference is only -6%. Under all other conditions, the STFC provides 25% better services than the non-adaptive fuzzy controller in terms of performance difference because the STFC further adjusts $\alpha K_{\Delta u}$

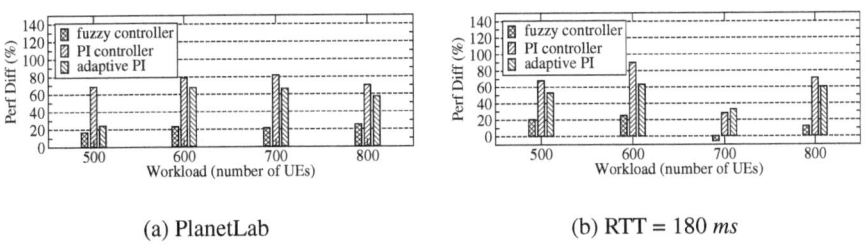

(a) PlanetLab   (b) RTT = 180 *ms*

Fig. 6. The performance comparison in PlanetLab and simulated networks

adaptively according to the transient behaviors of the Web server. Such tuning is important to compensate the effect of the process delay in resource allocation.

In comparison with the PI controller, the STFC achieves better performance even when the PI controller operates under its specifically tuned environment, which can be observed in Fig. 6(b). When the number of UEs is 700 and RTT is 180 *ms*, their performance difference is 28%. From Fig. 6 we observe that all performance differences of the PI controller are larger than 60% and the average is around 75%. The poor performance of the PI controller is due to its inaccurate underlying model. In the PI controller, we follow the approach in [10] and model the server as an $M/GI/1$ processor sharing system. It is known that the exponential inter-arrival distribution is unable to characterize the Web server [17]. Thus, the model is inaccurate. Similarly, although the adaptive PI improves upon the non-adaptive PI controller, it still has worse performance than the STFC and the fuzzy controller. Its average performance difference in relation to the STFC is around 50%. The poor performance of these two controllers is because they provide no means to compensate the effect of the process delay.

4.3   The Process Delay in Resource Allocation

Aforementioned, the process delay in resource allocation affects the performance of a controller. We have conducted experiments to quantify it. For brevity, we only present the results on simulated networks where the number of UEs was 700 and the RTT was 180 *ms*. Fig. 7(a) shows the percentage of requests finished within different numbers of sampling period after being admitted. Fig. 7(b) depicts corresponding cumulative distribution function of the service time, which is the time the Web server spends in processing requests. Comparing Fig. 7(a) and Fig. 7(b) we observe that, although over 95% of the requests are finished in 8 seconds after being admitted, only 77.8% of them are processed within the same sampling period when it is set to 8 seconds. Moreover, it also indicates that 22.2% of the measured response time are affected by the resource allocation performed more than one sampling periods ago. Consequently, the resource-allocation effect cannot be accurately measured promptly.

To provide QoS guarantees, however, the resource allocation in Web servers should be based on an accurately measured effect of previous resource allocation on client-

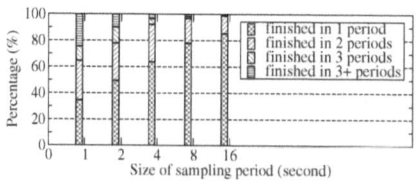
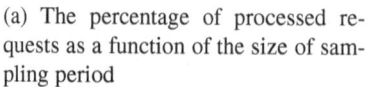
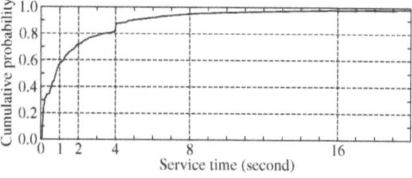

(a) The percentage of processed requests as a function of the size of sampling period

(b) The cumulative distribution function of service time

Fig. 7. The process delay in resource allocation

perceived QoS. It in turn controls the order in which client requests are scheduled and processed. The existing process delay has been recognized as one of the most difficult dynamic element naturally occurring in physical systems to deal with [21]. It sets a fundamental limit on how well a controller can fulfill design specifications because it limits how fast a controller can react to disturbances.

The process delay also affects the selection of an appropriate sampling period. Due to space limitation, we summerize our observation. From the results, we observe that the deviation decreases with the increase of the sampling period. It is because that the measured effect of resource allocation is more accurate using a large sampling period than a small one. When the sampling-period size continues to increase, the relative deviation turns to increases. It is because that, with the increase of sampling period, the processing rate of premium class is adjusted less frequently. Consequently, the eQoS becomes less adaptive to the transient workload disturbances. Based on the results, we set the size of sampling period to 4 seconds.

5   Related Work

Early work focused on providing differentiated services to different client classes using priority-based scheduling [2]. Although they are effective in providing differentiated services, they cannot guarantee the QoS a class received. To guarantee the QoS of a class, queueing-theoretic approaches have been proposed. The performance highly depends on the parameter estimation, such as the traffic variance, which is difficult to be accurate. To reduce the variance of achieved QoS, traditional linear feedback control has also been adapted [1, 24]. Because the behavior of a Web server changes continuously,, the performance of the linear feedback control is limited. In comparison, our approach takes advantage of fuzzy control theory to manage the server-resource allocation.

Recent work have applied adaptive control [10] and machine-learning [23] to address the lack of accurate server model. Although these approaches provide better performance than non-adaptive linear feedback control approaches under workload disturbances, the ignorance of the process delay limits their performance. Fuzzy control theory has also been applied in providing QoS guarantees [12, 16]. The objective of the STFC is different in that its focus is on providing end-to-end QoS guarantees. Moreover, the STFC explicitly addresses the inherent process delay in resource allocation.

6   Conclusions

In the paper, we have proposed a novel framework eQoS to providing end-to-end pageview response time guarantees. Within the framework, we have proposed a two-level self-tuning fuzzy controller, which does not require accurate server model, to explicitly addressing the process delay in resource allocation. The experimental results on PlanetLab and simulated networks have shown that it is effective in providing such QoS guarantees. They also demonstrated the superiority of the STFC over other controllers with much smaller deviations.

References

1. T. F. Abdelzaher, K. G. Shin, and N. Bhatti. Performance guarantees for Web server end-systems: A control-theoretical approach. *IEEE Transactions on Parallel and Distributed Systems*, 13(1):80–96, January 2002.
2. J. Almeida, M. Dabu, A. Manikutty, and P. Cao. Providing differentiated levels of service in Web content hosting. In *Proceedings of ACM SIGMETRICS Workshop on Internet Server Performance*, 1998.
3. P. Barford and M. Crovella. Generating representative web workloads for network and server performance evaluation. In *Proceedings of ACM SIGMETRICS*, 1998.
4. P. Barford and M. Crovella. Critical path analysis of TCP transactions. *IEEE/ACM Transactions on Networking*, 9(3):238–248, 2001.
5. N. Bhatti, A. Bouch, and A. Kuchinsky. Integrating user-perceived quality into Web server design. In *Proceedings of WWW*, 2000.
6. N. Bhatti and R. Friedrich. Web server support for tiered services. *IEEE Network*, 13(5):64–71, 1999.
7. C. Dovrolis, D. Stiliadis, and P. Ramanathan. Proportional differentiated services: Delay differentiation and packet scheduling. *IEEE/ACM Transactions on Networking*, 10(1):12–26, 2002.
8. M. E. Gendy, A. Bose, S.-T. Park, and K. G. Shin. Paving the first mile for QoS-dependent applications and appliances. In *Proceedings of IWQoS*, 2004.
9. F. Hernandez-Campos, K. Jeffay, and F. D. Smith. Tracking the evolution of Web traffic: 1995-2003. In *Proceedings of MASCOTS*, 2003.
10. A. Kamra, V. Misra, and E. Nahum. Yaksha: A self tuning controller for managing the performance of 3-tiered websites. In *Proceedings of IWQoS*, 2004.
11. J. Kaur and H. Vin. Providing deterministic end-to-end fairness guarantees in core-stateless networks. In *Proceedings of IWQoS*, 2003.
12. B. Li and K. Nahrstedt. A control-based middleware framework for quality of service adaptations. *IEEE Journal on Selected Areas in Communications*, 17(9):1632–1650, September 1999.
13. R. K. Mudi and N. R. Pal. A robust self-tuning scheme for PI- and PD-type fuzzy controllers. *IEEE Transactions on Fuzzy Systems*, 7(1):2–16, February 1999.
14. D. P. Olshefski, J. Nieh, and E. Nahum. ksniffer: Determining the remote client perceived response time from live packet streams. In *Proceedings of OSDI*, 2004.
15. K. Park, V. S. Pai, L. Peterson, and Z. Wang. CoDNS: Improving DNS performance and reliability via cooperative lookups. In *Proceedings of OSDI*, 2004.
16. S. Patchararungruang, S. K. halgamuge, and N. Shenoy. Optimized rule-based delay proportion adjustment for proportional differentiated services. *IEEE Journal on Selected Areas in Communications*, 23(2):261–276, February 2005.
17. V. Paxson and S. Floyd. Wide area traffic: The failure of possion modeling. *IEEE/ACM Transactions on Networking*, 3(3):226–244, June 1995.
18. L. Peterson, T. Anderson, D. Culler, and T. Roscoe. A blueprint for introducing disruptive technology into the internet. In *Proceedings of HotNets*, 2002.
19. L. Sha, X. Liu, Y. Lu, and T. F. Abdelzaher. Queueing model based network server performance control. In *Proceedings of RTSS*, 2002.
20. S. Shakkottai, R. Srikant, N. Brownlee, A. Broido, and K. Claffy. The RTT distribution of TCP flows in the Internet and its impact on TCP-based flow control. Technical report, The Cooperative Association for Internet Data Analysis (CAIDA), 2004.
21. F. G. Shinskey. *Process Control Systems: Application, Design, and Tuning*. McGraw-Hill, 4th edition, 1996.

22. J. Slottow, A. Shahriari, M. Stein, X. Chen, C. Thomas, and P. B. Ender. Instrumenting and tuning dataview—a networked application for navigating through large scientific datasets. *Software Practice and Experience*, 32(2):165–190, November 2002.
23. V. Sundaram and P. Shenoy. A practical learning-based approach for dynamic storage bandwidth allocation. In *Proceedings of IWQoS*, 2003.
24. J. Wei, X. Zhou, and C.-Z. Xu. Robust processing rate allocation for proportional slowdown differentiation on Internet servers. *IEEE Transactions on Computers*, 2005. In press.
25. M. Welsh and D. Culler. Adaptive overload control for busy Internet servers. In *Proceedings of USITS*, 2003.

Calculation of Speech Quality by Aggregating the Impacts of Individual Frame Losses

Christian Hoene, Sven Wiethölter, and Adam Wolisz

Technical University of Berlin, Germany
{hoene, wiethoel, wolisz}@tkn.tu-berlin.de

Abstract. Losing VoIP packets or speech frames decreases the perceptual speech quality. The statistical relation between randomly lost speech frames and speech quality is well known. In cases of bursty and rate-distortion optimized losses, a precise quality model is required to relate losses to quality. In the present paper, we present a model that is based on the loss impact - or the *importance* - of single speech frames. We present a novel metric to calculate the impact of the loss of multiple frames by adding the importance of the respective single frames. This metric shows a high prediction accuracy for distant losses. For losses following each other closely, we present an aggregation function which models the psychoacoustic post-masking effect. Our model helps to develop networking algorithms that control the packet dropping process in networks. For example, we show that a proper packet dropping strategy can significantly increase the drop rate while maintaining the same level of speech quality.

1 Introduction

In packet-based communication networks, such as the Internet, packet losses are a major source of quality degradation. This is true especially for real-time multimedia services over wireless links such as Wifi-VoIP. One would expect that the impact of VoIP packet loss[1] on speech quality is well understood. However, this is not the case because it is a highly interdisciplinary problem. Multiple "layers" have to be considered covering the loss process of IP-based networks, the behavior of speech codecs and frame loss concealment, the psychoacoustics of the human hearing, and even the cognitive aspects of speech recognition.

State of the art algorithms look up speech quality scores in tables, depending on the measured loss rate and the speech coding. Alternatively, these tables are modeled as linear equations or with neural networks [1]. However, the relation between mean packet loss rate and speech quality is only a statistical description

---

[1] Speech frames are compressed segments of speech which are generated by an encoder. VoIP packets carry one or multiple speech frames. Usually, a speech frames or VoIP packet carry a segment of speech, which has a length of 10, 20, or 30 ms.

H. de Meer and N. Bhatti (Eds.): IWQoS 2005, LNCS 3552, pp. 136–150, 2005.
© IFIP International Federation for Information Processing 2005

because the deviation for specific loss pattern can be high and depends on the content of the lost frames. Also, these relations are only valid for a specific loss pattern. For example, bursty losses (multiple VoIP packet or speech frame losses in a row) can have a different impact [2, 3] depending on the codec and the duration of the burst. Lately, rate-distortion optimized multimedia streaming or selective prioritization algorithms have been introduced [4, 5, 6], which control the loss process and select which media frames to drop. If losses cannot be avoided, they try to drop negligible instead of important media frames. Thus, they increase the service quality for a given loss rate. The loss rate can be rather high if only unimportant losses occur (refer to [7]). On the other side, losses of important frames degrade the speech quality highly.

In the same research context, a method has been developed and validated, which measures the *importance* of a single speech frame [8]. The importance of a speech frame is defined as the impact on the speech quality caused by a frame loss. In this paper we assume that we can use this method to determine the impact of one frame loss. Then, the question arises how the impact of multiple losses can be determined using the importance of single frame losses. The development of a novel metric or dimension of frame importance, which simply can be summed up to get an overall impact of multiple frame losses, is presented here.

The ITU-T P.862 PESQ algorithm [9, 10, 11] can assess the impact of one or multiple frame losses but works only for audio files and not on a speech frame level. It is an instrumental speech quality assessment tool, which simulates the human rating behavior of speech quality. It compares two speech samples – the original sample and the degraded versions, which might include coding and frame loss distortions – to calculate the mean option score (MOS) value. PESQ by itself cannot be directly applied on VoIP packets [12] and has a high computational delay and complexity, which inhibits its on-line and real-time application.

Thus, we remodel the internal behavior of PESQ algorithms using it for frame losses: We apply the algorithm which PESQ uses to aggregate signal distortions over time in order to accumulate frame loss distortions over time. This aggregation algorithm is also the basis for the novel importance metric, which allows adding the frames' importance linearly and thus has a low complexity. It shows a high prediction performance, if the losses are distant. If frame losses occur shortly one after the other, temporal auditory masking have to be considered. We develop a heuristic equation to model these effects. Overall, our approach shows a high correlation with instrumental speech quality measurements for many loss patterns.

The following paper first describes the required technical background. We also give an example showing the impact of the packet dropping strategy on the speech quality. Then, we present the approach on how to assess multiple speech frame losses. In the fifth chapter we compare our approach with the PESQ's speech quality predictions. Finally, we summarize this work and give an outlook to further research.

2   Background

2.1   PESQ

The Perceptual Assessment of Speech Quality algorithm predicts human rating behavior for narrow band speech transmission. It compares an original speech fragment with its transmitted and thus degraded version to determine an estimated mean option score (MOS), which scales from 1 (bad) to 5 (excellent). For multiple known sources of impairment (typical for analogue, digital and packetized voice transmission systems) it shows a high correlation (about $R = 0.93$) with human ratings. In the following we will describe some details of PESQ because they are required to understand the following sections.

Overview: PESQ transforms the original and the degraded signal input to internal representations of a perceptual model. If the degraded signal is not time aligned, e.g., due to jitter or delay, it is first adjusted to the original signal [10]. Next, the perceptual difference between the original signal and the degraded version is calculated [11] considering the human cognition of speech. Finally, PESQ determines perceived speech quality of the degraded signal (see Fig. 1).

Computation of the PESQ MOS Score: The final MOS score is simply a linear combination of so called normal and asymmetrical disturbance. In most cases, the output range will be a MOS-like score between 1.0 and 4.5, the normal range of MOS values found in human subjective experiments:

$$PESQ_{MOS} = 4.5 - 0.1 \cdot D_{indicator} - 0.0309 \cdot A_{indicator} \qquad (1)$$

with $D_{indicator}$ being the normal disturbance and $A_{indicator}$ being the asymmetrical disturbance. Before this final calculation the following processing steps are conducted:

Time-Frequency Decomposition: PESQ's perceptual model performs a short term FFT on the speech samples that have been divided into 32 ms *phoneme*. The phoneme overlap each other with 50% so that each position within the sample is covered by exactly two phonemes. PESQ calculates the spectral difference between orignal and degraded to calculate distortion of at given phoneme.

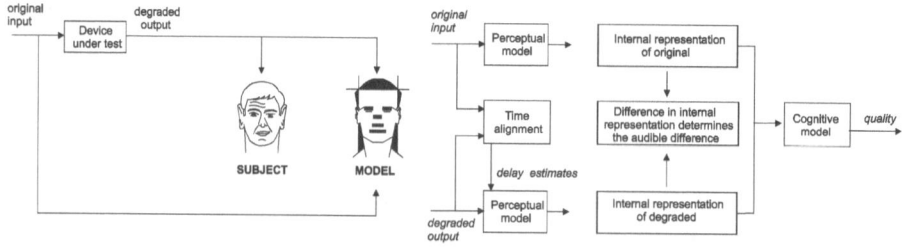

Fig. 1. Overview of the basic architecture of PESQ [9]

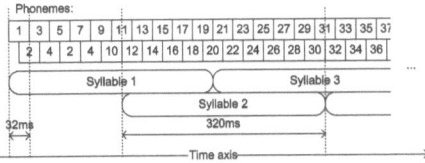

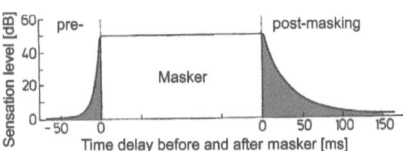

Fig. 2. PESQ: Structuring of the speech to phonemes (32 ms) and syllables (320 ms). The lengths presents have been chosen because they yield highest prediction performance

Fig. 3. Schematic drawing to illustrate and characterize the regions, in which pre- and post-masking occur (shaded areas) if a masker is present [14]

Asymmetric Effect: If high correlation between PESQ and subjective listening-only ratings [13] should be achieved, an asymetric effect has to be considered: Humans do not know the quality and spectrum of the original speech because they just hear the degraded speech. Actually, they compare the degraded speech with an immagetive original, which differs to the original by lacking curtain spectrum components. It is caused by the fact that the listener adapts to constant limitations of the transmitted signal spectrum. PESQ models this behavior and calculates separately two perceptual differences for both the normal and the asymmetric signals. Both disturbances are aggregated separately over time. Finally, they are combined.

Weighting of Disturbances over Time: PESQ uses a two layer hierarchy to group phonemes to *syllables* and to aggregate syllables over the entire sample length (Fig. 2). Twenty phoneme disturbances are combined to one syllable distortion with (2). Phonemes are aggregated with an exponent of 6 to model a cognitive effect: Even if only one phoneme is distorted, it is not possible to recognise the syllable anymore [15]. The authors of PESQ argue that this is a cognitive effect which needs to be considered for high prediction performance.

$$syllable_{indicator}^{AorD}[i] = \sqrt[6]{\frac{1}{20}\sum_{m=1}^{20} phoneme_{disturbance}^{AorD}[m+10i]^6} \qquad (2)$$

A syllable has the length of 320 ms. Similar to phonemes, syllables are also 50% overlapping and cover half of the previous and following syllables. The syllables are aggregated with (3) over the entire sample. Syllables are aggregated with an exponent of 2 because disturbances occurring during active speech periods are perceived stronger than those during silence [15].

$$AorD_{indicator} = \sqrt{\frac{1}{N}\sum_{n=1}^{N} syllable_{indicator}^{AorD}[n]^2} \qquad (3)$$

2.2   Temporal Masking

Zwicker and Fastl [14] describe temporal masking effects which characterize the human hearing: The time-domain phenomena pre- and post-masking plays an important role (Fig. 3). If faint sound follows shortly after a loud part of speech, the faint part is not heareable because it is masked. Also, if the maskee precedes the masker it vanishes.

If the temporal masking effect is applied to distortion values, the distinction between masker and maskee on the one side and between pre- and post masking the other side is difficult. If a frame got lost, it causes a distortion, resulting in a segment of speech which can be louder or fainter than the previous segment. If it is louder, the previous segment is pre-masked, if it is fainter, the loss is post-masked. Thus, if one considers only distortion, it is not possible to distinguish pre- and post-masking. Instead, the same amount of distortion can cause pre- or post-masking or can be effected itself by pre- or post-masking, depending on the loudness of the resulting speech segment.

This perceptual effect denoted as temporal masking had been considered as an addition to the PESQ algorithm. However, after implementing it, it never showed any improvements to the prediction performance of PESQ. Thus, it was not included.

2.3   Single Frame Loss and Importance

In [8], a measurement procedure was presented, which determines the impact of single frame losses. It is based on PESQ and consists of two speech quality measurements: First, a speech sample is encoded and decoded again. PESQ compares this degraded sample with the original to estimate the impact of the encoding process. Next, the same speech sample is encoded and one (or multiple frames) are dropped. Then, the encoded frames are decoded or concealed, depending whether the frames are lost. Again, PESQ calculates the MOS value. The impact of the frame loss is now identified by comparing the pure coding-degraded MOS value with the MOS value containing additionally the frame loss. The authors have conducted two million measurements with speech samples containing deliberately dropped packets. For example, Fig. 4 displays the distribution of MOS values, varying the sample content and the location of the lost packet in samples having a length of 8 s. The results show that the encoding has a large impact on the speech quality as well as the sample content (e.g., speaker and sentence). One can see that the *coding distortion* varies widely and depends on the sample content. Figure 4 shows also the impact of losing one and two speech frames. The *frame distortion* remains small.

Originally, PESQ has not been designed for measuring the impact of single packet losses and in such case works outside its specification [9]. Therefore this application has been verified with formal listening-only tests. Humans' subjective ratings and the predictions of PESQ have a cross correlation of R=0.94 [7]. PESQ therefore reflects well the single frame measurements.

In [8], an importance metric has been firstly introduced. It its defined as follows: If a sample is encoded, transmitted and decoded, the maximum achievable

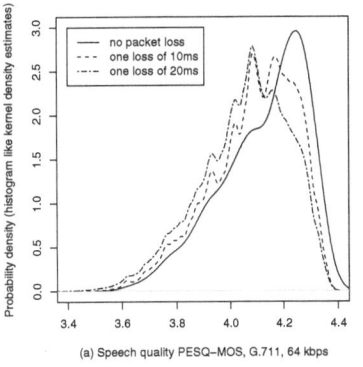

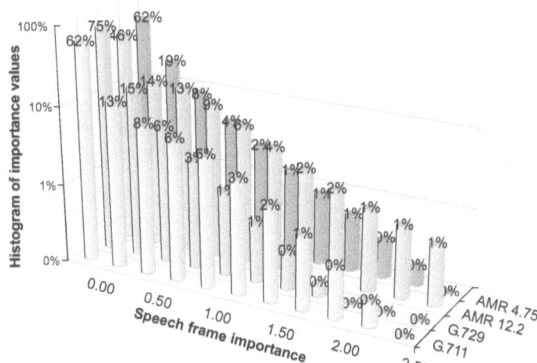

Fig. 4. Impact of coding distortion and packet loss on speech quality. The probability density functions (PDF) are displayed for varying sample contents

Fig. 5. Histogram of speech frame importance values during voice activity. Most speech frames are not important at all

quality of a transmission is limited by the coding performance, which depends on the codec algorithm, its implementation, and the sample content. Some samples are more suitable to be compressed than others (see Fig. 4). For a sample s, which is coded with the encoding and decoder implementation c, the quality of transmission is $MOS(s, c)$. The sample s has a length of $t(s)$ seconds. As explained above, the quality is not only degraded by encoding but also by frame losses. If such losses occur, the resulting quality is described by $\mathrm{MOS}(s, c, e)$. The vector e describes a loss event. The following empiric equation (4) describes how to calculate the importance. If this equation is applied on the data displayed in Fig. 4, one can see that most speech frames during voice activity are not important at all (Fig. 5).

$$\mathrm{Imp}(s, c, e) = (\mathrm{MOS}(s, c) - \mathrm{MOS}(s, c, e)) \cdot t(s) \qquad (4)$$

Still, one drawback remains. Equation 4 can only measure the effect of a single frame loss. If it is used to add the impact of two or more lost frames, it does not scale linearly with the number of frames [8]. Thus, the aim of this paper is to develop an "additive" metric.

3   Example: Frame Dropping Strategies

We have described a method to classify the impact of single and multiple frame losses. But how cam this be applied? In the following we assume a scenario in which we know the importance of each frame and in which we can control the loss process - e.g. which frames can be dropped. We assume that we can drop frames at any position and show, how the *frame dropping strategy* influence the speech quality.

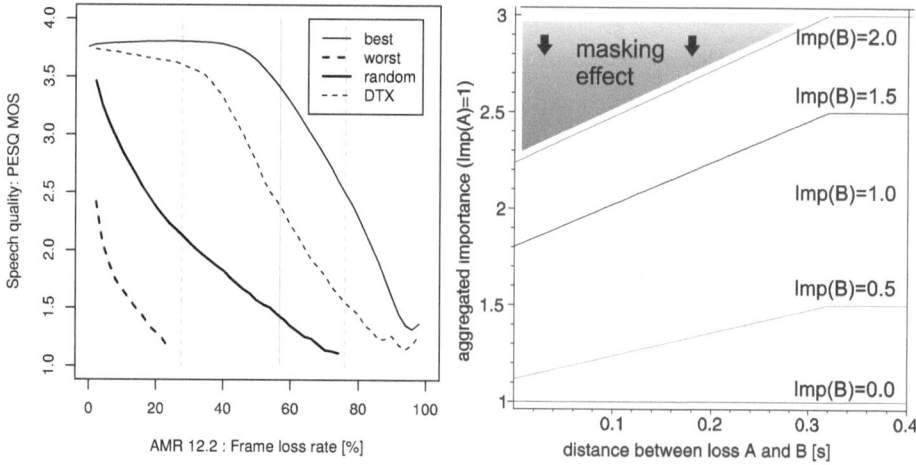

Fig. 6. Impact of dropping strategy on the speech quality. The gray, vertical lines refer the minimal, mean, and maximal percentage of silent frames in the sample set

Fig. 7. Behavior of Equation 12 depending on loss distance and importance

In our simulations, we increase the dropping rate from 0% to 100% in steps of 2% using adaptive-multi rate (AMR) coding at 12.2 kbit/s (other codecs give similar results). We use 832 different samples but consider only the mean MOS value over all sample variations. In Fig. 6 we have displayed the speech quality depending on the frame loss rate. If frames have to be dropped, which frames should be dropped? Classic approaches chose the frames randomly (line "random"). Discontinuous Transmission (DTX) algorithms detect the voice activity (VAD) to interrupt the frame generation. They reduce the transmission rate during inactive speech periods while maintaining an acceptable level of output quality. Thus, a DTX algorithm would first drop silent frames, and then active frames (line "DTX"). Using the metric of frame importance, we introduce two novel strategies: As a worst case we consider the dropping strategy that drops the most important frames first. The second called "best" loss strategy preferentially drops the less important frames, and only at high loss rates important frames are dropped. One can see that the "best" loss strategy performs better than the DTX and random case. In case of the worst strategy, the speech quality drops very fast.

4   Additive Metric

A metric that describes the importance of frames shall fulfil the following requirements: First, it should be easily deployable to quantify the impact of frame losses. Consequently, the loss distortion should be measurable with off-the-shelf instrumental measurement methods like PESQ (or any other successor). For example, it should be able to calculate the metric with two speech quality measurements: with loss and without loss. Second, the metric shall be one-dimensional. Of course, the distortions caused by frame loss can have many effects. However, it shall be modeled as a one-dimensional quality scale because this would simplify the development of algorithms that utilize this metric. Last, it should be possible to give a statement like "frame A and frame B are as important as frame C" or "frame A is three times more important than frame B". In a mathematical sense, this requirement is called additive property. It is of importance when frame loss impacts are to be applied in analytical contexts such as the rate-distortion multimedia streaming framework by Chou and Miao [6].

The development of such a metric is based on the idea to study the internal behavior of PESQ and to remodel it for frame losses. PESQ predicts the impact of frame loss rather well but is far too complex to be applied on a frame basis. Thus, a simpler model is required that only contains the issues that are relevant. The proposed approach is based on the following three principles. First, we assume that the importance of frames is known. For example, the method described in section 2.3 can be used for offline purposes. A real-time classification of frame importances is beyond the scope of this paper and is addressed in [16]. Second, if two or more frame losses have a distance of more than 320 ms, the importance values, as calculated by (10), can simply be added. Last, if two losses occur shortly after each other, then (12) is required to add the importance values. In the following it is described how we have developed this approach by remodelling PESQ's behavior.

Asymmetric effect: PESQ judges the impact of distortion with two factors, the asymmetric and the normal distortion. In case of frame loss, the overall coding spectrum, which influences strongly the asymmetric effect, is not changed because the impact of a frame loss is limited to the position of its loss and does not change the rest of the sample. Also, the asymmetric effect is mainly caused by the encoding and not by frame losses. Therefore it is reasonable to neglect the difference between asymmetric and normal distortion and consider just the sum of them.

Long-term aggregation: In general, the weighting of disturbances over time is determined as in PESQ. Thus, the syllable disturbances are added up as described in (3). Contrary, we consider disturbances of speech frames instead of syllables. The disturbance consists of coding as well as loss distortion as shown in (5). If frame losses are not present, the term $dist_{loss}[i]$ is zero.

$$sylablle_{indictor}[i] = dist_{coding}[i] + dist_{loss}[i]. \tag{5}$$

Combining (3) and (5) we can write

$$(AorD_{indicator})^2 = \frac{1}{N}\sum_{n=1}^{N}(dist_{coding}[n] + dist_{loss}[n])^2 \tag{6}$$

and transform (6) to (7):

$$
\begin{aligned}
&N \cdot (AorD_{indicator})^2 - \sum_{n=1}^{N} dist_{coding}[n]^2 \\
&= \sum_{n=1}^{N} \left(dist_{loss}[n]^2 + 2 \cdot dist_{coding}[n] \cdot dist_{loss}[n] \right)
\end{aligned}
\tag{7}
$$

As an approximation we combine both asymmetric and symmetric disturbances. Then, (1) can be simplified to:

$$
MOS = 4.5 - AorD_{indicator}
\tag{8}
$$

with $AorD_{indicator} = 0.1 \cdot D_{indicator} - 0.0309 \cdot A_{indicator}$. Combining (7) and (8), we get:

$$
\begin{aligned}
&\left((4.5 - MOS(s,c,e))^2 - (4.5 - MOS(s,c))^2 \right) N \\
&= \sum_{n=1}^{N} \left(dist_{loss}[n]^2 + 2 \cdot dist_{coding}[n] \cdot dist_{loss}[n] \right)
\end{aligned}
\tag{9}
$$

with $MOS(s,c)$ being the speech quality due to coding loss and $MOS(s,c,e)$ being the speech quality due to coding as well as frame loss. Equation 9 is the basis of our new importance metric. One can see that if a loss distortion does not overlap within one syllable, the distortions can simply be added. We define (10), which approximates a linear scale better than (4).

$$
\begin{aligned}
Imp(s,c,e) &= (cl - c) \cdot t(s) \\
\text{with } cl &= (4.5 - MOS(s,c,e))^2 \text{ and } c = (4.5 - MOS(s,c))^2
\end{aligned}
\tag{10}
$$

Short-term aggregation: For the short term aggregation, we first model the impact of two frame losses with two delta impulses at time t_a and t_b with the height of imp_a and imp_b representing the importance. If the distance $t_{width} = t_b - t_a$ is larger than 320 ms, adding of the importance values is done as described in the previous section. Otherwise, it is calculated as explained below.

First, we calculate the probability that both losses occur in the same syllable. We assume that syllables start at $0, 320, \ldots$ ms and have a length of $t_{syll} = 320$ like in PESQ. Because of the re-occurrence pattern of syllables, it is sufficient to consider only the period of $0 \leq t_a < t_{syll}$. The overlapping of syllables can be neglected, too. The probability that the two losses are within a syllable is

$$
\begin{aligned}
P_{in.syll}(t_{width}) &= \frac{1}{t_{syll}} \int_{t_a=0}^{t_{syll}} \left\{ \begin{array}{cc} 0 & \text{if } t_a + t_{width} \geq t_{syll} \\ 1 & \text{otherwise} \end{array} \right\} dt_a \\
&= \left\{ \begin{array}{cc} 0 & \text{if } t_{width} \geq t_{syll} \\ 1 - \frac{t_{width}}{t_{syll}} & \text{otherwise} \end{array} \right.
\end{aligned}
\tag{11}
$$

If two losses are within a syllable, PESQ adds them not with an exponent of $p = 2$ but with $p = 6$ (2). Because it is not simple to remodel PESQ's algorithm, we introduce the following heuristic function (Eq. (12) and Fig. 7), which shows a similar behavior as PESQ. For a loss distance longer than the length of a syllable, it simply sums up the importance values. If it is lower, the importance values are added but the sum is leveled with a factor $1 - P_{in.syll}$. Also, if the distance is short, we use an another addition, which sums up the square importance values. Again, this later addition is leveled by the probability of $P_{in.syll}$. Actually, we also tested to add cubics of importance values to model the effect of $p = 6$ but this solution did not let to higher correlation coeffiency.

$$add\left(imp_a, imp_b, t_{width}\right) =$$
$$\begin{cases} imp_a + imp_b & \text{if } t_{width} > t_{syll} \quad (12) \\ \left(imp_a + imp_b\right)\frac{t_{width}}{t_{syll}} + \sqrt{imp_a{}^2 + imp_b{}^2}\left(1 - \frac{t_{width}}{t_{syll}}\right) & \text{otherwise} \end{cases}$$

Equation 11 partially models the time-frequency masking effect, which causes a masking of minor distortions by nearby louder ones. However, PESQ models the temporal masking effect only in the statistical mean. PESQ's masking is stronger – or at least longer – than the pre- or postmasking effect. It can be seen if one compares Fig. 3 with 7. This observation explains why it was not necessary to add time masking effects to PESQ: It is already included.

5   Validation

We consider a scenario, in which frame losses occur randomly, and we determine the speech quality for a given frame loss rate. The same scenario has been conducted in [8] with the old metric based on (4). The experimental set-up is described briefly: We follow recommendation ITU P.833, conduct many instrumental speech quality measurements, and vary the coding, the sample, and the

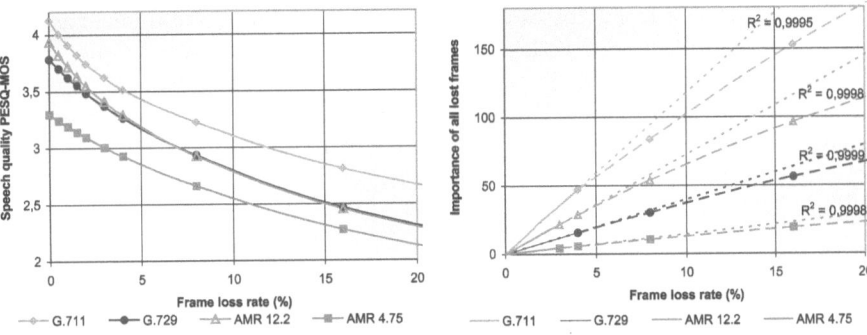

(a) Impact of random frame losses on speech quality

(b) Importance for many losses: measured (PESQ, slashed) and predicted (new metric, dotted)

Fig. 8. Impact of random frame losses on the speech quality. For loss rates (AMR <3%, ITU G.711/729 <4%) the correlation between measured and predicted importance is very high

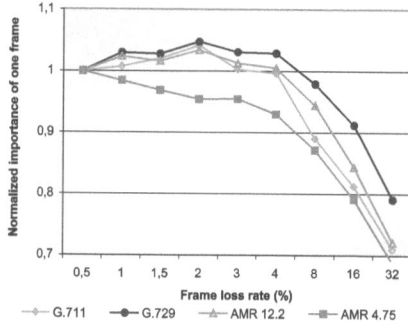
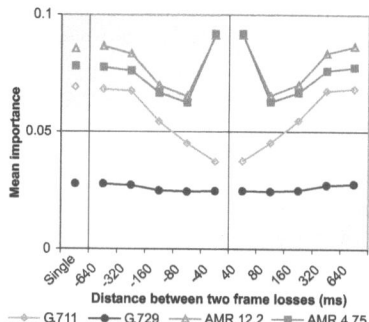

Fig. 9. Impact of loss rate on the mean, normalized importance using the new metric

Fig. 10. Mean importance of a single lost frame is given on the very left and the importance of the second lost frame is displayed in relation to its distance from the first lost frame

loss pattern: A speech sample is encoded, frame losses are enforced depending on the experimental requirements (e.g., random frame loss), the frames are decoded or concealed, and finally PESQ calculates the MOS value by comparing the original sample with the degraded version.

Figure 8a displays the relation between the rate of random frame losses and speech quality for different codecs: The higher the loss rate the worse are PESQ's speech quality ratings. Next, we calculate the importance of all frame losses (Fig. 8b). At a loss rate of 0% the importance value is 0. As long as the loss rate is low, the importance increases linearly with the loss rate.

If the impact of frame losses can be added, the following statement is valid: The overall importance of the loss of N frames can be calculated by multiplying the mean importance with N (13). In Fig. 9, the mean importance depending on the loss rate is displayed. For low loss rates the importance is a bit underestimated. In case of loss rate above 8%, it is clearly underestimated. One should note that in this experiment the masking is not considered.

$$Imp(s, c, l_{mean}) \cdot N = Imp(s, c, \{l_1, \ldots, l_N\}) \tag{13}$$

The next experiments reseembles the measurements of single frame losses described in [8], but this time we dropped two speech frames instead of one. Between both losses there is a lossless gap of 40, 80, 160, 320, or 640 ms. In Fig. 10 we display the importance averaged over all single frame losses, vertically sorted according to the encoding scheme and marked with Single on the horizontal axis. Also, we display the importance of the second frame l_2, if the first frame l_1 is lost already. The importance value is calculated using (14).

$$Imp(s, c, \{l_2 \mid l_1\}) = \Big((4.5 - MOS(s_i, c, \{l_1, l_2\}))^2 - \\ (4.5 - MOS(s_i, c, \{l_1\}))^2\Big) \cdot t(s) \tag{14}$$

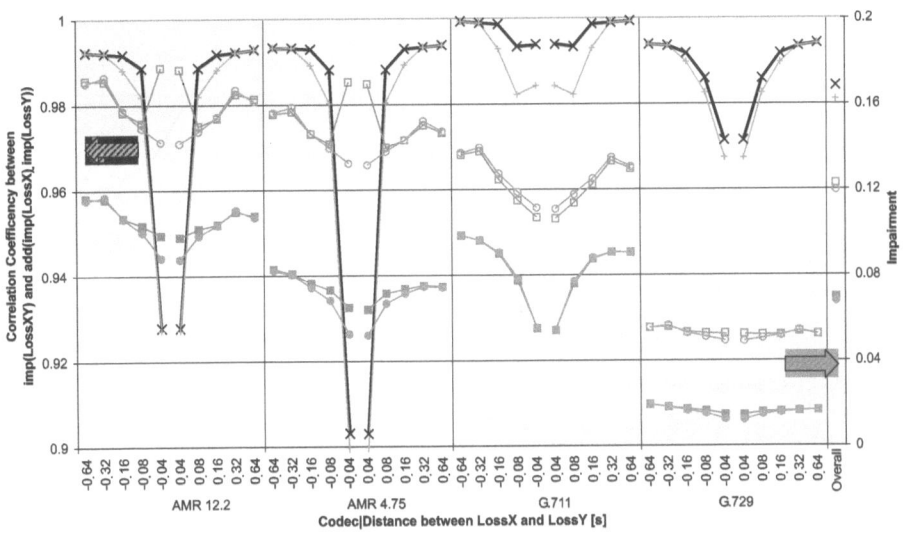

Fig. 11. Median and mean impairment due to two frames losses. Estimated with PESQ displaying $Imp(s, c, \{l_1, l_2\})$ and with our model: $add(Imp(s, c, l_1), Imp(s, c, l_2), t_{width})$. We also show the cross correlation between PESQ ratings and the rating of our model (R value). The R-without-masking compares PESQ with the long-term only aggregation function

Considering the G.711 results, one can see that the nearer the frame losses are, the lower the importance of a frame becomes. This effect can be explained with the temporal masking effect [14]. However, the mean importance for two AMR frame losses increases significantly, if the loss distance is 40 ms. We assume that this effect is due to a mismatch between the encoder's and decoder's internal state. The first loss results into to a desynchronized decoder. The applied loss concealment leads to a wrong prediction of frames' content. Since the de-synchronisation of the decoder can last for multiple following frames (up to 700 ms [16]), the mean impairment due to the concealment of the second loss can be significantly higher. This effect occurs only with the AMR codec, thus we will not consider it in this work any further.

Figure 11 displays the prediction performance of losing two speech frames compared to the sum of losing two individual frames. The correlation coefficient between the importance of the double loss case and the sum of both single loss case is calculated and displayed. The correlation for a distance of >320ms is about R$>$0.98 and drops down to a minimum of R=0.78 at a distance of 40ms. This effect can be explained with concealment and error propagation effects that are not modeled in our model.

In the next experiment we study the effect of bursty frame losses. We dropped one block of continuing speech frames within a sample length of 8 s. The du-

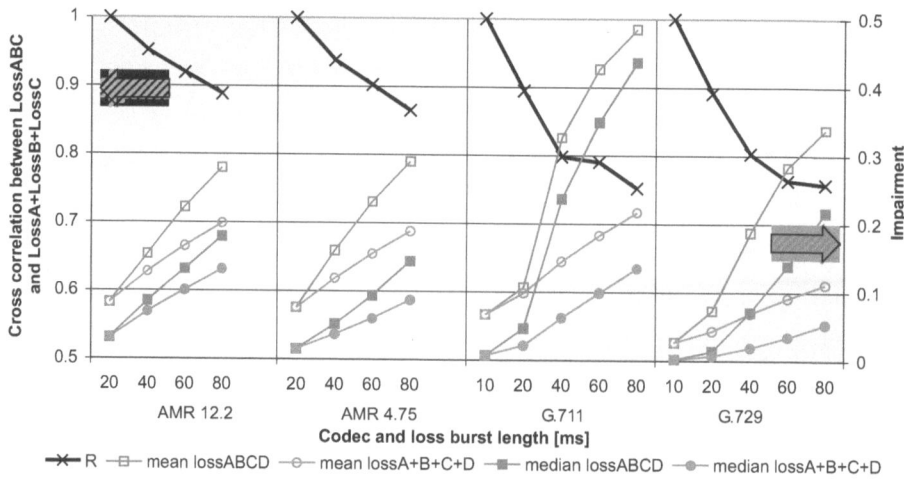

Fig. 12. Importance of a block of frame losses (red/square: PESQ, green/circle: our approach, black lines/cross: cross correlation R)

ration of the complete block was between 10 to 80 ms (in Fig. 12 the red lines marked with a square). Also we used our model to add the importance of the corresponding single frame loss (the green lines marked with a circle). To calculate the importance of the burst loss we use (15) with N being the number of continuously lost frames, pos the position of the first lost frame, and Imp^*_{pos} the importance of a frame loss at position pos.

$$Imp^*(N, pos) = \begin{cases} Imp^*_{pos} & \text{if } N = 1 \\ add\left(Imp^*(N-1, pos), Imp^*_{pos+N-1}, 0\right) & \text{if } N > 1 \end{cases} \quad (15)$$

The correlation (R) between PESQ and our model is displayed with black lines. The longer the loss burst, the worse the cross correlation. Our model give a lower impact of bursty losses as PESQ. This modelling is in line with the indications that PESQ displays an obvious sensitivity to bursty losses judging them worse than humans do [2].

6   Conclusion

This paper describes the impact of speech frames loss by considering their temporal relation. It is based on the concept of the *importance of speech frames* and models psychoacoustic aggregation behavior over time. Thus, our model covers an important aspect in the relation between speech frame losses and speech quality. Our model shows a high prediction accuracy for many loss patterns when compared to PESQ. Additionally, our time aggregation function has a very low complexity. However, before it can be fully applied, three issues have to be addressed:

First, the measurement of speech frame importance in [8] has a high computational complexity and delay. Thus, it cannot be applied online. We provide solutions in [16] that decrease delay and complexity at cost of a lower prediction accuracy. The question remains whether the lower prediction accuracy influences the performance of our time aggreation function.

Second, we compare the performance of our aggregation algorithm to the same PESQ algorithm, which we used to derivate and remodel our algorithm. We achieve a high prediction performance. However, it is still an open point how well our algorithm performs, if it is compared to subjective listening-only test results. The verification with databases containing subjective results is subjected of future studies.

Last, further studies are required to see how our metric scales at high loss rates. Definitely, the effects of concealment and error propagation play an important role if losses are frequent or bursty and need to be modeled.

Nevertheless, the given results contribute to research and standardization: First, they enable researchers developing communication protocols to model the impact of frame loss with a high accuracy. For example, it can be applied for algorithms that prevent frame loss burstiness. Second, this work provides also feedback to the developers of PESQ or similar algorithms, as it explains why PESQ does not require temporal masking: It was already included. Third, it identifies weaknesses of frame loss concealment algorithms (e.g. AMR). Last but not least, our work is directly intended for the standardization process of ITU-T P.VTQ, as it can been seen as an alternative or complementary algorithm to the ITU's E-Model, Telchemy's VQmon and Psytechnics' psyVOIP algorithms [17, 18], which relate VoIP packet loss and delay to service quality.

To show the relevance of the questions addressed in this paper, we demonstrate the impact of the packet dropping strategy on speech quality: Using the knowledge about frame importance, simulations and informal listening-only tests show that only a fraction of all speech packets need to be transmitted if (at least) speech intelligibility is to be maintained. Knowing the importance of speech frames might allow significant energy savings on wireless phones, because fewer packets need to be transmitted.

Acknowledgements

We like to thank A. Raake, J. G. Beerends and C. Schmidmer for their feedback, E.-L. Hoene for the revision of this paper, and last not least the reviewers for their excellent comments.

References

1. Mohammed, S., Cercantes-Perez, F., Afifi, H.: Integrating networks measurements and speech quality subjective scores for control purposes. In: Infocom 2001. Volume 2., Anchorage, AK, USA (2001) 641–649

2. Sun, L.: Subjective and objective speech quality evaluation under bursty losses. In: MESAQIN 2002, Prague, CZ (2002)
3. Jiang, W., Schulzrinne, H.: Comparison and optimization of packet loss repair methods on voip perceived quality under bursty loss. In: NOSSDAV. (2002) 73–81
4. Sanneck, H., Tuong, N., Le, L., Wolisz, A., Carle, G.: Intra-flow loss recovery and control for VoIP. In: ACM Multimedia. (2001) 441–454
5. Petracca, M., Servetti, A., De Martin, J.C.: Voice transmission over 802.11 wireless networks using analysis-by-synthesis packet classification. In: First International Symposium on Control, Communications and Signal Processing, Hammamet, Tunisia (2004) 587–590
6. Chou, P., Miao, Z.: Rate-distortion optimized streaming of packetized media. Technical Report MSR-TR-2001-35, Microsoft Research Technical Report, Redmond, WA (2001)
7. Hoene, C., Dulamsuren-Lalla, E.: Predicting performance of PESQ in case of single frame losses. In: MESAQIN 2004, Prague, CZ (2004)
8. Hoene, C., Rathke, B., Wolisz, A.: On the importance of a VoIP packet. In: ISCA Tutorial and Research Workshop on the Auditory Quality of Systems, Mont-Cenis, Germany (2003)
9. ITU-T: Recommendation P.862 - Perceptual Evaluation of Speech Quality (PESQ), an Objective Method for End-To-End Speech Quality Assessment of Narrowband Telephone Networks and Speech Codecs (2001)
10. Rix, A.W., Hollier, M.P., Hekstra, A.P., Beerends, J.G.: Perceptual evaluation of speech quality (PESQ), the new ITU standard for end-to-end speech quality assessment, part I - time alignment. Journal of the Audio Engineering Society **50** (2002) 755–764
11. Beerends, J.G., Hekstra, A.P., Rix, A.W., Hollier, M.P.: Perceptual evaluation of speech quality (PESQ), the new ITU standard for end-to-end speech quality assessment, part II - psychoacoustic model. Journal of the Audio Engineering Society **50** (2002) 765–778
12. Hoene, C., Wiethölter, S., Wolisz, A.: Predicting the perceptual service quality using a trace of VoIP packets. In: QofIS'04, Barcelona, Spain (2004)
13. Beerends, J.G.: Measuring the quality of speech and music codecs: An integrated psychoacoustic approach. presented at the 98th Convention of the Audio Engineering Society, preprint 3945 (1995)
14. Zwicker, E., Fastl, H.: Psychoacoustics, facts and models. Springer Verlag (1990)
15. Beerends, J.G., Stemerdink, J.A.: A perceptual speech-quality measure based on a psychoacoustic sound representation. Journal of the Audio Engineering Society **42** (1994) 115–123
16. Hoene, C., Schäfer, G., Wolisz, A.: Predicting the importance of a speech frame (2005) work in progress.
17. Telchemy: Delayed contribution 105: Description of VQmon algorithm. ITU-T Study Group 12 (2003)
18. Psytechnics: Delayed contribution 175: High level description of psytechnics ITU-T P.VTQ candidate. ITU-T Study Group 12 (2003)

Best-Effort Versus Reservations Revisited

Oliver Heckmann[1] and Jens B. Schmitt[2]

[1] KOM Multimedia Communications Lab, TU Darmstadt, Germany
[2] DISCO Distributed Computer Systems Lab, University of Kaiserslautern, Germany

Abstract. In this paper, we walk in the footsteps of the stimulating paper by Lee Breslau and Scott Shenker entitled "Best-effort vs. Reservations: A Simple Comparative Analysis"[1]. In fact, we finally follow their invitation to use their models as a *starting point* and *extend* them to reason about the very basic but still very much debated architectural issue whether quality of service (QoS) mechanisms like admission control and service differentiation are necessary or if overprovisioning with a single service class does the job just as well at lower system complexity. We analytically compare two QoS systems: a QoS system using admission control and a reservation mechanism that can guarantee bandwidth for flows respectively offers service differentiation based on priority queueing for two service classes and a system with no admission control and a single best-effort service class.

Keywords: Quality of Service, Network Architecture.

1 Prelude

The first set of models we use are based on those by Breslau and Shenker. They assume a single bottleneck and a single type of traffic (elastic, strictly inelastic or adaptive) using the bottleneck and then analyse the expected total utility by assuming a certain probability distribution for the number of flows. The main effects investigated with these models are admission control and bandwidth guarantees. As is common and good practice in sciences, we first reproduce the results of Breslau and Shenker and then give some further insights. The second set of models is an original contribution of this paper. Contrary to the other models, they analyse a given load situation and a *traffic mix consisting of elastic and inelastic flows* filling the link at the same time. By incorporating queueing theory and the TCP formula, the second set of models allows us to investigate more sophisticated utility functions and more realistic network behaviour than the first set. The main effects investigated with these models are scheduling and service differentiation.

2 On the Benefit of Admission Control

Shenker and Breslau [1, 7] analyse two fundamentally different QoS systems in their work:

H. de Meer and N. Bhatti (Eds.): IWQoS 2005, LNCS 3552, pp. 151–163, 2005.

1. A best-effort (BE) system without admission control where all flows admitted to the network receive the same share of the total bandwidth.
2. A reservation based QoS system with admission control, where only the flows are admitted to the network that optimally (w.r.t. total utility) fills the network. Their bandwidth is guaranteed by the system.

We start with a fixed load model that assumes a given traffic load for the network.

2.1   Fixed Load

The fixed load model from [7], also published in [1], assumes that there are a number of identical flows requesting service from a link with capacity C. The utility function $u(b)$ of a flow is a function of the link bandwidth b assigned for that flow with:

$$\frac{du(b)}{db} \geq 0 \; \forall b > 0, \, u(0) = 0, \, u(\infty) = 1 \tag{1}$$

A flow rejected by the admission control is treated as receiving zero bandwidth, resulting in zero utility. The link capacity is split evenly among the flows so that the total utility U of k admitted flows is given by $U(k) = k \cdot u(\frac{C}{k})$

If there exists some $\epsilon > 0$ such that the function $u(b)$ is convex but not concave[1] in the neighbourhood $[0, \epsilon]$, then there exists some k_{max} such that $U(k_{max}) > U(k) \; \forall k > k_{max}$. In this case, the network is overloaded whenever more than k_{max} flows enter the network; the system with admission control would yield the higher total utility because it could restrict k_{max}.

If the utility function $u(b)$ is strictly concave, then $U(k)$ is a strictly monotonically increasing function of k. In that case, the total utility is maximised by always allowing flows to the network and not using admission control.

Elastic Applications. typically have a strictly concave utility function as additional bandwidth aids performance but the marginal improvement decreases with b. Therefore, if all flows are elastic, the best-effort system without admission control would be the optimal choice.

Looking at the other extreme of the spectrum, there are **strictly inelastic applications** like traditional telephony that require their data to arrive within a given delay bound. Their performance does not improve if data arrives earlier, they need a fixed bandwidth $\tilde{b}$ for the delay bound. Their utility function is given by

$$u(b) = \begin{cases} 0 & b < \tilde{b} \\ 1 & b \geq \tilde{b} \end{cases} \tag{2}$$

which leads to a total utility of

$$U(k) = \begin{cases} 0 & k > C/\tilde{b} \\ k & k \leq C/\tilde{b} \end{cases} \tag{3}$$

---

[1] This rules out functions simple linear functions $u(b) = a_0 + a_1 \cdot b$ which would, by the way, also violate (1).

In this case, admission control is clearly necessary to maximise utility. If no admission control is used and the number of flows exceeds the threshold $C/\tilde{b}$, the total utility $U(k)$ drops to zero. The two extreme cases of elastic and strictly inelastic applications show that the Internet and telephone network architectures were designed to meet the needs of their original class of applications.

Another type are the **adaptive applications;** they are designed to adapt their transmission rate to the currently available bandwidth and reduce to packet delay variations by buffering. Breslau/Shenker propose the S-shaped utility function with parameter κ

$$u(b) = 1 - e^{-\frac{b^2}{\kappa+b}} \tag{4}$$

to model these applications. For small bandwidths, the utility increases quadratically $(u(b) \approx \frac{b^2}{\kappa})$ and for larger bandwidths it slowly approaches one $(u(b) \approx 1 - e^{-b})$. The exact shape is determined by κ.

For these flows, the total utility $U(k)$ has a peak at some finite k_{max} but the decrease in total utility for $k > k_{max}$ is much more gentle than for the strictly inelastic applications. The reservation based system thus has an advantage over the best-effort system, but two questions remain: The first is *whether that advantage is large enough to justify the additional complexity* of the reservation based QoS system and the second is, *how likely is the situation where $k > k_{max}$.* These questions are addressed in the next section with the variable load model.

2.2   Variable Load

Model. Breslau and Shenker [1] analyse the likelihood of an overload situation for the strictly inelastic and adaptive applications by assuming a given probability distribution $P(k)$ of the number of flows k. They use two models, a model with a discrete and one with a continuous number of flows k. We base our following analysis on the discrete model and on the algebraic load distribution. [1] also contains results for a Poisson and exponential load distribution, but they do not lead to fundamentally new insights.

For the *algebraic load distribution* $P(k) = \frac{\nu}{\lambda+k^z}$ the load decays at a slower than exponential rate over a large range. It has three parameters ν, λ and z^2. The algebraic distribution is normalised so that $\sum_{k=0}^{\infty} P(k) = 1$; we analyse $z \in \{2, 3, 4\}$.

Similar to [1], for the following analysis we choose the parameters of the probability distributions so that the expected number of flows $E(k) = \sum_{k=0}^{\infty} k \cdot P(k)$ is 100. For the utility functions, $\tilde{b} = 1$ in (2) and $\kappa = 0.62086$ in (4) as this parameter setting yields $k_{max} = C$ for both utility functions.

The two utility functions analysed should be seen as the extremes of a spectrum. The strictly inelastic utility function does not tolerate any deviation from the requested minimum bandwidth $\tilde{b}$ at all, while the adaptive utility function

---

[2] λ is introduced so that the distribution can be normalised for a given asymptotic power law z.

embodies fairly large changes in utility across a wide range of bandwidths above and below C/k_{max}.

The expected total utility $\overline{U}_{BE}$ of the best-effort system is

$$\overline{U}_{BE}(C) = \sum_{k=1}^{\infty} P(k) \cdot U(k) = \sum_{k=1}^{\infty} P(k) \cdot k \cdot u(\frac{C}{k}) \tag{5}$$

The QoS system can limit the number of flows to k_{max}. The expected utility $\overline{U}_{QoS}$ of the QoS system is $\overline{U}_{QoS}(C) = \sum_{k=1}^{k_{max}(C)} P(k) \cdot k \cdot u(\frac{C}{k}) + \sum_{k=k_{max}(C)+1}^{\infty} P(k) \cdot k_{max} \cdot u(\frac{C}{k_{max}(C)})$.

To compare the performance of the two QoS systems, the authors of [1] propose the bandwidth gap as a performance metric. The bandwidth gap is the additional bandwidth Δ_C necessary for the best-effort system so that the expected total utilities are equal: $\overline{U}_{QoS}(C) = \overline{U}_{BE}(C + \Delta_C)$

We propose a different metric: the unit-less **overprovisioning factor** OF. It puts the bandwidth gap in relation to the original bandwidth

$$OF = \frac{C + \Delta_C}{C} \tag{6}$$

The overprovisioning factor expresses the bandwidth increase necessary for a best-effort based QoS system to offer the same expected total (respectively average) utility as the reservation based one.

Evaluation. The overprovisioning factors for the strictly inelastic and the adaptive utility function and for the algebraic load distributions over a wide range of link bandwidths C are shown in Fig. 1. The reader is reminded of the fact that the expected number of flows $E(k)$ is 100.

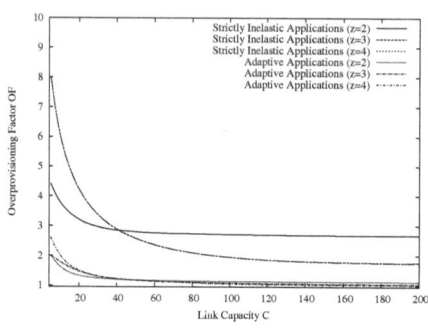

Fig. 1. Results

The algebraic load distribution decays slowly. The lower z, the slower the decay. For the inelastic applications, the very slow decay for $z = 2$ results in a significantly higher overprovisioning factor (2.70 if capacity equals demand and 2.67 if capacity equals twice the demand in the strictly inelastic case) than for the higher values of z (or for the exponential load distribution in [1], where the overprovisioning factor is around 2). For adaptive applications, the overprovisioning factor is close to one (between 1.05 and 1.14 if capacity equals demand).

The results here and in [1] show that the overprovisioning factor is close to unity for adaptive applications and significantly higher than unity for the inelastic applications. The link capacity significantly influences the performance of both QoS systems and the overprovisioning factor. The reservation based QoS system can provide significant advantages over the pure best-effort system in a well dimensioned network for strictly inelastic applications. For adaptive applications, the advantage is rather low in a well dimensioned network.

2.3 Summary and Conclusions

The analysis above respectively in [1] gives valuable insights but can also be criticised in some points:

- It assumes that only a single type of application utilises the network. If different applications with different requirements utilise a network at the same time, QoS systems can differentiate between them – e.g. by protecting loss sensitive flows or by giving delay sensitive flows a higher scheduling priority – and offer a further advantage over the best-effort system.
- The load distributions (Poisson, exponential, algebraic) used in [1] and above to derive the expected utility for a given bandwidth are not based on empirical studies.
- In addition, it is arguable whether the expected utility really represents the satisfaction of the customers with the network performance:
  If the network performance is very good most of the time but regularly bad at certain times (e.g. when important football games are transmitted), this might be unacceptable for customers despite a good *average* utility.

In the next section, we use a novel approach to avoid these drawbacks and shed more light on the comparison of the two QoS systems.

3 On the Benefit of Service Differentiation

When analysing a mix of different traffic types competing for bandwidth, it is not trivial to determine the amount of bandwidth the individual flows will receive and the delay it experiences. In this section, we present an analytical approach that – contrary to the previous approach – uses queueing theory and the TCP formula as a foundation to calculate the overprovisioning factor for a traffic mix of elastic TCP-like traffic flows and inelastic traffic flows.

3.1 Traffic Types

We assume that two types of traffic – elastic and inelastic – share a bottleneck link of capacity C. For **inelastic traffic**, we use index 1 and assume that there are a number of inelastic flows sending with a total rate r_1. The strictly inelastic traffic analysed in Section 2 did not tolerate any loss. Most multimedia applications, however, can tolerate a certain level of loss. For example, a typical voice transmission is still understandable if some packets are lost – albeit at reduced quality. We model this behaviour here by making the utility of the inelastic traffic degrading with the packet loss[3] and with excessive delay.

For the **elastic traffic,** we use index 2; it represents file transfer traffic with the characteristic TCP "sawtooth" behaviour: the rate is increased proportional to the round-trip time and halved whenever a loss occurs. We use a TCP formula to model this behaviour; the two main parameters that influence the TCP sending rate are the loss probability p_2 and the RTT respectively the delay q_2. We assume there are a number of greedy elastic flows sending as fast as the TCP congestion control is allowing them to send; their total rate is $r_2 = f(p_2, d_2)$. The utility of the elastic traffic is a function of its throughput.

3.2   Best-Effort Network Model

A best-effort network cannot differentiate between packets of the elastic and inelastic traffic flows and treats both types of packets the same way. The loss and the delay for the two traffic types is therefore equal $p_{BE} = p_1 = p_2$, $q_{BE} = q_1 = q_2$.

Let μ_1 be the average service rate of the inelastic flows, μ_2 the one for elastic flows, λ_1 the arrival rate of the inelastic traffic and λ_2 accordingly the arrival rate of the elastic traffic. The total utilisation ρ is then given by $\rho = \rho_1 + \rho_2 = \frac{\lambda_1}{\mu_1} + \frac{\lambda_2}{\mu_2}$ and the average service rate $\overline{\mu}$ by $\overline{\mu} = \frac{\rho_1\mu_1 + \rho_2\mu_2}{\rho_1 + \rho_2} = \frac{\lambda_1 + \lambda_2}{\rho_1 + \rho_2}$.

In the best-effort model, the loss probability p_{BE} is the same for both traffic types and can be estimated with the well-known $M/M/1/B$ loss formula for a given maximal queue length of B packets assuming Markovian arrival and service processes [2]: $p_{BE} = \frac{1-\rho}{1-\rho^{B+1}} \cdot \rho^B$.

For the queueing delay q_{BE} of the bottleneck link, the $M/M/1/B$ delay formula [2] is used: $q_{BE} = \frac{1/\overline{\mu}}{1-\rho} \cdot \frac{1 + B\rho^{B+1} - (B+1)\rho^B}{1-\rho^B}$.

The arrival rate λ_1 of the inelastic traffic is given by the sending rates r_1 of the inelastic flows (15) while the arrival rate λ_2 of the elastic traffic depends on the TCP algorithm and the network condition. There are several contributions like [5, 6] that describe methods for predicting the average long-term TCP throughput, depending on the loss and delay properties of a flow. For our high-level analysis, we are not interested in details like the duration of the connection establishment, etc. Therefore, we use the plain square-root formula of [3] for this analysis; it allows us to keep the complexity of the resulting model low:

$$\text{throughput} = \frac{\text{MSS}}{\text{RTT} \cdot \sqrt{2/3} \cdot \sqrt{p_2}} \tag{7}$$

with MSS as maximum segment size and RTT as the round trip time. RTT is assumed to be dominated by the queueing delay q_2. The throughput of the queue

---

[3] It can be seen as an intermediate application between the strictly inelastic and the adaptive traffic of Section 2.

can also be expressed as a function of the arrival process λ_2 and the loss probability p_2:

$$\text{throughput} = \lambda_2(1 - p_2) \tag{8}$$

Introducing parameter t that we call *flow size factor*, (7) and (8) can be simplified to $\lambda_2 = \frac{t}{q_{BE} \cdot \sqrt{p_{BE}}} \cdot \frac{1}{1 - p_{BE}}$ t encompasses the $MSS/\sqrt{2/3}$ part of (7) and part of the round-trip-time and is used to put the TCP flows in correct dimension to the inelastic flows which are dimensioned by their fixed sending rate r_1.

As λ_2 is a function of p_{BE} and q_{BE} and at the same time influences p_{BE} and q_{BE}, the network model is a non-linear equation system (see Model 1). It can be solved with standard methods.

3.3   QoS Network Model

To model a QoS system that differentiates between the inelastic and elastic traffic, we use priority queueing. The inelastic traffic receives strict non-preemptive priority in time and (buffer) space over the elastic traffic.

Using the *M/M/1* queueing model the expected waiting time $E(W_1)$ for a packet of an inelastic flow depends on the expected number of packets waiting to be served $E(L_1)$ and the residual service time of the packet currently in the queue. Because non-preemptive queueing is used, the latter can be a type 1 (inelastic flow) or type 2 (elastic flow) packet; because the exponential service time distribution is memoryless, the expected residual service time is $\sum_{i=1}^{2} \rho_i \frac{1}{\mu_i}$:

$$E(W_1) = E(L_1)\frac{1}{\mu_1} + \sum_{i=1}^{2} \rho_i \frac{1}{\mu_i} \tag{9}$$

By applying Little's Law [4] $E(L_i) = \lambda_i E(W_i)$, we get $E(W_1) = \frac{\sum_{i=1}^{2} \rho_i \frac{1}{\mu_i}}{1 - \rho_1}$.

To determine the average queueing delay q_1, we need the expected sojourn time $E(S_1) = E(W_1) + 1/\mu_1$: $q_1 = E(S_1) = \frac{1/\mu_1 + \rho_2/\mu_2}{1 - \rho_1}$.

For the second queue, the determination of the expected sojourn time is more complicated. The expected waiting time $E(W_2)$ and the sojourn time $E(S_2) = q_2$ for a packet of type 2 is the sum of

- the residual service time $T_0 = \sum_{i=1}^{2} \rho_i \frac{1}{\mu_i}$ of the packet currently in the queue because the queue is non-preemptive,
- the service times $T_1 = E(L_1)/\mu_1$ for all packets of priority 1
- and the service times $T_2 = E(L_2)/\mu_2$ for all packets of priority 2 that are already present waiting in the queue at the point of arrival of the new packet of type 2 and are therefore served before it
- plus the service times $T_3 = \rho_1(T_0 + T_1 + T_2)$ for all packets of priority 1 that arrive during $T_0 + T_1 + T_2$ and that are served before the packet of type 2 because they are of higher priority.

The waiting time is $E(W_2) = T_0 + T_1 + T_2 + T_3$, for the sojourn time respectively queueing delay the service time has to be added $q_2 = E(S_2) = E(W_2) + 1/\mu_2$.

By applying (9) and Little's Law [4] we get $q_2 = E(S_2) = \frac{(1+\rho_1) \sum_{i=1}^{2} \rho_i \frac{1}{\mu_i}}{(1 - \rho_1 - \rho_1 \rho_2)(1 - \rho_1)} + \frac{1}{\mu_2}$.

A packet of type 1 is not dropped as long as there are packets of type 2 waiting in the queue that could be dropped instead. With respect to loss, the arrival process 1 with arrival rate λ_1 thus experiences a normal $M/M/1/B$ queue with a loss probability for a packet of type 1 of $p_1 = \frac{1-\rho_1}{1-\rho_1^{B+1}} \cdot \rho_1^B$.

We make the simplifying assumption that λ_1 is small enough so the loss for queue 1 is negligible $p_1 \approx 0$. For the low priority queue, the loss probability is then given by

$$p_2 = \frac{(1 - \rho_1 - \rho_2)}{1 - (\rho_1 + \rho_2)^{B+1}} \cdot (\rho_1 + \rho_2)^B \cdot \frac{\lambda_1 + \lambda_2}{\lambda_2} \tag{10}$$

The first part of (10) represents the total loss of the queueing system; the second part $\frac{\lambda_1+\lambda_2}{\lambda_2}$ is necessary because the packets of type 2 experience the complete loss.

The priority queueing based QoS network model is summarised in Model 2, it is using the same parameters as Model 1. Like the best-effort network model, it is a non-linear equation system.

3.4   Utility Functions

Inelastic Traffic. The inelastic traffic represents multimedia or other real-time traffic that is sensitive to loss and delay. Therefore, the utility u_1 of the inelastic flows is modelled as strictly decreasing function of the loss probability p_1 and the deviation of the delay q_1 from a reference queueing delay q_{ref}: $u_1 = 1 - \alpha_p p_1 - \alpha_q \frac{q_1 - q_{ref}}{q_{ref}}$.

As a reference queueing delay q_{ref} we use the queueing delay (19) of the QoS network model as that is the minimum queueing delay achievable for this traffic under the given circumstances (number of flows, link capacity, non-preemptive service discipline, etc).

Elastic Traffic. The elastic traffic represents file transfer traffic. The utility of this traffic depends mostly on the throughput as that determines duration of the transfer. The utility u_2 is therefore modelled as function of the throughput d_2: $u_2 = \beta \cdot d_2 = \beta \cdot \frac{t}{q_2 \cdot \sqrt{p_2}}$.

We determine the parameter β so that $u_2 = 1$ for the maximum throughput that can be reached if $\lambda_1 = 0$; both network models lead to the same β if there is no inelastic traffic.

3.5   Evaluation

The default parameter values we use for the following evaluation are given in Table 1. The effect of parameter variation is analysed later. The motivation behind the utility parameter α_p is that the utility of the inelastic flows should be zero for 10% losses (if there is no additional delay); for the parameter α_q the motivation is that the utility should be zero if the delay doubles compared to the minimal delay of the QoS system. β is chosen so that the utility of the elastic

Table 1. Default Parameter Values for the Evaluation

Parameter	Value
μ_1	83.3 pkts/s
μ_2	same as μ_1
α_q	1
α_p	10
β	see Section 3.4
B	10 pkts
t	$t_0, 5t_0, 10t_0$
r_1	$[0, ..., 40]$ pkts/s
w_1	$[1, 2, 5]$
w_2	1

flow is 1 for the maximum throughput as explained in Section 3.4. During the evaluation we vary w_1, r_1 and t. For the choice of w_1, we assume that for the total utility evaluation, the inelastic flows are more important than the elastic flows because they are given priority over the elastic flows and it seems reasonable to expect users to also have a higher utility evaluation for one real-time multimedia flow (e.g. a phone call) than for a file transfer. An indication for that is the fact that the price per minute for a phone call nowadays is typically much higher than the price per minute for a dial-up Internet connection used for a file transfer. As evaluation metric we again use the **overprovisioning factor**[4].

Basic Results. The overprovisioning factors OF for different flow size factors[5] t and for different weight ratios $w_1 : w_2$ are depicted on the y-axis in the graphs of Fig. 2. The total sending rate r_1 of the inelastic flows is shown on the x-axis.

---

[4] For a given r_1 and t, we determine the solution vector (p_1, q_1, p_2, q_2) of the QoS network Model 2. The utility values $u_1 = f(p_1, q_1)$ and $u_2 = f(p_2, q_2)$ and the weighted average utility U_{ref} are derived from the solution vector with $w_1, w_2 > 0$:
$U_{ref} = \frac{w_1 u_1(p_1, q_1) + w_2 u_2(p_2, q_2)}{w_1 + w_2}$.
 The best-effort system based on Model 1 is overprovisioned by a factor OF. The bandwidth respectively service rates μ_1 and μ_2 are increased by that factor OF. Additionally, the buffer space B is increased by the same factor. U_{ref} is used as a reference value and OF is increased by a linear search algorithm until $U_{BE}(OF^*) = U_{ref}$.

[5] To derive an anchor point for t, we arbitrarily determine a t_0 that leads to $\rho_1 = 20\%$ and to $\rho_2 = 60\%$ using the QoS network model. This represents a working point with $\lambda_1 = 0.2 \cdot \mu_1$ with a total utilisation of 80%. Every fourth packet is a multimedia packet, creating a typical situation where a QoS system would be considered. If t is increased to $t = 5t_0$ and λ_1 kept constant, then the proportion of of multimedia packet to file transfer packet drops to 1 : 3.4. At the same time, the aggressiveness of TCP against the inelastic flows increases in the best-effort network model as can be seen in the evaluation results below (Fig. 2).

As can be seen from the graphs, the higher the ratio $w_1 : w_2$ is – that is, the more important the inelastic flows are for the overall utility evaluation – the higher the overprovisioning factor becomes. This can be expected, because for small overprovisioning factors the utility u_1 of the inelastic flows is smaller in the best-effort system than the QoS system where they are protected from the elastic flows because they experience more loss and delay. Thus, the higher u_1 is weighted in the total utility function U, the more bandwidth is needed in the best-effort system to compensate this effect.

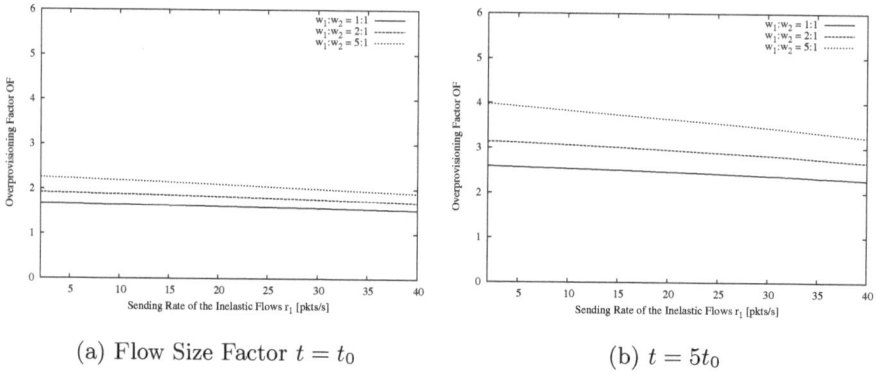

(a) Flow Size Factor $t = t_0$ (b) $t = 5t_0$

Fig. 2. Overprovisioning Factors for the Configuration of Table 1

Comparing the two graphs, it can be seen that as the flow size factor is increased more overprovisioning is needed. Increasing the flow size factor represents increasing the number of elastic (TCP) senders and the aggressiveness of the elastic flows. In the best-effort system where the inelastic flows are not protected, a higher flow size factor increases the sending rate of the elastic flows on cost of additional loss and delay for the inelastic flows that in return has to be compensated by more capacity leading to a higher overprovisioning factor.

Keeping the flow size factor constant, with an increase of the sending rate r_1 the overprovisioning factor decreases; the decrease is stronger the higher the flow size factor is. For a weight ratio of $w_1 : w_2 = 2 : 1$ for example the overprovisioning factor drops from $r_1 = 2$ to 40 by 12.0% for $t = t_0$ and 14.9% for $t = 5t_0$. This phenomenon can be explained the following way: When comparing the resulting utility values u_1 and u_2 of the QoS system with the best-effort system ($OF = 1$), the utility value of the inelastic flows u_1 drops because they are no longer protected. At the same time, the utility value of the elastic flows u_2 increases because they no longer suffer the full loss. The increase of u_2 is stronger than the decrease of u_1 the higher r_1 is, therefore for higher r_1 less overprovisioning is needed.

The following discussions – unless stated otherwise – are based on a weight ratio $w_1 : w_2 = 2 : 1$ and a flow size factor of $t = 5t_0$.

Different Bottleneck Resources. Increasing the buffer space B has two adverse effects; it decreases the loss rate and increases the potential queueing delay. An increase of B results in an increase of the overprovisioning factor OF. This is an indication that for the utility calculation, the queueing delay has a stronger effect than the loss rate. This is not surprising because for the $M/M/1/B$ formulas, the loss becomes quickly negligible for larger B.

To confirm this, we reduced the queueing delay effects by setting $\alpha_q = 0.05$ and repeated the experiment. Now, with an increase of B from 10 over 15 to 20 the adverse effect can be observed: the overprovisioning factor drops from 1.76 over 1.68 to 1.66 for $r_1 = 10$.

To conclude, the effect of the buffer size depends on the ratio of α_p to α_q in the utility function.

Next, the reference buffer space B and at the same time the bandwidth (respectively the service rates μ_1 and μ_2) are doubled; r_1 was increased accordingly.

Compared to the previous experiment, the overprovisioning factors only increased insignificantly for $t = 5t_0$. In the best-effort system – as can be seen from (14) – for large B, the queueing delay q_{BE} becomes inverse proportional to the service rate $\bar{\mu}$ and therefore the bandwidth. For large B, the loss p_{BE} exponentially approaches zero as can be seen from (13). Via (16), this leads to a massive increase the elastic rate λ_2 and overall utilisation ρ. This explains why the buffer space has a larger influence than the service rate. Similar arguments hold true for the QoS system.

3.6   Conclusions

The experiments of this section evaluated the relative performance advantage of a QoS system offering service differentiation over a plain best-effort system. The systems have two resources, buffer and bandwidth. We used two types of traffic – elastic and inelastic traffic – which share a bottleneck link. The evaluation is based on an aggregated utility function. Our results are overprovisioning factors that show how much the resources (bandwidth and buffer) of the best-effort system have to be increased to offer the same total utility that the QoS system provides.

Compared to the approach of Breslau and Shenker (Section 2), the overprovisioning factors of the models in this section are generally higher. This is explained by the fact that the models of Section 2 do not consider different traffic types sharing the bottleneck resources. Therefore, they miss one important aspect of QoS systems which is service differentation between flow classes.

In today's Internet the overwhelming part of the traffic is TCP based file transfer traffic. As realtime multimedia applications spread and are supported, their initial share of traffic will be low. In our models this can be represented by rather low sending rates r_1 (few inelastic flows) and a high flow size factor

t (many elastic flows). Interestingly, our results show that especially for this combination the overprovisioning factors are the highest. Therefore, to support the *emerging* realtime traffic applications, QoS architectures have their greatest advantages.

4   Caveat

Both sets of models in this paper necessarily have their limitations because they are based on analytical methods that by nature only allow a certain degree of complexity to be still solvable. The influence of the network topology has been neglected so far. Neither of the approaches uses a fully realistic traffic model that accounts for packet sizes, realistic variability of the packet interarrival times and so on.

Discussions may go on ...

Model 1. Best-Effort Network Model

---

r_1	Total sending rate of the inelastic flows [pkts/s] (given)
t	Flow size factor of the elastic flows [pkts] (given)
μ_1	Service rate of the inelastic traffic [pkts/s] (given)
μ_2	Service rate of the elastic traffic [pkts/s] (given)
B	Queue length [pkts] (given)
p_{BE}	Loss probability
q_{BE}	Queueing delay [s]
λ_1	Arrival rate of the inelastic traffic at the bottleneck [pkts/s]
λ_2	Arrival rate of the elastic traffic at the bottleneck [pkts/s]
ρ	Utilisation of the queue
$\overline{\mu}$	Average service rate [pkts/s]

Equations

$$\overline{\mu} = \frac{\lambda_1 + \lambda_2}{\rho} \tag{11}$$

$$\rho = \frac{\lambda_1}{\mu_1} + \frac{\lambda_2}{\mu_2} \tag{12}$$

$$p_{BE} = \frac{1 - \rho}{1 - \rho^{B+1}} \cdot \rho^B \tag{13}$$

$$q_{BE} = \frac{1/\overline{\mu}}{1 - \rho} \cdot \frac{1 + B\rho^{B+1} - (B+1)\rho^B}{1 - \rho^B} \tag{14}$$

$$\lambda_1 = r_1 \tag{15}$$

$$\lambda_2 = \frac{t}{q_{BE} \cdot \sqrt{p_{BE}}} \cdot \frac{1}{1 - p_{BE}} \tag{16}$$

Model 2. QoS Network Model

p_1	Loss probability of the inelastic flows
q_1	Queueing delay of the inelastic flows [s]
p_2	Loss probability of the elastic flows
q_2	Queueing delay of the elastic flows [s]
ρ_1	Utilisation of the queue with inelastic flows
ρ_2	Utilisation of the queue with elastic flows

Equation (15) and

$$\rho_1 = \lambda_1/\mu_1 \tag{17}$$

$$\rho_2 = \lambda_2/\mu_2 \tag{18}$$

$$q_1 = \frac{1/\mu_1 + \rho_2/\mu_2}{1 - \rho_1} \tag{19}$$

$$q_2 = \frac{(1 + \rho_1) \sum_{i=1}^{2} \rho_i \frac{1}{\mu_i}}{(1 - \rho_1 - \rho_1\rho_2)(1 - \rho_1)} + \frac{1}{\mu_2} \tag{20}$$

$$p_1 = \frac{(1 - \rho_1)}{1 - \rho_1^{B+1}} \cdot \rho_1^{B} \approx 0 \tag{21}$$

$$p_2 = \frac{(1 - \rho_1 - \rho_2)}{1 - (\rho_1 + \rho_2)^{B+1}} \cdot (\rho_1 + \rho_2)^{B} \cdot \frac{\lambda_1 + \lambda_2}{\lambda_2} \tag{22}$$

$$\lambda_2 = \frac{t}{q_2 \cdot \sqrt{p_2}} \cdot \frac{1}{1 - p_2} \tag{23}$$

References

1. Lee Breslau and Scott Shenker. Best-Effort versus Reservations: A Simple Comparative Analysis. In *Proceedings of the ACM Special Interest Group on Data Communication Conference (SIGCOMM 1998)*, pages 3–16, October 1998.
2. Leonard Kleinrock. *Queueing Systems – Theory*. Wiley-Interscience, New York, Vol. 1, 1975. ISBN: 0471491101.
3. T. V. Lakshman and U. Madhow. The Performance of TCP/IP for Networks with High Bandwidth-Delay Products and Random Loss. *IEEE/ACM Transactions on Networking*, 5(3):336–350, 1997.
4. J. D. Little. A proof of the queueing formula $l = \lambda w$. *Operations Research*, 9(3):383–387, March 1961.
5. M. Mathis, J. Semke, J. Mahdavi, and T. Ott. The Macroscopic Behavior of the TCP Congestion Avoidance Algorithm. *Computer Communication Review*, 27(3), July 1997.
6. J. Padhye, V. Firoiu, D. Towsley, and J. Kurose. Modeling TCP Throughput: A Simple Model and its Empirical Validation. In *Proceedings of the ACM Special Interest Group on Data Communication Conference (SIGCOMM 1998)*, pages 303–314, September 1998.
7. Scott Shenker. Fundamental design issues for the future internet. *IEEE Journal on Selected Areas in Communications*, 13(7):1176–1188, September 1995.

An Advanced QoS Protocol for Real-Time Content over the Internet

John Adams[1], Avril IJsselmuiden[2], and Lawrence Roberts[3]

[1] British Telecom, Martlesham Heath, Suffolk, UK
john.l.adams@bt.com
[2] IEM, University of Duisberg-Essen, 45326 Essen, Germany
avril@iem.uni-due.de
[3] Anagran, 2055 Woodside Road, Redwood City, CA 95061, USA
lroberts@anagran.com

Abstract. This paper describes an upgrade to network functionality aimed at the support of a mass-market home-based supply of QoS-sensitive content. We describe a new protocol that deals with congestion conditions that may arise when too many simultaneous QoS-sensitive flows compete for bandwidth at a network link. It provides a solution to enable certain flows to be guaranteed, by making others (typically the latest flow, or another flow selected because of policy reasons), the subject of focused packet discards. The business context and the protocol are described, and some simulation results from the model, are presented. The protocol has been the subject of discussion recently at ITU-T meetings, and ETSI meetings, and in January 2005 a new transfer capability based on this protocol was added to the draft ITU-T standard Y.1221, Traffic Control and Congestion Control in IP-based networks.

1 Introduction

This paper envisages a large proportion of broadband users becoming real-time content providers. This requires QoS to be added to the Internet. This would enable, for instance, talking / explaining sequences on a home movie while pausing and rewinding, as well as selling real-time content. The paper discusses a proposed solution to adding QoS to the Internet that can be fairly easily added on to what already exists. It applies to both mobile as well as fixed line services.

The protocol has been proposed to ITU-T SG12 [ITU-T 1–5], where it was discussed and provisional text agreed to be added to Recommendation Y.1221 [ITU-T 6]. A signalling protocol was also presented that is part of the total "QoS toolkit" that we are proposing, allowing applications to select the level of QoS control they need [ITU-T 7]. This signalling protocol is based on a more complex, end-to-end protocol for QoS in IPv6, using a hop-by-hop option and the Flow Label in IPv6. This has already been approved by the Telecommunications Industry Association (TIA 1039) [Roberts].

H. de Meer and N. Bhatti (Eds.): IWQoS 2005, LNCS 3552, pp. 164–177, 2005.
© IFIP International Federation for Information Processing 2005

In Section 2 we discuss the commercial and technical background to this idea; in section 3 we describe our protocol; in section 4 we describe and analyse the experiments performed to test our protocol; in section 5 we give our conclusions.

2   Commercial and Technical Background

The scenario of an end user that can connect to, potentially, many hundreds of thousands of content sites and purchase QoS-sensitive content causes a reconsideration of the business model, governing how money flows between the user, the service suppliers and content suppliers, and the QoS set-up and clear-down procedures. Some of these issues suggest a preference of one QoS architecture compared to others and will be outlined here.

Currently the end user may get QoS-sensitive content in different ways. For example, from an Internet Service Provider (ISP) product where the end user can see Internet content and, possibly, a content portal managed by the ISP. The ISP may provide QoS guarantees only on content purchased from within the portal, and the content suppliers would settle directly with the ISP.

Another method would be from the network access service provider, if they offer direct access to the Internet (i.e. the access provider assigns an IP address to the end user from its pool of addresses and the user selects services directly from different sites). The access provider may be vertically integrated so that its retail element also has content portal and only offers QoS guarantees on content selected from this portal.

However the needs of the user may encourage a new commercial model. It is envisaged that users will want to access any content site, including content on home-based businesses using residential broadband access; niche content where a site has established a reputation; or general content where a site is offering a highly competitive price. This new commercial model may trigger major changes in user behaviour on broadband, including new business opportunities for users to develop and sell niche content. In this model the user is not just looking for QoS guarantees on specific portal content but, more generally, on any QoS-sensitive content.

There are certain commercial conditions that are likely to apply to this scenario and have relevance to architecture. One case would be that when an end user has an ISP product for accessing Internet content, then there has to be a realistic commercial model that underpins any QoS guarantees that the ISP establishes with the access network provider.

There is a billing relationship for basic services between the end user and the ISP and, probably, an additional direct settlement between the user and content site. The ISP could seem excluded from all but basic services supply but could be brought into the commercial model more strongly if it charged for QoS establishment.

In this scenario the ISP could forward QoS requests from the content site towards the network access provider. The network access provider treats the ISP as a trusted source of such signals and bills the ISP for the QoS guarantees it establishes. In this case the network access provider is in the value chain for

QoS establishment. The ISP is also in the value chain if it, in turn, charges the user on a monthly basis on QoS flows consumed by that user. The user, in turn, needs to trust that the bills received each month only reflect what was wanted and consumed. This aspect needs controls on both unsolicited QoS content from a content site, and duration charges to truly reflect the actual duration of the content. This implies that either the ISP or network access provider takes steps with an untrusted content site (who has no charging incentive to send no unsolicited content or to clear down) to ensure that QoS guarantees are not charged for unwanted content or after the content flow has ceased.

We are proposing that the answer to these issues is a lightweight signalling protocol that puts minimum demands on the content site and more controls in the access provider network.

2.1   Comparisons with Other Methods

We next briefly discuss two existing well-known QoS methods, Intserv and Diffserv, to bring out areas where our protocol offers improvement.

Hard QoS quarantees can be provided by Intserv [Braden et al], or alternatively flows established using a SIP-based session control layer which is also responsible for checking, negotiating, reserving and committing network resources by communicating to the Connectivity and Media Resources components on a per-session basis. Assuming an over-provided core, not all network links need be checked. In Tables 1 and 2, we state some main advantages and disadvantages of both bandwidth manager established flows, and our protocol method. As shown, the former adds complexity and set-up delays. It may be hard to achieve a consistent realisation (standards and common profile settings) across multiple network hops. However different market segments could easily co-exist where one delivers content using hard guarantees (perhaps full-length movies) within a single service provider network and the other delivers content using our proposal allowing content from anywhere.

Diffserv [Carlson et al] allows for prioritisation of packets and would focus discards on best effort packets if congestion conditions exist at a potential congestion point. Furthermore if a significant proportion of traffic is best effort then the network may avoid discarding any QoS-sensitive packets. In the near term, Diffserv should be sufficient to support QoS-sensitive content enabling markets to be established. Diffserv would begin to fail when the proportion of QoS-sensitive traffic becomes high at a point where congestion cannot be avoided by discarding best effort packets. Conditions may differ from one micro-geography to the next so that one group of users on a DSLAM have started to consume content that is dominantly delay/ loss sensitive. Other groups on other DSLAMs may not have established the same pattern. But where such a group pattern becomes established they could all experience poor service if only reliant on Diffserv. Note that, between potential congestion points, Diffserv becomes an important support function for our flow state aware protocol (protecting packets marked as such, at the expense of best effort packets, along network links where there is sufficient network capacity and best effort traffic).

Table 1. Advantages of bandwidth manager established flows, and our protocol method

Type	Advantages
Bandwidth reservation via multiple bandwidth managers e.g. SIP-based	Hard guarantee on every accepted flow, except under network fault conditions.
Flow State Aware bandwidth Protection	Same low delay/loss as achieved by multiple bandwidth managers except for a target tiny fraction of flows (e.g. similar to PSTN network congestion target). Simplifies receiver set-up experience. No need to understand what bandwidth to reserve, as network deals with this complexity. Rate adjustments are easy for sending and receiving users. Set up delays should not normally be perceived. Very lightweight signalling to be standardised.

Table 2. Disadvantages of bandwidth manager established flows, and our protocol method

Type	Disadvantages
Bandwidth reservation via multiple bandwidth managers e.g. SIP-based	Receiving user experiences some complexity in successfully setting up an appropriate bandwidth reservation across multiple networks. Call set-up delay may be perceived as significant, especially for the case of viewing real-time content part way through a call. Changing the rate of a real-time flow may be perceived by the user as adding further complexity and additional set-up delay. Implementation complexity. Bandwidth management is likely to be implemented with different rules and in different ways in various network domains. It also requires an out-of-band signalling network that is potentially more complex to standardise.
Flow State Aware bandwidth Protection	New service experience where, very occasionally, the user can get service disruption and an apology message, instead of the more familiar call rejection message at the bandwidth reservation request stage. Will need commercial momentum to achieve standardisation, and mass deployment for an anywhere-to-anywhere service.

3 Our Proposed Protocol

Currently, when flows consist of different priority information, such as video and data, shapers use schemes such as Type of Service marking to distinguish flow content and discard packets of lower priority flows (typically the data flow) and protect the video flows [Wright et al]. However, the protocol proposed in this paper addresses the problem of equal priority flows causing congestion, and unable to slow down through the control of, for example, TCP. It protects certain connections by employing a protocol which comes into operation in moments of congestion, to focus discards on (typically) the most recent flows.

It is worth noting that a more complex, end-to-end protocol for QoS in IPv6, TIA 1039, has already been approved by the Telecommunications Industry Association. It uses a hop by hop option, and the Flow Label in IPv6 [Roberts]. Our protocol attempts to accomplish much the same functions, without the full end-to-end complexity, and also permits its use in IPv4 as well as IPv6. Our protocol envisages a new functional element that would be located at a BRAS. However, it could also operate equally well in other network locations, e.g. a Wi-Fi hotspot. With our protocol it is possible to:

- Admit VBR flows without being constrained to accept only a set of flows whose peak rates are less than the available capacity.
- Admit such flows without knowing the remaining capacity of the link.
- Admit flows without requiring a suspension of higher-level session control protocols.
- Provide guarantees to each of the admitted flows except under certain extreme traffic conditions, when selected flows will be targeted for packet loss, enabling other flows to continue without any loss or undesirable packet delays.

The protocol works on the principle that if congestion occurs, and packet discard is necessary, it is better to use focussed discard than arbitrary discard[Smith et al, Floyd et al, Romanow et al, Kawahara et al]. We apply this principle by making the latest flow(s) the subject of discard.

We propose a very simple signalling protocol consisting of a "Start Packet" appended at the head of a new flow of packets. The Start Packet also carries additional info, such as (if the application desires to signal this) the requested flow rate. A new diffserv class is used so that the new QoS mechanisms are not applied to legacy services, and this marking is carried in the Start Packet and subsequent data packets.

The network recognises that a new flow has started, because the flow is always preceded by a Start Packet. Having sent its Start Packet, there is no requirement for a flow to wait for any processing or acknowledgement of the Start Packet – it can immediately start transmitting actual QoS-sensitive data packets. However, as part of our proposed "QoS toolkit" the application can choose to wait for the Start Packet to traverse the network. As it does so, the requested rate may be reduced at Flow State Aware control points along the path. The receiving application then returns this via an acknowledgement packet directed towards the source (that may further indicate the receiver's willingness to accept this content). Finally the source may forward the Start Packet back again towards the receiver having accepted any reduced available rate or, if the network did nor reduce the rate, to reconfirm this information to all downstream Flow State Aware elements.

The basic principle is that the in-band Start Packet contains all the information necessary to identify the packets of any flow, e.g. source and destination addresses, flow label or port numbers. Subsequent data packets are examined and are able to be identified as belonging to that flow.

The "QoS toolkit" is aimed at two specific aspects of QoS that have different response time needs. The signalling protocol described above works within a slower response time that meets requirements at the beginning of flow establishment. There is also a second response time need that must work much faster and occurs during the lifetime of a flow. The reasons for this second, much faster response time occur when flows are re-routed. Another reason is that network utilisation is optimised for VBR traffic if admission control assumes a small probability of traffic overload is allowable. Such congestion instances would be handled by the fast response mechanism. We are also proposing a new simple QoS service to be available to the end user using just the fast response mechanism (i.e. without waiting for any acknowledgement to Start Packets). This QoS mode, albeit slightly less strict in its guarantee, may be sufficient to meet most needs of a residential mass-market for the supply of QoS-sensitive content.

The fast-response local QoS control maintains a "Drop Window". This is a register where flow IDs are stored. When a new flow starts, its flow identity enters this window, and whilst there, it is regarded as being the target of packet loss if congestion occurs. As new flows start up, the flow moves through the Drop Window, until eventually it is removed (by being overwritten), when certain conditions are satisfied. These conditions include:

- A flow cannot be removed from the Drop Window until x data packets have been forwarded belonging to that flow (where x is a parameter set by the network operator)
- A flow may not be removed from the Drop Window until there are y new flows added to the Drop Window (where y may be a constant or may vary so that the total number of flows in the Drop Window equals, say, 3 percent of the available capacity)

When a packet's ID is removed from the Drop Window, it becomes a guaranteed flow, (except under certain emergency traffic conditions to be discussed below). This means that, normally, there are no packets discarded from such a flow when the buffer starts to experience congestion.

Packet deletion will occur when either the output buffer, or a leaky-bucket representation of the load input and output rates triggers an alarm. Packets are only deleted if their flow identities match one of the identities in the Drop Window. When a packet is deleted for the first time on a flow since the latest onset of congestion, the protocol sends a new control packet forward towards the receiver, namely a Congestion Notification message. This advises the application resident in the customer's receiving equipment that a network congestion condition has occurred. An application may choose to continue receiving such data packets that are not deleted, or inform the source to close down or adjust the sending rate or level of forward error protection, etc. It may also indicate network conditions to the user.

The packet deletion mechanism will also inform a network billing function that flow discarding has commenced on a specific flow, if the charging arrangements require this information.

The probability that this diffserv class experiences congestion leading to packet loss is recommended to be based on the principles of forecasting and capacity planning, together with target probability values for the service. This is applied only to the traffic of this service class, which is assumed to be forecastable and constrained by pricing. This is similar to the way in which the PSTN capacity is planned, using Grade of Service as the target probability that a new call request will be blocked. On that basis, an end-user's frequency of experience of packet loss could be very low, even with the simple fast-response mode as the only mechanism invoked by the application using the QoS toolkit.

For the purposes of policing there is the need to have a second flow identity register, which maintains the identities of all guaranteed flows i.e. flows that are still active, but have exited the Drop Window. Policing ensures that flows cannot bypass the QoS mechanism by not supplying a Start Packet. However an important type of flow that does not deliberately by-pass the QoS mechanism is a mobile flow. After a flow has commenced, mobility can create the situation where data packets are re-routed along new paths that have not previously seen a Start Packet.

We advocate that policers are situated (as a minimum) at user-network interfaces (at both the network-to-user, and user-to-network directions). For mobile users this may be coincident with a base station. If a policer detects a flow which has apparently started without a Start Packet, the network generates and inserts a Start Packet into the flow, with default settings of application-defined fields. It is in the interest of the receiver and source applications to respond to this signal by completing a new 3-handshake signalling sequence as described in [ITU-T 7, Adams et al]. It may not be allowed to exit the Drop Window otherwise (adding another condition to the two bulleted items above).

Some instances of packet re-routing may occur that would not be detected if policers were only located at UNI's. Of course this problem could be solved by having policers at all network nodes. But we believe that network core nodes could support this new QoS service merely by appropriate scheduling of the new diffserv class. Any re-routings within this core would not need to be detected. Furthermore the fast-response mechanism would still apply without needing to implement the policer functionality at all Flow State Aware nodes.

The exit of a flow identity from the second policer flow identity register is through a timeout mechanism which looks for flows that have been inactive for a certain time. Clearly silence-suppressed voice is an example of an application that could trigger such a timeout, even though the call has not ceased. However, the UNI policing mechanism described above will re-trigger the inclusion of a flow identity (inserting it back in the Drop Window) if it had temporarily stopped and then started again after a silence period.

3.1   Detailed Description

The fast-response local QoS mechanism has four functionally separate blocks, and operates in one of three states: Normal, Delete or Emergency Delete. The Normal state indicates that all is well, and the buffer is experiencing no congestion; the Delete State indicates that the buffer is experiencing some congestion; and the Emergency Delete State indicates that the buffer is in a serious state of congestion.

As its name suggests, Emergency Delete mode is primarily aimed at rare events and unusual network conditions including re-routings following a link failure. It is expected that end users will not perceive any noticeable service deterioration due to Emergency discards.

The functionality of the four blocks is described next.

Packet Handler. The packet handler is responsible for either passing packets to the buffer, or for deleting them as necessary. If a Start Packet arrives, its ID is extracted and passed to the register for storage in the Drop Window. Start Packets themselves are always passed to the buffer, and are never the subject of deletion. We can summarise by saying that in:

- the Normal state, all packets are transmitted to the buffer;
- in the Delete state, some packets from flows in the Drop Window are deleted;
- in the Emergency state, packets from all vulnerable flows are deleted, and packets from a minimum number of previously guaranteed flows may also be deleted.

Buffer. The buffer is a finite space with two threshold points (Delete and Emergency) to signal congestion. More generally, a leaky bucket algorithm is performed that adds tokens at the same rate as arriving load and leaks possibly at a slightly slower rate than the buffer output. Different bucket fill-levels are used to indicate Delete and Emergency threshold points. It is assumed that packets are scheduled from the buffer using Expedited Forwarding.

Main Processor. The main processor controls management of the system state. It may also implement other functions, such as special customer policies for certain flows (e.g. flows which are guaranteed from the start and should not enter the vulnerable flows window), whether a customer is barred, or has exceeded their quota etc.

Register. The register is responsible for maintaining the Drop Window. When a new Start Packet has arrived, the flow is entered into the Drop Window. The ethos is that the most recent flow is the most vulnerable.As new flows start up, they move through the Drop Window until eventually they are able to leave (when certain conditions are satisfied), and they become guaranteed flows. In the Emergency state, a guaranteed flow may again be selected at random to return to the Drop Window.

4   Experiments

A simulation model was constructed with a number of CBR and VBR traffic generators attached. The model is able to run with the protocol active and inactive. In the inactive mode packets are discarded indiscriminately in the case of congestion. In the active state, the experiments should show that packet loss is focussed on a particular flow (or flows) which are in the Drop Window. Flows which have exited the Drop Window should show no packet loss.

We wanted to discover whether in fact the protocol would protect certain flows, as we intend it to do. The choice of protected flows is network-specific; in this paper, we describe how we protect older flows from newer flows which start up and cause congestion. The experiment parameters were engineered to allow 2 flows to exit the window, and 2 flows to remain in the window. Congestion is only caused by the start up of the 4th flow. The experiments are designed to discover whether in fact packet loss can then be focussed on only 1 flow (the 4th and last flow to start up), or on mainly this flow, with perhaps a little loss from the other flow still in the Drop Window. We also wanted to examine the effect that changing the buffer threshold points would have.

Traffic Generators. The protocol was set up with 4 traffic generators sending traffic to it, representative of different types of media, (described below). The generators start up at different times, producing clusters of packet arrivals (i.e. where packets from different flows arrive nearly together).

Representation	Type	Pkt Size (bytes)	Bandwidth
Voice	CBR	120	64 kbits
Media	CBR	680	3 Mbits
Media	CBR	680	6 Mbits
Gaming	VBR	680	3 Mbits

Reference Flow. The protocol was set up so that it could accommodate the first three flows (voice (64k), media 1 (3 Mbits), and gaming (3 Mbits)) to start, without any packet loss. These are the older flows which should be protected from the newest flow, which will cause congestion. The newest flow in these experiments is the fourth flow, media 2 (6 Mbits). This is the reference flow. When it arrives, the first 2 flows (voice and media1) leave the drop window, which leaves 2 flows (the reference flow, and gaming) in the drop window. The objective of the experiments was to focus loss, so that the reference flow would experience all or most of the loss as it was the last into the drop window, the gaming flow would experience none or a little loss (because it was still in the drop window and therefore vulnerable, although not so vulnerable as the reference flow), and medial and voice flows (the oldest flows) would experience no loss at all.

Parameters. The parameters which are changed for these experiments are the buffer size, and the threshold points. These parameters are set in packets, where a packet is 680 bytes.

Results. Experiments were run in sets of 5, using 5 different seeds, for a simulation period of 30 minutes each run. The average result from each set was calculated, using a confidence interval of 95 percent. Clearly, when the protocol is active, the setting of the threshold points will influence its performance. We need to perform a number of experiments in order to understand where the optimum or near optimum settings are, and how much the aggressiveness or weakness of the settings makes a difference to performance.

4.1   Protocol Off

Buffer Size 11. The first set of experiments were performed to verify that when there was no protocol in operation, congestion at the buffer would spread loss over the four flows. As expected, this was verified by the experiments. Figure 1(a) shows the absolute packet loss from each flow; clearly, packet loss is indiscriminate but relative to the transmission rate of the generator, and all 4 flows have suffered disruption.

4.2   Protocol On

Experiment 1 Buffer Size 11. The first set of experiments used the same buffer size as the experiments with the protocol turned off. The changeable parameters were the Buffer Threshold Points, which were set at 4 and 8 respectively. The results from this experiment show that the reference flow was the only steam to suffer disruption (Figure 1(b)). This is a promising initial result, as it shows that by using the protocol we can control and minimise the disruption caused by congestion.

Experiment 2 Buffer Size 11. In this experiment, we wanted to examine the difference when there was a gap of 2, and a gap of 3, between the buffer threshold points.

Figure 2(a) shows the results when there is a gap of 3 between the threshold points. The only flow to suffer disruption was the reference flow. The most aggressive setting of 2/5 produced a slightly larger loss than the other settings. From settings 3/6 to 7/10 the loss decreases at a steady pace.

Figure 2(b) shows the results when there is a gap of 2 between the threshold points. The most aggressive setting of 2/4 shows the same slightly larger loss as in the most aggressive setting in Figure 2(b); however, more interestingly is that

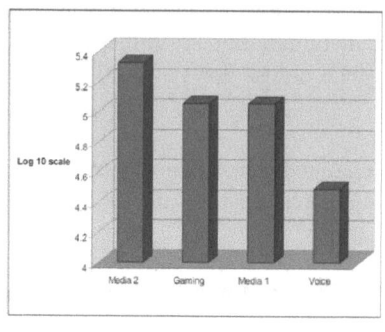
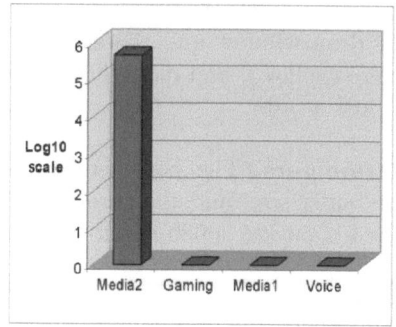

(a) Protocol Inactive   (b) Protocol Active

Fig. 1. A comparison of packet loss with the protocol active and inactive

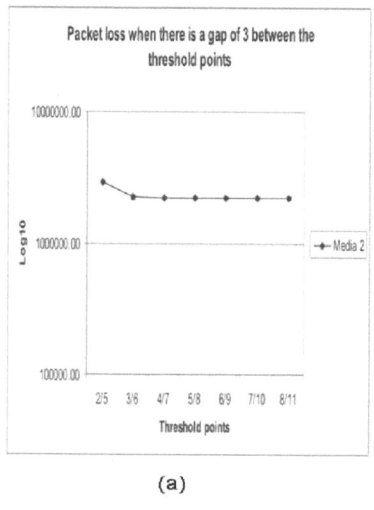
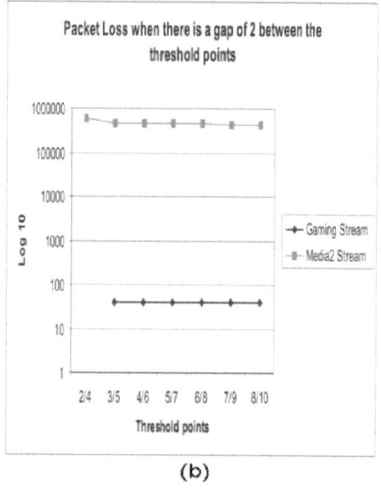

(a)   (b)

Fig. 2. A comparison of loss when there is a gap of 2 and 3 between the threshold points

from 3/5 up to 8/10, packet loss occurs not only from the reference flow, but also from the second most vulnerable flow (gaming).

It is unnecessary to lose packets from the gaming flow, as already shown in Figure 2(a). Here there is only loss from the targeted flow, and no buffer overflow, even when the settings are 8 and 11. We observed that when the settings were 9 and 11 there was buffer overflow (note that at these settings, the emergency delete state would never come into operation, because it is equivalent to the size of the buffer).

Experiment 3 Buffer Size 11. In this experiment, we fixed the second threshold point at 9, and moved the first threshold point, from 2 to 8 (Figure 3). So, for 6 experiments, there was a gap size of 3 or greater between the threshold points, and for 2 experiments there was a gap size of 2 and 1 between the threshold points. Interestingly, the first 6 experiments showed packet loss only from the reference flow; however, as soon as the gap went to 2, and then 1, there was also packet loss from the second most vulnerable flow. From this, and from experiment 2, we conclude that a gap of 3 or more between threshold points is always preferable to a gap of 2.

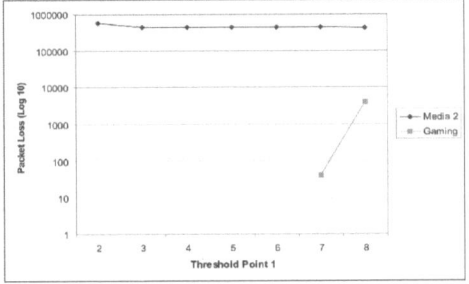

Fig. 3. Packet loss from the reference flow and the next most vulnerable flow, when Threshold point 2 remains fixed at 9, and Threshold point 1 moves from 2 to 8

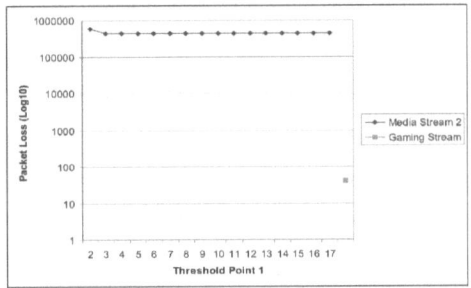

Fig. 4. Packet loss from a larger buffer, with a moving threshold point 1

Experiment 4 Buffer Size 20. In this experiment we wanted to observe the gain made by using a larger buffer, of size 20, and by setting the second threshold point high at 19, and moving the first threshold point. The results are shown in Figure 4. The results are identical to those obtained in Experiment 3. Whether the buffer size is 11 or 20, when the first threshold point is set at 2,3.., the results will be the same. Again, as shown in Experiment 3, when the gap between the threshold points is only 2 (i.e. 17 and 19), there is also loss from the next most vulnerable flow.

5   Conclusions

In this paper we presented a new QoS protocol for the Internet, which effectively enables certain flows to be guaranteed, and protected even during periods of congestion. The protocol was described, and results from the first experiments were presented, showing that it is able to be effective in focussing packet discard. Clearly, the settings of the buffer parameters, Threshold Points 1 and 2, are critical to obtaining the maximum efficiency – if the parameters are too aggressive, then flows will be unnecessarily disrupted; if the parameters are too relaxed, then buffer overflow will occur and discard will no longer be focussed and under the control of the protocol.

The results presented in this paper tested the Delete state of the protocol, under very controlled circumstances. A new version of the model with a larger number of generators was created, which loads the model so that the protocol was tested under conditions where Emergency state will be entered. These results, which were also very positive, may be seen in [Adams et al].

References

[ITU-T 1]   British Telecom contribution Service aspects on standards to support real-time content delivery over the Internet COM12 - D21 - E, International Telecommunications Union, Telecommunication Standardization Sector, Study Group 12, Geneva, 18-27 January, 2005

[ITU-T 2]   British Telecom contribution Commercial aspects on standards to support real-time content delivery over the Internet. COM12 - D19 - E, International Telecommunications Union, Telecommunication Standardization Sector, Study Group 12, Geneva, 18-27 January, 2005

[ITU-T 3]   British Telecom contribution: Functional aspects on standards to support real-time content delivery over the Internet COM12 - D20 - E, International Telecommunications Union, Telecommunication Standardization Sector, Study Group 12, Geneva, 18-27 January, 2005

[ITU-T 4]   British Telecom contribution: Proposal for a new IP transfer capability and future QoS studies. International Telecommunications Union, Telecommunication Standardization Sector, D-, Q4, 6,10,11,16, SG13, Geneva, Feb. 2004

[ITU-T 5]   British Telecom contribution: Delivery of assured QoS content in NGNs. International Telecommunications Union, Telecommunication Standardization Sector, D-, Q4, 6,10,11,16, SG13, Geneva, Feb. 2004

[ETSI]   British Telecom contribution: Delivering QoS from remote content providers. ETSI contribution TISPAN#01(03) TD132, Sophia Antipolis, Sept. 2004

[ITU-T 6]   ITU-T standard Y.1221: Traffic Control and Congestion Control in IP-based networks

[ITU-T 7]   British Telecom contribution: IP QoS Signalling. COM12-D22-
                     E, International Telecommunications Union, Telecommunication
                     Standardization Sector, Study Group 12, Geneva, 18-27 January,
                     2005
[Roberts]   Lawrence G. Roberts: IETF Draft of IPv6 QoS Signalling
                     http://www.packet.cc/IPv6Q-IETF-2A.htm. (Similar to TIA
                     1039)
[Braden et al]   R. Braden and D. Clark and S. Shenker: Integrated Services
                     in the Internet Architecture: An Overview. RFC 1633, Internet
                     Engineering Task Force, June 1994.
[Carlson et al]   M. Carlson and W. Weiss and S. Blake and Z. Wang and D. Black
                     and E. Davies: An Architecture for Differentiated Services. RFC
                     2475, December 1998.
[Adams and Smith]   J.L. Adams and A.J. Smith: Packet discard for broadband ser-
                     vices. European Patent Application No. EP 01 30 5209 Issue
                     June 2001.
[Wright et al]   S. Wright, T. Anschutz: QoS requirements in DSL networks.
                     GLOBECOM 2003 - IEEE Global Telecommunications Confer-
                     ence, no. 1, Dec 2003 pp. 4049-4053
[Smith et al]   A.J.Smith and C.J.Adams and A.G.Tagg and J.L. Adams: Use
                     of the Cell Loss Priority Tagging Mechanism in ATM Switches.
                     Proc ICIE '91, Singapore, December 1991.
[Floyd et al]   S. Floyd and V. Jacobsen: Random early detection gateways for
                     congestion avoidance. IEEE/ACM Transactions on Networking,
                     no. 4, August 1993, pp. 397-413.
[Romanow et al]   A. Romanow and S. Floyd: Dynamics of TCP Traffic over ATM
                     Networks. IEEE JSAC, V.13, N.4, May 1995, pp. 633–641.
[Kawahara et al]   K. Kawahara, K. Kitajima, T.Takine and Y. Oie: Performance
                     evaluation of selective cell discarding schemes in ATM networks.
                     Infocom '96, pp. 1054–1061, 1996.
[Adams et al]   J. Adams, L. Roberts and A. IJsselmuiden.: Changing the inter-
                     net to support real-time content supply from a large fraction of
                     broadband residential users. British Telecom Technology Jour-
                     nal, Special Issue on QoS, April 2005

Designing a Predictable Internet Backbone with Valiant Load-Balancing

Rui Zhang-Shen and Nick McKeown

Computer Systems Laboratory,
Stanford University,
Stanford, CA 94305-9030, USA
{rzhang, nickm}@stanford.edu

Abstract. Network operators would like their network to support current and future traffic matrices, even when links and routers fail. Not surprisingly, no backbone network can do this today: It is hard to accurately measure the current matrix, and harder still to predict future ones. Even if the matrices are known, how do we know a network will support them, particularly under failures? As a result, today's networks are designed in a somewhat ad-hoc fashion, using rules-of-thumb and crude estimates of current and future traffic.

Previously we proposed the use of Valiant Load-balancing (VLB) for backbone design. It can guarantee 100% throughput to *any* traffic matrix, even under link and router failures. Our initial work was limited to homogeneous backbones in which routers had the same capacity. In this paper we extend our results in two ways: First, we show that the same qualities of service (guaranteed support of any traffic matrix with or without failure) can be achieved in a realistic heterogeneous backbone network; and second, we show that VLB is optimal, in the sense that the capacity required by VLB is very close to the lower bound of total capacity needed by any architecture in order to support all traffic matrices.

1   Introduction

A network operator would like their backbone network to serve customers' demands at all times. But most networks have grown in an ad-hoc fashion, which – when considering failures and maintenance that frequently change the network – makes it impractical to systematically provision links so they have the capacity to carry traffic both during normal operation and under failures. To compensate, network operators tend to grossly over-provision their networks (typically below 20% utilization), because it is hard to know where new customers will join, what new applications will become popular, and when links and routers will fail.

It would help if we knew the traffic matrices the network will have to carry throughout its lifetime. Though the usual practice is to measure the current demand, and then extrapolate it to the future, the approach does not work for many reasons.

H. de Meer and N. Bhatti (Eds.): IWQoS 2005, LNCS 3552, pp. 178–192, 2005.

First, Internet traffic is hard to measure. The number of entries in a traffic matrix is roughly quadratic in the number of nodes, so it is usually impractical to obtain all the measurements directly. To estimate the traffic matrix from incomplete measurements, the best techniques today give errors of 20% or more [6] [9]. More importantly, the traffic demand fluctuates over time, and it is hard to determine when the *peak* usage of the network is. In practice, the "peak" is determined in an ad-hoc manner – by inspection, or some rules-of-thumb.

Second, even if we could accurately measure the current traffic matrix, it is hard to extrapolate to the future. Typically, estimates are based on historic growth rates, and adjusted according to marketing forecasts. But it's hard to predict future growth rates and what new applications will become popular. Even if the *total* growth rate is estimated correctly, the growth may not be uniform across the whole network, and the introduction of new applications may change traffic patterns. For example, peer-to-peer traffic has demonstrated how quickly usage patterns can change in the Internet. The widespread use of voice-over-IP and video-on-demand may change usage patterns again over the next few years. What's more, the growth rate does not take into account large new customers which may bring new demands. So network design has always used a wrong estimate of the future traffic matrix, and the designed network cannot guarantee to support the actual demand. It's therefore not surprising that operators so heavily over-provision their networks.

In summary, existing networks, which have evolved in an ad-hoc fashion, have unpredictable performance. With current design techniques, it is hard to design a network with throughput guarantees because it is impossible to obtain a good estimate of the future traffic matrix. Once built, a network may have to work with a range of traffic conditions, but it is unknown to network operators as to how to design a network for a wide range of traffic matrices.

We recently proposed Valiant Load Balancing (VLB) [10], so that backbone networks can be designed to give strong guarantees on the support for an arbitrary set of traffic matrices, even under failure, *and* operate at much higher utilization (and hence higher efficiency and lower cost) than today. We assume that each backbone node in the network, or Point-of-Presence (PoP), has constrained capacity, such as the aggregate capacity of the access network it serves, and design a backbone network to guarantee 100% throughput for *any* traffic matrix.

The limitations of designing a network for a specific traffic matrix, and the necessity to design for a wide range of traffic matrices, have been realized by some researchers recently, and a few schemes have been proposed [1] [5] [10] [7]. Most of these schemes use some type of load-balancing.

The VLB architecture makes the job of estimating the future traffic much simpler. While obtaining a traffic matrix estimation is hard, it is easier to measure, or estimate, the total amount of traffic entering (leaving) a backbone node from (to) its access network. When a new customer joins the network, we add their aggregate traffic rate to the node. When new locations are planned, the aggregate traffic demand for a new node can be estimated from the population that the node serves. While still not trivial, it is a lot easier than estimating the traffic from every node to every other node.

The Valiant load-balancing architecture has simple and efficient fault tolerance so that only a small fraction of extra capacity is required to guarantee service under a number of failures in the network. The failure recovery can be quick because no new paths need to be established on the fly.

In this paper, we extend the result of [10] to networks with arbitrary node capacities. We will focus on deriving the optimal capacity allocation in this network and leave fault tolerance for future work. The rest of the paper is organized as follows: Section 2 introduces the VLB architecture and the notation used in this paper; Section 3 derives the lower bound on the required capacity to support all traffic matrices and two load-balancing schemes which achieve capacity requirements close to the lower bound; We then relate our work to others' and conclude the paper.

2   Valiant Load-Balancing

The Valiant load-balancing architecture was first proposed by L. G. Valiant for processor interconnection networks [8], and has received recent interest for scalable routers with performance guarantees [2] [4]. Keslassy et al. proved that uniform Valiant load-balancing is the unique architecture which requires the minimum node capacity in interconnecting a set of identical nodes [3]. We applied the VLB architecture to designing a predictable Internet backbone which can guarantee throughput to all traffic matrices, and can tolerate a number of link and router failures with only a small amount of excess capacity [10]. We will re-introduce the architecture and re-state the relevant results here before extending it to the more general scenario in backbone network design.

2.1   Previous Results

Consider a network consisting of multiple backbone nodes, or PoPs, interconnected by long-haul links. The network is arranged as a hierarchy, and each PoP

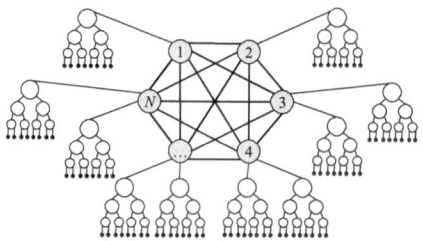

Fig. 1. A hierarchical network with N backbone nodes. The backbone nodes are connected by a (logical) full mesh, and each node serves an access network

connects an access network to the backbone (see Figure 1). For now, assume that there are N backbone nodes, and all of them are connected to access networks of the same aggregate capacity, r.

A full mesh of logical links of capacity $\frac{2r}{N}$ are established among the N backbone nodes. Traffic entering the backbone is load-balanced equally across all N two-hop paths between ingress and egress. A packet is forwarded twice in the network: In the first stage, a node uniformly load-balances each of its incoming flows to all the N nodes, regardless of the packet destination. Load-balancing can be done packet-by-packet, or flow-by-flow at the application flow level. Assume we can achieve perfect load-balancing, i.e., we can split traffic at the exact ratio we desire, then each node receives $1/N$-th of every node's traffic in the first stage. In the second stage, all packets are delivered to the final destination.

Uniform load-balancing leads to a guaranteed 100% throughput in this network. We consider the two packet forwarding stages. Since the incoming traffic rate to each node is at most r, and the traffic is evenly load-balanced to N nodes, the actual traffic on each link due to the first stage routing is at most $\frac{r}{N}$. The second stage is the dual of the first stage. Since each node can receive traffic at a maximum rate of r, and it receives $1/N$-th of the traffic from every node, the actual traffic on each link due to the second stage routing is also at most $\frac{r}{N}$. Therefore, a full-mesh network where each link has capacity $\frac{2r}{N}$ is sufficient to guarantee 100% throughput for any valid traffic matrix among N nodes of access capacity r.

This is perhaps a surprising result – a network where each pair of nodes are connected with a link of capacity $\frac{2r}{N}$ can serve traffic matrices where a node can send traffic to another node at rate r. This shows the power of load-balancing. Valiant load-balancing makes sure that each flow is carried by N paths, and each link carries a fraction of many flows, therefore a large flow is evened out by other small flows. If all the traffic were to be sent through direct paths, we would need a full-mesh network of link capacity r. Therefore load-balancing is $\frac{N}{2}$ times more efficient than direct routing. Although it may seem inefficient that every packet should traverse the network twice, it has been proved that in order to serve all traffic matrices in a network of identical nodes, the uniform Valiant load-balancing architecture provides the unique optimal interconnection pattern which requires the lowest capacity at each node [3]. An even more surprising result is that the VLB network only requires a small fraction of extra capacity in order to tolerate failures in the network [10].

A common concern with load-balancing is that packets may incur a longer delay. In a Valiant load-balanced network, propagation delay is bounded by traversing twice the network diameter. Within the continental US, it's been measured that this delay is well below 100ms, which is acceptable for all applications we know of. We believe that VLB gives a reasonable tradeoff of increased fixed propagation delay for improved predictability, and lower delay variance.

In this paper, we consider Valiant load-balancing in a more general and more realistic case – we remove the assumption that all access networks have the same capacity. Once the backbone network is no longer symmetric, the first stage load-balancing should no longer be uniform, and it is not clear what the optimal load-balancing scheme should be. In the rest of the paper, we will search for a scheme that is optimal in a similar sense as the uniform network case, i.e., a scheme which minimizes the interconnection capacity at each node.

2.2   Notations

We consider a backbone network consisting of $N \geq 3$ nodes of access capacities $r_1, r_2, \ldots, r_N$, where *access capacity* is the aggregate capacity of the access network a backbone node serves. This means, node i can initiate traffic to the other backbone nodes at a rate up to r_i, and can receive traffic from the other backbone nodes at a rate up to r_i. Without loss of generality, we assume that the nodes have been sorted according to decreasing access capacities, i.e., $r_1 \geq r_2 \geq \ldots \geq r_N$.

A traffic demand matrix Λ is an $N \times N$ matrix where the entry λ_{ij} represents the traffic rate from node i to node j. A *valid* traffic matrix is one such that no node is over-subscribed, i.e., $\sum_j \lambda_{ij} \leq r_i$, and $\sum_j \lambda_{ji} \leq r_i$, $\forall i$. We will only consider valid traffic matrices in this paper and our goal is to guarantee 100% throughput to *all* valid traffic matrices.

We start with a full-mesh interconnecting the N nodes, where the link capacity between node i and node j is represented by c_{ij}. Let C be the link capacity matrix $\{c_{ij}\}$. We are interested in finding the minimum values of c_{ij} that are required to serve all traffic matrices. If link$_{ij}$ is not needed, then we simply set c_{ij} to zero. We assume that a node can freely send traffic to itself without requiring any network resource, so we set $c_{ii} = \infty, \forall i$, and will not try to optimize them. Given any traffic matrix Λ, we can also set all its diagonal entries to zero.

The *interconnection capacity* of node i is the sum of the link capacities through which it connects to the other nodes, and is represented by $l_i = \sum_{j:j \neq i} c_{ij}$. The sum of all nodes' interconnection capacities is the *total interconnection capacity* of the network, and is represented by $L = \sum_{i=1}^{N} l_i = \sum_{(i,j):i \neq j} c_{ij}$. For convenience, let $R = \sum_{i=1}^{N} r_i$ be the *total access capacity* of all the nodes. We further define the *fanout* of node i to be $f_i = l_i/r_i$, the ratio of a node's interconnection capacity to its access capacity. Define the *network fanout* f to be the maximum fanout among all nodes, $f = \max_i f_i$.

Under these definitions, in the uniform network where every node has access capacity r, the optimal link capacities are $c_{ij} = \frac{2r}{N}$, for $i \neq j$. The interconnection capacity of a node is $l_i = \frac{2r}{N}(N-1), \forall i$, so the fanout of a node is $f_i = \frac{l_i}{r} = \frac{2(N-1)}{N}, \forall i$. Thus the network fanout is $f^u = \frac{2(N-1)}{N}$. The total interconnection capacity is $L = 2(N-1)r$ and the total access capacity is $R = Nr$.

3   Optimal Interconnect for a Heterogeneous Network

In this section we investigate the interconnection capacities required to serve any traffic matrix among N backbone nodes. To find the optimal interconnect, we can use the total capacity as the criteria and minimize L, or we can use the network fanout as the criteria and minimize f. Both may be of importance in network design. Minimizing the total capacity is more reasonable if the same amount of capacity costs the same in different places of the network. But by minimizing the network fanout, or the maximum fanout of all nodes, we try to make the fanouts of the nodes close to each other. This way, the interconnection capacity of a node is roughly proportional to its access capacity. This criteria is more sensible if the nodes in the network differ widely. The following lemma ties the two criteria together, and the minimum total capacity L gives a lower bound on the network fanout.

Lemma 1.

$$f = \max_i f_i = \max_i \frac{l_i}{r_i} \geq \frac{\sum_i l_i}{\sum_i r_i} = \frac{L}{R}$$

The inequality can be proved by induction and [11] has the details.

In the rest of this section, we will first derive the minimum total capacity required to serve all traffic matrices in any architecture, to give a lower bound on the network fanout. Then we propose a simple "gravity" load-balancing scheme which achieves a network fanout within a factor 2 of the lower bound. Finally we derive the minimum network fanout under oblivious load-balancing in the network, and show that it's within a constant factor 1.2 from the lower bound.

3.1   Minimum Total Capacity: Lower Bound on Network Fanout

Given a demand matrix Λ and we want to know whether an interconnection capacity matrix C can serve the demand. Load-balancing is allowed, so we do not require that $c_{ij} \geq \lambda_{ij}$ for all (i, j) pairs. For example, if there is not enough capacity from node s to node t to serve the demand, i.e., $c_{st} < \lambda_{st}$, we can send part of the flow through an alternative route, say, route s-k-t. Suppose we send amount x of flow$_{st}$ through route s-k-t, then the actual load carried on the network is Λ' which is obtained from Λ by subtracting x from λ_{st} and adding x to both λ_{sk} and λ_{kt}. We call this the *load-balancing transformation* of traffic matrix Λ, and the resulting matrix Λ' the *load matrix*. The traffic matrix Λ can be *served* by the capacity matrix C, if we can load-balance flows in Λ and obtain a load matrix Λ' such that $\lambda'_{ij} \leq c_{ij}, \forall i, j$.

Before we state the theorem of minimum total capacity, we prove the following lemma.

Lemma 2. *Load balancing cannot reduce the sum of the entries in the upper triangle of Λ, i.e., $\sum_{i<j} \lambda'_{ij} \geq \sum_{i<j} \lambda_{ij}$ for any load matrix Λ' obtained by load-balancing transformation of Λ. Same is true for the lower triangle.*

Proof. Suppose we route the amount x of flow$_{i_1 i_k}$, $i_1 < i_k$, through the route i_1-i_2-...-i_k. Then we subtract x from $\lambda_{i_1 i_k}$ and add x to each one of $\lambda_{i_1 i_2}, \lambda_{i_2 i_3}$, ..., $\lambda_{i_{k-1} i_k}$ to obtain the load matrix Λ'. Since $i_1 < i_k$, and $i_1, i_2, \ldots, i_k \in$

$\{1, 2, \ldots, N\}$, there must exist some $j : 1 \leq j \leq k - 1$ such that $i_j < i_{j+1}$. Thus the sum of the upper triangle of Λ does not decrease after the transformation, and we have $\sum_{i<j} \lambda'_{ij} \geq \sum_{i<j} \lambda_{ij}$. By induction, further load-balancing transformation will keep this inequality.

The proof for the lower triangle is similar.   □

Corollary 1. *A necessary condition for capacity matrix C to be able to serve traffic matrix Λ is*

$$\sum_{i<j} c_{ij} \geq \sum_{i<j} \lambda_{ij} \text{ and } \sum_{i>j} c_{ij} \geq \sum_{i>j} \lambda_{ij}. \tag{1}$$

The proof follows from Lemma 2 and the details are in [11].

Remark: The intuition of the above lemma is, if we line up the nodes from left to right according to their node numbers, then the upper triangle of the traffic matrix Λ represents the traffic that needs to go from left to right. No matter how we load-balance the demand, the amount of traffic that needs to be sent from left to right does not decrease. The upper triangle of the capacity matrix C represents the capacity that can carry traffic from left to right, and this has to be at least the amount of traffic that needs to be sent from left to right. Same is true for the traffic that needs to go the other direction.

Theorem 1. (minimum capacity) *In order to serve any valid traffic matrix among N nodes of capacities $r_1 \geq r_2 \geq \ldots \geq r_N$, the minimum total interconnection capacity required is $2(\sum_i r_i - \max_i r_i) = 2 \sum_{i=2}^{N} r_i$.*

Outline of proof. Necessity is shown by applying Corollary 1 to the following traffic matrix and its transpose:

$$\Lambda^{(1)} = \begin{pmatrix} 0 & r_2 & 0 & \ldots & 0 \\ 0 & 0 & r_3 & \ldots & 0 \\ \vdots & \vdots & & \ddots & \vdots \\ 0 & 0 & 0 & \ldots & r_N \\ 0 & 0 & 0 & \ldots & 0 \end{pmatrix}.$$

Sufficiency is shown by arranging the nodes in a "star" topology as in Figure 2. For details, please see [11].   □

Theorem 1 together with Lemma 1 gives a lower bound on the network fanout:

$$f \geq \frac{L}{R} \geq \frac{2(\sum_i r_i - \max_i r_i)}{R} = 2 \left(1 - \frac{r_1}{R} \right). \tag{2}$$

This lower bound can be less than 1 if $r_1 > \frac{R}{2}$, or equivalently, if $r_1 > \sum_{i=2}^{N} r_i$. This is the case when the largest node can initiate more traffic than all the other nodes combined can receive. But if we only allow valid traffic matrices, the largest node cannot initiate traffic at its maximum rate because that would overload some of the other nodes. So we can replace the capacity of node 1 with $\min(r_1, \sum_{i=2}^N r_i)$ and will not change any property of the network. This is equivalent to introducing 1 as another lower bound for f. Since the network fanout f is the maximum of all the nodes' fanouts, this lower bound of 1 can also be obtained by considering the smallest node, whose fanout has to be at least 1. So we now have the following:

Corollary 2. *In order to serve all valid traffic matrices, the network fanout of an interconnection network is lowered bounded by* $2\left(1 - \frac{\max_i r_i}{R}\right)$ *and 1, i.e.,*

$$f \geq \max\left(1, 2\left(1 - \frac{\max_i r_i}{R}\right)\right). \tag{3}$$

The lower bound on network fanout can be achieved in some cases. When $r_1 \geq \sum_{i=2}^N r_i$, a network fanout of 1 can be achievable by the star topology in Figure 2, where Node 1 has a fanout of at most 1 and the other nodes have a fanout of 1. But when $r_1 < \sum_{i=2}^N r_i$, the star topology does not minimize the network fanout. (The schemes presented in Sections 3.2 and 3.3 achieve better network fanouts.)

In the uniform case where all the nodes have the same capacity r, the lower bound in Equation (2) can also be achieved: $f^u = 2(1 - \frac{1}{N})$. So the uniform full mesh architecture minimizes the network fanout.

Both the uniform full mesh and the star topologies have a total interconnection capacity of $2r(N-1)$. So in order to minimize the total interconnection capacity of the network, both uniform full mesh and star topologies are optimal. But if the goal is to minimize the network fanout, the full mesh is the only topology that is optimal, as proved in [3]. From the network design point of view, the full mesh topology is better, because the star topology has many single points of failure, and it requires a lot of processing power from the center node. Therefore, we will use network fanout as the optimization criteria in designing the backbone network.

3.2   Gravity Full Mesh: 2-Approximation of Optimal Fanout

The star topology in Figure 2 does not give a good network fanout, because the node fanouts are $f_1 = \sum_{i=2}^N r_i/r_1$ and $f_i = 1$ for $i > 1$, and the fanout of

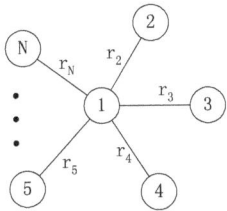

Fig. 2. The star topology which achieves the minimum total interconnection capacity. Node 1 has the highest access capacity

the center node can be large. For example, when all the nodes have the same capacity, we have $f_1 = N - 1$, which is much larger than the optimal network fanout $2(1 - \frac{1}{N})$.

We can easily obtain a much better network fanout by extending the load-balancing scheme of the uniform case. Suppose all the nodes' access capacities are integer multiples of some capacity "granularity" r, i.e., $r_i = k_i r$ for some integer $k_i, \forall i$. Then node i can be treated as k_i nodes of capacity r located together. Now if we count all the imaginary "nodes" of capacity r, there are $M = \sum_i k_i = \frac{R}{r}$ of them. Between each pair of such "nodes" should be a link of capacity $\frac{2r}{M}$. Now between the real nodes i and j, which are clusters of k_i and k_j imaginary "nodes", there should be $k_i \times k_j$ links of capacity $\frac{2r}{M}$, i.e.,

$$c_{ij} = \frac{2r}{M} k_i k_j = \frac{2r^2}{R} k_i k_j = \frac{2r_i r_j}{R}. \tag{4}$$

The link capacity between node i and node j is proportional to the product of capacities of the two nodes, therefore we call this the "gravity full mesh". Note that the capacity granularity r, which has dropped out of the expression in Equation (4), can be arbitrarily small, so we actually do not require any relationship among the nodes' capacities.

The load-balancing scheme in the gravity full mesh is: in the first stage traffic is spread proportionally to the capacity of the intermediate nodes, i.e., a proportion r_i/R of traffic is load-balanced to node i; in the second stage, traffic is delivered to the final destination. This network can be viewed as a uniform network of M nodes of capacity r, some of which have been clustered together, so the link capacities given in Equation (4) are sufficient to guarantee 100% throughput for any traffic matrix.

In the gravity full mesh, the fanout of node i is

$$f_i = \frac{l_i}{r_i} = \frac{\sum_{j \neq i} 2r_i r_j / R}{r_i} = 2\frac{\sum_{j \neq i} r_j}{R} = 2(1 - \frac{r_i}{R}).$$

So

$$f = \max_i f_i = 2(1 - \frac{\min_i r_i}{R}) = 2(1 - \frac{r_N}{R}) < 2. \tag{5}$$

The optimal network fanout f is at least 1 (Corollary 2), so we have obtained a 2-approximation to the optimal network fanout. In most cases, the approximation is much better than 2.

3.3   Minimum Network Fanout Under Oblivious Load-Balancing

We will now directly minimize the network fanout f, in the cases when the optimal network fanout is not easily known. In Section 3.1 we have shown that the minimum fanout $\min f = 1$ when $r_1 \geq \sum_{i=2}^{N} r_i$, so we will only consider the case when $r_1 < \sum_{i=2}^{N} r_i$ in this subsection.

If we want to find the optimal interconnection to minimize f, the load-balancing scheme should take into account all system information, such as traffic matrix and node capacities. Let $p_i^{st}(\Lambda)$ be the portion of the flow from node s to node t that is load-balanced to node i when the traffic matrix is Λ. By definition, $p_i^{st}(\Lambda) \geq 0$ and $\sum_i p_i^{st}(\Lambda) = 1$. In general, the traffic matrix may not be easily available to the nodes, and even if it is available, it can change with time. So we are only interested in the load-balancing schemes that are independent of the traffic pattern, i.e., we let $p_i^{st}(\Lambda) = p_i^{st}$.

Given the load-balancing ratios p_i^{st} and the traffic matrix Λ, we can calculate the amount of outbound traffic from node n:

$$T_n(\Lambda) = \sum_{i \neq n} \lambda_{ni} + \sum_{i,j \neq n} p_n^{ij} \lambda_{ij}. \tag{6}$$

The first sum is due to the traffic that originates from node n destined for the other nodes. The second sum is the amount of traffic that "passes by" node n, i.e., the traffic that is load-balanced to node n from the other nodes which node n needs to forward to the destination. The inbound traffic to node n has similar properties as the outbound traffic so we only need to consider one of them.

The network should support any valid traffic matrix, so the outbound link capacity of node n needs to be at least $\max_\Lambda T_n(\Lambda)$. Thus $\max_\Lambda T_n(\Lambda)/r_n$ gives a lower bound on the fanout of node n, and the lower bound is in terms of p_i^{st}. Since $f = \max_i f_i$, the maximum of these lower bounds gives a lower bound on the network fanout f. So we can formulate an optimization problem to find the values of p_n^{ij} which give the best lower bound on f, and if the lower bound is also achievable, we have found the optimal network fanout:

$$\text{minimize} \quad f = \max_n \{\max_\Lambda T_n(\Lambda)/r_n\}$$
$$\text{subject to} \quad p_i^{st} \geq 0, \sum_i p_i^{st} = 1, \forall s \neq t$$

where $T_n(\Lambda)$ is given by Equation (6). But the number of variables here is on the order of N^3, and the optimization problem is not easy to solve.

So we further simplify the load-balancing scheme and only consider *oblivious load-balancing*, where the load-balancing ratio is independent of the flow source and destination. That is, we set $p_n^{ij} = p_n$, and a proportion p_n of *every* flow is load-balanced to node n. We can find a closed form expression for $\min f$ under oblivious load-balancing schemes.

Theorem 2. *Under oblivious load-balancing schemes, the minimum network fanout f_o is*

$$f_o = \min f = 1 + \frac{1}{\sum_{j=1}^N \frac{r_j}{R - 2r_j}}, \tag{7}$$

if $\max_{i=1}^N r_i < \frac{R}{2}$; *and* $f_o = \min f = 1$ *if* $\max_{i=1}^N r_i \geq \frac{R}{2}$, *where* $R = \sum_{i=1}^N r_i$.

Proof. We will first show that the expression in Equation (7) is a lower bound, and then show that it is achievable. Some details are omitted here and can be found in [11].

Replacing p_i^{st} with p_i, we can rewrite Equation (6) as

$$T_n(\Lambda) = \sum_{i \neq n} \lambda_{ni} + \sum_{i,j \neq n} p_n \lambda_{ij} = (1 - p_n) \sum_{i \neq n} \lambda_{ni} + p_n \sum_{j \neq n} \sum_i \lambda_{ij}.$$

We maximize $T_n(\Lambda)$ over all valid traffic matrices:

$$\max_\Lambda T_n(\Lambda) = \max_\Lambda \left((1 - p_n) \sum_{i \neq n} \lambda_{ni} + p_n \sum_{j \neq n} \sum_i \lambda_{ij} \right) = r_n + p_n(R - 2r_n).$$

From $\max_\Lambda T_n(\Lambda)$ we can obtain a lower bound on f_n, which we denote by g_n:

$$g_n = \frac{r_n + p_n(R - 2r_n)}{r_n} = 1 + p_n \frac{R - 2r_n}{r_n}. \tag{8}$$

The maximum of these lower bounds is a lower bound of the network fanout: $f = \max_n f_n \geq \max_n g_n$.

The load-balancing ratios p_n satisfy $\sum_n p_n = 1$, so combining with Equation (8), we have the following equation for the lower bounds g_n:

$$1 = \sum_n p_n = \sum_n (g_n - 1) \frac{r_n}{R - 2r_n}. \tag{9}$$

This means that the positive linear combination of g_n is a constant (note that we only consider the case when $R > 2r_1$), so to minimize $\max_n g_n$, we must have $g_1 = g_2 = \ldots = g_n = g$, and Equation (9) gives

$$g = 1 + \frac{1}{\sum_n \frac{r_n}{R - 2r_n}}. \tag{10}$$

Equation (10) is a lower bound on f. We now show that this lower bound is achievable. Equation (8) gives the load-balancing probabilities: $p_n = (g - 1)\frac{r_n}{R - 2r_n}$. Consider the link from node i to node j. The traffic that traverses the link consists of two parts: the traffic that originates from node i and is load-balanced to node j of at most $r_i p_j$; and the traffic that is destined to node j and is load-balanced to node i of at most $r_j p_i$. So the link capacity required from node i to node j is $c_{ij} = r_i p_j + r_j p_i = (g - 1) \left(\frac{r_i r_j}{R - 2r_j} + \frac{r_i r_j}{R - 2r_i} \right)$.

With the link capacities given above, we can show $f_i = \frac{\sum_{j \neq i} c_{ij}}{r_i} = g$, which means $f = g$. This means that there exists a bandwidth allocation c_{ij} and oblivious load-balancing ratio p_n such that the lower bound g of the network fanout f is achieved. Therefore, under oblivious load-balancing schemes, $f_o = g = 1 + 1/\sum_j \frac{r_j}{R - 2r_j}$.

Although we have assumed that $r_1 < \sum_{i=2}^N r_i$ in the above derivation, the case $r_1 \geq \sum_{i=2}^N r_i$ can be analyzed by the same method. We first set $r_1 = \sum_{i=2}^N r_i$ because we only consider valid traffic matrices. Then from Equation (8), we obtain $g_1 = 1$ and $g_n \geq 1$ for $n \geq 2$. To minimize $\max_n g_n$, the optimal solution is $p_1 = 1$ and $p_n = 0$ for $n \geq 2$, in which case we obtain $g_n = 1, \forall n$, and $g = \max_n g_n = 1$. This gives the star topology and $f_o = 1$. $\square$

The network fanout given in Theorem 2 is always greater than one when $r_1 < \sum_{i=2}^N r_i$. This is because we want the network to support all traffic matrices. A

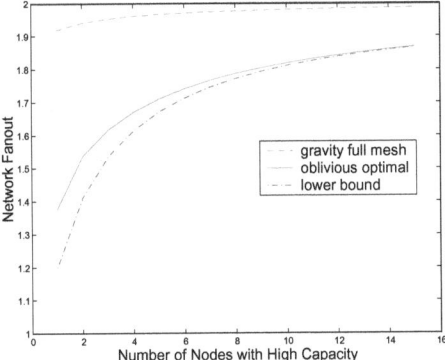

Fig. 3. A comparison of the optimal oblivious network fanout and the upper and lower bounds. The network has 16 nodes, and all nodes take either one of two capacities of ratio 10:1. The x-axis shows the number of nodes taking the higher capacity

network fanout of 1 can be achieved if the exact traffic matrix is known and we provision just enough capacity on each link to directly route the traffic. But if the traffic matrix changes, such a network may not provide throughput guarantees. In order to serve *all* valid traffic matrices, we need a minimum network fanout of more than 1, as proved in Theorem 1. In fact, it is a nice surprise that the capacity required to carry all traffic matrices is only less than twice the absolute minimum capacity required in a network, given the traffic matrix.

Note that the gravity full mesh presented in the last subsection is also an oblivious load-balancing scheme, so we expect that the optimal network fanout under oblivious load-balancing given by Theorem 2, is between the network fanout obtained by the "gravity full mesh" given in Equation (5), which we treat as an upper bound, and the lower bound for any architecture given in Corollary 2. We can verify this. Since all the nodes are sorted according to their access capacity, we have $\sum_j \frac{r_j}{R-2r_j} \leq \frac{\sum_j r_j}{R-2r_1} = \frac{R}{R-2r_1}$. So

$$f_o = 1 + \frac{1}{\sum_j \frac{r_j}{R-2r_j}} \geq 1 + \frac{R-2r_1}{R} = 2(1 - \frac{r_1}{R}).$$

That is, the optimal network fanout under oblivious load-balancing is greater than the lower bound. We can similarly show that

$$f_o = 1 + \frac{1}{\sum_j \frac{r_j}{R-2r_j}} \leq 2(1 - \frac{r_N}{R}).$$

In the uniform network case where all nodes have the same access capacity r, the lower and the upper bounds of the optimal network fanout become the same, thus we have $f^u = 2(1 - \frac{1}{N})$.

Now let's consider another example, a network of 16 nodes. The nodes take either one of two access capacities of ratio 10:1. We change the number of nodes with high or low capacities and plot the network fanout in Figure 3. We can see that the oblivious optimal fanout is very close to the lower bound. In fact, as will be shown next, the ratio is bounded by 1.2. So restricting ourselves to oblivious load-balancing does not cause a big loss in capacity efficiency, and we can simplify the load-balancing scheme greatly.

3.4   Oblivious Optimal Network Capacity and the Lower Bound

In the optimal oblivious load-balancing scheme, all the nodes have the same fanout, which is equal to the network fanout, so the total interconnection capacity in the network is $L_o = Rf_o$, where f_o is given by Theorem 2. The lower bound on the total capacity required by any network in order to serve all traffic matrices is given by Theorem 1: $L_l = 2(R - r_1)$, where node 1 has the highest access capacity amongst all N nodes. When $r_1 \geq \sum_{i=2}^{N}$, we have $L_o = L_l$, so we will only consider the case $r_1 < \sum_{i=2}^{N}$. Let α be the ratio of the minimum capacity in oblivious load-balancing and the lower bound for any network:

$$\alpha = \frac{L_o}{L_l} = \frac{R(1 + \sum_i \frac{1}{\frac{r_i}{R - 2r_i}})}{2(R - r_1)} = \frac{1 + \sum_i \frac{1}{\frac{r_i}{R - 2r_i}}}{2(1 - \frac{r_1}{R})}. \tag{11}$$

We study the value of α in this section.

We have shown that $L_o = Rf_o < 2R$ and $L_l > R$, so α is between 1 and 2. We'd like to find out the maximum value of α. Equation (11) shows that α is a smooth function of r_i, so the maximum value of α is achieved when

$$\frac{\partial \alpha}{\partial r_i} = 0, \forall i. \tag{12}$$

We can solve for the values of r_i^* from the above set of equations. But note that the variables $r_i, i = 2, 3, \ldots, N$, are completely symmetric in the equations, so in the solution, they should have the same value. Since α is only a function of the *ratios* of the r_i's, we let $r_2^* = r_3^* = \ldots = r_N^* = 1$. Now Equation (11) becomes

$$\alpha = \frac{1 + \frac{1}{\frac{r_1}{N - r_1 - 1} + \frac{N - 1}{r_1 + N - 3}}}{2 \frac{N - 1}{r_1 + N - 1}} = \frac{(N + r_1 - 1)(N - 2)}{N^2 - 2N + (r_1 - 1)^2}.$$

Now we solve for r_1^*: $\frac{\partial \alpha}{\partial r_1} = 0$ gives

$$r_1^* = 1 - N + \sqrt{2N(N - 1)} \tag{13}$$

and

$$\alpha^* = \frac{(N - 2)\sqrt{N(N - 1)}}{2N(\sqrt{2}(N - 1) - \sqrt{N(N - 1)})}. \tag{14}$$

As N increases, α^* increases and when $N \to \infty$, $\alpha^* \to \frac{1}{2}(\sqrt{2} + 1) \approx 1.207$. At the same time, $r_1 \to (\sqrt{2} - 1)N = 0.414N$. Thus, the ratio of the capacity required by optimal oblivious load-balancing and the capacity lower bound is upper bounded by Equation (14), which is at most 1.2. This shows that in order to serve all valid traffic matrices, oblivious load-balancing requires a total link capacity very close to the minimum total capacity required by any architecture.

4 Related Work

The papers by Applegate et al. [1] and Kodialam et al. [5] both studied using load-balancing to guarantee throughput for a wide range of traffic matrices, from a traffic engineering point of view. Given a capacitated network, they both compared the efficiency of providing service for all traffic matrices vs. for a specific traffic matrix. Applegate et al. [1] used maximum link utilization ratio as the performance measure and optimization criteria; Kodialam et al. [5] used the maximum traffic which can be carried by the network. The two measures are equivalent and a ratio of less than 2 was achieved in all their experiments.

Our paper looks at the problem from a network design point of view and tries to find the optimal capacity allocation. We analytically derived that in order to guarantee throughput for all traffic matrices, about twice as much capacity is required compared to the case when the exact traffic matrix is known. This result gives theoretical justification to the upper bound of 2 which has appeared in experiments.

Our work is also complimentary to the above two pieces of work. When designing a network from scratch, or expanding a network's capacity, our results provide guidelines to the optimal capacity allocation, and can lead the network to grow in an optimal direction. If a network has been built and cannot be changed on a short time scale, the traffic engineering approach can help utilize the network resources more efficiently and alleviate congestion in the network.

5 Conclusion

At first glance, it appears that the VLB architecture is inefficient (because it is based on a full mesh) and introduces long delays (because each packet traverses the network twice). But we believe these fears are probably unfounded. First, we can show that the network is surprisingly efficient – in fact, essentially the most efficient network that can support 100% throughput. We suspect that the actual deployed link capacity of such a network could be much lower than current networks that can make no such guarantees of service. Second, we believe that the additional delay is unlikely to be a problem to end-user applications. The additional delay is a fixed propagation delay, and so adds nothing to delay variation. In fact, given the efficiency of the network, the queueing delay (and hence delay variation) is likely to be lower than today.

We believe the Valiant Load-Balancing architecture opens up a new dimension in network design. It enables us to design efficient networks that can guarantee 100% throughput for any traffic matrix, and can continue to do so under a number of element failures. The load-balancing scheme is simple and easy to implement. What's more, as demonstrated in [10], the amount of excess capacity required for fault tolerance is surprisingly small. With VLB, we can build networks to efficiently provide high availability under various traffic conditions and failure scenarios.

Acknowledgment

We would like to thank Kamesh Munagala, Isaac Keslassy and Huan Liu for their insights and very helpful inputs.

References

1. D. Applegate and E. Cohen. Making intra-domain routing robust to changing and uncertain traffic demands: Understanding fundamental tradeoffs. In *Proceedings of the ACM SIGCOMM '03 Conference*, 2003.
2. C.-S. Chang, D.-S. Lee, and Y.-S. Jou. Load balanced Birkhoff-von Neumann switches, Part I: One-stage buffering. In *Proceedings of IEEE HPSR '01*, May 2001.
3. I. Keslassy, C.-S. Chang, N. McKeown, and D.-S. Lee. Optimal load-balancing. In *Proceedings of IEEE Infocom 2005*, March 2005.
4. I. Keslassy, S.-T. Chuang, K. Yu, D. Miller, M. Horowitz, O. Solgaard, and N. McKeown. Scaling Internet routers using optics. *Proceedings of ACM SIGCOMM '03, Computer Communication Review*, 33(4):189–200, October 2003.
5. M. Kodialam, T. V. Lakshman, and S. Sengupta. Efficient and robust routing of highly variable traffic. In *HotNets III*, November 2004.
6. A. Medina, N. Taft, K. Salamatian, S. Bhattacharyya, and C. Diot. Traffic matrix estimation: Existing techniques and new directions. In *Proceedings of ACM SIGCOMM '02*, Pittsburgh, USA, Aug. 2002.
7. G. Prasanna and A. Vishwanath. Traffic constraints instead of traffic matrices: Capabilities of a new approach to traffic characterization. *Providing quality of service in heterogeneous environments: Proceedings of the 18th International Teletraffic Congress*, 2003.
8. L. G. Valiant. A scheme for fast parallel communication. *SIAM Journal on Computing*, 11(2):350–361, 1982.
9. Y. Zhang, M. Roughan, C. Lund, and D. Donoho. An information-theoretic approach to traffic matrix estimation. In *Proceedings of ACM SIGCOMM '03*, pages 301–312. ACM Press, 2003.
10. R. Zhang-Shen and N. McKeown. Designing a predictable Internet backbone network. In *HotNets III*, November 2004.
11. R. Zhang-Shen and N. McKeown. Designing a predictable Internet backbone with Valiant load-balancing (extended version). *Stanford HPNG Technical Report TR05-HPNG-040605*, April 2005.

Preserving the Independence of Flows in General Topologies Using Turn-Prohibition

Markus Fidler[1], Oliver Heckmann[2], and Ralf Steinmetz[2]

[1] Centre for Quantifiable Quality of Service (Q2S), NTNU Trondheim, Norway
fidler@ieee.org
[2] Multimedia Communications Lab (KOM), TU Darmstadt, Germany
{heckmann, steimetz}@kom.tu-darmstadt.de

Abstract. Various elegant and powerful theories for network performance evaluation have to assume independence to be efficient. While traffic sources are often supposed to be independent, the implications of this assumption regarding flows in arbitrary networks are largely unknown. Recently, turn-prohibition was proposed to solve a related problem concerning feed-forward networks.

In this paper we extend the concept of turn-prohibition to address the issue of independence of flows in general topologies. To this end we evolve an algorithm which derives a set of critical turns that provide full connectivity while conserving the independence of flows up to multiplexing points. In an iterative procedure further turns are added to improve connectivity. The developed algorithm is proven and exemplified.

1 Introduction

Emerging quality of service architectures gave rise to various new approaches to network performance evaluation. Beyond classical queuing theory, for example [2, 8], methods like the theory of effective bandwidths, see [4, 11, 18] and references therein, and deterministic network calculus, for a comprehensive overview see [4, 12], were developed. Recently, network calculus extensions towards a probabilistic equivalent started to evolve, for example [3, 4, 6, 13, 17, 19].

Independence of flows is critical for the applicability, accuracy, and efficiency of a variety of these methods. While statistical multiplexing of independent flows is known to smooth out burstiness, dependent flows are still subject to worst-case analysis where bursts are cumulated. Yet, adequate preconditions that ensure independence have not been devised for general topologies. A related issue concerning feed-forward networks has recently been solved [7, 15, 16]. The feed-forward property facilitates inductive analyses, for example applying network calculus and its probabilistic extensions. While networks usually are not of a feed-forward type, turn-prohibiting algorithms [15, 16] have been developed, which allow modifying the routing [6] to ensure this property.

In this paper we extend the concept of turn-prohibition in a way such that arbitrary routing algorithms can generate paths that conserve the independence

H. de Meer and N. Bhatti (Eds.): IWQoS 2005, LNCS 3552, pp. 193–205, 2005.

of flows in general topologies. We apply a network model where routers are represented by vertices V and links and the belonging queuing and scheduling units by directed edges E. Bidirectional links are presumed and often displayed as such in figures, where each bidirectional link corresponds to two directed and opposing edges in E. For brevity and ease of presentation, we assume that the objective of the routing algorithm is to minimize the path length measured in hops. Traffic sources are expected to be uncorrelated, that is traffic flows are stochastically independent before entering the network. For clarity we distinguish between two conditions under which dependencies are created:

1. **Direct Dependencies:** Consider two flows i and j that pass a common queue. The flows i and j are dependent when leaving the queue.
2. **Indirect Dependencies:** Consider three flows i, j, and k. Let flows i and j traverse a queue and afterwards j and k traverse another queue. When leaving the queues, flows i and j respective j and k are directly dependent. Further on flow k depends via flow j indirectly on the properties of flow i.

Dependencies can further on be classified as plain or cyclic, where in the latter case a number of flows form a cycle of direct dependencies, such that the characteristics of a flow when leaving a queue indirectly depend on themselves. In the following we will introduce conditions under which dependencies cannot occur, namely the feed-forward property and unique dependency paths.

The remainder of this paper is organized as follows: Section 2 briefly recalls known methods to ensure the feed-forward property and introduces the concept of dependency graphs. In Sect. 3, we develop and prove an extended turn-prohibition algorithm that allows ensuring unique dependency paths. An example is discussed in Sect. 4 while Sect. 5 gives concluding remarks and recommendations for application.

2   The Feed-Forward Property

Definition 1 (Feed-Forward Property). *In a feed-forward queuing network the queues can be labeled in a way, such that whenever traffic flows from queue i to queue j this implies that $i < j$ [8]. That is the queues of a feed-forward network cannot form any cycles, respective it is impossible for traffic flows to create cyclic dependencies [4].*

Certain network topologies, for example sink-tree networks [4], are generally of a feed-forward nature. However, considering general topologies, few approaches are known which allow ensuring the feed-forward property. Among these are edge-prohibiting methods, for example based on spanning trees, and turn-prohibiting approaches, like up-down routing [15] and the turn-prohibition algorithm [16] where a directed turn (a, b, c) refers to the concatenation of two successive edges (a, b) and (b, c). Generally, turn-prohibiting methods may have significantly less performance impact then edge-prohibiting ones [16] since a prohibited turn only bans the combination of the belonging edges but not the edges themselves.

Here, we apply the turn-prohibition algorithm [16] and a related data structure referred to as dependency graph [5] respective turn network [7] which we briefly introduce in the following subsections.

2.1   Turn-Prohibition

The turn-prohibition algorithm [16] generally breaks all cycles in networks with bidirectional links. The steps of the basic version are summarized in Alg. 1 where Pre(.) denotes the set of predecessors of a vertex and Suc(.) the set of successors. Given a network graph $G = (V, E)$ with vertices V and edges E and an empty set of turns P, the algorithm inspects all turns around each of the vertices in increasing order of their degree that is the cumulated capacity of the connected edges. While inspecting a vertex, all turns around it are included in the set of prohibited turns P and the vertex and all adjacent edges are removed from the graph before the next vertex for inspection is determined.

Algorithm 1. Calculate prohibited turns P

Require: $G = (V, E), P = \emptyset$
   while $V \neq \emptyset$ **do**
      Select a vertex $b \in V$ with minimal degree
      for all $a \in \mathrm{Pre}(b), c \in \mathrm{Suc}(b), a \neq c$ **do**
         $P \leftarrow P \cup \{(a, b, c)\}$
      for all $a \in \mathrm{Pre}(b)$ **do**
         $E \leftarrow E \setminus \{(a, b)\}$
      for all $c \in \mathrm{Suc}(b)$ **do**
         $E \leftarrow E \setminus \{(b, c)\}$
      $V \leftarrow V \setminus b$

Figure 1 gives an example. In (a), four flows are displayed which create a cyclic dependency. In (b) and (c), turn-prohibition breaks this cycle. The vertices are investigated in the order of their labelling. No turns exist around vertex 0, thus vertex 0 and edges $(0, 2)$ and $(2, 0)$ are removed. The same applies for vertex 1. In

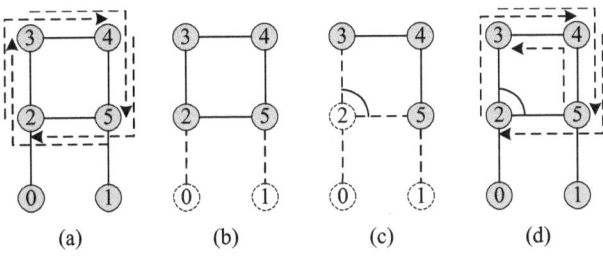

Fig. 1. Example application of turn-prohibition

case of vertex 2 the turns $(3, 2, 5)$ and $(5, 2, 3)$ are prohibited as indicated by the arc around vertex 2 before vertex 2 and the adjacent edges are removed from the graph. The following steps do not prohibit further turns. Finally in (d), shortest paths that do not utilize the prohibited turns are shown for the flows from the initial problem. Clearly turn-prohibition resolved the cyclic dependency.

2.2   Dependency Graphs

A structure which allows for efficient analysis of both cyclic and non-cyclic dependencies is the so-called dependency graph [5], also referred to as turn network [7] since it essentially consists of edges and turns. The graph of the turn network $G^* = (E, T)$ results from transformation of the initial network graph $G = (V, E)$ where edges become vertices and turns become edges. Thus, the notation of the set of predecessors $\text{Pre}(.)$ and successors $\text{Suc}(.)$ naturally extends to edges where it becomes $\text{Pre}((., .))$ and $\text{Suc}((., .))$ respectively. Since each edge in G respective vertex in G^* symbolizes a link including a queuing and scheduling unit, the edges in the graph G^* indicate dependencies that occur if traffic flows along the belonging turn in G. The transformation is summarized in Alg. 2.

Algorithm 2. Calculate dependency graph $G^* = (E, T)$

Require: $G = (V, E), T = \emptyset, \text{Pre}((., .)) = \emptyset, \text{Suc}((., .)) = \emptyset$
    for all $b \in V$ **do**
        for all $a \in \text{Pre}(b), c \in \text{Suc}(b), a \neq c$ **do**
        $T \leftarrow T \cup \{(a, b, c)\}$
        $\text{Pre}((b, c)) \leftarrow \text{Pre}((b, c)) \cup \{(a, b)\}$
        $\text{Suc}((a, b)) \leftarrow \text{Suc}((a, b)) \cup \{(b, c)\}$

Figure 2 shows the corresponding dependency graph for the example network in Fig. 1. The vertices are labeled by the source and destination vertices of the corresponding edges from Fig. 1 and whenever traffic can flow from one edge to another in Fig. 1, the corresponding turns are represented by edges in Fig. 2. The edges that correspond to the prohibited turns $(3, 2, 5)$ and $(5, 2, 3)$ are indicated by dotted lines. The dependency graph clearly shows the cyclic dependencies that are broken by prohibition of these turns.

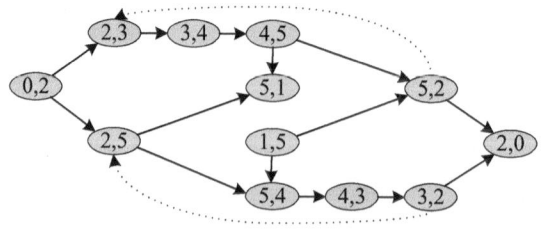

Fig. 2. Dependency graph after turn-prohibition

While allowing for a demonstrative analysis of dependencies, the turn network can immediately be applied for routing. In [7] it is shown that routing algorithms, like Dijkstra's algorithm, might not find optimal paths in a network with prohibited turns whereas optimal paths are found in the corresponding turn network from where they can be transformed back to the original network.

3   Unique Dependency Paths

Definition 2 (Unique Dependency Paths). *In a queueing network with unique dependency paths, traffic flows span at most one path from any queue i to any queue j. Flows span a path from queue i to queue j if a set of flows exists, where the first flow passes queue i, each pair of subsequent flows traverse at least one common queue, and the last flow passes queue j.*

A network which fulfills both, the feed-forward and the unique dependency path property, conserves the independence of initially independent flows until they are multiplexed. While the feed-forward property has been investigated for general topologies, we are not aware of corresponding methods regarding unique dependency paths. So far, many authors leave the problem open whereas few address the issue either by restricting the topology, for example applying sink-tree networks [4], or by assuming independence only at the ingress and dependence throughout the core of the network [3, 13].

Figure 3 (a) extends the example from Fig. 1 to show how indirect dependence can occur in a network without unique dependency paths. In the sequel we use the path of a flow as a synonym for the flow. The two flows $(0, 2, 5, 1)$ and $(0, 2, 3, 4)$ create a direct dependence at edge $(0, 2)$. Then, at edge $(3, 4)$ the flows $(0, 2, 3, 4)$ and $(3, 4, 5, 1)$ become dependent. Due to indirect dependence the flow $(3, 4, 5, 1)$ also depends on flow $(0, 2, 5, 1)$. Thus, when multiplexing flows $(3, 4, 5, 1)$ and $(0, 2, 5, 1)$ at edge $(5, 1)$ they are not independent. Obviously, the network does not have unique dependency paths since the chain of the two flows $(0, 2, 3, 4)$ and $(3, 4, 5, 1)$ – connected by the common edge $(3, 4)$ – spans a different path from edge $(0, 2)$ to edge $(5, 1)$ than flow $(0, 2, 5, 1)$.

An immediate though suboptimal solution to the problem is to use only edges that belong to a spanning tree where the shortest path spanning tree with root

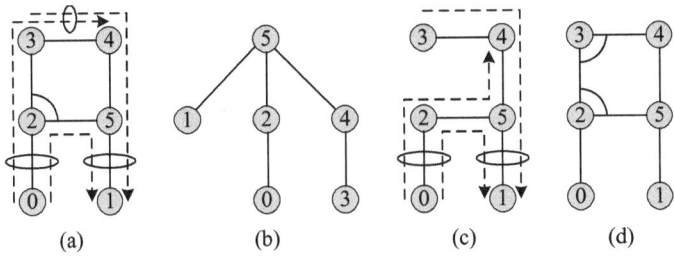

(a)   (b)   (c)   (d)

Fig. 3. Example application of extended turn-prohibition

vertex 5 is shown in Fig. 3 (b). Removing the edges $(2,3)$ and $(3,2)$ solves the problem as displayed in (c). However, a considerably better solution shown in (d) can be obtained as derived in the sequel where only the turns $(2,3,4)$, $(4,3,2)$, $(3,2,5)$, and $(5,2,3)$ but not the edges $(2,3)$ and $(3,2)$ have to be prohibited.

3.1   Extended Turn-Prohibition Algorithm

Our solution applies the turn-prohibition algorithm [16] to ensure the feed-forward property in a first step before switching over to the dependency graph. Certainly, the feed-forward property could also be ensured applying cycle-breaking methods to the dependency graph, however, the turn-prohibition algorithm is assumed to be efficient [16]. Our extended turn-prohibition algorithm derives a set of turns T' which can be used without violating the feed-forward and the unique dependency path properties. It comprises the following steps:

1. Apply Alg. 1 to the graph $G = (V, E)$ to calculate a set of prohibited turns P that ensure the feed-forward property.
2. Construct the shortest path spanning tree $SPST = (V, E')$ from the last vertex visited by turn-prohibition without using any of the turns in P and compute the dependency graph $SPST^* = (E', T')$ with Alg. 2.
3. Substitute nonessential turns – that are turns for which edges exist – by the respective edges using Alg. 3.
4. Add all remaining edges from the set E to $SPST^*$.
5. Incrementally add all turns which are not in P to $SPST^*$ if they do not violate the unique dependency path property according to Alg. 4.

Step 1 applies the known turn-prohibition algorithm [16] to derive a set of prohibited turns $P \subset T$ to ensure the feed-forward property.

In step 2 we identify a set of critical turns $T' \subseteq \{T \setminus P\}$ which are required to provide full connectivity among all vertices while ensuring unique dependency paths. A valid set T' is given by all turns that belong to the shortest path spanning tree rooted from the last vertex visited by the turn-prohibition algorithm which trivially ensures unique dependency paths. The shortest path spanning tree can for example be computed using Dijkstra's algorithm on the dependency graph $G^* = (E, T \setminus P)$ [7]. Figure 4 shows the dependency graph $SPST^*$ where the gray vertices correspond to the edges of the spanning tree in Fig. 3.

In step 3, Alg. 3 is applied to substitute turns by edges if applicable. Consider the initial network graph $G = (V, E)$ and the dependency graph of the shortest path spanning tree $SPST^* = (E', T')$. If there exist edges $(b, d) \in E$ and $(b, d) \notin E'$ and corresponding turns $(b, c, d) \in T'$, then the turns (b, c, d) are replaced by the edges (b, d) and for each turn $(a, b, c) \in T'$ respective $(c, d, e) \in T'$ a turn $(a, b, d) \notin P$ respective $(b, d, e) \notin P$ is added to T' to connect the edge (b, d).

In Fig. 3 no such turns exist, thus we investigate the modified example in Fig. 5. In (a), all turns belonging to the tree are indicated by arrows around vertices and two edges that do not belong to the tree are given by dashed lines; all turns that include these edges are assumed to be permitted. The result of the first iteration is shown in (b). The edges $(4,5)$ and $(5,4)$ replace the turns

Algorithm 3. Substitute nonessential turns

Require: $G = (V, E), SPST^* = (E', T'), P$
  repeat
    $T'' \leftarrow \emptyset$
    for all $b, c, d \in V, (b, c, d) \in T'$ **do**
      if $(b, d) \in E \setminus E'$ **then**
        $T''' \leftarrow \emptyset$
        for all $a \in V, (a, b, c) \in T'$ **do**
          $T''' \leftarrow T''' \cup \{(a, b, d)\}$
        for all $e \in V, (c, d, e) \in T'$ **do**
          $T''' \leftarrow T''' \cup \{(b, d, e)\}$
        if $T''' \cap P = \emptyset$ **then**
          $T' \leftarrow T' \setminus \{(b, c, d)\}, E' \leftarrow E' \cup \{(b, d)\}, T'' \leftarrow T'' \cup T'''$
    $T' \leftarrow T' \cup T''$
  until $T'' = \emptyset$

$(4, 6, 5)$ and $(5, 6, 4)$. Further on, the new edges are connected by turns $(1, 4, 5)$, $(5, 4, 1)$, $(2, 5, 4)$, and $(4, 5, 2)$. In the second iteration, shown in (c), the turns $(2, 5, 4)$ and $(4, 5, 2)$ are then replaced by the edges $(2, 4)$ and $(4, 2)$ which are connected by turns $(0, 2, 4)$, $(4, 2, 0)$, $(1, 4, 2)$, and $(2, 4, 1)$.

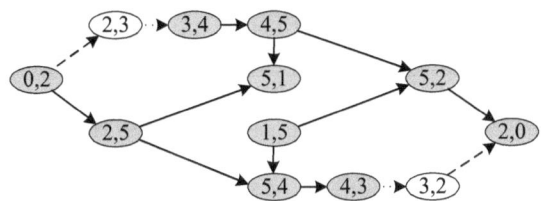

Fig. 4. Dependency graph after extended turn-prohibition

In step 4, all edges are added to the dependency graph $SPST^*$ since including edges without connecting turns does not create dependencies. In Fig. 4 these are the white vertices $(2, 3)$ and $(3, 2)$ which at this step are still unconnected.

Finally, in step 5 all turns not in P and not yet in T' are tested by Alg. 4 and added to T', if they do not violate the unique dependency path property. Preferably start with turns that are part of potential shortest paths between sparsely connected vertices. In Fig. 4 turns $(0, 2, 3)$ and $(3, 2, 0)$ can be added, whereas subsequently $(2, 3, 4)$ and $(4, 3, 2)$ fail the test and must not be used.

3.2   Proof of Correctness

Proposition 1. *The shortest path spanning tree $SPST$ from the last vertex visited by the turn-prohibition algorithm provides full connectivity among all vertices V without using any of the prohibited turns in P.*

Algorithm 4. Test uniqueness of dependency paths

Require: $G^* = (E, T)$
  for all $i \in E$ **do**
    $A \leftarrow \{i\}, B \leftarrow \{i\}$
    repeat
      $C \leftarrow \emptyset$
      for all $j \in B$ **do**
        $C \leftarrow C \cup \mathrm{Pre}(j)$
      if $A \cap C \neq \emptyset$ **then**
        The graph does not have unique dependency paths.
      $A \leftarrow A \cup C, B \leftarrow C$
    until $C = \emptyset$

A spanning tree that consists of bidirectional edges trivially provides full connectivity among all vertices. Note, however, that this is not an immediate result if certain turns are prohibited. Consider the spanning tree in Fig. 3 (b). If the turns $(5, 2, 0)$, $(0, 2, 5)$, $(5, 4, 3)$, and $(3, 4, 5)$ are permitted, the tree contains valid paths from the root vertex 5 to any other vertex and vice versa. This holds also if for example the turns $(1, 5, 2)$ and $(2, 5, 1)$ are prohibited, in which case the tree, however, does not contain any paths between vertices 1 and 2.

Proof. Let the vertices be numbered in the order of inspection by turn-prohibition starting with zero. Since the full version of the turn-prohibition algorithm preserves connectivity [16], the tree $SPST$ exists and there are valid paths in $SPST$ from the root vertex $n = |V| - 1$ to all other vertices and vice versa.

Yet, it remains to be shown that the tree $SPST$ provides connectivity among all of the remaining vertices. Clearly, since vertex n is the last vertex visited by turn-prohibition, there cannot be any prohibited turns around it. Thus, full connectivity among all direct children of the root vertex n is provided.

Consider a vertex i and a direct child of i with label j. If $j < i$ vertex j was removed from the graph G by the turn-prohibition algorithm before vertex i was inspected. Consequently, turns around vertex i originating from or destined

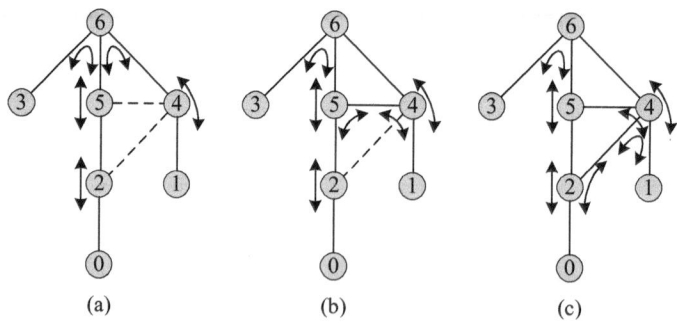

      (a)   (b)   (c)

Fig. 5. Shortest path spanning tree and substitution of turns

for vertex j cannot be prohibited. Thus, as long as children have smaller label values than parents, full connectivity among all vertices is ensured.

Let us now assume that a vertex with label i has a child with label j and $j > i$. In this case vertex i has been inspected by the turn-prohibition algorithm before vertex j and also before the root vertex n. If vertex i is a direct child of the root vertex n this, however, means that the turns (n, i, j) and (j, i, n) have been prohibited which means that vertex j cannot be a child of vertex i in contradiction to the assumption.

If vertex i is not a direct child of the root vertex, then either the parent vertex of i has a higher label $k > i$ in which case the same argumentation applies immediately, or it has a lower label $k < i$ in which case the above argumentation applies recursively for the parent vertex k. □

Proposition 2. *The substitution of nonessential turns by edges does not introduce new dependencies to the dependency graph $SPST^* = (E', T')$ and hence preserves unique dependency paths.*

Proof. Consider a turn $t = (b, c, d) \in T'$ that is substituted by an edge $s = (b, d) \in E \setminus E'$ where for each turn of type $(a, b, c) \in T'$ respective $(c, d, e) \in T'$ a turn $(a, b, d) \notin P$ respective $(b, d, e) \notin P$ is added to T'.

The substitution is one-to-one. Any path that includes the turn (b, c, d) with or without further connected turns of type (a, b, c) and (c, d, e) can be realized using the edge (b, d) or the turns (a, b, d) and (b, d, e) and vice versa.

Because there exists at most one dependency path between any two edges, all dependency paths that included t have to include s after substitution and all dependency paths that include s had to include t before substitution, provided s was not used before which is ensured by the condition $s \notin E'$.

Since all dependency paths that formerly included t and only these paths include s instead, the substitution does not introduce new dependencies. Again there exists at most one dependency path between any two edges and the proof applies inductively to all following iterations of the algorithm. □

4   Application to the DFN G-WiN Topology

In this section, we give an example applying our algorithm to the DFN G-WiN topology as of 2000 [10] that is shown in Fig. 6 (a). More recent topologies are available, see for example [9], however, the chosen topology reveals considerable complexity while still being useful for demonstrative purposes.

The level one nodes have been investigated by Alg. 1 in order of their numbering. Note that the unnumbered level two nodes fulfill the feed-forward property trivially. The resulting 7 bidirectional prohibited turns are marked by arcs in Fig. 6 (b). Further on, the edges that belong to the considered shortest path spanning tree rooted at the vertex with the highest label are indicated by solid lines compared to dashed lines that are edges which do not belong to the tree.

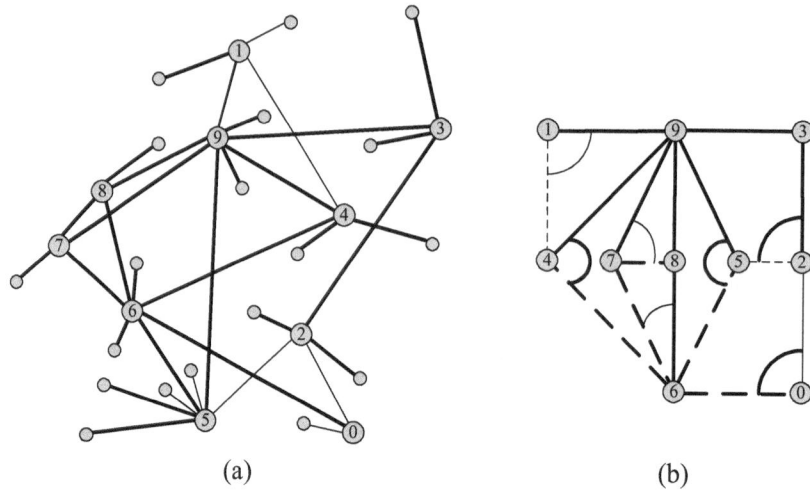

(a)   (b)

Fig. 6. G-WiN topology as of 2000, turn-prohibition, and spanning tree

Figure 7 shows the respective dependency graph where level two nodes and corresponding edges and turns are left out for clearness. Note, however, that given a level one node b, all edges (b, c) may share common predecessors (a, b) that are not displayed, where a is a level two node, respective all edges (a, b) may share common successors (b, c), where c is a level two node. While we take the first into account to ensure independence in the level one core, we ignore the latter such that flows when leaving the level one core may be dependent.

Solid lines in Fig. 7 indicate turns that belong to the graph after substitution of nonessential turns by edges. In the first iteration of Alg. 3 turns $(1, 9, 4)$ and $(4, 9, 1)$ have been substituted by edges $(1, 4)$ and $(4, 1)$ and turns $(8, 9, 7)$ and $(7, 9, 8)$ have been replaced by edges $(8, 7)$ and $(7, 8)$ which have been connected by turns $(6, 8, 7)$ and $(7, 8, 6)$. In the second iteration turns $(6, 8, 7)$ and $(7, 8, 6)$ have been substituted by edges $(6, 7)$ and $(7, 6)$.

The vertices in Fig. 7 that are marked grey correspond to edges that are part of the spanning tree in Fig. 6. The remaining vertices are marked white and all further turns that did not violate the unique dependency path property according to Alg. 4 are marked by dashed lines. The incremental procedure to add these turns started with turns that are part of potential shortest paths and processed these in the order of the numbering of the vertices, that is turns starting or ending at the vertex with the lowest index were tested first.

We find that of the 86 possible directed turns 14 have to be prohibited to ensure the feed-forward property and further 22 have to be prohibited to ensure unique dependency paths, thus 50 permitted turns remain. To ensure unique dependency paths the following bidirectional turns are prohibited: $(0, 2, 5), (0, 6, 8)$, $(1, 4, 9), (2, 5, 9), (4, 6, 5), (4, 6, 8), (5, 6, 7), (5, 6, 8), (6, 7, 9), (6, 8, 7), (7, 8, 9)$. Yet, only two paths with minimal hop count, $(0, 6, 8)$ and $(8, 6, 0)$, have to be

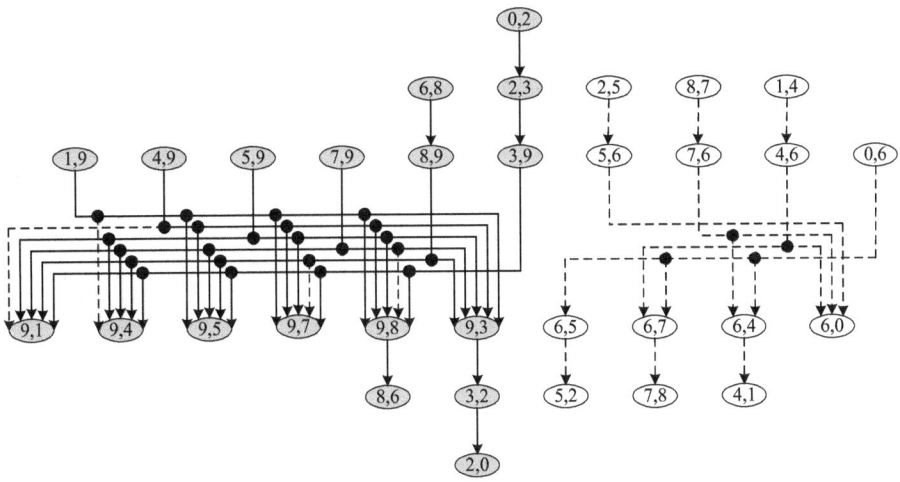

Fig. 7. G-WiN dependency graph

replaced by the longer paths $(0, 6, 7, 8)$ and $(8, 7, 6, 0)$, due to the prohibition of turns $(0, 6, 8)$ and $(8, 6, 0)$ to ensure independence in the level one core.

5   Concluding Remarks

A variety of powerful and elegant methods for network analysis rely on the assumption of independence of flows at multiplexing points. However, the correctness of this supposition is usually not investigated for specific topologies. To this end, we developed an extended turn-prohibition algorithm that ensures both the feed-forward and the unique dependency path property, under which flows that are independent at the ingress of the network retain this attribute throughout the core of the network until they are potentially multiplexed.

While the turn-prohibition approach is considered to be efficient [16], it clearly impacts routing performance. Yet, in case of the DFN G-WiN topology which can be considered to be challenging in this respect, we presented a solution where only one pair of shortest paths has to be replaced by paths with one additional hop to ensure independence in the level one core of the network.

Areas of application are for example emerging MPLS [14] networks with explicit routing and DiffServ [1] like aggregate service provisioning where turn-prohibition can be applied to compose a premium service with defined service guarantees. In this scenario, common best-effort traffic is unaffected and can still be routed along any path, thus providing an efficient solution.

A particular advantage of our analysis using dependency graphs is given in case of methods for performance analysis that make formulas available both for multiplexing independent and dependent flows, for example [6, 19]. In this case, individual decisions can be made, either to adapt the routing to ensure independence or to apply rules for multiplexing dependent flows, whenever the dependency graph indicates the necessity to do so, as in case of the outgoing links from level one to level two nodes in the G-WiN example.

Acknowledgements

This work was supported in part by an Emmy Noether grant of the German Research Foundation. The Q2S Centre of Excellence is appointed by the Research Council of Norway and funded by the Research Council, NTNU and UNINETT.

References

1. S. Blake, D. Black, M. Carlson, E. Davies, Z. Wang, and W. Weiss. *An Architecture for Differentiated Services*. RFC 2475, 1998.
2. G. Bolch, S. Greiner, H. de Meer, and K. S. Trivedi. *Queueing Networks and Markov Chains: Modeling and Performance Evaluation with Computer Science Applications*. Wiley, 1998.
3. R.-R. Boorstyn, A. Burchard, J. Liebeherr, and C. Oottamakorn. *Statistical Service Assurances for Traffic Scheduling Algorithms*. IEEE JSAC, 18(12):2651-2664, 2000.
4. C.-S. Chang. *Performance Guarantees in Communication Networks*. Springer, 2000.
5. J. Duato, S. Yalamanchili, and N. Lionel. *Interconnection Networks: An Engineering Approach*. Morgan Kaufmann, 2003.
6. M. Fidler. *Elements of Probabilistic Network Calculus Applying Moment Generating Functions*. Preprint Series of the Institut Mittag-Leffler, Sweden, 2005.
7. M. Fidler and G. Einhoff. *Routing in Turn-Prohibition Based Feed-Forwad Networks*. LNCS 3042, Springer, Proceedings of Networking, pp. 1168-1179, 2004.
8. B. R. Haverkort. *Performance of Computer Communication Systems: A Model-Based Approach*. Wiley, 1999.
9. O. Heckmann, M. Piringer, and R. Steinmetz. *On Realistic Network Topologies for Simulation*. Proceedings of the ACM Sigcomm Workshops, pp. 28-32, 2003.
10. G. Hoffmann. *G-WiN - the Gbit/s infrastructure for the German scientific community*. Elsevier Computer Networks, 34(6):959-964, 2000.
11. F. Kelly. *Notes on Effective Bandwidths*, Stochastic Networks: Theory and Applications, Royal Statistical Society Lecture Notes Series, 4:141-168, 1996.
12. J.-Y. Le Boudec and P. Thiran. *Network Calculus: A Theory of Deterministic Queueing Systems for the Internet*. Springer, 2001.
13. J. Liebeherr, S. D. Patek, and A. Burchard. *Statistical Per-Flow Service Bounds in a Network with Aggregate Provisioning*. Proceedings of IEEE Infocom, 2003.
14. E. Rosen, A. Viswanathan, and R. Callon. *Multiprotocol Label Switching Architecture*. RFC 3031, 2001.
15. M. D. Schroeder, A. D. Birrell, M. Burrows, H. Murray, R. M. Needham, and T. L. Rodeheffer. *Autonet: A High-speed, Self-configuring Local Area Network Using Point-to-point Links*. IEEE JSAC, 9(8):1318-1335, 1991.
16. D. Starobinski, M. Karpovsky, and L. Zakrevski. *Application of Network Calculus to General Topologies using Turn-Prohibition*. IEEE/ACM ToN, 11(3):411-421, 2003.

17. D. Starobinski and M. Sidi. *Stochastically Bounded Burstiness for Communication Networks*. IEEE TIT, 46(1):206-216, 2000.
18. D. Wischik. *The output of a switch, or, effective bandwidths for networks*. Queueing Systems, 32(4):383-396, 1999.
19. Q. Yin, Y. Jiang, S. Jiang, and P. Y. Kong. *Analysis of Generalized Stochastically Bounded Bursty Traffic for Communication Networks*. Proceedings of IEEE LCN, pp. 141-149, 2002.

Supporting Differentiated QoS in MPLS Networks

Roberto A. Dias[1], Eduardo Camponogara[2], and Jean-Marie Farines[2]*

[1] Federal Technology Center of Santa Catarina, Florianópolis, 88020-300, Brazil
[2] Federal University of Santa Catarina, C.P. 476, Florianópolis, 88040-900, Brazil
roberto@cefetsc.edu.br
{camponog, farines}@das.ufsc.br

Abstract. This paper proposes a new approach for providing different levels of QoS in IP networks over MPLS. The system's operator wishes to maximize the throughput of the high priority flows by choosing the less congested paths while taking care of the applications' requirements. These requirements give rise to an optimization problem that consists of finding resource-constrained shortest paths in a directed graph. The problem can be formally cast in mathematical programming and its solution can follow two directions: (i) a centralized, heuristic approach that aims at approximating the optimal solution in a fast and efficient way; (ii) a distributed approach that relies on Lagrangean relaxation to decompose the optimization problem in small subproblems and thereby divide the computational burden between distributed routers. By means of numerical analysis and simulation, this paper demonstrates the effectiveness of the proposed approaches and shows QoS improvements of the high priority flows.

1   Introduction

In a context of Internet expansion, Traffic Engineering (TE) can deliver a network operation that meets stringent QoS requirements of applications by optimizing the use of network resources. A key element to support TE in IP networks is the *Multiprotocol Label Switching* (MPLS) technology, to a great extent because MPLS implements explicit routing whereby data packets are transmitted in virtual paths denominated *Label Switched Paths* (LSPs). In this paper we propose a TE approach based on an optimization problem which consists of finding shortest paths in a directed graph, while respecting multiple constraints.

Further, the TE problem implements an admission control policy that, under circumstances of traffic congestion, favors the admission of high priority flows in detriment of low priority flows. However, the mathematical formulation of the TE operation renders a computationally hard problem (Section 2): the knapsack problem [1] can be easily reduced to the TE problem in polynomial

---

* This research was supported in part by CNPq (Brazil).

H. de Meer and N. Bhatti (Eds.): IWQoS 2005, LNCS 3552, pp. 206–218, 2005.

time. To circumvent both the computational hardness and the large size of typical instances, we propose two approaches: (i) a simple and effective centralized heuristic (Section 3); and (ii) the decomposition of the TE problem into a set of smaller subproblems to be solved distributively (Section 4).

2   Traffic Engineering Problem (TEP) Formulation

Our approach to service differentiation in MPLS networks is based on the formulation and solution of a *Traffic Engineering Problem* (*TEP*): the problem goal is throughput maximization of the flows transmitted by the communication network; the constraints are bandwidth limits and end-to-end maximum transmission delay; and a prioritization scheme is implemented to differentiate among service classes. Although our model can support an arbitrary number of priority levels, the numerical experiments herein use only two priority levels, which can be mapped in two classes of services: (i) *high priority class* which corresponds to premium applications; and (ii) *low priority class* which encompasses the best effort flows. Our model can cope with multiple classes of service which, in turn, can be mapped into service classes of the DiffServ architecture at ease.

The flows are forwarded in LSPs configured along paths connecting source and destination nodes, which adequately allocate bandwidth to avoid congestion. Path and bandwidth are subject to network constraints, as link bandwidth limitations and maximum end-to-end delays. Thus, the problem can be thought of as a *weighted maximum-flow multi-path problem subject to multiple constraints* [2] that, in its single-path form, renders an NP-Hard problem [3].

Our formulation of *TEP* also implements an admission control policy. Every flow forwarded in its respective LSP is labelled with a priority tag to indicate its importance. Under conditions of network congestion, the transmission rate of low priority flows can be reduced or, in extreme circumstances, dropped to zero to ensure QoS of high priority flows.

The bandwidths of the flow requests are discretized in levels that vary from a maximum desired value to zero, the latter one means the rejection of the request.

The network topology consists of a directed graph $G = (V, E)$, where $V = \{1, \ldots, N\}$ is the set of network nodes and $E \subseteq V \times V$ is the set of transmission links. The capacity of link (i, j) is μ_{ij} *Kbps*, and the time delay for transmitting data through this link is denoted by c_{ij}. The goal is to maximize the throughput weighted by the priority parameters. The variables define the paths and bandwidth levels for the LSPs. More specifically, $y_k^l \in \{0, 1\}$ takes on value 1 if the bandwidth level l is chosen for the kth LSP, while $x_{ij}^{kl} \in \{0, 1\}$ assumes value 1 if arc (i, j) appears in the path from the source to the destination node of the kth LSP when transmission level l is chosen.

The flow parameters are: (1) the number of LSP requests (K); (2) the source node of the kth LSP ($s_k \in V$); (3) the destination of the flow originated from s_k ($d_k \in V$); (4) the number of bandwidth levels of the kth LSP request (l_k);

(5) the transmission rate of the kth LSP forwarded in the lth level $(\lambda_k^l)^1$; (6) the maximum end-to-end transmission delay tolerated by the kth LSP (h_k); and (7) the priority of LSP k (δ_k), where high values mean high priority.

The constraints comprise the bandwidth limits of the links, the limits on transmission delay of the LSPs, and the connectivity constraints that ensure linkage between source and destination nodes. After introducing the terminology, we can formulate TEP in mathematical programming:

$$z = \text{Max} \quad \sum_{k=1}^{K} \sum_{l=1}^{l_k} \delta_k \lambda_k^l y_k^l \tag{1.1}$$

$$\text{S. to}: \sum_{l=1}^{l_k} y_k^l = 1, \qquad\qquad \forall k \in \mathcal{K} \quad (1.2)$$

$$\sum_{k=1}^{K} \sum_{l=1}^{l_k} \lambda_k^l x_{ij}^{kl} \leq \mu_{ij}, \qquad\qquad \forall (i,j) \in E \quad (1.3)$$

$$\sum_{l=1}^{l_k} \sum_{(i,j) \in E} c_{ij} x_{ij}^{kl} \leq h_k, \qquad\qquad \forall k \in \mathcal{K} \quad (1.4)$$

$$\sum_{\{j:(i,j) \in E\}} x_{ij}^{kl} - \sum_{\{j:(j,i) \in E\}} x_{ji}^{kl} = b_i^k y_k^l, \; \forall i \in V, \forall k \in \mathcal{K}, \forall l \in \mathcal{L}_k \quad (1.5)$$

$$x_{ij}^{kl} \in \{0,1\}, \qquad\qquad \forall (i,j) \in E, \forall k \in \mathcal{K}, \forall l \in \mathcal{L}_k \quad (1.6)$$

$$y_k^l \in \{0,1\}, \qquad\qquad \forall k \in \mathcal{K}, \forall l \in \mathcal{L}_k \quad (1.7)$$

where: $b_i^k = 1$ if $i = s_k$, $b_i^k = -1$ if $i = d_k$, and $b_i^k = 0$ otherwise. Further, $\mathcal{K}$ is a shorthand for $\{1, \ldots, K\}$ and $\mathcal{L}_k$ denotes the set $\{1, \ldots, l_k\}$. Expression (1.2) ensures that each LSP is configured in precisely one transmission level. Expression (1.3) imposes bandwidth constraints on the communication links. Expression (1.4) models the maximum delay limits of each LSP. Expression (1.5) spells out the connection-oriented constraints of LSPs (i.e., LSP k is configured along one path). Expressions (1.6) and (1.7) define the Boolean constraints of the decision variables.

3 Centralized Solution of TEP

This section shows a heuristic-based centralized solution for TEP called *purely heuristic procedure* (PHP). The steps of the PHP algorithm are detailed below.

Note that PHP forwards a set of flows in the MPLS network at a time, as opposed to approaches driven by one-by-one flow admission and forwarding [4]. By letting $N = |V|$ denote the number of vertices of G and $M = |E|$ denote

---

[1] We assume that the LSP levels are arranged in increasing order, that is, $\lambda_k^l < \lambda_k^{l+1}$ for $l = 1, \ldots, l_k - 1$, thus $\lambda_k^1 = 0$ is used to reject admission of the LSP request.

the cardinality of its edge set, it is straightforward to verify that the running time of PHP is $O(\sum_{k=1}^{K} l_k(N \log N + M))$ if we use Dijkstra's algorithm and a Fibonacci heap as the priority queue to compute shortest paths.

Purely Heuristic Procedure (PHP)

Let $\mathcal{L} = (k_1, \ldots, k_K)$ be a permutation of $\mathcal{K}$ s.t. $\delta_{k_j} \lambda_{k_j}^{l_{k_j}} \geq \delta_{k_{j+1}} \lambda_{k_{j+1}}^{l_{k_{j+1}}}, \forall j < K$

Let $t = 1$ be the iteration number

Let $G^t = G$ be the residual network modeling the remaining transmission capacity

Let $\Psi_H = \{x_{ij}^{kl}, y_k^l\}$ be the initial, candidate solution to TEP
    where $x_{ij}^{kl} = 0$ and $y_k^l = 0$ for all $k \in \mathcal{K}$, $(i,j) \in E$, and $l \in \mathcal{L}_k$

For $t = 1, \ldots, K$ do

    Let $k \leftarrow k_t$

    For $l = l_k, \ldots, 1$ and while a path has not been found do

        Use Dijkstra's algorithm to find a path p_k in G^t where (i,j)'s cost is:

        $c_{ij}^t = \infty$ if $\mu_{ij}^t < \lambda_k^l$, and otherwise $c_{ij}^t = c_{ij}$

        If a path p_k has been found and $\sum_{(i,j) \in p_k} c_{ij}^t \leq h_k$ then

            Setup LSP k to follow path p_k and update Ψ_H

            Reduce the capacity of G^t along p_k by λ_k^l units to obtain G^{t+1}

3.1   Using TEP for Dynamic Operations

This section aims to present a solution for the *Dynamic Traffic Engineering Problem* (referred to as $DTEP$). Our procedure consists of solving a sequence of TEP problems, $\{TEP_t\}$, which are instantiated over time as flow requests arrive at the computer network and other ones terminate. Consider the time iterate $t = 0$ and the first element TEP_0 of the series $\{TEP_t\}$. By solving TEP_0 with PHP, a solution $(x^{(0)}, y^{(0)})$ is obtained and implemented by the network: the network rejects every LSP request k whose transmission bandwidth allocation is zero, while forwarding the remaining LSPs with the chosen bandwidths along the prescribed paths. During the time interval that elapses while TEP_0 is solved and its solution is implemented, all of the requests received by the computer network are enqueued in a waiting list. These unprocessed requests will be reconsidered for admission when TEP_1 is solved.

3.2   An Experimental Analysis

To validate PHP as a viable procedure to solve TEP and assess the network operation quality resulting from the solution of $\{TEP_t\}$, we considered three experiments. *(i) Performance analysis:* it consists of the computation of the running time of PHP and the assessment of its solution quality for a representative instance of TEP, obtained by way of a comparison with the optimal solutions (or upper bounds computed via linear programming relaxation) produced by the CPLEX solver[2]. *(ii) Quality of service (QoS) analysis:* it is intended to evaluate

---

[2] ILOG CPLEX 9.0: Getting Started, ILOG Corporation, October, 2003.

the impact of PHP in a representative scenario as a computational tool for LSP request admission and routing; the analysis covers the typical QoS parameters of throughput and end-to-end transmission delay. *(iii) Admission control analysis:* its purpose is to evaluate admission-control parameters induced by the solution of a representative $DTEP$ instance with PHP.

Performance Analysis. The flows of the experiments were of *constant bit rate* (CBR) type and consisted of two priority types: *(i) low priority flows*: transmission rate between 20 and 150 Kbps with end-to-end delay constraint varying between 100 and 150 ms; *(ii) high priority flows*: transmission rate ranging from 380 to 870 Kbps with end-to-end delay constraint varying from 30 to 150 ms.

Each flow can be configured in one of 7 levels of transmission rate, i.e. $l_k = 7$ for $k = 1, \ldots, K$. The number of levels is an administrative decision that should take into account the traffic patterns. In our experiments, the use of 7 levels improved admission of low priority flows. The lowest level is set to zero Kbps, $\lambda_k^1 = 0$, which corresponds to rejecting the admission of the flow. The transmission rate of the subsequent levels increases exponentially up to the maximum desired transmission rate. The set of flow requests are generated randomly, according to a uniform distribution over the range of the parameters that define the requests. The optimal solution to each TEP instance was found by CPLEX solver, one of the leading optimization packages for mixed integer linear programming optimization. The network adopted for experimental analyses consists of 32 nodes and 18 transmission links, whose topology was taken from [4].

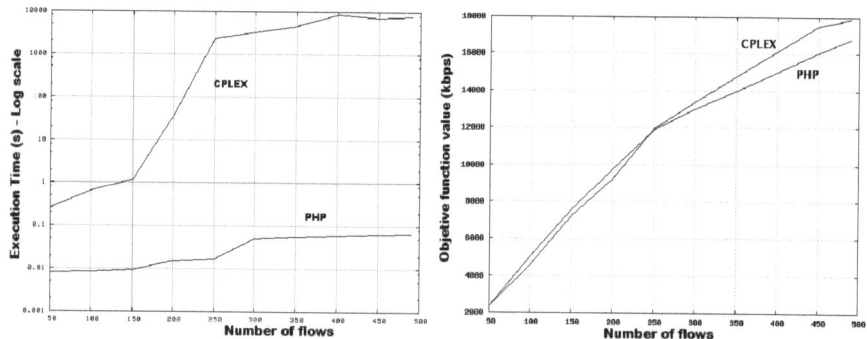

Fig. 1. Running time of PHP versus ILOG CPLEX for varying workloads (left) and quality of PHP solution compared with optimal solutions (right)

Figure 1 (left) gives the computation time[3] taken by PHP and CPLEX optimizer to solve a number of TEP instances in which we varied the workload (e.g. the number of flow requests). As expected, the computation time to obtain optimal solutions with CPLEX is high—TEP is an NP-Hard problem whose integer

---

[3] Note that the computation times are in logarithmic scale.

Table 1. QoS parameters for high priority flows

Flow Id	Throughput (Kbps)		Delay (ms)		QoS level
	Desired	Granted	Maximum	Incurred	
102	567	567	50	20	optimal
014	608	450	60	50	good
391	680	500	40	15	good
154	753	390	60	50	satisfactory

linear programming formulation has several decision variables and constraints. On the other hand, PHP is reasonably fast even for the largest instances.

Figure 1 (right) depicts the objective values of the solutions produced by PHP and CPLEX (optimal). The figure reveals that PHP can find nearly optimal solutions within a short time window, thereby supporting the claim that PHP can be effective at solving dynamic traffic engineering problems.

QoS Analysis. The purpose of the analysis herein is to assess the potential of PHP to solve $DTEP$. As a means to analyze simulation results qualitatively, we define three levels of QoS satisfaction: *(i) optimal*, when the maximum throughput is attained; *(ii) good*, when the throughput is at least 70% of the maximum; and *(iii) satisfactory*, when the throughput is at least 50% of the maximum. For a sample of the high priority flows, Table 1 shows the mean values of throughput and end-to-end transmission delay measured in the simulation time interval and compared with the respective maximum values. It is worth mentioning that the end-to-end delay constraints of all of the flow requests were not violated. The table shows that no delay violations are incurred to the high priority flows whose majority obtains good or optimal QoS level.

Admission Control Policy Analysis. Herein, we discuss some results regarding the admission control policy implemented by $DTEP$. In the experimental scenario, the mean of flow rejection in PHP solutions was small: about only 3% of the total number of flow requests were rejected, all of which had low priority.

The high priority flows were forced to wait less than 5 ms before being admitted by the network, which is sufficient time for PHP to find a solution to any problem of the sequence $\{TEP_t\}$ instantiated by $DTEP$. Around 3% of the low priority flows wait a time varying from 5 to 10 s before admission, but only about 12% of these low priority requests were dropped from the admission queue after 60 s due to time out.

The simulation results showed that the low priority flows experience a small QoS degradation under highly loaded operating conditions.

4   Distributed Solution of TEP

Heretofore, we have formulated the problem of operating a network as a series $\{TEP_t\}$ of problems, which are periodically solved to respond to the arrival and termination of LSP requests. Despite the fast speed of PHP, its reliance on central computations may become a liability with respect to fault tolerance, flexibility, and scalability. To this end, we will develop a framework to solve TEP_t approximately but distributively, whereby TEP_t is broken down in a set of decoupled Lagrangean subproblems. Section 4.1 deals with the decomposition rendered by relaxing constraints on bandwidth and maximum delay—this leads to a weaker decomposition but the subproblems are quickly solved with a modified Dijkstra's shortest-path algorithm. Section 4.2 addresses the decomposition obtained by relaxing only the bandwidth constraints—this decomposition is stronger and the computations can be carried out by distributed processes, but it entails solving singly constrained shortest-path problems which are NP-Hard.

4.1   Relaxing Bandwidth and Maximum Delay Constraints

By relaxing the bandwidth constraints (1.3) with Lagrangean multipliers $v = [v_{ij} : (i,j) \in E]$, $v \geq 0$, and the maximum delay constraints (1.4) with $w = [w_k : k \in \mathcal{K}]$, $w \geq 0$, we obtain the Lagrangean dual subproblem $L_1(v,w)$:

$$z_1(v,w) = \text{Max} \sum_{k=1}^{K} \sum_{l=1}^{l_k} \delta_k \lambda_k^l y_k^l + \sum_{(i,j) \in E} v_{ij} \left(\mu_{ij} - \sum_{k=1}^{K} \sum_{l=1}^{l_k} \lambda_k^l x_{ij}^{kl} \right) \quad (2.1)$$

$$+ \sum_{k=1}^{K} w_k \left(h_k - \sum_{l=1}^{l_k} \sum_{(i,j) \in E} c_{ij} x_{ij}^{kl} \right)$$

$$\text{S. to : constraints } (1.2), (1.5), (1.6), \text{ and } (1.7) \quad (2.2)$$

Variable v_{ij} acts as a penalty for bandwidth excess on arc (i,j), while w_k is the penalty for violation of the maximum transmission delay constraint on LSP k.

From the above formulation, it is evident that the variables of different LSPs are decoupled—the couplings originated from the constraints that now appear in the objective function, enabling us to search for LPS routes in parallel. Let $L(n) = \{k : s_k = n\}$ be the LSPs whose source node is n. Notice that $\bigcup_{n=1}^{N} L(n) = \mathcal{K}$. Then, we can break L_1 into a set $\{L_1(v,w,n)\}$ of subproblems, one for each $n \in V$, such that $L_1(v,w,n)$ is the restricted version of $L_1(v,w)$ including only the LSP requests originating from node n (the elements of $L(n)$). Let $z_1(v,w,n)$ denote the objective value of an optimal solution to $L_1(v,w,n)$.

It so happens that each subproblem $L_1(v,w,n)$ consists of a set of decoupled subproblems $L_1(v,w,n,k)$, namely a subproblem for each $k \in L(n)$ defined by:

$$z_1(v,w,n,k) = \text{Max} \sum_{l=1}^{l_k} \delta_k \lambda_k^l y_k^l - \sum_{l=1}^{l_k} \sum_{(i,j) \in E} (v_{ij} \lambda_k^l + w_k c_{ij}) x_{ij}^{kl} \quad (3.1)$$

$$\text{S. to : constraints } (2.2) \text{ restricted to all } l \in \mathcal{L}_k \quad (3.2)$$

Clearly, $z_1(v, w, n) = \sum_{k \in L(n)} z_1(v, w, n, k)$. An optimal solution to $L_1(v, w, n, k)$ can be obtained by computing l_k shortest paths with a modified Dijkstra's algorithm[4]. With a Fibonacci heap as priority queue, $L_1(v, w, n, k)$ can be solved in $O(l_k(N \log N + M))$ time. Thus, the router at node n can solve $L_1(v, w, n)$ in $O(\sum_{k \in L(n)} l_k(N \log N + M))$ time. Because $z_1(v, w)$ establishes an upper bound for z, the natural course of action is to solve the Lagrangean Dual:

$$LD_1 : z_1 = \text{Min } z_1(v, w) = \text{Min } \sum_{n \in V} z_1(v, w, n) + \sum_{k \in \mathcal{K}} w_k h_k + \sum_{(i,j) \in E} v_{ij} \mu_{ij}$$

$$= \text{Min } \sum_{n \in V} \sum_{k \in L(n)} (z_1(v, w, n, k) + w_k h_k) + \sum_{(i,j) \in E} v_{ij} \mu_{ij}$$

Although the Lagrangean dual LD_1 is not likely to produce a lower upper bound than linear relaxation of TEP (Section 10.2 of [1]), the dual solution tends to inherit features of the optimal solution to TEP, in that penalties are incurred for constraint violation. The issues that remain to be resolved are how we (approximately) solve LD_1 and whether the dual solution is satisfactory. Below, we present a distributed implementation of the subgradient algorithm [1] to solve LD_1 and thereafter assess the quality of the dual solutions numerically.

Distributed Subgradient Algorithm. The Lagrangean dual LD_1 is convex but nondifferentiable, making it unsuitable to apply efficient gradient-based procedures. The subgradient algorithm can be applied to solve LD_1, which can be viewed as a modified steepest-descent algorithm for nondifferentiable functions. The good news is that the subgradient algorithm can be implemented in a distributed fashion, not unlike the way the Lagrangean subproblem $L_1(v, w)$ can be solved distributively. Put simply, the subgradient algorithm uses the Lagrangean multipliers v_{ij} and w_k as penalty factors to discourage constraint violations: if the bandwidth constraint of a link (i, j) is not violated, then its Lagrangean multiplier v_{ij} is decreased by an amount that depends on the value of the subgradient; or else, the multiplier value is raised. The process is similar for the multipliers w_k. Iterations are performed until convergence is attained.

To implement the subgradient algorithm distributively, it suffices to have each network node i measuring the excess on bandwidth of each link (i, j) and broadcast this excess. This excess is the subgradient π_{ij} associated with the multiplier v_{ij}: v_{ij} will decrease if $\pi_{ij} < 0$ and increase otherwise. The multiplier θ_k for the delay constraint of an LSP k, $k \in L(n)$, can be computed locally by router n. A sketch of the distributed subgradient algorithm follows below.

Notice that $\pi_{n,j}^t$, as computed by router n, is the subgradient associated with arc (n, j): $\pi_{nj}^t = (\mu_{nj} - \sum_{k=1}^{K} \sum_{l=1}^{l_k} \lambda_k^l x_{nj}^{kl})$. At termination, the subgradient algorithm yields multipliers v and w that induce an upper bound $z_1(v, w)$ for z_1. The solution (x, y) to $L_1(v, w)$ is an approximate solution to TEP that, in the

---

[4] Notice that Dijkstra's algorithm can be applied because the cost of each arc (i, j) is given by $(v_{ij} \lambda_k^l + w_k c_{ij}) > 0$. If costs could be negative, then we would have to resort to slower Bellman-Ford's or Johnson's algorithm.

absence of constraint violation, is an optimal solution. Because the distributed subgradient algorithm is essentially a decentralized implementation of the standard subgradient algorithm, convergence to optimal Lagrangean multipliers can be ensured if certain rules for decreasing the step length δ^t are followed [1].

The Distributed Subgradient Algorithm

Let $t = 0$ be the iteration number, T be the max. number of iterations,
   $\epsilon > 0$ be a small constant, $\delta^t > 0$ be the initial decrement step,
   $v^t \in \mathbb{R}_+^M$ and $w^t \in \mathbb{R}_+^K$ be arbitrary Lagrangean multipliers
For $t = 1$ to T do
   Wait the routers coordinate to use the same values of t, δ^t, v^t, and w^t
   Each router n solves $L_1(v^t, w^t, n)$ to obtain a solution (x_n^t, y_n^t),
      where $x_n^t = [x_{ij}^{kl} : k \in L(n), l = 1, \dots, l_k, \forall (i,j) \in E]$ and
      $y_n^t = [y_k^l : k \in L(n), l = 1, \dots, l_k]$
   Let π^t be a subgradient for v^t, whereby each router n computes π_{nj}^t
      for all $(n,j) \in E$: π_{nj}^t is the excess on transmission in (i,j)
   Let θ^t be a subgradient for w^t. Each router n computes θ_k^t
      for all $k \in L(n)$: $\theta_k^t \leftarrow (h_k - \sum_{l=1}^{l_k} \sum_{(i,j) \in E} c_{ij} x_{ij}^{kl})$
   Let v^{t+1} be the next Lagrangean multip. for bandwidth. Each router n
      computes distributively: $v_{nj}^{t+1} \leftarrow \max\{0, v_{nj}^t + \delta^t \pi_{nj}^t\}$, $\forall (n,j) \in E$
   Let w^{t+1} be the next multipliers for maximum-delay. Each router n
      computes distributively: $w_k^{t+1} \leftarrow \max\{0, w_k^t + \delta^t \theta_k^t\}, \forall k \in L(n)$
   Let the routers obtain δ^{t+1} by decreasing δ^t and set $t \leftarrow t + 1$
   If $\delta^t < \epsilon$ then stop

Computational Experiments. We intend to evaluate the upper bounds from the approximate solutions to LD_1 and, last but not least, assess their quality as approximate solutions to TEP with respect to objective function, bandwidth constraint violation, and maximum delay. We adopted a decreasing schedule for the subgradient step whereby $\delta^0 = 2$ and $\delta^{t+1} = 0.9875\delta^t$. The initial multipliers v^t and w^t were selected at random within $[0, 10]$. The algorithm was allowed to iterate while $\delta^t \geq 10^{-6} = \epsilon$.

Table 2 depicts the results obtained with the (distributed) subgradient algorithm to the instances discussed in Section 3.2. For each instance, let $(\tilde{v}, \tilde{w})$ and $(\tilde{x}, \tilde{y})$ be the Lagrangean multipliers and solution to $L_1(\tilde{v}, \tilde{w})$, respectively. The 1st row gives the upper bound $z_1(\tilde{v}, \tilde{w})$. The 2nd row has the objective value induced by $(\tilde{x}, \tilde{y})$: $f(\tilde{y}) = \sum_{k=1}^{K} \sum_{l=1}^{l^k} \delta_k \lambda_k^l \tilde{y}_k^l$. The 3rd row gives the objective of the optimal solution to TEP. The 4th row gives the relative excess on bandwidth: $e_b(\tilde{x}) = [\sum_{(i,j) \in E} \max\{\sum_{k=1}^{K} \sum_{l=1}^{l_k} \lambda_k^l \tilde{x}_{ij}^{kl} - \mu_{ij}, 0\}] / [\sum_{k=1}^{K} \sum_{l=1}^{l_k} \sum_{(i,j) \in E} \lambda_k^l \tilde{x}_{ij}^{kl}]$. The 5th row gives the delay excess: $e_d(\tilde{x}) = \sum_{k=1}^{K} \sum_{l=1}^{l_k} \max\{\sum_{(i,j) \in E} c_{ij} \tilde{x}_{ij}^{kl} - h_k, 0\}$. The 6th row depicts the average computation time taken by the routers located at backbone nodes to run the subgradient algorithm.

From the table, we can infer that the objective value of the solutions produced by the subgradient algorithm are not significantly inferior to the optimal ones,

Table 2. Quality of the solution to the Lagrangean dual LD_1

Parameters	Number of LSP Requests (K)									
	50	100	150	200	250	300	350	400	450	490
$z_1(\tilde{v}, \tilde{w})$	2354	4539	7222	9503	12276	13178	14996	16430	17585	18020
$f(\tilde{y})$	2354	4539	7217	9227	11996	13178	14909	16200	16358	16995
Optimal objective	2354	4539	7217	9227	11955	13173	14771	16134	17150	17898
$e_b(\tilde{x})$ (%)	0	0	20.11	24.26	23.88	33.25	29.62	23.26	23.83	25.22
$e_d(\tilde{x})$	0	0	0	8	0	0	14	13	0	1
Comp. time (s)	0.215	0.324	1.418	1.986	2.451	2.923	3.505	3.994	4.483	4.870

and they can be attained far more quickly than using CPLEX. The results show that the excess on bandwidth capacity is significant, of the order of 23% of the total bandwidth allocation, while the excess on transmission delay is quite low.

4.2   Relaxing Bandwidth Constraints

Here we look into the decomposition of TEP yielded by relaxing only the bandwidth constraints (1.3). Given a set of Lagrangean multipliers $v = [v_{ij} \in \mathbb{R}_+ : (i,j) \in E]$ for bandwidth, the Lagrangean subproblem $L_2(v)$ can be cast as:

$$z_2(v) = \text{Max} \quad \sum_{k=1}^{K}\sum_{l=1}^{l_k} \delta_k \lambda_k^l y_k^l + \sum_{(i,j)\in E} v_{ij}\left(\mu_{ij} - \sum_{k=1}^{K}\sum_{l=1}^{l_k} \lambda_k^l x_{ij}^{kl}\right) \quad (4.1)$$

$$\text{S. to : constraints } (1.2),(1.4),(1.5),(1.6), \text{ and } (1.7) \quad (4.2)$$

As in the above developments, $L_2(v)$ consists of K decoupled subproblems of choosing the transmission level of each LSP k, y_k^l, and selecting a path from the source s_k to the destination d_k without exceeding maximum delay in transmission—the bandwidth capacity constraints were dualized and placed as penalty factors in the objective. First, let us break up $L_2(v)$ into N subproblems to be solved at each backbone node n, hereafter denoted by $L_2(v, n)$ whose optimal solution has value $z_2(v, n)$. Because a solution to $L_2(v)$ can be obtained by aggregating the solutions to the elements of $\{L_2(v, n)\}$, the objective value of the Lagrangean subproblem becomes: $z_2(v) = \sum_{n \in V} z_2(v, n) + \sum_{(i,j) \in E} v_{ij}\mu_{ij}$.

Continuing the problem break up, each $L_2(v, n)$ can be spliced into $|L(n)|$ decoupled subproblems, one for each $k \in L(n)$. Let $\{L(v, n, k)\}$ be the subproblems obtained by decomposing $L(v, n)$, with $L(v, n, k)$ defined by:

$$z_2(v, n, k) = \text{Max} \quad \sum_{l=1}^{l_k} \delta_k \lambda_k^l y_k^l - \sum_{l=1}^{l_k}\sum_{(i,j)\in E} v_{ij}\lambda_k^l x_{ij}^{kl} \quad (5.1)$$

$$\text{S. to : constraints } (4.2) \text{ restricted to all } l \in \mathcal{L}_k \quad (5.2)$$

The end result is the break up of $L_2(v)$ into a set $\{L_2(v, n, k) : n \in V, k \in L(n)\}$ of subproblems that can be solved asynchronously. The subset $\{L_2(v, n, k)\}$ is

Table 3. Quality of the solution to the Lagrangean dual LD_2

	Number of LSP Requests (K)							
Parameters	50	100	150	200	250	300	350	400
Upper bound $z_2(\tilde{v})$	2354	4539	7217	9283	12126	13455	14862	16336
Obj func $f(\tilde{y})$	2354	4539	7217	9227	11996	13379	14909	16107
Bandwidth excess $e_b(\tilde{x})$ (%)	0	5.68	18.15	34.24	40.48	46.79	30.29	21.97
Comp time (s)	88.62	95.50	144.25	183.12	237.37	287.62	339.37	385.25

solved by router n and the solution to $L_2(v)$ is obtained by combining the distributed solutions. Thus: $z_2(v) = \sum_{n \in V} \sum_{k \in L(n)} z_2(v, n, k) + \sum_{(i,j) \in E} v_{ij} \mu_{ij}$.

Calculating $z_2(v, n, k)$ entails solving l_k constrained shortest path problems. So $L_2(v, n, k)$ is an NP-Hard problem [5]. One way of solving $L_2(v, n, k)$ consists in computing l_k constrained shortest path with dynamic programming, one for each level of transmission of the kth LSP. Given the penalty vector v, a router node $n \in V$, an LSP $k \in L(n)$, and a transmission level $l \in \{1, \ldots, l_k\}$, the problem of finding a shortest path from s_k to d_k subject to the maximum delay constraint can be expressed recursively, provided that the parameters h_k are integers. Let $d(i, t, h)$ be the distance of a shortest path from node i to node d_k that contains at most t arcs and whose transmission delay is at most h. Having introduced this terminology, the recurrences can be stated as:

$$
\begin{cases}
d(i, 0, h) = +\infty, \; \forall i \in V - \{d_k\}, h = 0, \ldots, h_k \\
d(d_k, 0, h) = 0, \; h = 0, \ldots, h_k \\
d(i, t, h) = \min\{d(i, t - 1, h), \\
\quad \min\{v_{ij} \lambda_k^l + d(j, t - 1, h - c_{ij}) : (i, j) \in E, c_{ij} \le h\}\}, \\
\quad \forall i \in V, t = 1, \ldots, N - 1, h = 0, \ldots, h_k
\end{cases}
\tag{6}
$$

An optimal solution to $L(v, n, k)$ can be obtained by solving a set $\{L(v, n, k, l) : l = 1, \ldots, l_k\}$ of subproblems, where $L(v, n, k, l)$ is the problem $L(v, n, k)$ in which $y_k^l = 1$. It is straightforward to solve the recurrences (6) with dynamic programming to reach a solution to $L(v, n, k, l)$. For details on the steps of the dynamic programming algorithm, the interested reader can refer to [5].

The issues regarding the solution of LD_2 via a subgradient procedure and convergence to an optimal value z_2 are, in essence, identical to the ones raised in Section 4.1. To divide the computational burden of solving LD_2 among the routers, we can design a distributed subgradient algorithm by discarding the Lagrangean multipliers w of the preceding (distributed) subgradient algorithm, and solving $z_2(v)$ distributively in each step rather than $z_1(v, w)$.

Computational Experiments. We implemented the subgradient algorithm to solve LD_2 approximately. The numerical results reported in Table 3 provide evidence that the upper bound $z_2(\tilde{v})$ is tighter than $z_1(\tilde{v}, \tilde{w})$. However, the dual solution $(\tilde{x}, \tilde{y})$ induced by solving LD_2 is inferior to that obtained by solving

LD_1, namely the bandwidth violation is higher than that incurred by the solution to LD_1, and the computational cost far exceeds the cost of solving LD_1. An alternative to expedite the solution process is to resort to an approximate algorithm to solve $L_2(v, n, k, l)$ such as those from [6]. An alternative to reduce the duality gap is to solve the Lagrangean dual with the methods from [5].

5   Discussion and Concluding Remarks

Several works aim to solve similar network operating problems to ours. But the differences among the models, mainly in the order of LSP admission, prevents a quantitative comparison. In [7], the authors propose a load balancing scheme based on an admission control policy that considers only the link bandwidth capacity. But their proposal does not optimize the network performance. In [4], the authors deal with a generalization of a multi-objective shortest path problem subject to multiple constraints. To date, our developments do not handle multiple objectives but they can be extended as in [4]. In [8], the authors propose a distributed Lagrangean optimization approach to solve distributively a TE problem. However, they assume that the routes connecting source and destination nodes are given and they consider only constraints on link bandwidth, whereas we design paths and currently tackle link bandwidth and also transmission limits.

Our work has shown that the PHP framework attains a high degree of optimality, demanding low computational cost and being simpler than alternative algorithms for solving TE problems. Unlike other solution approaches, our framework implements an admission control policy to manage flows with different levels of priority.

The Lagrangean relaxation of the constraints on bandwidth and end-to-end transmission delay decomposed TEP into a set of smaller subproblems, $\{TEP_n\}$, one for each router n. The preliminary analysis of the distributed solution of $\{TEP_n\}$ has shown promise. The decomposition LD_1, obtained by dualizing bandwidth and end-to-end delay constraints, yielded tight upper bounds and was relatively fast to compute. The decomposition LD_2, obtained by dualizing only the bandwidth constraints, yielded tighter upper bounds but at the expense of higher computational cost and relying on a more complex, time-consuming dynamic programming algorithm. Two possibilities are the design of heuristics to keep the violations under limits and the application of multi-objective optimization algorithms, which would simultaneously maximize weighted throughput and minimize constraint violation.

References

1. Wolsey, L.A.: Integer Programming. John Wiley & Sons (1998)
2. Girish, M., Zhou, B., Hu, J.Q.: Formulation of the traffic engineering problems in MPLS based IP networks. In: Proc. IEEE ISCC. (2000)

3. Garey, M.R., Johnson, D.S.: Computers and Intractability: A Guide to the Theory of NP-Completeness. W. H. Freeman and Company (1979)
4. Banerjee, G., Sidhu, D.: Comparative analysis of path computation techniques for MPLS traffic engineering. Computer Networks **40** (2002) 149–165
5. Ziegelmann, M.: Constrained Shortest Paths and Related Problems. PhD thesis, Universitat des Saarlandes, Germany (2001)
6. Hassin, R.: Approximation schemes for the restricted shortest path problem. Mathematics of Operations Research **17** (1992) 36–42
7. Salvadori, E., Batiti, R.: A load balancing scheme for congestion control in MPLS networks. In: Proc. IEEE ISCC. (2003)
8. Xiaojun, L., Ness, S.B.: An optimization based approach for QoS routing in high bandwidth networks. In: Proc. IEEE INFOCOM. (2004)

Avoiding Transient Loops Through Interface-Specific Forwarding

Zifei Zhong[1], Ram Keralapura[2], Srihari Nelakuditi[1], Yinzhe Yu[3],
Junling Wang[1], Chen-Nee Chuah[2], and Sanghwan Lee[3]

[1] Department of Computer Science & Engineering,
University of South Carolina, Columbia, SC 29208, USA
{zhongz, srihari, wang257}@cse.sc.edu
[2] Department of Electrical & Computer Engineering,
University of California at Davis, Davis, CA 95616, USA
{rkeralap, chuah}@ece.ucdavis.edu
[3] Department of Computer Science & Engineering,
University of Minnesota, Minneapolis, MN 55414, USA
{yyu, sanghwan}@cs.umn.edu

Abstract. Under link-state routing protocols such as OSPF and IS-IS, when there is a change in the topology, propagation of link-state announcements, path recomputation, and updating of forwarding tables (FIBs) will all incur some delay before traffic forwarding can resume on alternate paths. During this convergence period, routers may have inconsistent views of the network, resulting in transient forwarding loops. Previous remedies proposed to address this issue enforce a certain order among the nodes in which they update their FIBs. While such approaches succeed in avoiding transient loops, they incur additional message overhead and increased convergence delay. We propose an alternate approach, *loopless interface-specific forwarding* (LISF), that averts transient loops by forwarding a packet based on both its incoming interface and destination. LISF requires no modifications to the existing link-state routing mechanisms. It is easily deployable with current routers since they already maintain a FIB at each interface for lookup efficiency. This paper presents the LISF approach, proves its correctness, discusses three alternative implementations of it and evaluates their performance.

1 Introduction

The widely used link state routing protocols such as OSPF and IS-IS distribute link states so that each router has a complete description of the network topology. When a link fails due to a faulty interface or a fiber cut [1], the nodes adjacent to the failure detect it and flood this change in link state to the rest of the network so that all the routers can recompute their routing tables. These routing table entries are then pushed onto Forwarding Information Base (FIB) at all line cards. Each of these steps – failure detection, link state propagation, routing table recomputation and FIB updates – incur some delay. Only after these steps

H. de Meer and N. Bhatti (Eds.): IWQoS 2005, LNCS 3552, pp. 219–232, 2005.

are complete, packets, for which the shortest paths to their destinations are affected by the failed link, are guaranteed to be forwarded correctly along the new alternate paths. The interval between the failure detection and the FIB updates at all the routers, is referred to as the *convergence delay*. During the convergence period, routers may have inconsistent views of the network and therefore can cause forwarding loops [2]. While these loops last for only a short time and their effect is mitigated by the TTL field in IP datagrams, they can still overwhelm high capacity links and render them unusable. Therefore, it is desirable to avoid any forwarding loops even if they are only transient.

Several remedies for the transient looping problem have been suggested in the literature [2,3,4,5,6][1] and an IETF working group has been addressing this issue [9]. Path locking with safe neighbors approach [2] categorizes routes into three types A, B, or C, and installs new routes for B and C types after a fixed configurable delay such that delay for type B is greater than delay for type C routes. While this approach decreases the likelihood of loops, it does not completely eliminate them. Moreover, it introduces additional delays in the installation of new routes compounding the convergence delay. A loop-free path-finding algorithm proposed in [3] blocks a potential loop when it detects that a loop can be formed. To achieve this, a router first reports to all its neighbors that its distance to reach the destination is infinity, and then waits for those neighbors to acknowledge its message with their own distances and predecessor information before updating its successor in the forwarding table. Recently, similar methods have been proposed in [4,5], where the forwarding table updates in the network are ordered such that a node updates its forwarding table only after all its neighbors that use the node to reach different destinations through the failed link update their forwarding tables. Although these schemes do avoid transient loops, they require additional messages to be exchanged among routers, to enforce the ordering of the updates of forwarding tables, resulting in increased convergence delay.

In this paper, we propose an alternate approach – *loopless interface-specific forwarding* (LISF) – that exploits the existence of one forwarding table per interface to avoid transient loops without requiring any changes to the existing link state routing mechanisms. When all the routers in a network have the same view of the network, there would not be a forwarding loop. Only in the presence of discrepancies in the views of different routers, a packet might get caught in a loop. In such a case, the packet would have arrived through an *unusual* interface of at least one of the routers involved in the loop. Therefore, a forwarding loop can be avoided if the packet were to be discarded in such a scenario rather than forwarded to the usual next hop. LISF does precisely that by selectively discarding packets that arrive through unusual interfaces. The key advantages of LISF are that it avoids transient loops without increasing the convergence delay

---

[1] Many other schemes have been proposed to deal with failures through fast local rerouting [7,5,8]. However, the focus of this paper is on schemes specifically designed for loop avoidance during convergence after a network-wide link state update.

and without employing any additional mechanisms to synchronize the forwarding table updates in different nodes.

The rest of this paper is structured as follows. In Section 2, we illustrate the problem of transient loops. Our LISF approach for avoiding forwarding loops and three possible implementations of it are described in Section 3. In Section 4, we prove that the proposed LISF methods prevent loops in case of symmetric single link failures. The results of our simulations evaluating the LISF methods are presented in Section 5. We finally conclude the paper in Section 6.

2   Transient Looping Problem and Existing Approaches

We now illustrate the occurrence of transient loops, discuss a recently proposed approach for avoiding them, and point out the need for an alternate approach.

We use an example to illustrate the problem of transient loops. Consider the topology shown in Fig. 1(a), where each directed link is labeled with its weight. For the purpose of illustration, let us assume that all the nodes have similar characteristics with a *failure detection time* of 50ms, a *failure notification time* between neighboring nodes of 100ms, and *route computation and update time* of 400ms at a node (100ms for nodes that are not affected by the failure).

Consider a scenario where link E−D fails at time 0s. We examine how this failure impacts the forwarding of packets from source node A to destination node D. Table 1 summarizes the routing events under the traditional OSPF and the corresponding changes in the packet's forwarding path from node A to node D. The resulting convergence delay (i.e., the total time for all the nodes in the network to converge after the failure) is 0.65s, and the service disruption time (i.e., the total time for which the service between A and D is disrupted due to the failure) is 0.55s. During the interval between the forwarding table updates in nodes E and F (i.e, between 0.45s and 0.55s), both the nodes have a different view of the network, resulting in a forwarding loop.

To avoid transient loops during the convergence after a planned link failure or an unplanned failure of a protected link, a method was proposed in [4] that

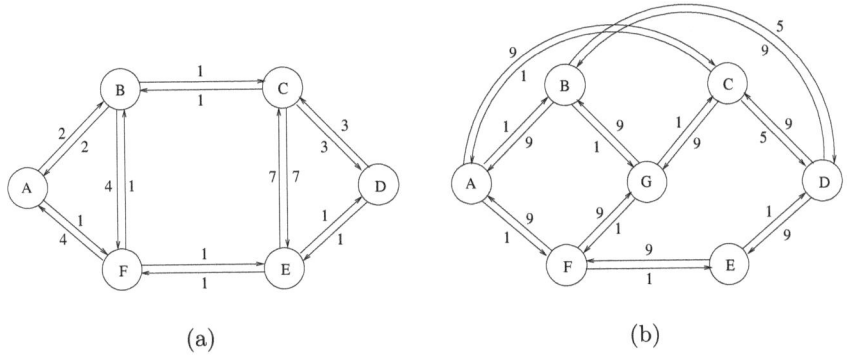

(a)   (b)

Fig. 1. Topologies used for illustration

Table 1. Summary of routing events under OSPF, ORDR, and LISF

	OSPF		LISF	ORDR	
Time	Events	A to D pkts	A to D pkts	Events	
0s	Failure of link E-D	A-F-E-drop	A-F-E-drop	Failure of link E-D	
0.05s	D,E: failure detected	A-F-E-drop	A-F-E-drop	D,E: failure detected	
0.15s	C,F: failure notified	A-F-E-drop	A-F-E-drop	C,F: failure notified	
0.25s	A,B: failure notified	A-F-E-drop	A-F-E-drop	A,B: failure notified	
0.35s	B: route update	A-F-E-drop	A-F-E-drop	B: route update	
0.45s	D,E: route update	A-F-E-F-...(**loop**)	A-F-E-F-**drop**		
0.55s	C,F: route update	A-F-B-C-D	A-F-B-C-D	C: route update	
0.65s	A: route update	A-B-C-D	A-B-C-D	A: route update	
1.05s				D: route update	
1.15s				F: route update	
1.65s				E: route update	

ensures ordered installation of forwarding table entries by exchanging messages between neighboring nodes. Here, we consider a similar approach (which we refer to as ORDR) for avoiding loops in case of unplanned failures (around 80% of all failures according to [1]) of unprotected links. The routing events under ORDR corresponding to Fig. 1(a) are shown in Table 1. Note that with this method, F updates its forwarding table 500 ms (assuming update time of 400 ms and the message propagation and processing time of 100 ms) after A updates its table. While this method avoids forwarding loops, its drawback is that it increases the network convergence delay. For the scenario discussed here, this method extends the convergence delay to 1.65s.

Our objective is to develop a scheme that combines the best features of OSPF and ORDR, i.e., low convergence delay and disruption time of OSPF and loop avoidance of ORDR. Such a scheme would ideally respond to the failure of E−D as shown in Table 1. Its behavior would be effectively similar to OSPF except that a packet is dropped if it would loop otherwise (as in the case of packets destined to D from F or E during the interval from 0.45s to 0.55s). Consequently, the ideal scheme would have the convergence delay of 0.65s and service disruption time of 0.45s while also avoiding forwarding loops. In the following sections, we present and evaluate a scheme that closely approximates this ideal behavior.

3   Our Approach

Our approach for avoiding forwarding loops is based on the notion of *interface-specific forwarding*, where a packet's forwarding depends on the incoming interface in addition to the destination address. In this section, we first briefly explain interface-specific forwarding and argue how it can be exploited to avoid loops. We then present three methods of computing interface-specific forwarding table entries and illustrate the differences between these methods in terms of loop avoidance and computational complexity.

3.1   Interface-Specific Forwarding

A packet in an IP network is traditionally routed based on its destination address alone regardless of its source address or the incoming interface. Therefore, a single forwarding table that maps a destination address to a next hop and an outgoing interface is sufficient for current routers to perform IP datagram forwarding. Nevertheless, routers nowadays maintain a forwarding table at each line card of an interface for lookup efficiency. However, all these forwarding tables at each interface are identical, i.e., these forwarding tables are interface-independent. For example, interface-independent forwarding tables at node B of Fig. 1(a) are as given in Table 2.

Instead of maintaining the same forwarding table at each interface, it is possible to avoid forwarding loops by making the entries of these forwarding tables *interface-specific*. Table 3 gives the possible set of interface-specific forwarding table entries at node B of Fig. 1(a). Each entry is marked with '−', **X**, or a nexthop node. The entries marked '−' are obviously never used. The entries marked **X** are not referenced normally, i.e., when there is no failure and all nodes in the network have the same consistent view. For example, in Fig. 1(a), a packet with destination D should not arrive at B from any of its neighbors since B is not the next hop for them. Similarly, B should not receive from A, a packet destined for F, since A is along the path from B to F. However, in the presence of link failures and inconsistent forwarding tables at different nodes (during the convergence period), a packet may arrive at a node through an unusual interface. Interface-specific forwarding enables special treatment of such packets that arrive through unusual interfaces without introducing any changes to the forwarding plane of the current network infrastructure. Here, we study how interface-specific forwarding can be exploited for the purpose of avoiding loops during the convergence period after a link state change in the network.

Table 2. Interface-independent forwarding tables at node B

		destination			
		A	C	D	E	F
interface	A→B	A	C	C	A	A
	C→B	A	C	C	A	A
	F→B	A	C	C	A	A

Table 3. Interface-specific forwarding tables at node B

		destination			
		A	C	D	E	F
interface	A→B	−	C	**X**	**X**	**X**
	C→B	A	−	**X**	**X**	A
	F→B	A	C	**X**	**X**	−

3.2   Loopless Interface-Specific Forwarding

It is clear that under link state routing, when all the routers in a network have the same view of the network, there would not be a forwarding loop. Only in the presence of discrepancies in the views of different routers, a packet might get caught in a loop. However, in such a case, under interface-specific forwarding, the packet would have arrived through an unusual interface of at least one of the routers involved in the loop. So a forwarding loop can be avoided if the packet were to be discarded in such a scenario rather than forwarded to the usual next hop. We refer to this approach of avoiding forwarding loops by selectively discarding packets that arrive through unusual interfaces as *loopless interface-specific forwarding* (LISF).

Ideally, a packet should be discarded by a router only if its forwarding would definitely result in a loop. However, with only its own local view of the network, a router cannot always determine the actual forwarding path of a packet with certainty. Therefore, the design challenge of LISF is to ensure loop freedom without unnecessarily discarding packets. In this paper, we study several implementation choices of LISF, ranging from conservative discarding of packets only if there would certainly be a loop otherwise but forwarding even if there could be a loop, to aggressively discarding of packets whenever there could be a loop even if there may not actually be a loop.

Before we proceed to present various LISF methods, we first introduce some notation that would help describe them. Let $\mathcal{G} = (\mathcal{V}, \mathcal{E})$ be the graph with vertices $\mathcal{V}$ and edges $\mathcal{E}$ representing the network. We use $\mathcal{R}_i^d$ to denote the next hop[2] from i to d in $\mathcal{G}$. Let $\mathcal{F}_{j \to i}^d$ denote the forwarding table entry, i.e., the next hop to d for packets arriving at i through the interface associated with neighbor j. We use $\mathcal{P}_i^d$ to refer to the shortest path from i to d given the graph $\mathcal{G}$. Similarly, the cost of the shortest path is denoted by $\mathcal{C}_i^d$.

We now present three different LISF methods. The difference between these methods lies in which of the entries marked **X** in Table 3 are set to $\ominus$, meaning *discard*. These methods are named according to the criterion they use to discard a packet. The operation of these methods, when a packet for destination d arrives at node i from neighbor j, is summarized in Table 4 and elaborated in detail below. It should be noted that, under LISF, a node i makes packet forwarding/discarding decisions based solely on its own view of the network.

PIPO. Discard a packet if its incoming and outgoing interfaces are the same, i.e., $\mathcal{F}_{j \to i}^d = \ominus$ if $j \in \mathcal{R}_i^d$.

PIPO discards a packet only when it arrives at a node from its next hop, i.e., along the reverse shortest path to the destination. It is the most conservative of all the methods listed here as it discards a packet only when there is a loop. Otherwise, without PIPO, in such a scenario, packets will ping-pong between two neighboring nodes. For example, in Table 5, a packet to destination D arriving

---

[2] Note that LISF works even with Equal Cost Multipath (ECMP) routing. But for ease of explanation, it is assumed that there is only one shortest path per destination.

Table 4. Differences in LISF methods in discarding a packet to d arriving at i from j

method	discard condition	discard criterion
PIng-POng (PIPO)	$j \in \mathcal{R}_i^d$	in and out interfaces are same
CYCLe (CYCL)	$j \in \mathcal{P}_i^d$	previous node along the path
NO Forward Progress (NOFP)	$\mathcal{C}_{\mathcal{R}_i^d}^d \geq \mathcal{C}_j^d$	no forward progress

Table 5. Interface-specific forwarding tables at B under different LISF methods

interface		destination A	C	D	E	F	destination A	C	D	E	F	destination A	C	D	E	F
	A→B	–	C	**C**	$\ominus$	$\ominus$	–	C	**C**	$\ominus$	$\ominus$	–	C	$\ominus$	$\ominus$	$\ominus$
	C→B	A	–	$\ominus$	A	A	A	–	$\ominus$	A	A	A	–	$\ominus$	A	A
	F→B	A	C	**C**	**A**	–	A	C	**C**	$\ominus$	–	A	C	$\ominus$	$\ominus$	–
		(PIPO)					(CYCL)					(NOFP)				

at B from C is discarded by PIPO since C is the next hop to D from B. PIPO is also the simplest since it incurs no additional overhead for computing interface-specific forwarding table entries beyond the currently used Dijkstra's algorithm for computing interface-independent forwarding tables. However, PIPO can ensure loop-freedom only when two nodes are involved in a loop, which is the case when links are *symmetric* (bidirectional with equal weights in both directions) and inconsistency in the views among routers is limited to a single link's state.

CYCL. Discard a packet if the previous node appears along the path from this node to the destination, i.e., $\mathcal{F}_{j \to i}^d = \ominus$ if $j \in \mathcal{P}_i^d$.

CYCL discards a packet when it arrives from a node which falls along the shortest path from this node to the destination. When the links are symmetric, CYCL behaves just like PIPO. Only when links are asymmetric and the resulting paths are asymmetric, the operation of CYCL could be different from PIPO. With a less stringent condition than PIPO, CYCL may discard a packet even when there may not actually be a loop, but at the same time, it can avoid some loops that are not avoided by PIPO. For example, in Table 5, a packet to destination E arriving at B from F is forwarded by PIPO to A resulting in a loop whereas it will be discarded by CYCL since F is along the shortest path from B to E. The computational complexity of CYCL is similar to that of PIPO as both require only a single shortest path tree computation.

NOFP. Discard a packet if there is no forward progress towards its destination from its previous hop to the next hop of this node, i.e., $\mathcal{F}_{j \to i}^d = \ominus$ if $\mathcal{C}_{\mathcal{R}_i^d}^d \geq \mathcal{C}_j^d$.

Table 6. Differences among LISF methods in discarding packets arriving at node B

from	to	failed link	PIPO	CYCL	NOFP
C	D	C−D	discard	discard	discard
F	E	F−E	forward to A	discard	discard
F	D	F−E	forward to C	forward to C	discard
C	E	C−D	forward to A	forward to A	forward to A

NOFP discards a packet if its previous hop is not farther from its destination than the next hop of this node. In such a case, there is a potential for a loop and NOFP discards such packets. For example, in Table 5, a packet to destination D arriving at B from F is discarded by NOFP since the cost from F to D is 2 whereas the cost from the next hop C is 3. This is in contrast to both PIPO and CYCL which forward the packet to C. While such discarding by NOFP seems unnecessary, NOFP can prevent more loops than PIPO and CYCL even when links are asymmetric and the state of multiple links change simultaneously. For example, in topology shown in Fig. 1(b), suppose link F−E failed. Further, assume that all nodes except nodes B and C are notified of the failure and their forwarding tables reflect the failure. In this scenario, under PIPO and CYCL, a packet from A to D is forwarded along a loop A−B−G−C−A−B···. On the other hand, under NOFP, it is discarded by B since, according to B's view, the cost of 3 from next hop G to D is not smaller than the cost from A to D which is also 3. The downside however is that, a straightforward method to implement NOFP requires a computation of $O(\frac{|\mathcal{E}|}{|V|})$ times Dijkstra on the average (to compute the shortest path trees rooted at each neighbor), whereas PIPO and CYCL have the same complexity as Dijkstra.

The difference between the actions of the above three methods is clearly evident in the presence of failures of links C−D and F−E in Fig. 1(a) as shown in Table 6. Here it is assumed that B is not yet aware of the failed links and the forwarding tables of B do not reflect the change. When only F−E fails, packets from F to D arriving at B are discarded by NOFP whereas PIPO and CYCL forward them along a loop-free path via C. Essentially these methods achieve different tradeoffs between loop-avoidance and packet-discarding, which can be summed up as follows.

- packet looping probability: PIPO ≥ CYCL ≥ NOFP
- packet discard probability: PIPO ≤ CYCL ≤ NOFP
- network convergence delay: PIPO = CYCL = NOFP

4   Proof of Loop-Free Property of LISF

We now prove that the LISF methods described in the previous section ensure loop-freedom when at most a single link state change is being propagated in a

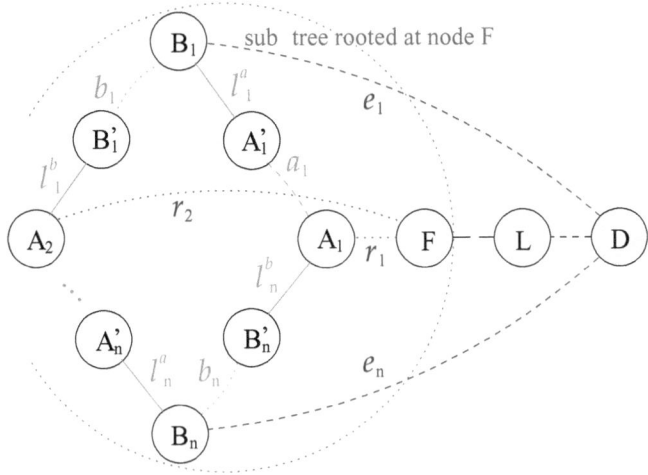

Fig. 2. Scenarios for illustrating loop-freedom under PIPO

network with symmetric links. It is clear that if PIPO is loop-free, other two methods are also loop-free since whenever PIPO discards a packet, they would too. Therefore, it suffices to provide the proof for PIPO which is given below.

We use the following notation in this section. Let $\mathcal{T}^D$ be the shortest path tree with undirected links rooted at a destination D. Note that this tree contains the shortest paths from every node to D since the links are symmetric. We use $S(i, \mathcal{T})$ to denote the subtree of $\mathcal{T}$ below the node i. Since the forwarding to a destination is independent of forwarding to other destinations, in the following we prove it for a destination D.

Theorem 1. *A packet destined for D will not loop under PIPO in case of the failure of a link ℓ.*

Proof. If $\ell \notin \mathcal{T}^D$, the forwarding path to D is the same with or without the failure of ℓ. Therefore, the forwarding to D is consistent at every node along the path and hence packets destined for D will not be caught in a loop due to the failure of ℓ. In the rest of the proof, it is assumed that $\ell \in \mathcal{T}^D$.

Let $\ell = F{-}L$ and F be the upstream node to L on the path from F to D as in Fig. 2. When ℓ is down, only those nodes in $S(F, \mathcal{T}^D)$ will be affected (i.e., all nodes outside the subtree will forward along the same path with or without F-L for destination D). Now consider a packet originating from any node in $S(F, \mathcal{T}^D)$. That packet may be forwarded to node F and then get rerouted, or get rerouted somewhere in $S(F, \mathcal{T}^D)$. Once the packet goes outside the subtree, it will be forwarded to D consistently. So the only possible loop is the one consisting of nodes which are all within $S(F, \mathcal{T}^D)$. Thus, to prove loop-freedom under PIPO, we only need to show that there will not be a loop within $S(F, \mathcal{T}^D)$.

Suppose there is a loop in subtree $S(F, \mathcal{T}^D)$. The loop must contain some nodes that are *aware* and some that are *unaware* of the failed link F$-$L. Pick an arbitrary node, A_1, in the loop that is aware of the failure. As shown in Fig. 2, suppose the packet starts from A_1 and is routed along zero or more "A" nodes (i.e., nodes that are aware of the failure and forward in consistence as A_1), and reaches A_1', the last "A" node in this stretch. A_1' forwards the packet to B_1, a node unaware of the failure. Note that from A_1 to B_1, the forwarding is consistent (with $\mathcal{P}_{A_1}^D (\mathcal{E} \setminus \ell)$). We use the dashed line to indicate this subpath of $\mathcal{P}_{A_1}^D (\mathcal{E} \setminus \ell)$. B_1 then reroutes the packet: instead of towards D via the dashed path, it forwards the packet via the dotted path towards B_1', i.e., it chooses $B_1 \rightsquigarrow B_1' \rightarrow A_2 \rightsquigarrow F \rightarrow L \rightsquigarrow D$. Similarly, the packet is rerouted at A_2, which intends to forward it to D through the next stretch of dashed path. This process continues until the packet is forwarded back to A_1 by $B_n (n \geq 1)$.

Now we show that there is a contradiction if such a loop exists. Note that in such a loop, any B_i can not forward a packet back to A_i' after getting the packet from A_i' (e.g., $A_{i+1}' \neq A_i'$), as the packet will get dropped under PIPO when being forwarded back to A_i'. Then consider the reroute decision at node $B_i (1 \leq i \leq n)$. Since the node B_i chooses the path $B_i \rightsquigarrow A_{i+1} \rightsquigarrow F$ over $B_i \rightsquigarrow A_{i-1} \rightsquigarrow F$, we have

$$\sum_{i=1}^{n-1} (b_i + l_i^b + r_{i+1}) < \sum_{i=1}^{n-1} (a_i + l_i^a + r_i) \tag{1}$$

$$b_n + l_n^b + r_1 < a_n + l_n^a + r_n \tag{2}$$

Adding them together, we have

$$\sum_{i=1}^{n} (b_i + l_i^b) < \sum_{i=1}^{n} (a_i + l_i^a) \tag{3}$$

Similarly, consider the rerouting decision made at node A_i. Since it chooses the path $A_i \rightsquigarrow B_i \rightsquigarrow D$ over the path $A_i \rightsquigarrow B_{i-1} \rightsquigarrow D$,

$$\sum_{i=1}^{n-1} (a_{i+1} + l_{i+1}^a + e_{i+1}) < \sum_{i=1}^{n-1} (b_i + l_i^b + e_i) \tag{4}$$

$$a_1 + l_1^a + e_1 < b_n + l_n^b + e_n \tag{5}$$

Adding them together, we get

$$\sum_{i=1}^{n} (a_i + l_i^a) < \sum_{i=1}^{n} (b_i + l_i^b) \tag{6}$$

Obviously, formula (6) above contradicts formula (3). Therefore, a forwarding loop is not possible under PIPO in case of a single link failure.

Using similar arguments as above, we can show that PIPO avoids forwarding loops during the convergence period after not only a failure but any change in the state of a link.

5   Performance Evaluation

In this section, we evaluate the performance of LISF methods and compare them against OSPF and ORDR. We first simulate single link failures and demonstrate that LISF methods prevent a significant number of loops that are possible under OSPF, and also have lower convergence delay than ORDR. We then experiment with scenarios of multiple failures to further study the tradeoffs of LISF methods between packet-discarding and loop-avoidance.

5.1   Single Link Failures

To evaluate LISF methods, we built a control plane simulator that emulates intra-domain routing dynamics in the presence of link failures and measures both service disruption (SD) time between different origin-destination (OD) pairs and network convergence (NC) time as presented in [10]. We use a Tier-1 ISP backbone (PoP-level) topology with 20 nodes and 42 links in our simulations which was used earlier in [10]. We assign OSPF link weights to different links by randomly picking integer values between 1 and 5. We consider both symmetric links where $X{\to}Y$ has the same OSPF weight as $Y{\to}X$, and asymmetric links where the OSPF weight for $X{\to}Y$ could be different from $Y{\to}X$. The forwarding table at each node includes entries for all the prefixes in the Internet. We assume that the rate of FIB update is 20 entries/ms and the number of prefixes is 161352. The other parameters in the simulator are set based on the findings in [11]. In every simulation run, we fail each link in the network exactly once. The results presented below represent the effect of all the link failures in a simulation run.

The total time during which a forwarding loop exists under OSPF is observed to be 11.851s, whereas LISF methods, as expected, have no loops in case of symmetric link failures. For the case of asymmetric link failures, OSPF has loops for a duration of 6.989s, while it is 0.056s for PIPO. In both cases, there are no loops under CYCL or NOFP. These results demonstrate the effectiveness

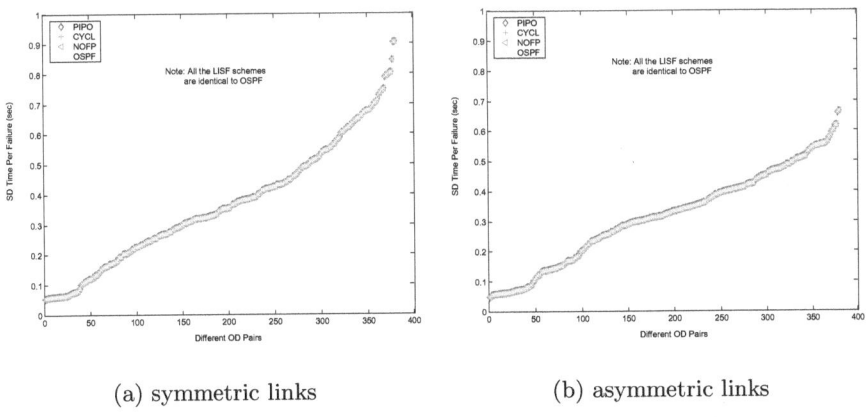

(a) symmetric links   (b) asymmetric links

Fig. 3. Average service disruption time per link failure for various O-D pairs

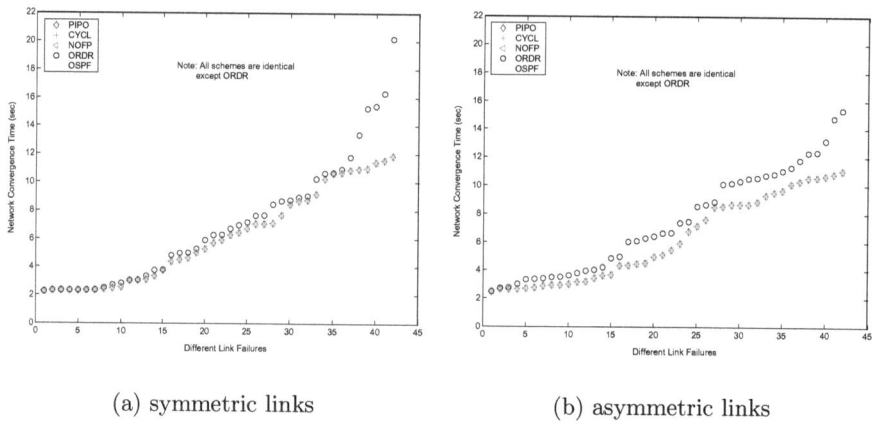

(a) symmetric links　　　　　　　　(b) asymmetric links

Fig. 4. Network convergence time due to various single link failures

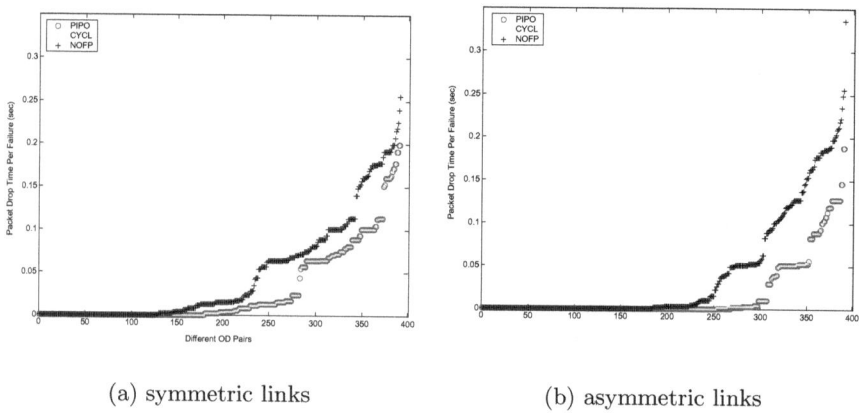

(a) symmetric links　　　　　　　　(b) asymmetric links

Fig. 5. Average packet discard time per link failure for various OD pairs

of LISF methods in avoiding loops. We proceed to show that this is achieved not at the expense of larger convergence delay or longer service disruption.

Figure 3(a) represents the average SD time experienced by all OD pairs due to a single link failure in this network with symmetric links. We can clearly see that the average SD time for a particular OD pair remains the same when LISF is implemented on top of OSPF. This shows that LISF does not add any extra SD time. Figure 3(b) shows a very similar behavior of average SD time for this network with asymmetric links.

Let NC time represent the total time taken for the network to converge after a link failure. Fig. 4(a) and Fig. 4(b) show the NC time due to different link failures for the backbone network with symmetric and asymmetric links respectively. Given that some nodes in the network have to wait for a longer time to update their FIBs under ORDR, it is easy to see that a network with ORDR exhibits higher NC times when compared to a network with LISF where no synchronization is needed between nodes for updating their FIBs.

Fig. 5(a) shows the packet discard times due to various LISF methods in the ISP network with symmetric links. As expected, with symmetric link failures, the packet discard times of PIPO and CYCL are identical, and NOFP is quite close to PIPO. A similar pattern is observed even with asymmetric links (Fig. 5(b)). However, the packet discard times under PIPO and CYCL are not identical due to the fact that more loops are avoided by CYCL compared to PIPO.

5.2   Multiple Link Failures

To further evaluate LISF methods, we simulated failures of multiple links and nodes. For this study, we did not use the control-plane simulator mentioned above as it can only handle single link failures. Instead, we used a simplified model to approximate link state propagation and route computation and FIB update times. It is assumed that link state propagation takes 1 time unit per hop and route computation and FIB update time is 3 units. We simulate single node failures and also simultaneous failures of 2 nodes, and also 2 links and 3 links. In each failure scenario, we forward a packet between every pair of nodes and count the number of node pairs for whom packets are undeliverable and also those that get caught in a loop.

Table 7. Comparison of LISF methods and OSPF in case of multiple failures

	looping probability				% of undeliverable node pairs			
failures	OSPF	PIPO	CYCL	NOFP	OSPF	PIPO	CYCL	NOFP
2 links	$10^{-2.3}$	$10^{-5.3}$	$10^{-5.3}$	0	5.9	5.9	5.9	6.2
3 links	$10^{-2.1}$	$10^{-4.9}$	$10^{-4.9}$	0	8.6	8.6	8.6	9.1
1 node	$10^{-3.0}$	0	0	0	4.3	4.3	4.3	4.4
2 nodes	$10^{-2.7}$	$10^{-3.7}$	$10^{-3.7}$	0	8.1	8.1	8.1	8.2

Table 7 shows the relative performance of different LISF methods and OSPF in terms of their ability to avoid loops and deliver packets. ORDR is not included here as it is not designed to deal with multiple failures. PIPO and CYCL yield identical performance since the links are symmetric. Compared to OSPF, loops are close to 1000 times less likely to happen with PIPO and CYCL, whereas no loops occur under NOFP. In terms of packet delivery, both PIPO and CYCL have the same performance as OSPF. The delivery ratio of NOFP is only slightly worse than OSPF. Considering that NOFP prevents loops without excessive discarding of packets, we believe LISF approach with NOFP method is a viable alternative for avoiding transient loops during the convergence of intra-domain routing schemes in IP networks.

6   Conclusions

In this paper, we proposed a simple interface-specific forwarding based approach called LISF to avoid transient forwarding loops during the network convergence periods. LISF approach selectively discards packets arriving through unusual interfaces when they are likely to be caught in a loop. We have demonstrated that LISF incurs no additional message overhead compared to OSPF and avoids forwarding loops like ORDR without increasing the network convergence time. We have presented several LISF methods and evaluated their performance. We observed that simple PIPO is effective in eliminating most of the loops and NOFP provides the best trade-off between packet-discarding and loop-avoidance.

References

1. Markopulu, A., Iannaccone, G., Bhattacharya, S., Chuah, C.N., Diot, C.: Characterization of failures in an IP backbone. In: Proc. IEEE Infocom. (2004)
2. Zinin, A.: Analysis and minimization of microloops in link-state routing protocols (2004) Internet draft, draft-zinin-microloop-analysis-00.txt, work in progress.
3. Garcia-Luna-Aceves, J., Murthy, S.: A path-finding algorithm for loop-free routing. IEEE/ACM Transactions on Networking **5** (1997)
4. Francois, P., Bonaventure, O.: Avoiding transient loops during IGP convergence in IP networks. In: IEEE Infocom. (2005)
5. Bryant, S., Filsfils, C., Previdi, S., Shand, M.: IP Fast Reroute using tunnels (2004) Internet draft, draft-bryant-ipfrr-tunnels-00.txt, work in progress.
6. Bryant, S., Zhang, M.: A framework for loop-free convergence (2004) Internet draft, draft-bryant-shand-lf-conv-frmwk-00.txt, work in progress.
7. Zhong, Z., Nelakuditi, S., Yu, Y., Lee, S., Wang, J., Chuah, C.N.: Failure Inferencing based Fast Rerouting for Handling Transient Link and Node Failures. In: Global Internet Symposium, Miami (2005)
8. Atlas, A.: U-turn alternates for IP/LDP fast-reroute (2005) Internet draft, draft-atlas-ip-local-protect-uturn-02, work in progress.
9. Routing Area Working Group: http://psg.com/ zinin/ietf/rtgwg (2004)
10. Keralapura, R., Chuah, C.N., Iannaconne, G., Bhattacharrya, S.: Service availability: A new approach to characterize IP backbone topologies. In: Proc. International Workshop on Quality of Service (IWQoS). (2004)
11. Iannaccone, G., Chuah, C.N., Bhattacharyya, S., Diot, C.: Feasibility of IP restoration in a tier-1 backbone. IEEE Network Magazine, Special Issue on Protection, Restoration and Disaster Recovery (2004)

Analysis of Stochastic Service Guarantees in Communication Networks: A Server Model

Yuming Jiang and Peder J. Emstad

Centre for Quantifiable Quality of Service in Communication Systems *
Department of Telematics
Norwegian University of Science and Technology (NTNU), Norway
ymjiang@ieee.org, peder@q2s.ntnu.no

Abstract. Many communication networks such as wireless networks only provide stochastic service guarantees. For analyzing stochastic service guarantees, research efforts have been made in the past few years to develop stochastic network calculus, a probabilistic version of (min, +) deterministic network calculus. However, many challenges have made the development difficult. Some of them are closely related to server modeling, which include *output characterization, concatenation property, stochastic backlog guarantee, stochastic delay guarantee*, and *per-flow service under aggregation*. In this paper, we propose a server model, called *stochastic service curve* to facilitate stochastic service guarantee analysis. We show that with the concept of stochastic service curve, these challenges can be well addressed. In addition, we introduce *strict stochastic server* to help find the stochastic service curve of a stochastic server, which characterizes the service of the server by two stochastic processes: an ideal service process and an impairment process.

1 Introduction

Many communication networks such as wireless networks only provide stochastic service guarantees. Due to the increasing deployment and application of such networks to support real-time and multimedia applications, which require QoS guarantees, the development of an information theory for stochastic service guarantee analysis in these networks has been identified as a *grand challenge* for future networking research [22]. Towards it, *stochastic network calculus*, the probabilistic generalization of (min, +) *(deterministic) network calculus* [6][5][14], has been considered as a fundamental and important step [17].

Many challenges have made stochastic network calculus difficult. Some of them are closely related to server modeling, which include *output characterization, concatenation property, stochastic backlog guarantee, stochastic delay guarantee*, and *per-flow service under aggregation*. In particular, the experience from

---

* "Centre for Quantifiable Quality of Service in Communication Systems, Centre of Excellence" is appointed by The Research Council of Norway and funded by the Research Council, NTNU and UNINETT. (http://www.ntnu.no/Q2S/)

H. de Meer and N. Bhatti (Eds.): IWQoS 2005, LNCS 3552, pp. 233–245, 2005.

the development of the (min, +) network calculus for deterministic service guarantee analysis tells that a server model with the following properties is desired:

- (P.1) **(Output Characterization)** The output of a server can be represented using the same traffic model as the input.
- (P.2) **(Concatenation Property)** The concatenation of servers can be represented using the same server model.
- (P.3) **(Service Guarantees)** The server model can be used to derive backlog and delay guarantees.
- (P.4) **(Per-Flow Service)** The service received by a flow in an aggregate can be characterized using the same server model.

For the (deterministic) network calculus, its *service curve* server model has all these properties (P.1) - (P.4).

For stochastic service guarantee analysis, to the best of our knowledge, no server model satisfying (P.1) - (P.4) has been available in the literature. The most widely used one, which we shall call *weak stochastic service curve*, was introduced by Cruz [9]. Although authors in [18] have adopted weak stochastic service curve as the server model and derived interesting results for stochastic service guarantee analysis, the weak stochastic service curve model, while having property (P.3), generally does not support properties (P.1), (P.2) and (P.4).

The purpose of this paper is to propose a server model having properties (P.1) - (P.4). The proposed model is called *stochastic service curve*. In the paper, we first introduce the idea behind extending (deterministic) service curve to weak stochastic service curve and stochastic service curve, and discuss the relationship between them. We then prove properties (P.1) - (P.4) for stochastic service curve. In addition, to help find the stochastic service curve of a stochastic server, we introduce the concept of *strict stochastic server*. In a strict stochastic server, the service behavior of the server is characterized by two stochastic processes: an ideal service process and an impairment process. This characterization is inspired by the nature of a wireless channel: data is sent and received when the channel is in good condition, and no data is sent or received when the channel is in bad condition or impaired. We prove that a strict stochastic server under some general impairment condition has a stochastic service curve.

2   Network Model and Background

2.1   Network Model and Notation

We consider a discrete time model, where time is slotted as $0, 1, 2, \ldots$. The traffic of a flow is represented by $A(t)$ denoting the amount of traffic generated by the flow in $(0, t]$. In addition, we use $A(s, t)$ to denote the amount of traffic generated by the flow in $(s, t]$. The service provided by a server is represented similarly. Particularly, we let $S(s, t)$ be the amount of service provided by the server to its input in $(s, t]$ and use $S(t)$ to represent $S(0, t)$. By convention, we let $A(0) = 0$, $S(0) = 0$, and $A(t, t) = 0$ and $S(t, t) = 0$ for all $t \geq 0$.

When we consider the input and output of a network node, we use A to represent the input , A^* the output and S the service. Wherever necessary, we use subscripts to distinguish between different flows, and use superscripts to distinguish between different network nodes. Specifically, A_i^n and A_i^{n*} represent the input and output of flow i from node n respectively, and S_i^n the service provided to flow i by node n.

For stochastic service guarantee analysis, we shall focus on backlog and (virtual) delay, which are defined as [5] [14]:

(i)   The backlog $B(t)$ at time $t(\geq 0)$ is $B(t) = A(t) - A^*(t)$;
(ii) The delay $D(t)$ at time $t(\geq 0)$ is $D(t) = \inf\{d \geq 0 : A(t) \leq A^*(t+d)\}$.

A function f is said to be wide-sense increasing if $f(s) \leq f(t)$ for all $s \leq t$ and to be wide-sense decreasing if $f(s) \geq f(t)$ for all $s \leq t$. We denote by $\mathcal{F}$ the set of wide-sense increasing functions defined for $t \geq 0$ with $f(t) = 0$ for $t < 0$; $\bar{\mathcal{F}}$ the set of wide-sense decreasing functions defined for $t \geq 0$ with $f(t) = +\infty$ for $t < 0$. By definition, $A(t)$ and $S(t)$ belong to $\mathcal{F}$ and are additive, i.e. $A(s,u)+A(u,t) = A(s,t)$ and $S(s,u)+S(u,t) = S(s,t)$ for all $0 \leq s \leq u \leq t$.

The convolution of two functions f and g, denoted by $f \otimes g$, is defined as

$$f \otimes g(x) = \min_{0 \leq y \leq x}[f(y) + g(x - y)]. \tag{1}$$

If both f and g belong to $\mathcal{F}$, (1) is the same as the (min, +) convolution [14] and many properties of it have been proved [14]. These properties include: *closure property*, i.e. $\forall f, g \in \mathcal{F}$, $f \otimes g \in \mathcal{F}$; *commutativity*, i.e. $\forall f, g \in \mathcal{F}$, $f \otimes g = g \otimes f$; *associativity*, i.e. $\forall f, g, h \in \mathcal{F}$, $(f \otimes g) \otimes h = f \otimes (g \otimes h)$. In this paper, we shall use (1) also for functions in $\bar{\mathcal{F}}$. Similarly, we can prove the following properties of $\otimes$ for functions in $\bar{\mathcal{F}}$ [14]:

Lemma 1. *Basic properties of $\otimes$ in $\bar{\mathcal{F}}$:*

- **Closure property:** $\forall f, g \in \bar{\mathcal{F}}$, $f \otimes g \in \bar{\mathcal{F}}$.
- **Commutativity:** $\forall f, g \in \bar{\mathcal{F}}$, $f \otimes g = g \otimes f$.
- **Associativity:** $\forall f, g \in \bar{\mathcal{F}}$, $(f \otimes g) \otimes h = f \otimes (g \otimes h)$.
- **Monotonicity:** $\forall f_1, f_2, g_1, g_2 \in \bar{\mathcal{F}}$, if $f_1 \leq f_2$ and $g_1 \leq g_2$, $f_1 \otimes g_1 \leq f_2 \otimes g_2$.

We now present the definitions of *(deterministic) arrival curve* and *(deterministic) service curve* used in *(deterministic) network calculus* (e.g. [14]).

Definition 1. *A flow is said to have an arrival curve $\alpha \in \mathcal{F}$ iff for all $0 \leq s \leq t$, there holds*

$$A(s,t) \leq \alpha(t - s). \tag{2}$$

Definition 2. *A server is said to provide service curve $\beta \in \mathcal{F}$ to its input A, iff for all $t \geq 0$, its output A^* satisfies*

$$A^*(t) \geq A \otimes \beta(t). \tag{3}$$

Literature results show that service curve has all the properties (P.1) - (P.4) (e.g. see [14]). The concept of service curve, its these properties, together with the concept of arrival curve have helped the development of the (min, +) deterministic network calculus [6] [7] [8] [13] [5] [14].

2.2   Background on Stochastic Service Guarantee Analysis

Many applications, such as Internet video and audio, can tolerate some delay and loss, and may only require stochastic service guarantees. In addition, many networks such as wireless networks only provide stochastic service guarantees. Because of these, stochastic service guarantee analysis has become an increasingly important issue and attracted a lot of research attention in recent years. Towards it, *stochastic network calculus*, the probabilistic generalization of *deterministic network calculus* has been considered as an important step and several attempts have been made [23] [15] [21] [9] [3][16][18][2].

Most of these attempts assume deterministic server and have focused on the extension or generalization of arrival curve to the stochastic case. These extensions have generally resulted in two versions of stochastic arrival curve, which are called *traffic-amount-centric (t.a.c) stochastic arrival curve* and *virtual-backlog-centric (v.b.c) stochastic arrival curve* respectively [12]. A representative special case of t.a.c stochastic arrival curve is Exponentially Bounded Burstiness (EBB) [23] and its generalization Stochastically Bounded Burstiness (SBB)[21]. There are two limitations with t.a.c stochastic arrival curve, as investigated in [24] [16]. One is the difficulty in applying t.a.c stochastic arrival curve to the network case; the other is t.a.c stochastic arrival curve cannot be directly used to derive stochastic backlog and delay guarantees. To overcome these difficulties, t.a.c stochastic arrival curve needs to be converted to v.b.c stochastic arrival curve, or requires some additional restriction on traffic (e.g. [16]). In contrast, v.b.c stochastic arrival curve does not have these limitations. A representative special case of v.b.c stochastic arrival curve is generalized Stochastically Bounded Burstiness (gSBB)[24] (also called stochastic smoothness constraint in [9]). Under deterministic server assumption, v.b.c stochastic arrival curve has been used to analyze stochastic backlog and delay guarantees in both single node and network cases [18][12]. In addition, it is shown in [12] that many well-known types of traffic can be readily represented using v.b.c stochastic arrival curve. In this paper, we adopt v.b.c stochastic arrival curve as the traffic model.

Definition 3. *A flow is said to have a* virtual-backlog-centric (v.b.c) *stochastic arrival curve* $\alpha \in \mathcal{F}$ *with bounding function* $f \in \bar{\mathcal{F}}$, *denoted by* $A \sim_{vb} \langle f, \alpha \rangle$, *iff for all* $t \geq 0$ *and all* $x \geq 0$, *there holds*

$$P\{\max_{0 \leq s \leq t}\{A(s,t) - \alpha(t-s)\} > x\} \leq f(x). \tag{4}$$

The following result introduced in [20] [5] [12] can be used to find the v.b.c stochastic arrival curve of a flow:

Lemma 2. *Suppose* $a(t) \equiv A(t) - A(t-1)$ *is stationary and ergodic. Then, if* $E\{a(1)\} < r$, *there holds, for all* $t \geq 0$ *and* $x \geq 0$,

$$P\{W(t;r) > x\} \leq P\{W(t+1;r) > x\} \leq \cdots \leq P\{W(\infty;r) > x\}, \qquad (5)$$

where $W(t;r) \equiv \max_{0 \leq s \leq t}[A(s,t) - r(t-s)]$ *and* $W(\infty;r)$ *denotes the steady state of* $W(t;r)$ *as* $t \to \infty$.

Note that $\max_{0 \leq s \leq t}[A(s,t) - r(t-s)]$ can be interpreted as the queue length at time t of a virtual single server queue (SSQ) with service rate r fed with the same traffic [24][12]. Then, the monotonicity property implies that if the traffic of the flow is stationary and ergodic, the steady-state queue length distribution of the SSQ can be used as the bounding function $f(x)$. Consequently, if the steady-state queue length distribution of a flow in a SSQ is known, then it has a v.b.c stochastic arrival curve $A \sim_{vb} \langle f, \alpha \rangle$ with $f(x) = P\{q > x\}$, the steady state compliment queue length distribution. With these, many well-known types of traffic, including Poisson, Markov Modulated Process, effective bandwidth, α−stable, etc., can be shown to have v.b.c stochastic arrival curves [12].

While many attempts have been made for stochastic traffic modeling and analysis as discussed above, only a few have considered stochastic server and stochastic service guarantee in networks of such servers [15][9][18][16]. Essentially, the stochastic server models proposed or used in these attempts can be mapped to the following model, which we call *weak stochastic service curve* and is based on a stochastic server model used in [9]:

Definition 4. *A server* S *is said to provide a* weak stochastic service curve $\beta \in \mathcal{F}$ *with bounding function* $g \in \tilde{\mathcal{F}}$, *denoted by* $S \sim_{ws} \langle g, \beta \rangle$, *iff for all* $t \geq 0$ *and all* $x \geq 0$, *there holds*

$$P\{A \otimes \beta(t) - A^*(t) > x\} \leq g(x). \qquad (6)$$

Comparing Definition 4 with Definition 2, it is clear that weak stochastic service curve is an intuitively simple generalization of (deterministic) service curve. One can easily verify that if a server has a deterministic service curve β, it has a weak stochastic service curve $S \sim_{ws} \langle 0, \beta \rangle$. In addition, the Exponentially Bounded Fluctuation (EBF) model proposed in [15] is a special case of weak stochastic service curve with an exponential form bounding function. The stochastic server model *effective service curve* used in [16] can also be verified to be a special case of weak stochastic service curve.

In [9], [18] and [16], some results have been derived based on weak stochastic service curve. The difference between them is that while [16] uses t.a.c stochastic arrive curve as the traffic model, [18] and [9] use v.b.c stochastic arrive curve. In addition to backlog and delay at a single node, [18] has considered the network case. Nevertheless, weak stochastic service curve generally does not have properties (P.1), (P.2) and (P.4) as to be explained in the remarks in the next section.

3   Stochastic Service Curve

In this section, we first investigate the duality principle of service curve, which is the idea behind the generalization of service curve to its probabilistic versions. We then introduce a new stochastic server model, called *stochastic service curve*. Stochastic service guarantee analysis is further conducted based on the new server model. Particularly, properties (P.1) - (P.4) are proved for stochastic service curve.

3.1   Definition of Stochastic Service Curve

The following result presents the duality principle of service curve. Its proof is trivial and can be found from [11].

Lemma 3. *For any constant* $\sigma \geq 0$, $A \otimes \beta(t) - A^*(t) \leq \sigma$ *for all* $t \geq 0$, *if and only if* $\max_{0 \leq s \leq t}\{A \otimes \beta(s) - A^*(s)\} \leq \sigma$ *for all* $t \geq 0$, *where* $\beta \in \mathcal{F}$.

By letting $\sigma = 0$, the first part of Lemma 3 defines a service curve β. In this case, Lemma 3 implies that if a server has service curve β or $A^* \geq A \otimes \beta(t)$, then there holds $\max_{0 \leq s \leq t}[A \otimes \beta(s) - A^*(s)] \leq 0$ and vice versa. It is in this sense we call Lemma 3 the *duality principle of service curve*.

Comparing the first part of Lemma 3 with Definition 4, one can find that the former is the basis for generalizing service curve to weak stochastic service curve. Based on the second part of the duality principle of service curve, we define the following stochastic server model, called *stochastic service curve* [1]:

Definition 5. *A server S is said to provide a* stochastic service curve $\beta \in \mathcal{F}$ *with bounding function* $g \in \bar{\mathcal{F}}$, *denoted by* $S \sim_{sc} \langle g, \beta \rangle$, *iff for all* $t \geq 0$ *and all* $x \geq 0$, *there holds*

$$P\{\max_{0 \leq s \leq t}[A \otimes \beta(s) - A^*(s)] > x\} \leq g(x). \tag{7}$$

Stochastic service curve implies weak stochastic service curve, since we always have $A \otimes \beta(t) - A^*(t) \leq \max_{0 \leq s \leq t}[A \otimes \beta(s) - A^*(s)]$ for all $t \geq 0$. Formally,

Lemma 4. *If a server provides stochastic service curve* $S \sim_{sc} \langle g, \beta \rangle$, *then it also provides weak stochastic service curve* $S \sim_{ws} \langle g, \beta \rangle$.

---

[1] In [1], *service curve with loss* is defined. It should be noticed that this definition is different from Definitions 4, 5 and 6 here. In a service curve with loss network element, packets are dropped if their deadlines assigned via the (deterministic) service curve are not met. However, in a network element with weak stochastic service curve or stochastic service curve or strict stochastic service curve, packets are allowed to violate their deadlines if they would be given such deadlines via the corresponding (deterministic) service curve.

3.2   Properties of Stochastic Service Curve

We now study Properties (P.1) - (P.4) for stochastic service curve. For proving these properties, we need the following result. For random variables X and Y, there holds

$$P\{X + Y > x\} \leq f_X \otimes f_Y(x) \qquad (8)$$

where $f_X(x) = P\{X > x\}$ and $f_Y(x) = P\{Y > x\}$. The proof of (8) can be found from the literature (e.g. [9][19][2]). With the monotonicity property of $\otimes$, if $P\{X > x\} \leq f(x)$ and $P\{Y > x\} \leq g(x)$, we get from (8) that

$$P\{X + Y > x\} \leq f \otimes g(x). \qquad (9)$$

Theorem 1. (Output) *Consider a server fed with a flow. If the server provides stochastic service curve $S \sim_{sc} \langle g, \beta \rangle$ to the flow and the flow has v.b.c stochastic arrival curve $A \sim_{vb} \langle f, \alpha \rangle$, then the output of the flow from the server has a v.b.c stochastic arrival curve $A^* \sim_{vb} \langle f^*, \alpha^* \rangle$ with $\alpha^*(t) = \max_{s \geq 0}[\alpha(t + s) - \beta(s)]$ and $f^*(x) = f \otimes g(x)$.*

Proof. Note that the output up to time t cannot exceed the input in $[0, t]$, or $A^*(t) \leq A(t)$. We now have,

$$\max_{0 \leq s \leq t}[A^*(s, t) - \alpha^*(t - s)]$$
$$= \max_{0 \leq s \leq t}[A^*(t) - A^*(s) - \alpha^*(t - s)] \leq \max_{0 \leq s \leq t}[A(t) - A^*(s) - \alpha^*(t - s)]$$
$$= \max_{0 \leq s \leq t}[A(t) - A \otimes \beta(s) - \alpha^*(t - s) + A \otimes \beta(s) - A^*(s)]$$
$$\leq \max_{0 \leq s \leq t}[A(t) - A \otimes \beta(s) - \alpha^*(t - s)] + \max_{0 \leq s \leq t}[A \otimes \beta(s) - A^*(s)] \qquad (10)$$

in which,

$$\max_{0 \leq s \leq t}[A(t) - A \otimes \beta(s) - \alpha^*(t - s)]$$
$$= \max_{0 \leq s \leq t}[A(t) - \min_{0 \leq u \leq s}[A(u) + \beta(s - u)] - \alpha^*(t - s)]$$
$$= \max_{0 \leq s \leq t} \max_{0 \leq u \leq s}[A(t) - A(u) - \beta(s - u) - \alpha^*(t - s)] \leq \max_{0 \leq s \leq t} \max_{0 \leq u \leq s}[A(u, t) - \alpha(t - u)]$$
$$\qquad (11)$$
$$= \max_{0 \leq u \leq t} \max_{u \leq s \leq t}[A(u, t) - \alpha(t - u)] = \max_{0 \leq u \leq t}[A(u, t) - \alpha(t - u)] \qquad (12)$$

where the step (11) follows because $\alpha^*(t - s) = \max_{\tau \geq 0}[\alpha(t - s + \tau) - \beta(\tau)] \geq \alpha(t - u) - \beta(s - u)$.

Applying (12) to (10), since $S \sim_{sc} \langle g, \beta \rangle$ and $A \sim_{vb} \langle f, \alpha \rangle$, or $P\{\max_{0 \leq s \leq t}[A \otimes \beta(s) - A^*(s)] > x\} \leq g(x)$ and $P\{\max_{0 \leq u \leq t}[A(u, t) - \alpha(t - u)] > x\} \leq f(x)$, we then get from (9), $P\{\max_{0 \leq s \leq t}[A^*(s, t) - \alpha(t - s)] + \min_{s \geq 0}[\beta(s) - \alpha(s)] > x\} \leq f \otimes g(x)$, from which the theorem follows.

Remarks: (i) Note that in (10), its right hand side has a term $\max_{0 \leq s \leq t}[A \otimes \beta(s) - A^*(s)]$. If the server only has weak stochastic service curve, what is known is $P\{A \otimes \beta(s) - A^*(s) > x\} \le g(x)$ and it is hard to find $P\{\max_{0 \le s \le t}[A \otimes \beta(s) - A^*(s)] > x\}$ that is critical for proving (P.1). This explains why weak stochastic service curve does not have property (P.1), if the input is modeled with v.b.c stochastic arrival curve.

(ii) If α is subadditive, following similar steps as in the above proof, we can prove that the output also has v.b.c stochastic arrival curve $A^* \sim_{vb} \langle f \otimes g(x + \min_{t \ge 0}[\beta(t) - \alpha(t)], \alpha \rangle$.

Theorem 2. (Concatenation) *Consider a flow passing through a network of N nodes in tandem. If each node $n(= 1, 2, \ldots, N)$ provides stochastic service curve $S^n \sim_{sc} \langle g^n, \beta^n \rangle$ to its input, then the network guarantees to the flow a stochastic service curve $S^* \sim_{sc} \langle g^*, \beta^* \rangle$ with $\beta^*(t) = \beta^1 \otimes \beta^2 \otimes \cdots \otimes \beta^N(t)$ and $g^*(x) = g^1 \otimes g^2 \otimes \cdots \otimes g^N(x)$.*

Proof. We shall only prove the two-node case, from which the proof can be easily extended to the N-node case. For the two-node case, the output of the first node is the input of the second node, so, $A^{1*}(t) = A^2(t)$. In addition, the input of the network is the input to the first node, or $A(t) = A^1(t)$, and the output of the network is the same as the output of the second node, or $A^* = A^{2*}$, where $A(t)$ and A^* denotes the input to and output from the network respectively. We then have,

$$\max_{0 \le s \le t}[A \otimes \beta^1 \otimes \beta^2(s) - A^*(s)] = \max_{0 \le s \le t}[(A^1 \otimes \beta^1) \otimes \beta^2(s) - A^{2*}(s)]. \quad (13)$$

Now let us consider any s, $(0 \le s \le t)$, for which we get,

$$
\begin{aligned}
&[(A^1 \otimes \beta^1) \otimes \beta^2(s) - A^{2*}(s)] - X^1(t) - X^2(t) \\
&\le (A^1 \otimes \beta^1) \otimes \beta^2(s) - A^{2*}(s) - X^1(s) - X^2(s) \\
&\le \min_{0 \le u \le s}[A^1 \otimes \beta^1(u) + \beta^2(s - u)] - \max_{0 \le u \le s}[A^1 \otimes \beta^1(u) - A^2(u)] - \max_{0 \le u \le s}[A^2 \otimes \beta^2(u)] \\
&\le \min_{0 \le u \le s}[(A^1 \otimes \beta^1(u) + \beta^2(s - u)) - (A^1 \otimes \beta^1(u) - A^2(u))] - \max_{0 \le u \le s}[A^2 \otimes \beta^2(u)] \\
&= \min_{0 \le u \le s}[A^2(u) + \beta^2(s - u)] - \max_{0 \le u \le s}[A^2 \otimes \beta^2(u)] \\
&= A^2 \otimes \beta^2(s) - \max_{0 \le u \le s}[A^2 \otimes \beta^2(u)] \le 0. \quad (14)
\end{aligned}
$$

where $X^i(t) \equiv \max_{0 \le u \le t}[A^i \otimes \beta^i(u) - A^{i*}(u)]$, $i = 1, 2$.

Applying (14) to (13), we obtain

$$\max_{0 \le s \le t}[A \otimes \beta^1 \otimes \beta^2(s) - A^*(s)] \le \max_{0 \le u \le t}[A^1 \otimes \beta^1(u) - A^{1*}(u)] + \max_{0 \le u \le t}[A^2 \otimes \beta^2(u) - A^{2*}(u)], \quad (15)$$

with which, since both nodes provide stochastic service curve to their input, the theorem follows from (9) and the definition of stochastic service curve.

Remark: In deriving (14), we have proved $[(A^1 \otimes \beta^1) \otimes \beta^2(s) - A^{2*}(s)] \le \max_{0 \le u \le s}[A^1 \otimes \beta^1(u) - A^{1*}(u)] + \max_{0 \le u \le s}[A^2 \otimes \beta^2(u) - A^{2*}(u)]$ for all $s \ge 0$. However, if we want to prove concatenation property for weak stochastic service curve, we need to prove $[(A^1 \otimes \beta^1) \otimes \beta^2(s) - A^{2*}(s)] \le [A^1 \otimes \beta^1(s) - A^{1*}(s)] + [A^2 \otimes \beta^2(s) - A^{2*}(s)]$ for all $s \ge 0$, which is difficult to obtain and does not hold in general. This explains why weak stochastic service curve does not have property (P.2).

The following lemma presents stochastic backlog and stochastic delay guarantees, or property (P.3), provided by a server with weak stochastic service curve. Its proof can be found from [11] and similar results can be found from the literature (e.g. see [9] [18]). Since stochastic service curve implies weak stochastic service curve as stated by Lemma 4, Theorem 3 follows from Lemma 5.

Lemma 5. *Consider a server fed with a flow. If the server provides weak stochastic service curve $S \sim_{ws} \langle g, \beta \rangle$ to the flow and the flow has v.b.c stochastic arrival curve $A \sim_{vb} \langle f, \alpha \rangle$, then, for all $t \geq 0$ and all $x \geq 0$, (1) $P\{B(t) > x\} \leq f \otimes g(x + \min_{t \geq 0}[\beta(t) - \alpha(t)])$, and (2) $P\{D(t) > x\} \leq f \otimes g(\min_{s \geq -x}[\beta(s + x) - \alpha(s)])$.*

Theorem 3. (Service Guarantees) *Consider a server fed with a flow. If the server provides stochastic service curve $S \sim_{sc} \langle g, \beta \rangle$ to the flow and the flow has v.b.c stochastic arrival curve $A \sim_{vb} \langle f, \alpha \rangle$, then*

- *The backlog $B(t)$ of the flow in the server at time t satisfies: for all $t \geq 0$ and all $x \geq 0$, $P\{B(t) > x\} \leq f \otimes g(x + \min_{s \geq 0}[\beta(s) - \alpha(s)])$;*
- *The delay $D(t)$ of the flow in the server at time t satisfies: for all $t \geq 0$ and all $x \geq 0$, $P\{D(t) > x\} \leq f \otimes g(\min_{s \geq -x}[\beta(s + x) - \alpha(s)])$.*

Finally, the following theorem presents per-flow service under aggregation or property (P.4) for stochastic service curve.

Theorem 4. (Per-Flow Service) *Consider a server fed with a flow A that is the aggregation of two constituent flows A_1 and A_2. Suppose the server provides stochastic service curve $S \sim_{sc} \langle g, \beta \rangle$ to the aggregate flow A.*

- *If flow A_2 has (deterministic) arrival curve α_2, then the server guarantees stochastic service curve $S_1 \sim_{sc} \langle g_1, \beta_1 \rangle$ to flow A_1, where, $g_1(x) = g(x)$; $\beta_1(t) = \beta(t) - \alpha_2(t)$.*
- *If flow A_2 has v.b.c stochastic arrival curve $A_2 \sim_{vb} \langle f_2, \alpha_2 \rangle$, then the server guarantees to flow A_1 weak stochastic service curve $S_1 \sim_{ws} \langle g_1', \beta_1' \rangle$, where, $g_1'(x) = g \otimes f_2(x)$; $\beta_1'(t) = \beta(t) - \alpha_2(t)$.*

Proof. For the output, there holds $A^*(t) = A_1^*(t) + A_2^*(t)$. In addition, we have $A^*(t) \leq A(t)$, $A_1^*(t) \leq A_1(t)$, and $A_2^*(t) \leq A_2(t)$. We now have for any $s \geq 0$,

$$A_1 \otimes (\beta - \alpha_2)(s) - A_1^*(s) = \min_{0 \leq u \leq s}[A(u) + (\beta - \alpha_2)(s - u) - A_2(u)] - A^*(s) + A_2^*(s)$$

$$\leq [A \otimes \beta(s) - A^*(s)] + A_2(s) - \min_{0 \leq u \leq s}[A_2(u) + \alpha_2(s - u)]$$

$$= [A \otimes \beta(s) - A^*(s)] + \max_{0 \leq u \leq s}[A_2(u, s) - \alpha_2(s - u)]. \quad (16)$$

For the first part, with (16), we have

$$\max_{0 \leq s \leq t}[A_1 \otimes (\beta - \alpha_2)(s) - A_1^*(s)] \leq \max_{0 \leq s \leq t}[A \otimes \beta(s) - A^*(s)] + \max_{0 \leq s \leq t} \max_{0 \leq u \leq s}[A_2(u, s) - \alpha_2(s - u)].$$

$$(17)$$

Since A_2 has deterministic arrival curve α_2 and $A_2(u, s) \leq \alpha_2(s - u)$ for all $0 \leq u \leq s$, we hence have $\max_{0 \leq s \leq t} \max_{0 \leq u \leq s}[A_2(u, s) - \alpha_2(s - u)] \leq 0$, with which, $\max_{0 \leq s \leq t}[A_1 \otimes (\beta - \alpha_2)(s) - A_1^*(s)] \leq \max_{0 \leq s \leq t}[A \otimes \beta(s) - A^*(s)]$. Then, the first part follows from the definition of stochastic service curve.

For the second part, we further get from (16) that

$$A_1 \otimes (\beta - \alpha_2)(s) - A_1^*(s) \leq \max_{0 \leq u \leq s}[A \otimes \beta(s) - A^*(s)] + \max_{0 \leq u \leq s}[A_2(u, s) - \alpha_2(s - u)] \quad (18)$$

with which, $S \sim_{sc} \langle g, \beta \rangle$ and $A_2 \sim_{vb} \langle f_2, \alpha_2 \rangle$, the second part follows from (9).

Remark: Theorem 4 proves that a flow in an aggregate receives a stochastic service curve from a stochastic server when other flows in the aggregate have deterministic arrival curve. If other flows in the aggregate only have v.b.c stochastic arrival curve, what has been proved is that the flow only receives weak stochastic service curve. The difficulty in proving stochastic service curve for the flow can be found from (17), where $P\{\max_{0 \leq s \leq t} \max_{0 \leq u \leq s}[A_2(u, s) - \alpha_2(s - u)] > x\}$ is difficult to obtain from the given assumptions for the second part of Theorem 4. Nevertheless, we believe Theorem 4 can be readily used for stochastic service guarantee analysis in many network scenarios. One is the single node case. With Theorem 4 and Lemma 5, per-flow stochastic backlog and delay guarantees can be derived for the single node case. Another scenario is the analysis of Differentiated Services (DiffServ) in wireless networks. Under DiffServ, the Expedited Forwarding (EF) class is deterministically regulated and usually put at the highest priority level. In this scenario, Theorem 4 sheds some light on deriving stochastic service curve and stochastic service guarantees for DiffServ Assured Forwarding (AF) that is given lower priority than EF.

4   Strict Stochastic Server

In this section, we introduce *strict stochastic server* to help find the stochastic service curve of a stochastic server, which is inspired by an intuition.

In wireless networks, the behavior of a wireless channel is most simply revealed by the following intuition. The channel operates in two states: "good" and "bad". If the channel condition is good, data can be sent from the sender to the receiver at the full rate of the channel; if the condition is bad, no data can be sent. The bad channel condition has various causes such as noise, fading, contention, etc, which in all we shall call *impairment*.

Inspired by the above intuition, we use two stochastic processes to characterize the behavior of a stochastic server. These two processes are (1) an *ideal service process* $\hat{S}$ and (2) an *impairment process* I. Here, $\hat{S}(s, t)$ denotes the amount of service that the server would have delivered in interval $(s, t]$ if there had been no service impairment, and $I(s, t)$ denotes the amount of service, called *impaired service*, that cannot be delivered in the interval to the input due to some impairment to the server. Particularly, we have that the actually delivered service to the input satisfies, for all $t \geq 0$,

$$S(t) = \hat{S}(t) - I(t), \quad (19)$$

where $\hat{S}(t) \equiv \hat{S}(0,t)$ and $I(t) \equiv I(0,t)$ with $\hat{S}(0) = 0$ and $I(0) = 0$ by convention. It is clear that $\hat{S}, I$ are in $\mathcal{F}$ and additive.

We now define *strict stochastic server* as follows:

Definition 6. *A server S is said to be a* strict stochastic server *providing* strict stochastic service curve $\hat{\beta}(\cdot) \in \mathcal{F}$ *with impairment process I to a flow iff during any backlogged period $(s,t]$, the output $A^*(s,t)$ of the flow from the server satisfies*

$$A^*(s,t) \geq \hat{\beta}(t-s) - I(s,t).$$

In the rest, we assume $\hat{\beta}$ is additive and has the form of $\hat{\beta}(t) = \hat{r}t$. In addition, we assume the impairment process $I(t)$ is $(\sigma(\theta), \rho(\theta))$-upper constrained, a model that was initially used in [4] to characterize stochastic behavior of traffic, whose definition is as follows:

Definition 7. *A stochastic sequence I, $I \equiv \{I(t), t = 0, 1, 2, \ldots\}$ with $I(0) = 0$, is said to be $(\sigma(\theta), \rho(\theta))$-upper constrained (for some $\theta > 0$), iff for all $0 \leq s \leq t$*

$$\frac{1}{\theta} \log E e^{\theta(I(t) - I(s))} \leq \rho(\theta)(t-s) + \sigma(\theta). \tag{20}$$

The following result shows that if the impairment process $I(t)$ is $(\sigma(\theta), \rho(\theta))$-upper constrained, a strict stochastic server has a stochastic service curve. Due to space limitation, the proof is omitted and can be found from [11].

Theorem 5. *Consider a strict stochastic server providing strict stochastic service curve $\hat{\beta}(t) = \hat{r} \cdot t$ with impairment process I to a flow. Suppose I is $(\sigma(\theta), \rho(\theta))$-upper constrained. Then, the server provides to the flow a stochastic service curve $S \sim_{sc} \langle \beta, g \rangle$, where $\beta(t) = p\hat{r} \cdot t$ and $g(x) = \frac{e^{\theta \sigma(\theta)}}{(1 - e^{\theta(\rho(\theta) - (1-p)\hat{r})})^2} e^{-\theta x}$ with any p, $(0 \leq p < 1)$, satisfying $(1-p)\hat{r} > \rho(\theta)$.*

Remark: The definition of strict stochastic server is based on the intuition on the behavior of a wireless channel, which provides a simple approach to characterize this behavior. Theorem 5 proves the stochastic service curve of a strict stochastic server, with which and the analysis in the previous section, stochastic service guarantees can be derived for networks of strict stochastic servers. In addition, in [4] [5], many well known processes such as Markov Modulated Processes have been proved to be $(\sigma(\theta), \rho(\theta))$-upper constrained. Note that these processes have also been used in the literature for characterizing a wireless channel (e.g. [9] [10]). We hence believe our results are useful for stochastic service guarantee analysis in such networks.

5   Conclusion

In this paper, we introduced a new server model, called *stochastic service curve*, for stochastic service guarantee analysis. We have proved that stochastic service curve has properties (P.1)-(P.4), which are crucial for stochastic service guarantee analysis and the development of stochastic network calculus. In addition, we have proposed the concept of *strict stochastic server* to help find the stochastic service curve of a stochastic server. In a strict stochastic server, the service is characterized by two stochastic processes: an ideal service process and an impairment process. The impairment process provides a simple approach to model the impairment experienced by a server, which is typical in wireless networks.

While property (P.4), i.e. per-flow service under aggregation, has been proved for stochastic service curve, it is based on the assumption that other flows in the aggregate are deterministically upper-bounded. It would be interesting to prove stochastic service curve for property (P.4), when the other flows in the aggregate are only stochastically upper-bounded. Future work could hence be conducted to design traffic and server models to have properties (P.1)-(P.4) without additional assumptions on traffic or server.

References

1. S. Ayyorgun and R. L. Cruz. A composable service model with loss and a scheduling algorithm. In *Proc. IEEE INFOCOM'04*, 2004.
2. S. Ayyorgun and W. Feng. A systematic approach for providing end-to-end probabilistic QoS guarantees. In *Proc. IEEE IC3N'04*, 2004.
3. A. Burchard, J. Liebeherr, and S. D. Patek. A calculus for end-to-end statistical service guarantees. Technical report, CS-2001-19, University of Virginia, 2002.
4. C.-S. Chang. Stability, queue length, and delay of deterministic and stochastic queueing networks. *IEEE Trans. Automatic Control*, 39(5):913–931, May 1994.
5. C.-S. Chang. *Performance Guarantees in Communication Networks*. Springer-Verlag, 2000.
6. R. L. Cruz. A calculus for network delay, part I: network elements in isolation. *IEEE Trans. Information Theory*, 37(1):114–131, Jan. 1991.
7. R. L. Cruz. A calculus for network delay, part II: network analysis. *IEEE Trans. Information Theory*, 37(1):132–141, Jan. 1991.
8. R. L. Cruz. Quality of service guarantees in virtual circuit switched networks. *IEEE JSAC*, 13(6):1048–1056, Aug. 1995.
9. R. L. Cruz. Quality of service management in integrated services networks. In *Proc. 1st Semi-Annual Research Review, CWC, UCSD*, June 1996.
10. M. Hassan, M. M. Krunz, and I. Matta. Markov-based channel characterization for tractable performance analysis in wireless packet networks. *IEEE Trans. Wireless Communications*, 3(3):821–831, May 2004.
11. Y. Jiang and P. J. Emstad. Analysis of stochastic service guarantees in communication networks: A server model. Technical report, Q2S, NTNU, April 2005.
12. Y. Jiang and P. J. Emstad. Analysis of stochastic service guarantees in communication networks: A traffic model. Technical report, Q2S, NTNU, Feb. 2005.
13. J.-Y. Le Boudec. Application of network calculus to guaranteed service networks. *IEEE Trans. Information Theory*, 44(3):1087–1096, May 1998.
14. J.-Y. Le Boudec and P. Thiran. *Network Calculus: A Theory of Deterministic Queueing Systems for the Internet*. Springer-Verlag, 2001.
15. K. Lee. Performance bounds in communication networks with variable-rate links. In *Proc. ACM SIGCOMM'95*, pages 126–136, 1995.
16. C. Li, A. Burchard, and J. Liebeherr. A network calculus with effective bandwidth. Technical report, CS-2003-20, University of Virginia, November 2003.

17. J. Liebeherr. IWQoS 2004 Panel Talk: Post-Internet QoS Research, 2004.
18. Y. Liu, C.-K. Tham, and Y. Jiang. A stochastic network calculus. Technical report, ECE-CCN-0301, National University of Singapore, December 2003.
19. Y. Liu, C.-K. Tham, and Y. Jiang. Conformance study for networks with service level agreements. *Computer Networks*, 2005. in press.
20. R. M. Loynes. The stability of a queue with non-independent inter-arrival and service times. *Proc. of the Cambridge Philosophical Society*, 58(3):497–520, 1962.
21. D. Starobinski and M. Sidi. Stochastically bounded burstiness for communication networks. *IEEE Trans. Information Theory*, 46(1):206–212, Jan. 2000.
22. Workshop Attendees. Report of the National Science Foundation Workshop on Fundamental Research in Networking, April 2003.
23. Q. Yaron and M. Sidi. Performance and stability of communication networks via robust exponential bounds. *IEEE/ACM Trans. Networking*, 1:372–385, June 1993.
24. Q. Yin, Y. Jiang, S. Jiang, and P. Y. Kong. Analysis on generalized stochastically bounded bursty traffic for communication networks. In *Proc. IEEE LCN'02*, 2002.

Preemptive Packet-Mode Scheduling to Improve TCP Performance[*]

Wenjie Li[1], Bin Liu[1], Lei Shi[1], Yang Xu[1], and Dapeng Wu[2]

[1] Department of Computer Science and Technology, Tsinghua University,
Beijing 100084, P. R. China
{lwjie00, shijim, xy01}@mails.tsinghua.edu.cn
liub@mail.tsinghua.edu.cn
[2] Department of Electrical & Computer Engineering,
University of Florida,
Gainesville, Florida 32611-6130, USA
wu@ece.ufl.edu

Abstract. Recent Internet traffic measurements show that 60% of the total packets are short packets, which include TCP acknowledgment and control segments. These short packets make a great impact on the performance of TCP. Unfortunately, short packets suffer from large delay due to serving long data packets in switches running in the packet mode, i.e. a packet is switched in its entirety. To optimize TCP performance, we apply a cross-layer approach to the design of switching architectures and scheduling algorithms. Specifically, we propose a preemptive packet-mode scheduling architecture and an algorithm called preemptive short packets first (P-SPF). Analysis and simulation results demonstrate that compared to existing packet-mode schedulers, P-SPF significantly reduces the waiting time for short packets while achieving a high overall throughput when the traffic load is heavy. Moreover, with a relatively low speedup, P-SPF performs better than existing packet-mode schedulers under any traffic load.

1 Introduction

Input queueing packet switches are widely employed in state-of-the-art core routers, such as Cisco 12000 series core routers [1], the Tiny-Tera [2] and the BBN router [3]. In these switches, a buffering scheme called virtual output queueing (VOQ) is typically deployed. In VOQ, an input port maintains one separate buffering queue for each output port. VOQ entirely eliminates the head-of-line (HOL) blocking in input queueing switches, and even achieves 100% throughput with appropriate scheduling algorithms, such as iSLIP [4], iLPF [5] and DRRM [6]. All of these algorithms

---

[*] This work was supported by NSFC (No. 60173009 and No. 60373007), China 863 High-tech Plan (No. 2002AA103011-1 and No. 2003AA115110), China/Ireland Science and Technology Collaboration Research Fund (CI-2003-02) and the Specialized Research Fund for the Doctoral Program of Higher Education of China (No. 20040003048).

H. de Meer and N. Bhatti (Eds.): IWQoS 2005, LNCS 3552, pp. 246–258, 2005.

operate on a fixed time slot, which is defined as the duration of a cell (a fixed-size segment). This kind of scheduling is generally called cell-mode scheduling.

In cell-mode scheduling, IP packets are segmented into cells at an input port, then these cells are switched independently from input ports to their destination output ports, and finally IP packets are reassembled at each output port. Since cells from different input ports may be interleaved with cells of other packets when switching, virtual input queueing (VIQ) is deployed to reassemble IP packets. VIQ requires lots of logical buffers when the switch has many ports and multiple priority queues. In recent years, researchers have proposed another architecture called packet-mode scheduling. In packet-mode scheduling, scheduling algorithms consider all the cells of a packet as one scheduling unit and grants an input port continuously until the last cell of a packet. Meanwhile, a granted input port sends cells of the same packet in the acknowledged VOQ. Packet-mode scheduling simplifies the switching architecture, removes the reassembly buffer, and reduces the delay for reassembling packets at an output port. Furthermore, packet-mode scheduling does not bring about performance penalty from the perspective of user's QoS [7][8].

Although packet-mode scheduling may be more attractive due to the fact that variable-size packets are processed in routers, we find that packet-mode scheduling results in large delay for short packets because of the continuous transferring of other long data packets. This is not a simple fairness problem among packets of variable sizes, because short and long packets carry different types of traffic. We analyze a real Internet trace called Auckland-II from National Laboratory for Applied Network Research (NLANR) [9], and obtain that the fraction of Transmission Control Protocol (TCP), User Datagram Protocol (UDP) and other protocol packets are about 86.5%, 12.8% and 0.7%, respectively. This obviously demonstrates that TCP is the dominant transport protocol in Internet, and it is invaluable to study how to optimize TCP protocol. In Auckland-II the fraction of packets not more than 64 bytes is about 60% of overall packets. Of those short packets, TCP data packets are only about 3.9% and others are TCP ACKs and TCP control segments, such as SYN, FIN and RST. TCP ACKs can be piggybacked in TCP data packets, but in practice piggybacking seldom occurs because most applications do not send data in both the forward and reverse directions simultaneously [10][11]. Blocking short packets will cause lots of TCP retransmissions due to the timeout of TCP ACKs, and thus wastes the network bandwidth by resending the same data packet twice or more. Moreover, the round-trip time (RTT) of TCP flows has a significant variability [12]. TCP performance can be improved by greatly reducing the congestion delay for short packets, while not or slightly increasing the delay for long data packets.

Differentiated Services (DS) model [13] deals with different priority flows, rather than packets within the same TCP flow. Some DS-based works [14][15] have addressed the problem of blocking TCP ACK segments, and the preferential scheduling of variable-size TCP flows has been also proposed [16]. Different from these works, we do the research from the perspective of switching architectures and scheduling algorithms in core routers, and our main objective is to reduce the delay for short packets. One approach is to retain the architecture of general packet-mode scheduling, but grant short packets first when both short and long packets at the heads of VOQs compete for the same output port. However, through simulations we obtain that this approach cannot significantly improve the performance of short packets. This is because short packets are mainly blocked by long packets that are ahead of them in the same VOQ, rather than by cells at the heads of other VOQs. Then we turn to consider another approach called Short Packets First (SPF) [17]. SPF buffers short and long packets into separate VOQs, and then always schedules short packets first without preempting the transferring of long packets. SPF can achieve 100% throughput and substantially reduce the average packet waiting time for short packets as well as overall packets.

In this paper, to lower the buffering complexity of SPF and improve the performance of SPF further, we propose a new scheduling algorithm called preemptive short packets first (P-SPF). In P-SPF, at an input port all short packets (regardless of destination output ports) are buffered in one separate FIFO queue, but they can preempt the transferring of long packets. P-SPF eliminates the VOQs for short packets in [17] and reduces its buffering complexity. Furthermore, P-SPF achieves even lower delay for short packets than SPF, and this greatly benefits TCP flows because TCP ACK segments and control segments are treated as short packets (see Section 2 for details). P-SPF achieves an overall throughput of 94% with respect to a real traffic model. With a moderate speedup, P-SPF performs better than other packet-mode scheduling algorithms under any traffic load.

The rest of this paper is organized as follows. Section 2 describes the preemptive packet-mode scheduling architecture and studies the criteria of classifying short and long packets to avoid the out-of-sequence problem for TCP data packets. Section 3 illustrates the iterative scheduling process of P-SPF. Section 4 analyzes the performance of P-SPF using standard queueing theory. Section 5 presents simulation results under a model based on the real measurement in Internet. Finally, the concluding remarks are given in Section 6.

2 Logical Architecture for P-SPF

In this section we describe the preemptive packet-mode scheduling architecture, and study the criteria of classifying short and long packets to avoid the out-of-sequence problem within a TCP data flow.

2.1 Preemptive Packet-Mode Scheduling Architecture

Fig. 1 shows the logical architecture of preemptive packet-mode scheduling, where N is the port number. When an IP packet arrives at an input port, it will be segmented into one or more cells by the segmentation module. The buffer manager module is responsible for buffering cells into *IFIFO_S* for short packets or *VOQ_k* for long packets, where k is the packet's destination port number. The input scheduler module monitors the status of *IFIFO_S* for short packets and all the VOQs for long packets, sends connection requests for both short and long packets to the switch scheduler, and then transfers the head cell in *IFIFO_S* or *VOQ_k* when it receives an acknowledgment for short packets or one for long packets. The switch scheduler module executes

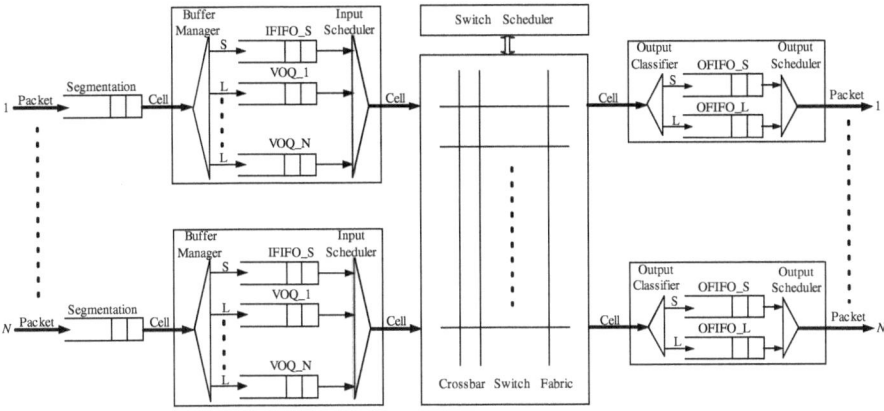

Fig. 1. Preemptive packet-mode scheduling architecture

the preemptive packet-mode scheduling algorithm, and then reconfigures the crossbar switch fabric in the corresponding time slot.

At an output port, the output classifier module dispenses cells of short and long packets into *OFIFO_S* and *OFIFO_L*, respectively. Once a short packet or all the cells of a long packet have been transferred to an output port, the output scheduler module will send short and long packets to the external link. The output scheduler does not preempt the transferring of any packets to the link, but sends short packets first when the link is available.

2.2 The Criteria of Classifying Short and Long Packets

In many studies, the cell size of 64 bytes is adopted as a compromise between the utilization of switching bandwidth and the convenience of switching and scheduling. In this paper we also choose 64 bytes as the switching cell size[1].

For TCP data flows with mixed short and long packets, preempting the transferring of long packets may occasionally cause out-of-sequence of data packets within a TCP flow. Although this phenomenon is allowed [18] and does exist in Internet owing to local parallelism in routers and links [19], we still develop the criteria of classifying short and long packets, which can guarantee the sequence of TCP data packets.

Criteria: a packet is classified as a short packet if and only if the two conditions are both satisfied: 1) the packet size is not more than 64 bytes; and 2) it is a UDP packet or a TCP non-data packet (i.e. a TCP packet but not containing any data). Otherwise, a packet is classified as a long packet.

The criteria can be easily implemented in a network processor when performing the layer-4 flow classification. The IP header length, IP total length and protocol can

---

[1] In switches for IPv6 routers, the cell size will be a little larger.

be extracted from the IP header. If the protocol field indicates that the encapsulated payload is a TCP packet, the TCP header length field will be obtained from the TCP header. If IP total length equals IP header length plus TCP header length, we say that this packet is a TCP non-data packet.

3 P-SPF Scheduling Algorithm

P-SPF is an iterative packet-mode scheduling algorithm. The scheduling of P-SPF in each time slot is composed of two parallel processes: scheduling for short packets and scheduling for long packets. Let N denote the port number. An input port i ($1 \le i \le N$) maintains one pointer $IP_L(i)$ for long packets. An output port j ($1 \le j \le N$) has two pointers: $OP_S(j)$ for short packets and $OP_L(j)$ for long packets. We will present the scheduling for short packets as well as for long packets as follows.

The scheduling for short packets, whose sizes are only one cell, is relatively simple.

Step 1. *Input Request.*
Each input port, where *IFIFO_S* is not empty, sends a connection request to its head cell's destination output port.
Step 2. *Output Grant.*
Each output port j grants a request for short packets using the round-robin schedule with the highest priority pointer $OP_S(j)$, and then updates $OP_S(j)$ to the one next to the granted input port (modulo N).

In the scheduling for long packets, input ports and output ports have two states.

1) *Free* state: no cells or the last cell of a packet is transferring;
2) *Busy* state: the port is occupied by the transferring of a packet except its last cell.

The scheduling for long packets involves three iterative steps.

Step 1. *Input Request.*
Each *free* input port sends connection requests for long packets at the heads of VOQs to their destination output ports.
Step 2. *Output Grant.*
If an output port has received requests for short packets while serving a long packet, it will break the current transferring of long packets and grant short packets. If not, a *busy* output port continues to grant its matched input port. If a *free* output port j has received multiple requests for long packets, it will grant the one which appears next in a fixed round-robin schedule starting from the highest priority input port with the pointer $OP_L(j)$. If and only if output port j's acknowledgment is accepted by an input port in step 3, the pointer $OP_L(j)$ is updated to the one beyond the granted input port (modulo N).
Step 3. *Input Accept.*
If input port i receives multiple grants for long packets from output ports, it will accept the one, saying k, which appears next in the round-robin schedule from $IP_L(i)$, and then update $IP_L(i)$ to the one next to output port k (modulo N).

Newly matched *free* input and output ports will update their states to *busy* when the size of granted packet is larger than one cell, and still stay in *free* when the packet has just one cell. *Busy* input and output ports are set to *free* state when they have sent out and received the last cell of a packet, respectively.

Because of the simultaneous scheduling for short and long packets, an input port may accept at most two acknowledgments: one for short packets and the other for long packets. In this scenario, the input port will send the short packet in the current time slot, and then cells of the acknowledged long packet immediately if receiving no acknowledgment for short packets in the following time slots.

4 Performance Analysis

Under admissible traffic, we mainly study the performance closely related to the switch fabric, which includes the delay in waiting queues and that of traversing the switch fabric.

Packet delay: the time interval between the departure time at an output port and the arrival time at an input port for the same packet.

Packet service time: the time a packet occupies the switch fabric.

Packet waiting time: the duration when a packet stays at an input port.

We focus on an output port, take this output port as a queueing server, and define the following symbols.

1) λ_s, λ_l and λ : the packet arrival rate of short, long and overall packets.

2) ρ_s, ρ_l and ρ : the offered load of short, long and overall packets.

3) $E(S_s)$, $E(S_l)$ and $E(S)$: the average packet service time for short, long and overall packets.

4) C_V : the coefficient of variation of the packet service time.

5) $E(W_s)$, $E(W_l)$ and $E(W_p)$: the average packet waiting time for short, long and overall packets in P-SPF. In general packet-mode scheduling, the average packet waiting time for overall packets is denoted by $E(W_G)$.

6) G : preemptive gain, which is defined as the ratio of the average packet waiting time for overall packets in general packet-mode scheduling and that in P-SPF.

4.1 Packet Waiting Time Estimation of P-SPF

By queueing theory, we can give an intuitive and quantitative estimation on the average packet waiting time. In input queueing switches, there are two types of conflicts: one at each output port, and the other at each input port. When an output port receives multiple requests from different input ports, only one request can be granted. Similarly, when an input port receives multiple grants from different output ports, only one grant can be accepted. To estimate the average packet delay with a queueing model, we neglect the conflicts occurring at each input port. This means that in the following theoretical analysis we assume that an input port can accept multiple grants and can send more than one cell in one time slot. As in [7], the analysis results are reasonably accurate for low to medium load.

The service model of short packets is identical to the input queueing model in [20]. From its simulations we deduce that when the offered load is low it is accurate to use an output queueing model to characterize the average delay in the input queueing model. Let $\overline{W}$ denote the average waiting time of cells in the output queueing model, and from [20] we have

$$\overline{W} = \frac{N-1}{N} \times \frac{p}{2(1-p)} \; ,$$

(1)

where p is the probability that a cell arrives at a particular input port.

In fact, the offered load of short packets in Internet is generally less than 0.1 (See the simulation model in Section 5 for details), so using (1) we get

$$E(W_S) = \frac{N-1}{N} \times \frac{\lambda_S}{2(1-\rho_S)} \; .$$

(2)

When $N \to \infty$, $E(W_S) = \dfrac{\lambda_S}{2(1-\rho_S)} \; .$

(3)

In P-SPF, short packets can preempt the transferring of long packets, and we use the preemptive priority queueing model [21] to estimate the approximate delay for long packets. We have

$$E(W_l) = \frac{1}{1-\rho_s} \times \left[E(S_l) + \frac{\lambda_S E(S_S^2) + \lambda_l E(S_l^2)}{2(1-\rho)} \right] - E(S_l) \; ,$$

(4)

$$E(W_P) = \frac{\lambda_S}{\lambda} E(W_S) + \frac{\lambda_l}{\lambda} E(W_l) = \frac{1}{\lambda(1-\rho_s)} \left[\frac{1}{2}\lambda_S^2 + \rho_s\rho_l + \lambda_l \frac{\lambda E(S^2)}{2(1-\rho)} \right] \; .$$

(5)

In general packet-mode scheduling, packets are served without being interleaved with cells of other packets. Consequently, general packet-mode scheduling algorithm corresponds to the M/G/1 FCFS queueing model [7][22], so we can get

$$E(W_G) = \frac{(1+C_V^2)\rho E(S)}{2(1-\rho)} \; .$$

(6)

Combining (5) with (6), we get the preemptive gain

$$G = \frac{E(W_G)}{E(W_P)} = \frac{(1+C_V^2)(1-\rho_s)\rho^2}{(1-\rho)\lambda_S^2 + 2(1-\rho)\rho_s\rho_l + \lambda_l\lambda E(S^2)} \; .$$

(7)

4.2 The Maximum Overall Throughput of P-SPF

The preemption of short packets will break the matched connections between input and output ports for long packets. Fig. 2 shows such an example. In the current time slot, two matches for long packets are established. Then a short packet destined to O_A arrives at I_A, the new matching for this short packet will break the two previous

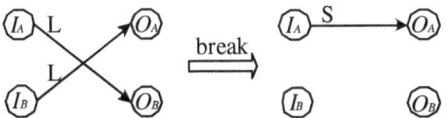

Fig. 2. An example of a broken match

matches and make output port O_B tewmporarily hanged up in the next time slot. As a result, the bandwidth of O_B is wasted and the overall throughput is degraded.

We focus on the output port O_B and define two probability events.

1) $A_s(O_B)$: a short packet with the destination port O_B arrives at an input port.
2) $A_s(I_A)$: a short packet arrives at input port I_A .

When a long packet is transferring to O_B, it will be blocked if both $A_s(I_A)$ and *not* $A_s(O_B)$ occur. Therefore, the probability that O_B is blocked can be represented as

$$P_r\left(A_s\left(I_A\right)\cap\overline{A_s\left(O_B\right)}\right)=P_r\left(\overline{A_s\left(O_B\right)}\left|A_s\left(I_A\right)\right.\right)\times P_r\left(A_s\left(I_A\right)\right)=\left(1-\frac{\lambda_S}{N}\right)^{N-1}\times\left(1-\frac{1}{N}\right)\times\lambda_S . \tag{8}$$

When $N \rightarrow \infty$, we obtain

$$P_r\left(O_B \text{ is blocked}\right)=\lambda_S \ell^{-\lambda_S} . \tag{9}$$

Let T_{max} denote the maximum achievable throughput of P-SPF, and then T_{max} can be figured out as follows:

$$T_{max} =1-P_r\left(O_B \text{ is blocked}\right)=\begin{cases}1-\lambda_S\left(1-\dfrac{1}{N}\right)\left(1-\dfrac{\lambda_S}{N}\right)^{N-1} & N<\infty \\ 1-\lambda_S \ell^{-\lambda_S} & N=\infty\end{cases} . \tag{10}$$

Assuming $\lambda_S = 0.0686$, we can obtain $T_{max} = 0.936$ when $N =\infty$, and $T_{max} = 0.940$ when $N = 16$. The result is consistent with the simulation solution in Section 5.

5 Simulations

We build a simulated switch model and run one million time slots. The switch size is 16×16, i.e. $N = 16$. *ON-OFF* model is used to simulate the packet arrival process.

OFF state: no packets arrive in this state. *OFF* state is modeled by the geometric distribution, and the probability that *OFF* state ends is fixed to a parameter, which determines the offered load at an input port.

ON state: packets are generated in this state. In *ON* state, destinations of arrival packets are uniformly distributed over all output ports. *ON* state ends when the packet is transferred completely.

We omit the process of padding packets whose sizes are not integral times of the cell size, and then use the TRIMODEL to describe the distribution of packet sizes.

TRIMODEL(a, b, c, P_a, P_b): Packet sizes are chosen equal to either a cells with probability P_a, or b cells with P_b, or c cells with $1 - P_a - P_b$. In the simulations, we set the parameter $a = 1$, $b = 9$, $c = 24$, $P_a = 0.559$ and $P_b = 0.200$, i.e. the packet sizes are 64, 576 and 1536 bytes, respectively. These 64-byte packets are short packets and others are long data packets. The model is consistent with the real Internet traffic reported in [7][10][11], so TRIMODEL(1, 9, 24, 0.559, 0.200) is a relatively accurate model to describe the real packet size distribution in Internet.

Under general packet-mode scheduling, we simulate 4-iSLIP [4], maximum size matching (MSM), maximum weight matching with the weight of cell age (MWM-CA) and maximum weight matching with the weight of queue length (MWM-QL) [23]. The reason for choosing 4-iSLIP is its high performance and practicality, and the reason for choosing MSM, MWM-QL and MWM-CA is that they are the most typical algorithms used in the theoretical analysis. We also modify MSM, MWM-QL and MWM-CA to function in preemptive packet-mode scheduling, and call the modified algorithms P-MSM, P-MWM-QL and P-MWM-CA, respectively. These algorithms work similarly to P-SPF, except that they use MSM, MWM-QL and MWM-CA to schedule short packets first and then schedule long packets among the unmatched input/output ports.

5.1 Performance on the Maximum Throughput

Table 1 shows the maximum throughput of these selected algorithms under general packet-mode and preemptive packet-mode scheduling. The results in Table 1 show that all these algorithms under general packet-mode scheduling can achieve approximate 100% throughput, and under preemptive packet-mode scheduling, the maximum throughput is 94%. When an input port is under full utilization, we can get the arrival rate of short packets:

$$\lambda_S = \frac{aP_a}{aP_a + bP_b + cP_c} = 0.0686 \ . \tag{11}$$

Therefore, the simulated throughput equals what we have obtained from (10).

5.2 Delay Performance of Preemptive Packet-Mode Scheduling

The maximum benefit of P-SPF is for short packets, and Fig. 3 shows the average packet waiting time for short packets. In general packet-mode scheduling, the waiting time for short packets is very large. This is mainly because short packets have to wait behind those long packets that require a large service time. In preemptive packet-mode scheduling, it is observed that the average packet waiting time for short packets is approximately zero, no matter under P-SPF, P-MSM, P-MWM-CA or P-MWM-QL. This means that the blocking probability of short packets is low, i.e. short packets will get served immediately after they arrive at an input port. Throughout the simulations we get the maximum length of $IFIFO\_S$ is less than 7 cells. By preempting the transferring of long packets, the waiting time for short packets falls drastically, especially when the offered load is high. In other words, the preemption provides a fast switching path for short packets.

Table 1. Throughput of simulated scheduling algorithms

Algorithms	Throughput	Algorithms	Throughput
4-*i*SLIP	0.996	P-SPF	0.940
MSM	0.997	P-MSM	0.940
MWM-QL	0.997	P-MWM-QL	0.940
MWM-CA	0.998	P-MWM-CA	0.940

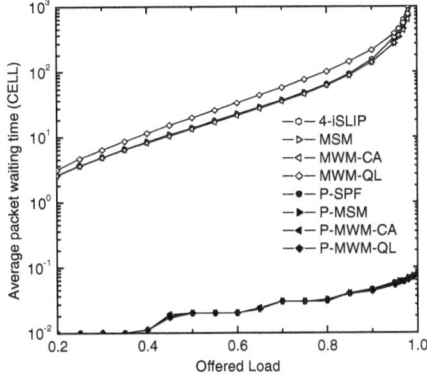 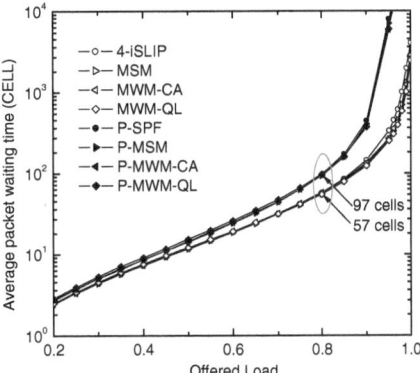

Fig. 3. Average packet waiting time for short packets

Fig. 4. Average packet waiting time for long packets

In preemptive packet-mode scheduling, the first priority and preemption of short packets may increase the average packet waiting time for long packets. Fig. 4 shows the average packet waiting time for long packets. When the offered load is less than 0.8, the performance degradation of long packets is much small. E.g., when the offered load is 0.8, the average packet waiting time for long packets is about 40 cells larger than that in general packet-mode scheduling. The absolute time is less than that transferring a maximum-size Ethernet packet (24 cells) twice at the line rate. As a conclusion, the increased delay for long packets can be almost ignored when the line rate is high, such as 10 Gb/s or 40 Gb/s. When the offered load is greater than 0.8, the difference of average packet waiting time for long packets between general and preemptive packet-mode scheduling becomes a little larger.

Fig. 5 shows the simulation results on the average packet delay for overall packets with the offered load from 0.2 to 1.0. The four curves of preemptive packet-mode scheduling algorithms overlap almost everywhere. This shows that P-SPF can achieve the performance of maximum weight matching under the simulated Internet traffic. When the offered load is less than 0.85, the performance of preemptive packet-mode scheduling is better than that in general packet-mode scheduling. When the offered load is larger than 0.85, the performance of preemptive packet-mode scheduling begins to degrade with the increase of the offered load. This is the limitation of the

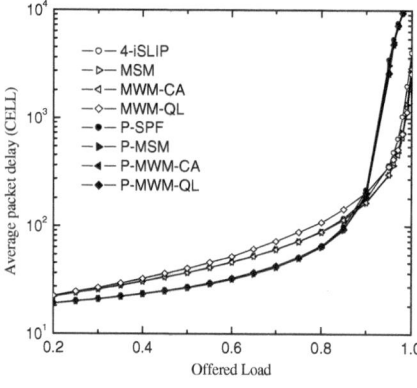 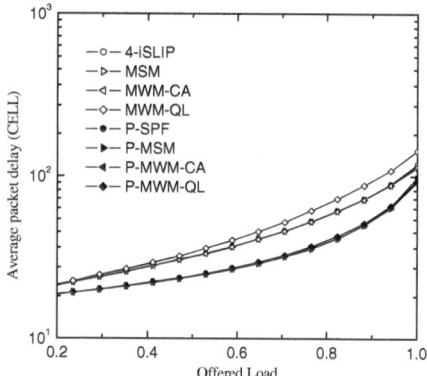

Fig. 5. Average packet delay for overall packets

Fig. 6. Average packet delay for overall packets with the speedup of 1.176

overall throughput of 94%, which can be improved further with the approach discussed in next subsection.

5.3 To Improve the Delay Performance of P-SPF

We deploy rather a small speedup to improve the throughput and reduce the delay for overall packets in P-SPF further. In Fig. 5 we get that when the offered load is lower than 0.85, P-SPF will always perform better than general packet-mode scheduling algorithms. Therefore, the speedup of 1.176 (1/0.85) can always guarantee the advantages of P-SPF.

Fig. 6 shows the average packet delay for overall packets, where all the simulated scheduling algorithms are with the speedup of 1.176. By comparing Fig. 6 with Fig. 5, we can see that the overall packet delay in P-SPF is greatly reduced under heavy offered load. E.g., when the offered load is 1.0, the average packet delay for overall packets is less than 100 cells in P-SPF, and this value is much large in Fig. 5 without the speedup. In real router designs, such a low speedup is easy to implement in hardware. E.g., to deal with 10 Gb/s links, with the mature 3.125 Gb/s high-speed serial link (HSSL) technology, four serial links can achieve the speedup of 1.25.

6 Conclusions

In this paper, we consider the packet-mode scheduling in input queueing switches and propose a scheduling algorithm called P-SPF. Compared to the general packet-mode schedulers, P-SPF can provide lower delay for short packets, resulting in an improved performance of upper layer protocols, such as TCP.

This is achieved by the following mechanisms and features. First, we took a cross-layer approach in the design of switching architectures and scheduling algorithms.

Second, we proposed a preemptive packet-mode scheduling architecture. Compared to general packet-mode scheduling architecture, the added cost of P-SPF is one FIFO queue for short packets at each input port and that at each output port; the FIFO size is very small and hence the increased cost is negligible. Third, P-SPF is practical and its complexity is almost the same as iSLIP. Fourth, with the low speedup of 1.176, P-SPF always performs better than existing packet-mode scheduling schemes. Last but not the least, P-SPF can significantly reduce the average packet waiting time for short packets, which greatly benefits TCP flows.

Furthermore, most real time voice over IP (VoIP) traffic in UDP flows is of short packets, so lowering the delay for these short packets will also upgrade the QoS of VoIP traffic and provide a better way to support VoIP in backbone networks. This exciting topic will be researched in future works.

References

1. McKeown N.: Fast Switched Backplane for a Gigabit Switched Router. Business Commun. Review, vol. 27, no. 12, (1997) 1-30
2. McKeown N., Izzard M., Mekkittikul A., Ellersick W., Horowitz M.: Tiny Tera: a Packet Switch Core. IEEE Micro, vol. 17, no. 1, (1997) 26-33
3. Partridge C., et al.: A 50-Gb/s IP Router. IEEE/ACM Trans. Networking, vol. 6, no. 3, (1998) 237-248
4. McKeown N.: The iSLIP Scheduling Algorithm for Input-Queued Switches. IEEE/ACM Trans. Networking, vol. 7, no. 2, (1999) 188-201
5. Mekkittikul A., McKeown N.: A Practical Scheduling Algorithm to Achieve 100% Throughput in Input-Queued Switches. IEEE INFOCOM 1998, (1998) 792-799
6. Chao H.J.: Saturn: a Terabit Packet Switch Using Dual Round-Robin. IEEE Commun. Magazine, vol. 38, no. 12, (2000) 78-84
7. Marsan M.A., Bianco A., Giaccone P., Leonardi E., Neri F.: Packet-Mode Scheduling in Input-Queued Cell-Based Switches. IEEE/ACM Trans. Networking, vol. 10, no. 5, (2002) 666-678
8. Ganjali Y., Keshavarzian A., Shah D.: Input Queued Switches: Cell Switching vs. Packet Switching. IEEE INFOCOM 2003, (2003) 1651-1658
9. The Auckland-II trace, National Laboratory for Applied Network Research (NLANR), http://pma.nlanr.net/Special/
10. Thompson K., Miller G.J., Wilder R.: Wide-Area Internet Traffic Patterns and Characteristics. IEEE Network, vol. 11, no. 6, (1997) 10-23
11. Fraleigh C., et al.: Packet-level Traffic Measurements from the Sprint IP Backbone. IEEE Network, vol. 17, no. 6, (2003) 6-16
12. Aikat J., Kaur J., Smith F.D., Jeffay K.: Variability in TCP Round-trip Times. ACM SIGCOMM Conference on Internet Measurement Workshop 2003, (2003) 279-284
13. Blake S., Black D., Carlson M., Davies E., Wang Z., Weiss W.: An Architecture for Differentiated Services. IETF RFC 2475, (1998)
14. Papagiannaki K., Thiran P., Crowcroft J., Diot C.: Preferential Treatment of Acknowledgment Packets in a Differentiated Services Network. IWQoS 2001, Springer-Verlag Lecture Notes in Computer Science, vol. 2092, (2001) 187-201
15. Wang H.N., Shin K.G.: Transport-aware IP Routers: a Built-in Protection Mechanism to Counter DDoS Attacks. IEEE Trans. Parallel and Distributed Systems, vol. 14, no. 9, (2003) 873-884

16. Rai I.A., Biersack E.W., Urvoy-Keller G.: Size-Based Scheduling to Improve the Performance of Short TCP Flows. IEEE Network, vol. 19, no. 1, (2005) 12-17
17. Li W.J., Liu B.: SPF: to Improve the Performance of Packet-Mode Scheduling. Elsevier Computer Commun., in press, (2005)
18. Baker F.: Requirements for IP Version 4 Routers. IETF RFC 1812, (1995)
19. Bennett J.C.R., Partridge C., Shectman N.: Packet Reordering is not Pathological Network Behavior. IEEE/ACM Trans. Networking, vol. 7, no. 6, (1999) 789-798
20. Karol M., Hluchyj M., Morgan S.: Input Versus Output Queueing on a Space-Division Packet Switch. IEEE Trans. Commun., vol. 35, no. 12, (1987) 1347-1356
21. Allen A.O.: Probability, Statistics, and Queueing Theory with Computer Science Applications. New York Academic Press, New York (1978)
22. Wolff R.W.: Stochastic Modeling and the Theory of Queues. Prentice-Hall Inc., Englewood Cliffs, NJ USA (1989)
23. Mckeown N., Mekkittikul A., Anantharam V., Walrand J.: Achieving 100% Throughput in an Input-Queued Switch. IEEE Trans. Commun., vol. 47, no. 8, (1999) 1260-1267

Edge-Based Differentiated Services

Henrik Lundqvist, Ignacio Más Ivars, and Gunnar Karlsson

Laboratory for Communication Networks,
KTH, the Royal Institute of Technology,
Electrum 229 164 40 Kista, Sweden
{henrik.lundqvist, nacho, gk}@imit.kth.se

Abstract. Network quality of service is traditionally thought to be provided by a combination of scheduling in the network nodes to enforce a capacity sharing policy and traffic controls to prevent congestion that could annihilate that policy. The work presented herein is instead based on an end-to-end argument: A capacity sharing policy is enforced by traffic controls in the hosts at the edges of the network, without any scheduling support in the network. Our proposal is to add a feed-forward control at the transport layer to provide a service that is better suited to conversational and streaming applications than the batch-oriented transfer mode provided by TCP. The paper presents the control and its evaluation: We compare the sharing of capacity between traffic classes and study the loss rate seen by admitted streams. The outcome is that the new control adds a distinctly different service to the service offered by TCP for the Internet.

1 Introduction

Conversational and streaming services need quality assurances in the Internet. Most of these services convey audio-visual data that have inherent rates, determined by rate-distortion tradeoffs in the encoding of signals from the different information sources. Human perception places a limit on the amount of delay that is acceptable for communication. For conversational services, it is the well-established mouth-to-ear delay of 150 to 200 ms that need be respected as well as the adjoining lip-to-mouth synchronization of moving images that roughly lies within the range of ±100 ms [12]. Furthermore, human perception favors consistency. The network should hence allow a session to complete when started without noticeable changes in quality which could annoy the user or which might render the session useless.

Since TCP congestion control is not adequate for streaming and conversational services, we propose to add a second congestion control to the transport layer of the IP protocols to provide a consistent quality. The throughput should with high probability be at a level that exceeds the bit rate of the stream. Thereby, we make the quality of service assurance into a delay-loss tradeoff that can be made outside the network [11].

The congestion control we propose is a probe-based admission control, which the authors have proposed in several prior publications [3][4][5]. However, it has hitherto been combined in the classical manner with network scheduling for providing

H. de Meer and N. Bhatti (Eds.): IWQoS 2005, LNCS 3552, pp. 259–270, 2005.

isolation between traffic classes as well as between probes (flow establishment attempts) and ongoing flows. Section 2 in this paper describes how this probe-based admission control works and how it can be used to provide resource sharing with TCP along a network path without any differentiation in the network. The two controls are supposed to provide different types of services, and it is important to note that the two service classes have incomparable characteristics and can therefore not be judged better or worse in any general sense: Only for a given application can it be said that one or the other class is the best.

Section 3 contains a description of how FEC can be added to separate the loss requirement of the applications from the loss rate in the network, and how the parameters of the FEC and the admission control should be set. In Section 4 simulations are used to evaluate the scheme in terms of fairness and the provided quality. Finally, the conclusion of the evaluation of the proposal is given in Section 5.

The work presented herein is an extension and evaluation of the initial proposal presented in [1]. The proposal by Roberts and Oueslati-Boulahia for flow aware networking gives the rationales for the classification of traffic into a stream class and a batch class, and it gives the general properties of the classes [2]; the basic idea of providing two different classes that cannot be ranked in goodness is akin to the alternative best effort proposal by Hurley et alii [9]. The suggested implementations of these two proposals are however entirely network centric. Our proposal is the antithesis of the TCP friendly rate control of Floyd et alii [7] in the sense that we do not promote rate adaptation per stream, but allow streams to be inelastic, when admitted into the network; the probe-based admission control ensures that the aggregate of admitted streams is responsive to congestion in a way that is fair to TCP. There is a time-scale separation that need be recognized: TCP reacts fast to congestion but will also quickly capture capacity that becomes available, while the stream class will be slower to react both to congestion and to available capacity. So, the services provided by the TCP congestion control and the probe-based congestion control are clearly different.

2 Probe-Based Admission Control

Probe-based admission control can be performed without any support from the network. A new flow can only be established after probing the path across the network to the receiver and determining that the network state is acceptable. A probe is a stream of packets that is sent at a constant rate, R_{UDP}, which is equal to the peak rate of the variable-rate flow. The contents of the probe packets may be control data for the flow, such as encoding and flow parameters. The receiver may furthermore use the constant-rate probe-packet stream for clock synchronization and for allowing the jitter removal control system to settle into steady state. The details of the probe-based admission control are described in [4].

The receiver acknowledges received probe packets, which allows the sender to estimate the loss probability for the path, denoted by p. The important criterion is when to accept a flow. Our policy bases the decision on the estimation of an equivalent TCP sending rate:

$$r_{TCP} = \frac{MSS}{RTT} \sqrt{\frac{C}{p}}, \qquad (1)$$

where C is a constant related to the throughput of TCP, RTT is the round trip time and MSS is the maximum segment size, measured in bits. The constant C is often set to 1.5, but the exact value depends on details in the TCP parameters, such as whether delayed acknowledgements are used. In this context C can be used to tune the sharing between UDP and TCP, and it has been chosen to 1.0 in the simulations in this paper based on some experimental evaluation. The flow may be established when the probe rate is below the equivalent TCP rate, $R_{UDP} < r_{TCP}$, and rejected otherwise. (An admission policy based on comparing the probe loss to a fixed threshold is included in the evaluation of ref. [1].)

3 Parameter Setting

In this section we investigate how the loss requirement of an application can be met when the loss rate in the network for an accepted flow would exceed the tolerance of the application. By using forward-error correction, it is possible to achieve a separation between the loss probability seen by the application and the loss probability of the network. We assume that the application has a certain requirement on the data rate, the maximum tolerable delay and loss. For example, an audiovisual application may use the rate-distortion and loss-distortion functions to determine the total distortion at a given loss probability and data rate. Depending on the desired quality, the data rate and the maximum loss requirement are determined. Using knowledge about the admission policy it is also possible to find good combinations of data rate and loss requirement, p_{req}, for given distortion requirements.

The parameters of the error correction are set statically for a flow to values that give the highest chance of admittance while not being unfair to the TCP traffic. In order to achieve this we make use of the TCP throughput equation again. From (1) the loss probability, p_{eq}, that corresponds to a certain bit rate, R_{UDP}, can be found to be:

$$p_{eq} = \frac{MSS^2 C}{RTT^2 R_{UDP}^2} \qquad (2)$$

Equation (2) shows how the admission threshold for the probe based admission control can be set when the MSS and the RTT are already known. By comparing p_{eq} and p_{req} we can deduce which one sets a lower requirement on the loss probability and use that as admission threshold. The only information required for this is the RTT and the MSS, which therefore must have been estimated beforehand, for example using ICMP echo requests and path-MTU discovery. As it turns out, measurement of the RTT may in fact not be necessary: In Section 4.6 we will introduce a compensation for the delay that will be used in the admission policy. It means that the parameters of the FEC will not depend on the RTT. For now, assume that the RTT and MSS are known, however.

The probe-based admission control can only give probabilistic guarantees about the quality of a flow, therefore it is important to include margins that ensures that the loss rate will be sufficiently good. In principle it would be desirable to have a guarantee that an admitted flow should experience a lower loss rate than the specification, with a given probability. However, since that depends on the future development of the loss rate and the length of the flow it is not feasible. A better solution is to ensure that the loss rate on the probed path does not exceed the required loss rate with a certain probability. We base the loss-probability estimate on the assumption that the measured loss is normally distributed for the probes, and use a 95 percent confidence level [3]. The assumption of normal distribution is motivated by central limit arguments, which are valid since we choose the probe long enough for the admission threshold. If FEC is not taken into account, the loss threshold for the admission process including margin can be written as:

$$P_{m\,arg} = P_{req} - z_R \sqrt{\frac{P_{req}(1 - P_{req})}{N_{probe}}},$$ (3)

where z_R is the R-percentile for a normal distribution and N_{probe} is the number of packets in the probe. The resulting p_{marg} will hence be significantly lower than the loss requirement p_{req}. Without FEC the admission threshold would have to be set to the minimum of p_{marg} and p_{eq}.

To evaluate the gain of FEC the packet losses are assumed to be uncorrelated. Even though the real loss process is correlated the simulations will show that this assumption is sufficiently good for our purposes. We consider block codes, such as Reed-Solomon codes, with erasure decoding so that the number of recoverable losses per block is the same as the number of added redundant packets. The number of lost packets in a block is geometrically distributed and the loss rate after FEC can be calculated for a given block length of N data packets and M redundant packets:

$$P_{packetloss} = \sum_{i=M+1}^{N+M} \binom{N+M}{i} p^i (1-p)^{N+M-i} \frac{i}{N+M}.$$ (4)

The last factor in (4) is the fraction of lost packets; it converts the block loss rate to packet loss rate. The block length is determined by the delay tolerance of the application as dR_{UDP}/P_{size}, where d is the delay and P_{size} is the size for UDP packets (we assume equal packet size).

After recovering losses with FEC the remaining loss rate from (4) should be lower than p_{req} with 95 percent probability. Therefore the 95 percent confidence interval is added to the admission threshold level p_{eq}.

$$p_{FECm\,arg} = P_{eq} + z_R \sqrt{\frac{P_{eq}(1 - P_{eq})}{N_{probe}}}.$$ (5)

When $p_{FECmarg}$ is used to determine the residual loss rate after FEC from (4), the probability that the actual loss rate is too high to provide low enough residual loss rate is lower than five percent.

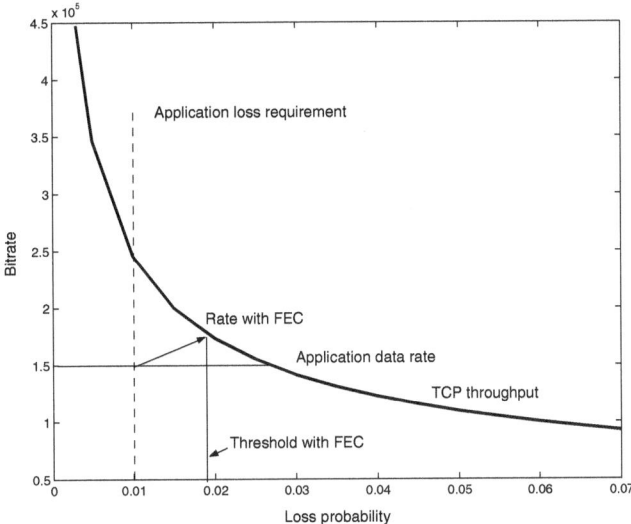

Fig. 1. When FEC is added the total rate is increased until it corresponds to a rate on the TCP throughput curve where the application requirement is met

The procedure for setting the amount of redundancy and the admission threshold is illustrated in Fig. 1. The source starts by using equation (2) to calculate the loss rate that corresponds to the peak data rate. If p_{eq} from (2) is higher than p_{marg} from (3), then the flow must use FEC. The source may first count on adding one redundant packet to each block; the corresponding increase in sending rate leads to a new value for p_{eq} which is calculated from (2). Using p_{eq} the loss rate including margin, $p_{FECmarg}$, is calculated from (5), and the packet loss rate after decoding can be calculated from (4). If this is higher than the loss requirement, another redundant packet is added and the calculations are repeated. This is iterated until the loss rate after decoding is lower than what the application demands. In Fig. 1 this means that the admission threshold p_{eq} will be on the TCP throughput curve and the angle of the arrow will be determined by the block length, i.e. the delay tolerance of the application.

4 Simulation Results

All results presented in the paper are from simulations with NS-2. The experimental settings have been chosen to provide insight into the characteristics of the scheme without adding unnecessary complexity.

4.1 TCP Fairness

A first simulation experiment aims at evaluating the fairness between TCP and streaming UDP traffic. For this purpose a single bottleneck topology with a capacity of 20 Mb/s and a one-way propagation delay of 50 ms is simulated. The first traffic scenario consists of 30 long-lived TCP Newreno flows and a varying number of constant bit rate UDP flows. The UDP flows use a probe length of one second, have a loss requirement of one percent and a net throughput of 200 kb/s. Following the procedure described in Section 3, FEC is added with three redundant packets per 20 data packets, hence resulting in a 230 kb/s total rate. The UDP flows arrive as a Poisson process and have an exponentially distributed flow length with average 50 s. In Fig. 2 the expected throughput per flow for TCP and UDP is plotted as a function of the loss rate in the network with 95 percent confidence intervals indicated. The expected goodput per UDP flow is calculated as the net sending rate times the admission probability which decreases at high loss rates due to the high probability of blocking, whereas the TCP throughput for each flow is decreased as the congestion control reacts to the packet losses. Despite of these differences in mechanisms the result is that the expected throughput is similar for both traffic types. The main difference is that TCP gets a higher throughput when the load on the network is low, since TCP will be using up the extra capacity, whereas admitted UDP flows have no need to use a higher rate than the peak rate R_{UDP}.

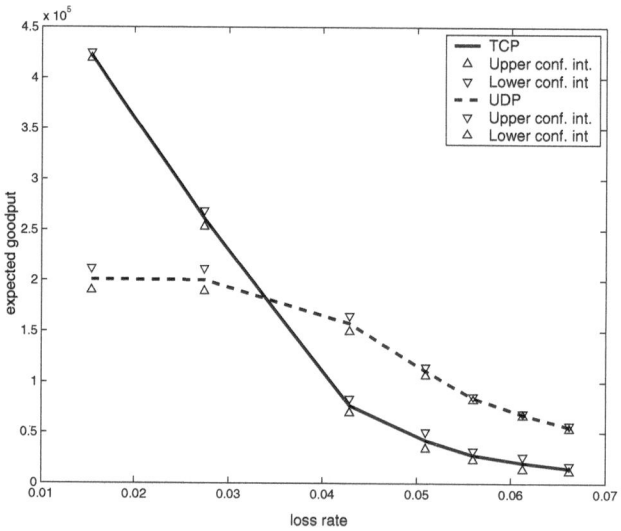

Fig. 2. The expected throughput of each TCP and UDP session decrease at similar rates as the number of UDP sessions increase. The decrease in expected UDP rate is due to higher blocking probability

Note that the sharing of TCP and UDP can be changed by modifying the parameter C in (1), for example a higher value for C results in lower blocking probability for UDP traffic. Note also that the sending rate for UDP is actually 15 percent higher when redundancy is included. It can also be seen from Fig. 2 that the shape of the curves are different, the TCP throughput is essentially convex as opposed to the expected UDP throughput, hence no perfect fairness can be defined. Furthermore, the sharing between UDP and TCP flows also depends on the traffic mix and the properties of the loss process [15]. Therefore, the targeted fairness between TCP and UDP should be such that neither of the services always gets a higher throughput over a wide range of parameters. Hence, for a specific application it should be favorable to use the intended service class.

4.2 FEC Gain

To evaluate the effect of FEC we simulate a single link topology with different offered traffic loads and evaluate the loss rate with and without FEC. The scenario is essentially the same as in the first simulation with 30 TCP flows and an increasing number of UDP flows that can tolerate a packet loss rate of maximum one percent. The offered UDP load is varied from 25 percent to 300 percent of the link capacity by increasing the arrival rate of UDP flows, however, some of the flows will be rejected. Fig. 3 shows that the loss rate of the flows can be reduced so that they achieve a sufficient quality as long as the offered UDP load is not higher than 150 percent of the link capacity. Without FEC the loss rate would on average be higher than the acceptable level. To simplify the comparison of UDP with and without FEC there is no 95 percent confidence level here, otherwise an even higher load would be tolerable without causing too high loss for the applications. This also has the effect of changing the FEC parameters so that only 10 percent redundancy is added, rather than 15 in the previous section. With the 95 percent confidence level the problem is that the acceptance probability without FEC is very low. Fig. 3 also shows that at high load some

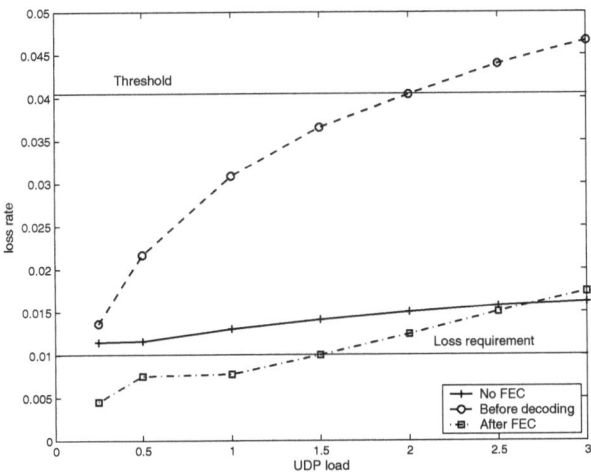

Fig. 3. The loss rate can be reduced to a level that is acceptable to the application by adding FEC. The curve with the highest loss rate is with FEC before decoding, i.e. the loss rate in the network, and the lowest is with FEC after decoding. Without FEC more sessions are rejected, hence the loss rate in the network is lower than with FEC

flows will be admitted even though the loss rate is actually higher than the threshold, this is due to the estimation inaccuracy in the probing process. Note that the loss rate after FEC does not increase significantly between 50 and 100 percent offered UDP load. This is not an effect of simulation inaccuracy; the efficiency of FEC depends on the correlation of the loss process and the degree of multiplexing, which in turn depends on the traffic. As the share of UDP traffic increase at the expense of TCP the losses are less correlated and FEC becomes more efficient.

4.3 Fairness Between Applications with Different Requirements

The choice of FEC parameters and threshold described in Section 3 does not only define the fairness between TCP and UDP flows. It also provides a way of defining fairness between real-time flows with differing requirements on loss rate, data rate and delay. The method described results in an admission threshold that determines the admission probability of a flow. To illustrate this, a traffic scenario with eight different UDP classes has been investigated. In Table 1 the rate, loss requirement and the FEC block length are given for the different classes. The FEC block length follows directly from the delay requirements of each application. Class 3 has the largest delay budget allocated for FEC in this example, the delay is 200 ms for a packet size of 188 bytes. From the three given parameters, the number of redundancy packets per block and the admission threshold are calculated. Note that due to the 95 percent confidence level, the threshold is lower than the required loss rate also for class 2 where no redundancy is added. The blocking probability for each of the classes is found from the simulation. As expected the blocking probability follows the admission thresholds so that the most demanding flows are least likely to be admitted. The last column in Table 1 shows the percentage of the admitted flows that experience a higher loss rate than their requirement. Clearly, almost all the flows get their required quality.

Table 1. Parameters and simulation results for UDP flows with differing requirements. Failed corresponds to admitted flows that get a higher loss probability than the requirement. The 95 percent confidence intervals are less than 3% for blocking rate and less than 1% for failed flows

Class	Rate (kb/s)	Loss req. %	Block lgth.	Thr. %	Red. pkts	Block prob. %	Failed %
0	500	0.5	40	0.8	2	98	0
1	500	2.0	-	1.4	0	80	0
2	300	0.5	10	1.8	2	55	0
3	300	0.5	40	2.2	3	29	0.4
4	300	2.0	10	2.1	1	34	0
5	300	2.0	40	2.3	2	24	0
6	100	0.5	10	10.2	5	0	0.1
7	100	2.0	10	11.7	4	0	0

4.4 Time Dynamics

As has already been noted in previous sections, the properties of the loss process have an impact both on the TCP throughput and on the FEC efficiency. Furthermore, the time dynamics of the channel impacts both the estimation of the loss rate and how well the loss estimate of the probe works as a predictor for the loss rate during the flow. In Fig. 4 the loss process for a typical simulation has been plotted, measured as loss average over 50 ms, one and three seconds respectively. The simulated scenario is the same as in Section 4.1 with 30 UDP flows and an average offered UDP load of 20 Mb/s. The first observation is that the average time between loss epochs is around 0.5 seconds; this depends on both the RTTs of the TCP flows, the buffer size and the number of TCP flows. Hence the typical time between loss epochs can vary significantly in more heterogeneous scenarios, but a first conclusion is that a probe time shorter than one second is inappropriate. With a probe length of one second the loss estimate can vary significantly, as can be seen from the one second mean. The three second mean gives a better estimate of the long term loss rate in the network as can be seen from the smoother curve. However, the experienced probe loss is used to make a decision regarding the whole duration of the flow and it might not be meaningful to make a very accurate estimation of the momentary loss rate. For flows with a long life time it can be expected that the loss rate will vary due to fluctuations in the load. Hence, to limit the probing delay at the start of a new session it would be reasonable to choose a probe length between one and three seconds. Further investigations of the effect of probe length and session length can be found in [15].

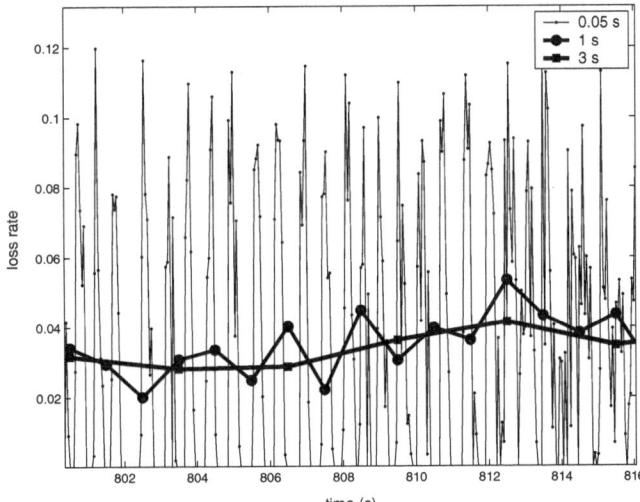

Fig. 4. The loss process has a very bursty behavior on short time scales and a probe length of at least one second is required to get a reasonable estimate of the loss rate

4.5 The Importance of Delay

One objective of the service differentiation is that the chances of getting a flow accepted should mainly depend on the desired rate and loss levels of the application and on the loss rate of the path. To evaluate this we use a topology with two bottlenecks where the capacity of the links is 20 Mb/s. Although it is not a complex network, it serves the purpose of illustrating the service differentiation in a more realistic way than a 'dumb-bell' topology. The traffic in the network consists of combinations of long-lived TCP flows and TCP controlled smaller file transfers (mice).

To investigate the effect of the delay we consider a topology with six different paths: P1-P6. Paths P1 and P2 both have two bottleneck links, the difference between them is that P1 has a one-way propagation delay of 50 ms and P2 has 100 ms. The first bottleneck of P1 and P2 is shared with P3 and P5, whereas the second bottleneck is shared with P4 and P6. P3 and P4 both have a one-way propagation delay of 50 ms while P5 and P6 have 100 ms. On each of the six paths there are ten persistent TCP flows, and on the paths P3 to P6 there are TCP mice contributing 0.5 Mb/s on each of the paths. The offered UDP load corresponds to four Mb/s per path, or equivalently to a total of 40 percent of the link capacity, consisting of flows of 200 kb/s with a loss requirement of one percent. The results in Table 2 reveals that the blocking rate is higher for the path with longer delay but lower loss rate, than for the path with two bottlenecks and low delay. This is due to the comparison with TCP, since TCP throughput depends heavily on the RTT. With a delay of 50 ms the UDP source can add 3 redundancy packets to a block of 20 data packets and get a resulting admission threshold of 4 %. The paths that experience a 100 ms one-way delay can only add one redundant packet and get an admission threshold of 1.2 %. This is an undesirable effect that follows from the definition of fairness by comparison with TCP. This can be seen from the fact that the throughput of the TCP flows and the blocking probability of UDP on the different paths follow the same pattern. For TCP the effect is a consequence of the window based congestion control, and should not necessarily be considered as a problem. However, feed-forward admission control does not have the same issues regarding stability as the feedback congestion control of TCP, therefore the effect is inappropriate for UDP.

Table 2. The results for paths with different delays show that the UDP flows are not affected by the delay. The 95 percent confidence intervals are smaller than 3% for the blocking rate, 0.05% for the path loss, 1% for failed flows and less than 10 kb/s for the TCP throughput

	P1, 50 ms	P2, 100 ms	P3/P4, 50ms	P5/P6, 100ms
Blocking probability	4 %	100 %	0 %	30 %
Path loss	2.5 %	-	1.1 %	1.1 %
Loss rate (after FEC)	2.3 %	-	0 %	0 %
TCP throughput per flow	380 kb/s	180 kb/s	590 kb/s	250 kb/s

4.6 Delay Compensation

To avoid the undesirable RTT dependence we can consider a hypothetical TCP flow using segment sizes proportional to the round-trip delay. This would cancel the RTT dependence in the TCP throughput equation (1). Of course, if we modify the admission threshold accordingly, there is no guarantee that the policy is fair to TCP anymore. As could be seen in Section 4.1 it is not possible to guarantee perfect fairness between TCP and UDP, therefore it makes sense not to let the TCP comparison impair the fairness criterion between different UDP flows.

With this modification, equation (2) would change to

$$p_{eq} = \frac{T}{R_{UDP}^2},$$
(6)

where T is a constant. For example, if we would use a hypothetical segment size of 500 bytes for the path with 50 ms one-way delay and 1000 bytes for the path with one-way delay 100 ms, T would be equal to 1.6×10^9. With this modification the service received by UDP sessions does not depend on the RTT [15].

This new admission policy is independent of the RTT and the MSS of TCP. Therefore, there is no need to estimate the RTT before choosing the FEC parameters, as mentioned in the Section 3.

There are of course other possible criteria that can be used, which do not have to be related to TCP fairness at all. In that case the admission threshold does not have to be inversely proportional to the square of the sending rate.

5 Conclusions

We have presented an entirely edge-based scheme for providing service differentiation to streaming and elastic traffic. Probe-based admission control is used to make streaming traffic TCP friendly without a need for per-flow rate control. Even though the two traffic controls work on different time scales simulations show that there is a reasonable fairness between TCP and streaming traffic. Furthermore, we address two problems with TCP fairness: The loss rate in the network may not be acceptable to the application at equilibrium and the TCP fairness depends on parameters that are not relevant to the streaming traffic.

The first of these problems is addressed by FEC, which is added in a way that does not discriminate against TCP traffic.

The second problem is addressed by modifying the admission policy not to take the round-trip time into account, but still to maintain TCP fairness on the average. Since the policies not only define fairness between TCP and UDP, but also between UDP flows with differing requirements, it is important to use a policy that is not too closely tied to the TCP throughput equation when it impairs the fairness between UDP flows.

In our future work we intend to analyze and optimize the parameters of the probing process to further improve the stability, fairness and isolation between flows. Furthermore, the scheme will be evaluated on larger scale networks and over longer time scales to provide more realistic conclusions about the performance.

We conclude from our evaluation that the proposed scheme can offer useful differentiated services for a wide range of network scenarios, as exemplified in the paper. It is our belief that this is an appropriate first step towards quality service for conversational and streaming applications over the Internet.

References

1. G. Karlsson, H. Lundqvist and I. Más Ivars, "Single-Service Quality Differentiation," Proc. IEEE IWQOS, Montreal, Canada, June 7-9, 2004.
2. J. W. Roberts and S. Oueslati-Boulahia, "Quality of Service by Flow Aware Networking," in Phil. Trans. of The Royal Society of London, series A, vol. 358, no. 1773, August 2000.
3. V. Fodor (née Elek), G. Karlsson, and R. Rönngren, "Admission Control Based on End-to-End Measurements," Proc. IEEE INFOCOM, Tel-Aviv, Israel, March 26-30, 2000.
4. I. Más Ivars and G. Karlsson. "PBAC: Probe–Based Admission Control", Proc. QoFIS, Coimbra, Portugal, Sept. 2001.
5. I. Más Ivars, V. Fodor and G. Karlsson, "Probe-Based Admission Control for Multicast," Proc. IWQOS, Miami Beach, May 2002.
6. P. Key, L. Massoulié, A. Bain and F. Kelly, "Fair Internet traffic integration: network flow models and analysis," to appear in Annals of Telecommunications, special issue on teletraffic. Available at URL http://research.microsoft.com/users/lmassoul/annals-telecom.ps
7. S. Floyd, M. Handley, J. Padhye and J. Widmer, "Equation-based congestion control for unicast applications," Proc. ACM SIGCOMM, Stockholm, Sweden, 2000.
8. E. Kohler and S. Floyd, "Datagram congestion control protocol (DCCP) overview," URL http://www.icir.org/kohler/dcp/summary.pdf.
9. P. Hurley, M. Kara, J. Y. Le Boudec and P. Thiran, "ABE: Providing a Low-Delay Service within Best Effort" IEEE Network Magazine, Vol. 15, No. 3, May 2001.
10. J. Padhye, V. Firoiu, D. Towsley and J. Kurose, "Modeling TCP Reno performance: a simple model and its empirical validation," IEEE/ACM Trans. on Networking, Vol. 8, Issue 2, April 2000.
11. G. Dán, V. Fodor, "Quality Differentiation with Source Shaping and Forward Error Correction," in Proc. MIPS, Naples, Italy, Nov. 18-21, 2003.
12. R. Steinmetz, "Human perception of jitter and media synchronization" IEEE Journal on Selected Areas in Communications, Vol. 14, No. 1, Jan. 1996.
13. M. Roughan, A. Erramilli, D. Veitch, "Network Performance for TCP Networks Part 1: Persistent Sources", International Teletraffic Congress, ITC 17, 2001.
14. P. Frossard, "FEC Performances in Multimedia Streaming", IEEE Comm. Letters, Vol. 5, No 3, March 2001.
15. H. Lundqvist, I. Mas, G. Karlsson, "Edge-based Differentiated Services", Technical Report, KTH, April 2005. URL: http://web.it.kth.se/~hen/EBDS_TR.pdf

Processor Sharing Flows in the Internet

Nandita Dukkipati[1], Masayoshi Kobayashi[2], Rui Zhang-Shen[1], and Nick McKeown[1]

[1] Computer Systems Laboratory,
Stanford University,
Stanford, CA 94305-9030, USA
{nanditad, rzhang, nickm}@stanford.edu
[2] System Platforms Research Laboratories,
NEC Corporation, Japan
m-kobayashi@eo.jp.nec.com

Abstract. Most congestion control algorithms try to emulate processor sharing (PS) by giving each competing flow an equal share of a bottleneck link. This approach leads to fairness, and prevents long flows from hogging resources. For example, if a set of flows with the same round trip time share a bottleneck link, TCP's congestion control mechanism tries to achieve PS; so do most of the proposed alternatives, such as eXplicit Control Protocol (XCP). But although they emulate PS well in a static scenario when all flows are long-lived, they do not come close to PS when new flows arrive randomly and have a finite amount of data to send, as is the case in today's Internet. Typically, flows take an order of magnitude longer to complete with TCP or XCP than with PS, suggesting large room for improvement. And so in this paper, we explore how a new congestion control algorithm — Rate Control Protocol (RCP) — comes much closer to emulating PS over a broad range of operating conditions. In RCP, a router assigns a single rate to all flows that pass through it. The router does not keep flow-state, and does no per-packet calculations. Yet we are able to show that under a wide range of traffic characteristics and network conditions, RCP's performance is very close to ideal processor sharing.

1   Introduction

Congestion control algorithms try to share congested links efficiently and fairly among flows. In the absence of information such as the size, round trip time (RTT) and path of each flow, it is natural to share a congested link equally among all flows. In fact, if the routers in the Internet had unlimited buffering, and if it was simple to emulate Processor Sharing (PS), then the solution to the congestion problem would be simple: Let a source send data at maximum rate, and use a PS scheduler to share link bandwidth equally among flows.

But routers have limited buffers, and per-flow scheduling is non-trivial. And so congestion control algorithms send feedback to the source to limit the amount of traffic admitted into the network, allowing simple FIFO queuing in the routers. Most notably, TCP's congestion control mechanism provides feedback by dropping packets (or through explicit congestion notification); and is quite successful at emulating processor sharing in a static scenario when a fixed number of flows have an infinite amount of

H. de Meer and N. Bhatti (Eds.): IWQoS 2005, LNCS 3552, pp. 271–285, 2005.

data to send[1]. But in practice flows arrive randomly, and transfer a finite amount of data. Simple experiments with *ns-2* indicate that with typical Internet flow sizes, TCP does not come close to emulating processor sharing. For example, Figure 1 compares TCP (as well as XCP, which we'll discuss shortly) with ideal PS, in case of Poisson flow arrivals with pareto distributed flow sizes. The left plot compares the mean duration of flows (how long they take to complete) as a function of flow size. The values for PS are computed analytically [7] [2] and show that flows would complete an order of magnitude faster than for TCP.

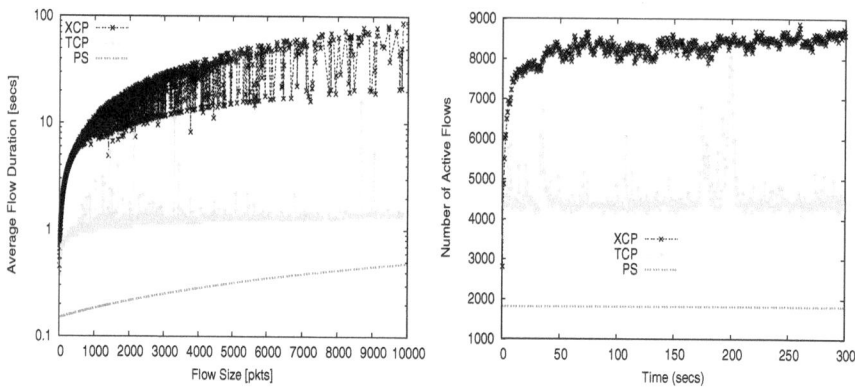

Fig. 1. The plot on left shows the average flow duration versus flow size under TCP and XCP from a simulation with Poisson flow arrivals, flow sizes are pareto distributed with mean = 30 pkts (1000 byte/pkt) and shape = 1.4, link-capacity = 2.4 Gbps, RTT = 100 ms, offered load = 0.9. The plot on right shows the the number of active flows versus time. In both plots the PS values are computed from analytical expressions

There are several reasons for the long duration of flows with TCP. First, it takes "slow-start" several round trip times to find the fair-share rate. In many cases, the flow has finished before TCP has found the correct rate. Second, once a flow has reached the "congestion-avoidance" mode, TCP adapts slowly because of additive increase. While this was a deliberate choice to help stabilize TCP, it has the effect of increasing flow duration. We'll see later that we can design stable congestion control algorithms that don't require additive increase. A third reason TCP flows last so long is because of buffer occupancy. TCP deliberately fills the buffer at the bottleneck, so as to obtain feedback when packets are dropped. Extra buffers mean extra delay, which add to the duration of a flow.

Our plots also show eXplicit Control Protocol (XCP) [2]. XCP is designed to work well in networks with large bandwidth-delay products. The routers provide feedback,

---

[1] We assume here that all flows have the same RTT. TCP approximately shares bandwidth as $\frac{K}{RTT\sqrt{p}}$ where p is loss probability and K is a constant [1].

[2] Flow duration in PS = RTT + $\frac{L}{C(1-\rho)}$, L is flow length, C is link capacity, ρ is offered load.

in terms of incremental window changes, to the sources over multiple round trip times, which works well when all flows are long-lived. But as our plots show, in a dynamic environment XCP can increase the duration of each flow even further relative to ideal PS, and so there are more flows in progress at any instant.

The goal of our work is to identify a simple and practical congestion control algorithm that emulates processor sharing irrespective of traffic characteristics and network conditions. Our approach is very different from TCP and XCP. Instead of incremental window changes in every round trip time, we want to know if there is an explicit rate that the router can give to the flows so as to emulate processor sharing. Furthermore, we would like to achieve this without per-flow state, per-flow queues, or per-packet calculations at the routers.

2   Rate Control Protocol (RCP): An Algorithm to Achieve Processor Sharing

2.1   Picking the Flow Rate

We are going to address the following question:

Is there a rate that a router can give out to all flows, so as to emulate processor sharing?
If the router has perfect information on the number of ongoing flows at time t, *and* there is no feedback delay between the congested link and the source, then the rate assignment algorithm would simply be:

$$R(t) = \frac{C}{N(t)}$$

where $R(t)$ is the rate given out to the flows by the router at time t [3], C is the link capacity and $N(t)$ is the number of ongoing flows at time t. But the router does not know $N(t)$ and it is complicated to keep track of. And even if it could, there is a feedback delay and so by the time $R(t)$ reached the source, $N(t)$ would have changed. So, we propose that the routers have an adaptive algorithm that updates the rate assigned to the flows, to approximate processor sharing in the presence of feedback delay, without any knowledge of the number of ongoing flows. RCP is a particular heuristic designed to approximate PS. It has three main characteristics that makes it simple and practical:

1. The flow rate is picked by the routers based on very little information (the current queue occupancy and the aggregate input traffic rate).
2. Each router assigns a *single* rate for all flows passing through it.
3. The router requires no per-flow state or per-packet calculations.

2.2   The Algorithm

The basic RCP algorithm operates as follows.

1. Every router maintains a single fair-share rate, $R(t)$, that it offers to all flows. It updates $R(t)$ approximately once per RTT.

---

[3] The sources are informed at what rate to transmit. We will shortly see how this is done.

2. Every packet header carries a rate field, R_p. When transmitted by the source, $R_p = \infty$ or the desired sending rate. When a router receives a packet, if $R(t)$ at the router is smaller than R_p, then $R_p \leftarrow R(t)$; otherwise it is unchanged. The destination copies R_p into the acknowledgment packets, so as to notify the source. The packet header also carries an RTT field, RTT_p, where RTT_p is the source's current estimate of the RTT for the flow. When a router receives a packet it uses RTT_p to update its moving average of the RTT of flows passing through it, d_0.
3. The source transmits at rate R_p, which corresponds to the smallest offered rate along the path.
4. Each router periodically updates its local $R(t)$ value according to Equation (1) below.

Intuitively, to emulate processor sharing the router should offer the same rate to every flow, try to fill the outgoing link with traffic, *and* keep the queue occupancy close to zero. We want the queue backlog to be close to zero since otherwise if there is always a backlog then at any instant, only those flows which have their packets in the queue get a bandwidth share, and the other flows do not. This does not happen in ideal PS where at any instant every ongoing flow will get it's fair share. The following rate update equation is based on this intuition:

$$R(t) = R(t - d_0) + \frac{[\alpha(C - y(t)) - \beta\frac{q(t)}{d_0}]}{\hat{N}(t)} \tag{1}$$

where d_0 is a moving average of the RTT measured across all packets, $R(t - d_0)$ is the last updated rate, C is the link capacity, $y(t)$ is the measured input traffic rate during the last update interval (d_0 in this case), $q(t)$ is the instantaneous queue size, $\hat{N}(t)$ is the router's estimate of the number of ongoing flows (i.e., number of flows actively sending traffic) at time t and α, β are parameters chosen for stability and performance.

The basic idea is: If there is spare capacity available (i.e., $C - y(t) > 0$), then share it equally among all flows. On the other hand, if $C - y(t) < 0$, then the link is oversubscribed and the flow rate is decreased evenly. Finally, we should decrease the flow rate when the queue builds up. The bandwidth needed to drain the queue within an RTT is $\frac{q(t)}{d_0}$. The expression $\alpha(C - y(t)) - \beta\frac{q(t)}{d_0}$ is the desired aggregate change in traffic in the next control interval, and dividing this expression by $\hat{N}(t)$ gives the change in traffic rate needed per flow.

RCP doesn't exactly use the equation above for two reasons. First, the router cannot directly measure the number of ongoing flows, $N(t)$, and so estimates it as $\hat{N}(t) = \frac{C}{R(t-d_0)}$. Second, we would like to make the update rate interval (i.e., how often $R(t)$ is updated) a user-defined parameter, τ. This is in case we want to drain a filling queue more quickly than once per RTT. The update interval is actually $T = \min(\tau, d_0)$ since we want it to be at least equal to average RTT, d_0. The desired aggregate change in traffic over one average RTT is $\alpha(C - y(t)) - \beta\frac{q(t)}{d_0}$, and to update the rate more often than once per RTT, we scale this aggregate change by T/d_0. And, $\hat{N}(t) = C/R(t-T)$. Then the equation becomes:

$$R(t) = R(t - T)[1 + \frac{\frac{T}{d_0}(\alpha(C - y(t)) - \beta\frac{q(t)}{d_0})}{C}] \qquad (2)$$

2.3   Understanding the RCP Algorithm

How good is the estimate $\hat{N} = C/R$?   When the router updates the rate, it knows precisely the spare capacity and the queue size it needs to drain. So the accuracy of the algorithm depends on how well C/R estimates $N(t)$.

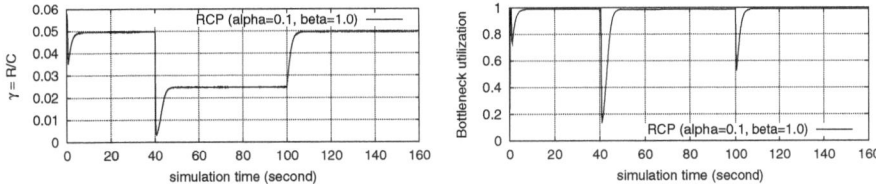

Fig. 2. The time evolution of RCP rate factor $\gamma(t) = R(t)/C$ and measured bottleneck utilization under long-lived flows. At $t = 0$, 20 flows start; at $t = 40$s, 20 more flows start; at $t = 100$s, 20 flows finish. In each case, $C/R(t)$ converges to $N(t)$

In the simplest scenario with only long-lived flows, $C/R(t)$ converges to the correct number of flows, N. An example is shown in Figure 2 where 20 flows start at time $t = 0$ and 20 more flows start at time 40, and 20 flows complete at time 100. In each case, $C/R(t)$ converges to $N(t)$. The values of α and β only affect the rate of convergence; we will examine the stability region for α and β shortly.

When flows are not long-lived, $C/R(t)$ can still be a good estimate of the number of active flows. In particular, when flows correspond to current Internet conditions (Poisson flow arrivals, pareto flow size distributions, and mean flow size $E[L]$ is close

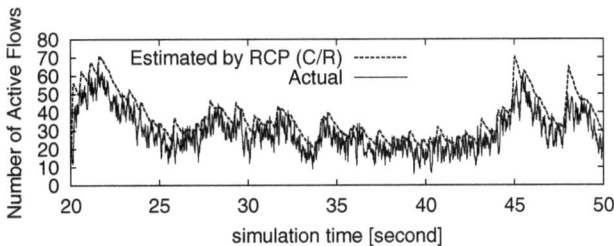

Fig. 3. Comparison of the number of measured active flows and the estimate (C/R). Bottleneck capacity, $C = 10$Mb/s, RTT = 50ms, flow arrival rate = 400 flows/sec, and flow sizes are pareto with mean = 25 pkts (1000 byte/pkt) and shape parameter is 1.2

to or greater than bandwidth×RTT), then $C/R(t)$ is a good estimate. It is a smoothing estimate of $N(t)$ since flows arrive and depart quickly and $N(t)$ changes rapidly. An example of this case is shown in Figure 3.

When $E[L] \ll$ bandwidth × RTT, most of the flows fit in the bandwidth-delay "pipe" and most do not have sufficient data to send for an entire round trip. In this case $C/R(t)$ represents an "effective" number of flows, $N_e(t) < N(t)$, where each flow has at least a round trip time worth of data to send. Underestimating the flows (and hence increasing the rate for each flow) is actually the right thing to do because when each flow has less than an RTT of data to send, giving exactly $C/N(t)$ to each flow means the pipe will never be filled.

Stability and Convergence: Stability of RCP depends on it's parameters α and β. We can think about RCP stability under the following two very different regimes:

1) Deterministic scenario of long-lived flows: In this scenario with N long-lived flows the equilibrium state of the RCP system is: R_e (equilibrium rate) $= C/N$ and q_e (equilibrium queue) $= 0$. We find that, if perturbed, the system will return to stability so long as α, β are within the stable region shown in Figure 4. There are two regions shown in the figure: a) The stable region obtained by Bode and Nyquist analysis of the linearized system. Details of the linear stability analysis are given in the technical report [3]. b) Stable region of the non-linear system. The real system is non-linear in nature, the most important one being the queue saturation at $q = 0$. In general while doing the stability analysis of congestion control protocols such as TCP, this non-linearity is ignored since the equilibrium point is away from it. The same is not true of the RCP system. Shown in Figure 4 is also the stable region obtained by simulations and phase portraits of this nonlinear system. Using tools from non-linear control theory, we obtained a precise characterization of the non-linear stable region and it matches well with our simulated region. The details of the non-linear analysis can be found at [4].

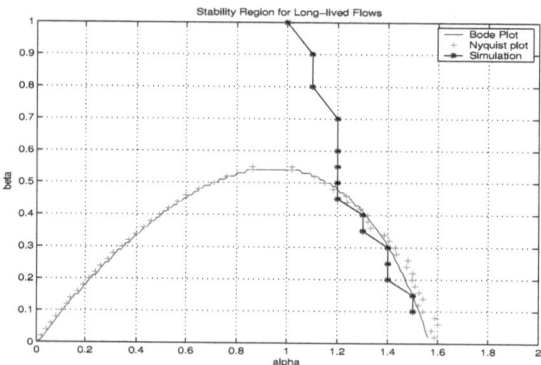

Fig. 4. Region enclosed by the solid curve is the stability region obtained via Bode and Nyquist analysis. The region to the left of the $'-*'$ line is the stability region of the non-linear system obtained from simulations and phase plane method

The two key points of the stability analysis are: First, the derived stability conditions for (α, β) guarantee global stability in the sense that irrespective of the initial conditions, (R_0, q_0), the system always converges to the equilibrium point; and second, we can make the system stable by choosing α and β *independent* of link RTT, capacity and number of flows. Although these results are proved to hold true incase of a single bottleneck link, our simulations in [3] indicate that they also hold true in a network scenario with multiple bottlenecks.

2) Stochastic scenario with random flow arrival times and flow sizes: In this case, convergence of $R(t)$ in the same sense as for long-lived flows is less meaningful because the input conditions are changing. Further, as discussed before we do not always want $R(t)$ to be equal to $C/N(t)$ exactly: If $N(t)$ is very large but each of the flows has very little traffic to send (less than a RTT) then we actually want to underestimate $N(t)$ and thereby give a higher rate to each flow, since if we give $C/N(t)$ exactly to each flow we will never fill up the link.

What would be more meaningful would be convergence in the stochastic sense like $E[N(t)]$ (mean number of flows) and $E[D(l)]$ (mean flow completion time for flow of length l) converge to finite equilibrium values. Proving such a result rigorously is a notoriously hard problem specially for non-linear delayed feedback systems such as RCP. The same is true for TCP, XCP and other algorithms. A large number of simulations indicate that under a variety of dynamic situations (like different flow arrival distributions, different flow size distributions, offered load, link capacities, round trip times...) RCP's performance in terms of $E[N(t)]$ and $E[D(l)]$ converges to that under ideal processor sharing for a wide range of $(\alpha, \beta) > 0$. These simulations are shown in section 3 and a more exhaustive set is in [3].

The convergence of RCP's performance measures $E[D(l)]$ (and $E[N(t)]$) to that of processor sharing is independent of the initial value of $R(t)$ chosen. The simulations support this. For any particular simulation we observe that $R(t)$ sweeps over the entire space (min-rate, link-capacity), depending on the conditions on the link. Any point could have been the starting point of the experiment. An example to illustrate this is shown in Figure 5. Notice that $R(t)$ takes a wide range of values depending on the input conditions. Starting with different initial values of $R(t)$ will give different sample

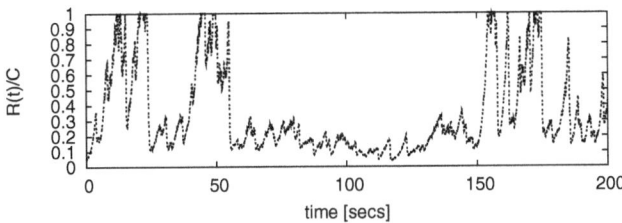

Fig. 5. The figure shows the normalized rate, $R(t)/C$ versus time for Poisson flow arrivals with pareto distributed flow sizes. Bottleneck capacity, $C = 150$ Mb/s, RTT = 100ms, offered load = 0.7, mean flow size = 30 pkts (1000 byte/pkt) and shape parameter is 1.2. Initial rate, $R(0) = 0.05C$. $R(t)$ sweeps over it's entire range depending on the input conditions

paths of the stochastic processes $N(t)$ and $D(l)$, but the key point is the underlying statistical properties $E[N(t)]$ and $E[D(l)]$ converge to that in processor sharing.

Given that the algorithm is stable for a wide range of $(\alpha, \beta) > 0$, we picked those values for the RCP system to maximize performance for a wide range of traffic and network conditions.

Round Trip Time Estimation: Every packet passing through the router carries the source's estimate of it's RTT. The router uses this to update the moving average, d_0, as follows:

$$d_0 = gain \times RTT_{packet} + (1 - gain) \times d_0^{last}$$

where gain $= 0.02$. The running average gives an estimate of the average RTT across all packets passing through the router. This skews the RTT estimate towards flows which have a larger number of packets. This is what is desired since the flows with a large number of packets will last many RTTs and will determine the stability of the control loop. The control loop stability depends less on the short flows which finish within one or just a few RTTs.

We find from our large number of simulations that RCP is robust to the RTT distribution of the flows. An example is shown in section 3.3 where flows with RTT ratios up to two orders of magnitude co-exist on a single link and RCP successfully emulates processor sharing.

Handling Packet Losses: RCP retransmits lost packets just like TCP. Losses were rare events for RCP in all our simulations, which is not surprising since RCP drives the queue towards empty. A queue only builds up because of the short term "mistakes" in rate estimation, resulting from the feedback delay and the small amount of information the algorithm is working with. Although the current form of RCP in Equation (2) does not explicitly account for losses, we note that it can easily do so by replacing $q(t)$ with $q(t)+$ (number of packet losses in interval T) – i.e. this would have been the queue we wanted to drain if we had enough buffering to accept the lost packets.

Comparison with XCP: Both XCP and RCP try to emulate processor sharing among flows, which is why their control equations are similar. The manner in which they converge to PS is quite different; the main difference between XCP and RCP is in the kind of feedback that flows receive. XCP gives a window increment or decrement over the current window size of the flow (which is small for all newly starting flows). At any time XCP flows could have different window sizes and RTTs and therefore different rates. XCP continuously tries to converge to the point where all flows have the fair-share rate, by slowly reducing the window sizes of the flows with rates greater than fair-share and increasing windows of the flows with rates less than fair-share (while avoiding over-subscription). New flows start with a small window, and the convergence could take several RTTs especially if there is little or no spare capacity. If the flows arrive as a Poisson process with heavy-tailed flow sizes, then most of the flows finish by the time they reach their fair share. In RCP, all flows (new and old) receive the same rate feedback which is their *equilibrium* rate. This helps flows finish quickly. We will see in Section 3 that this difference between RCP and XCP contributes to a big difference in their performance.

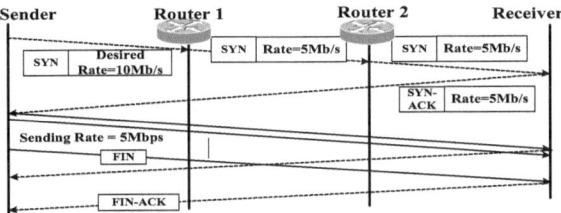

Fig. 6. The SYN message sent by the source indicates the rate at which it wants to send the flow (which could be infinite). As detailed in the last section, each router maintains a single rate, $R(t)$, that it assigns to all flows. As the message passes through the network, if the current rate $R(t)$ at a router is lower than the value in the SYN packet, the router overwrites it. When the SYN packet reaches its destination, it has the lowest rate corresponding to the most congested link along the path. This value is sent back to the source in the SYN-ACK message to set the starting rate. When the flows last longer than an RTT then they are periodically and explicitly told a new rate by the network. This rate is piggy-backed on the data and the ACK messages

XCP is computationally more complex than RCP since it gives different feedback values to each flow, and involves multiplications and additions for every packet. RCP maintains a single rate for all flows and involves no per-packet computation. [4]

2.4 RCP for the Internet

This is an outline of how RCP can be implemented in the Internet. We assume that – as with TCP – flows continue to have the connection set-up phase to establish state at both ends of the connection. This allows the initial rate to be calculated during the initial handshake by piggy-backing on the SYN and SYN-ACK messages. This is very important for short-lived flows, which could last less than one RTT. Current feedback-based algorithms do not work well for short-lived flows, yet most flows in the Internet are of this type [5]. An example of the RCP startup mechanism is illustrated in Figure 6.

3 RCP Performance

3.1 Simulation Setup

In this section we study RCP's performance using ns-2 [6] (Version 2.26) augmented with RCP end-host and queue modules.

We compare the performance of RCP with processor sharing, TCP and XCP. We are primarily interested in the average flow completion time (AFCT) [5]. Flow completion

---

[4] The router uses the RTT information in the packets to update its RTT estimate – our stability analysis and simulations indicate that it is sufficient for the router to have a "rough" estimate of the feedback delay, and so it can even just sample a few packets and update its estimate of RTT.

[5] We will use the term "flow" here to represent the packets corresponding to a particular application flow.

time (FCT) is defined as the time from when the sender sends a SYN packet until the receiver receives the last packet of the flow, i.e. FCT = 1 RTT for the connection set-up plus the duration of the data transfer. For elastic flows this is arguably the most important performance metric. We will use RTPD to abbreviate *round-trip propagation delay*. AFCT is the average of FCT over all flows for the simulation run. Note that $AFCT \geq 1.5RTPD + \frac{E[L]}{C}$. This is because (ignoring queuing delay) the minimum FCT for any flow of size L is: 1 RTPD for SYN/SYN-ACK and (1/2 RTPD + L/C) for the data transfer. The analytical expression for FCT of a flow of size L under processor sharing is [7]:

$$FCT_{PS} = 1.5\ RTPD + \frac{L}{C(1 - \rho)} \tag{3}$$

where ρ is the offered load and C is the link capacity. We will use Equation (3) to compute the PS values for our simulation setups. As secondary measures, in [3] we are also interested in the link utilization, and the average number of ongoing or active flows – which in PS can be simply computed by Little's Law: $E[N] = \lambda \times FCT_{PS}$ where λ is the flow arrival rate.

We assume the usual rule-of-thumb that a router's queue equals the bandwidth-delay product, i.e., link capacity multiplied by maximum RTPD of flows passing through it. We also assume that packets are dropped from the tail of the queue. Our simulations are run until the performance measures converge. In all simulations so far, we have not seen any packet drops with RCP and XCP. There are packet drops with TCP.

Equation (2) is the rate update equation used in the RCP router. The RCP parameters are: Control period, $T = \min(10ms, d_0)$ and $\alpha = 0.1, \beta = 1.0$. For TCP, we used TCP Reno module in *ns-2* with an initial window size of two packets. The *ns-2* implementation of XCP (Version 1.1) is publicly available [8], and the parameters are set as in the paper [2].

All data packets are 1000 bytes and the control packets (SYN, SYN-ACK, FIN) are 40 bytes. Unless otherwise mentioned we will assume that flows arrive as a Poisson process with rate λ and flow sizes are pareto distributed [5, 9]. The offered load on a link is $\rho = \lambda E[L]/C$. In our simulations we vary the network and traffic parameters from one extreme to the other and observe how RCP, TCP and XCP compare with PS.

3.2   When Traffic Characteristics Vary

In this section our goal is to find out if RCP's performance is close to PS under different traffic characteristics. All simulations in this section are done with a single bottleneck link in the network.

Average Flow Completion Time vs. Flow Size: In this section we will observe the AFCT of RCP, XCP and TCP for an entire range of flow sizes in a particular simulation setup chosen to represent high bandwidth-delay product ($C \times$ RTPD) environment. This is the scenario that often differentiates the performance of protocols.

- Setup: C = 2.4 Gbps, RTPD = 100 ms, ρ = 0.9, pareto distributed flow sizes

AFCT is plotted against flow size in the top two graphs of Figure 7. The AFCT of RCP is close to that of PS and it is always lower than that of XCP and TCP. For flows up to 2000 pkts, TCP delay is 4 times higher than in RCP, and XCP delay is as much as 30 times higher for flows around 2000 pkts. Note the logscale of the y-axis.

With longer flows (> 2000 pkts), the ratio of XCP and RCP delay still remains around 30, while TCP and RCP are similar. For any fixed simulation time, not only was RCP better for the flows that completed, but it also finished more flows (and more work) than TCP and XCP.

The third graph in Figure 7 shows the maximum delay for a given flow size. Note that in RCP the maximum delay experienced by the flows is also very close to the average PS delay. With all flow sizes, the maximum delay for RCP is smaller than for TCP and XCP. TCP delays have high variance, often ten times the mean.

The results above are representative of the large number of simulations we performed. Now let's see why these protocols have such different delays.

RCP vs. TCP: In figure, 7 the TCP delay for most flows follows the *Slow-start* curve. The delay in TCP slow-start for a flow of size L is $[log_2(L+1)+1/2] \times RTPD+L/C$ (excluding the queuing delay). With RCP the same flows get a jump-start because the routers set a higher initial rate close to what they would have gotten with PS. Hence their delay is close to PS. This is clear from the time evolution of a typical flow, as shown in Figure 8 (left plot).

Next, consider the TCP flows which deviate from the Slow-start curve. These flows experienced at least one packet drop in their lifetime and entered the additive increase, multiplicative decrease (AIMD) phase. Once a flow is in the AIMD phase, it is slow in

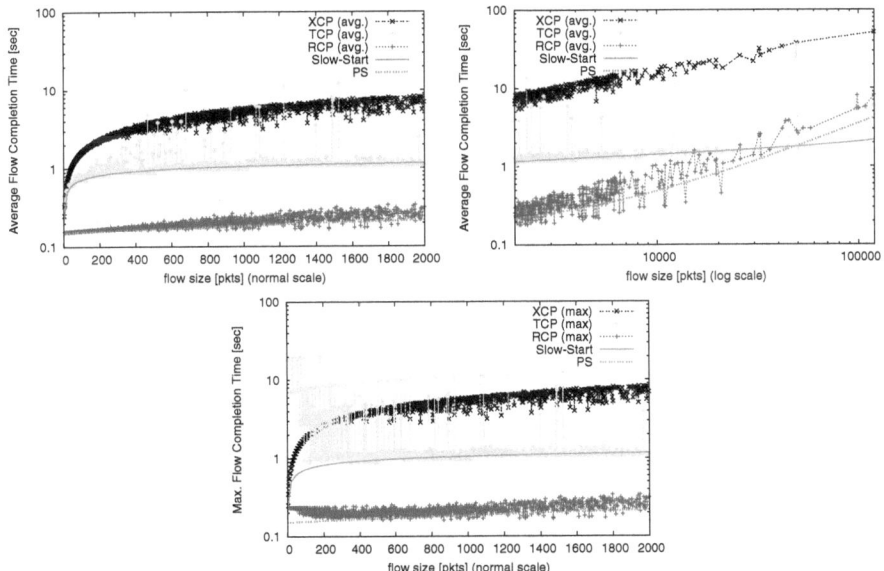

Fig. 7. AFCT for different flow sizes when $C = 2.4$ Gb/s, RTPD=0.1s, and $\rho = 0.9$. Flows are pareto distributed with $E[L] = 25$ pkts, shape = 1.2. The top left plot shows the AFCT for flow sizes 0 to 2000 pkts; the top right plot shows the AFCT for flow sizes 2000 to 10^5 pkts; the bottom plot shows the maximum flow completion time among all flows of the particular size

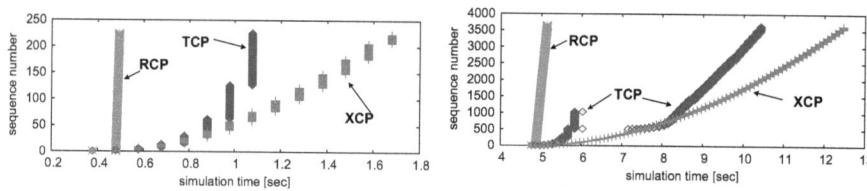

Fig. 8. Time evolution of the sequence numbers of two flows under TCP, XCP and RCP, chosen from the simulation set up of Figure 7. The flow size in the left plot is 230 pkts, and in the right plot is 3600 pkts

catching up with any spare capacity and therefore lasts longer than it needs to. RCP on the hand is quick to catch up with any spare capacity available and flows finish sooner. An example of the time evolution of a flow is shown in Figure 8 (right plot).

RCP vs. XCP: The time evolution of XCP for two sample flows is shown in Figure 8. XCP is slow in giving bandwidth to the flows, giving a small rate to newly starting flows. It gradually reduces the window sizes of existing flows and increases the window sizes of the new flows, making sure there is no bandwidth over-subscription. It takes multiple RTTs for most flows to reach their fair share rate (which is changing as new flows arrive). Many flows complete before they reach their fair share rate. In general, XCP stretches the flows over multiple RTPDs, to avoid over-subscribing the link, and so keep buffer occupancy low. On the other hand, RCP tries to give the equilibrium rate to every flow based on the information it has so far, at the expense of temporary bandwidth over-subscription.

When mean flow size increases: Figure 9 compares AFCT when mean flow size gets longer. Flow sizes are pareto distributed and the mean flow size is varied from 30 pkts (equals $\frac{1}{1000} \cdot C \cdot RTPD$) to 30,000 pkts (equals $C \cdot RTPD$). The left plot shows the AFCT averaged over flows with $< 7,000$ pkts and the right one is for flows $\geq 7,000$ pkts. [6]

There are two points to take away from the graph:

1. The AFCT of RCP is close to PS irrespective of the mean flow size
2. The performance of XCP and TCP is reversed as the mean flow size increases: when the mean flow size is small, XCP performs far worse than TCP (for flows with > 7000 pkts) and as the mean flow size gets larger, XCP's performance gets closer to PS while TCP deviates further from it – see right plot of Figure 9.

XCP vs. TCP: The reversal in performance of XCP and TCP is also clearly illustrated in Figure 10. The top left plot shows a snap shot of the AFCTs for $E[L] = 30$ pkts and the other two plots are for $E[L] = 30000$ pkts. In the bottom plot the AFCT

---

[6] We consider these two different ranges because, with a pareto distribution, there are many more short flows than long flows. Just taking the average AFCT over all flows is more representative of the short flows than the long flows.

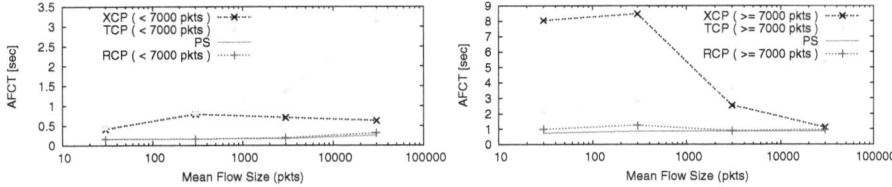

Fig. 9. Comparison of AFCT as the mean flow size increases. Flows are pareto distributed with shape 1.2 and the mean flow size varies as shown on x-axis. $C = 2.4$ Gb/s, RTPD $= 0.1$s and $\rho = 0.8$. The left plot shows the AFCT for flows with < 7000 pkts vs. mean flow size; the right plot shows the AFCT for larger flows (> 7000pkts) vs. mean flow size

of TCP flows is more than an order of magnitude higher than in PS – this is due to the well known problem with TCP in high bandwidth delay product environments i.e., long flows are unable to catch up with spare bandwidth quickly after experiencing a loss. XCP and RCP are both close to PS. On the other hand, for small flows, XCP's performance is worse than TCP's because XCP is conservative in giving bandwidth to flows, especially to newly starting flows. This unnecessarily prolongs flows and so the number of active/ongoing flows begins to grow. This in turn reduces the rate of new flows, and so on. Our many simulations showed that new flows in XCP start slower than with Slow Start in TCP.

We observe from a large number of simulations that the trends in flow completion times observed above for RCP, TCP and XCP hold true for other traffic characteristics

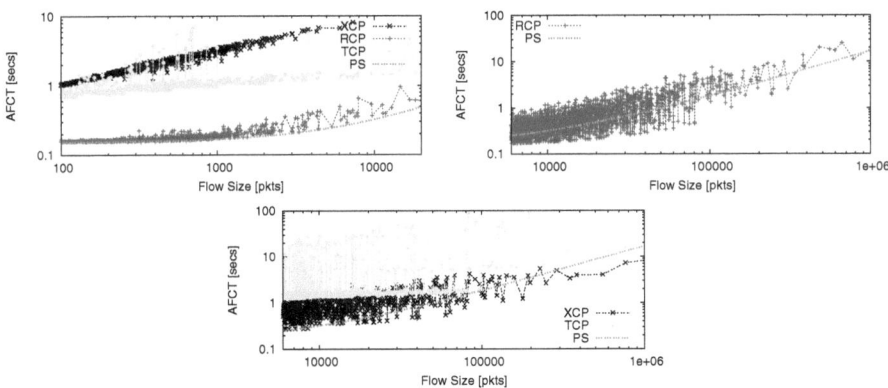

Fig. 10. Comparison of AFCT as the mean flow size increases. The simulation set up is the same as in Figure 9. The top left graph shows the AFCT vs. flow size when $E[L] = 30$; the top right (RCP) and bottom graph (TCP, XCP) show the AFCT vs. flow size when $E[L] = 30000$ pkts. RCP does close to PS irrespective of mean flow size. The performance of XCP and TCP are reversed with the increase in the mean flow size

such as different flow size distributions, as the offered load varies, and under different non-poisson flow arrival time distributions. Simulation results for these are in [3].

3.3   When Network Conditions Vary

In this section we explore how well the congestion control algorithms match PS under different network conditions. We show one particular scenario here when flows with widely different round trip times share a common bottleneck link. Simulations for other network conditions such as varying bottleneck link capacities, RTTs, increasing number of bottleneck links are shown in [3]. In each case, we find that RCP matches PS closely for a single bottleneck. In case of multiple bottlenecks, RCP achieves max-min fairness.

Flows with different round-trip times: All three congestion control schemes depend on feedback to adjust the window size and/or sending rate. If different flows have shorter round trip times, we do not want them to benefit at the expense of others.

To explore this effect we simulated flows that share a common bottleneck link, but with different RTPDs. The round-trip delay of the common bottleneck link is 0.01 s and its capacity is 640Mb/s. Arriving flows are classified into ten groups. Flows in the same group have the same end-to-end RTPD, and each group has an RTPD of 0.02, 0.04, ..., 0.18, or 0.2s. All groups have the same flow arrival rate and total $\rho = 0.9$.

Figure 11 shows the AFCT for these different groups of flows. The x-axis is each group's RTPD. For each RTPD, RCP is close to PS, suggesting that RCP is not biased in favor of flows with shorter RTPD.

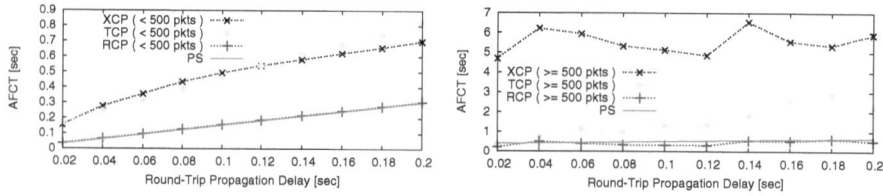

Fig. 11. Comparison of RCP, TCP and XCP when flows with different RTPDs coexist on a single bottleneck of $C = 0.64$ Gb/s. Flows arrive as a Poisson process with pareto distributed flow sizes, $E[L] = 25$ pkts, shape = 1.2. RTPD of flows vary from 0.02s to 0.2s. The left figure is the AFCT of flows with flow size ≤ 500 pkts and the right figure shows the AFCT for flows with size > 500 pkts

4   Conclusion

TCP's congestion control mechanisms work well in a static network with only long-lived flows. With long lasting flows, small mistakes in control do not lead to a big drop in performance. This is no longer true in a dynamic environment with random flow arrivals and arbitrary amounts of data to send. We saw in this paper the unnecessary number of round trip times taken by the TCP slow-start and AIMD algorithm to find the fair-share rate. Often, the flow has finished before the fair-share rate has been found. Unfortunately, making the network faster does not help, because the flow duration is dominated by the propagation delay. The same is true for XCP.

It is the premise of this paper that it is better to design congestion control algorithms to closely emulate processor sharing. This way the algorithm scales naturally with link capacities, RTTs and other network conditions. The performance is invariant of the flow size distribution – so it will not matter what mix of flows applications generate. Flows will complete sooner for a broad range of network and traffic conditions.

RCP is designed to be a practical way to emulate processor sharing, and appears to come very close to doing so under a broad range of conditions, and allows flow to complete much faster than with TCP or XCP.

References

1. S.B. Fredj, T. Bonald, A. Proutiere, G. Regnie, J.W. Roberts, "Statistical Bandwidth Sharing: A Study of Congestion at Flow Level," In *Proceedings of ACM Sigcomm 2001*, San Diego, August 2001.
2. D. Katabi, M. Handley, and C. Rohrs, "Internet Congestion Control for High Bandwidth-Delay Product Networks," In *Proceedings of ACM Sigcomm 2002*, Pittsburgh, August, 2002.
3. N. Dukkipati, M. Kobayashi, R. Zhang-Shen, N. McKeown, "Processor Sharing Flows in the Internet," *http://yuba.stanford.edu/rcp/*, Stanford HPNG Technical Report TR04-HPNG-061604.
4. H. Balakrishnan, N. Dukkipati, N. McKeown and C. Tomlin, "Stability Analysis of Switched Hybrid Time-Delay Systems – Analysis of the Rate Control Protocol," *http://yuba.stanford.edu/rcp/*, Stanford University Department of Aero/Astro Technical Report.
5. M. E. Crovella and A. Bestavros, "Self Similarity in World Wide Web Traffic: Evidence and Possible Causes," In *IEEE/ACM Transactions on Networking*, Vol. 5, No. 6, December 1997.
6. The Network Simulator, http://www.isi.edu/nsnam/ns/
7. W. Wolff, "Stochastic Modeling and the Theory of Queues," PrenticeHall, 1989
8. *ns-2* code for Explicit Control Protocol, *http://ana.lcs.mit.edu/dina/XCP/*
9. V. Paxson and S. Floyd, "Wide Area Traffic: The Failure of Poisson Modeling," In *IEEE/ACM Transactions on Networking*, 3(3):226-44, June 1995.

A Practical Method for the Efficient Resolution of Congestion in an On-path Reduced-State Signalling Environment

András Császár, Attila Takács, and Attila Báder

TrafficLab, Ericsson Telecommunication Hungary,
Laborc utca 1., Budapest, Hungary, H-1037
{Andras.Csaszar, Attila.Takacs, Attila.Bader}@ericsson.com

Abstract. Currently, the standardisation of on-path signalling protocols is going on within the Next Steps in Signalling (NSIS) Working Group of the IETF. NSIS is responsible for the definition of a general IP signalling protocol. The first use case of the proposed protocol is flow-level resource management. One of the considered reservation methods, reduced-state mode, is based on the Resource Management in DiffServ (RMD) framework. Since it relies only on per-class state information in interior routers, it has a number of benefits including scalability, low complexity, and low memory consumption. However, the price of simplicity is decreased efficiency in case of exceptional situations. The most demanding task for RMD is the handling of congestion that may occur after a failure resulting in re-routing of flows onto a new path. Resolving a suddenly evolved overload without per-flow states is a highly non-trivial task. We present a low complexity mechanism which easily handles the undesirable situation, and we give guidelines to set the parameters of our scheme based on worst-case calculations.

1 Introduction

In the IETF the NSIS working group [1] is responsible for standardising a general IP signalling protocol for flow-level resource management as the first use case. A *flow* is a series of packets transmitted during a session of a specific application by a specific host. For example, the flow could be the packet series of a streaming audio or video session but an FTP file transfer will also generate a packet flow. The task of a flow-level resource management protocol is to implement admission control. That is, it has to decide whether the network has enough free resources to accommodate both the new and the previously admitted flows.

The intention of the NSIS QoS application (QoS-NSLP [2]) is to re-use, where appropriate, the protocol mechanisms of RSVP [3], while at the same time applying a more general signalling model suiting other, possibly simpler, resource management schemes as well. Currently, the working group considers implementing two models, a *stateful* and a *reduced-state* realisation. These terms reflect

H. de Meer and N. Bhatti (Eds.): IWQoS 2005, LNCS 3552, pp. 286–297, 2005.

the complexity of interior nodes in a domain. The stateful solution store per-flow state information in interior nodes suiting the IntServ/RSVP QoS model. On the other hand, the reduced-state solution relies on aggregated, per-class states in interior nodes, and only edge nodes are permitted to dispose of per-flow states. This mode implements the DiffServ/RMD model, where RMD stays for Resource Management in Diffserv [4, 5, 6, 7].

RSVP, RMD, and the new QoS-NSLP are on-path resource management protocols because they all reserve resources, typically bandwidth, in a hop-by-hop manner. Before admitting the flow, a signalling message is sent between the two end-points. On every hop, this signalling message requests admission and reserves the resources if admitted. The admission decision for a link is generally very simple. If the sum of the newly arriving bandwidth request and the sum of admitted reservations is smaller than or equal to a pre-defined *admission threshold*, the new request is admitted and its reservation is added to the sum. The difference between a stateful and a reduced-state solution is coming from what kind of states are available and established by the signalling message in interior nodes.

In previous papers [6, 7] the authors argued that under normal circumstances in a high-speed network with many flows the reduced-state mode is preferable over stateful operation. The reason is that a reduced-state protocol poses less processing and storage capacity requirements to core routers and it has a smaller protocol overhead, while the achievable performance is similar.

However, there is an exceptional situation where per-flow states give an advantage to stateful protocols. This situation occurs when routing protocols re-direct flows from their original path to alternative paths. This might happen as a reaction to node or link failure. In general, on-path resource reservation protocols face the problem that the admission of re-routed flows to the new path is uncertain for example because there is not enough bandwidth to accommodate all re-routed flows. If this is the case *severe congestion* occurs [7, 8, 9].

We devote this paper to the severe congestion handling procedure of RMD. We detail the problem of severe congestion in Section 2. Then we focus on congestion handling mechanisms in Section 3, and introduce our improved solution. In Section 4 we present a worst-case model for the configuration of the proposed method. Finally, we conclude the paper.

2   Severe Congestion: Problem Description

Severe congestion is considered as an undesirable state, which may occur as a result of a route change. Typically, routing algorithms are able to adapt and change their routing decisions to reflect changes in the topology (e.g., link or node failures) and traffic volume. In such situations the re-routed traffic will follow a new route. Nodes located on this new path may become overloaded, severe congestion may occur, since they suddenly might need to support more traffic than their capacity. The resource management protocol in reaction to severe congestion has to

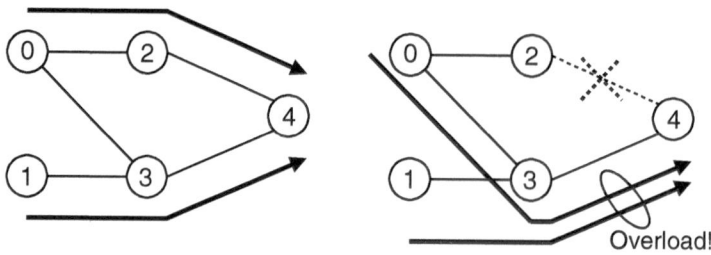

Fig. 1. Severe congestion example

terminate[1] some flows on the congested path in order to ensure proper QoS for the remaining flows.

Figure 1 shows an example scenario. First, the traffic distribution was such that the upper and lower paths were both utilised under normal conditions. After a link failure, the traffic of the upper path was suddenly re-directed to the $0 - 3 - 4$ path without immediately initiating reservation requests to decide on the admission of the traffic to this new path. The joint load on link $3 - 4$ is higher than the admission threshold, hence a mechanism is needed to recover to an acceptable load rather than to accept QoS degradation. The incoming traffic volume has to be decreased by means of terminating flows so that if a flow remains admitted after congestion handling, it has to be given the full previously reserved bandwidth.

Generally, stateful resource reservation protocols like RSVP or YESSIR [10] store the destination address for all flows in their database. If the routing protocol announces which destination address have been assigned a new path, the reservation protocol can easily identify the re-routed flows. Then, it can try to re-reserve the needed resources for all these flows on the new path. For example, in Fig. 1 router 0 can initiate a new reservation for all flows headed towards destination address 4. If this new reservation fails, the refused flows will be terminated within a round-trip time (RTT) when the source node or the domain's ingress edge node is informed. In RSVP this feature is called *Local Repair*. This approach is advantageous since the whole procedure is as quick as it can get, the reaction starts as soon as the routing protocol re-directs the flows and finishes within a RTT. Additionally, Local Repair also re-reserves the resources for as many of the re-routed flows as possible according to the admission threshold (i.e., only the excess part of the traffic is terminated).

The above procedure is based on per-flow states. However, due to the absence of per-flow states in interior nodes, a reduced-state protocol is not able to distinguish the re-routed flows from those ones that were originally traversing that path. Similarly to RSVP, RMD or the RMD-based QoS-NSLP of NSIS

---

[1] Flow termination may mean to stop the flow, or to re-map it to a lower-quality (e.g., best-effort) class. In any case, the originally agreed resources are not guaranteed any longer.

use the soft-state principle to keep reservations up-to-date: if flows do not refresh their reservation within periodical intervals (30 seconds by default), their
reservations time out. Considering re-routing, this means that the re-directed
flows are going to try to refresh their reservation maximum within a refresh
interval, when the excess flows that are above the *admission threshold* can be
terminated.

However, during this time the quality of flows may be violated seriously,
e.g., packet drops may occur. Hence, reduced-state protocols need an alternative
mechanism, which is able to handle severe congestion quickly. Since resource
reservation is foreseen to be applied to streaming traffic, primarily to VoIP applications, the expectation is to be able to handle severe congestion within a
few hundred milliseconds so that the users of not terminated calls do not realise
quality degradation.

3   Severe Congestion Handling

In [8] the authors gave a solution for severe congestion handling for the original, stand-alone RMD protocol. In this paper we are describing an enhanced,
more precise solution to be used for the reduced-state NSIS QoS-NSLP
protocol.

With reduced-state protocols, severe congestion in the communication path
has to be notified to the edge nodes, since core nodes do not have per-flow
identification and so cannot initiate flow termination. Edge notification is done
by the following mechanism (see Fig. 2).

After re-routed packets arrive (1) core routers estimate the overload of the
link by measuring arriving traffic (2) with a fixed measurement interval (S).
If the estimated bandwidth is higher than the predefined admission threshold,
denoted by T, the router concludes severe congestion. After that, the core router

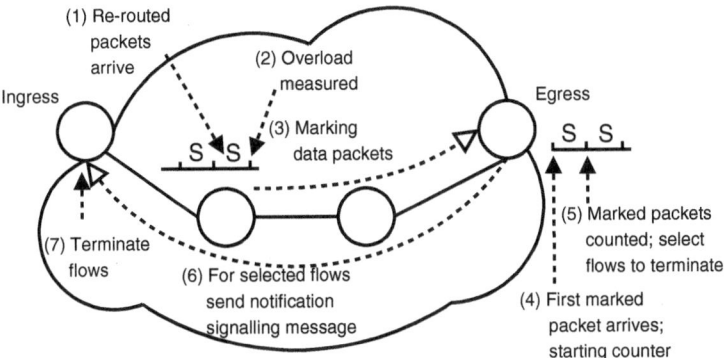

Fig. 2. Basic severe congestion handling mechanisms of RMD

informs the edge nodes about the amount of the estimated overload by marking[2] (3) regularly dequeued user data packets. The number of marked packets encodes the amount of overload. As an example, let us suppose that after a measurement interval the router estimated an arrival rate R, and $R > T$. The estimated overload is $R - T$ (e.g., in bytes per seconds). The core node transforms this metric to a number of bytes to mark as $B = (R - T) \cdot S$. The core router will mark that many leaving packets the total size of which corresponds to B, while a new bandwidth measurement cycle begins. With this procedure the core node can manage to encode and signal the amount of overload to the egress nodes without relying on per-flow information.

After receiving the first marked packet (4), every egress node counts the number of received marked bytes with counting interval S. After this (5), egress nodes transform the counted marked bytes back to an overload bandwidth value as follows. Let $\mathcal{E}$ denote the set of egress routers receiving marked packets. B_e is the amount of marked bytes counted by egress routers ($e \in \mathcal{E}$). Then $\frac{B_e}{S}$ gives the amount of overload seen by egress router e. Note that if marked packets are not dropped than the summarised overload bandwidth seen by all affected egress routers is the same as the overload estimated on the core node:

$$\sum_{\forall e \in \mathcal{E}} B_e = M \;\Rightarrow\; \sum_{\forall e \in \mathcal{E}} \frac{B_e}{S} = R - T.$$

After calculating $\frac{B_e}{S}$, any egress router e chooses a set of flows to terminate which will resolve the calculated overload. Preferably, the flows to be terminated are randomly selected among the flows that passed the congested link.

For every chosen flow, the egress sends back a congestion report (6) signalling message to the ingress node of the flow, requesting it to terminate the connection.

A shortcoming in the original RMD solution was how the egress identifies the set of flows that were passing through the congested node in order to select some of them to terminate. Trivially, ending an arbitrary flow that has a different route (i.e., did not contribute to the overload) makes no sense. The previous solution can only choose from those flows that received marked packets. However, the network operator may wish to choose flows for termination not only from those that received marked packets but from all flows involved in the congestion. E.g., within a voice traffic class the operator may prefer emergency calls over regular phone calls even though accidentally only the packets of the emergency calls got marked.

We propose to rely on an enhanced stamping procedure of the interior node. The previously explained procedure to encode and signal overload value is only slightly modified. The key idea is, to stamp all other packets in the congested node that are not carrying encoded overload information with a new *affected* stamp. That is, a packet can have three stamping states: *none*, *encoded*, and *affected*, respectively. The stamping can be done with the help of two bits in the

---

[2] Setting a bit in the header, or changing the DiffServ code-point to a domain specific administrative code-point, etc.

packet header, e.g., the Explicit Congestion Notification (ECN) bits (described in [11]), or by separating two bits from the DiffServ Code Point (DSCP). Another solution is if the network operator locally assigns for every traffic class two other DSCPs, which are interpreted at its egress nodes as encoded or affected stamps.

3.1 Solving the Over-Reaction

The severe congestion handling algorithm defined in the original RMD concept (described in the previous section) has a major shortcoming which needs to be addressed to get an efficient solution.

The problem is over-reaction. With over-reaction we refer to the case when more flows are terminated than necessary by the congestion handling algorithm. This effect can be seen as an "undershoot" in the link utilisation graph of the affected links. This is highly undesirable as the result is lot of terminated flows (e.g., VoIP calls) and poor network utilisation after the congestion.

The reason of the over-reaction is the delayed feedback included in the congestion handling control loop. Since marking is done in core nodes, the decisions is made at egress nodes, and termination of flows are done in ingress nodes, a significant delay may be introduced until the overload information is learned by ingress nodes. The delay consists of the trip time of data packets from the congested core node to the egress, the counting interval in the egress (S), and the trip time of the explicit signalling messages from egress to ingress (see Fig. 2). Moreover, until the overload decreases at the congested core node an additional trip-time from ingress to the core must expire. This is because immediately before the congestion notification and flow termination the ingress may have sent out packets in the flows that were selected for termination. That is, a terminated flow may contribute to the congestion for a trip-time from the ingress to the core node. Considering all the delays involved we get that signalling the congestion has no influence on the overload for as long as $S + \text{RTT}$, where RTT is the round-trip time. However, with the original congestion handling method core nodes continue marking the packets until the measured utilisation falls below the congestion threshold. Thus, it can happen that the necessary number of flows are already being terminated but the core node still signals overload to the egress as shown in Fig. 3. This way, at the end more flows will be terminated than necessary.

To solve the problem of over-reaction a memory needs to be introduced in the core nodes keeping track of the signalled overload in a couple of previous measurement intervals. At the end of a measurement period before signalling the overload, the actual measured overload should be decreased with the sum of already signalled overloads stored in the memory since that overload is already being handled in the severe congestion handling control loop.

We propose to use a sliding window to store previously marked overloads. The memory consists of an integer number of cells. At the end of every measurement interval, the newest calculated overload is pushed into the memory, and the oldest cell is dropped. If R denotes the measured data rate at the end of a measurement period, T is the admission control threshold, and M_i is the ith

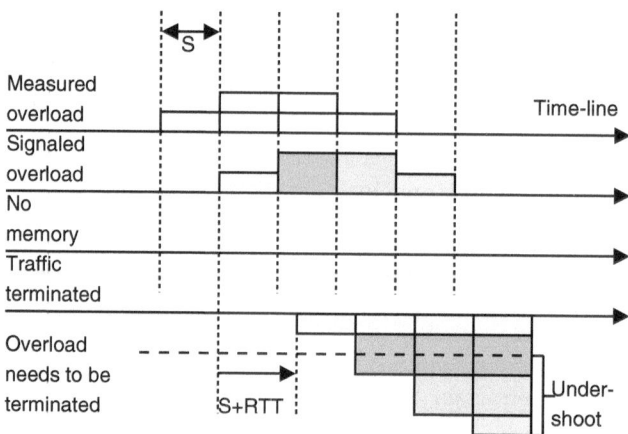

Fig. 3. Severe congestion handling without memory

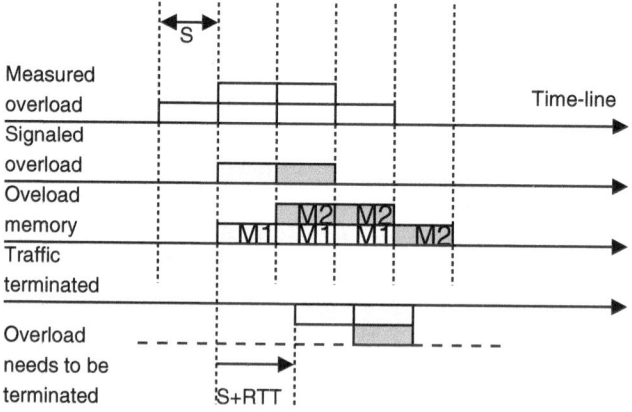

Fig. 4. Severe congestion handling with the proposed method

memory cell ($i \in [1..N]$), then at the end of every measurement interval the considered overload, as shown in Fig. 4, is the following:

$$\hat{R} = R - T - \sum_{i=1}^{N} M_i .$$

Next, the memory is updated as:

$$M_i := M_{i+1} \ \forall i = 1..(N-1), \text{ and } M_N := \hat{R} .$$

As discussed earlier, the time until a congestion signal (marked packets) affects the overload is $S + \text{RTT}$. To make sure that already handled congestion signals do not cause over-reaction, the number of memory cells must be set according to:

$$N = \lceil \frac{S + \text{RTT}}{S} \rceil = 1 + \lceil \frac{\text{RTT}}{S} \rceil.$$

While S is the measurement period which is unique in the domain, flows are likely to have different RTT values. To guarantee the elimination of over-reaction considering all flow, the operator should overestimate the required memory cells using the maximal RTT should in the calculation.

4   Worst-Case Model for Configuring the Parameters of the Congestion Handling Method

This section addresses the joint configuration of the number of memory cells (N) and the length of the measurement interval S, the two parameters of our severe congestion handling method. Our dimensioning tool is based on a worst-case severe congestion handling model. The model has been implemented as a simplified simulator that in a step-by-step manner calculates the load of the congested link at the end of every measurement interval. The model has three parameters; i) the measurement interval (S), ii) the maximal round-trip time ($\text{RTT}_{\max}$), and iii) the number of memory cells (N).

For the dimensioning two aspects of severe congestion handling are considered. The volume of over-reaction and the time needed to resolve the congestion (handling time). First, eliminating over-reaction is necessary to keep network utilisation high even after a congestion occurred. Second, having a fast solution that resolves congestion within a few hundred milliseconds is essential for a resource management protocol being considered for deployment in a high-resilience carrier-grade network.

Undershoot is the volume of the unnecessarily terminated flows in percent of the threshold. If after congestion the load sinks back right to the admission threshold, undershoot is zero; however, if the load decreases to zero, i.e., all flows are terminated, undershoot is 100%. Handling time is defined as the time between the arrival of the first re-routed packet on the given link up to the arrival of the last packet of the last terminated flow at the link.

The simulator evaluates the worst-case where all flows are supposed to have the maximal RTT, i.e., the flow termination process will need in all cases the maximal $S + \text{RTT}_{\max}$ amount of time. The result is that the highest possible undershoot and the longest handling time is calculated.

First of all, we point out that regarding the worst-case calculation of the volume of over-reaction the particular values of S and RTT are irrelevant, only the ratio of these ($\frac{RTT}{S}$) affects the results. Intuitively, by having $S < \text{RTT}$, multiple measurements are carried out during the feedback of congestion. Hence, congestion is detected fast but over-reaction is more likely to occur. On the other hand, if $S > \text{RTT}$, the feedback delay is low compared to the slow measurements, hence for the price of higher handling time over-reaction will not be a likely phenomenon. Further consideration is left to the reader.

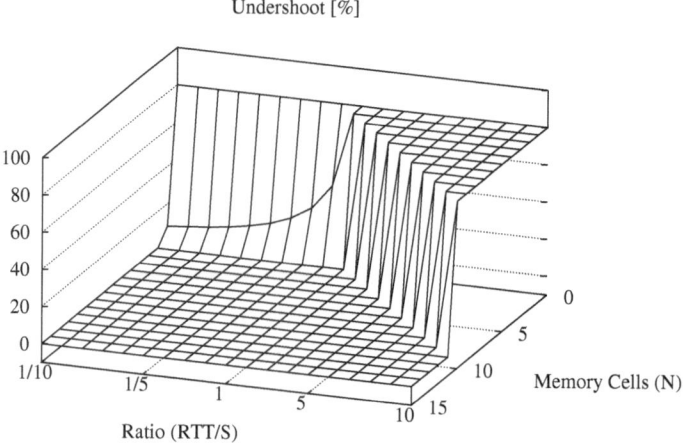

Fig. 5. Undershoot occurrance with different parameters

Figure 5 shows the dependence of the worst-case over-reaction from the number of memory cells (N) and the ratio of RTT and S. The figure shows that if $N \geq 1 + \lceil \frac{\text{RTT}}{S} \rceil$, over-reaction is eliminated in all cases. Without memory, the algorithm will always over-react ($N=0$). An important message of the figure is that one needs the less memory cells the higher value the ratios takes. That is, the higher S is compared to $\text{RTT}_{\max}$. To reduce processing and storage requirements in core routers, this would speak for configuring S to at least the maximal round-trip time, where only two memory slots are needed.

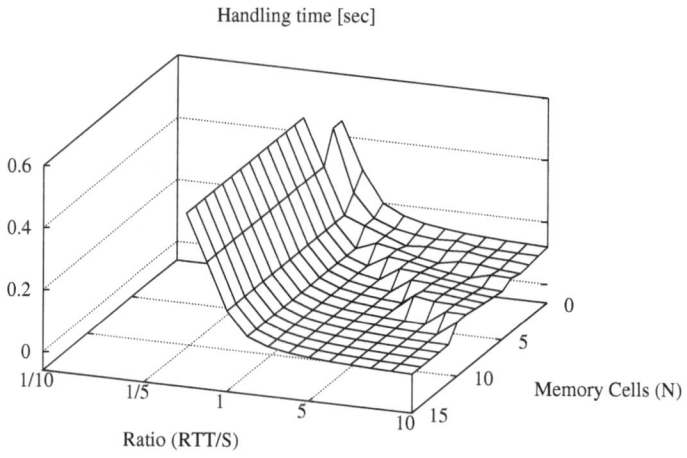

Fig. 6. Congestion handling time with different parameters

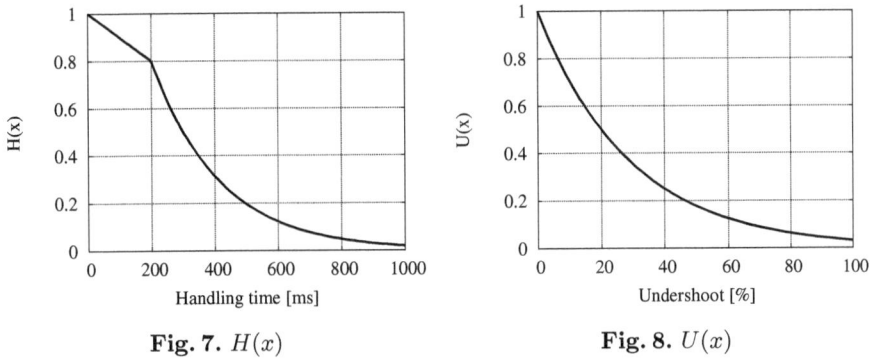

Fig. 7. $H(x)$ **Fig. 8.** $U(x)$

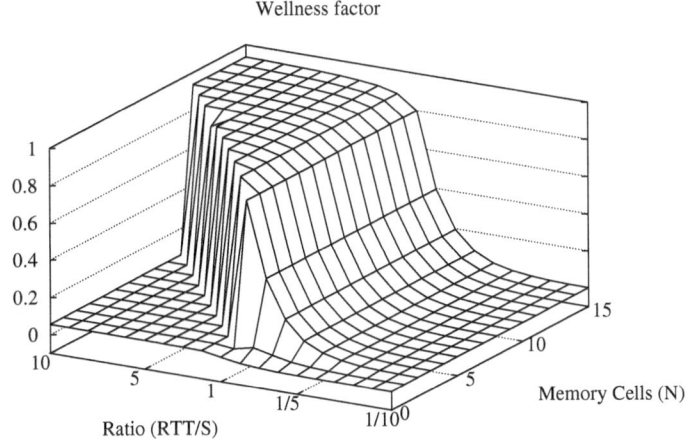

Fig. 9. Wellness factor with different parameters

On the other hand, increasing the measurement period will result in increased handling time. Figure 6 shows the results for a maximal RTT of 50 milliseconds. It shows that adding memory cells has little influence on handling time. Opposed to over-reaction, Fig. 6 also shows that choosing higher S has bad influence onto the handling time. However, by considering both figures one can see that there are parameter setups where both handling time and undershoot are low. To quantify this observation we defined a wellness function ($W(.)$) which formalises our precedence relation between low over-reaction and low handling times. The measure is $W(h, u) = H(h) \cdot U(u)$, where h is the handling time, u is the undershoot. Function $H(.)$ is shown in Fig. 7 and $U(.)$ in Fig. 8 respectively. By formalising the functions $U(.)$ and $H(.)$ we had the following assumptions. First, naturally we need a method which do not over-reacts severely. Hence we selected an exponential measure which punishes high over-reactions radically. Second, we would like fast congestion handling but basically any value, say, below 200 ms is fairly acceptable. Hence in this region we have a linear relation between handling time and $H(.)$. However, if resolving the congestion takes more time the utility of such configurations is exponentially degrading.

The resulting wellness function is shown in Fig. 9[3]. It shows that the preferred setups should be lower S values with more memory cells. However, we should focus on the lower left edge of the highest plane. At this edge we have those configurations that need the least amount of memory cells and at the same time can have the highest possible measurement period. This way, we get for example, that if the maximal RTT is 50 ms, then, e.g., the $S=50$ ms and $N=2$ or $S=25$ ms and $N=3$ configuration reflect two good setups where handling time is below 200 ms and no over-reaction evolves. This way, using the worst-case calculations along with the wellness function we can select an appropriate S and N value based on the estimated RTT_{max} which will yield a proper configuration for the proposed congestion handling method.

5   Conclusion

As the last performance gap between stateful and reduced-state resource management protocols we addressed the issues of failure recovery with reduced-state resource management protocols, specifically with the RMD-based operation mode of the QoS-NSLP protocol, which is currently being specified in the NSIS working group of the IETF. We highlighted the problem of severe congestion as the result of re-routing, and we introduced a low complexity solution. We also investigated the efficiency of the proposed method with worst case calculations.

The given calculations can be used to configure the parameters of the severe congestion handling algorithm. As a guideline we derived that the ratio of the measurement period (S) and the RTT of the flows has a great influence on congestion handling precision. We found that fast handling time can be achieved when $\frac{S}{RTT} \leq 1$. However, in this case over-reaction (more flows are terminated than necessary) occurs. Introducing a small local memory in the handling algorithm reduces and even eliminates the undershoot without increasing handling time. Using our method and dimensioning equations a low severe congestion handling time without any undershoot can be achieved.

References

1. Hancock, R., Freytsis, I., Karagiannis, G., Loughney, J., den Bosch, S.V.: Next steps in signaling: Framework. Internet Draft draft-ietf-nsis-fw, IETF (2004) Work in progress.
2. den Bosch, S.V., Karagiannis, G., McDonald, A.: NSLP for quality-of-service signaling. Internet Draft draft-ietf-nsis-qos-nslp, IETF (2004) Work in progress.

---

[3] Note that this figure has a different angle from previous ones.

3. Braden, R., Zhang, L., Berson, S., Herzog, S., Jamin, S.: Resource reservation protocol (RSVP) – version 1 functional specification. RFC 2205, IETF (1997)
4. Báder, A., Westberg, L., Karagiannis, G., Kappler, C., Phelan, T.: RMD-QOSM - the Resource Management in Diffserv QoS model. Internet Draft draft-ietf-nsis-rmd, IETF (2005) Work in progress!
5. Karagiannis, G., Báder, A., Pongrácz, G., Császár, A., Takács, A., Szabó, R., Westberg, L.: RMD – a lightweight application of NSIS. In: Proc. of the Networks 2004, Vienna, Austria (2004)
6. Westberg, L., Császár, A., Karagiannis, G., Marquetant, A., Partain, D., Pop, O., Rexhepi, V., Szabó, R., Takács, A.: Resource management in diffserv (RMD): A functionality and performance behavior overview. In: Proc. of PfHSN 2002, Berlin, Germany, (2002)
7. Császár, A., Takács, A.: Comparative performance analysis of RSVP and RMD. In: Proc. of the QoFIS 2003, Stockholm, Sweden, (2003)
8. Császár, A., Takcs, A., Szabó, R., Rexhepi, V., Karagiannis, G.: Severe congestion handling with resource management in diffserv on demand. In: Proc. of the Networking 2002, Pisa, Italy, (2002)
9. Császár, A., Takács, A., Szabó, R., Henk, T.: State correction after re-routing with reduced state resource reservation protocols. In: Proc. of the Globecom 2004, Dallas, TX, USA, (2004)
10. Pan, P., Schulzrinne, H.: YESSIR: a simple reservation mechanism for the internet. ACM SIGCOMM Computer Communication Review **29** (1999)
11. Ramakrishnan, K., Floyd, S., Black, D.: The addition of explicit congestion notification (ECN) to IP. RFC 3168, IETF, Network WG (2001)

Case Study in Assessing Subjective QoS of a Mobile Multimedia Web Service in a Real Multi-access Network

Tiia Sutinen[1] and Timo Ojala[2]

[1] VTT Electronics, Kaitoväylä 1, 90571 Oulu, Finland
Tiia.Sutinen@vtt.fi
[2] MediaTeam Oulu, University of Oulu,
P.O.Box 4500, FI-90014 University of Oulu, Finland
Timo.Ojala@ee.oulu.fi

Abstract. This paper presents an empirical task-based user evaluation, which was carried out for the purpose of assessing the subjective QoS of a mobile multimedia web service in a real multi-access network environment comprising of WLAN and GPRS networks and automatic mobility management with Mobile IP. Subjective quality ratings were collected from 20 test users to obtain a distribution representing the service quality experienced by the subjects. The obtained results show that even though the service usability in GPRS domain was barely satisfactory, this type of automatic utilization of multiple access networks with some enhancements can be considered as a potential access method for mobile services.

1 Introduction

Increasing availability of multiple access technologies and multi-mode user terminals makes it possible for mobile Internet users to utilize the advantages of the different technologies by dynamically routing traffic always via the best available access network. This is referred to as multi-access. Depending on the characteristics of the available access networks, however, vertical handovers can introduce substantial changes in the QoS. Even if the operation of user applications and ongoing communication sessions could be preserved during the handover with different mobility and handover management mechanisms, it still might cause the subjective application quality to degrade to an unacceptable level in the user's opinion.

This work has a two-fold motivation. First, the aforementioned technology push has created environments with multiple access networks (e.g. GPRS, EDGE, UMTS and WLAN), and mobile terminals with multiple radio interfaces (e.g. Nokia 9500, Motorola CN620, and Qtek 9090). Thus, in terms of technology the road is paved for introducing new service scenarios relying on utilization of multi-access networks.

The second motivation is the correlation between market pull and user experience. A positive/negative user experience of a service or an application has high impact on its commercial success. Therefore, it is imperative to evaluate the usability of a new service to expose any factors that might hamper the user experience. Since most mobile services are interactive systems, their true evaluation can be carried out only empirically [10].

H. de Meer and N. Bhatti (Eds.): IWQoS 2005, LNCS 3552, pp. 298–312, 2005.

The novel contribution of this work is an empirical task-based user evaluation of the end user QoS of a mobile multimedia service in the real environment of use involving a real multi-access network comprising of WLAN and GPRS networks and automatic mobility management by Mobile IP.

Related work is scarce, as published studies on QoS in multi-access networks (e.g. [22]) do not include a concrete empirical evaluation of end user QoS in a real-world realization of the proposed QoS architecture, but report performance characterizations by simulations if any. The Moby Dick project [8] developed an IP-based QoS architecture for multi-access networks, but the results of the six months real environment field trial advertised on the project's web site are not yet available in form of scientific publications. The VHO project [19] has developed prototype services based on vertical handover in a multi-access network, but the available publications do not include any user evaluations of the services.

This paper is organized as follows. In section 2 we describe the ABC (Always Best Connected) concept and its realization with a heterogeneous network comprising of multiple access networks, together with relevant mechanisms for mobility and handover management. In section 3 we discuss various methods for assessing subjective application layer quality of service. Section 4 reports our case study on assessing end user QoS in a heterogeneous network, and section 5 concludes the paper.

2 Inter-technology Mobility

2.1 ABC – Always Best Connected

The different access technologies available today may differ even significantly from each other in terms of bandwidth, coverage, cost of the connectivity, etc. Also the set of networks accessible to a mobile user varies from area to area as depicted in Figure 1. Further, it is acknowledged that no single technology, either today or most likely in the future, can provide optimally all the qualities demanded in a network connection [9], including for instance tetherless connectivity, ubiquitous access, and above all sufficient bandwidth for future applications. Thus, multi-access, which enables the mobile user to utilize the different access networks in a dynamic fashion by routing his/her connections through the best available network in any location, is a widely accepted scenario for the near future [9], [18].

A new concept of staying always best connected (ABC) has thus emerged. The goodness of a network connection can be defined based on various criteria, including QoS parameters, personal preferences, device capabilities, application requirements, operator or corporate policies, and available network resources. The basic idea is to optimally combine the advantages of the different technologies (e.g. the wide coverage of cellular networks and the large bandwidth of occasional WLAN hot spots) and the chosen set of criteria can be used to build algorithms that automatically maintain an optimal connection to the used services. The required functionalities recognized for an ABC service include access discovery, access selection, authentication, authorization and accounting (AAA) support, mobility management, profile handling, and content adaptation [4].

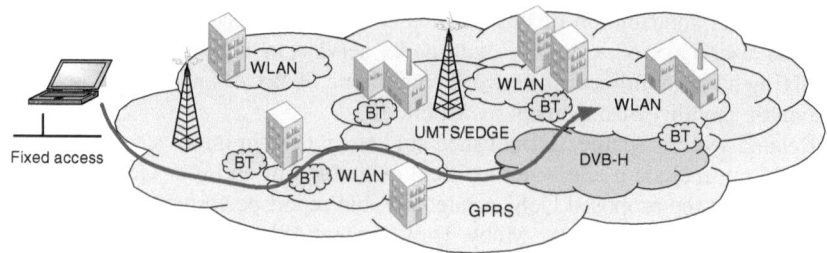

Fig. 1. Multiple access networks in different places

Mobility in a heterogeneous network environment is referred to as inter-technology roaming, where the roaming user's network connection can be transferred either horizontally between points of access belonging to the same technology (horizontal handover) or vertically between points of access belonging to different network technologies (vertical handover) [12]. The realization of inter-technology roaming comprises of mobility management and vertical handover support, which we discuss next from the viewpoints relevant to the case study presented in section 4.

2.2 Mobility Management

To enable host mobility in IP networks calls for a mechanism capable of hiding the changing of the host's IP address from the upper layers whenever it roams from one addressing domain to another (i.e. location transparency). For this purpose several mobility management protocols and other mechanisms have been developed [1]. Our work focuses on network layer mobility and specifically on Mobile IP.

Mobile IP is currently the dominant macro-mobility protocol. That is it enables a mobile terminal to keep its IP address constant while roaming from one administrative domain to another, but it relies on the subnetwork to provide the micro-mobility support (e.g. access technology specific scheme, possibly combined with some micro-mobility management protocol to enhance mobility management efficiency and QoS [1]). There are two versions of Mobile IP: Mobile IPv4 (MIPv4) and Mobile Ipv6 (MIPv6). Since the mobility management solution used in the case study presented in this paper is based on MIPv4, we describe only its operation here.

Mobile Ipv4 (defined in RFC 3344) [14] extends the Ipv4 protocol. It enables constant delivery and reception of data packets regardless of the changing location (i.e. IP address) of the user terminal (named mobile node or MN). This is achieved by associating the MN with two addresses: a home address, which is the MN's statically allocated IP address in its home network, and a care-of address (CoA), which is the node's temporary IP address while in a foreign network. In standard MIPv4, the correspondent node (CN) knows only the MN's home address, and to route packets accordingly between the two entities, Mobile IP uses home and foreign agents. A home agent (HA) is a router in the MN's home network and it is responsible for maintaining the relation (binding) between the MN's two addresses. The HA intercepts all traffic headed to the MN's home address and whenever the MN is outside its home network, the HA forwards the traffic by tunneling to the MN's valid CoA. Depending on the Mobile IP implementation, the CoA can be either the address of a local router (i.e. foreign agent or FA) or a local address obtained by the MN itself (e.g. though DHCP or PPP). In the latter case, FA functionality is included in the MN and the MN is said to have a co-located CoA. Supporting MIPv4 operation in today's Internet however requires additional mechanisms such as Reverse Tunneling (RFC 2344) and NAT Traversal for Mobile IP (RFC 3519).

2.3 Vertical Handover Support

In multi-access, handovers are not triggered just to maintain an ongoing connection but also to ensure that the user always receives the best available service and that the user preferences are met. Thus, in order to achieve an optimal handover management solution for heterogeneous networks requires not only assessing the capabilities of the available networks but also taking the user preferences and application requirements into account. This requires additional mechanisms, referred to as vertical handover support here.

In multi-access handovers can be classified as imperative and alternative based on their urgency [21]. Imperative handovers are triggered whenever the current link becomes unusable, i.e. for example when the link quality (measured e.g. in received signal strength or RSS) drops below a certain level. Alternative handovers on the other hand are triggered to get better access to the used services and therefore do not possess such urgency. The criteria for alternative handovers include QoS (i.e. the new link provides more bandwidth, smaller delay, etc.) or AAA related reasons (e.g. using the new network is cheaper).

Practical handover control solution for multi-access is a mobile-controlled handover (MCHO) scheme with automatic handover management [21]. The automatic handover triggering may be based on policies derived from user specified criteria (e.g. use WLAN if link quality > 10%, else use GPRS). Manual control is regarded as a way for the user to intercept the automatic handover process if needed.

Finally the applications place requirements on the handover performance: and they can be classified according to the type of handover management they require (i.e. fast, smooth, and normal handovers) [18], [21].

3 Application Layer Quality of Service

3.1 Defining Quality of Service

Quality of Service (QoS) is an overarching term covering different parts of end-to-end service quality. The general definition of QoS provided by the International Telecommunication Union (ITU) [5] is that QoS is *"the collective effect of service performance, which determines the degree of satisfaction of a user of the service"*. Different people and communities nevertheless interpret QoS differently, and at least the following viewpoints of QoS can be distinguished: QoS requirements of a user, QoS perceived by the user, QoS offered or planned by a provider, and QoS delivered or achieved by the provider [15]. We are discussing QoS in the user's point of view.

There are two main aspects of QoS: subjective and objective [16]. Subjective QoS essentially is the user's overall perception of service quality, that is, it is the user's opinion whether a service is working satisfactorily or not. Subjective QoS is often difficult to be specified with objective measures, at least in a way meaningful for users, and thus user-perceived quality is often expressed also non-technically [2]. Objective QoS then refers to the technical aspects of QoS, and can be specified with quantitative measures. Figure 2 illustrates different scopes of QoS (i.e. application QoS and network QoS) in a client-server communication scenario [16].

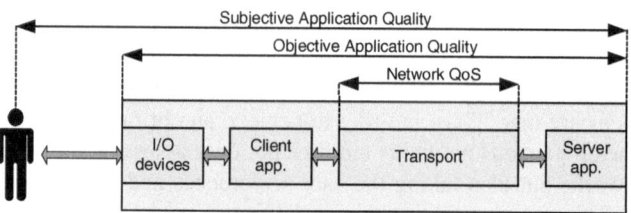

Fig. 2. Scopes of Quality of Service

3.2 Subjective Application Quality

User's Perception. The network QoS parameters, such as bandwidth, delay, jitter and packet loss, are not necessarily applicable to express subjective QoS, since a user has a high-level perspective over application performance, rather than an in-depth conception of details of the underlying implementation and operation of the network service [6]. Therefore, application quality and its variation need to be expressed in terms that describe user-perceivable effects, instead of their causes in the end-to-end transmission path. It should be noted also that subjective application quality deterioration is not solely caused by network QoS fluctuations, but is attributable to numerous other factors, including characteristics of the ongoing task (e.g. urgency), application's incompatibility with the operating system, application or protocol malfunction, disturbing factors in usage environment (e.g. faulty equipment), and so forth [7].

User-Level QoS Requirements. In the user's point of view, QoS requirements are those that are visible to him/her [6]. Thus, it is the user application that leads the main role in determining the user's QoS requirements, although neither does it dictate them solely. The salience of different quality criteria is influenced also by the goal of the interaction, and the ideal QoS profile of an application consequently varies with the task performed [3]. Three general categories for user-level QoS requirements (defined in [6]) are discussed here: criticality, cost, and security.

The criticality comprises of user-level QoS requirements characterized by the application type and data transmission (e.g. QoS metrics for a telephony service are communications continuity and voice quality). Depending on the application type, usage context, previous experience, and personal preferences, a user may consider several factors in order to come into a positive or a negative judgment of the used application or service [6], [7], [15], including service availability, session continuity, response time, throughput, reliability, media quality (video rate, video smoothness, picture detail, etc.), operability (e.g. an easy-to-use UI), etc.

Cost then represents the money value the user is charged when using a service. It is very important for the user to be able to distinguish whether the service generates costs to him/her and on what is the charging based, e.g. transmitted data (bits) or connection duration (seconds).

Finally, security requirement has several types such as confidentiality, integrity, digital signature capability, and authentication [6], and their necessity depends on the nature of the communications. Also where in the end-to-end delivery path (i.e. network, application or service) security is implemented is relevant: for instance, unless security is implemented in the application or in the service a vertical handover may jeopardize the security of the communications (e.g. when roaming to a WLAN).

It is clear that all the user-level QoS requirements can be compromised in a vertical handover as the characteristics of the underlying network connection may change even drastically. How vertical handovers affect the user experience of a service is discussed in section 4.

Methods for Measuring Subjective Application Quality. Two principal approaches for subjective application quality assessment exist: user study methods and objective measurements. The user study methods include, e.g. Mean Opinion Scores (MOS), continuous assessment, Task Performance Measures (TPMs), and qualitative methods [3]. Objective measurements, on the other hand, rely on measurement of some application quality metric(s) (e.g. Peak-Signal-to-Noise-Ratio (PSNR) for video) [20]. We chose to use MOS in our user study to collect the subjects' opinions of the experienced service quality. In short, MOS enables performing controlled assessment of subjective QoS with untrained subjects and controlled levels of quality [3]. The method employs a 5-point scale, according to which subjects judge the experienced quality after conducting a task. The given ratings are then averaged across the subjects to get the final MOS.

4   Case Study in Assessing Subjective QoS in a Heterogeneous Network

The purpose of the presented case study was to evaluate how host mobility in a heterogeneous network environment affects usability and subjective quality of different web-based services. The case study was organized as a task-based user evaluation, where test users conducted a set of predefined tasks in the real environment of use involving a multi-access network with automatic mobility management realized with a Mobile IP implementation.

4.1   Multi-access Network

The main access networks available to a mobile user in Oulu region are GPRS/EDGE, UMTS, and WLAN. In this study, the Octopus GSM/GPRS network [11] and panOULU WLAN network [13] were used. panOULU is a public access network based on IEEE 802.11a/b technology and provides free-of-charge wireless Internet access in different parts of the city. Host mobility between the two networks was enabled with Secgo Mobile IP, a commercial product based on the Mobile IPv4 standard. Secgo's solution has two system components: Secgo Mobile IP server, which in our setup is used to provide the home agent functionality, and Secgo Mobile IP client, which implements the mobile node functionality.

In our setup presented in Figure 3, the Secgo MIP server application was running on a Linux computer located in a local area network (denoted OPOY's network in the figure), of which public IP addresses are provided by Oulun Puhelin Plc. (OPOY). During the testing, the MN never roams to its home network. The panOULU WLAN and the Octopus GPRS network are the visited domains, in which the MN uses a co-located CoA, that is, there are no FAs deployed in either network. As shown in the figure, the roaming user's Internet connection was always routed via the home network and thus the location of the HA is optimal in terms of routing delay.

The MN has a public home address in the OPOY's network (i.e. 212.50.147.109) but the used care-of addresses are always private addresses since both panOULU WLAN and Octopus GPRS are located behind a NAT. Due to the presence of firewalls and NAT devices both reverse tunneling and NAT traversal are used. The MIP client is configured so that WLAN had a higher priority than GPRS and a WLAN-to-GPRS handover occurred if the link's signal quality dropped below 20%. To avoid the ping-pong effect the link reselection quality was set higher, i.e. the MN did not roam back to WLAN unless the quality of the link was higher than 40%.

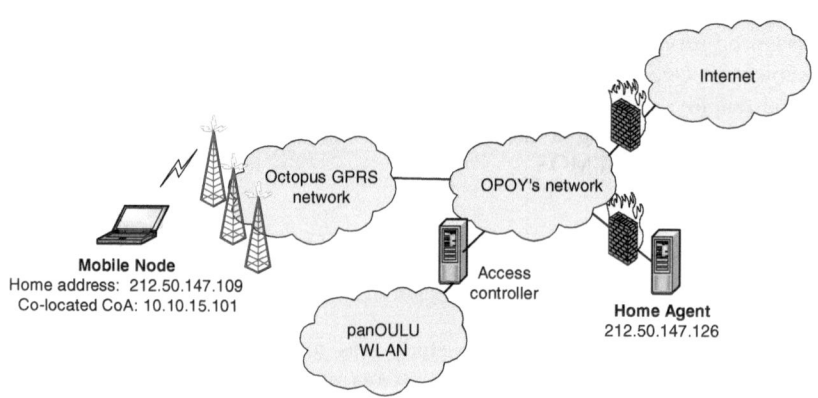

Fig. 3. Test network topology

4.2 Device Setup

Since Secgo MIP client is only available for Windows 2000/XP and Linux (≥2.2), the choice of the user terminal was limited to a laptop computer. The devices used during the testing included a laptop (IBM ThinkPad R40) and a PDA (Fujitsu Siemens PocketLOOX 610 BT/WLAN), which was connected to the laptop with an USB cable. The laptop's network interfaces included an integrated IEEE 802.11 WLAN radio (Intel PRO Wireless LAN) and Nokia D211 multi-mode card, which was used for GPRS access. The communication between the two devices was enabled with

ActiveSync v3.7.1 application that was set to a pass-through mode, i.e. the traffic emanating from the PDA was sent by using the laptop's IP address. Applications running on the laptop computer included Secgo MIP client v3.0.6 and Ethereal 0.10.6, configured to monitor HTTP traffic passing through the Mobile IP virtual network adapter. The PDA ran PocketPC2003 OS and Pocket Internet Explorer web browser.

4.3 Tasks

The user study was organized into tasks that were based on using the Digital Oulu Cultural Database web service (abbreviated DOK). DOK offers different types of services, including browsing of XHTML pages, searching for cultural objects, downloading multimedia presentations of the objects (text, images, and audio and video files), and streaming audio and video. The image and video content in DOK are adapted separately for different device types: desktop/laptop computers, PDAs, and Nokia S60 and S40 mobile phones. The user device is identified at the server-side from the received HTTP request message. Since access-based adaptation is not supported and the same user device will be used throughout the test, the test users will receive the same sized content regardless of the underlying access network.

There were two types of tasks (listed in Table 1). A Type 1 task comprised of browsing XHTML pages consisting of 2-4 small objects (approx. 1-20 KB in size). The pages contained text and/or image(s). A Type 2 task involved downloading of a video file (approx. 2 MB in size).

Table 1. Tasks performed during the test

Task ID	Access Network	Task Type
1	WLAN	1 (text+image)
2	WLAN	1 (text+image)
3	GPRS	1 (text+image)
4	GPRS	1 (text+image)
5	WLAN	2 (video)
6	GPRS	2 (video)
7	GPRS/WLAN	1+2 (text+image+video)

The users were asked to walk a given route around the city of Oulu and perform the different tasks. The route was carefully defined so that in the first six tasks only one access is used, whereas in the last task the users could move around freely in a specified area where vertical handover(s) were likely to occur. This way it was ensured that the users were exposed to as controlled levels of QoS as possible.

The subjects were told prior to the testing that they will be using different access networks during the test. However, they were not provided with any information of the used access networks while conducting the test. Thus, the users had a complete transparency to roaming in the sense that they did not have to modify any settings or connect to any access networks before they were able to use the services.

4.4 Data Collection

The test includes both subjective and objective evaluation of application layer QoS. Research data was collected with questionnaires and both client-side and server-side logging of user sessions.

Subjective user data was collected with three questionnaires: A pre-test questionnaire gathering background information, a questionnaire filled during the test with task-specific questions of the service's operation in different situations (including quality ratings), and a final questionnaire filled in a debriefing session. The questionnaire filled during the test included a scale for subjective evaluation of the experienced level of QoS. After conducting a task the users were asked to assess the service's quality according to the six-point Likert scale defined in Table 2. A six-point scale was used instead of the traditional five-point to avoid vague results [17].

Table 2. The six-point Likert scale used in evaluating subjective application quality

Score	Description
1	Excellent: "The service worked impeccably."
2	Good: "The service worked well, I noticed only few deficiencies."
3	It was all right: "The service worked sufficiently well considering the purpose of use."
4	Somewhat poor: "The operation of the service was a bit annoying, but I would use the service anyway."
5	Unsatisfactory: "I would use the service only if it was absolutely necessary."
6	Unusable: "I could not use the service at all."

In addition to the MOS scores, users' experiences were collected in the questionnaires with open ended questions and questions associated with 1-7 rating scales. This is simply because MOS scores can convey only a limited amount of information of the experienced service quality, e.g. it does not reveal any information of the reasons behind the given evaluations.

Objective measurement data was collected by capturing user traffic with Ethereal and Secgo MIP client's log at the client side. This allowed clocking actual download times, and to map this them to the subjective evaluations. The available data was sufficient for determining which access network was used at a given point of time, but not for making precise measurements of the performance of the vertical handover.

4.5 Test Users

Altogether 20 test users participated in the study. All of the participants were Finnish and 50% of them were men and 50% women. Majority of the users were quite young: 30% (6) were 20-24, 60% (12) were 25-34, one subject (5%) was 35-44, and one decided not to report his/her age. The professional background of the test users grouped by field is: 40% IT professionals or students, 15% data processing science teaching staff or researchers, 25% economics teaching staff or researchers, and 20%

other. All the subjects use at least some kind of an Internet service (basically e-mail and web browsing) more or less daily, and use mainly fixed access technologies.

Test users were asked to familiarize themselves with the UI, content, and operation of DOK beforehand. It was assumed that if the users were familiar with the service to begin with, they would not focus so much on the content or UI related issues that remain more or less static throughout the test. Since 35% of the subjects reported that they had never used a PDA before, they were also given an opportunity to try out the device before the test.

4.6 Main Results

The results consist of MOS ratings representing the experienced levels of QoS in each task, qualitative data providing more information of the user experiences, and objective measurements of the service's operation.

Subjective QoS Evaluations. The distributions of the QoS evaluations on the six-point Likert scale (Table 2) in each task are presented in Figure 4. According to the obtained results in the Type 1 tasks, the service worked very well via WLAN access but with GPRS the service can be considered as barely satisfactory.

After conducting each task the users were asked to compare the experienced service quality with the previous task. Interestingly, only 65% of the users reported that they had noticed degradation in the service quality relative to the previous task when conducting Task 3, i.e. the first Type 1 task that was performed using GPRS after conducting Tasks 1 and 2 (and a Type 2 task 5) via a WLAN connection.

In the two Type 2 tasks, the users were asked to assess the quality of a video file download. The size of the video files downloaded was 1.9 MB and the first video download was done via a WLAN connection (Task 5) and the second via a GPRS connection (Task 6). The users were in general very pleased with the quality (speed) of the first download, whereas the second received very low ratings: 30% of the subjects considered the service quality to be "Somewhat poor", 45% "Unacceptable", and 15% "Unusable". Also in Task 6, 60% of the subjects had interrupted the video download themselves, thus it can be considered practically unusable.

The users were in general pleased with quality of the video presentation. The obtained results indicate however that offering files of this size to be downloaded over GPRS is not practical in this type of a service. Whether streaming services would perform better in this case will be studied in future work.

In Task 7, the users were asked to move while using the service in an area where vertical handover(s) are likely to occur. In this task 35% of the users reported that they had noticed no changes in the service quality, 40% had noticed the quality to change once, and 25% had noticed 2-3 changes in the service quality. The number of vertical handovers per usage session is presented in Figure 5.

However, the open-ended questions reveal that the reported occurrences of quality changes were not always correlated with the occurrences of vertical handovers. Only 30% of the subjects had written that they had noticed a clear improvement in the service quality – mainly when downloading the video but a couple of users had also noticed some quality variation in other parts of the service, as well. 65% of the users had not noticed that their location had any effect on the service quality and one subject (5%) gave no answer.

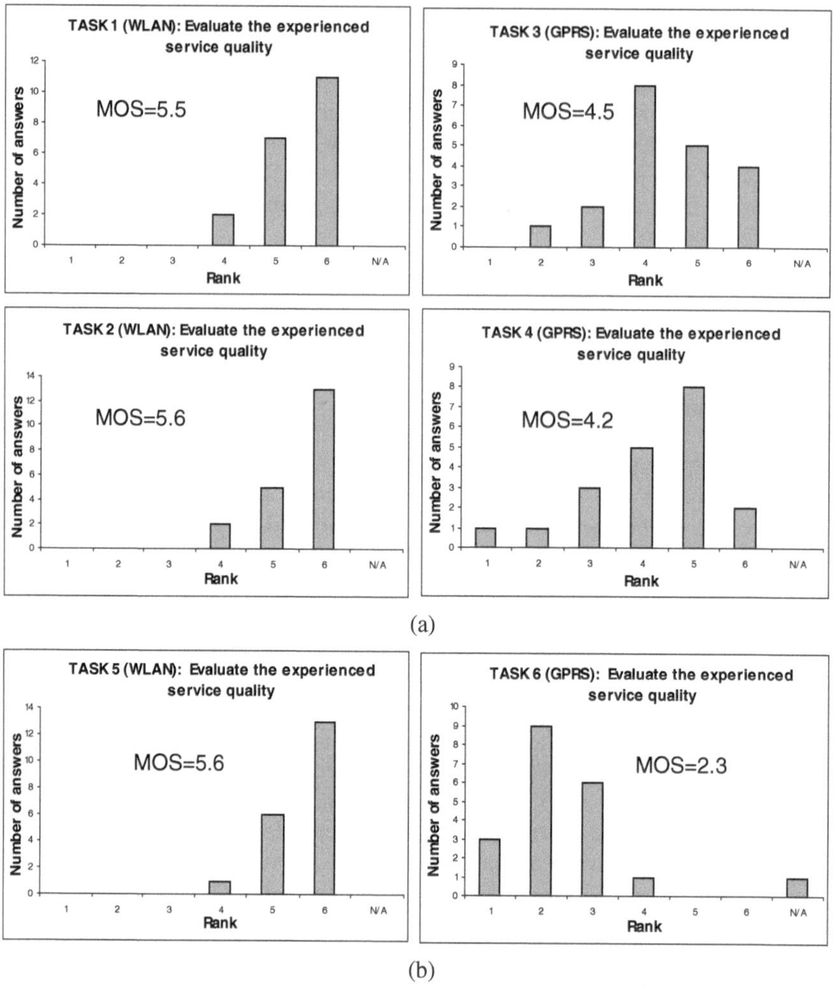

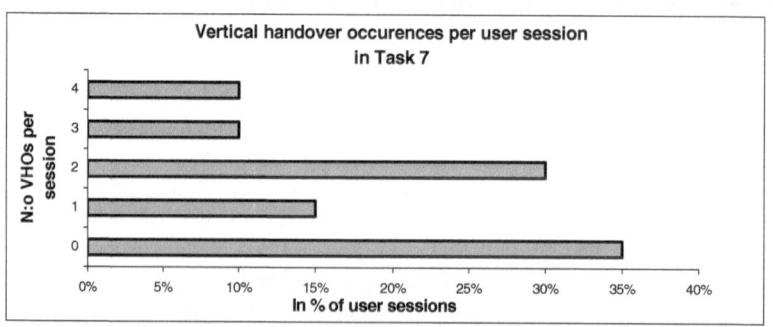

Fig. 4. Subjective evaluations in (a) Type 1; and (b) Type 2 tasks

Fig. 5. Vertical handovers per user session

The fact that the users missed most of the vertical handover instants is due to the properties of the used service and the task realization. Using a web-browsing service is not continuous and thus small changes in the quality are difficult to perceive. Also the period of time, during which the other access network was used after a handover was in some cases so short that the user did not even download anything before a handover in the reverse direction had already occurred. Also using two types of services (i.e. basic browsing and video downloads) in a same task was a bit confusing; many of the users understood poor video downloading performance as a change in quality since the basic browsing had worked well or least satisfactorily in their opinion, even if GPRS was used all the time. To obtain proper results in this scenario would require the usage of a service that generates a continuous traffic pattern (e.g. streaming). Due to these problems, MOS ratings could not be used for the analysis of the experienced service quality in this task, and thus the following comments are solely based on the gathered qualitative data.

Changes that increased the service's operational speed were considered very positive but changes in the opposite direction were irritating to the subjects. The subjects who had noticed a clear improvement in speed at some point of the video download in Task 7 were positively surprised. However, in these cases it is highly probable that the subjects let the downloading proceed slowly at first due to the test situation and this way they were able to experience the effect of the handover. In general, after experiencing the slow video download speed in Task 6 most subjects were very eager to interrupt the download in this task as they noticed that it was so slow again. Thus, to be of any use the downward vertical handover has to take place in the beginning of the download of a large file. But without getting any information of anticipated handovers the user does not have any means to predict the situation and will most likely discard the download as unusable as soon as he/she becomes frustrated with it.

In all of the tasks, there were no significant differences in the given ratings between technically oriented and novice users. Reasons for this may be well-defined test scenarios or the familiarity of the used service types (i.e. browsing and file download) to the users.

Acceptability of QoS Variations. After completing the tasks the users were asked to assess the degree of the experienced QoS variation in the two types of task on scale 1 (imperceptible) – 7 (high). The chart in Figure 6 shows that video download introduced high subjective QoS variations, which is expected. The chart in Figure 7 depicts the users' assessment on how acceptable the QoS variation experienced during the test was.

There is a high variation in the obtained results. To summarize the opinions obtained from the open ended question related to this evaluation, the acceptability of fluctuating QoS was not only dependent on the degree of the variation but also on the type of the used service: basic browsing was expected to work impeccably all the time whereas some variation can be tolerated in the video download due to the novelty of the technology in the mobile domain of usage, and how usable the service was under the poorest QoS: browsing over GPRS was still operable whereas downloading the video over GPRS was not reasonable.

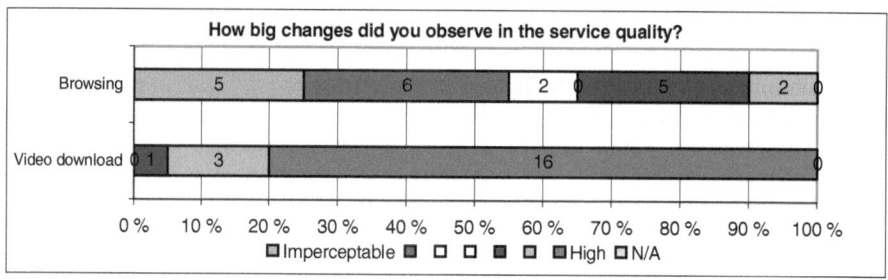

Fig. 6. Degree of the experienced QoS variations in different task types

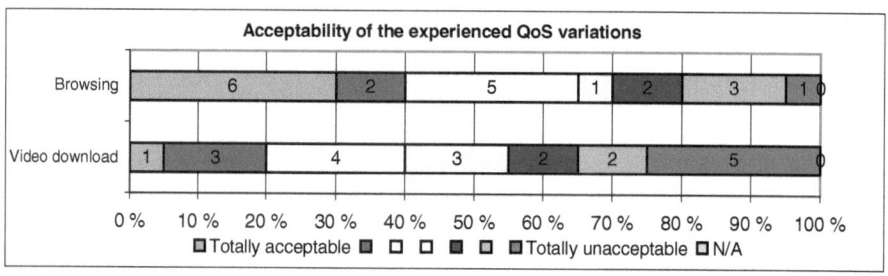

Fig. 7. Acceptability of the experienced QoS variations

User Viewpoint on Inter-technology Roaming. After completing the test the users were given a short description of the characteristics of WLAN and GPRS networks followed by few questions related to inter-technology roaming.

Based on the chart shown in Figure 8 the users clearly understood the advantages of the multi-access capability. As expected, WLAN connection (fast and free-of-charge but small coverage) was preferred to GPRS (slow, chargeable, and ubiquitous coverage), but it was acknowledged that service availability is more important than the characteristics of the underlying access network.

A majority of the users would utilize inter-technology roaming if their mobile device had such a capability. The fact that using GPRS is not free-of-charge was the main argument against transferring the user's connection automatically from one access network to another. However, notifying the user or asking for his/her consent when roaming to a chargeable connection was considered sufficient in this case.

The subjects were also asked how the selection of the access network and handover management should be carried out. The preferred roaming solution was automatic handover management (90% of the answers) complemented with some sort of notification or other solution that enables the user to be aware with which access network he/she is using at any time (required by 60% of the users). Only two subjects preferred manual control of vertical handovers. It should be noted however that in this study the users did not get to try manual network switching.

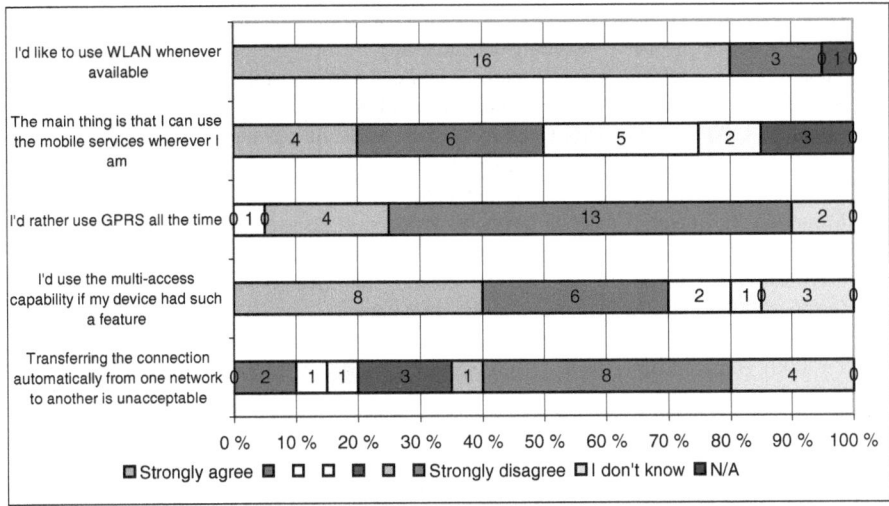

Fig. 8. Users' opinions on inter-technology roaming

5 Discussion

We presented an empirical task-based user evaluation of the end user QoS of a web service in a multi-access network utilizing automatic mobility management between WLAN and GPRS networks by Mobile IP. The empirical results and feedback from test users show that this type of a multi-access network combined with automatic mobility management offers a promising setting for provisioning future mobile multimedia services.

Future work will focus on addressing the limitations of the present study. The Mobile IP client needs to be ported to the actual mobile device. Services involving streaming data have to be included in the evaluation, as they are good candidates for future services in multi-access networks. Other access network technologies might be considered, as well. Further, solutions for service adaptation and user feedback need to be studied to obtain better user experience in heterogeneous networks.

References

1. Banerjee N, Wei W & Das SK (2003) Mobility Support in Wireless Networks. IEEE Wireless Communications 10(5):54-61.
2. Bouch A, Kuchinsky A, & Bhatti N (2000) Quality is in the Eye of the Beholder: Meeting Users' Requirements for Internet Quality of Service. CHI Letters 2(1).
3. Bouch A, Sasse MA & DeMeer H (2000) Of Packets and People: A User-centered Approach to Quality of Service. Proc. Eighth International Workshop on Quality of Service, Pittsburgh, PA, 189-197.
4. Gustafsson E & Jonsson A (2003) Always Best Connected. IEEE Wireless Communications 10(1):49-55.

5. ITU-T Recommendation E.800 (08/94) Terms and definitions related to quality of service and network performance including dependability.
6. Jamalipour A. (2003) The Wireless Mobile Internet: Architectures, Protocols, and Services. John Wiley & Sons Ltd., West Sussex, UK.
7. Miras D (2002) A Survey of network QoS needs of advanced Internet applications, http://qos.internet2.edu/wg/apps/fellowship/Docs/Internet2AppsQoSNeeds.pdf
8. Moby Dick Project (2004) http://ist-mobydick.org.
9. Mohr W (2002) Heterogeneous Networks to Support User Needs with Major Challenges for New Wideband Access Systems. Wireless Personal Communications 22:109-137.
10. Newman W & Lamming M (1995) Interactive System Design. Addison-Wesley.
11. Octopus (2004) http://www.mobileforum.org/octopus/.
12. Pahlavan K, Krishnamurthy P, Hatami A, Ylianttila M, Makela, J-P, Pichna R & Vallstron J (2000) Handoff in Hybrid Mobile Data Networks. IEEE Personal Communications 7(2):34-47.
13. panOULU (2004) http://www.panoulu.net.
14. Perkins CE (1998) Mobile IP: Design Principles and Practices. Addison-Wesley, USA.
15. Räisänen V (2003) Implementing Service Quality in IP Networks. John Wiley & Sons, West Sussex, UK.
16. Scaefer C, Enderes T, Ritter H & Zitterbart M (2002) Subjective Quality for Multiplayer Real-Time Games. Proc. First Workshop on Network and System Support for Games, Braunschweig, Germany, 74-78.
17. Serif T, Gulliver SR & Ghinea G (2004) Infotainment Across Access Devices: the Perceptual Impact of Multimedia QoS. Proc. ACM Symposium on Applied Computing, Nicosia, Cyprus, 1580- 1585.
18. Sun J & Sauvola J (2004) Mobile IP Applicability: When Do We Really Need It? Proc. 2004 International Conference on Parallel Processing Workshops, Montreal, Canada, 116-123.
19. VHO Project (2004) http://www.cs.hut.fi/~pmrg/VHO.html.
20. Wang Z, Banerjee S & Jamin S (2003) Studying Streaming Video Quality: From an Application Point of View. Proc. o11th ACM International Conference on Multimedia, Berkeley, CA, 327-330.
21. Zhang W, Jaehnert J & Dolzer K (2003) Design and Evaluation of a Handover Decision Strategy for 4th Generation Mobile Networks. Proc. IEEE Vehicular Technology Conference, Orlando, FL, 3:1969-1973.
22. Zhuang W, Yung-Sze Gan Y-S, Loh K-J & Chua K-C (2003) Policy-based QoS-management architecture in an integrated UMTS and WLAN environment. IEEE Communications Magazine 41(11):118-125.

WXCP: Explicit Congestion Control for Wireless Multi-hop Networks

Yang Su and Thomas Gross

Department of Computer Science, ETH Zurich,
Zurich Switzerland

Abstract. TCP experiences serious performance degradation in wireless multi-hop networks with its probe-based, loss-driven congestion control scheme. We describe the Wireless eXplicit Congestion control Protocol (WXCP), a new explicit flow control protocol for wireless multi-hop networks based on XCP. We highlight the approaches taken by WXCP to address the difficulties faced by the current TCP implementation in wireless multi-hop networks. Simulations with ns-2 show that WXCP outperforms current TCP implementations in terms of efficiency and fairness.

1   Introduction

With the progress in wireless technology, wireless networks become a potential candidate for constructing a broadband wireless backbone to provide ubiquitous low cost Internet connection [11, 2]. We need an efficient transport protocol for this new network architecture that should also deal with multi-hop networks and their variants (e.g., meshes).

Currently, the most widely-deployed TCP implementation is TCP Reno and its variations. However, recent studies have shown that TCP Reno suffers fairness and efficiency problems in wireless ad hoc network environment [9, 16, 8, 18]. There are several reasons for those problems.

1. TCP couples congestion control with reliability control. It detects congestion by packet loss events. Packet loss is strongly correlated to congestion in wireline networks but not a reliable congestion signal in wireless networks, where packet loss can also be introduced by medium related errors [6] and mobility related routing failures [9].
2. TCP relies on the AIMD (Additive-Increase Multiplicative-Decrease) adjustment of its congestion window to converge to a fair sharing of network bandwidth. It cannot acquire spare bandwidth efficiently after re-routing events [16, 5].
3. The throughput of multi-hop wireless networks is highly dependent on the traffic load. When traffic load increases over some threshold, the link error rate increases, and throughput drops down. TCP's flow control aims to fill the bottleneck interface queue and often puts too many packets into the network. [13, 8].

H. de Meer and N. Bhatti (Eds.): IWQoS 2005, LNCS 3552, pp. 313–326, 2005.
© IFIP International Federation for Information Processing 2005

We attempt to improve the performance of the transport protocol in wireless multi-hop networks by designing a new congestion control scheme that tackles the second and third problems. Our solution adopts an explicit congestion control architecture where intermediate stations make congestion estimations and send rate feedback to senders. The senders adjust their transmit rate based on the received rate feedback. This protocol called WXCP (Wireless eXplicit Congestion Control Protocol) is inspired by XCP (eXplicit Congestion control Protocol) [12], a window-based explicit congestion control scheme designed for high bandwidth-delay networks. We integrate a number of mechanisms, both at intermediate stations and the sender, to adopt XCP to the wireless network environments. At intermediate stations, WXCP makes more precise estimation of congestion conditions than current approaches and computes the rate feedback based on multiple congestion metrics. By using explicit rate feedback instead of probing the available bandwidth, WXCP flows are able to converge to a transmission state where better throughput is achieved. At the same time, WXCP flows converge to the equilibrium more quickly than TCP. In addition, loss discovery and pacing mechanisms are introduced at the sender to deal with the tiny window and burst problem.

The rest of the paper is organized as follows. Section 2 discusses the related work. In Section 3, we describe the design of WXCP in details. Section 4 contains an evaluation of the protocol. We conclude the paper in Section 5.

2   Related Work

WXCP is an extension of XCP, which was developed for high bandwidth-delay product networks [12].

Many research contributions address improving TCP performance or design new schemes for reliable data transmission over multi-hop wireless networks.

1. A first group of approaches is based on end-to-end measurement. Wang and Zhang [17] explore the approach to improve TCP performance by detecting and responding to out-of-order packet delivery events. Fu et al. [7] present a TCP-friendly transport protocol that tries to distinguish events such as mobility-introduced disconnection, reconnection, high out-of-order delivery ratio, or channel error from network congestion by performing multi-metric joint identification for packet and connection behaviors based on end-to-end measurements.

2. Several researchers have attempted to improve the performance of reliable data transmission in wireless networks by using explicit feedback from the routing layer. Holland and Vaidy [9] investigates the effects of link breakage due to mobility on TCP performance and propose an explicit link failure notification technique (ELFN). Chandran et al. [4] present a similiar mechanism called TCP-Feedback. Liu and Singh [15] introduce a thin layer between transport and underlying routing layers which deals with explicit

notifications from intermediate stations and shields TCP from the underlying behavior of an ad hoc network.

These approaches [15, 17, 7, 4, 9] improve the performance of TCP by distinguishing *congestion related* packet losses from packet losses caused by *medium errors* or *routing failures*. They solve the first problem listed in Section 1.

3. Recently, researchers also proposed to use explicit rate feedback from intermediate stations to deal with the second and third problems in Section 1. Sundaresan et al. [16] present a rate-based transport layer protocol called ATP. In ATP, the sender adjusts its transmission rate based on explicit rate feedback from the bottleneck station. Chen et al. introduce EXACT (EXplicit rAte-based flow ConTrol), which adapts the rate-based feedback framework of ATM's ABR (Available Bit Rate) congestion control to ad hoc networks [5]. Our scheme, which shares the same target and also makes use of explicit rate feedback, differs from these approaches in that we deploy window-based congestion control instead of pure rate-based congestion control at the sender. In contrast to [5], intermediate stations in WXCP do not maintain per flow information. Therefore implementation and deployment of WXCP are much simplified. [16] also does not maintain per-flow information, but it does not take into account the spatial characteristics of the wireless medium, whereas WXCP maintains time fairness instead of throughput fairness among flows to different next hop stations. Consequently WXCP achieves an higher aggregate throughput.

3   Explicit Congestion Control Protocol for Wireless

3.1   Motivation

In this paper, we make two assumptions about the MAC protocol: 1. It is based on CSMA/CA. 2. Unicast packets are acknowledged. As shown in [19], it is challenging to apply XCP to shared media wireless networks. To accurately calculate feedback, the XCP router must know the precise link capacity in advance. However, in shared media wireless networks, all the stations contend for the media. The true output capacity is changing depending on the contention traffic load. XCP takes the link capacity at interface to compute the rate feedback. That introduces capacity overestimation with which XCP will generate inflated feedback, the senders will send more than the link can transfer, and the queue will build up. Instead of using a fixed interface capacity, WXCP estimates how much capacity that it has fair access to by locally monitoring the channel conditions at intermediate stations. In addition, at the sender, loss discovery and pacing mechanisms deal with the tiny window and burst problem.

In the rest of this section, we describe congestion metrics used to estimate the available capacity and calculate the rate feedback. Then we present the design of WXCP for intermediate stations and for the sender.

3.2   Congestion Metrics

WXCP uses three metrics to measure the state of resource usage and the level of congestion at a station: *available bandwidth, interface queue (IFQ) length and average link layer retransmission (ALR)*.

We use available bandwidth to represent how much network capacity is still available. The less bandwidth is available, the more probable it is that congestion will happen. Available bandwidth can be estimated based on local observation without exchange of additional control packets. If the estimation is made periodically, channel free time represents network capacity still available during the estimation period. To convert channel free time to a rate, we need the link layer throughput. Since the wireless medium condition at different locations might be different, link layer throughput to different neighboring stations might also be different. Hence, although the same channel is used, the available bandwidth estimation to different destination stations might be different. The available bandwidth we use in WXCP is the average available bandwidth of all the paths.

If the estimation period is T, average available bandwidth B is:

$$B = \frac{T_{free} \cdot bw}{T} \tag{1}$$

where T_{free} is channel free time during period T; bw is the average link layer throughput to all the different destinations. The model can be implemented with the IEEE 802.11 DCF MAC protocol, where CSMA/CA mechanism is used to control multiple stations visiting the same channel. By monitoring the radio state, we can get T_{busy}, which is the sum of "time used by station itself", "physical carrier sense time", and "virtual carrier sense time" during the observation interval T. Then, T_{free} can be computed as $T - T_{busy}$. In IEEE 802.11 DCF, any non-broadcasting data packet is always companied with an acknowledgment packet. bw is an average of each link layer throughput measurement sample, which is computed as:

$$\frac{s_j}{t_t - t_r} \tag{2}$$

where s_j is the size of packet j, t_t is the time when the packet is delivered to the MAC layer, t_r is the time when the corresponding ACK packet is received.

The second metric is the state of the output interface queue (IFQ). When the input traffic rate is greater than the output rate, packets start to be buffered in IFQ and the length of the queue increases. When the queue is full, further packets coming to the queue are dropped. TCP uses this event to infer the existence of congestion in the network.

Because of the hidden terminal problem [1], without any coordination, sender contends for a channel around the receiver against stations out of its sensing range, but still in the receiver's sensing range. If the hidden traffic comes from the flow itself, it is the well-known self-interference. When a flow puts too many packets in the network, self-interference happens, transmission delay increases and throughput drops down. By adjusting the transmission rate, a flow can change the degree of self-interference. However the length of a sender's IFQ is not sensitive enough to detect this condition [20]. Hence, we use the average link layer retransmission (ALR) from successfully transmitted packets as the third congestion metric to detect the degree of self-interference.

There are many noise sources for using ALR to sense self-interference, because packet losses in wireless ad hoc networks are caused not only by self-interference but also by other kinds of wireless medium errors (such as interference due to multi-path reflection and signals from other kind of sources, attenuation and path dispersion[21, 6]) and route failures. It is difficult to distinguish self-interference from other kinds of wireless medium errors. It is possible that when network experiences severe wireless medium errors, a station gets a number of high retransmissions and hence infers the existence of a high degree of self-interference, but in fact, there is no self-interference at all. In this case, a transmission protocol that uses this metric becomes too conservative. WXCP deals with this problem by following the convention of TCP implementations that keep the minimum CWND greater or equal to one packet. From Section 3.4 and Section 4, we see that a CWND of one packet is close to the optimal value for most network settings. In the worst case, when severe wireless medium errors happen and WXCP senses the self-interference incorrectly, it can at least work with a CWND of one and achieve reasonable performance.

3.3   Explicit Congestion Feedback Computation in WXCP

In WXCP, intermediate stations make congestion control and fairness control decisions separately, based on flow information carried in data packet headers and the estimation of congestion metrics described in the last section. Because in wireless networks, link layer throughputs over different paths are different, to achieve higher overall throughput, the WXCP fairness controller maintains time fairness instead of throughput fairness among flows. Every control interval T, which is the average of RTT of all the flows over this station, WXCP calculates the aggregate feedback:

$$\Phi = \alpha \cdot \frac{T \cdot B}{n+1} - \beta \cdot Q_{ifq} - \zeta \cdot Retry_{avg} \tag{3}$$

where B is the estimation of available bandwidth that is shared by n neighboring stations and the station itself. n can be obtained by counting the number of different sources from packets overheard during the last control interval. Q_{ifq} represents the minimal length of interface queue observed during the control interval. $Retry_{avg}$ represents the average ALR from successfully transmitted packets over all the destination stations during last control interval. α, β, ζ are constants.

When aggregate feedback is positive, we want to increase the active time of all flows by the same amount. Thus Δt_i, the change of active time of any flow i, will be proportional to the same constant. Assume that flow i flows over path k with link layer throughput bw_k. Since Δt_i is proportional to the change in throughput of the flow $\Delta throughput_i$, and inversely proportional to link throughput bw_k (i.e., $\Delta t_i = \frac{\Delta throughput_i \times T}{bw_k}$), the change of throughput of flow i is proportional to the link layer throughput of the path. In addition, the change in congestion window of flow i is the change in its throughput multiplied by its RTT. Hence, the change in the congestion window of flow i should be proportional to the flow's RTT and link layer throughput,(i.e., $\Delta cwnd_i \propto rtt_i \times bw_k$).

The total change in congestion window of a flow is the sum of the per-packet feedback it receives. The expected number of packets from flow i seen by the router in a control interval T is proportional to the congestion window of the flow $cwnd_i$ and inversely proportionally to its round trip time rtt_i and packet size s_i (i.e., $\frac{T}{rtt_i} \times \frac{cwnd_i}{s_i}$). Thus, per-packet positive feedback p_i is given by:

$$p_i = \xi_p \cdot bw_k \cdot \frac{rtt_i^2 \cdot s_i}{cwnd_i} \tag{4}$$

where ξ_p is a constant. Since the total increase of the aggregate traffic rate is equal to the sum of the increase in the rate of all flows in the aggregate, ξ_p can be derived as:

$$\xi_p = \frac{\Phi}{T \cdot \sum^L bw_k \cdot \frac{rtt_i \cdot s_i}{cwnd_i}} \tag{5}$$

where L presents all the flows over the station. Similarly, we compute the per-packet negative feedback when the aggregate feedback is negative. In this case, we want the decrease in the active time of flow i to be proportional to its current active time (i.e., $\Delta t_i \propto t_i$). At the same time, t_i is proportional to $throughput_i$ and inversely proportional to bw_k. Δt_i is proportional to $\Delta throughput_i$ and inversely proportional to bw_k. It can be derived that the decrease in the throughput of flow i is proportional to its current throughput (i.e., $\Delta throughput_i \propto throughput_i$), which is the same as XCP. From XCP [12], per-packet negative feedback n_i is given by:

$$n_i = \xi_n \cdot rtt_i \cdot s_i \tag{6}$$

Constant ξ_n can be derived as:

$$\xi_n = \frac{\Phi}{T \cdot \sum^L s_i} \tag{7}$$

3.4   Loss Discovery

As with XCP, a WXCP sender maintains a congestion window of the outstanding packets, $cwnd$, and an estimate of the round trip time, rtt. On packet departure, the sender fills its current $cwnd$ and rtt into the packet header. Whenever a new acknowledgment arrives, the sender adjusts its $cwnd$ according to $feedback$ contained in the acknowledgment:

$$cwnd = max(cwnd + feedback, s) \tag{8}$$

where s is the packet size. In addition to feedback, WXCP also responds to losses in the similar manner to TCP.

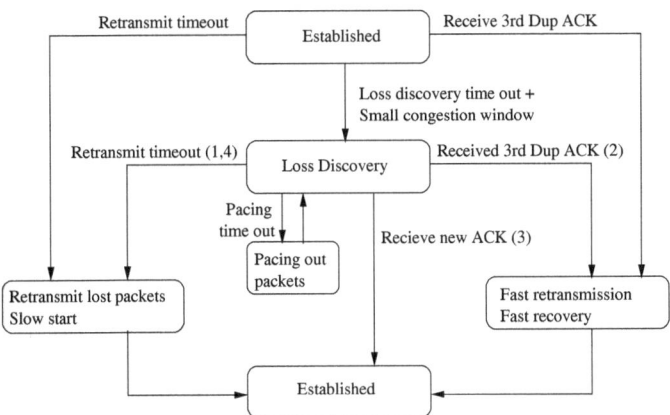

Fig. 1. State machine for WXCP sender

[14, 3] show that when TCP works with a small congestion window the window size limits the number of returning ACKs the sender may receive. Because TCP requires three duplicate ACKs to trigger fast retransmission, small windows may prevent these algorithm from being effective.

WXCP keeps the congestion window with a size close to the optimal value where better throughput is achieved. As shown in [8], the optimal window size for window-based flow control over multi-hop wireless ad hoc networks remains a small value (e.g., smaller than 5) in most of network settings. To avoid unnecessary timeouts, a WXCP sender needs to put enough packets into the network to make a decision about current packet loss pattern. Hence we introduce loss discovery state into sender side WXCP state machine. The basic idea is that when the congestion window is small, if there is no new ACK received and there are not enough duplicated ACKs returned, instead of waiting for a retransmission timeout, the sender switches from window-based control to rate-based control with reduced transmission rate. As shown in Figure 1, two timers, loss discovery timer and pacing timer, are added to sender side implementation. Every time when the retransmission timer is set, the loss discovery timer is also set with timeout period equal to current smoothed RTT estimation. If there is no packet lost, and RTT over the path does not increase dramatically, the loss discovery timer will not time out before it is reset. Otherwise, when a loss recovery timeout happens, the current congestion window size is checked. If the congestion window is smaller than the threshold W_{min}, the sender enters the loss discovery state. In loss discovery state, packets are paced out with a rate that is half to the current transmission rate (e.g., $\frac{cwnd}{2 \cdot RTT}$). The sender keeps reducing the transmission rate to half when it paces out a CWND of packets. During loss discovery period, CWND remains unchanged. RTT estimation is updated as normal. As shown in Figure 1, the sender exits the loss discovery state under the following conditions:

1. There have already been W_{min} packets inserted in the network but still no new ACKs returned, and the number of duplicated ACKs is less than 3. Now it is reasonable to infer that most of the packets are lost and the network is in congestion. The sender will stop injecting new packets into the network and wait for a retransmission timeout.
2. Sender receives 3 duplicated ACKs. This situation indicates that there are packets lost. Sender quits loss discovery state and starts fast retransmission and fast recovery.
3. Sender receives new ACKs. There are no packets lost and there is no congestion present in the network.
4. Retransmission timer expires. If RTT of the path is large, it is possible that the retransmission timer times out before packets in the network are increased to W_{min}. In this case, the sender enters retransmission timeout state and retransmits lost packets in the same manner to TCP.

3.5   Pacing

Window-based transmit schemes have the advantage that they make use of the ACK self-clock instead of relying on a fine grained timer. They also have the drawback that they introduce bursts when many ACKs are received and the sender sends out back-to-back packets. Those packets would interfere with each other over the wireless medium. To smooth this burst, a pacing mechanism is introduced into the window-based WXCP sender. We define B_t as maximum tolerable burst. The WXCP sender shapes its outgoing traffic by B_t. Normally, when it has available congestion window space W_a, the sender tries to send as much packets as W_a allows. In WXCP, the sender checks B_t. If $W_a < B_t$, packets are sent out as usual, otherwise, packets belonging to one congestion window are paced out with rate $\frac{cwnd}{rtt}$, where $cwnd$ is current congestion window, rtt represents the last RTT sample. As soon as one of the acknowledgments for paced out packets is received, the pacing phase ends. Further packets are sent out with ACK self clocking.

3.6   Discussion of Parameter Settings

1. **Loss discovery threshold W_{min}:** When its congestion window reaches this threshold, the WXCP connection is considered to be resilient to timeout and always works with window-based rate control. When its congestion window is below the threshold, the WXCP connection operates in the loss discovery state to reduce unnecessary timeout. In this paper, we set the threshold to be 7 packets.
2. **Maximum tolerable burst B_t for pacing:** B_t represents the burst that a WXCP connection wants to tolerate in the network. To minimize the self-contention, we set its value to 2.
3. **Parameters for intermediate stations:** There are three parameters concerning the algorithms at intermediate stations. α controls the allocation of available bandwidth to WXCP flows. Its value is between 0 and 1. With

large α, WXCP increases its rate quickly to fill the available bandwidth. To reduce the transmission delay, WXCP tries to keep both short IFQ and low self-interference at intermediate stations, which are controlled by β and ζ. Hence, these three parameters must be set to balance the increased protocol responsiveness to available bandwidth with the increased delay from queuing at IFQ and self-interference. Currently we set α, β, ζ to 0.20, 0.11 and 67. A detailed discussion of parameters setting can be found in [20].

4   Evaluation

4.1   Experimental Setup

All the experiments in this paper rely on simulation. Unless explicitly mentioned, all simulations use the configuration described here. The simulation platform that we use is the ns-2 simulator (version 2.27). We use TCP Newreno as the basis for comparison. In all the experiments, we use FTP as application traffic, AODV as routing protocol and at the MAC layer, the IEEE 802.11 DCF MAC protocol with RTS/CTS enabled. Channel bandwidth is 2Mbps. The effective transmission range is 250 meters, and the interference range is about 550 meters. The active simulation time is 120s.

4.2   Chain Topology

To provide insight into the protocol's baseline behavior, we investigate the performance of WXCP with stationary chain topologies where stations are arranged in a chain and two adjacent stations are 200 meters apart. We repeat the experiments with the length of chain changing from 1 hop to 16 hops. Each simulation runs for 140 seconds. From 5s to 125s, an FTP traffic flows over the chain from the first station to the last station.

1. **Throughput.** We present overall throughput data over 120s simulation for TCP and WXCP with packet size of 1000 bytes in Figure 2. Each plot

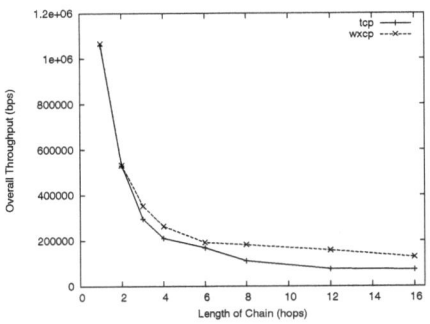

Fig. 2. Comparison of overall throughput of TCP and WXCP over chain topology

Table 1. Average congestion window over chain topology

Hops	TCP	WXCP	Ideal
1	120.6	2.0	1.0
2	86.7	1.9	1.0
3	31.0	1.8	1.0
4	7.3	1.8	1.0
6	7.9	2.0	1.5
8	8.3	3.0	2.0
12	8.8	5.0	3.0
16	9.7	6.7	4.0

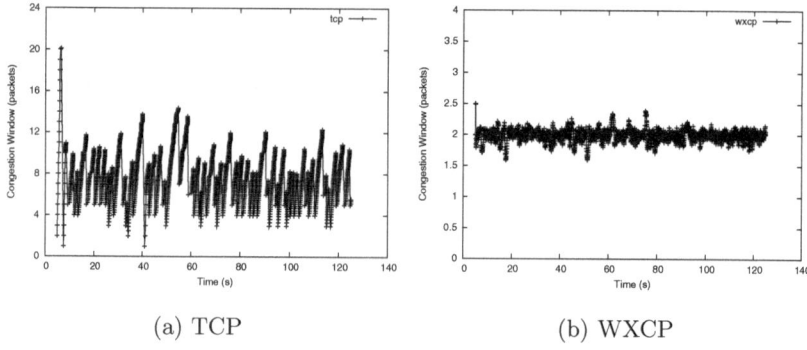

(a) TCP   (b) WXCP

Fig. 3. Instantaneous congestion window vs. time

presents the average result of 10 independent simulations running with different random seeds. We observe that WXCP achieves the same throughput as TCP in short chain scenarios (less than 3 hops) and realizes a 10% to 25% throughput improvement over chains with medium length (3 to 7 hops). When it operates over long chains (more than 8 hops), WXCP can achieve 34% to 110% more throughput than TCP. Due to different per-packet overhead, the transport protocols achieve different throughput when using different packet sizes. However, as shown in [20], both protocols, TCP and WXCP, change their behavior in a similar way. Hence, in the following experiments, we only show the results when the packet size is 1000 bytes.

2. **Congestion window.** From [8], we know that in multi-hop wireless networks, for window-based flow control, there exists a value for window size such that spatial channel reuse is maximized. This window size results in best channel utilization and consequently highest throughput. In the chain topology, optimal throughput is achieved when the window size is $h/4$ packets, h is number of hops, if the impact of ACK packets is omitted. The reason is that stations can only transmit concurrently with stations 4 hops away without interference. Table 1 shows the average congestion window of WXCP, TCP and $h/4$ for chains of different lengths. We observe that by estimating the channel condition more accurately, WXCP keeps the congestion window to a reasonable size, whereas TCP makes the estimation by using the AIMD adjustment of its congestion window. This behavior of TCP leads to too many packets in flight. These packets interfere with each other and finally hurt performance. For TCP over shorter paths (1 or 2 hops), chances for packets from one flow to interfere with each other is small. Hence, although TCP's CWND is far from the optimal value, it still can achieve a throughput close to WXCP, as shown in Figure 2. In Figure 3 we present snapshots of the instantaneous congestion window for TCP and WXCP in a 6-hop chain. The vibration of TCP's congestion window is due to its frequent packet loss. In contrast, WXCP shows a relatively stable behavior.

3. **Packet loss.** Figure 4(a) shows the number of packets dropped at the MAC layer; this number presents the degree of contention for the wireless medium. It includes all kinds of packets dropped at the MAC layer (MAC layer control packets, routing layer control packets, and data packets). Packet loss at the MAC layer does not always introduce packet loss observed by the transport protocol, because of the local error control mechanism of IEEE 802.11. We observe that in short chains there are fewer packets dropped at the MAC layer using WXCP than using TCP. This result shows that WXCP can keep the channel in a lower contention state while achieving a little better throughput than TCP. When the length of the chain increases, the number of packet losses at the MAC layer for WXCP approaches the number for TCP. However, WXCP achieves much higher throughput than TCP. From Figure 4(b), which shows the number of packets lost at MAC layer per successfully transmitted packet, we conclude that WXCP maintains lower contention for the wireless medium than TCP.

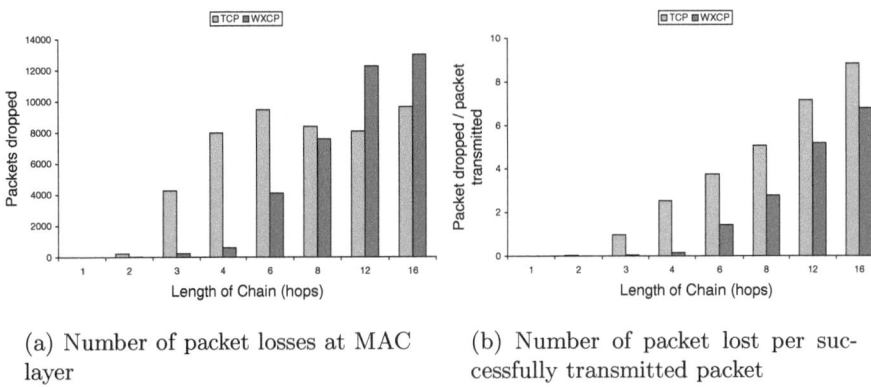

(a) Number of packet losses at MAC layer

(b) Number of packet lost per successfully transmitted packet

Fig. 4. Packet loss at MAC layer

To study the interaction between WXCP flows, we create two WXCP flows from station 0 to the last station in the chain. The flows share the same path. These simulations are repeated with TCP flows in the same setting. Figure 5 shows the aggregate overall throughput. Depending on network configuration, WXCP achieves 1% to 97% improvement over TCP. At the same time, different flows sharing the same path are expected to obtain nearly the same throughput. In this paper, we use the coefficient of variation as fairness index; this value will be 0 under fair allocation of resources [10]. Table 2 shows the comparison of fairness between TCP and WXCP. Each number represents the average coefficient of the variation of throughput. We observe that WXCP guarantees better fairness among two flows over networks with a chain topology than TCP.

While the scenarios discussed thus far comprise static traffic loads, to investigate the performance of WXCP's rate adaptation mechanism in the event of

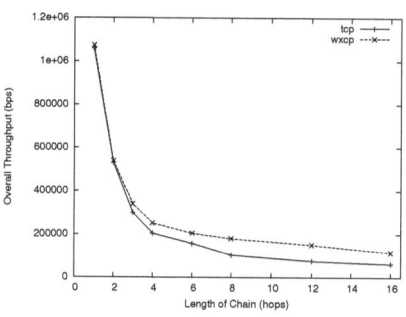

Fig. 5. Aggregate overall throughput of two flows over chain topology

Table 2. Average coefficient of variation of throughput over chain topology

Hops	TCP	WXCP
1	0.0007	0.0005
2	0.0018	0.0004
3	0.8985	0.0003
4	0.1336	0.0009
6	0.1097	0.0004
8	0.1132	0.0157
12	0.1620	0.0368
16	0.1122	0.0281

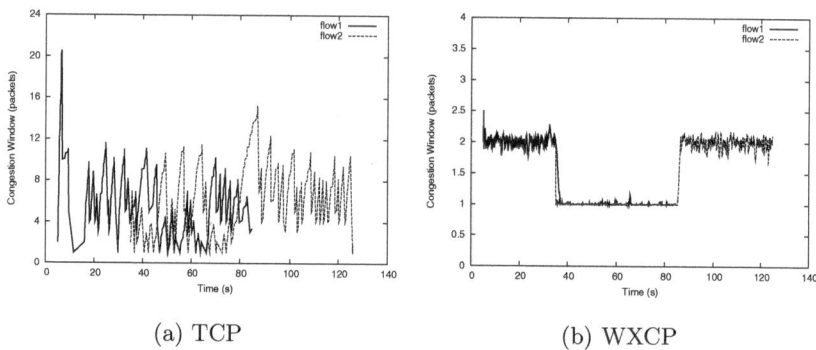

(a) TCP   (b) WXCP

Fig. 6. Instantaneous congestion window dynamics

network traffic dynamics, we conduct an experiment over a 6-hop chain with two flows $f1$ and $f2$. $f1$ exists in the interval between 5s and 85s, while $f2$ exits in the interval between 35s and 125s. The instantaneous congestion windows of the two WXCP flows are presented in Figure 6(b). We observe that after the arrival of $f2$, the two flows converge to the fair sharing of available channel capacity in a short time. After $f1$ leaves, $f2$ is able to catch up to the total available capacity again. The corresponding instantaneous congestion window dynamics for two TCP flows is shown in Figure 6(a). It can be seen that when flow $f2$ joins, the two flows cannot converge to a stable fair sharing of bandwidth. Instead the congestion windows oscillate. When $f1$ leaves, $f2$ is unable to properly catch up to the available capacity.

4.3 Grid Topology

To evaluate WXCP in more complex topologies, we create a stationary wireless ad hoc network whose nodes are arranged in a 13×13 grid topology as shown in Figure 7. For TCP and WXCP, we run 2, 4, 6, 8,10 and 12 flows respectively.

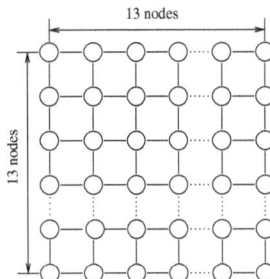

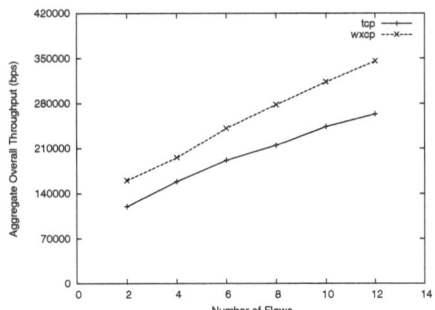

Fig. 7. Grid topology

Fig. 8. Aggregate overall throughput vs. Number of flows over grid topology

In each of these cases, flows are spaced evenly in two directions (top-to-down and left-to-right). The aggregate throughput is summarized in Figure 8. In all cases, WXCP increases throughput by about 23% to 34% relative to TCP.

5   Concluding Remarks

WXCP is an explicit congestion control protocol for wireless multi-hop or ad hoc networks. In WXCP, based on the estimation of multiple congestion metrics, intermediate stations maintain an estimate of congestion conditions and explicitly notify flows about their available bandwidth. As a result, WXCP flows are able to catch the available bandwidth quickly and precisely. WXCP also integrates a new loss recovery algorithm at the sender to deal with the potential small-window problem companied with window-based transfer. Simulation results show that WXCP outperforms TCP in terms of both efficiency and fairness.

References

1. Allen, D.: Hidden Terminal Problems in Wireless LAN. IEEE 802.11 working Group paper 802.11/93-xx
2. Bahl, V.: Self-Organizing Neighborhood Wireless Mesh Networks. Microsoft mesh network homepage
3. Balakrishnan, H. and Padmanabhan, V. and Seshan, S. and Stemm, M. and Katz, R.: TCP behavior of a busy internet server: Analysis and improvements. Proceedings of IEEE INFOCOM, 1998
4. Chandran, K. and Raghunathan, S. and Venkatesan, S. and Prakash, R.: A Feedback-based Scheme for Improving TCP Performance in Ad Hoc Wireless Networks. Proceedings of ICDCS, 1998
5. Chen, K. and Nahrstedt, K. and Vaidya, N.: The Utility of Explicit Rate-Based Flow Control in Mobile Ad Hoc Networks. Proceedings of IEEE WCNC, 2004

6. Eckhardt, D. and Steenkiste, P.: Measurement and Analysis of the Error Characteristics of an In-Building Wireless Network. Proceedings of ACM SIGCOMM, 1996

7. Fu, Z and Greenstein, B. and Meng, X. and Lu, S.: Design and Implementation of a TCP-Friendly Transport Protocol for Ad Hoc Wireless Networks. Proceedings of IEEE ICNP, 2002

8. Fu, Z. and Zerfos, P. and Luo, H. and Lu, S. and Zhang, L. and Gerla, M.: The Impact of Multi-hop Wireless Channel on TCP Throughput and Loss. Proceedings of IEEE INFOCOM, 2003

9. Holland, G. and Vaidya, N.: Analysis of TCP Performance over Mobile Ad Hoc Networks. Proceedings of ACM Mobicom, 1999

10. Jain, R. and Chiu, D. and Hawe, W.: A Quantitative Measure of Fairness and Discrimination for Resource Allocation in Shared Computer System. Technical Report TR-301, Digital Equipment Corporation, 1984

11. Karrer, R. and Sabharwal, A. and Knightly, E.: Enabling Large-scale Wireless Broadband: The Case for TAPs. Proceedings of the 2nd Workshop on Hot Topics in Networks (Hot-Nets II), 2003

12. Katabi, D. and Handley, M. and Rohrs, C.: Congestion Control for High Bandwidth-Delay Product Networks. Proceedings of ACM SIGCOMM, 2002

13. Li, J. and Blake, C. and Couto, D. and Morris, R.: Capacity of Ad Hoc Wireless Networks. Proceedings of ACM MOBICOM, 2001

14. Lin, D. and Kung, H.T.: TCP Fast Recovery Strategies: Analysis and Improvements, Proceedings of IEEE INFOCOM, 1998

15. Liu, J. and Singh, S.: ATCP: TCP for Mobile Ad Hoc Networks, IEEE Journal on Selected Areas in Communications, 2001

16. Sundaresan, K. and Anantharaman, V. and Hsieh, H-Y. and Sivakumar, R.: ATP: A Reliable Transport Protocol for Ad-hoc Networks, Proceedings of ACM MOBI-HOC, 2003

17. Wang, F. and Zhang, Y.: Improving TCP Performance over Mobile Ad-Hoc Networks with Out-of-Order Detection and Response, Proceedings of ACM MOBI-HOC, 2002

18. Xu, K. and Gerla, M. and Qi, L. and Shu, Y.: Enhancing TCP Fairness in Ad Hoc Wireless Networks Using Neighborhood RED, Proceedings of ACM MOBICOM, 2003

19. Y.G. Zhang and Henderson,T: An Implementation and Experimental Study of the eXplicit Control Protocol (XCP), Proceedings of IEEE INFOCOM, 2005

20. Su, Y. and Gross, T.: WXCP: Explicit Congestion Control for Wireless Multi-Hop Networks, Technical Report, ETH Zurich, Feb.2005

21. Eckhardt, D. and Steenkiste, P.: Improving Wireless LAN Performance via Adaptive Local Error Control, Proceedings of IEEE ICNP, 1998

A Non-homogeneous QBD Approach for the Admission and GoS Control in a Multiservice WCDMA System[*]

Ioannis Koukoutsidis[1], Eitan Altman[1], and Jean Marc Kelif[2]

[1] INRIA, 2004 Route des Lucioles, BP 93,
06902 Sophia Antipolis Cedex, France
{gkoukout, altman}@sophia.inria.fr
[2] France Telecom R&D, Rue du Général Leclerc,
92794 Issy-les-Moulineaux Cedex 9, France
JeanMarc.Kelif@francetelecom.com

Abstract. We consider a WCDMA system with real time (RT) calls that have dedicated resources, and data non-real-time (NRT) calls that share system capacity. We apply reservation of some resources for the NRT traffic and assume that this traffic is further assigned the resources unused by RT calls. The grade of service (GoS) of RT traffic is also controlled in order to allow for handling more RT calls during congestion periods, at the cost of degraded transmission rates. We consider both the uplink and downlink, and derive performance evaluation results regarding user-perceived QoS parameters, namely the blocking rates of RT calls and sojourn time of NRT calls. On what concerns the bandwidth-sharing policy of NRT traffic, we compare WCDMA behavior in the presence of a high data rate scheme. Finally, we extend our results to cover NRT admission control schemes and examine blocking behavior and transfer times of NRT traffic.

1 Introduction

In this paper, we are interested in analyzing resource sharing between RT (real time) and NRT (non-real time) traffic in a cellular CDMA network, as well as the attained QoS (quality of service) and GoS (grade of service). A classical approach widely used in wireless networks is based on adaptively deciding how many channels (or resources) to allocate to calls of a given service class, based on a measure of capacity. In CDMA, capacity is rather a complex combination of cell parameters and channel conditions, being mostly interference-limited [4],[14]. However, existing models ([5],[8]) allow us to obtain the resources required by transmissions of a given class with a given GoS, both in the uplink as well as the downlink of a CDMA system.

RT traffic (conversational, streaming) has stringent QoS requirements with regards to transmission rate and/or duration. On the other hand, NRT traffic (transfer of files, web browsing, etc.) has no guaranteed bit rate and is apt for a processor-sharing setting. Based on these principles, we design the admission and rate control scheme. User-centric QoS parameters of interest are primarily the blocking probabilities for RT calls

---

[*] This work was supported by a CRE research contract with France Telecom R&D and by the EuroNGI network of excellence.

H. de Meer and N. Bhatti (Eds.): IWQoS 2005, LNCS 3552, pp. 327–340, 2005.

and expected sojourn times for NRT calls. We use the inflected term 'call' to refer also to the sending of NRT data, including connectionless services. Further, the term 'GoS' refers specifically to the rate of transmission. We allow downgrading of this rate for RT calls during congestion epochs (i.e. having in mind adaptive real-time compression algorithms, or tolerable loss of quality). Overall, the proposed control policy combines admission control together with GoS control for both RT and NRT traffic. Fairness in transmission rate between users of the same service class is considered as a basic building block of the access mechanism.

This work is a follow-up of [5],[8] in which NRT traffic was scheduled using a time-sharing approach, as is the case in the High Speed Downlink Packet Access (HSDPA) system [13],[7]. This allowed to derive a tractable mathematical model based on a homogeneous QBD (Quasi Birth-Death) process [12],[11]. In this paper, we consider the standard case with simultaneous transmissions in a cell. The system analyzed then cannot be evaluated anymore with a homogeneous QBD and we present a more involved analysis based on a non-homogeneous QBD. A numerical investigation is conducted and key performance measures are computed.

2   Background: Computing the Transmission Rates

The analysis is based on radio models for the downlink (DL) and uplink (UL) introduced in [8],[5]. For completeness we recall in this section the derivation of capacities and transmission rates.

2.1   Downlink

Let there be S base stations. The minimum power received at a mobile k from its base station l is determined by a condition concerning the signal to interference ratio, which should be larger than some constant

$$(C/I)_k = \frac{E_s}{N_0} \frac{R_s}{W} \Gamma, \tag{1}$$

where E_s is the energy per transmitted bit of type s, N_0 is the background noise density, W is the spread bandwidth, R_s is the transmission rate of the type s call, and Γ is a constant related to shadow fading and imperfect power control (cf. [5]).

Let $P_{k,l}$ be the power transmitted to mobile k from base station l. Assume that there are M mobiles in cell l; the base station transmits at a total power $P_{tot,l}$ given by $P_{tot,l} = \sum_{j=1}^{M} P_{j,l} + P_{CCH}$, where P_{CCH} corresponds to the power transmitted for the orthogonal common control channels (CCH). Note that this last term is not power controlled and is assumed not to depend on l. Due to multipath propagation, a fraction α_k of the received own cell power is experienced as intracell interference (non-orthogonality factor). Let $g_{k,l}$ be the attenuation between base station l and mobile k. Denoting by $I_{k,inter}$ and $I_{k,intra}$ the intercell and intracell interferences, respectively, we have

$$\frac{C}{I}\bigg|_k = \frac{P_{k,l}/g_{k,l}}{I_{k,inter} + I_{k,intra} + N},$$

where N is the receiver noise floor (assumed not to depend on k), $I_{k,intra} = \alpha_k \cdot (P_{CCH} + \sum_{j \neq k} P_{j,l})/g_{k,l}$ and $I_{k,inter} = \sum_{j=1,j \neq l}^{S} P_{tot,j}/g_{k,j}$. Define

$$F_{k,l} = \frac{\sum_{j=1,j \neq l}^{S} P_{tot,j}/g_{k,j}}{P_{tot,l}/g_{k,l}},$$

i.e. the ratio between the received intercell and intracell power. It then follows that

$$\beta_k = \frac{P_{k,l}/g_{k,l}}{(F_{k,l} + \alpha_k)P_{tot,l}/g_{k,l} + N}, \tag{2}$$

where $\beta_k = \frac{(C/I)_k}{1+\alpha_k(C/I)_k}$. We then consider two service classes, that will correspond to RT and NRT traffic. Let $(C/I)_s$ be the target SIR ratio for mobiles of service class s with a corresponding value of β_s. Let there be in a given cell M_s mobiles of class s. Using an average approximation[1], we substitute $F_{k,l}$, $g_{k,l}$, α_k by their sample averages over all $k = 1, \ldots, M$. We denote these as F, G, α. We consider these parameters to be the same for all service groups. Then (2) gives the following value for $P_{tot,l}$ (we omit the index l):

$$P_{tot} = \frac{P_{CCH} + NG\sum_s \beta_s M_s}{1 - (\alpha + F)\sum_s \beta_s M_s}. \tag{3}$$

Further assuming that the power for the common channels is a fraction of the total power, $P_{CCH} = \psi P_{tot}$ and defining the downlink loading as $Y_{DL} = \sum_s \beta_s M_s$, this gives

$$P_{tot} = \frac{NG\sum_s \beta_s M_s}{Z_2}, \quad \text{where} \quad Z_2 = (1 - \psi) - (\alpha + F)Y_{DL}. \tag{4}$$

Thus the maximum base station output power determines the maximum loading supported by the system. According to the power limitation of the base station, one poses the constraint $Z_2 \geq \epsilon$ for some $\epsilon > 0$. Consequently, we can define the system's capacity as $\Theta_\epsilon = 1 - \psi - \epsilon$, and the capacity required by a connection to be $\Delta(s) := (\alpha + F)\beta_s$. Combining this with (1) and substituting the expression for β_s we get the throughput of a connection s, that "uses" a capacity $\Delta(s)$.

$$R_s = \frac{\Delta(s)}{\alpha + F - \alpha\Delta(s)} \times \frac{N_0 W}{E_s \Gamma}. \tag{5}$$

A similar analysis can be followed to derive an expression in the case where macrodiversity is implemented in the downlink (cf. [10]).

---

[1] This is a standard approximation for downlink models, see [6, 7]; further, as was performed in [6], the accuracy of the single parameters can be improved by curve fitting, based on actual measurements for the total base station output power.

2.2   Uplink

We briefly recall the capacity notions from the case of the uplink from [5]. Define for $s = 1, 2$,

$$\tilde{\Delta}_s = \frac{E_s}{N_0} \frac{R_s}{W} \Gamma, \text{ and } \Delta'(s) = \frac{\tilde{\Delta}(s)}{1 + \tilde{\Delta}(s)}. \tag{6}$$

The power that should be received at a base station originating from a type s service mobile in order to meet the QoS constraints is given by Z_1/Z_2 where $Z_1 = N\Delta'(s)$ and $Z_2 = 1 - (1 + f) \sum_{s=1,2} M_s \Delta'(s)$ (N is the background noise power at the base station, f is some constant describing the average ratio between inter- and intracell interference, and M_s is the number of mobiles of type s in the cell). Here in order to maintain an equal rate, the smallest maximum received power amongst all mobiles in the cell determines the maximum uplink loading. Again, to avoid that Z_2 becomes too close to zero one imposes the constraint $Z_2 \geq \epsilon$ for some $\epsilon > 0$. We can thus define the system's capacity as $\Theta_\epsilon = 1 - \epsilon$, and the capacity required by a connection of type $s = 1, 2$ to be $\Delta(s) = (1 + f)\Delta'(s)$. Combining this with (6) we get

$$R_s = \frac{\Delta(s)}{1 + f - \Delta(s)} \times \frac{N_0 W}{E_s \Gamma}. \tag{7}$$

3   Admission and Rate Control

We consider that there exists a capacity L_{NRT} reserved for NRT traffic. The RT traffic can use up to a capacity of $L_{RT} := \Theta_\epsilon - L_{NRT}$. We introduce GoS by providing RT calls with a variable transmission rate. In such a case, we may allow more RT calls at the expense of a reduced transmission rate.

Assume more generally that the set of available transmission rates for RT traffic has the form $[R^{min}, R^{max}]$. Note that $\Delta(RT)$ is increasing with the transmission rate. Hence the achievable capacity set per RT mobile has the form $[\Delta^{min}, \Delta^{max}]$. The maximum number of RT calls that can be accepted is $M_{RT}^{max} = \lfloor L_{RT}/\Delta^{min} \rfloor$. We assign full rate R^{max} (and thus the maximum capacity Δ^{max}) for each RT mobile as long as $M_{RT} \leq N_{RT}$, where $N_{RT} = \lfloor L_{RT}/\Delta^{max} \rfloor$. For $N_{RT} < M_{RT} \leq M_{RT}^{max}$ the capacity of each present RT connection is reduced to L_{RT}/M_{RT} and the rate is reduced accordingly.

We next describe the rate control scheme for NRT calls. We consider that NRT calls make use of the reserved system capacity, as well as any capacity left over from RT calls. Thus the available capacity for NRT calls is a function of M_{RT} as follows:

$$C(M_{RT}) = \begin{cases} \Theta_\epsilon - M_{RT}\Delta^{max}, & \text{if } M_{RT} \leq N_{RT}, \\ L_{NRT}, & \text{otherwise.} \end{cases}$$

In [8],[5], the capacity $C(M_{RT})$ unused by the RT traffic (which changes dynamically as a function of the number of RT connections present) was fully assigned to a single NRT mobile, this being time-multiplexed rapidly so that the throughput is shared equally between the present NRT mobiles. This modeling is consistent with a fair implementation of a high data rate scheme. Specifically, schemes such as HDR [1], corresponding to the CDMA 1xEV-DO standard, and its 3GPP counterpart HSDPA [13] have been proposed for the downlink in order to achieve higher transmission rates. These schemes implement a complex scheduler which evaluates channel conditions and pending transmissions for each connection, using additionally fast retransmission and multicoding to improve throughput. The scheduling decisions permit the system to benefit from short-term variations and allow most of the cell capacity to be allocated to one user for a very short time, when conditions are favorable.

The modeling in this optimum scenario follows a homogeneous QBD approach, as the transmission rate is independent of the number of on-going NRT sessions. Here we consider the standard case where transmissions are simultaneous and available capacity is split equally between the NRT calls, in a fair rate sharing approach. Then according to the previous analysis and assuming that channel conditions do not change substantially, the total transmission rate R_{NRT}^{tot} of NRT traffic for the downlink and uplink depends on the number M_{RT} of RT calls as well as the number M_{NRT} of NRT calls and is given respectively by

$$DL: \quad R_{NRT}^{tot}(M_{NRT}, M_{RT}) = \frac{M_{NRT}C(M_{RT})}{M_{NRT}(\alpha + F) - \alpha C(M_{RT})} \times \frac{N_0 W}{E_s \Gamma},$$

$$UL: \quad R_{NRT}^{tot}(M_{NRT}, M_{RT}) = \frac{M_{NRT}C(M_{RT})}{M_{NRT}(1 + f) - C(M_{RT})} \times \frac{N_0 W}{E_s \Gamma}.$$

The expression for the downlink with macrodiversity is similarly derived, albeit being more cumbersome.

4   Traffic Model and the LDQBD Approach

We assume that RT and NRT calls arrive according to independent Poisson processes with rates λ_{RT} and λ_{NRT}, respectively. The duration of an RT call is exponentially distributed with parameter μ_{RT}. The size of an NRT file is exponentially distributed with parameter μ_{NRT}. RT call durations and NRT file sizes are all mutually independent. Note that since their mean duration is fixed, the evolution of RT calls is not affected by the process of NRT calls and can be studied independently as an Erlang loss system. However, the departure rate of NRT calls depends on the current number of RT and NRT calls:

$$\nu(M_{NRT}, M_{RT}) = \mu_{NRT} R_{NRT}^{tot}(M_{NRT}, M_{RT}).$$

The number of active sessions in the downlink and uplink models can be described as a *non-homogeneous* or *level-dependent* (LD) QBD process, and we denote by Q its generator. Upon a stable system, the stationary distribution π is calculated by solving $\pi Q = 0$, with the normalization condition $\pi e = 1$ where e is a vector of ones of proper dimension. The vector π represents the steady-state probability of the two-dimensional process lexicographically. We may thus partition π as $[\pi(0), \pi(1), \ldots]$ with $\pi(i)$ for level i, where the levels correspond to the number of NRT calls in the system. We may further partition each level into the number of RT calls, $\pi(i) = [\pi(i, 0), \pi(i, 1), \ldots, \pi(i, M_{RT}^{\max})]$, for $i \geq 0$. In (i, j), j is referred to as the *phase* of the state. The generator Q is given by

$$
Q = \begin{bmatrix} B & A_0 & 0 & 0 & \cdots \\ A_2^1 & A_1^1 & A_0 & 0 & \cdots \\ 0 & A_2^2 & A_1^2 & A_0 & \cdots \\ & & & & \\ 0 & 0 & \ddots & \ddots & \ddots \end{bmatrix} \tag{8}
$$

where the matrices B, A_0, A_1^i, and A_2^i are square matrices of size $(M_{RT}^{\max} + 1)$. The matrix A_0 corresponds to an NRT connection arrival, given by $A_0 = \mathrm{diag}(\lambda_{NRT})$. The matrix A_2^i corresponds to a departure of an NRT call and is given by $A_2^i = \mathrm{diag}(\nu(i, j); 0 \leq j \leq M_{RT}^{\max})$. The matrix A_1^i corresponds to the arrival and departure processes of RT calls. A_1^i is tri-diagonal as follows:

$$
A_1^i[j, j+1] = \lambda_{RT},
$$
$$
A_1^i[j, j-1] = j\mu_{RT},
$$
$$
A_1^i[j, j] = -\lambda_{RT} - j\mu_{RT} - \lambda_{NRT} - \nu(i, j).
$$

Of course, A_1^i is properly modified on the boundaries $j = 0$, $j = M_{RT}^{max}$. We also have $B = A_1^i + A_2^i$. Due to the special structure of the matrix, this is independent of i.

As in the QBD case, there exist matrix-geometric methods to calculate the equilibrium distribution of a LDQBD process. These involve the solution of a system of matrix recurrence equations (see e.g [11]). However, the number of states is often so large that the solution becomes untractable. For this reason, algorithmic approaches are usually sought. Here we use an extension of a method introduced in [3] for a finite non-homogeneous QBD process. The implementation is simple and converges to the equilibrium distribution in a relatively small number of steps. Details of the algorithm are deferred to the Appendix.

5   Numerical Evaluation

In this section, the major performance evaluation results that reflect user-perceived QoS are presented for a system with integrated RT and NRT calls. First the uplink and downlink performance is analyzed and the system bottleneck is determined. Comparisons are then carried out against our model of the high data rate scheme in WCDMA. Continuining, we explore the extent to which intercell interference can deteriorate system behavior. Finally, numerical results are extended to the case of an NRT call admission control scheme.

5.1   Setting

Here we address the values of parameters used in the numerical evaluation. Common CDMA performance evaluation parameters (such as chip rate, energy-to-noise requirements, interference factors, etc.) are derived from equipment capabilities and field tests. The parameters initially used for the numerical evaluations in our setting are as follows:

- Chip rate: $W = 3.84$ Mcps
- Transmission rate of RT mobiles: max 12.2 kbps, min 4.75 kbps
- E_{RT}/N_0: Uplink 4.2 dB, Downlink 7.0 dB (12.2 kbps voice)
- E_{NRT}/N_0: Uplink 2.2 dB (64 kbps data), Downlink 5.0 dB (144 kbps data)
- Average RT call duration: $1/\mu_{RT} = 125$ sec
- Mean NRT session size: $1/\mu_{NRT} = 160$ kbits
- Arrival rate of calls: $\lambda_{RT} = \lambda_{NRT} = 0.4$
- Interference factor: Uplink $f = 0.73$, Downlink $F = 0.55$
- Non-orthogonality factor: $\alpha = 0.64$
- Fraction of power for CCH channels: $\psi = 0.2$

The traffic characteristics for RT and NRT calls are chosen to correspond to heavy traffic conditions, whereupon performance evaluation must focus. We assume a chip pulse is rectangular, so that the chip rate equals the spread bandwidth. The parameter Γ, which accounts for shadow fading in the calculation of the system capacity, has been incorporated in the E_b/N_0 targets. These are set here according to §12.5 of [7] (3GPP performance requirements for a slow moving user, Tables 12.26, 12.27). Values are greater in the downlink, the reason being smaller receiver sensitivity and antenna gain in the mobile units. In addition, antenna diversity is not usually assumed in the downlink. We have also made the simplifying assumption that these values remain approximately constant for different transmission rates. This generally holds when the same type of modulation is used for all rates [9].

5.2   Uplink and Downlink Performance

Here we study the behavior in the uplink and the downlink of the WCDMA system. For RT traffic, the major performance metric is the blocking probability of a new call, since QoS bounds are otherwise guaranteed. This is calculated and shown graphically in Fig. 1(a), for different values of the L_{NRT} threshold. As anticipated, the probability of rejection increases as more capacity is reserved for NRT calls. In the case of NRT traffic, performance evaluation results are portrayed in Fig. 1(b). Here, quality of service is manifested essentially by the time it takes to complete the document transfer, i.e. the mean sojourn time in the system. The behavior of NRT traffic reflects the general admission and rate control policy modeled previously: given the same NRT file size distribution and in availability of a lot of resources, the NRT calls that "come into" the system transmit at a higher rate and then leave. Therefore, the corresponding sojourn time can be smaller. On the other hand, if there are only few resources, the NRT calls that join in transmit at a very low rate and stay in the system longer. In that sense, Fig. 1(b) shows the improvement in NRT traffic transfer time as the capacity reserved for it increases.

These results also permit to see the trade-off relationship between the performance of RT and NRT transmissions. However, we remark that although NRT improvement through capacity reservation comes at the expense of RT traffic, a region of L_{NRT} values can be selected where performance is satisfactory for both service classes. For

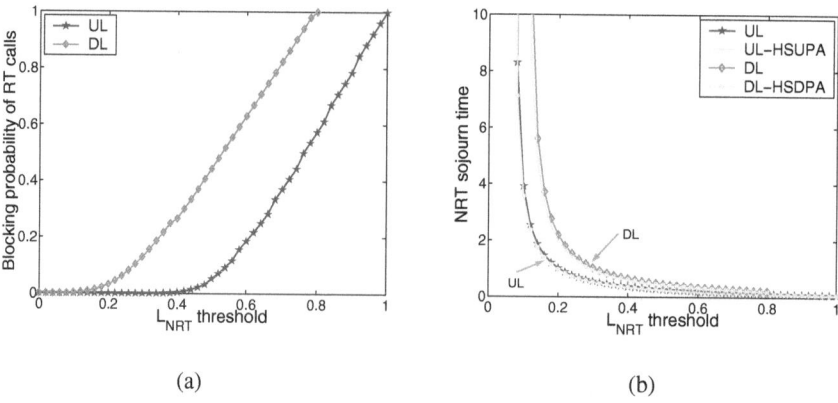

Fig. 1. RT call blocking probability (a) and mean NRT sojourn time (b) vs. L_{NRT} reservation, in the UL and DL cases. Comparison with high data rate services in (b)

example, in the results here a good operating region for both service classes can be chosen near $L_{NRT} = 0.2$ in the DL and between $0.2 \leq L_{NRT} \leq 0.4$ in the UL.

We also make the following observations regarding the determination of the system bottleneck. Although the downlink enjoys less interference, this can be largely eclipsed by the increased E_b/N_0 ratios that require more capacity for a given transmission rate, and the expended power for CCH channels. This is substantiated in the results here and is evidence that, with user mobility and intracell interference due to non-orthogonal channels, the downlink may be the bottleneck even with symmetric traffic transferred on both sides. On the other hand, further numerical evaluations can show that the UL is usually bottlenecked for static users and a smaller non-orthogonality factor. Of course one should keep in mind that in reality, with time-varying channel and traffic conditions, both sides may be the bottleneck at one time or another.

An ergodicity condition is essential for stability in the theoretical case of an un-bounded number of NRT calls. As shown in Fig. 1(b), below a certain value of the L_{NRT} threshold (approximately[2] $L_{NRT} \approx 0.1$ in the DL case), the sojourn time tends to infinity and the system becomes unstable. That is, below a certain capacity the NRT transmission rate becomes too small, which leads to a very high number of such calls in the system. In the system under consideration, the stability condition is [11]:

$$\mu_{NRT} \cdot \mathbb{E}R_{NRT}^{tot} > \lambda_{NRT}. \qquad (9)$$

Here the calculation of $\mathbb{E}R_{NRT}^{tot}$ is problematic, since it also depends on the number of NRT calls which is unbounded. However, we observe that as $M_{NRT} \rightarrow \infty$, the total transmission rate reaches a limit in both the UL and DL cases. Therefore, the non-homogeneous LDQBD process converges to a homogeneous QBD process. Moreover, the departure rates of NRT calls in the LDQBD process are greater for smaller levels, and always greater than those of the limiting process. It can be formally shown that sta-

---

[2] A granularity of 10^{-2} is taken in the numerical results.

bility conditions are the same for both processes, i.e. it suffices to check the ergodicity of the limiting homogeneous process. The general theorem is deferred to the Appendix; due to limited space, only a sketch of the proof is presented. Interested readers may refer to the complete version in [10].

For NRT calls, Fig. 1(b) also presents a comparison of the standard WCDMA behavior with that of the scheme similar to HSDPA, mentioned in § 3. We also consider the corresponding scheme in the uplink —analogously named HSUPA (which has recently been added in 3GPP Release 6 [7]). An attainable performance improvement is then apparent under system congestion conditions, namely very high load or very small allocated capacity. Indeed, in terms of the mean sojourn time, Fig. 1(b) shows that the outperformance of the time-scheduling approach is non-negligible for small NRT reserved capacity. In the numerical results obtained, the difference reached up to 80 sec in the uplink, for $L_{NRT} \approx 0.06$.

5.3   Impact of the Interference Expansion Factor

As CDMA capacity is primarily limited by interference, we would like to know to what extent this affects system behavior. Here numerical results are taken by varying the ratio of received intercell-to-intracell power, F in the downlink. This is the analog of the ratio of intercell-to-intracell interference in the uplink. A more perceptive term for such ratios is the *interference expansion factor*. Increasing values of F can then be seen as increased intercell interference.

Numerical results are portrayed in Fig. 2. The value of the interference expansion factor depends on the traffic distribution of interfering cells and may well assume values greater than unity [15]; however we take selected values until $F = 1$ for our test cases here. We may deduce that intercell interference has a significant impact on performance. Concerning the blocking probability of RT calls in Fig. 2(a), for smaller values of F an initially good performance is observed; for the smallest value $F = 0.1$, the loss

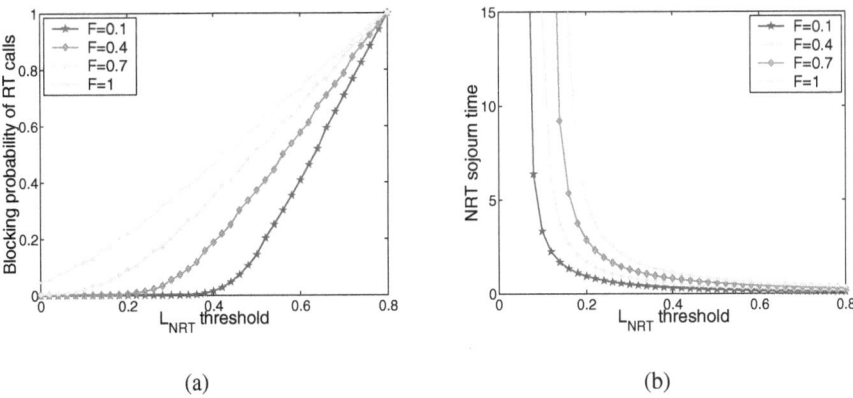

Fig. 2. RT call blocking probability (a) and mean NRT sojourn time (b) vs. L_{NRT} reservation, for different values of the interference ratio, F, in the downlink

rate remains insignificant until $L_{NRT} < 0.4$. However, blocking severely increases for higher interference ratio; for $F = 1$, a blocking probability of $P_B = 5 \cdot 10^{-2}$ occurs even for no allocated NRT capacity and is almost linearly increased to the value of 1 as the L_{NRT} threshold increases. The NRT behavior is similarly affected. We observe in Fig. 2(b) that the mean transfer time is greater as interference increases, as well as that the instability region is larger.

The deteriotation of system behavior in all cases is due to the fact that more power, and hence more capacity is required by users to overcome interference. This means less resources available –even for the lowest quality RT calls– and smaller transfer rates for NRT sessions. Naturally, the same observations carry over to the uplink. Further, an analogous situation –due to power control– occurs in the uplink and downlink in case of increased intracell interference, and we expect similar observations to carry over to this case.

5.4   NRT Call Admission Control

Even though best-effort applications are considered to be elastic, we have seen that under a small reserved capacity and high loads, NRT rate calls can suffer severe performance degradation, in terms of very large transfer times. This could lead to unwanted reneging, as a result of user impatience. Hence setting an upper bound on the number of admitted NRT sessions is required to ensure some minimal QoS in these cases.

The setting of an upper bound introduces call blocking for NRT traffic. Since we have assumed Poisson arrivals, the blocking probability of an incoming NRT call is

$$P_B = Pr\{M_{NRT} = (M_{NRT}^{max})\} = \sum_{j=0}^{M_{RT}^{max}} \pi(M_{NRT}^{max}, j).$$

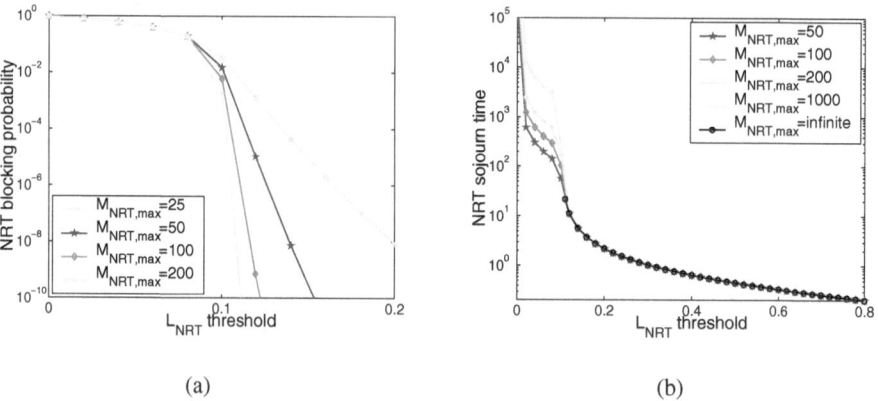

(a)   (b)

Fig. 3. NRT admission control scheme. NRT call blocking probability (a) and mean sojourn time (b) vs. L_{NRT} reservation, for different allowed maximum number of NRT calls (downlink)

Then the average sojourn time of an NRT session can be calculated using Little's law, considering the portion of NRT calls that are admitted into the system:

$$T_{NRT}^{soj} = \frac{E[M_{NRT}]}{\lambda_{NRT}(1 - P_B)}. \tag{10}$$

The impact of the number of allowed NRT calls is considered in the numerical evaluations of Fig. 3. Algorithm *Finite LDQBD* (Appendix A) is used to calculate the stationary distribution.

We observe in Fig. 3(b) that restricting access for data transmissions on the CDMA link can improve performance in critical congestion regions where resources for this traffic are limited. For example, for a resource reservation $L_{NRT} \approx 0.1$ and $M_{NRT}^{max} = 100$ we have $T_{NRT}^{soj} = 104$ s, which decreases by more that 45% if we restrict to $M_{NRT}^{max} = 50$. This improvement is traded-off with an increase in blocking probability for new calls; as anticipated, lowering the maximum number of admitted NRT calls increases blocking (Fig. 3(a)). However, we reason that this effect must be largely mitigated due to the fact that NRT calls then spend less time in the system. In any case, from a QoS perspective, ensuring acceptable quality to users already in the system is more important.

6   Summary and Conclusions

We end by recapitulating the major conclusions drawn from this research. The performance of an integrated CDMA system with RT and NRT classes of traffic is determined by the actual traffic load, E_b/N_0 requirements for each class, as well as interference and physical power limitations. Besides that, the actual system behavior and QoS parameters are mirrored through the admission and rate control scheme applied. Here, we have studied a system with adaptive-rate RT calls and elastic NRT traffic. The general admission control scheme allows NRT calls to benefit from periods of low or intermittent RT traffic to attain an improved performance.

QoS management is introduced by varying the amount of capacity reservation for elastic traffic. Both for the uplink and downlink, it has been shown that capacity reservation can offer significant performance improvement to NRT sessions, at the expense of increased blocking of RT calls. However, the amount of reservation need not be very high; for the test cases considered, a reservation around 20% of the total capacity vastly improves the NRT performance, while not significantly harming RT behavior.

In case of overload conditions, the behavior of the system can severely degrade. High data rate methods such as HSDPA, which employ a complex scheduling of the different user transmissions each making use of the whole available resources, can then reduce congestion and improve performance. Additionally, the impact of interference should be carefully considered in the choice of a capacity reservation.

Finally, admission control on elastic traffic might also be imperative to reduce the service time of NRT calls under high load conditions. In this scope, we have demonstrated how the setting of an admission control policy on NRT traffic allows a trade-off between the number of calls allowed and the QoS offered to those served.

References

1. Bender, P., Black, P., Grob, M., Padovani, R., Sindhushayana, N., Viterbi, A.: CDMA/HDR: A bandwidth-efficient high-speed wireless data service for nomadic users. IEEE Communications Magazine **38** (2000) 70–77
2. Brandt, A., Last, G.: On the pathwise comparison of jump processes driven by stochastic intensities. Mathematische Nachrichten **167** (1994) 21–42
3. Gaver, D.P., Jacobs, P.A., Latouche, G.: Finite birth-and-death models in randomly changing environments. Advances in Applied Probability **16** (1984) 715–731
4. Gilhousen, K.S., Jacobs, I.M., Padovani, R., Viterbi, A.J., Weaver, A., Jr., Wheatley C.E.: On the capacity of a cellular CDMA system. IEEE Transactions on Vehicular Technology **40** (1991) 303–312
5. Hegde, N., Altman, E.: Capacity of multiservice WCDMA networks with variable GoS. In Proc. of IEEE WCNC (2003)
6. Hiltunen, K., De Brarnardi, R.: WCDMA downlink capacity estimation. In Proc. IEEE VTC-Spring (2000) 992–996
7. Holma H., Toskala, A. (eds.): WCDMA for UMTS: Radio access for third generation mobile communications. John Wiley & Sons, 3rd Ed. (2004)
8. Kelif, J.M., Altman, E.: Admission and Gos control in multiservice WCDMA system. In Proc. ECUMN, LNCS 3262 (2004) 70–80
9. Kim, S.-L., Rosberg, Z., Zander, J.: Combined power control and transmission rate selection in cellular networks. In Proc. IEEE VTC-Fall (1999) 1653–1657
10. Koukoutsidis, I., Altman, E., Kelif, J.M.: A non-homogeneous QBD approach for the admission and GoS control in a multiservice WCDMA system. INRIA Research Report No. RR–5358 (2004)
11. Latouche, G., Ramaswami, V.: Introduction to matrix analytic methods in stochastic modeling. ASA-SIAM (1999)
12. Neuts, M.F.: Matrix-geometric solutions in stochastic models: an algorithmic approach. The John Hopkins University Press (1981)
13. Parkvall, S., Dahlman, E., Frenger, P., Beming, P., Persson, M.: The high speed packet data evolution of WCDMA. In Proc. 12th IEEE PIMRC (2001)
14. Viterbi, A.M., Viterbi, A.J.: Erlang capacity of a power-controlled CDMA system. IEEE J. Selected Areas in Communications **11** (1993) 892–900
15. Viterbi, A.J., Viterbi, A.M., Zehavi, E.: Other-cell interference in cellular power-controlled CDMA. IEEE Transactions on Communications, **42** (1994) 1501–1504

Appendix

A   LDQBD Algorithms

Consider the transition probability matrix for a LDQBD process as in § 4 but with a finite number of levels, K. Clearly we have only matrices A_2^K, A_1^K in the last level, with $A_1^K[j,j] = -\lambda_{RT} - j \cdot \mu_{RT} - \nu(K,j)$. We use the following algorithm from [3] to calculate the steady state distribution. The algorithm consists of the following steps:

Algorithm *Finite LDQBD* :

1)   Compute the stochastic S_i matrices using the following recursion:

$$S_0 = B,$$
$$S_n = A_1^n + A_2^n(-S_{n-1}^{-1})A_0, \quad 1 \leq n \leq K.$$

2) Find the stationary distribution of the S_K stochastic matrix by solving

$$\pi_K \cdot S_K = 0,$$
$$\pi_K \cdot e = 1.$$

3) Recursively compute the remaining stationary distributions

$$\pi_n = \pi_{n+1} \cdot A_2^{n+1} \cdot (-S_n^{-1}), \quad \text{for } 0 \leq n \leq K-1.$$

4) Renormalize to obtain the steady-state distribution

$$\pi = \frac{\pi}{\pi \cdot e}.$$

In order to solve the infinite system, the objective is to find a value for the number of level K^* such that $\pi(k) \approx 0 \ \forall \ k > K^*$. Thus we may extend the previous algorithm as follows:

> **set** $K^* = K_{init}$
> **while** $\pi(K^*) \cdot e > \epsilon$
> $\quad K^* = K^* + h,$
> $\quad$ **run** algorithm *Finite LDQBD*
> **end**

The values of ϵ, h define the tolerance and step size, respectively and determine the accuracy and rate of convergence of the algorithm. An appropriate value of K_{init} can be readily available from runs in the finite case, which give an indice on how big the number of levels should be. Provided the system is stable, the algorithm will converge to the steady-state distribution.

B   Ergodicity Theorem

Theorem 1. *Consider a stochastic irreducible LDQBD process $X(t)$ whose submatrices $Q_0^{(k)}$, $Q_1^{(k)}$, $Q_2^{(k)}$ converge to level independent submatrices Q_0', Q_1', Q_2' of a homogeneous QBD process $X'(t)$ as the level number $k \rightarrow \infty$. It holds that $Q_0^{(1)} < Q_0^{(2)} < \cdots < Q_0'$ and $Q_2^{(1)} > Q_2^{(2)} > \cdots > Q_2'$, $\forall \ k \in \mathbb{Z}^+$. Transitions rates in $Q_1^{(k)}$, Q_1' are identical within the same level. Then, if the homogeneous QBD process $X'(t)$ is ergodic, so is the non-homogeneous LDQBD process $X(t)$. Conversely, if process $X'(t)$ is not ergodic with a positive expected drift, i.e. $d = \pi Q_0' e - \pi Q_2' e > 0$, process $X(t)$ is also not ergodic.*

Proof (sketch). We first proceed to show that $X(t) \leq_{st} X'(t)$, i.e. that $X'(t)$ stochastically dominates $X(t)$. Let $(E, \leq)$ be a countable partially ordered set, and a set $F \subseteq E$ which is $\leq$-increasing. Denote by $q(i, j)$, $q'(i, j)$ the transition intensities of $X(t)$, $X'(t)$, respectively, where $\sum_{j \neq i} q_{ij} < \infty$ and $\sum_{j \neq i} q_{ij}' < \infty \ \forall \ i, j \ \in E$. Then from [2] $X(t) \leq_{st} X'(t)$ if and only if the following conditions hold, for all $x \leq y$ in E and all increasing sets, F:

(i) if $x, y \in F$, $\sum_{z \notin F} q(x, z) \geq \sum_{z \notin F} q'(y, z)$

(ii) if $x, y \notin F$, $\sum_{z \in F} q(x, z) \leq \sum_{z \in F} q'(y, z)$.

We define the partial order relation $(<)$ by $(i, j) < (k, l)$ if $((i < k) \wedge (j \leq l)) \vee ((i \leq k) \wedge (j < l))$. It is then easy to show that our system satisfies conditions (i) and (ii), considering that transitions have the same structure and are *skip-free* in each direction. Therefore $X(t) \leq_{st} X'(t)$. Then considering the recurrence times σ_ℓ, σ'_ℓ to the *smallest*[3] state $\ell = (0, 0)$, we may prove that $E[\sigma_\ell] \leq E[\sigma'_\ell]$, from which we conclude that if $X'(t)$ is ergodic, both mean recurrence times are finite and $X(t)$ is also ergodic.

In the reverse part, we show that there exists a modified QBD process $X''(t)$ which is not ergodic and for which holds $X''_t \leq_{st} X^L_t$, where X^L_t is the *truncated* LDQBD for levels $k \geq L$, obtained by rerouting transitions from level L to $L - 1$ back to L. Then, using again mean recurrence times, we show that X^L_t is not ergodic from which we can also establish that the original LDQBD process is not ergodic. □

---

[3] Note that due to the partial order here, the 'smallest' state is defined as $\ell = \{x \in E : \nexists x' \neq x \text{ with } x' > x\}$.

Part III

Short Papers

Quality of Service Authentication, Authorization and Accounting

Tseno Tsenov and Hannes Tschofenig

Siemens AG, Otto-Hahn-Ring 6, Munich 81739, Germany
tseno.tsenov@mytum.de,
hannes.tschofenig@siemens.com

Abstract. Proper authorization is essential for a QoS signaling protocol. The policy control of future QoS signaling solutions is expected to make use of existing AAA infrastructure for computing the authorization decision. In this paper, we point to two approaches for QoS authorization (based on COPS and Diameter) and present possible extensions and directions for future work.

1 Introduction

To meet the Quality of Service (QoS) requirement for applications such as Voice-over-IP in a heavily loaded network, packets belonging to real-time application must be identified and segregated from other traffic to ensure that the bandwidth, delay, and loss rate requirements are met. This requires explicit reservation techniques. In addition to the verification of resource availability, authentication and authorization of the requests are required, especially in an environment where the endpoints are not trusted. A variety of QoS protocols exist, including RSVP [1] and the NSIS QoS NSLP [3]. In this paper, we present a short overview of the framework, proposed solutions and future work.

2 Framework

Policy control for QoS signaling is conceptually organized as illustrated in Fig. 1. Network elements through which application flows need to pass, a cloud of Policy/AAA servers and an Authorizing entity/PDP are shown. A resource request sent by the end host is intercepted at a router along the path. This router will offload the authorization decision to the AAA backend infrastructure. The request will, for example, be routed to the home network, where the home AAA server will return a decision. Not all of the routers are policy-aware since policy enforcement is likely to be concentrated on the borders of an administrative domain.

2.1 COPS Usage for RSVP

RFC 2749 [2] is a part of a framework for policy-based control over admission control decisions for QoS signaling using RSVP. The Common Open Policy Service (COPS) protocol is used to exchange policy information between a Policy Decision

H. de Meer and N. Bhatti (Eds.): IWQoS 2005, LNCS 3552, pp. 343–345, 2005.

Point (PDP) and a set of RSVP routers (Policy Enforcement Points, PEPs). At the event of incoming RSVP request, the entire RSVP message is encapsulated in COPS REQ message and sent to the PDP. The PDP is assumed to implement the same RSVP functional specification as the PEP and share the RSVP state. A decision is taken at the PDP, based on the policy data object and other objects from the RSVP message.

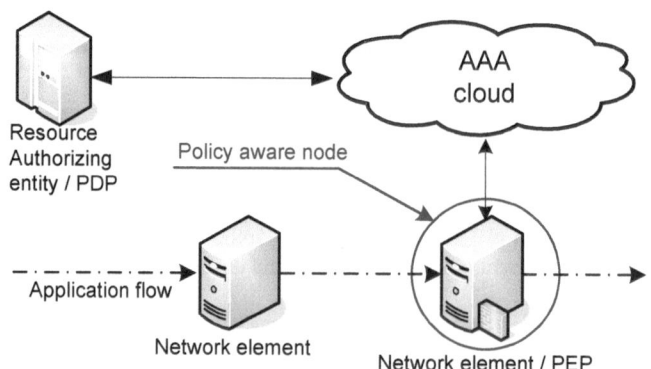

Fig. 1. Policy Control Architecture

2.2 NSIS QoS NSLP and Diameter QoS Application

The Diameter QoS application, in contrast to COPS, might be used by QoS NSLP capable nodes along the path of a given application flow to contact an authorizing entity/application server, located somewhere in the network, providing an AAA service of the reservation request [5]. This allows for a wide variety of deployment models. Extending the Diameter protocol includes the use of new mandatory AVPs and Command-Codes that are required to enable QoS authorization.

A generalized QoS parameter format is used by the Diameter QoS application (taken from the NSIS QSPEC template [6]) that allows the Diameter QoS application to be combined with virtually all QoS signaling protocols. An authorizing server would use the QoS parameters in addition to an authorization token included in the QoS-Authorization Request message to make a decision. After a positive authorization decision, the router starts an accounting session. Session termination may be initiated by both sides. Possible causes might be a NSIS tear down message, loss of bearer report, insufficient credits or session termination at the application layer.

3 Extended QoS Authorization

With the support for one-pass authentication methods (including authorization tokens/Kerberos tickets [8]) not all deployment scenarios can be addressed adequately. Existing QoS protocols currently lack the support for a generic three party authorization model that includes support for:

– Challenge-Response-based Authentication and Key Agreement (AKA),
– EAP-based Authentication and Key Agreement (AKA)

These two approaches show the tradeoff between the flexible choice of AKA protocols and complexity. EAP provides a high degree of flexibility with a certain amount of inefficiency and complexity (see [5]). Both approaches provide better security properties than a token-based approach [7] due to the active involvement of the end host and better integration into existing network architectures regarding key distribution.

Beyond adding new payloads, it is essential to evaluate the security implications of the three party exchange as part of the keying framework.

4 Summary and Outlook

Unlike the approach followed with RSVP, where the entire RSVP message is encapsulated into a COPS message, the Diameter QoS application includes only the relevant fields from a QoS NSLP message, avoiding the overhead of transmitting irrelevant objects for the AAA infrastructure. Together with a generic QoS format, the Diameter QoS application is less dependent on a particular QoS signaling protocol or a particular QoS model. Diameter plays an important role for accounting and charging in an inter-domain environment and is therefore ideally suited for QoS authorization. Many of the functions provided by Diameter are lacking in COPS. A number of security related open issues have been identified (see [4] and [5]).

References

[1] Braden, R.: Resource ReSerVation Protocol (RSVP) – Version 1 Functional Specification. RFC 2205 (Proposed Standard) (1997) Updated by RFCs 2750, 3936.

[2] Herzog, S.: "COPS Usage for RSVP", RFC 2749, January 2000.

[3] Van den Bosch, S., Karagiannis, G., McDonald, A.: NSLP for Quality-of-Service signaling. Internet draft (draft-ietf-nsis-qos-nslp-06), work in progress (2005)

[4] Alfano, F., McCann, P., Tschofenig, H.: Diameter Quality of Service Application. Internet draft (draft-alfano-aaa-qosprot-02), work in progress (2005)

[5] Tschofenig, H., Kross, J.: Extended QoS Authorization for the QoS NSLP Internet draft (draft-tschofenig-nsis-qos-ext-authz-00), work in progress (2004)

[6] Ash, J., Bader, A., Kapper, C.: QoS-NSLP QSpec Template, Internet-Draft (draft-ietf-nsis-qspec-03), work in progress, February 2005

[7] Hamer, L., Gage, B., Kosinski B., Shieh H.: Session Authorization Policy Element. RFC 3520 (2003)

[8] Baker, F., Lindell, B., Talwar M.: RSVP Cryptographic Authentication. RFC 2747 (2000)

Preliminary Results Towards Building a Highly Granular QoS Controller

Cristian Koliver[2] and Jean-Marie Farines[1]

[1] University of Caxias do Sul , C.P. 1352, Caxias do Sul, RS, Brazil 95001-970
[2] Federal University of Santa Catarina, C.P. 476, Florianopolis, SC, Brazil 88040-900

Abstract. In this paper, we describe a function to be used in a video distribution tool with user-driven QoS control. Controller acts based on this function whose dimensions are bit rate, QoS level and quality. Our results show an alternative for reducing the function construction cost.

1 Introduction

QoS adaptation mechanisms are often based on control systems. The controller initiates some corrective action in order to bring the observed parameters back to the acceptable ranges (e.g., packet loss rate between 5 and 10%), usually changing the multimedia stream bit rate by degrading one QoS parameter from the application layer (e.g., reducing video frame rate, or resolution or the quantization factor value of the encoder, for live data applications). Thus, quality is dealt as an one-dimensional phenomenon, neglecting that under user' perspective, changes in one dimension can influence the perception of the others. This simplification is mainly due to the lack of a compressed video quality assessment in terms of dynamically changeable QoS parameters of the application layer. We believe that the construction of controllers supporting highly granular quality imposes a mapping bit rate↔QoS level↔quality, where a QoS level is a combination of values of several application layer QoS parameters and quality is quantified by an objective measure. The advantage of highly granular quality controllers is to get a smooth QoS adaptation and the best quality according to end-users when shaping the multimedia stream to the available bandwidth.

2 Quantifying Quality

In [1], we describe a general framework for QoS adaptation. The framework is based on using a table containing *QoS levels*. A *QoS level* L is a n-tuple $< \rho_1, \rho_2, ..., \rho_n >$ representing a combination of values of the n QoS parameters from the application layer. Associated to each QoS level, there is the bit rate (B) needed for supporting it and the *quality degree* ($Q\hat{o}S$), a metric used to quantify the quality of QoS levels in agreement with user's perception. Therefore, each entry of the table is a $(n + 2)$-tuple $< \rho_1, \rho_2, ..., \rho_n, Q\hat{o}S, B >$. The

H. de Meer and N. Bhatti (Eds.): IWQoS 2005, LNCS 3552, pp. 346–348, 2005.

value of $Q\hat{o}S$ is obtained using the quality degree function $\mathcal{Q}oS : P \mapsto [0,1]$ ($P = P_{\rho_1} \times P_{\rho_2} \times ... \times P_{\rho_n}$). For the QoS level $L_j =< \rho_{1_j}, \rho_{2_j}, ..., \rho_{n_j} >$, $Q\hat{o}S_j = \mathcal{Q}oS(\rho_{1_j}, \rho_{2_j}, ..., \rho_{n_j})$. By $\mathcal{Q}oS$, QoS adaptation mechanisms can select the (theoretically) best combination of application QoS parameters values for a given network bit rate. The definition of a choice criterion is important since different L's can have similar requirements of bit rate representing completely distinct qualities.

A key step of our framework is the QoS levels quality assessment by subjective tests, that might be very time-consuming, depending on the cardinality of P ($|P|$), even after discarding many QoS levels. Note that the more P_{ρ_i} sets considered, the less user' perception to QoS level change (QoS adaptation) during the multimedia application session. For example, let just three QoS parameters: video frame rate, whose domain goes from 10 fps to 30 fps, pixel depth (number of colors), with three values (8, 16, and 24 bits/pixel) and the DC accuracy (8, 9, 10 and 11 bits/pixel). In this case, we would have to perform $k \times 252$ quality evaluations, since $|P| = 21 \times 3 \times 4 = 252$. k is the number of tests for objective tests or human subjects for subjective tests. In this paper, we propose an approach for reducing the complexity of $\mathcal{Q}oS$ construction from $P_{\rho_1} \times P_{\rho_2} \times ... \times P_{\rho_n}$ to $P_{\rho_1} + P_{\rho_2} + ... + P_{\rho_n}$ without loosing accuracy.

3 Reducing Evaluations

Due to the cost of quantifying the quality considering as many QoS parameters as possible, we have developed an alternative approach based on using *utility functions* [2] for each QoS parameter. A utility function is a bidimensional function which associates a utility degree (in fact, a measure of quality), between 0 and 1, to each value of a QoS parameter from users' preferences. Thus, for an application QoS parameter ρ_i, the utility function is $v_{\rho_i} : P_{\rho_i} \mapsto [0,1]$ ($i = 1, 2, ..., n$).

For building $\mathcal{Q}oS$ from utility functions, let $v_{\rho_1}, v_{\rho_2}, ..., v_{\rho_n}$ be the utility functions and let $\omega_{\rho_1}, \omega_{\rho_2}, ..., \omega_{\rho_n}$ be the weights of the QoS parameters $\rho_1, \rho_2, ..., \rho_n$ of the application layer ($\sum_{i=1}^{n} \omega_{\rho_i} = 1$). For a QoS level $L_j =< \rho_{1_j}, \rho_{2_j}, ..., \rho_{n_j} >$, the quality degree function is $\mathcal{Q}oS(< \rho_{1_j}, \rho_{2_j}, ..., \rho_{n_j} >) = v_{\rho_1}(\rho_{1_j}) \times \omega_{\rho_1} + v_{\rho_2}(\rho_{2_j}) \times \omega_{\rho_2} + ... + v_{\rho_n}(\rho_{n_j}) \times \omega_{\rho_n}$. For the example of Sect. 2, using this approach, we would have to perform $k \times (21 + 3 + 4)$ quality evaluations rather than $k \times 21 \times 3 \times 4$.

Methodology. In order to check if the utility functions-based approach provides a $\mathcal{Q}oS$ function similar to the one provided by exhaustive evaluations, we have performed a number of quality evaluations using a specially developed interface for that. Each test image (initially, only a talking head-type clip) was exhibited during ten seconds, in randomized order, and the total evaluation did not exceed 30 minutes, in order to avoid test subject's starvation. The interface generates log files containing additional information such as: test subject's name, test subject's skill, date, initial time, final time, sort of interface, and so on. Such data will permit further information related to result variations, not addressed

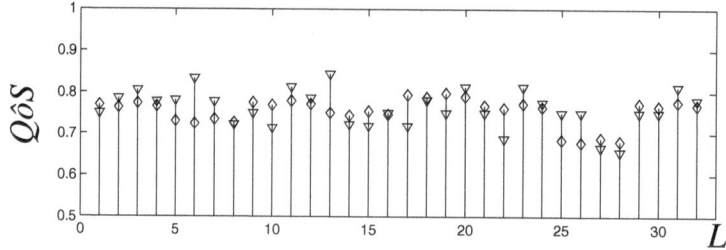

Fig. 1. Quality degrees: exhaustive tests × utility functions ($\omega_F = 0.7; \omega_D = 0.3$))

in this paper. Five different test subjects have performed 600 evaluations. We have restricted the QoS parameters to video frame rate, whose domain is $F = \{10, 12, 15, 23.976, 24, 25, 29.97, 30\}$ and the DC accuracy ($D = \{8, 9, 10, 11\}$). Therefore,$P = \{< 10, 8 >, < 12, 8 >, ..., < 29.97,\ 11 >, < 30, 11 >\}$ ($|P| = 32$).

Results. Graphic of Fig. 1 shows two resulting QoS. Each point in x axis represents a QoS level L_i ($L_i \in P$); y axis represents $QoS(L_i)$. Diamond-marked points are the quality degrees got from v_F and v_D ($QoS(< F_j, D_j >) = 0.7 \times v_F(F_j) + 0.3 \times v_D(D_j)$); triangle-marked points are the quality degrees got from exhaustive evaluations. The difference between values, in the worst case, is around 17%. Note that QoS is simplified, not including B_i ($i = 1, 2, ..., n$).

4   Conclusion

In this paper, we described an approach for quantifying video quality by a function (QoS) whose dimensions are bit rate, QoS level, and quality. Our preliminary results showed that we can reduce the quality quantification cost needed to build QoS by using several utility functions rather than exhaustive evaluations. However, the accuracy of this approach is strongly related to the correct weights assessment to QoS parameters. The current work include the implementation of a video distribution tool with a QoS controller based on using RTCP protocol [3] whose bit rate adjustment is done by using QoS.

References

1. Koliver, C., Farines, J.M., Nahrstedt, K.O.: QoS Adaptation Based on Fuzzy Theory. In Wang, L., ed.: Soft Computing for Communications. Springer-Verlag (2004) 245–267
2. Krasic, C., Walpole, J.: QoS Scalability for Streamed Media Delivery. Technical Report CSE-99-011, Oregon Graduate Institute os Science and Technology, Oregon, USA (1999)
3. Sisalem, D., Schulzrinne, H.: The Direct Adjustment Algorithm: a TCP-Friendly Adaptation Scheme. In: 1st International Workshop Quality of Future Internet Services (QofIS'2000), Berlin, Germany (2000)

Concept of Admission Control in Packet Switching Networks Based on Tentative Accommodation of Incoming Flows

Kenta Yasukawa[1], Ken-ichi Baba[2], and Katsunori Yamaoka[1]

[1] Tokyo Institute of Technology, Ookayama 2-12-1-S3-68, Meguro, Tokyo, 152-8552 Japan
[2] Osaka University, Yamaodaoka 1-1, Suita-shi, Osaka, 565-0871 Japan

Abstract. We propose a novel admission control strategy called the Tentative Accommodating and Congestion Confirming Strategy (TACCS). The main idea is to accommodate incoming flows tentatively and confirm congestion after a certain period. TACCS makes it possible to control admission without collecting resources information in advance. Our simulation results demonstrated that TACCS enabled a domain to control admission without a centralized management agent.

1   Introduction

Admission control is becoming an essential technique for Internet Protocol (IP) networks to provide full-fledged multimedia streaming services. The integrated services (Intserv) or the differentiated services (Diffserv), which were standardized by the Internet Engineering Task Force (IETF), can be used to achieve admission control in IP networks. However, these architectures achieve this based on the same idea as the concept of circuit switching networks, i.e., a signaling-based resource reservation.

In circuit switching networks, reserved resources cannot be used by other connections until these are released, even if no data is transferred using it. The concept of packet switching networks was originally produced for eliminating such inefficiency in circuit switching networks and to gain the effect of statistical multiplexing. Considering such background to producing the concept of packet switching networks, we notice that the resource reservation based idea leads packet switching networks back to the same problems as those of circuit switching networks. Therefore, we insist on that strict resource reservation is not adequate for packet switching networks and should not be aimed. Based on this point of view, we propose a new admission control scheme which does not strictly allocate resources to each flow and does not guarantee QoS for them, but prevents congestion by controlling admission of newly incoming flows.

2   Concept of Tentative Accommodation

Where resources are not strictly allocated to each flow, it is generally necessary for controlling admission to determine the resources remaining after new incoming flows have been accommodated. However, in general packet switching networks, it is difficult to achieve this because of the following.

H. de Meer and N. Bhatti (Eds.): IWQoS 2005, LNCS 3552, pp. 349–352, 2005.

1. It is necessary to observe the resources in every node or link and to know the network topology and the complete routing information in the domain.
2. It is necessary to determine not only the remaining bandwidth for every link but also the remaining power of each node's packet-processing unit.

Moreover, in general packet switching networks, whether remaining resources are sufficient or not cannot be determined only by the bit-rate of incoming traffic but also depends on the probabilistic distribution of packet arrival. This means that the queueing delay or packet loss probability cannot be estimated even though the mean amount of remaining resources is determined. Furthermore, although the distribution of packet arrival could be determined by observing incoming traffic, it is still difficult to predict the distribution after new incoming flows have been accommodated. Therefore, we can see that it is difficult to achieve strict admission control taking all these things into consideration with the signaling-based idea in packet switching networks.

Having considered these things, we propose the Tentative Accommodating and Congestion Confirming Strategy (TACCS). Let us assume that Congestion Detect Agents (CDAs) are installed on bottlenecked points in a domain and these can observe the number of dropped packets (Fig. 1). Let us also assume CDAs advertise this information to ingress nodes at certain intervals by multicasting. Based on the information from CDAs, ingress nodes control admission as follows in TACCS. When flows arrive at a domain,

(1) Ingress nodes tentatively accommodate them and assign a higher drop precedence than for previously accommodated flows (tentative accommodation).
(2) After receiving information from the CDAs, ingress nodes check whether packets with a higher drop precedence have been dropped or not (congestion confirmation).
    (2)-a If packets with a higher drop precedence have been dropped, ingress nodes decide tentatively accommodated flows caused the congestion and drop them.
    (2)-b Otherwise, the ingress nodes accommodate them and reduce their drop precedence to the same level as the previously accommodated flows.

Note that we here assume flows are multimedia streaming flows and these are isolated from best effort traffic such as TCP flows.

The drop precedence is a differentiation between packets. The higher the drop precedence, the more packets with this designation are dropped when congestion occurs. By utilizing this mechanism, accommodated flows are protected from being affected by tentatively accommodated flows. With the Diffserv architecture, drop precedences are achieved by marking different Diffserv Code Points (DSCPs) for packets and utilizing Multilevel Random Early Detection (MRED) schemes on routers. For the purposes of drop precedence in TACCS, we recommend using the Multilevel Drop Tail (MDT) instead of MRED because we found that MDT can more effectively protect packets with lower drop precedence from ones with higher ones than MRED in previous work [1].

The main premise behind TACCS is that it is easy to know whether congestion is occurring after incoming flows have been accommodated by observing the queue length in the nodes' packet buffer or the number of dropped packets although it is difficult to predict in advance. Its benefits are summarized as follows. Since tentative accommodation of new incoming flows enables to generate the same situation as if they had been accommodated, it is possible to control admission reflecting the remaining bandwidth,

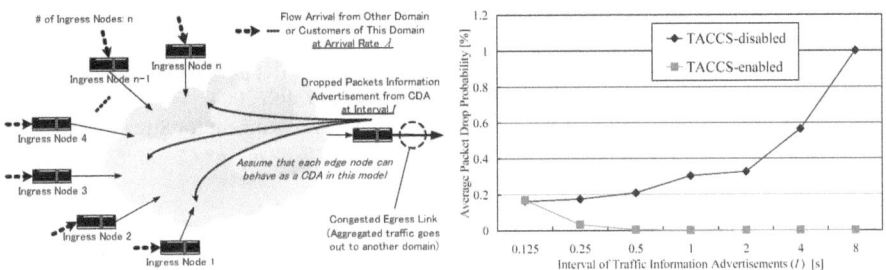

Fig. 1. System Image

Fig. 2. Average Packet Drop Probability

the remaining power in each node's packet-processing unit, and the properties of packet arrival, without collecting resource information in advance. Moreover, the recognition of each flow or a centralized management agent are both unnecessary with TACCS.

3   Evaluation

For confirming the effects of TACCS, we simulated same kind situation as in Fig. 1 and compared TACCS enabled case with a case where only traffic advertisements were done without TACCS.

Figure 2 shows the results. In this figure, the x-axis represents the interval of traffic advertisements from CDAs and the y-axis is the average drop probability of the accommodated flows. We can see from Fig. 2 that congestion could be avoided and the packet drop probability was maintained a low level in the case of TACCS-enabled. This means that TACCS enables a network domain to control admission even though each ingress node independently admit incoming flows without a centralized management agent.

4   Conclusion

We proposed TACCS, which could control admissions reflecting the properties of packet arrival without collecting resources information in advance. To investigate the characteristics of TACCS further and reveal guidelines for configuring parameters, we will mathematically analyze TACCS in future work. The future work also involves to compare TACCS with signaling-based schemes and to study issues of CDA placement. After these, we will integrate TACCS into a dynamic class assignment method for stream flows [2] which we proposed in our previous work.

Acknowledgements

Parts of this research were supported by the International Communications Foundation (ICF) of Japan.

References

1. K. Yasukawa, K. Baba, and K. Yamaoka, "Drop Precedence Mapping on Dynamic Class Assignment Method," *in Proc. of CSNDSP 2004*, pp. 416–419, Jul. 2004.
2. K. Yasukawa, K. Baba, and K. Yamaoka, "Dynamic Class Assignment for Stream Flows Considering Characteristics of Non-stream Flow Classes," *IEICE Trans. on Communications*, Vol. E87-B, No. 11, pp. 3242–3254, Nov. 2004.

Improving Uplink QoS of Wifi Hotspots

Benjamin Bappu and June Tay

Networks Research Centre, British Telecommunications, Adastral Park,
Martlesham Heath, Ipswich, IP53RE, UK
{Benjamin.Bappu, June.Tay}@bt.com

Abstract. Hotspots providers (using IEEE 802.11 Wireless LAN, also known as WiFi) are looking into ways to increase revenue from their service and improve customer satisfaction/experience. We propose a practical two-hop relaying scheme, managed by the Access Point (AP) to increase aggregate data throughput. We argue that controlled and incentives based collaboration among nodes and AP can improve overall QoS and hence the driving force for making relaying commercially viable.

1 Introduction

Relaying is where nodes communicate with their immediate neighbours to relay information for another node (to an AP in our scenario), with power control to minimize interference and/or maximize throughput. We propose a simple and practical two hop relay scheme where the AP centrally manages all nodes.

Consider a hotspot scenario: Node x situated at the edge of the hot-spot's ring of influence may be connected to the hotspot at a lower power transmission (due to its limited battery life left in his portable device) or lower transmission rate due to high interference. Node r who sits between node x and the hotspot could share power by acting as a relay and improve overall QoS. In doing so, a relay node can help to increase the throughput of the link since it may adapt to a higher data rate due to lower interference (e.g. nearer to AP). In highly concentrated (or busy) areas, an AP can preclude low data rate associations with distant nodes in an attempt to minimize delays (i.e. improve aggregate throughput of the busy network). However, using relays, benefits (i.e. aggregate throughput is proportional to revenue) are gained for both the hotspot provider and distant nodes. Related work such as [1] and [2] offer complex and impractical solutions for relaying in Wifi hotspots. They also do not consider the economic aspect of relaying (e.g. providing incentives) in their architectures, which we believe is essential to make relaying commercially successful. Ideally we want a scheme that benefits both the network operator, user and complies with standards.

In this paper, we introduce and briefly discuss our new research work on a simple handshaking protocol for selecting the best relay, incentive mechanisms and QoS issues for Wifi hotspots.

H. de Meer and N. Bhatti (Eds.): IWQoS 2005, LNCS 3552, pp. 353–355, 2005.
© IFIP International Federation for Information Processing 2005

2 Handshaking Protocol for Hot-Spots

Our initial design assumes that an AP always transmits at maximum power. Nodes within range can either reply to the AP directly using maximum power or through relaying via intermediate nodes using reduced power. Our approach requires the AP to build a virtual table of nodes corresponding to their signal strength that can be used to determine the appropriate relay node. One of the difficulties here is the location awareness of the nodes.

Let's say that it takes 100mW (an equivalent of 20dB) to transmit for a distance of 100 metres from AP to node x. Cisco has stated some theoretical calculations on estimating outdoor ranges and indoor ranges of wireless links [3]. In an outdoor wireless link scenario, the coverage distance doubles for every increase of 6dB (9dB for indoors). Similarly, the coverage in RF transmit power is reduced to half for every decrease of 6dB. To transmit from node x to AP takes 100mW. If node r is employed to do relaying, node x can therefore reduce its coverage distance (or range) by half. For outdoor wireless link condition, node x would take 25mW (14dB) to transmit to node r and with node r taking another 25mW to transmit to AP. In total, it takes 50mW (for indoors its 25mW).

Therefore, we can achieve a savings of 50% - 75% in terms of transmit power usage when using relaying excluding overheads such as relay reception power, relay protocol etc. Theoretically, in the best case, when high transmission rates are selected, using 802.11g, we can achieve 27Mbps throughput (x→r→AP), which is considerably better than 2Mbps (x→AP) at low transmission rate.

To identity the best relay, lets assume that node x is associated to the AP using a low transmission modulation rate (at 1Mbps). There are two possible ways to save power using a relay node. One is to use reduced power to transmit to a relay and the other to use the same power, but a high rate (e.g. 54Mbps) via the relay. In the latter case, you save power by reducing transmission time. Most importantly, an appropriate relay needs to be identified. We propose the following technique:

- Node x sends a relay request message at full power and low rate. All nodes, including AP will be aware of this request.
- Node x re-sends a relay request message at a reduced power (e.g. 50%) and high rate. AP may not be able to receive/decode this message successfully. However, nodes that receive this second message and if they are close to AP, would reply with a accept request message at full power. This is to ensure that AP and nearby nodes knows the relay.
- AP will choose the appropriate relay (assuming there is more than one) based on the power tables and policy (such as relay reliability and fair incentive distribution etc).
- Upon confirmation, Node x sends data at reduced power and/or at high rate. Relay node forwards data to AP.
- AP sends ACKs to Node x directly. Note that in this multi-hop scheme, all nodes are always within range of AP's maximum power.

The distance a signal can be transmitted depends on a various number of factors such as antenna gains, transmitter power and receiver sensitivity etc. Received signal strength is a measurement that is the difference between transmission signal strength minus path loss. In our scheme, the AP chooses a relay by checking from its table to select the node that is capable of being a relay based on it being able to fulfill a minimum received signal strength and it uses less transmit power than the other relay nodes. Only nodes that are within range of high data rate can be selected as relays.

To provide incentives each node has to be registered with a hotspot provider. This simplifies the management of security and incentives for relays. Nodes that are willing to share power must register with AP, and successfully close the session in order to gain benefits from AP. If a relay node disappears, timeout occurs, and this is followed by a new relay node being appointed by the AP. One way to provide incentives would be to credit a percentage of relayed message data to the relay account, when a successful transaction occurs. Any node sharing less than a pre-negotiated amount of time will not get any incentives. This also precludes malicious relay nodes. However, an unintentional disruption (e.g. movement, system crash, severe interference) to relaying may also result in this penalty. A relay rating policy may be used by the AP to rate relays based on their past performance.

3 QoS Issues and Summary

The described relay scheme should be QoS aware for optimal performance. For instance, in a real-time application, how do we minimize latency and jitter for node x when a relay node is used to forward uplink traffic? If the relay node prioritises different flows (locally), how should the AP police this to ensure fairness? One simple approach is to ensure that a relay node behave like two nodes, when relaying is enabled. That is, the contention window is halved, giving a much higher opportunity to access the AP for node x and relay node's own data. Alternatively the relay node could map individual flows according to the service differentiation (i.e. EDCA) as specified in the upcoming IEEE 802.11e. Or perhaps, the scheduling and admission control should be done at the AP to ensure minimal delays for distant nodes that require certain QoS guarantees. This makes it less complex for nodes, but likely incurs inefficient use of the wireless spectrum (e.g. retransmission of dropped/delayed packets of other nodes).

In addition, we have not considered the effect of mobility. Our approach assumes that nodes (including relays) intending to participate in this hybrid mode needs to be in a fixed location for at least the duration of the session.

References

1. Hao Zhu, and Guohong Cao, On Improving the Performance of IEEE 802.11 with Relay-Enabled PCF, Kluwer Academic Publishers, Mobile Networks and Applications, 9, 423-434, 2004.
2. Seungjoon Lee, Suman Banerjee and Booby Bhattacharjee, The Case for a Multi-hop Wireless Local Area Network, Infocom 2004.
3. Cisco RF Power Values. Document ID: 23231,
    http://www.cisco.com/warp/public/102/wlan/powervalues-23231.html, 2004

Resilient State Management in Large Scale Networks

Yangcheng Huang and Saleem N. Bhatti

Department of Computer Science, University College London,
London WC1E 6BT UK
{y.huang, s.bhatti}@cs.ucl.ac.uk

Abstract. This paper describes, briefly, ongoing research on resource reservation state management, including research motivations and initial design.

1 Introduction

A fundamental challenge in designing protocols in large scale networks is how to manage a large amount of state information to deal with failures but with acceptable cost in protocol overhead. In the Resource reSerVation set-up Protocol (RSVP) [1], a soft state mechanism has traditionally been used to achieve state consistency, but its high overhead makes it infeasible for large-scale deployment [8]. This research is to propose a framework for reservation state management to maximize RSVP's performance, including reliability in delivering control messages and resilience in restoring state from inconsistency while minimizing protocol overhead and complexity.

2 Motivations

The standard RSVP [1] takes a soft-state approach in its design. In order to maintain its state information, RSVP nodes send periodic RSVP refresh messages for each existing RSVP session. In the absence of refresh messages, the RSVP state information would automatically time out and be deleted. The original RSVP relies heavily on a soft-state approach in state maintenance, including: 1) detecting state inconsistency and recovering from internal state corruption and failure; periodic PATH and RESV refresh messages contain state information for each existing RSVP session; a RSVP node verifies its RSVP state with refresh messages to detect/recover state errors; 2) achieving reliability in control message delivery; PATH and RESV state installation messages are transmitted as best-effort traffic under the assumption that any loss of control messages would be recovered from periodic refresh messages.

However, soft state mechanisms may not be the best choice because:

- The communication overhead due to such periodic refreshes increases linearly with the number of active RSVP sessions [6];
- In some RSVP extensions [2] [6], a timer mechanism is widely deployed to achieve robustness and resilience. However, different extensions may have correlations and conflicts in timer configuration. For example, the timer interval of a Srefresh (summary refresh) message should be longer than that of standard refresh

H. de Meer and N. Bhatti (Eds.): IWQoS 2005, LNCS 3552, pp. 356–358, 2005.
© IFIP International Federation for Information Processing 2005

message; when a standard refresh message is sent, a corresponding summary refresh should not be sent during the same refresh period [2];

– Recent efforts [3] in state mechanisms show that a simple soft state approach does not compete with a mixed hard/soft state approach in performance: "a soft-state approach coupled with explicit removal substantially improves the degree of state consistency while introducing little additional signalling message overhead" [3]. Further efforts in analyzing and improving its performance are desirable.

3   Towards a Resilient State Management Framework

3.1   Internal Failure Detection Based on State Consistency Arbiter

Existing methods for internal state corruption detection are based on soft-state synchronization, such as refresh messages in standard RSVP [1] and neighbouring state verification mechanisms in RSVP extensions [6] [7]. To reduce dependence on soft state mechanism, we propose an asynchronous state consistency verification mechanism in which no periodic state updating is required; state consistency verification only happens when there are state changes; once state inconsistency is detected, state recovery process will be initiated. The mechanism is described as follows.

State consistency arbiter could be any node in or outside the RSVP session. The role of an arbiter is to listen to state updates from every RSVP node, simulate the global state of the RSVP session and detect inconsistency. In the absence of inconsistencies, it works in silent mode: only collecting state digests from RSVP nodes. Once inconsistency is detected, the arbiter either notifies the RSVP node to initiate state recovery/synchronization, or create a corrected state digest and transmit it to all nodes.

Whenever detecting any state change, every RSVP node computes a digest for all active RSVP sessions and sends the digest to the arbiter; when receiving digest information from a RSVP node, the arbiter compares the digest information with other digest information it already holds to judge the consistency.

The state digest mechanism in this approach is similar with that in state compression [6]. The key difference between the state compression and arbiter architecture is that the former adopts a soft state mechanism and sends periodic state digests to neighbouring RSVP nodes, while the latter adopts asynchronous state verifying methods and sends state digests to a centralized arbiter only when state is changed. Compared with state verification through exchanging neighbouring nodes' state information, this approach has a global view of RSVP sessions and could solve the problem of simultaneous failure among neighbouring nodes.

3.2   Dynamic Refresh Timer

In existing soft state protocols, the values of the timer intervals are chosen by "matching empirical observations with desired recovery and response times" [4]. The fixed-intervals mechanism has no consideration of network status in terms of failure rate; it adapts neither to the wide range of link qualities that exist in large scale networks, nor to fluctuations in rate of failure occurrence over time.

We propose an adaptive approach in which values of timer intervals adapt dynamically to real-time link status based on failure feedback. The essential mechanisms required to realize this dynamic timer approach are: 1) fast failure detection and reporting mechanisms to signal end hosts to adjust timer intervals; 2) dynamic adjustment of a sender's refresh rate so that state failure can be recovered very quickly after it occurs, whilst overhead is kept low when there is no error.

3.3 Reliable Control Message Delivery

Loss of control messages may cause delay in RSVP setup or state inconsistency [9]. So, it is desirable that RSVP control messages are reliably delivered. However, we argue that per-session ACK-based mechanism [2] [5] are costly and inefficient to handle, causing bursts of RSVP requests, especially for short RSVP sessions.

We propose a summary acknowledgement scheme (S_ACK), which guarantees control message delivery for a list of RSVP sessions. In our scheme, we verify the delivery of trigger messages after multiple messages have been transmitted.

4   Conclusions and Current Status

This paper describes briefly ongoing PhD research on state management; simulations and experiments are being carried out; therefore more results will be available soon.

References

1. L. Zhang, S. Deering, D. Estrin, S. Shenker, D. Zappala: RSVP: A New Resource Reservation Protocol. IEEE Network, Vol. 7, Sept. 1993
2. L. Berger, et al: RSVP Refresh Overhead Reduction Extensions. RFC 2961, April 2001
3. Ping Ji, Zihui Ge, Jim Kurose, Don Towsley: A Comparison of Hard-state and Soft-state Signaling Protocols. Proc. ACM SIGCOMM, 2003
4. P. Sharma, et al: Scalable timers for soft state protocols. Proc. IEEE Infocom, Japan, 1997
5. P. Pan, H. Schulzrinne: Staged Refresh Timers for RSVP. Proc. IEEE Globecom, 1997
6. L. Wang, et al: A New Proposal for RSVP Refreshes. Proc. IEEE ICNP, 1999
7. D. Awduche, et al: RSVP-TE: Extensions to RSVP for LSP Tunnels. RFC 3209, Dec 2001
8. A. Mankin, et al: Resource ReSerVation Protocol (RSVP) Version 1 Applicability Statement: Some Guidelines on Deployment. RFC2208, Sept 1997
9. O. Komolafe, J. Sventek: An Evaluation of RSVP Control Message Delivery Mechanisms. Proc. IEEE HPSR, Phoenix, Arizona, USA, April 2004

Performance Analysis of Wireless Scheduling with ARQ in Fast Fading Channels

Hwee Pink Tan

EURANDOM, Eindhoven University of Technology,
P.O. Box 513, 5600 MB,
Eindhoven, The Netherlands
tan@eurandom.tue.nl

Abstract. We develop a Markov model to study the performance of opportunistic scheduling for downlink data transmissions with type-II packet-combining hybrid ARQ in a multirate cellular network for a fast fading environment. For a two-user scenario with two feasible transmission rates, there exists an operating region within which opportunistic scheduling maintains its scheduling gain over round-robin scheduling. In ongoing work, we seek to extend the analysis of the model as well as generalize the model to a multi-user scenario.

1 Introduction

Emerging multirate cellular networks are envisaged to provide high-rate data services to mobile users. Various opportunistic scheduling approaches (e.g., [1]) were proposed recently that transmits to the user with the best or relatively-best according to the predicted feasible transmission rate so as to maximize channel efficiency. However, transmission errors may occur due to the inaccuracy of feasible rate prediction. For the seamless operation of higher layer protocols (e.g., TCP) over such a network, link-layer protocols such as ARQ (automatic repeat request) are used to improve the transmission reliability through packet retransmissions. Assuming perfect prediction, while the same probability of packet success is maintained at every transmission attempt with pure ARQ, hybrid type-II packet-combining ARQ (e.g., [2]) combines the soft decision values of previous noisy copies to improve the probability of packet success.

While opportunistic scheduling and ARQ have mostly been studied separately, few works have emerged recently that considered the problems collectively. While pure ARQ is considered in [3], packet-combining ARQ is considered in [4]. The assumption of a slow fading channel is crucial in both works, where the assumptions of perfect feasible rate prediction in [3] and constant user channel over the analysis interval in [4] are justified.

In this paper, we develop an analysis model for opportunistic scheduling with packet-combining ARQ in a fast fading environment. In such an environment, the analysis becomes more complex since the probability of decoding failure also depends on the feasible rate. Numerical results show that under certain conditions, opportunistic scheduling actually loses its scheduling gain over round robin scheduling, which is channel-unaware.

H. de Meer and N. Bhatti (Eds.): IWQoS 2005, LNCS 3552, pp. 359–361, 2005.

2   System Model and Assumptions

We consider the downlink slotted transmission from a single base station to M mobile users, where each fixed-size time slot is allocated to one user and the data flow corresponding to each mobile user is continuously backlogged. We characterize the channel condition of user j in terms of (a) its *feasible* transmission rate (bits/slot), t_j^f, where $t_{min} \leq t_j^f \leq t_{max}$, and (b) the resulting probability of decoding failure, p_j^e, if it transmits. We consider a fast fading channel, where t_j^f is uniformly distributed over $[t_{min}, t_{max}]$ and independent in each slot.

To characterize the mechanism of packet-combining ARQ, let $t_{r_j,j}^a$ denote the *actual* transmission rate of user j at the $(r_j + 1)^{th}$ transmission attempt. For the first attempt (r_j=0), user j transmits at $t_{0,j}^a$ corresponding to the predicted feasible rate. For a fast fading channel, $t_{0,j}^a$ and t_j^f are identically distributed.

However, if the first attempt fails, subsequent transmissions ($r^j > 0$) occur at the same rate as the previous attempt, i.e., $t_{r_j,j}^a = t_{r_j-1,j}^a$, and we expect the probability of decoding failure to be reduced with r_j, i.e., if $p_j^e = \alpha$ for r_j=a, then:

$$p_j^e < \alpha \quad \text{if } r_j > a \tag{1}$$

In addition to Eq. (1), it is reasonable to assume that if $p_j^e = \beta$ for $t_{r_j,j}^a = t_j^f$, then the following properties should hold:

$$p_j^e \begin{cases} > \beta, \, t_{r_j,j}^a > t_j^f; \\ \leq \beta, \, t_{r_j,j}^a < t_j^f. \end{cases} \tag{2}$$

Hence, we propose the following model for p_j^e that satisfies both Eq. (1) and (2):

$$p_j^e = \begin{cases} (1 + \frac{t_{\max(r_j-1,0),j}^a - t_j^f}{t_{max} - t_{min}})\delta \cdot 0.5^{r_j}, & r_j < r_{max}; \\ 0, & r_j = r_{max}. \end{cases} \tag{3}$$

where r_{max} is the retransmission threshold such that if $r=r_{max}$, the transmission is always successful, and δ is a constant that indicates channel quality, $0 \leq \delta \leq \frac{1}{2}$, so that $0 \leq p_j^e < 1$. We note that Eq. (3) is also applicable to pure ARQ.

We consider an opportunistic scheduling mechanism which selects the mobile user m^* with the lowest probability of decoding failure for transmission so as to maximize the overall system throughput, i.e.,

$$m^* = \arg \min_{1 \leq j \leq M} p_j^e \tag{4}$$

round-robin scheduler is also considered as a comparison benchmark.

3   Performance Evaluation

According to Eq. (4), to determine m^* in each slot i, it is necessary to compute $p_j^e \, \forall \, j$, which in turn depends on the values of r_j and $t_{\max(r_j-1,0),j}^a$. By defining x_j

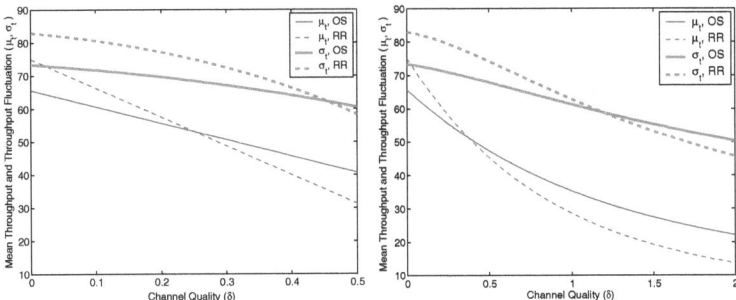

Fig. 1. Performance comparison of Opportunistic and Round-Robin Scheduling for two-user scenario in a fast fading channel with $t_{min}=100$ and $t_{max}=2t_{min}$ for various δ with (left) pure and (right) packet-combining $(r_{max}=2)$ ARQ

$= (r_j, t^a_{\max(r_j-1,0),j})$ as the state variable for user j in any slot, we can model the scheduling and ARQ mechanism as a Markov chain. By analyzing the Markov model, we can derive the throughput distribution for each user.

We evaluate the mean throughput (μ_t) as well as throughput fluctuation (σ_t) of opportunistic scheduling (**OS**) and round-robin scheduling (**RR**) with pure and packet-combining ARQ for a two-user scenario with two feasible transmission rates. The results are shown in Fig. 1 for $t_{min}=100$ and $t_{max}=2t_{min}$.

We note that for sufficiently large δ, $\mu_t^{OS} > \mu_t^{RR}$, i.e., **OS** maintains its scheduling gain over **RR** as expected. However, as δ is reduced below some threshold δ^{μ_t}, this scheduling gain is lost. Similarly, there exists a corresponding threshold for throughput fluctuation (denoted by δ^{σ_t}) such that when $\delta < \delta^{\sigma_t}$, the throughput of **OS** is less jittery than that of **RR** and vice versa. Since $\delta^{\mu_t} < \delta^{\sigma_t}$, we can define the region $\delta^{\mu_t} \leq \delta \leq \delta^{\sigma_t}$ where **OS** is the preferred scheduling scheme with higher and less jittery throughput; beyond this region, there is a trade-off between **OS** and **RR** in terms of μ_t and σ_t.

References

1. Liu, X., Chan, E.K.P., Shroff, N.B.: Opportunistic Transmission Scheduling with Resource-Sharing Constraints in Wireless Networks. *IEEE Journal of Selected Areas in Communications*, 19(29):2053-2064, October 2001.
2. Harvey, B.A., Wicker, S.B.: Packet Combining Systems Based on the Viterbi Decoder. *IEEE Transactions on Communications*, 42(4):1544-1557, April 1994.
3. Issariyakul, T., Hossain, E.: Channel-Quality-Based Opportunistic Scheduling with ARQ in Multi-Rate Wireless Networks: Modeling and Analysis, *Submitted to IEEE Transactions on Wireless Communications*, 2004.
4. Huang, J., Berry, R., Honig, M.L.: Wireless Scheduling with Hybrid ARQ, *38th Conference on Information Sciences and Systems*, March 2004.

Privacy and Reliability by Dispersive Routing

Haim Zlatokrilov and Hanoch Levy

School of Computer Science Tel-Aviv University, Tel-Aviv, Israel

Abstract. The traditional single (shortest) path routing paradigm leaves sessions vulnerable to a variety of security threats, especially eavesdropping. We propose to overcome this via dispersive routing, conducted over multiple paths. This increases significantly the costs inflicted on an attacker who wishes to eavesdrop or conduct DoS attack on network sessions by hijacking network links (or routers)[1].

1 Introduction

The traditional single (usually shortest) path routing leaves sessions vulnerable to attacks along the route. Attackers may eavesdrop sessions as well as maliciously drop their fragments (causing denial-of-service (DoS) attack), on nodes or links along the path. The approach proposed in this work is to enhance privacy and reliability by adding additional layer of protection. While encryption is a good defense against attackers that managed to eavesdrop an entire session, the dispersion of session fragments over multiple paths can prevent the attacker from conducting a meaningful eavesdropping or significant malicious dropping[2] in the first place.

Our model is based on the assumption that each link is associated with some adversary hijacking cost. This cost is based on parameters such as physical link properties (e.g. wire or wireless), geographic location, etc. We study the problem of shipping session fragments in a way that will force the attacker to invest at least a predefined minimal effort to conduct a successful attack. We look at the worst-case scenario, assuming the attacker is familiar with the exact dispersion strategy and knows the path taken by each fragment. Comprehensive study of this problem with several extensions, such as finding minimal number of paths and limiting paths' length, will be presented in [4].

Dispersing session fragments over multiple paths can be implemented in a variety of methods such as: IP tunneling, implementation in overlay or MPLS networks, etc. We assume that the Security Traffic Manager (STM) can plan and execute the transmission of session fragments regardless of the underlying machinery. We focus on the context of a single session and neglect bandwidth constraints, assuming that session's bandwidth requirements[3] are very small in comparison to network capacity.

---

[1] This work was partially supported by Israeli Science Foundation grant 235/03 and by Euro NGI network of excellence.
[2] We will use the term *dropping* both for eavesdropping and malicious dropping attacks.
[3] Dispersion techniques are also known to increase network efficiency as discussed in [3].

H. de Meer and N. Bhatti (Eds.): IWQoS 2005, LNCS 3552, pp. 362–365, 2005.

Sending session fragments over several paths might cause degradation in QoS due to jitter and out-of-order effects, but in some scenarios can also enhance QoS [1].

1.1 A Brief Demonstration of the Problem

Consider the network depicted in Fig.1-a, where the numbers represent link hijacking costs. The STM's goal is to transfer a session of 10 fragments from s to t, such that the attacker will be forced to invest at least cost of 5 units in order to drop 8 fragments. If the fragments are directed as shown in Fig.1-b or Fig.1-c, the attacker will be able to drop 8 fragments at the cost of 4 units by hijacking links $s{\to}a$ and $a{\to}t$ (or link $b{\to}t$ in Fig.1-c). Using the dispersion strategy depicted in Figure.1-d will keep the session safe.

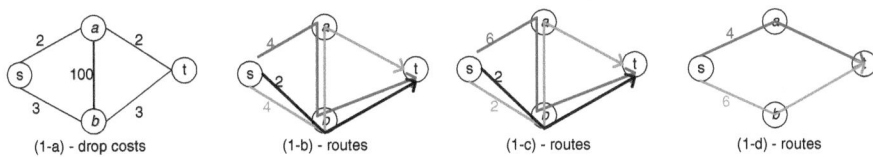

Fig. 1. An example of the STM's problem. (1-a) - network structure and link costs. (1-b) and (1-c) - bad assignment of fragments over the paths (the numbers depict the number of assigned fragments over the paths). (1-d) – a good assignment which protects the session

1.2 The Attacker's Problem

INSTANCE: Graph $G(V,L)$, cost c_l for all links $l \in L$, a set p_i, $i = 1..K$, of paths from s to t, the path taken by each of N fragments and a parameter P. Let $\gamma_i^j = 1$, denote that fragment j is sent over path p_i, otherwise $\gamma_i^j = 0$ (Clearly $\sum_{j=1}^{N}\sum_{i=1}^{K}\gamma_i^j = N$).

QUESTION: Find a set of edges $L' \subseteq L$, such that $\sum_{l \in L'} c_l$ is minimized and the number of unique[4] fragments on L' is greater than or equals to $P \cdot N$.

Lemma 1: *The attacker's problem is NPC even with identical link costs for any $0 < P \le 1$. The attacker's problem has a $(1 + ln(|V|))$-approximation by a greedy algorithm.*

1.3 The STM's Problem

INSTANCE: Graph $G(V,L)$, cost c_l for all links $l \in L$, source and destination nodes (s and t respectively), a parameter $0 < P \le 1$ and a constant $C > 0$.

QUESTION: Find a set of paths U from s to t and an assignment of N fragments to the paths such that: There exists no set of links L', obeying $\sum_{l \in L'} c_l < C$, that captures $P \cdot N$ fragments.

---

[4] A fragment is counted only once, even if the attacker drops it several times.

We prove that the STM's problem in general is at least NP-hard. Nonetheless several special cases (covering large set of parameters) of the problem can be solved in a polynomial time.

1.4   The STM's Problem with Either $P=1$ or $P<1$ and Identical Cost Links

We propose simple polynomial time algorithms solving these cases of STM's problem, where the number of session fragments obeys $N>C/c_{min}$ (c_{min} is the minimal cost link). If no solution exists the algorithms fail. The algorithms are based on finding max-flow and translating costs to number of fragments to be sent on paths. The complexity of these algorithms is identical to that of the max-flow algorithm.

1.5   The STM's Problem with $P<1$ and Non-identical Cost Links

We show that the problem is at least NP-hard. We propose a heuristic for the STM's problem possessing the following properties (C' denotes the minimal cost cut):

- If the attacker's budget $C>C'$, the attacker can always prevail and the algorithm stops.
- If $C < P \cdot C'$, a solution that guarantees that the STM prevails is found.
- Otherwise, if $P \cdot C'< C < C'$, it is not clear whether a valid solution exists. Several enhancement heuristics can be used in that case. Validating the solution in that case, which is the attacker's problem, is NPC.

1.6   Simulation Results

Fig.2 demonstrates the increase in the attacker's required dropping budget as a function of node degree. This is achieved by running the *STM's Algorithm* and computing the capturing cost (*heuristic's solution* curve). The simulations were conducted on random graphs with random edge costs in the range of 1-5 and $P=0.8$. The plot depicts the averaged results. The *max single path cost* curve stands for the maximal dropping cost in case of single path routing. The *min cost cut* curve stands for the budget for which the attacker will always prevail. The figure demonstrates that implementing the *STM's algorithm* can dramatically increase the dropping cost in comparison to single path routing, up to the cost $P \cdot C'< C < C'$

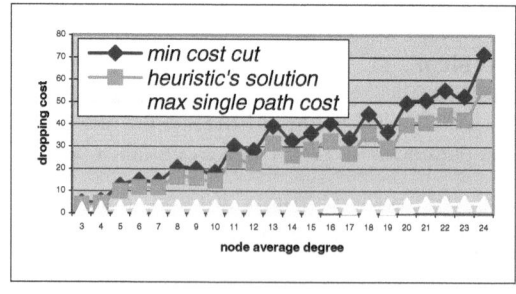

Fig. 2. increase in attacker's dropping budget

References

1. H. Zlatokrilov, H.Levy, "The Effect of Packet Dispersion on Voice Applications in IP Networks", in Proc. of IEEE INFOCOM'04, Hong-Kong.
2. S. Bohacek, J. P. Hespanha, K. Obraczka, J. Lee, C. Lim, "Enhancing Security Via Stochastic Routing", In Proc. of the 11th IEEE ICCCN, May 2002.
3. Patrick P. C. Lee , V. Misra , and D. Rubenstein. "Distributed Algorithms for Secure Multipath Routing", in Proc. of IEEE INFOCOM, March 2005, Miami, FL, USA.
4. H. Zlatokrilov, H. Levy, "Session Security enhancement by traffic dispersion", forthcoming.

Distributed Online LSP Merging Algorithms for MPLS-TE

Li Lei and Srinivas Sampalli

Faculty of Computer Science, Dalhousie University,
Halifax, NS B3H 1W5, Canada
{llei, srini}@cs.dal.ca

Abstract. Merging of Label Switched Paths (LSPs) saves label space and reduces processing time in routers. We introduce two distributed merging algorithms for online LSP merging.

1   Introduction

As the size of the MPLS network [1] increases, the large label space becomes a big performance concern [2]. Labels can be saved by merging conventional point-to-point (p-t-p) LSPs to form Multipoint-to-Point (m-t-p) LSP trees [1], as shown in Figure 1.

The optimization of LSP merging problem is NP-hard [5]. Previous proposed merging schemes [4] [5] require a central control and global route information and suffer from performance degradation in online use [5]. In this paper, we describe two fully distributed online LSP merging algorithms.

2   Distributed LSP Merging Algorithms

We abstract the LSP control and management as general message passing processes. We also assume only local information is available at each route.

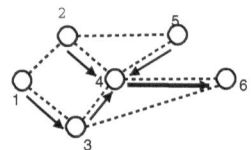

Fig. 1. LSPs merging example

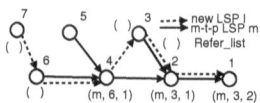

Fig. 2. Example of on the fly merging

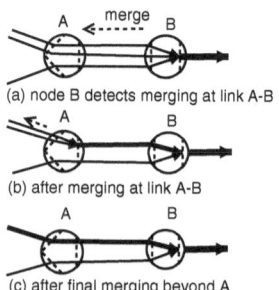

(a) node B detects merging at link A-B

(b) after merging at link A-B

(c) after final merging beyond A

Fig. 3. Example of upstream wave merging

H. de Meer and N. Bhatti (Eds.): IWQoS 2005, LNCS 3552, pp. 366–368, 2005.
© IFIP International Federation for Information Processing 2005

The *on the fly merging algorithm* requires two messages, *request* and *resv*. The procedure *REQUEST* collects merging information along the route, as shown in Figure 2. The procedure *RESV* assigns to the new LSP l the same label as that of selected LSP m rather than a new one. The normal label distribution process resumes after the *refnode* specified in the reference entry. This algorithm rapidly merges a new LSP into an existing LSP but unable to merge all possible LSPs.

```
 1: procedure REQUEST(reflist)
 2:    for all entry i ∈ reflist do
 3:       if port_out(i) = port_out(l) then
 4:          hop(i) + +
 5:       else
 6:          remove entry i
 7:       end if
 8:    end for
 9:    N ← {LSP m|port_out(m) = port_out(l) ∧ port_in(m) ≠ port_in(l)}
10:    for all LSP j ∈ N do
11:       if qos(j) = qos(l) then
12:          reflist ← reflist ∪ {j}, hop(j) ← 1, refnode(j) ← itself
13:       end if
14:    end for
15: end procedure
16: procedure RESV(reflist)
17:    if reflist ≠ φ then
18:       m ← reference LSP in reflist
19:       if refnode = itself then
20:          clear reflist
21:          assign l a new label
22:       else
23:          assign l the same lables as m
24:          modify the bandwidth reservation of m
25:       end if
26:    end if
27: end procedure
```

Algorithm 1. On the fly merging algorithm

The *upstream wave merging algorithm* detects and merges all possible LSPs starting from the egress nodes. It requires two messages *merge* and *release*. The procedure *DETECT* finds merging opportunities starting from the egress nodes. The procedures *REMAP* and *RELEASE* illustrate the merging operation, as shown in Figure 3.

3   Conclusion and Future Work

In this paper, we propose two distributed LSP merging algorithms for MPLS-TE. Currently, we are in the progress of simulating our algorithms. LSP merging

```
 1: procedure DETECT
 2:     for every output port r do
 3:         OUT ← {all outgoing labels to r}
 4:         for every input port s do
 5:             for every label i ∈ OUT do
 6:                 IN_i ← {all LSPs from s to outgoing label i}
 7:             end for
 8:             if(|IN_i| > 1) send message merge(IN_i) to node s
 9:         end for
10:     end for
11: end procedure
12: procedure REMAP(LSP set M, message source node s )
13:     l ← LSP which has the minimal label in M
14:     for all LSP j ∈ M − {l} do
15:         label_out(j) ← label_out(l)
16:         bandwidth(l) ← bandwidth(l) + bandwidth(j)
17:     end for
18:     send message release(M) to s
19: end procedure
20: procedure RELEASE(LSP set M)
21:     remove NHLFEs for all LSP l ∈ M
22: end procedure
```

Algorithm 2. Upstream wave merging algorithm

may affect other fields of traffic engineering, such as preemption. Integration of tess algorithms with ours previously proposed preemption scheme [3] is a work for further study. Extending MPLS signaling protocols for LSPs merging also requires more attention.

References

1. E. Rosen, A. Viswanathan, and R. Callon, *Multiprotocol Label Switching Architecture*, IETF, RFC-3031, January 2001.
2. H. Hummel and J. Grimminger, *Hierarchical LSP*, IETF Internet Draft, draft-hummel-mpls-hierarchical-lsp-00.txt, March 2002, work in progress
3. L. Lei and S. Sampalli, *Backward connection preemption in multiclass QoS-aware networks*, Proceeding of 12th IEEE IWQOS, page(s):153-160, June 2004
4. H. Saito, Y. Miyao, and M. Yoshida, *Traffic Engineering using Multiple Multipoint-to-Point LSPs*, Proceeding of IEEE INFOCOM 2000, Page(s): 894-901 vol.2, March 2000.
5. S. Bhatnagar, S. Ganguly and B. Nath, *Creating Multipoint-to-point LSPs for Traffic Engineering*, Proceeding of IEEE HPSR Workshop 2003, page(s): 201-207, June 2003

Implicit Flow QoS Signaling Using Semantic-Rich Context Tags

Roel Ocampo[1,2], Alex Galis[2], Hermann de Meer[3], and Chris Todd[2]

[1] Department of Electrical and Electronics Engineering, University of the Philippines,
Diliman, Quezon City, 1101 Philippines
[2] Department of Electronic and Electrical Engineering, University College London,
Torrington Place, London WC1E 7JE, U.K.
[3] Faculty of Mathematics and Computer Science, University of Passau,
94032 Passau, Germany

Abstract. An important feature of future context-aware and adaptive networks would be the ability to provide QoS to user flows. Our approach enables end-hosts and other devices to expose and provide context information to the network to support underlying QoS mechanisms, including adaptation. We discuss the key elements of our approach and demonstrate its use in an experimental scenario.

1   Introduction

Current proposals for providing QoS in networks often expect end-hosts to either explicitly signal their requirements and undertake resource reservation, or for them to have sufficient knowledge about the underlying QoS model in order to map application flows to existing QoS classes. While QoS signaling messages may contain detailed description of QoS characteristics and requirements of a flow [1], they are often not sufficient to paint a "big picture" that better describes the desired interaction between the user and the network.

In this paper we briefly describe some aspects of our on-going work, which explores the application of concepts and techniques in *context awareness* to networks, particularly through the use of context tags that describe flow context. Although we envision a wide range of applications for context tags, we will focus here on their possible use in implicitly signaling the QoS characteristics and requirements of network flows.

2   The Context of a Flow

Our definition of flow context is derived from the domain of pervasive and ubiquitous computing [2]. We define the context of a network flow as any information that can be used to characterize its situation, including information pertaining to other entities and circumstances that give rise to or accompany its generation at the source, affect its transmission through the network, and influence its use

H. de Meer and N. Bhatti (Eds.): IWQoS 2005, LNCS 3552, pp. 369–371, 2005.
© IFIP International Federation for Information Processing 2005

at its destination. This includes not only the intrinsic, low-level characteristics of a flow, but also the nature of the applications, devices, and the activities, intentions, preferences and identities of the users that produce or consume the flow.

From a QoS perspective, flow context may be used in the following ways: (1) to decouple end-hosts and applications from the underlying domain-specific QoS model, (2) to provide or expose additional information about the flow to the network in an explicit way to facilitate flow classification for QoS purposes, (3) to trigger QoS adaptation directly on the flow, and (4) to identify and label suspicious and malicious flows, or those that are in violation of QoS contracts.

3   Tagging Flows with Context

Our approach consists primarily of tagging network flows with context information. The following are the key elements of this approach:

1. *Architecture.* Context sensing is performed in a distributed fashion, at end-hosts and network devices such as middleboxes. Context tags are then assembled and injected along the path of the flow and are intercepted and processed by devices downstream. This may lead to a control or management action, a service, or an adaptation function being triggered within an attached forwarding device such as a router. End-hosts may also process context tags.
2. *Tag structure.* Tags are formatted using Extensible Markup Language (XML) [3] and transported within UDP datagrams. The IP packet header contains the IP Router Alert Option as described in RFC 2113 and RFC 2711 [4].
3. *Tag aggregation.* Tag processing also results in the aggregation of information coming from multiple tags accumulated over time, or from multiple flows, resulting in higher-level context information that provides a more complete contextual description of a single flow or a flow aggregate (macroflow).
4. *Flow context ontology.* Declarative semantics within an ontology encode contextual relationships and properties, and facilitate the use of reasoning within the tag aggregation process. They likewise provide a means by which QoS characteristics and requirements may be inferred from context.

4   Experimental Scenario

Figure 1 illustrates the use of context tags for QoS adaptation in a simple experimental scenario. (A) A user, initially allocated 500 kbps, views a video stream. (B) The context tag within the stream results in a new bandwidth allocation of 1.5 Mbps, allowing the video stream to rise to its characteristic level of around 850 kbps. (C) The user requests an additional video stream with a higher priority. (D) The combined traffic saturates the bandwidth allocation, resulting in degraded video for both streams. (E) Receipt of the new context tag and aggregation allows the streams to be prioritized, and the network further adapts

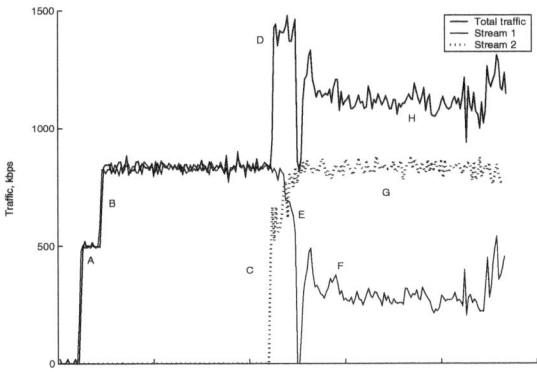

Fig. 1. Inbound traffic on end-host

by applying transcoding on the lower-priority stream. (F) The lower priority stream now operates at a lower average bitrate after transcoding, while the higher priority stream occupies its natural traffic level (G). (H) The total bandwidth consumed stays well within the 1.5 Mbps allocation.

5   Conclusion and Future Work

The ability to provide QoS to flows in a manner that decouples end-hosts from the underlying QoS model is an important aspect of context-aware and adaptive networks. We have demonstrated using a simple experimental scenario how context tags may implicitly signal QoS requirements. Work is ongoing on the further development of the flow context ontology and its dynamic linkage with the tag processing and aggregation component of our architecture.

Acknowledgment. This paper describes work partially undertaken in the context of the E-NEXT - IST FP6-506869 project, which is partially funded by the Commission of the European Union. The views contained herein are those of the authors and do not necessarily represent those of the E-NEXT project. Roel Ocampo acknowledges support from the Doctoral Fellowship Program of the University of the Philippines.

References

1. L. Zhang, S. Deering, D. Estrin, S. Shenker, and D. Zappala. RSVP: A New Resource ReSerVation Protocol. *IEEE Network*, September 1993.
2. A. K. Dey, D. Salber, and G. D. Abowd. A Conceptual Framework and a Toolkit for Supporting the Rapid Prototyping of Context-Aware Applications. *Human-Computer Interaction (HCI) Journal*, 16 (2-4), 2001
3. T. Bray, J. Paoli, C.M. Sperberg-McQueen, E. Maler, and F. Yergeau (editors). Extensible Markup Language 1.0 (Third Edition). *W3C Recommendation 04 February 2004*, http://www.w3.org/TR/REC-xml
4. D. Katz. IP Router Alert Option. *Request for Comments 2113*, February 1997.

Using IP as Transport Technology in Third Generation and Beyond Radio Access Networks

Attila Báder[1], Lars Westberg[2], and Georgios Karagiannis[3]

[1] Traffic Lab, Ericsson Research, P.O. Box 107, Budapest, Hungary, H-1300
[2] Ericsson Research, Torshamnsgatan 23, SE-16480, Stockholm, Sweden
{attila.bader, lars.westberg}@ericsson.com
[3] University of Twente, P.O. Box 217, 7500 AE Enschede, the Netherlands
g.karagiannis@utwente.nl

Abstract. This paper discusses the motivation for developing a new QoS signaling protocol for IP-based Radio Access Networks. It describes the main characteristics of these networks and the special requirements imposed by these characteristics on QoS signaling solutions.

1 Introducing IP Transport in Radio Access Networks: Motivation

Due to its flexibility and cost efficiency, IP transport is gradually introduced in different parts of third generation and beyond cellular networks, including their Radio Access Network (RAN).

The discussion related to the introduction of the IP technology in radio access networks is valid for all types of cellular systems, i.e., GPRS and IMT2000 (e.g. CDMA2000 and UMTS). For reasons of clarity, we will only focus on the Universal Mobile Telecommunication System (UMTS). Third generation and beyond cellular networks consist of access and core networks. In case of the UMTS Terrestrial RAN (UTRAN), see Figure 1, the boundaries are the radio base stations (i.e., Node Bs) and the Radio Network Controllers (RNCs) [1]. The Node B provides the radio channel coding/decoding and transmission/reception function for User Equipments (UE) in its coverage area called cell. The RNC controls the radio resources (the radio channels and the connections) of a number of Node Bs. The RNC is also responsible for controlling the soft handover combining and splitting between streams from different Node Bs belonging to the same User Equipment. Furthermore, the RNC is responsible for the allocation of transport resources within the RAN. The Mobile Switching Centre (MSC) and Media Gateway (MGW) are used for circuit-switched services towards other User Equipments and external circuit-switched networks. The SGSN and GGSN entities provide support for packet switched services towards User Equipments, including mobility management, access control and control of packet data protocol contexts. In addition, the GGSN provides inter-working with external packet-switched networks such as the public Internet.

The IP technology can be considered as an open transport architecture that can run on top of many various link layer techniques, such as Ethernet, SDH, ATM. The

H. de Meer and N. Bhatti (Eds.): IWQoS 2005, LNCS 3552, pp. 372–374, 2005.

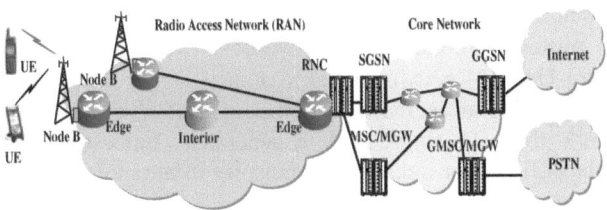

Fig. 1. Third generation cellular network scenario

choice of the link layer techniques is completely transparent to the higher layers, making it possible to use several solutions at the same time. Ethernet for example can be cost efficient choice in a metropolitan area.

Considering that IP is already used in the transport part of the UMTS core network, if IP will also be used in the transport part of the UTRAN, then one single network management system can be used for both UMTS core and radio access network (full IP network). Due to the auto-configuration capabilities of IP updating the network to higher traffic volume or wider coverage is simpler than e.g. in case of ATM network.

Using IP-based transport within the UTRAN, gives operators an opportunity to upgrade their transport network to a packet-based one. When compared with a traditional STM-based system, the gain is seen in the statistical multiplexing of traffic. As a tradeoff, an efficient QoS solution has to be developed for IP based RAN.

2   Characteristics of RANs and Imposed QoS Requirements

The characteristics of the RAN impose special requirements on the resource reservation protocol that is used within the RAN. The main characteristics of radio access networks are the following:

Very often the transmission in a RAN contains a relatively high volume of expensive leased lines [3].

The fact that Node Bs are spread over a large geographic area and in general far away from the backbone typically results in high cost of the transmission links. Therefore, efficient bandwidth utilization in UTRAN is essential.

A majority of the traffic transported on the transmission links of UTRAN are radio frames, which are short data segments that are transmitted by the Node B on a given radio channel and given time slots [4,5]. The traffic is, therefore, very sensitive both for delay and jitter. The QoS requirement is especially strict for voice traffic that is usually dominating in the networks.

Due to the mobility, and in order to efficiently utilize the radio resources, the UTRAN supports frequent handover procedures between radio channels and Node Bs. Supporting soft handover (between Node Bs controlled by the same RNC) in 3G network releases, puts the most demanding requirements on the resource reservation protocol.

In the early phase of 3G networks the voice traffic dominates in the network. By introducing HSDPA (High Speed Downlink Packet Access) service, the bandwidth demand increases rapidly and the UTRAN transport network may become the main bottleneck of the UMTS network.

- A potential UTRAN network is large, consisting of several hundred Node Bs that are generating an increasing number of traffic volume over the lifetime of the network. Even if a single Node B generates a modest traffic volume, the total amount of flows for radio frame transport in the radio access network is significantly large.

Though several other QoS solutions can be applied for IP-based RAN, signaled QoS is fairly the most effective in such a dynamic environment. The special characteristics of RANs arises the need to identify the requirements of a resource reservation signaling protocol that can be used within IP based UTRAN:

- The resource reservation between the edges of the RAN, see Figure 1, is imposed by radio specific functions, and not by the end-to-end resource reservation signaling. Therefore, the resource reservation in the UTRAN may be different from the QoS solutions in the other part of the network. If the resource reservation in the UTRAN is part of an end-to-end resource reservation protocol, the protocol should support edge-to-edge reservations as well. Support is also necessary for bi-directional unicast reservations for delay-sensitive traffic, due to the nature of the radio frame traffic flows [4, 5].
- The peak bit rate of the multi-rate radio channels is selected on-demand [6]. To efficiently utilize the bandwidth of the expensive transmission links used for radio frame transport, over-provisioning is in general not feasible and, therefore, the protocol would be used for on-demand reservation.
- At each handover event, the resource reservation may be reinitiated. As a consequence of the frequent handover, the resource reservation protocol will be used very frequently and needs to be fast.
- Due to the large number of flows and high traffic that have to be supported within the UTRAN, the protocol needs to be scalable.

The NSIS working group in IETF develops a QoS signaling protocol that takes into account the above requirements [2]. The Resource Management in Diffserv Quality of Service Model, whichcan be used within the NSIS protocol suite, is especially suitable for large-scale RAN applications [7].

References

1. 3GPP TS 25.401: "UTRAN Overall Description".
2. Brunner, M., "Requirements for Signaling Protocols" IETF Request for Comments 3726.
3. Bjarhov, M., Friberg, C., "GSM network solutions for new-growth markets", Ericsson Review, Issue nr. 01, 2004.
4. 3GPP TS 25.104: "UTRA (BS) FDD; Radio transmission and Reception".
5. 3GPP TS 25.105: "UTRA (BS) TDD; Radio transmission and Reception".
6. 3GPP TS 26.093: "Source Controlled Rate operation ".
7. A. Bader, L. Westberg, G. Karagiannis, C. Kappler, T. Phelan, H. Tschofenig: "RMD-QOSM – The Resource Management in Diffserv Quality of Service Model. " Internet draft, work in progress, Feb. 2005.

Closing the Gap Between Industry, Academia and Users: Is There a Need for QoS in Wireless Systems ?

Gábor Fodor, Karim El-Malki, and David Partain

Ericsson AB, Stockholm, Sweden
{Gabor.Fodor, Karim.El-Malki,
David.Partain}@ericsson.com

Abstract. In this short paper we make the point that although there may be a gap between academic and industrial research in the area of quality of service (QoS), this gap can be narrowed. In order for this to happen, it is important that the academic and industrial players jointly make an effort to better understand business drivers and end user needs and analyze how networks are used and how they are likely to evolve. That is, understanding the key drivers (the "why"-s) in the QoS area is the key in bringing academic and industrial research (that aims to answer the "how"-s) closer to each other.

1   Introduction

The convergence of the tele/datacommunications, computer and consumer electronics industry offers players in these areas opportunities for expanding their sales and profit, but also the threat of being marginalized. While it is difficult to predict the winners, we believe that those who understand key research challenges and invest in the "right" research and development (R&D) projects have an advantage. Therefore, understanding the reasons behind the different directions taken in industrial and academic research is of interest for both of these groups.

The "industry-academia gap" cannot be understood and overcome without analyzing the relationship between industry players and the actual end users. The downtrend in the data- and telecommunications market in the past years has brought industry players to focus on delivering technology tailored to immediate customer (for example large telecommunications operator) needs. This has contributed to widening the gap in some areas between the industry and the academia. This effect has been exacerbated by efforts devoted by the industry (along with the networking research community) to technologies that did not prove successful in terms of end user deployment. The lesson learned is that the research community should be taking a step back and take a realistic look at how networks are used and how they are likely to evolve [1], [2]. Specifically, in the area of wireless QoS solutions, it seems especially important that the driving factors are well identified. This is because sophisticated QoS techniques tend to tempt researchers (notably the performance evaluation community) to propose far too complex architectures and algorithms that are not justified by end user requirements.

H. de Meer and N. Bhatti (Eds.): IWQoS 2005, LNCS 3552, pp. 375–378, 2005.
© IFIP International Federation for Information Processing 2005

2   QoS and Price Differentiation in Wireless Mobile Systems

We are currently witnessing a rapid growth of the wireless voice and data market. This in turns results in an increasing traffic volume over wireless network segments both in the local and wide area and both in private and public environment.[1]

The vast majority of IP networks is lightly loaded, and there are research data available that indicate that it will remain that way for the foreseeable future. In addition, overprovisioning helps to eliminate the need to maintain state information in the network, which helps in keeping the network architecture as simple as possible [4].

As IP meets the wireless world, the debate whether overprovisioning is a viable solution for QoS is still open. On one side, the proponents of open spectrum argue that spectrum itself is not such a scarce resource as many believed so far [5]. Also, the success of wireless local area networks, basically without any support for QoS differentiation mechanisms seemed to reinforce the argument that providing application level QoS is technically possible over best effort networking technologies. On the other side, the WLAN community has also recognized the technical benefits of supporting traffic differentiation over the air interface and started work on QoS within the 802.11 standards suite (802.11e). Also, claims about the abundance of spectrum resources remain questionable (just think of the tight regulatory policies, the narrowness of the ISM bands, and the price GSM operators in Europe had to pay for licences). Third generation cellular networks employ sophisticated QoS management and make very efficient use of spectrum resources, be they based on the wideband code division multiple access (WCDMA) or the cdma2000 standards suite. 3G network operators are interested in QoS mechanisms, because they help reduce operational and capital expenditures and facilitate the timely introduction of new services.

Finally, the emergence of beyond 3G architectures and the integration of various multiple access technologies over scarce wireless spectrum opens new exciting issues on the design of QoS architectures, which need to include resource management mechanisms at various levels (admission control, scheduling, routing when multi-hop wireless networks are considered, differentiated channel access mechanisms and priority support, etc.) to either differentiate the treatment encountered by different services and traffic categories, as well as provide adequate service quality on an end-to-end basis.

3   Radio Resource Management: Admission Control or Session Drop ?

The management of radio resources (RRM) involves a number of related areas, including power control, admission control, channel allocation, load balancing, hand-over management and packet scheduling. Early works on RRM issues mainly focused on applications that can be characterized in terms of some resource requirements. The prime objective of the RRM functions is to maximize the number of accommodated applications (predominantly voice). With the advent of IP services, adaptive and rate

---

[1] In this section we reuse parts of [3].

controlled applications have gained increasing attention, stimulating a number of research contributions in the area of joint rate- and power control (see [6] for an overview and extensive literature survey). Rate adaptive applications are attractive because of two main reasons. First, such applications tend to perform well over various networks employing different QoS mechanisms (including best effort networks). Also, being rate adaptive is a kind of exception handling when such applications run across "provisioned bandwidth" and congestion occurs due to, for instance, a failure situation.

There are arguments for decreasing the role and complexity of admission control techniques and to complement them with rate adaptation and autonomous or network enforced session drop based solutions. These types of discussions and debates strongly resemble those discussed by the Internet community [7] and call for research both in the architecture and performance evaluation areas. It is however not clear whether these solutions are indeed viable (just think of the issue that enforced session termination is perceived much more negatively by users than session blocking by some admission control mechanism). Also, relaxing the admission control mechanisms may make the network vulnerable to denial of service attacks and can result in extreme unfairness between "well behaving" and greedy users.

4   Conclusions

In this short paper we addressed the issue of the "research gap" between academic and industry players in the area of wireless QoS. We made the point that this gap cannot be overcome without understanding the main drivers for wireless QoS solutions before devising and debating the actual QoS architectures and algorithms. We expect that wireless resources will remain more scarce than wireline resources which calls for some form of QoS handling.

Acknowledgments

We would like to thank Göran Malmgren and Reiner Ludwig, both from Ericsson, for their comments on an early version of this material. We also thank the anonymous reviewers for their thoughtful comments.

References

1. A. Odlyzko, "Telecom Dogmas and Spectrum Allocations", *http: //www.dtc.umn.edu/ ~odlyzko*, Jun 20, 2004.
2. A. Odlyzko, "The Evolution of Price Differentiation in Transportation and Its Implciations for the Internet", *Review of Network Economics*, Vol. 3, Issue 3, September 2004.
3. A. Ahmad, G. Bianchi, L. Bernstein, G. Fodor, G. Pujolle, Lee Bu Sung and Yu-Dong Yao, "QoS Support and Service Differentiation n Wireless Networks - Guest Editorial", *International Journal of Communication Systems*, Vol. 17, No. 6, 2004.
4. B. Frankston, "At the Edge", *http://www.frankston.com/public/writing.asp?name=attheedge*

5. "Open Spectrum Frequently Asked Questions", *http://www.greaterdemocracy.org/ OpenSpectrumFAQ.html*

6. M. Xiao, N. B. Shroff and E. K. P. Chong, "Resource Management in Power-controlled Cellular Wireless Systems", *Wireless Communications and Mobile Computing*, Wiley, 2001; 1:185-199

7. S. Floyd and J. Kempf, "IAB Concerns Regarding Congestion Control for Voice Traffic in the Internet", *ITEF RFC 3714*, March 2004.

Why QoS Will Be Needed in Metro Ethernets

Rainer Baumann and Ulrich Fiedler

Computer Engineering and Networks Laboratory,
Swiss Federal Institute of Technology,
ETH-Zentrum, Gloriastrasse 35,
CH-8092 Zurich, Switzerland
{baumann, fiedler}@tik.ee.ethz.ch

Abstract. Emerging Metro Ethernets create new opportunities to converge data and telephony services. However, to connect legacy telephony
equipment, networks have to meet customary QoS requirements even at
the presence of bursty data cross traffic. We show with analytical evaluation and simulation results that without appropriate mechanisms the
QoS requirements cannot be met.

1 Introduction

Recent developments create new opportunities to converge data and telephony
services. The emerging deployment of fiber fosters the proliferation of Metropolitan Gigabit Ethernets. Thus a major aspect of interest is to employ these networks to connect legacy private branch exchanges (PBX) and GSM base stations
to the core telephony network. This protects investments in existing infrastructure and creates new revenues for network providers. However, to implement this
convergence, these networks have to be configured in a way that customary QoS
requirements for telephony, which are significantly more stringent than the ones
for VoIP, can be met. This is a crucial problem given that the data cross traffic in
these networks is bursty. This burstiness can cause excessive queueing delay and
frame losses due to buffer overflow [1]. Moreover, the burstiness of data traffic
in these networks is known to be self-similar. This means that there is very little
smooth out when aggregating the traffic over time which in turn means that
buffering has little effect in mitigating the burstiness. However, it is also known
that the burstiness is caused by the heavy-tail in the distribution of transfer
sizes which is known to be bounded due to the limitation of file sizes in popular
operating systems [1]. Since Gigabit Ethernets operate at very fast transmission
rates, the problem whether Metropolitan Gigabit Ethernet can accommodate
the burstiness of expected traffic patterns becomes real.

Therefore in this paper, we review the problem whether it is reasonable to
expect that TDM E1 telephony traffic can be run on Metropolitan Gigabit Ethernets. We conduct a simulation study combined with an analytical evaluation
to show that QoS requirements (in terms of delay and loss) as defined by the
Metro Ethernet Forum [2] cannot be met even when data traffic utilization is as
low as 1%.

H. de Meer and N. Bhatti (Eds.): IWQoS 2005, LNCS 3552, pp. 379–381, 2005.

2   Simulation Setup

We use OpNet modeler as our simulation environment. Modeler is a discrete event simulator that offers hierarchical network models and has a focus on layer two. We model the encapsulated TDM E1 telephony traffic that carries the signal of 32 telephony channels as a 5.1 Mbit/s stream. We generate the self-similar data cross traffic offline with a set of 100'000 superposed On/Off sources and inject the traffic into the simulation. On-times are heavy-tailed since the corresponding transfer size distribution is Pareto with 12 kByte average, 4.1 GByte maximum and tail index 1.2. Off-times follow a Pareto distribution with 1025 seconds average and tail index 1.2. We have verified that the data traffic generated has Hurst parameter 0.9. Since each switch has to meet the QoS requirements for delay and loss, we focus on representing the most congested switch (see figure 1 for the simulation topology). For QoS requirements, we refer to the Metro Ethernet Forum[2]. This essentially says that the fraction of E1 TDM frames that are delayed over 25ms or lost must be less than $8.75 \cdot 10^{-7}$. This is significantly more stringent than the requirements for VoIP (see [3]). Switches are configured to use FIFO queueing and tail drop. Buffer capacities are limited to 500 frames, 1000 frames, 1MB, 2MB, respectively. This choice is due to the Metro Forum's delay requirement of 25ms.

3   Overview of Results

First, we give an analytical evaluation to show that data frames in our simulation can overflow at frequencies that likely degrade the QoS of the E1 TDM traffic. Second, we present simulation results that account for effects that ameliorate the negative effect of frequent data frame overflows on E1 TDM traffic such as the lock-out of large data frames in favor of small E1 TDM frames in the switch buffer.

The frequency with which data frames overflow in the switch can be estimated as follows: We take the transfer size distribution from the On/Off model to estimate which fraction of transfers cause buffer overflows[1]. Then, we infer the expected frequency of data frame overflows given that the On/Off sources generate 106.6 transfers per second (see [5] for the math). For a buffer size of 1 MByte 0.056 percent of the transfers cause buffer overflows. ¿From this we expect that data frames overflow every 16.7 seconds. For a buffer size of 2 MByte the corresponding numbers are 0.024 percent and 39.0 seconds. If E1 TDM frames overflow at comparable rates, QoS is degraded.

Second, we present results of 2:47 hours simulation runs for 16 seeds each. We find that limiting the number of frames in the buffer, as currently done in most deployed switches, degrades QoS. Limiting to 500 frames, 1000 frames, and 2MB only one out of 16 runs, respectively three out of 16 runs in the later two cases, meet the requirements for delay and loss. When limiting the buffer at 1MB, all

---

[1] see [4] why percentiles lead to meaningful expected values.

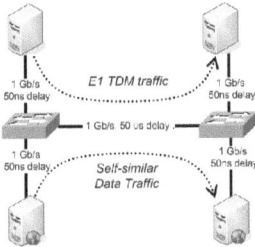

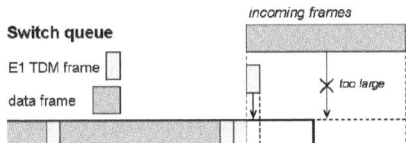

Fig. 1. Topology   **Fig. 2.** Lock-out phenomenon

16 simulation runs meet the QoS requirement. However, this can be explained with the fact that 1500 byte large data frames are locked-out at the tail of a full buffer queue although there is remaining buffer capacity for 78 byte small E1 TDM frames (see figure 2). We denote that our simulation over-estimates the effect of this phenomenon since almost all data frames generated by the On/Off sources in our simulation are 1500 bytes large. This has to do with the way superposition is done. For detailed results refer to [5].

4   Conclusion

In this paper, we have given an analytical evaluation and simulation results that indicate that Metro Forum's QoS requirements for telephony traffic cannot be met when switch buffers are configured to limit the number of frames as currently done in practice. Even when limiting the buffer size instead of the number of frames, QoS may not be achieved despite the fact that large data frames are locked-out at the tail of a full buffer queue where as there is still buffer capacity for small telephony frames. We thus conclude that it is necessary to consider QoS support mechanisms such as priorization as defined in IEEE 802.1p. This may lead to a break through in deploying QoS support mechanisms, since Metropolitan Gigabit Ethernets are usually managed by a single provider, which significantly simplifies deployment.

References

1. Park, K., Willinger, W.: Self-Similar Network Traffic and Performance Evaluation. John Wiley & Sons, Inc. (2000)
2. Metro Ethernet Forum: Introduction to Circuit Emulation Services over Ethernet (2004)
3. Fiedler, U., Huang, P., Plattner, B.: Towards Provisioning Diffserv Intra-Nets. Lecture Notes in Computer Science **2092** (2001)
4. Fiedler, U., Plattner, B.: Using Latency Quantiles to Engineer QoS Guarantees for Web Services. Lecture Notes in Computer Science **2707** (2003)
5. Rainer Baumann and Ulrich Fiedler: Why QoS will be needed in Metro Ethernets. TIK Report 215, ETH Zurich (2005)

Research Issues in QoS Provisioning for Personal Networks

Weidong Lu, Anthony Lo, and Ignas Niemegeers

CWPC, Delft University of Technology, Delft, The Netherlands
{W.Lu, A.Lo, I.Niemegeers}@ewi.tudelft.nl

Abstract. This paper outlines our ongoing research in providing personal networks (PNs) with QoS support. Research challenges and directions for the QoS provisioning in heterogeneous and dynamic PN environments are presented in two interrelated aspects: the traditional end-to-end QoS provisioning and the QoS support in PN self-organization.

1 Introduction

Personal network (PN) [1] [2] as a user-centric enabler for future wireless communications, starts from the user and extends the user's personal area network (PAN) to a global coverage of his personal devices and services in his home, car and office etc. as well as other foreign networks and services regardless of their geographical locations. Figure 1 illustrates an network abstraction of a PN. The PAN depicted in the thick circle is called Core-PAN, which is intimately associated with the person and is regarded as the heart of the PN. The extension of Core-PAN to different networks and services is made available via either ad hoc networks or infrastructure-based networks including UMTS networks and the Internet with wireless access points (APs) as depicted in Figure 1.

The need for provisioning of QoS for PNs inherits from the IP networks for providing real-time multimedia services. Furthermore, QoS provisioning in PN becomes more challenging and complex due to the heterogeneity and dynamism

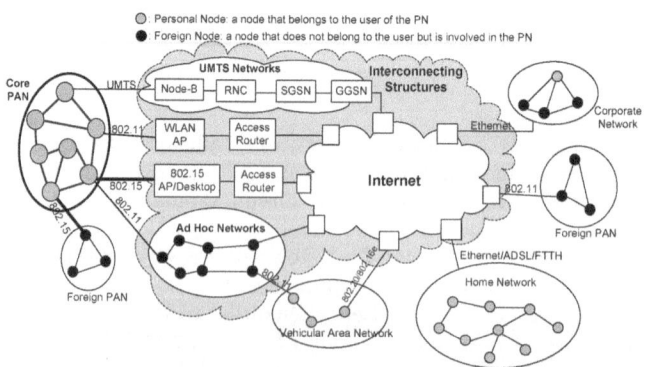

Fig. 1. A network abstraction of a personal network

H. de Meer and N. Bhatti (Eds.): IWQoS 2005, LNCS 3552, pp. 382–384, 2005.
© IFIP International Federation for Information Processing 2005

characteristics of PNs. The *heterogeneity* of PNs lies in that mobile devices in a PN are heterogeneous in functionalities, computational and battery capacities and may be equipped with heterogeneous wireless technologies with different coverage ranges. Networks that are involved in PNs are also heterogeneous including ad hoc networks, wireless access to the Internet, the Internet and UMTS networks etc. Moreover, heterogeneous devices, wireless technologies and networks are complementary to each other and could cooperate with each other in a PN to best meet the user's demands and QoS requirements of applications. The *dynamism* of PNs inherits from ad hoc networks where mobile nodes move around and communicating with each other. However, the dynamics become more severe in PNs due to the mobility and cooperation in heterogeneous PN environments. For example, communications in a PN may switch between different interfaces, devices and networks frequently to achieve the best performance.

2   Research Issues in QoS Provisioning for PNs

In this section, we will discuss the challenges that the heterogeneity and dynamism may pose to the QoS provisioning for PNs from the following two aspects. We will briefly address some challenges in end-to-end QoS provisioning and focus on the discussions of self-organization, a new form of QoS in PNs.

End-to-end QoS Provisioning. The end-to-end QoS provisioning in wired networks and self-organized ad hoc networks has been studied extensively over the years. However, several issues are still challenging for PNs. First is the unification of QoS parameters for heterogenous networks and QoS domains. Second is the end-to-end admission control and resource reservation in the heterogeneous and dynamic PN environments involving ad hoc networks, wireless access to the Internet and the Internet itself. Third is the QoS routing, a multiple constraints routing that dynamically determines the network path which satisfies the given constraints. The static QoS routing problem has been solved in practise but the QoS routing in dynamic PN environments is still under investigation.

QoS Support in Self-Organization of PNs. In addition to the traditional end-to-end QoS provisioning, new issues in QoS delivery for PNs lies in the self-organization of a PN, which refers to as the process in which the internal organization of the PN and the establishment of communications among nodes inside the PN are performed automatically and without or with minimal human intervention. Typical self-organization functions include device discovery, address-autoconfiguration and duplicated address detection (DAD), route discovery, mobility management, resource discovery, and context discovery, etc [3]. Self-organization functions need to be performed in a timely fashion to adapt to the dynamics of PNs.

Discovery functions play important roles in self-organization of PNs. Devices discovery and route discovery are related to the formation of PANs and PNs. The latency introduced in these discovery processes may be very high. For example, the device discovery latency of Bluetooth technology is in the range of 3 to 10 seconds. Mechanisms need to be investigated to minimize the latency of discovery functions so that the formation of a PN is accomplished promptly. In addition, context discovery (context awareness) facilitates the cooperation in Core-PAN to achieve better QoS. For example, every mobile node in Core-PAN should be aware of the status of ongoing connections inside Core-PAN by context discovery. When there is no ongoing session, mobile nodes could turn to sleep mode and perform device and route discovery less frequently to save energy. On the other hand, when there is any ongoing communication, mobile node need to be active and perform discovery functions frequently to search for possible alternative route to the Internet so that when the QoS requirement can not be meet on one path, for example due to handover or link failure, alternative path can be selected to forward packets. The context of Core-PAN could also be its location and mobility. Mobility, for example, can be utilized to determine the proper gateways and interfaces to be selected to setup communications. If the mobility of Core-PAN is high, it is preferable to choose long distance UMTS connections to setup communication instead of short range 802.15 or 802.11 technologies.

Another key function in self-organization is mobility management which allows mobile nodes such as nodes in Core-PAN remain reachable while moving around. The network layer mobility solution, Mobile IP, is considered appropriate to provide mobility across heterogeneous networks. However, handover processes, especially vertical handovers between heterogeneous wireless technologies and networks may still result in a significant degradation of QoS. In order to solve this problem, end-to-end resource reservation need to be re-established on the new path after handover using QoS signalling such as RSVP. Moreover, mechanisms need to be investigated to minimize the handover latency in the dynamic PN environments. For example, to minimize the delay caused by the simultaneous movement of both ends during communications.

3   Conclusions

This paper discussed research issues in provisioning of QoS for PNs from two aspects: traditional end-to-end QoS in heterogeneous and dynamic PN environments and the self-organization of PNs which is a new form of QoS. In the future, we are going to investigate and provide new solutions for the research issues highlighted in this paper for QoS provisioning in PNs.

References

1. I.G. Niemegeers and S.M. Heemstra de Groot: Research Issues in Ad-Hoc Distributed Personal Networking. Wireless Pers. Commun. 26, August (2003) 149–167
2. Martin Jacobsson et al.: A Network Layer Architecture for Personal Networks, in IST MAGNET International Workshop, Nov. (2004)
3. W. Lu, A. Lo, and I. Niemegeers: On the Dynamics and Self-organization of Personal Networks. IST MAGNET International Workshop, Nov. (2004)

RSVP Standards Today and the Path Towards a Generic Messenger

Xiaoming Fu[1] and Jukka Manner[2]

[1] Telematics Group, Institute for Informatics, University of Goettingen
[2] Department of Computer Science, University of Helsinki

1 Introduction to the Base Standard and Its Extensions

The Resource Reservation Protocol (RSVP) specified in RFC2205[1] has evolved from ST-II (RFC1819) to provide end-to-end QoS signaling services for application data streams. Hosts use RSVP to request a specific quality of service (QoS) reservation from the network for particular application flows. RSVP maintains and refreshes reservation states in routers for a requested QoS application flow. By original design, RSVP fits well into the framework of the Integrated Services (IntServ) of RFC2210 with certain modularity and scalability.

The fundamental concepts of RSVP include soft state management, two-pass signaling message exchanges, receiver-based resource reservation, and separation of QoS signaling from routing. Most of the functionality designed into RSVP has emerged from the original goal to support multicast reservations: the (multicast) receiver-based resource reservation, reservations styles and reservation merging, and soft state to support changes in the multicast routing tree.

RSVP was originally designed to support real-time applications over the Internet. Over the past several years, a tremendous demand for multicast-capable real-time applications, which many people had envisioned to be a killer application that could benefit from network-wide deployment of RSVP, has never materialized. Instead, RSVP-TE (RFC3209), an RSVP extension for traffic engineering, has been widely deployed by a large number of network providers to support label distribution in MPLS networks. GMPLS RSVP-TE (RFC3473) further extends RSVP-TE, by enabling the provisioning of data-paths within networks supporting a variety of switching types including packet and cell switching networks, layer two networks, TDM networks and photonic networks.

Various other extensions have been designed to extend the use of RSVP. RFCs 2379 and 2380 define RSVP over ATM implementation guidelines and requirements to interwork with the ATM UNI 3.x/4.0. RFC2996 introduces a DCLASS Object to carry DSCPs in RSVP message objects. The Null Service Type in RFC2997 allows applications to identify themselves to network policy agents using RSVP, and leaves resource allocations up to the network policies.

RFC2746 allows RSVP to make reservations across all IP-in-IP tunnels, basically, by recursively applying RSVP over the tunnel portion of the path. RFC2207 extends RSVP by using the IPsec SPI in place of the UDP/TCP-like

---

[1] All RFC documents available from `http://www.ietf.org/rfc/rfcNUMBER.txt`.

H. de Meer and N. Bhatti (Eds.): IWQoS 2005, LNCS 3552, pp. 385–387, 2005.
© IFIP International Federation for Information Processing 2005

ports. As RFC2205 leaves the policy component open, later RFCs 2749, 2750, and 3181 specify POLICY_DATA objects, handling of RSVP policy events by COPS-aware nodes, and a preemption priority policy. RFC2961 describes mechanisms to reduce processing overhead of refresh messages, eliminate the state synchronization latency incurred when an RSVP message is lost and, refreshing state without the transmission of whole refresh messages. Aggregation of reservations is specified in RFC3175. RSVP diagnostic messages are defined in RFC2745 to collect and report RSVP state information.

2   Analysis of the Current RSVP

A good signaling protocol should be transparent to the applications. RSVP has proven to be a very well designed protocol. However, it has a number of fundamental protocol design issues that requires more careful re-evaluation.

The design of RSVP was originally targeted at multicast applications. The result is that the message processing within nodes is somewhat heavy, mainly due to flow merging. Still, merging rules should not appear in the specification as they are QoS-specific. Also, the QoS objects should be more general.

From the security point of view, RSVP does provide the basic building blocks to protect the messages from forgery and modification in various deployment environments. However, current RSVP security mechanisms do not provide non-repudiation and protection against message deletion; the two-way peer authentication and key management procedures are still missing.

Domains not supporting RSVP are traversed transparently by default. Unfortunately, like other IP options, RSVP messages implemented by way of IP alert option may result in themselves being dropped by some routers. Also, RSVP does not support message fragmentation and reassembly at protocol level. If the size of an RSVP message is larger than the link MTU, e.g., from carried large security-related objects, the message may be fragmented by IP. However, RSVP routers simply cannot detect and process message fragments.

The state machine of RSVP is complex, mainly due to the focus on multicast, which complicates message processing and per-session state maintenance. Moreover, the order and existence of objects can vary, which increases the complexity in message parsing and internal message and state representation. RFC2961 tries to lower the bandwidth consumption of RSVP, and provide better reliability. However, a lot of effort has to be spent on per-session timer maintenance, message retransmission (e.g., avoid message bursts), and message sequencing.

Although RSVP uses soft state mechanism and is independent of underlying routing protocols, a mobile node's movement may not properly trigger a reservation refresh for the new path and a mobile node may be left without a downlink reservation up to the lifetime of the refresh timer. This can happen because only Path messages can repair the routing path of the reservation messages, and a receiving node must wait for a Path message from the sender. Furthermore, RSVP does not work properly when the mobile node's IP address changes, since the filters will not identify the flow that had a reservation.

Moreover, to be useful, RSVP needs support from both communicating end hosts, and the underlying network. In many deployment scenarios, it would be most beneficial, if a reservation could be applied to only the local domain. Ideas from different points of view have been discussed in the IETF, e.g., the RSVP Proxy and the Localized RSVP.

It is expected that the development of future signaling protocols should learn from the lessons of existing ones. A thorough evaluation of Internet QoS signaling protocols can be found in *Analysis of Existing Quality of Service Signaling Protocols*, Internet Draft (work in progress), December 2004.

3   Path Towards a Generic Messenger

As observed in RFCs 3234 and 3724, the rise of various middleboxes including QoS boxes and stateful packet filter firewalls, has put in question the general applicability of the end-to-end principle. Unlike SIP (RFC3261), which is designed under an architecture with registrars and proxies for end-to-end session level signaling between both communication endpoints, middleboxes require session-related state installation and maintenance along the communication path. Due to the variety of middleboxes, there has been a strong need for a generic signaling service for delivery of control information into these boxes. A big question is, can RSVP be changed to handle present and tomorrow's deployment scenarios and requirements? In our view, the new signaling requirements, with network security requirements, and with MTU problems, will prevent a direct re-use of the existing RSVP. A new, generic messenger is needed: the protocol must be catered primarily for unicast applications, must be able to handle reliable and secure messaging, message packing, the MTU problem, small triggered message volumes, and changes in IP addresses and effective re-routing during the lifetime of a reservation. Moreover, moving a signaling protocol for QoS resource reservations into a generic messenger can provide much adoption. Towards this, several design choices have been identified in the IETF NSIS Working Group:

- The messenger is separated from signaling applications, dedicates to message delivery, and is responsible for only transporting signaling data into relevant middleboxes.
- It decouples the discovery of next signaling hop and signaling message transport, which allows rich security protocol for transport while keeping the discovery component rather simple.
- It reuses reliable transport protocols, such as TCP and SCTP, which also support fragmentation and other features, as well as unreliable ones, for message transport depending on the application requirements and availability.

Given the amount of legal RSVP implementations, the transition path from RSVP to such a generic messenger may be gradual. For example, if fragmentation or strong security for signaling messages is not required, unreliable transport and coupling next hop discovery within signaling message transport can still be used as in RSVP, especially in intra-domain cases.

QoS in Hybrid Networks – An Operator's Perspective

Aiko Pras[1], Remco van de Meent[1], and Michel Mandjes[2]

[1] University of Twente, The Netherlands
{pras, meent}@cs.utwente.nl
[2] Center for Mathematics and Computer Science, The Netherlands
michel.mandjes@cwi.nl

Abstract. The goal of this paper is to foster discussions on future directions for QoS related research. The paper takes the viewpoint of an operator; as an example it presents the topology, capacity and expected usage of the next generation research network within the Netherlands, called SURFnet6. In that network the traffic from normal and demanding users gets separated; the mechanism to realize this is lambda switching. The key method to assure performance is overprovisioning; there is no need to use DiffServ or IntServ.

1 Introduction

Since many years Quality of Service (QoS) is an important research topic. In literature, QoS has been defined as "providing service differentiation and performance assurance for Internet applications" [1]. Traditionally, QoS research relied on frameworks like IntServ and DiffServ to achieve its goals. The Internet hype, which led to a gross overinvestment in transmission capacity, and the subsequent collapse of the bubble, require us to rethink these frameworks, however. In the last five years we've witnessed a growth of available backbone capacity that exceeded the growth of Internet usage, which remained stable at approximately 100% per year [2]. As a result, prices went down considerably; for the costs of a few kilometres highway, it is now possible to create a nation-wide backbone in the Tbps range. Backbone link capacity need therefore no longer be regarded as a scarce resource.

Section 2 of this paper discusses the consequences of these developments for the next generation of the Dutch research network, called SURFnet6. It shows how service differentiation and performance assurance will be realized in that network. Section 3 provides the conclusions and identifies some remaining QoS related research challenges.

2 SURFnet6

The organization responsible for the Dutch research network is SURFnet. The first generation of their network was installed in the early eighties of the previous century and installation of the sixth generation started at the end of 2004. The main idea

H. de Meer and N. Bhatti (Eds.): IWQoS 2005, LNCS 3552, pp. 388–391, 2005.

behind this new network is to take advantage of the dark-fibre infrastructure that has recently become available, and to use lambda switching to separate the traffic generated by demanding users from that of normal users. In the next subsections the topology, capacity and expected usage of that network will be discussed.

2.1 Topology

It is exactly five years back that the Internet hype reached its top. At that time it was impossible to rent dark-fibre. Since there was a common believe that Internet usage would explode, many organizations started to install their own fibre infrastructure. In the year 2000 the cost of digging fibre trenches was in the range of 50 to 100 euro / meter. Soon after the collapse of the Internet bubble, it became clear that there had been an over-investment in fibre capacity. As a result of this over-investment, a significant part of the available fibre capacity remained unused. The owners of the fibre infra-structure were subsequently forced to change their business models and, as a result, it is now possible to rent dark-fibre from multiple parties. The prices for dark-fibre are, in rural areas, in the range of a few euros per meter (for a 15 years lease period). Also digging costs went considerably down to around one-fifth of the original costs. These developments made it possible for SURFnet to acquire a dedicated fibre infrastructure for the new SURFnet6 research network (Figure 1). The length of this infrastructure is around 5300 km, which is comparable to the size of the Dutch rail and highway infrastructure.

Fig. 1. Topology

2.2 Capacity

With Coarse Wave Division Multiplexing (CWDM), which is a relative cheap technology, it is possible to use 16 wavelengths on a single fibre pair. If OC-48 is used, the resulting capacity becomes 40 Gbps. Besides some CWDM rings in metro areas, SURFnet will use the more advanced Dense Wave Division Multiplexing (DWDM) on five individual rings of dark fibre pairs, with a capacity up to 720 Gbps per fibre pair per ring. Note that some links within SURFnet6 will not consist of a single fibre pair, but of multiple pairs. Hundreds of such pairs may be included within a single duct.

2.3 Usage

The usage of SURFnet6 is expected to keep on doubling every year [3]. Two kinds of users can be distinguished:

- Normal users, who use the network for web surfing and email exchange. Some of these users will also participate in P2P networks and watch Internet videos.
- Demanding users, who would like to exchange data at Gigabit speed for longer periods of time. Examples of such users are physicists, who perform nuclear experiments, and astronomers, who correlate data from different radio telescopes (like LOFAR).

To assure performance, no special measures are required for the normal users; there is no need for relatively complex mechanisms like DiffServ and IntServ. As explained in the previous subsection, the issue is not a lack of link capacity between network nodes. Rather the issue is the complexity of the nodes themselves, which should be kept at a minimum. Contrary to what some researchers claim, overprovisioning may be a viable method to assure performance!

For demanding users the situation is somewhat different; the amount of data that these users exchange may be such that, without special measures, performance for normal users can no longer be guaranteed. For that reason traffic from the relatively small number of demanding users will be separated from that of normal users. The mechanism to realize this separation is lambda switching. Dedicated optical path connections are established between these demanding users, using dedicated DWDM colours. This separation has the additional advantage that demanding users are free to operate dedicated high-speed transport protocols; such protocols could disturb the correct operation of the 'normal' TCP protocol and should therefore not be mixed with normal TCP traffic on top of a single IP network. It is important to note that optical path establishment is not limited to the Netherlands, but via NetherLight [5] and the Global Lambda Integrated Facility (GLIF) [6] it is already possible to reach major parts of Europe, the US, Canada, the Far East as well as Australia.

3 Conclusions and Remaining QoS Challenges

Since link capacity will continue to grow faster than the capacity of routers, SURFnet doesn't see a need for IntServ and DiffServ. Our belief is that the shift towards optical networks should also lead to a shift in thinking about QoS: instead of ensuring QoS at a fine level of granularity (packets and flows), QoS should be ensured at an aggregate level (provisioning of links and optical paths). In [4], for example, a study is described that balances overprovisioning and resource demands by looking at peak usage at (small) time scales that correspond to users' perception of QoS. The results may be used to determine whether investments in link upgrades are warranted or may be postponed without sacrificing performance. Although the study focuses on access links, the ideas could also be extended to a network wide setting. Also automatic lambda management may be an interesting topic for research: when is it worthwhile to setup and use a lightpath between two points in the network, and how can this be done automatically?

Acknowledgement

We would like to thank Erik-Jan Bos, Jan van Oorschot (both SURFnet) and Remco van Mook (Virtu Secure Webservices) for their input, comments and valuable information.

References

1. W. Zhao, D. Olshefski and H. Schulzrinne: Internet quality of service: An overview, Technical Report CUCS-003-00, Columbia Univ., Computer Science Dept., Feb. 2000
2. A. M. Odlyzko: Internet traffic growth: Sources and implications, in: Optical Transmission Systems and Equipment for WDM Networking II, Proc. SPIE, vol. 5247, 2003
3. SURFnet Annual report, 2003, http://www.surfnet.nl/staging/attachment.db?349156
4. R. v.d. Meent, A. Pras, M.R.H. Mandjes, J.L. van den Berg, F. Roijers, L.J.M. Nieuwenhuis, P.H.A. Venemans: Burstiness predictions based on rough network traffic measurements, Proceedings of the 19th World Telecommunications Congress (WTC/ISS 2004), Seoul, Korea, September 2004
5. NetherLight home page, http://www.netherlight.net/
6. GLIF home page, http://www.glif.is

QoS for Aggregated Flows in VPNs

Pratik Bose, Dan Voce, and Dilip Gokhale

Lockheed Martin Integrated Systems & Solutions,
22300 Comsat Drive, Clarksburg, MD USA, 20871

Abstract. Aggregation of flows is a natural consequence of the transition of flows across multiple network domains. The quality of service that is provided to an aggregated flow is dependent on a sufficient set of individual flow characteristics correctly transformed in to the aggregated flow characteristics. VPN routers at the boundary of the private networks encrypt information within the data packets of a flow and flow characteristics are no longer visible to the interface domain. This document describes the challenges faced by QoS mechanisms to provide quality of service to secure aggregated flows.

1 Introduction

A simplified view of heterogeneous networks being designed today consists of high data rate (in Gbps) user networks which connect to backbone network service providers. The user networks are expected to consist of both wireless and optical infrastructure. A typical characteristic of the user networks is the presence of Virtual Private Network (VPN) routers which encrypt data intended for authenticated user network peers prior to injecting it into the backbone network. The backbone networks provide transport to these encrypted and encapsulated data packets to other user networks where peer VPN routers decrypt the information for end hosts.

The Quality of Service (QoS) is provided to the user network for typical parameters such as delay, delay variation, packet loss, throughput and service Availability. At the edge of the user network and backbone network microflows are aggregated based on flows which share similar parameters. The key issue is offering network service guarantees for one or more elevated classes of traffic for these encrypted flows. As evident, the user network must provide sufficient information to the backbone network about the QoS desired for the encrypted flow. Another key issue is to preempt lower priority flows to accommodate higher priority flows.

2 Shortcomings in Current Architectures

2.1 Differentiated Services

The DiffServ architecture naturally aggregates different application data into an IP flow with a single DSCP (for ex, voice data is typically marked with the Expedited Forwarding DSCP). The aggregate of say, all voice flows in the backbone network using the DSCP does not provide sufficient information to distinguish between different application data types and the priority of a microflow within an aggregate.

H. de Meer and N. Bhatti (Eds.): IWQoS 2005, LNCS 3552, pp. 392–394, 2005.

Different recommendations have been made to provide higher QoS fidelity in the DiffServ architecture. These primarily have been based on traffic conditioning using additional parameters such as the source and the destination address of the flow; assigning additional DSCPs to distinguish between applications and flow priorities; congestion notification and bandwidth management

These methods however, do not provide sufficient guarantees that may be required by the user network for certain critical flows.

2.2 IntServ, RSVP and Aggregate RSVP

The IntServ framework was developed to provide QoS guarantees on a per-microflow basis. The key building blocks to an IntServ architecture are (a) admission control and (b) a resource reservation protocol that performs resource reservation once a flow is admitted. This model is extended to support the mapping of QoS classes to a DSCP in Aggregate RSVP

Aggregation with RSVP combining the aggregation of DiffServ is described in RFC 3175 which proposes a scheme to aggregate multiple RSVP reservations across a transit region (called an aggregation region) into a single reservation request.

2.3 Flow Based Networking

[1] proposes a new QoS signaling standard for use within IPv6 to permit the complete specification of the Quality of Service of a flow (or a group of flows) in-band in a hop-by-hop option field. This permits the QoS to be setup in real time by router hardware without a separate signaling message structure like RSVP. The QoS request and response are incorporated into the data flow packet headers so that the QoS can be setup during the first round trip.

3 QoS Challenges for Secure Aggregated Flows

The key challenges in providing QoS for secure aggregate flows using any of the architectures described in section 2 are as follows:

1. Signaling mechanisms between networks should sufficiently describe the desired QoS parameters without compromising the security of the flow.
2. Sufficient information must be provided to each network to enable the following QoS functions: Packet classification; Metering and shaping; Queue scheduling and management; and Priority and preemption.
3. The capability of VPN routers should be expanded such that these routers can participate in the QoS functions described in 2 above. The current capabilities of VPN routers are limited in this arena and secure flows are implemented as tunneled aggregates between VPN sites.
4. MLPP [2] defines a prioritized flow handling service where the relative importance of flows allows higher priority flows at the expense of lower priority flows. RSVP provides a capability to signal priority preemption elements as defined in [20]. Preemption is applicable to emergency services as required by civilian and military networks.

5. The trust model of secure aggregation deems the network edge as an appropriate place to condition traffic. Traffic conditioning in the backbone may provide greater DiffServ QoS fidelity. However traffic conditioning in the backbone suffers from scalability issues.

6. QoS integration with the security model that is implemented by networks is necessary. Changes in VPN routing, authentication and encryption may affect the QoS of related flows. QoS functions must be capable of adapting to such changes emanating from the security function.

7. Scalability of an integrated QoS-security model also offers challenges that need to be addressed. As an example ARSVP can provide a combination of QoS aggregation and secure flow aggregation at VPN boundaries.

3.1 Emerging Solutions

[3], [4] and [6] are examples of emerging solutions that address some of the requirements outlined in Section 3. [3] presents an architectural framework for nested VPN routers which participate in QoS signaling. [4] defines RSVP signaling at an IPSec router which can aggregate flows based on DSCP and security associations at the router. Further work is required to meet or exceed the requirements of QoS aggregation in secure networks.

4   Conclusion

A key consideration for heterogeneous networks of today and tomorrow is to support for QoS for secure aggregated flows. The applicability of different QoS approaches to the secure aggregate flows was described and their relative strengths and weaknesses with respect to meeting the functional requirements were evaluated. The optimal QoS solution must meet the challenges described in this paper and address the issues and constraints highlighted in this paper.

References

[1] Lawrence G. Roberts, "QoS Signaling for IPv6 QoS Support", TR-34.1.7/04.03.25.04, March 2004.
[2] International Telecommunications Union, "Multilevel Precedence and Preemption (MLPP)", ITU-T Recommendation I.255.3, 1990.
[3] Fred Baker and Pratik Bose "QoS Signaling in a Nested Virtual Private Network" draft-baker-signaled-preemption-01.txt
[4] F Le, Faucheur et. al "Aggregate RSVP reservations for IPSec tunnels"
[5] Herzog – RFC 3181 - Signaled Preemption Priority Policy Element, October 2001
[6] James Polk et. al – "A Resource Reservation Extension for the Reduction of Bandwidth of A Reservation Flow" – draft-polk-tsvwg-rsvp-bw-reduction-00.txt.

Supporting Mission-Critical Applications over Multi-service Networks

C. Christou[1] and M. Davenport[2]

[1] Booz Allen Hamilton, 8283 Greensboro Drive, McLean, VA, USA 22102
[2] Booz Allen Hamilton, 5220 Pacific Concourse Drive, Los Angeles, CA, USA 90045
{christou_chris, davenport_michael}@bah.com

Abstract. Future government IP networks must satisfy mission-critical QoS requirements that are introduced by high-priority customers. A prime example includes the Multi-level Precedence and Preemption (MLPP)-like requirements. This paper will focus on the challenges in satisfying these needs in future government IP networks.

1 Introduction

Government organizations, to save on long-term operational expenditures, have begun migrating services (i.e., voice, video, mission critical applications) to a single IP-based infrastructure. For example, the US Department of Defense (DoD) has outlined its intent to transition to IPv6 by 2008, facilitating its transformation to net-centric operations [1]. Therefore, the demand for converged services over IP networks to support critical operations introduces new challenges. Future networks will need to support a MLPP-like service which was offered over legacy circuit-based networks. In addition, future designs will have to provision these services over wireless networks, introducing challenges when trying to guarantee service. Finally, the architecture should be balanced with the security requirements that must be simultaneously satisfied.

2 QoS for Mission Critical Applications over Wireless Networks

The first step for developing QoS requirements for any network involves enumerating the types of applications that will be transported over the infrastructure and categorizing them into Service Classes. Although the Service Classes defined for the Internet in [2] apply to government users, some applications that are not necessarily unique to government users but are mission-critical to their communities could include telemetry, command and control, and high quality video/imagery. In these cases, special service classes might be required. However, the uniqueness of these applications is an area requiring further study.

Additional requirements related to QoS exist that are unique to the military and mission-critical networks. As discussed in [3], MLPP is a service currently offered in

H. de Meer and N. Bhatti (Eds.): IWQoS 2005, LNCS 3552, pp. 395–397, 2005.
© IFIP International Federation for Information Processing 2005

legacy circuit networks, providing commanders the ability to allow for the communication of high precedence calls during times of crisis. In general, MLPP offers the ability for high precedence calls (e.g., flash) to preempt lower precedence ones (e.g., routine) during times of congestion. Future IP networks will need to support this service not only for telephony, but for other inelastic and elastic services as well. Several architectures, including those mentioned in [3] and [4], have been proposed to satisfy both QoS and MLPP requirements. Most importantly, the use of QoS signaling protocols to provide service guarantees and admission control in support of inelastic services and MLPP is a strong consideration. Nevertheless, in trying to assess the applicability of these architectures to future systems, the performance characteristics of future networks must also be considered. Most importantly, military and humanitarian missions will increasingly rely on wireless networks, including satellite IP-based networks and Mobile Ad-hoc Networks (MANETs), for their communications needs. Therefore, QoS mechanisms must be applied carefully to these diverse infrastructures to ensure that MLPP-like services, and service quality in general, are provided.

With respect to satellite networking, the use of Demand Assigned Multiple Access (DAMA) techniques are increasing due primarily to the gains that can be achieved through bandwidth sharing for multiple connected regions. However, there are issues with this increased use due not only to their high Bit Error Rate (BER) but also the instability of the BER. For example, the provisioning of guaranteed services could result in a reduction in RF link utilization, which could be extremely costly considering the limitations of RF communications with respect to capacity. For MANET communications, the fact that they have dynamic topologies with limited security make the provisioning of signaling mechanisms/guaranteed service much more challenging due to routing instabilities and variable bandwidth. Therefore, further analysis is needed to determine whether a signaled approach is a viable solution for wireless networks while understanding whether the utilization for providing guarantees is too costly.

3   QoS and Levels of Assurance

In addition to supporting policy requirements (e.g., MLPP), future networks will also require high levels of information assurance (IA) with respect to authentication, integrity, and protection. Therefore, these separate IA, QoS, and policy requirements present a common tradeoff: one must provide functionality to end users while preserving a secure infrastructure. With IP networks implementing IP encryption and authentication closer to the network edge, providing high levels of QoS for end-to-end guarantees becomes increasingly difficult. As proposed in [3], one can leverage the Resource Reservation Protocol (RSVP) to offer MLPP services over IP networks . However, depending on the policy and security requirements, end-to-end RSVP signaling may not be permitted across all networks. Even in cases where QoS signaling is allowed, individual domains must implement strong Authentication and Authorization mechanisms if accepting resource requests from external networks. In addition, the security risks associated with including information in data plane packet headers must be considered. Therefore, the QoS architecture that is applied across networks may differ depending on the security requirements—in some cases network engineers may have more flexibility in the functionality that is permitted. However, for more sensitive cases, the mechanisms that are applied may be more limited due to more heightened security risks.

4 Conclusion

In this paper we addressed the trend towards migrating all services to a single IP-based infrastructure. Examples of this trend include the US DoD's current transition to an IPv6-based infrastructure. The challenges outlined in this paper include: supporting IP QoS over multiple environments and the integration of IA and QoS. In particular for government IP networks, they must not only satisfy end user performance requirements but also provide MLPP-type services for high priority users. However, providing QoS with MLPP becomes difficult due to the types of networks that will be deployed. For example, the approach to addressing the issues in wireless environments must take into account the dynamic nature of mobile and satellite IP networks. In addition, regardless of the network over which converged services will be deployed, strict IA requirements must be taken into consideration. As these next generation networks mature, organizations such as the Internet Engineering Task Force must continue to develop additional standards, new approaches, and new analysis techniques to provide an architecture which balances these special needs and maximizes utilization for all environments.

References

1. Kraus, Marilyn (2003) *DoD Transition to IPv6*. In: US IPv6 Summit 2003, 8-11 Dec 2003, Washington D.C. http://www.6journal.org/archive/00000057/01/Marilyn_Kraus.pdf
2. J. Babiarz, K. Chan, F. Baker (2004) *Configuration Guidelines for DiffServ Service Classes*. draft-baker-diffserv-basic-classes-04.
   http://www.ietf.org/internet-drafts/draft-baker-diffserv-basic-classes-04.txt
3. F. Baker and J. Polk (2005) *Implementing MLPP for Voice and Video in the Internet Protocol Suite*. draft-ietf-tsvwg-mlpp-that-works-00. http://www.ietf.org/internet-drafts/draft-ietf-tsvwg-mlpp-that-works-00.txt
4. M. Pierce and S. Silverman (2005) *Multi-Level Expedited Forwarding Per Hop Behavior (MLEF PHB)*. draft-silverman-tsvwg-mlefphb-02.txt. http://www.ietf.org/internet-drafts/draft-silverman-tsvwg-mlefphb-02.txt.

Author Index

Lecture Notes in Computer Science

For information about Vols. 1–3439

please contact your bookseller or Springer